W9-ABF-797

20.95
67p

WITHDRAWN

Salem Academy and College
Gramley Library
Winston-Salem. N.C. 27108

SECOND EDITION

News Reporting
and Writing

PN
4781
.N34
1985

SECOND EDITION

News Reporting and Writing

The Missouri Group:

Brian S. Brooks
George Kennedy
Daryl R. Moen
Don Ranly

School of Journalism
University of Missouri at Columbia

Salem Academy and College
Gramley Library
Winston-Salem, N.C. 27108

St. Martin's Press   New York

Library of Congress Catalog Card Number: 83–61604
Copyright © 1985 by Brian S. Brooks, George Kennedy,
Daryl R. Moen, and Don Ranly
All Rights Reserved.
Manufactured in the United States of America.
98765
fedcba
For information, write St. Martin's Press, Inc.,
175 Fifth Avenue, New York, N.Y. 10010

cover design: Darby Downey
cover photo: Woodfin Camp & Associates

ISBN: 0–312–57205–0

Acknowledgments and copyrights continue at the back of the book on pages 547–548, which constitute an extension of the copyright page.

Acknowledgments

p. 7: Front page of the Longview Daily News, reproduced by permission.

p. 8: Front page of the Lakeland Ledger, reproduced by permission.

p. 9: Front page of the Columbia Missourian, reproduced by permission.

p. 53: Excerpted news story by Tom Uhlenbrock reprinted by permission of United Press International.

p. 65: Front page of USA Today, reproduced by permission.

pp. 78–79: News story reprinted by permission of United Press International.

p. 84: Excerpt originally appeared in *Playboy* magazine: Copyright 1980 by *Playboy*.

pp. 86–87: Excerpted news story reprinted by permission of the Columbia Missourian.

p. 101: Excerpted news story reprinted by permission of the Columbia Missourian.

p. 150: Obituary reprinted by permission of the Columbia Missourian.

p. 169: Excerpted news story reprinted by permission of the Milwaukee Sentinel.

p. 169: Excerpted news story reprinted by permission of the Cleveland Plain Dealer.

p. 170: Excerpted news story reprinted by permission of the St. Petersburg Times.

pp. 171–172: Excerpted news story reprinted by permission of The Boston Globe.

pp. 172–173: News story reprinted by permission of the Columbia Missourian.

p. 186: Excerpted news story reprinted by permission of the San Jose Mercury.

p. 187: Excerpted news story reprinted by permission of the San Jose Mercury.

p. 188: Excerpted news story reprinted by permission of the San Jose Mercury.

Preface

Like the first edition of *News Reporting and Writing*, this revised and expanded second edition is intended to be, above all, useful.

It begins at the beginning, explaining what news is and why accuracy and fairness are essential in reporting and writing. The section that teaches the basic techniques for news gathering and writing includes an expanded chapter on the most common reporting technique—interviewing—and a new discussion on the newest technique—searching computer data bases.

After presenting the basics, the book shows students how to handle increasingly complex stories, how to write those stories effectively and how to move into specialized reporting. The chapter on business and consumer reporting has been expanded in recognition of the increasing importance of that specialty. The concluding chapters cover law and ethics. The law chapter contains most recent important cases. The expanded ethics chapter provides a sound framework and suggests approaches to solving journalism's toughest and most common ethical problems.

The second edition reflects the thorough testing the book has received during five years of use in basic and advanced reporting classes at the University of Missouri School of Journalism and in more than 300 other schools and departments. Also as a result of that experience, we have written a separate workbook to provide more and better exercises.

We think that this second edition, even more than the first, is helpfully organized, clearly written and complete. We have continued our stress on good writing, both in the content of the book and in its style. We have followed the wire service style used by nearly all newspapers. The updated appendix includes the most commonly used sections of the wire service stylebooks.

We want to thank our colleague Dale Spencer, a journalist and lawyer, who revised his chapter on law, and James K. Gentry, director of Missouri's business journalism program, who revised the chapter on business and consumer reporting. We are grateful, too, to our many colleagues across the country who provided us with helpful comments and suggestions for this second edition: Anantha Babbili, Texas Christian University; Gail Barwis, Marquette University; Thomas Beell, Iowa State University; Peter Benjaminson, SUNY—Binghamton; Richard Bergeman, Linn-Benton Community College; James M. Bernstein, Michigan State University; Shirley Biagi, California State University—Sacramento; Michael Bugeja, Oklahoma State University; Rosalie Carroll, University of Arizona; Paula A. Cashdollar, Community College of Rhode Island; Lawrence Clancy, Russell Sage Junior College of Albany; Patrick Connolly, Rock Valley College; Walter G. Cowan, University of New Orleans; Diana D'India, Framingham State College; John C. Donahue, Purdue University; Glenn C. Doty, SUNY—New Paltz; John Dunn, University of Michigan—Ann Arbor; Jerry W. Elam, Broward Community College; C. A. Fleming, Oklahoma State University; E. Fraas, Western Kentucky University; Jerome Greenfield, SUNY—New Paltz; Max K. Hall, Broward Community College; Susan Harrigan, SUNY—Binghamton; Mary Hires, County College of Morris; Beatrice Hirschl, Duquesne University; Sharon Hoover, Alfred University; William E. Huntzicker, University of Wisconsin—River Falls; Arnold H. Ismach, University of Minnesota—Minneapolis; DeWayne B. Johnson, California State University—Northridge; James Joseph, Troy State University; L. D. Kennedy, Campbellsville College; Stephen K. Koski, Mary of the Plains College; Paul Krakowski, Duquesne University; Kim Landon, Utica College; Tahree Lane, University of Michigan—Ann Arbor; Jae-Won Lee, Cleveland State University; John Luter, University of Hawaii; Sue Maloney, Duquesne University; Merlin R. Mann, Abilene Christian University; Raleigh Mann, University of North Carolina—Chapel Hill; Mary Marcus, East Texas State University; Lois Matthews, Eastern Michigan University; W. M. Mecklenburg, Duquesne University; David Merves, Broward Community College; James McKinley, University of Missouri—Kansas City; David C. Nelson, Purdue University; Hank Nuwer, Clemson University; Rosemary Parker, Michigan State University; Elise Parsigian, University of Michigan—Ann Arbor; Jon Ramsey, Skidmore College; William J. Roach, University of Northern Florida; James R. Ross, University of Pittsburgh; Jon Sacks, Broward Community College; Michael Salwen, Michigan State University; Herman Scheiding, Foothill College; Lawrence Schneider, California State University—Northridge; George J. Searles, Mohawk Valley Community College; Kathleen Burton Shores, Pepperdine

University; Diane Silver, Michigan State University; Sarah Snyder, University of Michigan—Ann Arbor; Stanley Soffin, Michigan State University; Harlan S. Stensaas, Oral Roberts University; Susan Stock, Union County College; Stephen Turner, Milwaukee Area Technical College; Larry K. Uffelman, Mansfield State College; Kenneth G. Vance, Indiana State University—Evansville; John B. Webster, Purdue University; Jean Gaddy Wilson, Missouri Valley College; Eleanor S. Wright, Eastern Michigan University; and Ernest Wyatt, Georgia Southern College. We thank our students—past and present—whose work we've drawn on to illustrate the principles of the book and from whom we've learned. Our wives, Anne, Robin, Nancy and Joan, have been full partners in this project.

Brian S. Brooks   Daryl R. Moen
George Kennedy   Don Ranly

Contents

ix

SECOND EDITION

News Reporting and Writing

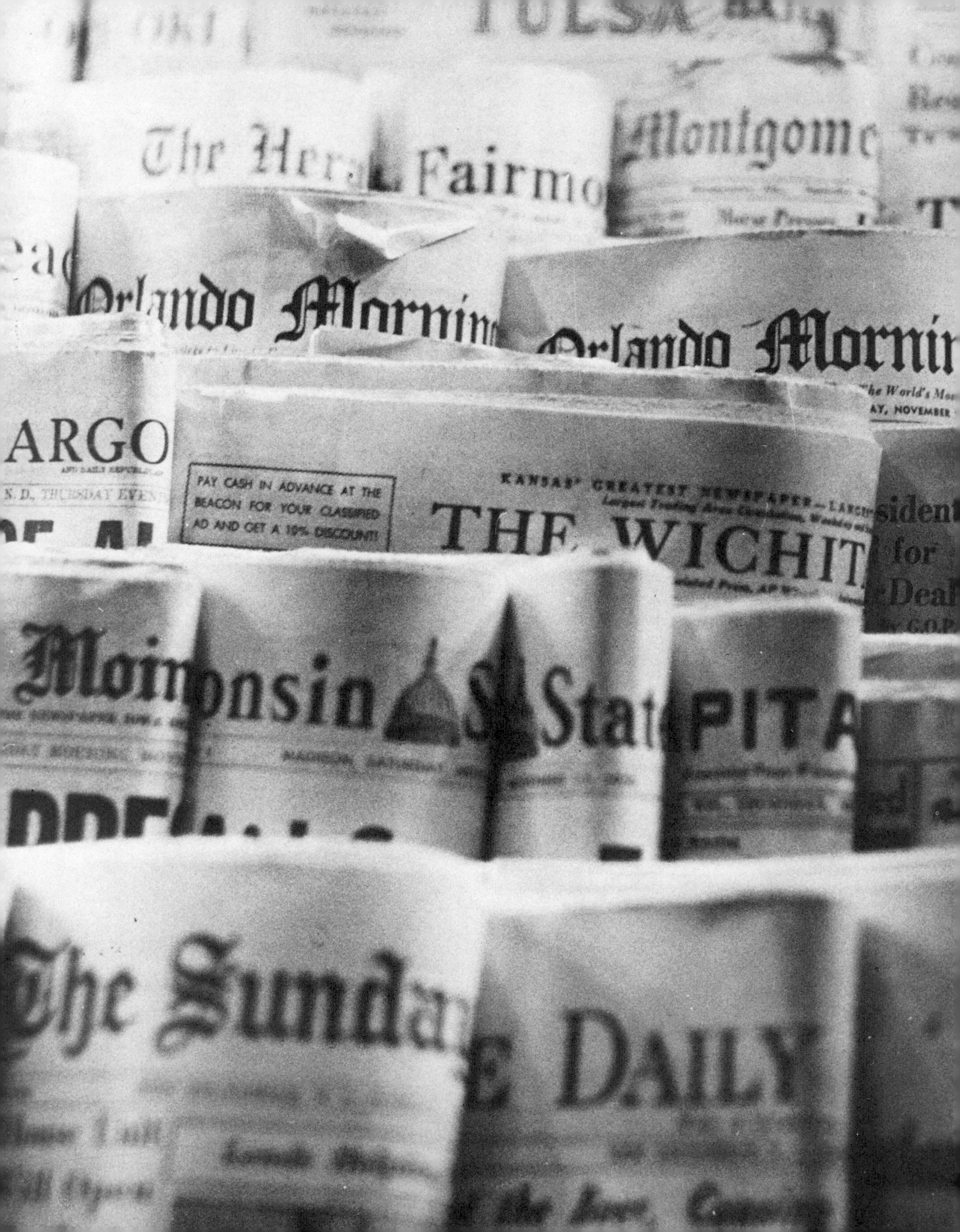
TULSA
The Hera
Fairmo
Montgome
Orlando Mornin
Orlando Mornin
ARGO
PAY CASH IN ADVANCE AT THE BEACON FOR YOUR CLASSIFIED AD AND GET A 10% DISCOUNT!
KANSAS' GREATEST NEWSPAPER
THE WICHIT
sident
for
Deal
Moin
onsin
Stat
PITA
The Sunda
DAILY

PART ONE

Introduction to the News

1

The Nature of News

For Dan Rather, the most important news of January 10, 1984, was the re-establishment of diplomatic ties between the United States and the Vatican. That story led the "CBS Evening News." Following it was a report on the first visit to the United States of the Chinese premier.

The Daily News of Longview, Washington, had both stories on its front page that afternoon, but the News gave more space to a story about the arrival of computers in the classrooms of a local school district and to a story about plans for dredging from the Cowlitz River debris left over from the eruption of Mount St. Helens.

The Ledger of Lakeland, Florida, also had the Vatican and China stories on its front page the next morning but gave more prominence to a gunman's rampage in a courtroom in Orlando, not far away.

The Columbia Missourian of Columbia, Missouri, put the Vatican story on Page 5. The top story on the front page was a report on how local schools plan to improve programs. The other front-page stories, all local, included an economist's forecast of good times for local farmers and a story about conflict between city and county governments over money for bridge repairs.

Only the shooting story, among the dozens of local stories for which the three newspapers found room, rated a few seconds on the network that day.

Look at almost any day, and the pattern will be the same. What's news in Longview or Lakeland or Columbia is usually of little interest to the networks, or even to papers and stations 50 miles away. In short, there is no single, universally accepted definition of "news."

News is what newspapers print, what newscasts announce. News is made up of facts, but not every fact is news. News is usually about people, but not every person is newsworthy. News is an account of what is happening in the world, but only a tiny fraction of any day's events is ever reported.

Even trained editors assessing stories that evoke broad interest often reach sharply different conclusions about the value of such stories as news. A study published in 1983 found that over seven days 100 daily newspapers published 514 different stories. Only 11 of those stories appeared in as many as half the newspapers.

Still, there are broad areas of agreement among professional journalists about what kinds of things are most likely to be news. As a reporter, you need to know what those areas are to help you decide what is a story and what is not, what questions to ask, which facts are the most important, what to cover and what to let pass.

In this chapter you will learn:

1. The traditional criteria for judging news value that experienced reporters and editors use to determine the importance and interest of a story.
2. How the range of stories to which these criteria are applied is broadening.
3. How sources of news are changing.
4. Why accuracy and fairness are the two most important characteristics of any story.

Traditional Criteria of News Value

The traditional criteria of news value are those that generations of journalists have used to decide which sets of facts make up news stories and which stories are better than others. The most important criteria of news value, and what they mean to you as a reporter, are:

1. *Audience.* Like snowflakes, no two audiences are identical. So the same story may be of much more importance or interest to one audience than to another.
2. *Impact.* How many people the news affects and how seriously it affects them determine its importance as news. So does the extent to which the information may be useful.
3. *Proximity.* Usually, the same event is bigger news if it happens in your town than if it is 1,000 or even 10 miles away.
4. *Timeliness.* Today's news is stale tomorrow. Given the speed of broadcast reports, however, many newspapers and magazines now concentrate more on telling how and why something happened and less on telling when it happened.

5. *Prominence.* Names don't always make news. Still, thousands of Americans chop wood or ride horseback without attracting attention. When Ronald Reagan did either, it was news. He was past 70 years old and president of the United States.

6. *Unusualness.* The unusual makes news. Charles Lindbergh and Sandra Day O'Connor were news because they were first. The bizarre makes news, too. A 19th-century editor decreed that "when a dog bites a man, that's not news; but when a man bites a dog, that's news." The principle, if not the example, still applies.

7. *Conflict.* Most reporters spend most of their time covering conflict — whether wars, politics, crime or sports.

In varying proportions, these factors help reporters and editors judge the news value of a story. And the news value, in turn, determines whether a story is displayed at the top of the front page, tucked away next to the want ads or left out altogether.

AUDIENCE

One factor that weighs heavily in judgments of news value is the nature of the audience being addressed. Unlike the other criteria of news value, this one has nothing to do with the event itself; rather it is the backdrop against which reporters and editors consider questions of news value.

Details of a new federal program for the aged are more likely to make the front page of the St. Petersburg (Fla.) Times than that of the Lawrence (Kan.) Journal-World. St. Petersburg is a haven for retirees. Lawrence is a college town. Similarly, the Des Moines (Iowa) Register devotes much more reporter time and news space to agriculture than does the Miami Herald, which pays closer attention to stories of Cuban politics and personalities.

You need to keep something else in mind about your readers: Most of them probably differ substantially from you in background, interests, age, education and outlook on the world. Therefore, what seems interesting or important to you may not be viewed that way by your readers.

Newspaper readers generally are people with homes to maintain, children to educate, taxes to pay. They usually have roots in their community and obligations and interests that reflect those roots. You are likely to be younger, better educated, more liberal and less bound up with family and community. You must bridge that gap.

The strongest bridge is a keen awareness of and concern for the interests of your readers. A good rule of thumb to follow, when covering city hall or the capitol, is: People are most concerned about things that affect their lives directly. A big part of the journalist's job is figuring out what these things are and what the effects may be.

Newspapers and broadcasters alike study their audiences regularly for guidance. The most common tool used in such studies is the survey, which can reveal not only the characteristics of the people in the audience — including age, sex, education and income — but also what kinds of news these people need and want. Another research tool being used with growing frequency is the "focus group." This differs from the survey in that small groups of people are engaged in detailed discussion rather than having many people answer brief questionnaires. The two approaches can be used together to yield information that is both broad and deep.

Knowing your audience helps in weighing the other criteria.

IMPACT

The most important criterion for determining news value is impact — how many people in your audience will be affected and how directly. Let's look at the papers from Lakeland, Longview and Columbia to see how their editors judged the impact of one day's news (see Figures 1.1, 1.2 and 1.3).

Few events have the visceral impact of sudden death. That is the topic of the top story in the Lakeland Ledger. The impact of a visit from the premier of China is less immediate, but Ledger editors judged it important, probably because of its long-range implications for world peace. The same rationale may explain the nearly equal prominence given the re-establishing of full diplomatic ties with the Vatican.

Longview editors rated the China story most important, but gave major display to stories whose impact is closer to home. The dredging of a much-choked river protects important fisheries and alleviates flooding threats. Computers in the classroom will shape the future of the area's children.

Schools are especially important in a college town such as Columbia, where education is the leading industry as well as the key to the future. Columbia is surrounded by 100 miles of farmland in all directions, so the economic health of agriculture touches many lives. The same is true, of course, of taxes.

The *impact* of news, then, depends on:

1. How much of the audience is affected.
2. How direct the effect is.
3. How immediate the effect is.

Figure 1.1 Front Page of the Longview (Wash.) Daily News for January 10, 1984.

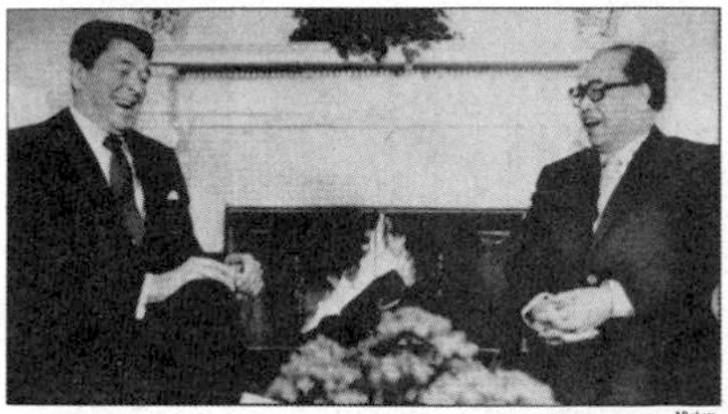

President Reagan shares a chuckle with Chinese Premier Zhao Ziyang

AP photo

Chinese premier warns of obstacles as talks begin

WASHINGTON (AP) — Chinese Premier Zhao Ziyang told President Reagan today that a continued improvement in relations between their two countries is marred by "difficulties and obstacles." He said relations have become more friendly but have been marked by "ups and downs."

Reagan, welcoming Zhao in arrival ceremonies on the South Lawn of the White House, said that while differences remain, the two countries "stand on common ground" in searching for peace and "opposing expansionism and interference" in the affairs of other nations.

Zhao, the head of government and the highest-ranking Chinese com-

Post-Mao premier: Page A3

munist official ever to visit the United States, praised the U.S.-Chinese progress in cultural, scientific, technological and economic areas.

"But it should be conceded that the growth of the Sino-U.S. relation is far below the level it should have attained," he said.

U.S. officials, who spoke about the trip on the condition they not be identified by name, played down expectations that a potent strategic alliance can soon be forged between Peking and Washington to balance the military might of the Soviet Union.

However, "I won't deny that in dealing with the Soviet Union it is helpful for them to see China and the United States cooperating, especially on the problem of Soviet expansionism," the senior U.S. official said.

In advance of his trip here, the Chinese premier announced he would not repeat Chinese insistence on an immediate halt of U.S. arms sales to Taiwan, a step apparently intended to avoid unnecessary public disputes. But the Chinese government also made known that Zhao, maintaining China's independent and non-aligned stance, did not intend to "kowtow" to Reagan administration officials.

THE DAILY NEWS

Tuesday, January 10, 1984 | Longview, Washington | 25 Cents

Corps plans more Cowlitz river dredging

By Andre Stepankowsky
The Daily News

Record November rains washed so much sediment into the Cowlitz River that the Army Corps of Engineers this morning announced a $9 million dredging project to keep Castle Rock from flooding.

However, the project to dredge 3 million cubic yards of silt only will maintain the status quo, not increase flood

Kelso, Castle Rock back flood plan: Page B1

protection. The new "emergency" work will begin in about two weeks.

John Durum, Cowlitz-Toutle river restoration coordinator for the Portland District of the Corps, said it is impossible to mobilize dredges to do more dredging than the Corps plans between now and March, the "critical" flooding period on the Cowlitz.

By the way the Corps measures flood protection, the city's dikes protect 3,000 Castle Rock residents from a 50-year storm flow — one with a one-in-50 chance of occuring annually.

Without the additional dredging, the Corps estimates that with normal rainfall, flooding odds would increase to one in 10 by March as the Toutle washes more silt into the Cowlitz. The silt fills the river's channel, reducing its capacity to carry water.

Longview and Kelso remain protected from more than a 100-year storm flow — one with a one in 100 annual odds. Lexington has slightly less than 100-year protection.

Since fall, the Corps has spent $13.1 million dredging 5 million cubic yards of silt from the Cowlitz between Horseshoe Bend and the mouth of the Toutle River.

That project was supposed to have provided 100-year protection for Castle Rock. But the Corps today said that November rains were so heavy — 200 percent of normal — that the project did not accomplish its goal, even through the Corps expanded its three dredging contracts to dredge more silt.

Also, the debris accumulated in the Cowlitz despite a $4.3 million Toutle Corps dredging project to catch some debris before it reached the Cowlitz. Castle Rock might be in a much more serious position without that work, which so far has removed 2 million cubic yards of debris.

The Corps announcement today underscores the persistence and seriousness of the problem with sediment, which comes off a massive 17-mile long deposit of debris Mount St. Helens created in the north fork of the Toutle River.

The work will be paid under a specially authorized Cowlitz-Toutle dredging project Congress passed last summer that requires the Corps to maintain 100-year protection levels. Durum said he doesn't know why more work wasn't done earlier to prevent flood protection levels from falling below that level at Castle Rock.

Bids for the work, which will involve dredging between river miles 14 and 20, will be opened next Tuesday. The Cowlitz River bridge at Castle Rock is at river mile 17.

Views of the News

By Dick Pollock
Associate Editor

Priorities ridiculous

SHAKING fists in the directon of the head man of the Corps of Engineers in Washington, D.C., has been a favorite local pastime. "Why can't they," the reasoning goes, "get their act together? There are lives at stake out here."

But is our pot calling their kettle black? We don't have our act together, either.

An agreement is needed on a way to reduce the chances of our being wiped out — quickly, by a wall of watery mud from Spirit Lake, or slowly, by sediment eroding from the Toutle Valley.

The main hang-up concerns Spirit Lake water. Should the water be kept in the Toutle River drainage, its natural place, or be diverted into the Lewis River drainage? It is possible Spirit Lake water won't "smell" right to salmon and steelhead as they approach the Lewis River where their spawning grounds and hatcheries are.

County Commissioner Walt Church, speaking for his constituents in the Woodland area, as he is expected to do, is voting against any plan that would divert the water into the Lewis.

There was a phrase in the county proposal that said it would not oppose a diversion into the Lewis if tunnels into the Toutle River are found unsafe. In other words, Commissioner Church opposes diversion into the Lewis River even if it means the Toutle Valley, Castle Rock, Lexington and so on are placed in danger. Those close to the situation in Washington, D.C., say the difference of opinion will delay a solution, maybe by a year.

If such a breakout occurs because a solution is delayed, the Cowlitz Valley would be full of mud. Railroad and highway traffic between Portland and Puget Sound could be cut off for months. Woodland, and everyone else around here, would be on a dead-end road

Please see Views, Page A2

'Terminal' health

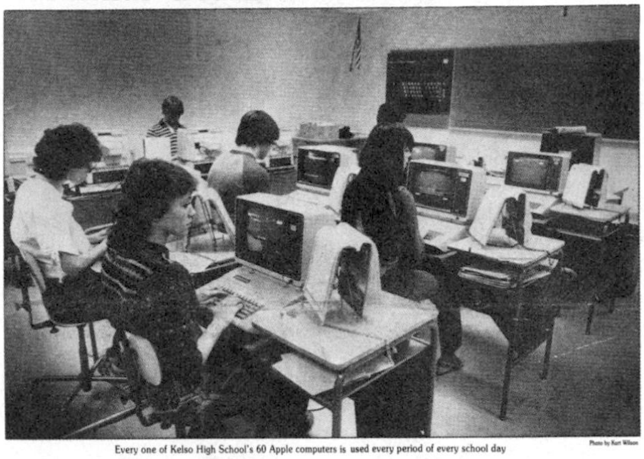

Every one of Kelso High School's 60 Apple computers is used every period of every school day

Photo by Kurt Wilson

Computers transform Kelso's typing classes

By Steve Twedt
The Daily News

Typewriting classes in Kelso High School's business and office education department have undergone a strange metamorphosis.

In rooms where typing keys once clattered, there now sit 52 Apple IIE computer terminals, glowing quietly while students almost imperceptibly glide their hands over the keyboards.

Gone is the clattering of keys, the shuffling of papers and the ring of carriage returns. They are replaced by a network of wires carrying a transfusion of energy to each computer from an unseen Corvus hard disc computer. The students, fully absorbed in the operation of the machine before them, appear connected to the machines as well.

Call this metamorphosis a case of "terminal" health.

Since September, Kelso High has pioneered one of the state's most far-reaching approaches to "keyboarding," the 1980's equivalent to Typing I.

Its innovation is not so much in its technology or even instruction. Its innovation is in its size — a total of more than 60 terminals (the department had 12 terminals from last year), serving better than 325 students during any one semester. According to school district officials, the Kelso computer-business education program is now the largest in Washington or Oregon.

That means, says Rob Fieldman, the district's director of vocational programs, that all students going through Kelso High can elect to spend a minimum of 90 hours working on a computer before they graduate.

"Where some districts would have 20 computers total, we have 60 in the business section alone. We are able to get a huge number of students exposed to this area," Fieldman said.

At a price of nearly $1,000 per machine, collecting 52 computers is nearly impossible without taking a megabyte out of a school district's budget. So Kelso, and Fieldman, asked the state superintendent's office to buy the computers to become part of the school's vocational education program. The state came through last spring and the computers arrived one week before school began.

"We felt that we were ready to move into that type of a program because we had staff that was able to teach it," Fieldman said. Meanwhile, the 70 or so electric typewriters are now being used for junior high typing classes.

So far, Kelso High's computer terminals have been used solely for keyboarding classes. But once the high school gets junior high grads with typing experience, the computers will be used for more advanced classes like accounting. A word processing course is already planned for the coming semester.

Department chairman Seppo Soderman believes the computers already have proved their worth. Students seem to be more attentive in the keyboarding classes, he said, and a greater cross section of the student body is signing up than for standard typing.

"It's OK for a macho-type person to come in and take the class now," he said. "And it's OK for those who were strictly academic before."

The students say the computers are easier to operate than typewriters and are a good preparation for careers or writing college papers.

"It seems like you can type faster," said senior Jeff Bryant.

The demand for the class is so high that three of the department's five teachers gave up their preparation period to teach an additional keyboarding class. Every computer is used every period of every class day.

The teachers, despite the extra workload, like the computers because the students' work is better (mistakes are easier to correct with the computers) and machine maintenance is less.

With typewriters, said teacher Sharon Kaighin, "the repairman was out here two days a week. It was not because of mischievous misuse. It was just wear and tear."

Also, she said, students who arrive three weeks into a semester can still catch up by using special self-teaching computer programs.

"Usually anyone who comes in that late is doomed," she said.

The students like such features as the easy-to-press keys and a mechanism that can instantly tell them their typing speed. More than that, they know the little video boxes are like having insurance, whether they eventually go into programming or simply use their computer ability as a back-up skill.

With student demand for computer classes still growing, it should not be long before the machines become as common in schools as dog-eared textbooks and dirty chalk trays. Eventually, business classes may change beyond recognition to anyone who graduated before 1975.

"I heard a student the other day say, 'Have you ever tried to type on a manual machine?' " said Kelso business teacher Bev Laulainen. "I think (the computers) spoil them a little bit. But they like it."

United States establishes full diplomatic relations with Vatican

WASHINGTON (AP) — The United States established full diplomatic relations with the Vatican today for the first time in 117 years, a decision President Reagan made after concluding that the benefits outweigh lingering Protestant opposition.

John Hughes, the State Department spokesman, said the move was made "to promote the existing mutual friendly relations" between the two and should result in "obviously better communications." He said it is effective immediately.

"We will have the same channel of communciations as 107 other countries that recognize the Vatican," he said. Hughes also said recognition was done now because it was thought "this was the appropriate time to do it."

Hughes said he didn't think public opinion was against the move.

He also argued it wouldn't violate the Constitutional separation of church and state because "for a long time we recognized the Holy See as having an international personality distinct from the Roman Catholic Church." The Holy See is responsible for the Vatican, which Hughes described as "a sovereign city state."

Pope John Paul II heads the Holy See as well as the Roman Catholic Church.

Navy chief: Punish officers who were to blame for Beirut bombing

NEW YORK (AP) — Navy Secretary John F. Lehman Jr. has recommended reprimanding officers accused of command failures that contributed to the October truck-bombing of the Marine headquarters in Lebanon, The New York Times reported today.

Disciplinary letters, though short of courts-martial, would block further advancement and be tantamount to terminating the officers' careers, the Times reported, quoting unidentified sources.

It said Lehman made the recommendation to Defense Secretary Caspar Weinberger on Monday, over the opposition of some top Navy officers and after "heated" and "intense" debate.

Lehman, touring U.S. naval operations in Europe, was in Naples, Italy, today, where a spokesman, Capt. Jimmy Finkelstein, said, "The secretary would not have any comment on it (the report)."

It was not known whether Lehman had recommended disciplinary letters for both Navy and Marine officers, or how high in the chain of command the letters might reach, the newspaper reported.

President Reagan on Dec. 27 said that if there were blame for the bombing, "it properly rests here in this office and with this president." Officials said Reagan's remarks precluded courts-martial but not disciplinary letters.

Figure 1.2 Front Page of the Lakeland (Fla.) Ledger for January 11, 1984.

AM
AT A GLANCE

LHS band cancels trip to Vienna. 1B

Wake up to the facts on yawning. 1C

Mocs turn one over to UCF. 1D

Local

Black tenants at the Redwood Apartments in Lake Alfred claim attempts to evict 13 families are racially motivated and part of continuing harassment. 1B.

Florida Commissioner of Agriculture Doyle Conner came to Lakeland Tuesday, not to inspect frostbitten oranges, but to make sure the state's push for achievement benefits both vocational and collegebound students. 1B.

Touting a successful administration as public defender, Winter Haven native Jerry Hill announced his candidacy Tuesday for state attorney of the 10th Judicial Circuit, which includes Polk, Hardee and Highlands counties. 2B.

Summary

The Supreme Court, possibly signaling a toughened stand against illegal aliens, made it easier Tuesday for the government to deport foreign citizens -- even though they have remained in the United States for a long time. 4A.

Druse leader Walid Jumblatt said Tuesday that key issues remained unresolved in the plan to separate the country's warring factions and that no agreement could be expected soon. 6A.

President Reagan said Tuesday his Task Force on Food Assistance has presented the nation with a challenge "by reminding us that in this land of plenty, there can be no excuse for hunger." 12A.

Air Florida has paid off a $33 million loan from its largest lender and is seeking a major infusion of cash from a "mystery investor" that would become the controlling shareholder, the airline's chairman said Tuesday. 4B.

Rejecting pleas from mothers of youths killed by drunken drivers, a House committee Tuesday defeated a bill to raise Florida's drinking age from 19 to 21. 8B.

Today

Wednesday, January 11, 1984 — Today is the 11th day of the year with 355 days remaining . . . On this date: In 1963, the United States and the Soviet Union began talks in New York on a possible treaty to limit nuclear tests . . . In 1770, the first rhubarb was shipped to America from London by Benjamin Franklin . . . In 1861, Alabama seceded from the Union . . . In 1913, the first sedan-type automobile, a Hudson, went on display at the 13th Automobile Show in New York City . . . And in 1964, Panama suspended diplomatic relations with the United States after clashes between Panamanian students and U.S. troops in the Canal Zone . . . Five years ago: The surgeon general said there was "overwhelming proof" that cigarette smoking causes lung cancer, heart disease and a host of other serious ailments . . . One year ago: Owner George Steinbrenner introduced Billy Martin as the new manager of the New York Yankees, proclaiming the start of a "new era for the third time." . . . NBC board chairman Grant Tinker is 58 years old. Actor Rod Taylor is 54. . . . Quote for today: "I like work. It fascinates me. I can sit and look at it for hours." — Jerome K. Jerome, English humorist (1859-1927).

Weather

Cloudy and colder with highs near 60 to mid-60s. Details, 2A.

Tip of the day

Can't get ketchup out of a new bottle? Insert a drinking straw, push to bottom and then remove. Enough air will be admitted to start the ketchup flowing.

Action Line	2C	Entertainment	9D
Astrology	7D	Legals	3C
Business	4B	Life/Style	1C
Classified	3C	Local	1B
Comics	6D, 7D	Obituaries	3C
Conversation	10D	Sports	1D
Crossword	6D	Stocks	5B
Editorial	10A	Television	8D

The Ledger

25¢

Wednesday, January 11, 1984, Lakeland, Florida, Vol. 78, No. 81

Gunman kills one in court spree

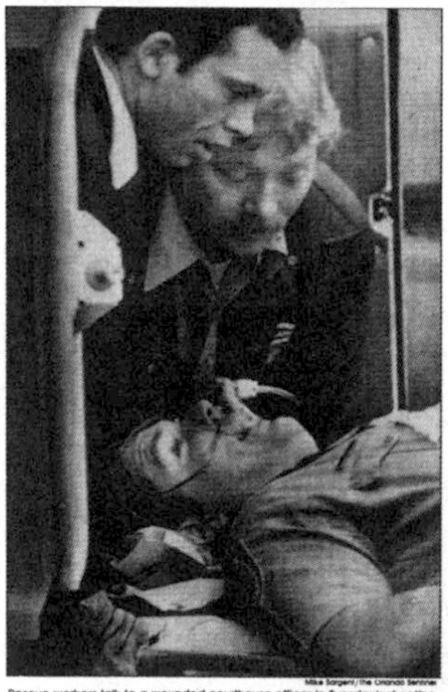

Mike Sargent/The Orlando Sentinel

Rescue workers talk to a wounded courthouse officer in Tuesday's shooting at the Orange County courthouse in downtown Orlando.

Ledger wire services

ORLANDO — Every weekday for the last three months, Thomas Provenzano went to the court clerk's office at the Orange County courthouse and asked to see the case file from his disorderly conduct arrest in August.

Every day, Provenzano, 34, would stand at the counter and slowly thumb through the file for 10 or 15 minutes, then return the folder and leave.

"We never called him by his name, because we pulled his file so much we knew the number," said Bob Wolfe, manager of the misdemeanor division of the clerk's office. "We always called him 5611."

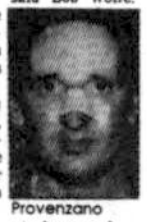

Provenzano

Provenzano was usually very calm, but he was glassy-eyed and often wore the same clothes for several days in a row.

"Something told me to keep a close eye on this guy," Wolfe said.

On Tuesday, Provenzano didn't go to the court clerk's office. He was scheduled to stand trial, and the clerk's office sent his case file to a judge's office on the fourth floor of the courthouse.

Just before 10:30 a.m., workers in the first-floor clerk's office heard several gunshots. Wolfe said the first thing they thought about was Provenzano.

"Two of my girls stood up when they heard the shots," Wolfe said. "All they said was, 'That had to be 5611.'"

Police said Provenzano, carrying three firearms, shot and killed a bailiff and seriously wounded another bailiff and a corrections officer before being wounded himself.

Police said they had no idea why.

They said Provenzano was waiting to be arraigned when the shooting erupted at mid-morning in the crowded courthouse.

Sheriff Lawson Lamar called the shooting "obviously premeditated" but said he was "not going to speculate on a motive at this time."

County Judge Lee Conser told reporters he believed he was Provenzano's intended target.

One of the court officers, William Arnold Wilkerson, 60, was killed by a shotgun blast in the hallway outside the courtroom. The other two, bailiff Harry Dalton, 53, and county corrections officer Mark Parker, 19, were reported in critical condition with head wounds.

Provenzano was reported in stable condition with a gunshot to the chest.

See Court on Page 8A

Polk County courthouses 'vulnerable'

By Paul Saltzman
The Ledger

BARTOW — Tuesday's shooting spree at the Orange County courthouse has Polk County court officials worried about a repeat here.

"One of the things that always troubles us when something like this happens is the copycat thing," said William A. Norris Jr., chief judge for the 10th Circuit Court.

"We have vulnerability, yes," said Frank Hustin, who supervises the 20 bailiffs who provide security at the three courthouses spread around downtown Bartow.

Tuesday morning, the Orange County Sheriff's Department said Thomas H. Provenzano, 34, a Winter Park man being arraigned on two misdemeanor charges of resisting arrest, grabbed a bailiff's gun and opened fire in an Orlando courtroom, killing one.

Little security exists at the Bartow courts to stop a similar shooting, Norris and Hustin said, though neither could recall any courtroom violence in the past 11 years but for minor scuffles.

See 'It on Page 8A

Vatican, U.S. seal full ties

By R. Gregory Nokes
The Associated Press

WASHINGTON — The United States and the Vatican established full diplomatic relations Tuesday after a break of 117 years, a move the State Department said should bring "obviously better communications" between Washington and the headquarters of the Roman Catholic Church.

President Reagan's decision, reflecting his eagerness to bolster his administration's standing with the Catholic hierarchy under Pope John Paul II, encountered considerably milder opposition from Protestant circles than when similar moves were attempted in the past.

Reagan nominated William Wilson, an old friend and California real estate developer, to be ambassador to the Vatican, subject to Senate confirmation. Wilson has been Reagan's personal representative to the Vatican since 1981.

See Protestant on Page 8A

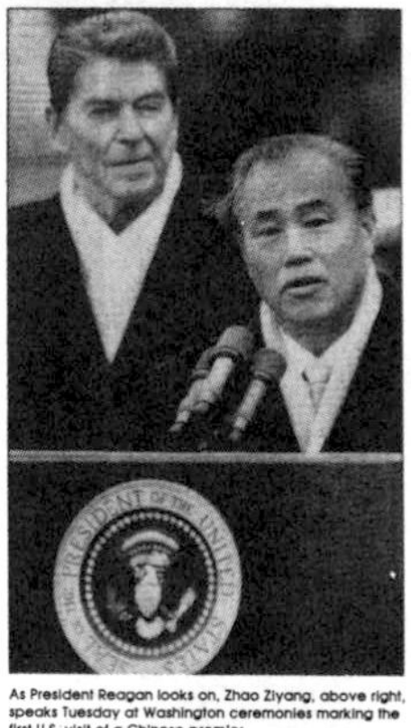

As President Reagan looks on, Zhao Ziyang, above right, speaks Tuesday at Washington ceremonies marking the first U.S. visit of a Chinese premier.

Taiwan issue lurks behind China talks

By Michael Putzel
The Associated Press

WASHINGTON — President Reagan said Tuesday the United States and China "stand on common ground" in the quest for peace and opposition to Soviet expansionism, but Premier Zhao Ziyang says the relationship "is far below the level it should have attained."

After welcoming Zhao to the White House, Reagan and China's highest ranking official met in private for a two-hour discussion that U.S. officials said was dominated by the sensitive issue of U.S. support for Taiwan.

A senior American official, who briefed reporters only on the condition that he not be identified, said Reagan "was candid about the fact that we take seriously the question of commitments to old friends."

"We would be kidding ourselves if we think that this issue was ever going to simply disappear," the official added.

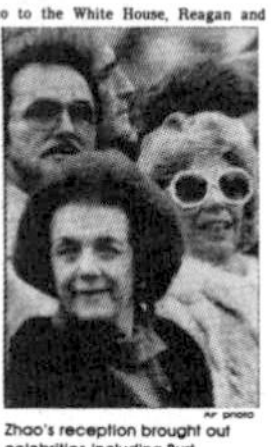

AP photo

Zhao's reception brought out celebrities including Burt Reynolds, Gregory Peck and Dinah Shore.

Although the United States has withdrawn diplomatic recognition of Taiwan as the legitimate government of the Chinese mainland, it has continued to supply arms to the Nationalist-ruled island while insisting that its future be determined peacefully, with the participation of both China and Taiwan.

The Chinese consider the continuing U.S. role in Taiwan to be direct interference in their internal affairs.

Reagan nonetheless sought to stress areas where the two leaders could agree. Zhao, the first Chinese premier ever to visit the United States, said there had been "ups and downs" in relations between Washington and Peking and that "difficulties and obstacles' still exist.

On Zhao's arrival for three days of talks, Reagan acknowledged that "differences between our two countries" exist, but assured his guest that "we stand ready to nurture, develop and build upon the many areas of accord to strengthen the ties between us."

"We stand on common ground in opposing expansionism and interference in the affairs of independent states," Reagan said.

The U.S. briefing official said Reagan and Zhao also discussed the Soviet military buildup in the Far East, Moscow's involvement in Cambodia and the Soviet occupation of Afghanistan.

See China on Page 8A

Kissinger campaigning for himself

Analysis

By James McCartney
Knight News Service

WASHINGTON — The Kissinger commission report on Central America, now thoroughly leaked to the press, is a blueprint for a stronger U.S. commitment and deeper U.S. involvement in the region.

It is probably pretty close to what President Reagan was hoping for last July when the commission was appointed — a detailed rationale and argument for the hard-line anti-communist policy he has pursued for three years.

But the report, to be made public formally today, also may be one of the longest, and most ambitious, job application letters of all time — for Henry Kissinger.

Many of Kissinger's friends (such as former White House national security adviser Brent Scowcroft) as well as his enemies (such as biographer Seymour Hersh) believe that Kissinger has used

See Kissinger on Page 8A

Also watching as the U.S. and China try to strengthen their relations was Soviet Ambassador to the U.S. Anatoliy Dobrynin, at right. Reagan alluded to the Soviets when he said China and the U.S. "stand on common ground in opposing interference in the affairs of independent states."

AP photos

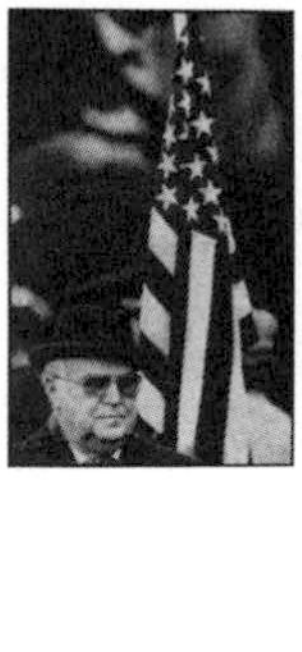

Plane facts

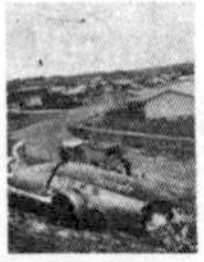

A Canadian owned DC-3 cargo plane crashed into an embankment along Interstate 70 Tuesday night, only narrowly missing homes in a St. Louis suburb. Both the pilot and copilot were hospitalized after the crash. FAA offcials are still investigating. See page 16A.

Cookie scouts

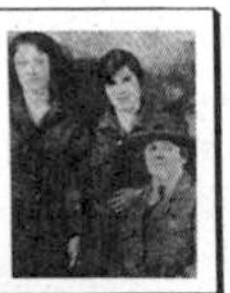

Girl Scout cookies have been around almost since Juliette Low first founded the Girl Scouts in 1912. Anticipating new stockpiles of the tasty morsels, some former scouts have compiled their favorite dessert recipies that put the flavorful cookies to work. See page 1B.

Reunion

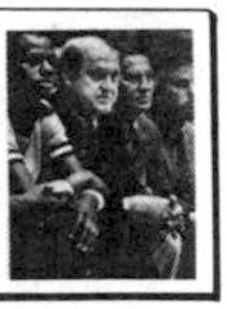

It will be a reunion of sorts for Missouri basketball coach Norm Stewart when the Tigers play Northern Iowa tonight. Stewart, who has won more than 400 games during his career, broke into collegiate coaching with Northern Iowa. See Page 7A.

Columbia Missourian 75

1908-83

76th Year — No. 101 | Good Morning! It's Wednesday, January 11, 1984 | 8 Sections — 50 Pages — 25 Cents

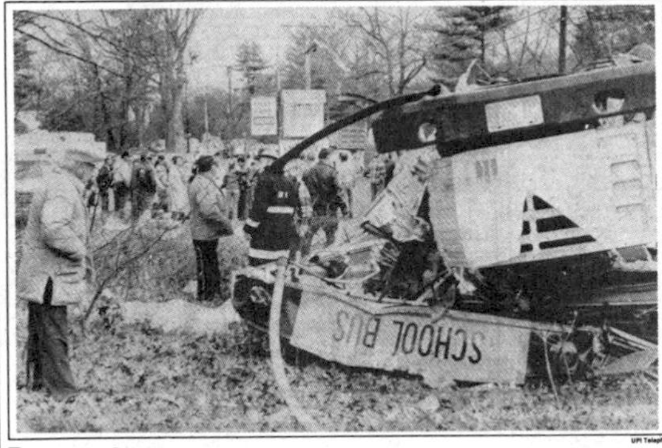

UPI Telephoto

Bus tragedy A collision between a tractor-trailer truck and a kindergarten school bus in Rehoboth, Mass., left both drivers dead and 15 youngsters injured, two seriously. The truck skidded into the path of the bus, flipping the two vehicles into a field.

Columbia schools seek to strengthen programs, policies

By Lydia Locklin
Missourian staff writer

In the wake of national criticism aimed at public education, the Columbia public school system has decided to address some of its shortcomings.

The Board of Education is eyeing a proposed list of new and extended programs that many say will strengthen the school system. The suggestions encompass everything from increased graduation requirements to a pre-hiring exam for prospective teachers.

Superintendent Russell Thompson discussed the proposed changes during Monday's board meeting. Some were picked from "A Nation At Risk," the National Commission on Excellence in Education's report on the sad state of public education in America.

Thompson said the school program is scrutinized yearly for improvements, but the review this year was more intense because of the derogatory national report. When the national report was released last spring, Columbia school officials initiated a rash of meetings, polls and panel discussions on the state of local education.

"You have to be aware that you don't throw the baby out with the bath," Thompson cautioned board members. The important end of any improvement is what happens in the classroom — not the improvement itself, he said.

First on the list were tougher local high school graduation requirements. Current requirements call for 3 units English, 2 social studies, 1 math, 1 science, 1 fine arts, 1 practical arts, 1.5 physical education and 10.5 electives. The new plan would remove three units of electives and dole them among mathematics, science and social studies.

"This is a reasonable goal," Thompson said. "It does obviously cut down on the amount of electives they can take."

At least one teacher of a music course — one of the electives that could lose a few students due to the change — doesn't mind. Rich Hadfield, Rock Bridge High School's band director, said there are enough electives to go around.

"We're talking about three electives in the course of four years," he said of the units that will be lost under the new system.

It won't hurt enrollment, he said. "It's going to make a student a lot more selective about his electives."

The call for tougher graduation requirements stems from a nationwide trend of falling standardized test scores among college bound high school seniors. Although Columbia students' scores were above average, nationwide SAT and ACT averages have fallen 43 points and .7 points in the last 10 years.

Graduation requirements could be toughened immediately, said Eliot Battle, director of pupil personnel services. But the improvements are only suggestions — they must endure months of scrutiny before any decisions are made.

Thompson said the board should act on a portion of the recommendations within 60 days.

Some of the recommendations will be a problem to carry out due to money shortages.

The sixth grade computer pro-

See STUDY, Page 20A

City may seek county money for bridges

By Nancy Gingrich and Tammy Resler
Missourian staff writers

INSIGHT

The City of Columbia will have to bridge a communication gap if it hopes to get a share of funds earmarked for repairing spans in Boone County.

Funds for bridge repair in the county were generated through a $7.5 million county bond issue approved by voters in 1979. The city would like to use some of the remaining $1.3 million to repair bridges within the city limits. The only problem is that the city has never bothered formally to request a share of the funds.

"How do you respond without someone asking?" Boone County Southern District Judge Kay Roberts wonders.

Besides, the county's bond issue doesn't include the city, Roberts says. So there are no guarantees that the request will be approved if the city does ask the county for money. When the bond issue was first discussed, the county asked the city to see if it wished to estimate the amount it needed for repairs and to be included. The city declined, she says, so the $7.5 million figure did not include money needed for city bridge repairs.

County Public Works Director Bob Hagerty agrees with Roberts that the bond issue was intended primarily for rural bridges. Bond issues passed by voters only can be used for the stated purpose, Hagerty says. Therefore, public hearings would need to be held before the city could use county funds.

"I'm sure the public would feel if the money is there then they (the city) should use it," he says. "Of course, that's speculation on my part."

The bridge improvement question on the 1979 ballot states that the funds were to be used for repair of county bridges. It does not specify that the funds were to be used only on rural county bridges outside the city limits.

City officials think the 1979 bond issue definitely includes the city, whose citizens pay approximately 65 percent of all Boone County property taxes. The county cannot exclude the city from matters concerning Boone County as a whole.

"I think some elected officials are confused about Columbia and Boone County being one and the same," Fourth Ward Councilman Pat Barnes says.

Boone County residents who happen to live within the city limits, therefore, are taxed twice for bridge repairs in Columbia, Barnes says. In addition to paying their share of the Boone County bridge bond issue, Columbians also are paying taxes toward a $6.37 million city bond issue passed in April 1982 to repair streets and bridges within the city limits.

This bond issue was only for designated streets and bridges, however, and does not settle the question of county funds being used for repairs within the city limits.

Barnes brought up the issue of county funding for bridge repairs inside the city limits at the Dec. 19 City Council meeting. The council was discussing proposed reconstruction of the bridge on Rock Quarry Road over Hinkson Creek. Barnes directed the city staff to approach the county about funding the repairs even though the 1982 city bond issue specifically targets the Rock Quarry bridge as one for repair.

"I've raised the question several times," Barnes says, "but not seriously." No directive was issued previously to the staff to seek county funds, he says. But the city's public works director, Ray Beck, says he now intends to approach the county regarding the Rock Quarry bridge repair.

The city staff has proposed that Rock Quarry Road be straightened and widened and the 50-year bridge spanning Hinkson Creek be rebuilt. Beck said the bridge now only allows vehicles of five tons or less to cross and is unsafe for heavy emergency vehicles and full school buses. Fire trucks also have had to circumvent the bridge when answering some calls in the area.

Opponents of the proposed realignment say it would damage the Grindstone Nature Area. Citizens living in the area pointed out at the Dec. 19 meeting that the city could not show statistics of accidents on the bridge and asked that the bridge be rebuilt without the major realignment proposed by the city.

Barnes sees no reason why the left-over funds from the county bond issue could not be used on the city bridges, including Rock Quarry. "The funds are sitting dormant and not being used for anything," he says.

Originally a three-year project, the county bond issue was passed to repair 69 span bridges and 35 culverts in Boone County. Seventy span bridges have been completed, Hagerty says.

Half a million of the left-over funds was switched to a debt-reduction fund to pay off the bonds sooner, Boone County Treasurer Kay Murray says. Because an additional $1.3 million is still in the fund, the project was expanded to include 125 more culverts. Ninety culverts now are finished with the rest to be completed within the next three years.

Missourians reported in favor of tax increases

By Gunilla Faringer
Missourian staff writer

While the the Missouri Legislature is wrestling with the state's declining finances and its own unwillingness to raise taxes, there is evidence that a slight majority of Missourians are in favor of increased taxes.

Nine times in the last 10 years, Missourians have voted on statewide tax and financial issues. In those nine referenda, the median vote — or mid-point of the results of the nine referenda — was 51 percent in favor of higher taxes. The figures come from an study conducted by two University faculty members.

The study, an investigation into attitudes toward tax actions in Missouri, was conducted by David Leuthold, professor in political science, and John Ballard, state specialist in governmental affairs. The finding of the median 51 percent vote for higher taxes was based on referenda in which Missouri voters five times voted for higher taxes or authorization of bond sales, while on four occasions they voted against.

Concerning city and county sales tax votes, more than three-quarters of these elections statewide resulted in voter approval since such taxes were authorized in 1969. Surveys have confirmed the public's positive attitudes toward sales taxes, which are regarded as fair and desirable, because everybody pays the same rate. On the other hand, many political leaders regard the sales tax as regressive and inappropriate, the academics' report says.

Analysis of statewide election results also shows public support for earmarked taxes. Programs receiving tax funding have included conservation and environment, education and industrial and economic

See EDUCATORS, Page 20A

Economist predicts good year for local farmers

By Chris Fennewald
Missourian staff writer

It looks to be a flip-flop year for Missouri crop and livestock farmers. Consider:

Prospects for agriculture appear fair for the first half of the year, but murky for the second half.

The first six months should be good ones for crop farmers, but bad ones for livestock producers. That prognosis could reverse during the second six months.

But according to Harold Breimyer, University extension economist, Missouri farmers can look forward to some year-long good news. They should be getting higher prices than the national average for both grains and livestock.

Glen Grimes, also a University extension economist, said central Missouri farmers usually receive prices a little higher than the national average.

"We have the potential for better hog and possibly better cattle prices," Grimes said.

According to Breimyer, the first-half outlook will be influenced by a combination of the effects of the Payment-in-Kind (PIK) program and the 1983 drought. Both PIK and the drought cut back yields of fall-harvested crops and boosted their price.

For the second half of the year, the size of plantings and prospects for the year's crops will dominate the price picture.

"The fear in farming circles," Breimyer said, "is that producers of corn, sorghum, and soybeans will over-respond to the improved prices of this winter and plant 'fencerow to fencerow,' but we have no survey data on just how many farmers feel that way."

If that happens, increased supply will cause prices to drift downward. Two of the crops, corn and soybeans, are important commodities for Missouri farmers.

Grimes said nationally there will be an estimated 7.8 billion bushels of corn on hand in 1984 with a price of $2.65 per bushel. The soybean crop is estimated to be 2.2 billion bushels giving an estimated price of $6.60 per bushel, and the wheat crop is estimated at 2.45 billion bushels with a average estimated price per bushel of $3.35.

Bushel estimates are based on the 1984 production year. Price estimates are based on each crop's marketing year. The marketing year for wheat is June 1 to May 31; for soybeans, Sept. 1 to Aug. 31; and for corn, Oct. 1 to Sept. 30.

In the first half of 1984, wheat will be abundant. There is potential for a adequate carryover stock of 1.4 billion bushels of wheat nationally in 1984, said Grimes.

Feed grains and soybeans, however, will be in shorter supply and thus higher priced than a year before, said Breimyer. He also noted that feeding margins for cattle and hogs will likely remain favorable for a number of months.

"Government programs probably will not do a great deal to reduce crop acreages in 1984," said Breimyer. "After the costly 1983 experience, the 1984 programs are modest. Moreover, direct government payments are unlikely to supplement farmers' incomes as much in 1984 as they did in 1983."

In fitting the livestock forecast in with the Missouri livestock scene, Grimes said hog prices will not be as good as a year ago in the first quarter of '84 and will only equal 1983 prices in the second quarter. It is in the final two quarters of the year when hog prices will be much better than in 1983.

"Here, the weather and the number of sows bred will be determing factors," said Grimes.

For Missouri feeder cattle, Grimes said prices in the first half of 1984 will do as well as last year. For the second half of 1984, farm operators should look for prices to be better than the same half of 1983 if they have normal weather, said Grimes.

"The biggest risk is what the weather will do," he said. "If it will be normal, (Missouri) farmers will have a better year than in 1983. But it doesn't look like a record year."

Figure 1.3 Front Page of the Columbia Missourian for January 11, 1984.

Figure 1.4 Proximity. Renovation of the Ritz-Carlton Hotel in Boston was important news there, but it wouldn't be newsworthy anywhere else.

PROXIMITY

The health of Columbia, Mo., schools has little interest for readers in Longview, Wash. Similarly, it is a safe bet that few people in Lakeland, Fla., ever heard of the Cowlitz River. They are unlikely to care whether it is dredged. Even the shooting spree in Florida, though it made the network news, rated only Page 3 in Columbia and got no mention in Longview.

But local news isn't necessarily the most important news. War in the Middle East, for example, is a bigger story than many things that happen in the Midwest, even for a paper in Columbia. Its impact, immediate and potential, is great. In the case of events of similar magnitude, however, the closer they are, the more newsworthy they are likely to be.

Proximity is less important than impact in determining news value, but it means that:

1. Among stories of roughly equal importance, the one nearest your audience is the most newsworthy.
2. Some stories are of interest and news value only in the community in which they occur.

TIMELINESS

Look at the first paragraph of the story about the Chinese premier as it appeared in Longview.

WASHINGTON (AP) — Chinese
Premier Zhao Ziyang told President
Reagan today...

The Daily News, an afternoon paper, tries to get that word "today" into every possible story.

The papers in Lakeland and Columbia are published in the morning. That may mean that readers already have heard a story, even if just in bulletin form, the night before. So the time element is less important. Notice the shooting story in the Ledger, for example. Only in the sixth paragraph is the day of the event mentioned.

With news, the fresher the better. Reporters and editors, newspapers and broadcast stations, compete to be first with a big story. Much of the material on this morning's front page or on the evening news will rate only brief mention, or none at all, as different events capture the eye and the imagination tomorrow.

Timeliness isn't everything, though. No print reporter can hope to compete with broadcast colleagues in sheer speed. If an event is important enough, the broadcaster can be on the air with it in minutes. Tomorrow's newspaper won't be out until tomorrow.

So newspaper and magazine journalists have come to concentrate less on the "when" of a story and more on the "why" and "how." Though they still want to cover the story in the next day's or next week's issue, these reporters and editors look less at the clock and more at the content. Often, both print and broadcast journalists will report as many details of an event as possible under the pressures of the clock, and then — a few hours or days later — return with a *backgrounder*, analysis that puts those details in context and explains what they mean.

Some good stories have little or no time element. Look, for instance, at the "Insight" story on our page from the Missourian.

The City of Columbia will have to
bridge a communication gap if it
hopes to get a share of funds earmarked for repairing spans in Boone
County.

The issue is continuing. It was important yesterday and will be tomorrow. Indeed, many of the most important issues in any day's news are perennial — war and peace, life and death, wealth and poverty, East and West.

Even some stories that could and should have been timely retain their impact when belatedly reported. One of the most famous and most important stories of the Vietnam war era — the story of the massacre of civilians at the village of My Lai — was not written until a year after it happened. Details of secret FBI files on President

Salem Academy and College
Gramley Library
Winston-Salem, N.C. 27108

John F. Kennedy got, and deserved, front-page headlines when they were released in 1983, 20 years after his death.

Timeliness means that:

1. Your audience wants and needs its news as quickly as possible.
2. Sheer speed, however, often is less important than thoroughness and explanation.
3. The time to tell a good story is as soon as you can, whether that is five minutes or five years after it happens.

PROMINENCE

"Names makes news," goes the cliché. Well, sometimes they do. Even when they don't, editors go to considerable lengths to get them, and the faces that go with them, into the paper or onto the screen. Many newspapers print names-if-not-news columns under a variety of titles, such as "People in the News." The doings, even though inconsequential, of film stars, rock singers or the widow of former President Kennedy are of interest to many readers because the names are known.

The same presumed interest fuels gossip columns and most of what passes for reporting from Hollywood. Dozens of magazines and weekly tabloids are devoted to satisfying that interest and little else.

Still, it indisputably is news when a university president is arrested for drunken driving or a famous singer dies or a presidential contender is divorced. Most people are interested in the private lives of public figures.

Often it can be argued, and sometimes demonstrated, that a weakness for whiskey, say, or the love of money affects a person's public as well as private life. In recent years the latter has proved the undoing of a half-dozen congressmen caught in the FBI's Abscam investigation, as well as a vice president of the United States.

But difficult questions for journalists arise when the connections between private acts and public prominence are not so clear. For example, is a public official's drinking problem news if there is no evidence that it has interfered with his or her work? Traditionally the answer of most reporters has been no. Increasingly, however, the answer is changing because private vices may sometimes provide useful insights into the character of public figures.

To take another example, suppose you learn that the mayor of your town is a homosexual. Is that a story? Many journalists would argue that it is not. But suppose that his preference is for boys under the age of 12. That becomes a more difficult issue to resolve.

To sum up, *prominence* usually adds news value because:

Figure 1.5 Prominence.
Woody Allen is a
celebrity, so his
activities attract
reporters—and readers.

1. Many people, including many journalists, are keenly interested in the offstage lives of public figures.
2. The unofficial actions, whether praiseworthy or deplorable, of public officials often yield insight into their character.

UNUSUALNESS

The first flight to the moon was big news. So was Sandra Day O'Connor's appointment as the first woman justice of the Supreme Court. Neither had ever been done before. The last voyage of the ocean liner Queen Elizabeth was big news, too. It would never be done again.

"Firsts," "lasts" and "onlys" have been staples of newspapers since the 19th century. So have stories of freak occurrences and scientific — or pseudoscientific — phenomena. The National Enquirer, the biggest-selling weekly in America, fills its pages with such tales. But it was not the National Enquirer that sponsored the expedition in search of the fabled Loch Ness monster. It was The New York Times.

The Times, the National Enquirer and the country weekly that prints a photograph of a locally grown turnip bearing a resemblance to Winston Churchill are all motivated by the same compelling force

Figure 1.6 Unusualness.
When two American astronauts were the first to float freely in space in February 1984, the uniqueness of the event made it newsworthy.

— winning and maintaining readership. A daily diet of crisis, corruption and conflict demands leavening with a little entertainment. Oddity is a part of the human experience, just as tragedy is.

There is an element of the unusual in nearly every newsworthy event. Indeed, one definition of news might be "a deviation from the usual."

There is no story of man biting dog on any of our front pages, but there is a picture of an upside-down school bus in the Missourian and a shooting victim on the floor of a courtroom in the Ledger. Both pictures have emotional impact, at least in part because the scenes are unexpected.

Thus, *unusualness* makes news because:

1. Unusual or unexpected events capture the imagination, provide a moment's diversion and lighten the gloom of much of the rest of the day's news.
2. Strange events and people are part of life. Only the bounds of good taste should limit journalists' efforts to describe fully and fairly the world around them.

CONFLICT

Nearly every story in each of the three front pages is a story of conflict. The shooting in Florida is the most graphic example. Other stories tell of more complex, but not less real, conflict. The stories about the Chinese premier's arrival, for example, stress the disagreements between the two nations and the size of the stakes in the talks to come. In the Missourian, local school officials are responding to national criticism of education, a continuing source of conflict. City and county governments are arguing over money, another recurring theme.

Conflict is a central feature of most news. Sometimes it is physical, as in war or sports. Sometimes it is more subtle or sophisticated. Political conflict falls into this category, though it may lead to physical struggle. Social and economic conflict may also produce bloodshed, though most often they too are fought with words.

But if conflict makes news, it also raises great problems for journalists. One of the most common and best-founded criticisms of American journalists is that we try to report too many stories as simple, straightforward tales of conflict. Journalists often are accused of operating with a "police beat" or "sports page" mentality — categorizing the good guys and the bad guys, insisting that every conflict has a winner and a loser. Too often we are guilty as charged.

One of the most important functions of journalists in a democratic society is to make complex events understandable. Reporters must translate jargon into standard English and try to get at real causes and real effects. The pursuit of this unquestionably worthy goal can, however, produce questionable results.

Look, for example, at the stories of the Chinese premier's visit. In the Daily News, the restrictions of space force the treatment of tangled issues and complicated history in far too few words to produce real understanding. The Ledger story comes closer to capturing the complexities involved.

Often, the most important stories of conflict are also the most complex. Often, it is difficult to know even what the real questions are. The answers usually are far from simple. Sometimes there aren't any answers, or none we can discover.

It is vital, then, that you seek to understand the nature of the conflict you are covering. It almost certainly is more complicated than is apparent at first glance. It is vital, too, that you avoid oversimplification while seeking clarity. Clarity leads to understanding; oversimplification makes understanding impossible.

Conflict is a quality of news that must be handled carefully because:

1. It is present, sometimes in subtle forms, in most important news.
2. Its true causes and most likely effects often are unclear even to the participants. When the combatants know what they are fighting over, they may seek to keep the issues obscured.
3. Right is seldom on only one side — and may not be on either.
4. Even after the battle is over — if it ever ends — it isn't always possible to tell who won. Sometimes nobody does.

Changing Standards of News Value

These traditional criteria for judging what is news and what isn't continue to be applied by print and broadcast journalists alike, but the range of issues and events to which the criteria are applied is broadening significantly. Creed Black, then president of the American Society of Newspaper Editors, wrote in 1983:

> If we can believe what we tell each other at our seminars and conventions, most American editors now agree that "news" is no longer just an account of what has happened since yesterday's paper was published. Underlying trends, particularly in the area of social changes, also claim and deserve our attention....
>
> Most of us would also agree, however, that we don't do as well as we should in identifying and reporting these trends. The traditional patterns of covering and editing the news are strong, and old habits take time to break.

Black was writing an introduction to a study of newspaper coverage of women's issues. The study, conducted at George Washington University, offers some suggestions that are likely to be increasingly important for journalists trying to keep up with society's changes. The suggestions include these three:

1. Human news, emerging social issues that affect the lives of many, must be defined as newsworthy.
2. The effect of change, of new or proposed laws, of court decisions, on the daily lives of readers should be part of the new definitions of news. Such stories need explaining, telling readers how they will be affected, as well as how society will be affected.
3. Sensitivity must be developed on issues and problems that may not interest an editor or reporter but may be of great interest, even assistance, to readers.

An even more influential study, first reported in 1979 and updated in 1984, shows both change and continuity in the needs of
readers and the demands on journalists. "Changing Needs of Changing Readers" was both its title and its substance. Its author was
Ruth Clark. Its findings have helped shape the content of hundreds
of newspapers. The 1979 report emphasized the importance to readers of the quality, the style, of their lives. Lifestyle journalism, already an important part of most newspapers, became even more
popular. One of the new favorites was the how-to-cope story, intended to help readers with everything from buying a new car to
handling stress. A flood of consumer stories has appeared, with
such topics as developments in health care, changes in tax laws and
information about the quality of goods and services. Another staple
of lifestyle journalism is the examination of people's lives, celebrities and ordinary people alike, in search of insights to illuminate the
human condition.

Many critics worried that these "soft" stories were crowding
"real" news out of newspapers and off the air. What the critics
failed to see was that lifestyle stories, while often lacking the conflict and immediacy of more traditional journalism, usually possess
the most important quality of news — impact.

Five years later, Ruth Clark was suggesting that the changing
readers had changed again. The emphasis on self-fulfillment that
characterized the 1970s is giving way, she reported, to a greater concern with the world outside, as the Americans of the 1980s realize
that neither resources nor opportunity is unlimited. Readers of the
1980s seem less interested in advice columns and entertainment,
more interested in "hard" news. But what kind of hard news? Certainly not just the simple accounts of what happened yesterday,
which often can be provided more quickly and conveniently by radio
or television. Clark sees new interest among newspaper readers in
such topics as economics, local government and international affairs — "news that helps them understand the world they live in." In
other words, news with impact.

A 1982 survey conducted for the Newspaper Readership Project
supports Clark's assessment. Asked what they usually read or look
at in the paper, 89 percent of newspaper readers questioned replied
"news about the local community." Ranking second, with 86 percent, was news about the economy. Third, with 84 percent, was
world news. Then came news about local politics or government, 74
percent; the calendar of local events, 61 percent; obituaries, 53 percent; and sports news about local schools, colleges or clubs, 51 percent.

It seems a good guess, then, that despite shifts in emphasis, the
audiences of the next 10 years will be demanding of journalists in-

sightful stories about social trends and explanatory stories about grocery prices, stories that clarify the politics of Central America and the politics of the city council, stories built on hard fact and told in human terms. Reporters and editors in 1990 probably will be applying much the same criteria of news value that their predecessors of 1970 and 1950 used, but they'll be applying those criteria to more complex issues.

Another good guess is that the journalists of 1990 will have to be better educated and better trained than their predecessors, able to dig more deeply and write more compellingly, if the changing needs of changing readers (and viewers and listeners) are to be met.

Changing Sources of News

As the traditional subjects of news are changing and broadening, so are the traditional sources of news.

The main traditional sources of news are people who are close to the centers of power in society — government officials, business leaders and the advisers, aides and public-relations functionaries who surround them. Most reporters still spend most of their time dealing with people who hold and exercise power — whether governmental power, political power or business power. The sought-after assignments still are those requiring reporting on the power centers with direct impact on a widespread audience — the White House, the state capitol, city hall, the school board, business and labor.

All of these power centers are what might be called "official" sources. All of them are part of the formal power structure of society. Official sources wield power — and influence lives — because of their positions as elected or appointed public officeholders or as controllers of economic power.

As journalists' ideas of what makes up news have broadened, the range of important sources has expanded, too. We have come to realize that many of the forces with greatest impact on audiences, and on us, are outside the formal power structure.

The civil rights movement that captured public attention in the early 1960s probably forced the dawning of that realization. Martin Luther King Jr., Stokely Carmichael, H. Rap Brown, Medgar Evers, Ralph Abernathy — men who held neither public office nor corporate positions — dominated the news and changed the nation. Since then Americans have witnessed the black power movement, the youth movement, the women's movement, the consumer movement, the environmental movement, the anti-nuclear movement. The stories of these social forces meet most of the traditional standards of news value. Conflict is clear, oddity and prominence are common, nothing could be more timely or proximate. Impact is staggering.

But the sources are different. Government and business officials cannot tell these stories. Indeed, the institutions they represent are often opposed to the new newsmakers. So if reporters are to tell nontraditional stories, they must find and evaluate nontraditional sources. The George Washington University study referred to previously offers some guidelines that can be applied to reporting on any topic.

1. Take the time to read current, authoritative publications in the field. Finding these is much easier than it used to be since computerized data bases have become easily accessible. (See Chapter 2 for further details.) Any university library, many public libraries and a growing number of news organizations offer almost instantaneous computer searches of comprehensive indexes, usually with experts available to help you and usually for only a small fee.

2. Make sure human sources are qualified and reliable. The publications often will suggest some experts you can interview. With other people, especially those who present themselves as spokesmen, ask about their credentials and their experience.

3. Look for equally qualified sources on all sides of the issue you're exploring. Perhaps the best-known and most-quoted opponent of the Equal Rights Amendment is Phyllis Schlafly. But is she really as qualified as, for example, former Rep. Martha Griffiths, chief sponsor of the amendment in the House of Representatives?

4. The more tangled and emotional the issue, the more important it becomes to try to get behind rhetoric to fact. Simple reporting of charge and countercharge, which most journalists once saw as their role, is giving way to a search for the substance of the arguments.

5. False and misleading statements should be analyzed and exposed for what they are. That rule applies to statements of presidents of the United States, corporation heads and citizen activists alike.

The best journalists already are applying these guidelines.

Accuracy and Fairness

The goal that the guidelines are intended to help bring within reach has seldom been expressed any better than in a phrase used by Bob Woodward of The Washington Post. Woodward was defending in court an investigative story published by the Post. The story, he said, was "the best obtainable version of the truth."

A grander-sounding goal would be "the truth," unmodified. But Woodward's phrase, while paying homage to the ideal, recognizes the realities of life and the limitations of journalism. After centuries of argument, philosophers and theologians have been unable to agree on just what truth is. Even if there were agreement on that basic question, how likely is it that Phyllis Schlafly and Martha Griffiths would agree on the "truth" about the ERA, or that the Catholic Church and the Planned Parenthood organization would agree on the "truth" about abortion, or that Ronald Reagan and Walter F. Mondale would agree on the "truth" about the state of the American economy?

In American daily journalism, that kind of dispute is left to be fought out among the partisans on all sides, on the editorial pages and in commentaries. The reporter's usual role is simply to find and write the facts. The trouble is, that turns out often to be not so simple.

Sometimes, it's hard to get the facts. The committee searching for a new university president announces that the field of candidates has been narrowed to five, but the names of the five are not released. Committee members are sworn to secrecy. What can you do to get the names? Should you try?

Sometimes, it's hard to tell what the facts mean. The state supreme court refuses to hear a case in which legislators are questioning the constitutionality of a state spending limit. The court says only that there is no "justiciable controversy." What does that mean? Who won? Is the ruling good news or bad news, and for whom?

Sometimes, it's even hard to tell what is a fact. A presidential commission, after a year-long study, says there is no widespread hunger in America. Is the conclusion a fact? Or is the fact only that the commission said it? And how can you determine whether the commission is correct?

Daily journalism presents still more complications. Usually, as a reporter you have only a few hours, at most a few days, to try to learn as many facts as possible. Then, even in such a limited time, you may accumulate information enough for a story of 2,000 words, only to be told that there is space or time enough for 1,000 or fewer.

When you take into account all these realities and limitations, you can see that just to reach the best obtainable version of the truth is challenge enough for any journalist.

How can you tell when the goal has been reached? Seldom, if ever, is there a definitive answer. But there are two questions every responsible journalist should ask about every story before being satisfied: Is it accurate? Is it fair?

Accuracy is the most important characteristic of any story, great or small, long or short. Accuracy is essential in every detail. Every name must be spelled correctly; every quote must be just what was said; every set of numbers must add up. And that still isn't good enough. You can get the details right and still mislead unless you are accurate with context, too. The same statement may have widely different meanings depending on the circumstances in which it was uttered and the tone in which it was spoken. Circumstance and intent affect the meaning of actions, as well. You will never have the best obtainable version of the truth unless your version is built on accurate reporting of detail and context.

Nor can you approach the truth without being fair. Accuracy and fairness are related, but they are not the same. The relationship and the difference show clearly in this analogy from the world of sports:

The umpire in a baseball game is similar, in some ways, to a reporter. Each is supposed to be an impartial observer, calling developments as he sees them. (Of course, the umpire's job is to make judgments on those developments, while the reporter's is just to describe them.) Television has brought to sports the instant replay, in which a key development, say a close call at first base, can be examined again and again, often from an angle different from the umpire's view. Sometimes, the replay shows an apparent outcome different from the one the umpire called. A runner who was ruled to be out may appear to have been safe instead. The difference may be due to human error on the umpire's part, or it may be due to the difference in angle, the difference in viewpoint. Umpires recognize this problem. They try to deal with it by obtaining the best possible view of every play and by conferring with their colleagues on some close calls. Still, every umpire knows that an occasional mistake will be made. That is unavoidable. What can, and must, be avoided is unfairness. The umpire must be fair, and both players and fans must believe he is fair. Otherwise, his judgments will not be accepted; he will not be trusted.

There are no instant replays in news. There are, however, different viewpoints from which every event or issue can be observed. Each viewpoint may yield a different interpretation of what is occurring and of what it means. There is also, in journalism as in sport, the possibility of human error, even by the most careful reporters.

Fairness requires that you as a reporter try to find every viewpoint on a story. Hardly ever will there be just one; often there are more than two. Fairness requires that you allow ample opportunity for response to anyone who is being attacked or whose integrity is being questioned in a story. Fairness requires, above all, that you make every effort to avoid following your own biases in your reporting and your writing.

The goals of accuracy and fairness often are summed up as journalistic objectivity. The concept of objectivity has been a controversial one. Critics have argued that it is impossible for any human being to be truly objective, that no one can escape the influence of biases. Some critics have complained that objectivity permits only a mechanistic recording of events, with no concern for context and little room for judgment by reporters or editors. The criticisms became so heated in the 1960s and early 1970s that even many journalists who believed in the concept looked for another term to describe it. One possible alternative is "professional detachment."

By any name, the goal of most print and broadcast journalists remains the one outlined in 1947 by the Hutchins Commission on freedom of the press, "a truthful, comprehensive and intelligent account of the day's events in a context which gives them meaning." It is a goal that is not always reached. You can approach it if you strive for accuracy and fairness. Remember that the public deserves, and expects, no less than the best obtainable version of the truth.

Suggested Readings

Bogart, Leo. "Press and Public." Hillsdale, N.J.: Lawrence Erlbaum Associates, 1981. An analysis of the changing patterns of newspaper readership by one of the leading researchers in the field.

Schudson, Michael. "Discovering the News." New York: Basic Books, 1978. Subtitled "A Social History of American Newspapers," this well-written study traces the development of objectivity in American journalism.

Journalism Reviews: Any issue of the Columbia Journalism Review, the Washington Journalism Review, the Quill or the Bulletin of the American Society of Newspaper Editors offers reports and analyses of the most important issues of contemporary journalism.

2

Inside the News Room

Walker Lundy, executive editor of the Tallahassee (Fla.) Democrat, once wrote of the changes that have transformed American news rooms since the early 1970s:

> In the pre-computer days, the news room was a cacophony of banging manual typewriters, clacking, ringing wire machines and grouchy old men yelling, "Copy!" and "Boy!"
>
> No one suggested the noise level be reduced. You simply learned to shut it out. Today, however, except for the ringing telephones and an occasional "beep" from an offended (computer) terminal that has been asked to do something it doesn't, the news rooms of America are as quiet as publishers' offices. And reporters complain to the city editor that it's too noisy.
>
> "Noisy?" the city editor responds incredulously. "You should have worked here in the old days."
>
> "Oh, no," chorus the 24-year-old reporters. "Not those stories again."

Computers *have* created major changes in news rooms, but other factors have contributed to changes in the news room environment, too. During much of the first half of the 20th century, news rooms were populated primarily by white men with high school diplomas but no college education. Today, women are found on every reporting staff, and it is increasingly common to find them in positions as editors, managing editors and city editors. Blacks, Hispanics and other minorities, while underrepresented in journalism even today, make up ever larger percentages of the staffs of newspapers, magazines, and radio and television stations. College-trained reporters are now the norm, not the exception, in American news rooms, despite the complaints of some editors that journalism education leaves much to be desired.

"I am a journalism dean who confesses there is much that is subpar in journalism education today," Ed Mullins of the University of Alabama wrote in Presstime, the magazine of the American Newspaper Publishers Association. "I also am a product of journalism education and the newspaper industry (reporter, copy editor, executive) and have seen our educational programs *and* our field become more professional over the last 25 years."

No matter how much old-timers reminisce about the "good old days," few would want to return to the pre-computer era of copy pencils, paper copy and crusty old city editors who smoked cheap stogies and quaffed great quantities of gin between editions. Newspapers have entered the computer era, staffs have become more representative of society as a whole, and the level of professionalism has increased. The same can be said of magazines, radio and television. The profession of journalism, and the public, are better served because of those changes.

Despite assertions that the news room now resembles the office of a publisher — or an insurance company — more than the news room in the heyday of Charles Dana, the renowned editor of the New York Sun in the latter half of the 19th century, it still is an exciting place to be. Through it pass the stories of modern man's successes and failures, the chronicles of triumphs and tragedies. It is the place, perhaps more than any other, where the pulse of the community, if not the nation, can be taken. It is an exciting place to be for those with inquisitive minds. It is exciting work, but it is not easy work. Writes H. D. "Doc" Quigg, a senior editor for United Press International who has covered many of the big stories of the past half century:

> For those of you who are considering taking up reporting, I can tell you at least one heartening thing that I suspect is not much emphasized when you study the craft: There is a wonderful camaraderie in being a reporter. Lasting friendships are made with colleagues and competitors.

He cautions, however:

> Despite the promise of the computer to enable you to sit in your office or home and communicate with faraway places, at least one thing probably won't become obsolete over the next quarter century. That's footwork, the reporter's key to talent, to accomplishment. The telephone is a fine instrument, as are all its electronic grandchildren. However, they just don't — not yet — bring you the smell of a thing.

Good reporters can sniff out a story on the telephone, but leg work — literally transporting oneself to the scene of a news story — is the key to the success. It also helps if you understand the environment in which you operate. You should become acquainted with your fellow reporters. They can help you find the computer terminal and the coffeepot, the police station and the payroll window. You can draw upon their experience in digging out a story. They can teach you to use the *morgue*, the newspaper's reference library where background information for a story may be obtained. And they can give you tips on how to win the confidence of your editors. Until you have that confidence, your contribution to the newspaper will be limited.

Learn who your editors are and what they do. Learn through whose hands a news story passes, at least until the last editor presses a key on a computer terminal to send that story to a typesetting machine. Learn how the newspaper is produced and how you, as a reporter, fit into that process.

Your editors will look for solid reporting coupled with good writing, the primary assets of a good reporter. But they also will look for things that may not seem as important, including how well your copy is prepared. If it is filled with typing, spelling and grammatical errors, an editor may deduce that you are sloppy in your work habits. That may lead to distrust of your reporting ability and diminished confidence in you.

It is essential, then, that you learn to use the equipment at your disposal, which usually includes a *VDT*, or *video display terminal*, as quickly as possible after starting to work. Like the telephone, the VDT is one of the tools of your trade. You must learn to use them all.

The production of a newspaper is a remarkable accomplishment involving a unique combination of human beings and machines in a race against the clock. This chapter will introduce you to some of those involved and describe how they do their jobs. Using this as a background, you should study your newspaper when you begin work.

In this chapter you will learn:

1. How newspapers, and their editorial departments in particular, are organized.
2. How copy flows from one editor to the next.
3. How copy is prepared.
4. What tools may be available to help you do your job.

Newspaper Organization

Chuck Haga, city editor of the Grand Forks (N.D.) Herald, wrote in the Bulletin of the American Society of Newspaper Editors:

The managing editor and I were interviewing a job applicant, an earnest young man who wanted to be a reporter. "How would you go about covering city hall?" we asked him.

"Well," the young man said, "first I'd find out where it is."

That young man undoubtedly did well in journalism; learning one's beat is important for a beginner. Also of importance is learning about the news room and the people who are part of it.

Strangely, news rooms often are places where communication leaves much to be desired. One editor of a small daily in the Midwest conducted a survey of new reporters and was told: "Operation (of the news room) could be improved considerably if communications were increased. Sometimes the standards differ from editor to editor."

One journalism graduate wrote a former professor and urged that in the future more time be spent discussing what the young reporter called "news room politics." He wrote:

Human behavior is not a hands-off topic for classroom discussion. Reporters need to be taught that news room politics is not just a game of favoritism. If favoritism exists, it is earned.

The message was clear: Work hard, do a good job and sooner or later you will be rewarded with the best assignments.

No one can describe the situation you will face in your first news room; no two are alike. Similarly, no two editors are alike. All have their likes and dislikes, their foibles and idiosyncrasies.

No two newspapers are organized exactly alike, either. Large dailies with large staffs obviously operate differently from small ones with small staffs. There are enough similarities, however, to make some observations about key personnel and their functions.

TOP MANAGEMENT

Publisher. This title often is assumed by the newspaper's owner, although some *chains* or *groups* — corporations that own two or more newspapers — designate as publisher the top-ranking local executive. The publisher presides over the entire newspaper operation but usually concentrates on financial matters and leaves editorial decisions to the editors. Unless you work at a weekly or small daily newspaper, as a reporter you seldom will see or work with the publisher.

General Manager. Usually the general manager is responsible for advertising, circulation and production. In some chains, however, the general manager serves as the top-ranking local executive and may have a voice in editorial matters. As a reporter, you will have only limited contact with the general manager.

THE EDITORIAL DEPARTMENT

Editor. Most newspaper *editorial departments*, or *news rooms*, are headed by an editor in chief, often known simply as the editor. The editor is responsible for the editorial content of the newspaper, including everything from comics to news stories to editorials. Unless you begin work as a reporter at a weekly or small daily newspaper, you will have little contact with the editor. The editor's influence is exerted through those who report directly to that editor, usually the managing editor and the editorial page editor.

Editorial Page Editor. This is the person charged with producing the editorial page, and, at large newspapers, an *op-ed page.* (The op-ed page draws its name from its position in the paper — opposite the editorial page.) Opinion — that of the newspaper, its columnists and its readers — usually is confined to these two pages. Traditionally the editorial function has been separated from news gathering to distinguish clearly between fact and opinion.

As a reporter you probably will have contact with the editorial page editor only when questioned about something you covered that will be the subject of an editorial. Reporters deal with fact, not opinion, although occasionally they may be asked to write analytical articles.

Managing Editor. Primary responsibility for news-gathering operations is in the hands of the managing editor. The managing editor is the highest-ranking person who makes frequent appearances in the news room. Because of that, the managing editor is the highest-ranking editor with whom you, as a reporter, will have frequent contact.

The managing editor makes decisions about placement of major stories in the newspaper. Frequently the managing editor does the hiring, prepares the news room budget and makes most of the editorial department policy decisions (in consultation with the editor on major decisions). At larger newspapers the managing editor may have one or more assistants who share those responsibilities.

News Editor. This editor has supervisory control of the *copy desk*, where final editing of stories is done, pages are designed and headlines are written. Working for the news editor are *copy editors*, specialists who polish the wording of stories. They check verifiable information, including the spelling of names and the accuracy of addresses, and write headlines. They also may crop and size photographs and other artwork, lay out pages and work directly with the composing room to make sure that stories fit the space available.

At a small daily newspaper the news editor may serve as the copy desk chief, who designs pages and determines how stories are dis-

Figure 2.1 The National Desk at the New York Times. Large newspapers, such as the New York Times, often have separate desks responsible for news gathering and copy editing.

played. At a large newspaper he or she may direct the placement of stories, and a separate desk chief may carry out those instructions.

Some newspapers, mostly small ones, have universal copy desks to handle all news copy. Many large newspapers have separate desks that handle both the gathering and editing of various categories of news — city, state, national and international (see Figure 2.1). Others have a single desk to handle all such news but maintain specialized departments for sports, entertainment and lifestyle stories, each with its own copy editors.

Whatever the form, the copy desk plays an important role in production of the newspaper. It is charged with enforcing deadlines so that the newspaper is produced on time. Deadlines affect everyone in the news room, including you, the reporter. Even so, you will have little direct contact with the copy desk. Deadline pressures are enforced through the city editor (see below). Only when a copy editor questions what you have written is there likely to be direct contact. Even then, the question may be channeled through the news editor to the city editor.

Despite the infrequent contact, it is important for you to develop an appreciation of what the news editor and the copy desk crew accomplish. They polish writing and correct errors that if printed may embarrass you, particularly if your byline is on the story in question.

City Editor. Known at some papers as the metropolitan or metro editor, the city editor supervises the reporters who gather local news. This editor directs the city desk, which may be shared with one or more assistant city editors. The city desk is the hub of the news room because of its importance; local news is the primary news product of most newspapers.

As a reporter you will work directly for the city editor and the assistant city editors. They will give you assignments and follow your progress from the time you begin to gather information until the story is written, edited and sent to the copy desk for final editing and a headline. The city editor often acts as devil's advocate, questioning you about the accuracy of your story and the way you have written it.

The city desk also serves as a primary link to the public because it answers inquiries about news stories. After the initial contact is made there, you may be assigned to act on a complaint or tip.

The city desk maintains a *futures file*, a chronological collection of newspaper clippings, letters, public relations releases and notes to remind editors of upcoming events or stories that require follow-up. This file often is the source of stories you are assigned to cover. As a reporter you should keep a similar file of your own to remind you to follow stories you covered earlier. Never rely upon the futures file for this purpose; notes and clippings can be misplaced easily.

Large newspapers may have editors whose jobs parallel that of the city editor but who deal with areas other than the city and its suburbs. State desks, national desks and international desks are ex-

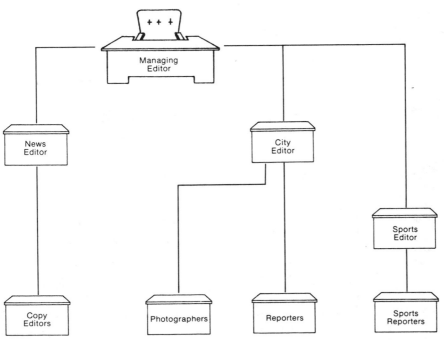

Figure 2.2   Typical News Room Organization of the Small Daily Newspaper.

amples. They are directed by editors who are charged with gathering, compiling and editing news in those areas. Feature editors, sports editors, business editors and Sunday editors may operate still other desks.

If, as a reporter, you are assigned to one of those desks, you will find that the editor in charge of that desk functions much like the city editor. Your job will be affected by the type of news you cover, but your relationship with the editor of your desk will be similar in any situation. Obviously, as a reporter you will work most closely with the editor of your desk and his or her assistants. But you must understand the functions of the other editors who scrutinize your work.

OTHER DEPARTMENTS

Figure 2.3 Typical News Room Organization of the Medium-Sized Daily Newspaper.

You also should realize that the editorial department is but one of several departments that work as a team to produce the newspaper (see Figure 2.4). Most newspapers have advertising, business, circulation and production departments. Some have separate departments to handle promotions, public relations and personnel matters as well.

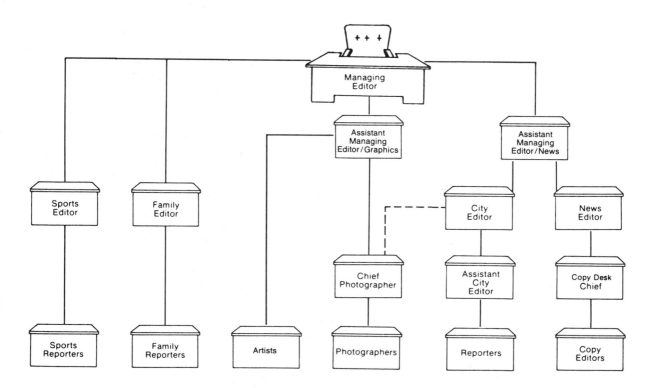

Advertising	Business	Circulation	Editorial	Production
Local Display	Accounting	Mail Room	City Desk	Composing
Classified	Billing	Delivery	Copy Desk	Platemaking
National	Credit	Rural	Photography	Camera
Advertising Art	Payroll	City	Graphics/art	Data Processing
Ad Research	Credit Union		Library	Maintenance
Ad Promotion	Labor Relations		Sports	Press
Public Relations			Family	
		Carriers*	Other Desks	
		Vendors*		

* Outside contractors not employed by newspaper.

The *advertising department* generates most of the newspaper's income, from which your salary is paid. Most advertising departments are divided into display and classified sections, which correspond to the two major forms of advertising. Large newspapers also may have advertising art and research sections, and they may separate display advertising into local and national sections.

The *circulation department* is charged with distributing the newspaper and is the second leading source of newspaper income. Only occasionally will the circulation department affect your job as a reporter. One such occasion is during periods of bad weather or on holidays, when the circulation manager asks for earlier news deadlines to allow more time for delivery of the newspaper.

The *business department* handles billing, accounting and related functions. It manages the payroll, group insurance plans and other benefits, and only in that capacity will you have frequent contact with it.

The *production department*, as its name implies, is responsible for transforming the creative work of reporters, editors and advertising salespeople into the finished product — the newspaper. The composing room, where type is set and pages are assembled, the platemaking section and the pressroom are all parts of the production department.

Large newspapers may subdivide these departments further. Regardless of the newspaper's organization, all the functions mentioned are vital in producing a newspaper, from the nation's smallest weekly to its largest daily. As a reporter you play an important role in producing the newspaper. You are a part of a team.

It is important that you understand how that team works. Because most editors realize this, you can expect to be taken on a tour of the newspaper plant soon after you are hired. If no one offers such a tour, ask for it.

Figure 2.4 Major Departments of the Typical Newspaper and their Subsections.

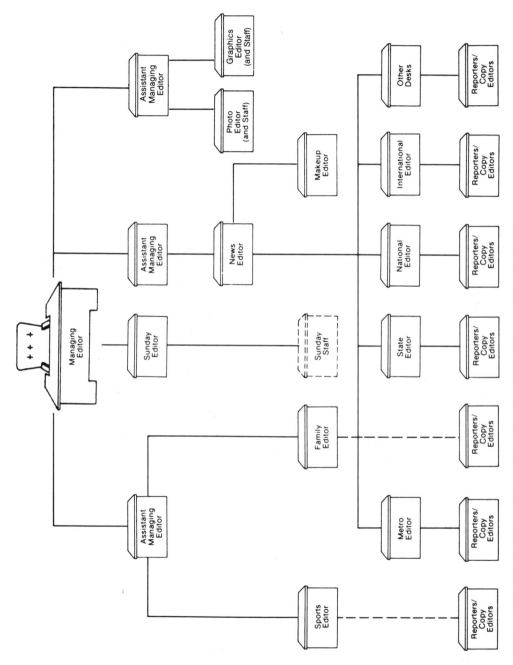

Figure 2.5 Typical News Room Organization of the Metropolitan Daily Newspaper.

Copy Flow

If learning how your newspaper is produced is important, so, too, is learning how the news room works. You should learn what happens to a story as it makes its way through the hands, or, more commonly, the VDT *queues*, of several editors.

At first glance, the flow of copy through an editorial department seems simple enough. You write your story and transfer it to the city desk queue, the electronic equivalent of an in-basket. There the city editor reads it and makes necessary changes. Then it is sent electronically to the copy desk, where it is edited again. The story is assigned a position in the newspaper, and a headline is written. Finally, an editor presses a key on the VDT keyboard to send your story to a typesetting machine in the composing room. This simple copy flow pattern exists at most newspapers, whether that newspaper uses VDTs or still does things the old-fashioned way with typewriters and paper copy. Indeed, electronic copy flow patterns in most cases merely duplicate the pre-computer copy flow patterns of newspapers. Despite the seeming simplicity of the pattern, many decisions can be made along the way that make the process much more complicated than it appears at first glance.

When the city editor receives your copy, that editor must read it and make some initial decisions: Is there missing information? Does the story need to be developed? Does it need more background? Are there enough quotes? Are the quotes worth using? Does the *lead*, or opening, need to be polished? Have you chosen the right lead or should another angle be emphasized? Is the story important? Is it useful, interesting or entertaining? Is there, in fact, some reason for publishing it? If it is important, should the managing editor and news editor be alerted that a potential Page One story is forthcoming? Each time a city editor reads a story for the first time, these questions and more come up. The city editor is expected to answer them quickly; there is no time for delay.

After making those initial decisions, the city editor confers with you and gives directions on changes to be made. If the changes are minor ones, simply rewriting a section of the story or inserting additional information will suffice. If the changes are more substantial, involving additional interviews with sources or major rewriting, your job is more difficult.

When those changes are made, you resubmit your story to the city editor, who reads the revised version and edits it more carefully. Your work may be finished after you answer a few remaining minor questions. Or, if the city editor is still unhappy with it, another rewrite may be ordered.

You can expect frustration in the process. Often an assistant city editor reads your story first and gives instructions on how it is to be revised. When your rewrite is submitted, the city editor or another assistant may do the editing, resulting in the need for more changes and yet another rewrite. This can be discouraging, but such a system has its merits. Generally, a story is improved when more than one editor handles it. Each sees gaps to be filled, and varied viewpoints usually lead to an improved story.

At some point in the process, ideally at the outset, editors will decide whether to order a photograph to accompany your story. This once was done almost as an afterthought by editors, who considered photos mere decoration to break up the type of a newspaper page. Now, progressive newspapers realize that photos, artwork, charts and graphs are forms of communication with tremendous reader appeal. Photo editors and graphics editors, often with the authority of an assistant managing editor, work closely with the city editors to ensure that visual opportunities are not missed. Finding reporter-photographer teams assigned to a story from the outset is increasingly common.

It is important that you develop a good working relationship with the staff photographers. In recent years newspapers have become increasingly aware of the importance of making the photographer a full partner in the news-gathering process. Rather than shackle the photographer with precise instructions about how to take a picture to accompany your story, relate what the story is about and let the photographer make suggestions. Remember that your expertise is in written communication; the photographer's expertise is in visual communication.

When the story and photograph are ready, the city desk may submit them to the news editor, who decides where they are to be placed in the newspaper. Often this decision is made in consultation with the city editor, the managing editor or an assistant managing editor.

The story then may be handed to the copy desk chief, who designs the page on which the story and picture are to appear. That editor orders a headline for your story and transfers the package to a copy editor, still known at some newspapers by the antiquated term "copyreader."

The copy editor asks many of the same questions about your story that the city editor asks. Have you selected the right lead? Does the writing need to be polished? Have you chosen the correct words? Primarily, though, the copy editor checks for misspelled words, adherence to style, grammatical errors, ambiguities and errors of fact. The copy editor reworks a phrase here or there to clarify your meaning but is expected to avoid major changes. If major changes are nec-

Individual	Action
Reporter	Gathers facts, writes story, verifies its accuracy, forwards to city editor
City Editor*	Edits story, returns to reporter for changes or additional detail (if necessary), forwards story to news editor
News Editor*	Decides on placement of story in newspaper, forwards story to copy desk chief for implementation of instructions
Copy Desk Chief	Prepares page dummy that determines story's length, setting and headline size, forwards to copy editor
Copy Editor	Polishes writing of story, checks for missing or inaccurate detail, writes headline, returns to copy desk chief for final check
Copy Desk Chief	Verifies that story is trimmed as necessary and that correct headline is written, transmits story to typesetting machine.

Figure 2.6 Typical News Room Copy Flow Pattern.

* Or assistant

Note: At any point in the process, a story may be returned to an earlier editor for clarification, amplification or rewriting.

essary, the copy editor calls that to the attention of the news editor. If the news editor agrees, the story is returned to the city editor, and perhaps to you, for yet another revision.

When the copy editor is satisfied with the story, work begins on the headline. The size of the headline ordered by the copy desk chief determines how many characters or letters can be used in writing it. Headline writing is an art. Those who are able to convey the meaning of a story in a limited number of words are valuable members of the staff. The quality of the copy editor's work can have a significant impact on the number of readers who will be attracted to your story. If the headline is dull and lifeless, few will; if it sparkles, the story's exposure will be increased.

The copy editor also may write the cutline, or caption, that accompanies the picture. At some newspapers, however, this is done by the reporter or at the city desk. Large newspapers may have a photo desk to handle cutlines as well as picture cropping and sizing.

When finished, the copy editor transfers the story to the copy desk chief, who must approve the headline and may check the editing changes made by the copy editor. When the desk chief is satisfied, the story and headline are transferred to the composing room, where the creative effort of writers and editors is transformed into type. The picture is sent to another section of the production department for processing.

The size of the newspaper may alter this copy flow pattern substantially. At a small newspaper the jobs of news editor, copy desk chief and copy editor may be performed by one person. Some small dailies require the city editor or an assistant to perform all the tasks normally handled by the copy desk.

News room copy flow patterns have been designed with redundancy in mind. Built into the system is the goal of having not one editor, but several, check your work. Through repeated checking, editors hope to detect more errors — in fact and in writing style — to make the finished product a better one.

In this sense editors work as gatekeepers. They determine whether your work measures up to their standards. Only when it does is the gate opened, allowing your story to take the next step in the newspaper production process.

Copy Preparation

Since 1970 remarkable changes have transformed the American news room from a citadel of 19th-century methods into a showcase of space-age technology. Manual typewriters have been replaced by

VDTs. Reporters and editors use them to produce stories that subsequently are typeset at speeds of more than 1,000 lines per minute.

In a few news rooms reporters still produce copy on typewriters, but they are modern, electric models designed to produce a high-quality typescript that can be "read" or "scanned" by a machine called an *optical character reader (OCR).* OCRs work with high-energy laser beams, once known only as lethal weapons in science fiction thrillers. This process, popular in the 1970s, is fading from use because it is cumbersome. Reporters must type relatively clean copy, and editors are limited in making changes.

A few American reporters still use manual typewriters to produce copy that will be retyped by a compositor. Traditional copy preparation with a typewriter is most often used when a portable VDT is not available or when writing for a publication other than your own.

The origins of modern newspaper technology can be traced to reductions in the American space program. When astronaut Neil Armstrong became the first man to walk on the moon on July 20, 1969, an American dream was realized and a 10-year obsession with accomplishing that feat ended. Subsequent reductions in the staff of the National Aeronautics and Space Administration forced many space-age computer technicians and engineers to find jobs in the private sector. As a result, space technology was used to benefit various industries, among them newspapers.

Those technicians realized that tremendous savings were possible in the newspaper industry if the reporter's typing effort could be used to operate typesetting machines. That would eliminate the redundant process of having another employee retype the story in the composing room.

Video display terminals, already used in other industries, were well-suited for this task. They were first installed at newspapers in the early 1970s, and they brought about the most significant changes in newspaper production since the invention of Ottmar Mergenthaler's linecaster. No longer are reporters and editors involved in production only to the extent that they are required to meet deadlines. Reporters have become vital links in the production process because they have assumed the role of typing copy that ultimately will be used in typesetting.

The face of American news rooms has changed dramatically, and most reporters and editors have adapted well. They like the change to electronic editing because they have more control over what appears in the newspaper. The composing room is almost eliminated as a source of errors. Spurring the change, of course, is what the technicians realized from the outset: Money can be saved. Publishers are able to reduce the number of composing room workers and save thousands of dollars in labor costs.

A few of the more than 1,700 daily newspapers in this country are still in the process of converting to the new technology. The result is that you, as someone studying to become a journalist, must be familiar with both new and old methods.

THE TRADITIONAL PROCESS

A reporter using the traditional process writes stories on a typewriter with low-quality paper, often newsprint. The reporter usually makes at least two carbon copies. The reporter submits the original and one carbon copy to the city desk. The original is edited and eventually finds its way to the composing room, where a compositor transforms it into type. The city desk and the reporter keep carbon copies in case the original is lost or they need to refer to the piece later. The assembled sheets of newsprint and carbon paper are known as *books*.

After inserting a book in the typewriter, you must type identifying information in the upper-left-hand corner. The minimum information includes your name, the date and a story *slug*, an identifying word that will remain with the article throughout the production process. The slug should give some indication of the story's subject matter. An article about a city council meeting, for example, may use the slug "council."

The first line of the article should appear no less than one-third down the page. This practice allows room at the top for the city editor or an assistant to insert your byline, if one is used. It also allows room for the city desk and copy desk editors to insert information such as typesetting instructions, headline specifications and, in some cases, the headline itself.

Articles are written on one side of the paper only and should be double- or triple-spaced, depending on the newspaper's practice. If there is insufficient space for the article on one sheet of paper — one *take* as it is commonly called — type "more" at the end of the last complete paragraph that will fit. A take should never end in the middle of a sentence or in the middle of a paragraph because such a practice can complicate typesetting. Takes of an article often are set by different compositors and pieced together once the type is set. That task becomes difficult, if not impossible, if a take ends in mid-sentence.

The second take of copy should be treated similarly with these exceptions:

1. The date can be eliminated.
2. The slug should be followed by a dash and the words "first add." A first add is equivalent to the second page of a manu-

Jones

5-11

Council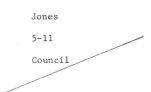

The Springfield City Council voted today to abandon plans
to widen West Ash Street, the city's major east-west thoroughfare.

The council voted 6-1 to delay the project indefintely
in the face of widespread citizen opposition. Councilman Ed
Pƒerez cast the dissenting vote.

"This decision is a major victory for historic
preservation," said Wilman Lindendorf, chairman of Citizens
to Preserve West Ash, a group formed last month to oppose the
project. "There are some houses along that street of historical
interest and widening the street from two lanes to four would
have destroyed the lawns in front of them and diminished their
value."

A preliminary survey by the State Office of Historical
Preservation showed earlier this month that widening the street
could harm the "historical character" of the neighborhood.
The final report probably will not be issued until next year,
but several council members said the preliminary study convinced
them the project should be abandoned.

 (MORE)

Figure 2.7 First Take of a Story. The reporter writes his or her name, the date and the story slug at the top. The top third of the page is left blank for editing instructions, and "MORE" at the bottom indicates there are additional takes.

Figure 2.8 The Second and Last Take of a Story. The slug and "first add" at the top identify the piece, and "30" indicates the end of the story.

COUNCIL -- first add

    Fifth Ward Councilwoman Jane Trevor said she was not convinced the city had studied alternatives to widening the street. "There is some indication that widening West Elm would be less disruptive," she said.

    Sixth Ward Councilman Giuseppi Grimaldi agreed. "We want to be certain we have the best solution to the east-west traffic problem, and I'm not convinced we know what that is."

-30-

script. Some newspapers prefer to use numerical designations, so, depending on the practice at your newspaper, the second page would contain the slug "council — first add" or "council — 2."

3. There is no need to leave the top third of the page blank.

If the article is lengthy, you may need a "second add," "third add" and so forth. The end of the story should be marked by "30," "#" or "END." All information for editors and production personnel should be circled. That indicates the material is for information only and should not appear in print.

Writing an article this way is simple because perfect manuscripts are unnecessary. In fact, they are rare. The main requirement is that editors and compositors be able to read and understand what you have written. Because several people must read the copy, neatness is essential. For that reason, several rules governing copy preparation have evolved:

1. Never correct typing errors by backspacing and typing over a character. Instead, cross out the error with a pencil and re-type, or strike over the entire word and retype.
2. Never use a hyphen at the end of a typewritten line. This can lead to confusion because a compositor may think the hyphen is to be inserted in the typeset copy.
3. Correct simple errors, such as transposed characters, with copy editing marks. These symbols differ from proofreading marks, which are used to mark corrections in typeset copy. (See Figures 2. 9 and 2.10.)
4. If a section of an article is difficult to read because of numerous corrections, retype it. Corrected paragraphs, for example, can be pasted over difficult-to-read copy. Rubber cement is best for such pasting.

THE VDT PROCESS

Writing a story on a video display terminal can be a pleasure, and those who switch from the traditional method to VDTs seldom want to change back. VDTs are keyboards with attached television-like screens that display information as it is typed. They are similar to the home computers now found in many North American households. The terminal screen substitutes for the paper copy produced by a typewriter. Corrections, deletions and insertions can be made easily and quickly, and the writer has the advantage of working with

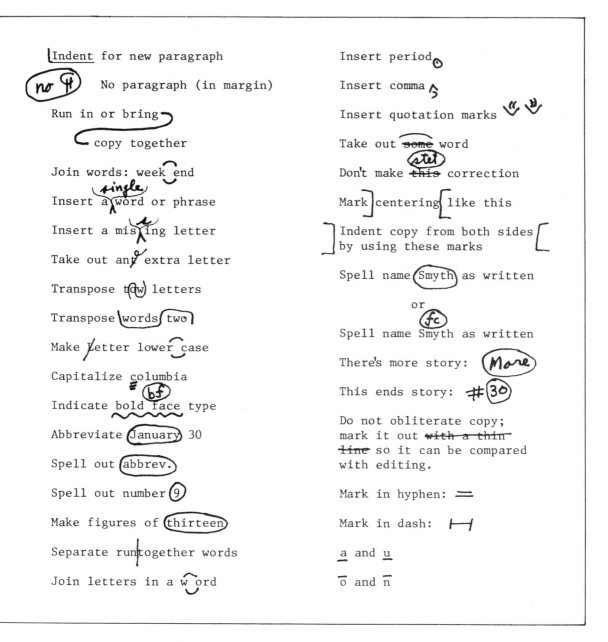

Figure 2.9 Copy Editing Symbols.

clean copy at all times. There are no strikeovers or handwritten insertions.

As you strike a key and the character appears on the VDT screen, it is stored on disk by a computer, called a *controller*, to which the VDT is attached by cable. The controller allows you to store your story for later retrieval or to send it to your editor.

Symbol	Description	Symbol	Description
∧	Insert at this point.	ⱱⱱ	Space evenly.
⊥	Push down space.	◠	Close up entirely.
ℓ	Take out letter, letters or words.	⊏	Move to left.
ꝰ	Turn inverted letter.	⊐	Move to right.
ⓛⓒ	Set lowercase.	⊔	Lower letter or word.
ⓦⓕ	Wrong font letter.	⊓	Raise letter or word.
ⓘⓣⓐⓛ	Reset in italic type.	*out, see copy*	Words are left out.
ⓡⓞⓜ	Reset in roman (regular) type.	∥	Straighten lines.
ⓑⓕ	Reset in bold face type.	⑨	Start new paragraph.
⊙	Insert period.	*no ⑨*	No paragraph. Run together.
⩑	Insert comma.	ⓣⓡ	Transpose letters or words.
⩘	Insert semicolon.	⑦	Query; is copy right?
H	Insert hyphen.	⊢	Insert dash.
ⱱ	Insert apostrophe.	☐	Indent 1 em.
ⱱ ⱱ	Enclose in quotation marks.	☐☐	Indent 2 ems.
≡	Replace with a capital letter.	☐☐☐	Indent 3 ems.
#	Insert space.	*stet*	Let it stand.

Learning to operate a VDT is more complicated than learning to use a typewriter because there are more keys with which to contend. In addition to the standard typewriter keyboard layout, there are keys to control the *cursor*, a rectangle of light that indicates your position in the text. Still other keys control computer functions such as routing the story from desk to desk. Newspapers usually provide training for newcomers as they join the staff. Because many companies manufacture VDTs for newspapers, there is little standardization.

Once the keyboard is mastered and you become accustomed to seeing your story on a VDT screen rather than on paper, the rest is simple. Mistakes can be corrected as you write simply by moving the cursor backward and striking over the incorrect letters. By striking the insert key, characters, words, sentences, paragraphs and even larger blocks of type can be inserted at any point in the text. Sentences and paragraphs can be moved with similar ease.

Each terminal screen displays about 14 lines of text. As more space is needed, lines disappear from the screen but are stored in the memory of the computer. You simply depress a key to move forward or backward to any part of the story.

Once you are satisfied with your article, you can make a paper printout of it by depressing another key. This printout replaces the carbon copy in the traditional process and can be used for later reference.

With yet another key you transmit your article to the controller and assign it to the editor's queue. The editor can instruct the VDT

**Figure 2.10
Proofreading Symbols.**

Figure 2.11 Reporter at VDT. Reporters at many newspapers now write their stories directly on video display terminals (VDTs).

Figure 2.12 Closeup of VDT Screen. The advantage of writing and editing copy on a VDT is that the copy is always easy to read. There is no need to interpret handwritten insertions or corrections.

to provide a *directory*, or index, of stories awaiting attention. When it is time to process your story, the editor simply strikes another key and the story appears on the screen for editing. The article moves from editor to editor in this way until finally it is sent electronically to the typesetter, much as a voice travels over telephone lines.

Tools to Help You

A wise reporter wastes no time learning where the morgue, or newspaper reference library, is located. The morgue and the people who operate it can be of immense help to a reporter. Background information on literally thousands of people and topics will be available in a good newspaper library. Typically, morgues have subject files, biographical files and photo files. The librarian can show you how to use the morgue at your newspaper.

A good morgue will contain a variety of reference books that may be of great help to you. These may range from an encyclopedia to Bartlett's Familiar Quotations and from an almanac to Who's Who in America. Check to see what reference materials are available in your library. Then you will know where to turn for information that can enhance your story.

Many morgues are being converted to electronic data bases. With the best of the library storage and retrieval systems, a reporter can summon information from the data base while sitting at a VDT in the news room. With other systems, it may be necessary to use a terminal in the morgue. Some newspapers have not yet converted their own morgues to electronic data bases but have purchased access to systems that contain data from The New York Times, national magazines and other sources. Popular data bases for such use include Dialog, the Source and CompuServe. The latter two carry the complete wires of United Press International and the Associated Press, respectively, but do not serve as a form of archival storage of such information. Data from the wire services is retained in the data base for a matter of hours, then purged to make space for more up-to-date material. Other material available through Dialog, the Source and CompuServe is more permanent and can be used to enhance your stories.

Typically, data found in such data bases comes in the form of references to articles in newspapers and magazines (see Appendix II). A reporter for the Columbus (Ohio) Dispatch, for example, found eight data-base citations when researching reports that a doctor accused of income tax evasion was connected to an offbeat religious order. At the Louisville (Ky.) Courier-Journal, reporters used several data bases to produce a 1,600-item bibliography that was useful in producing a 30-part series on toxic waste dumps. At the Providence (R.I.) Journal, a science reporter found data on herpes and a drug called Lysine by searching a data base called Medline. Such searches are both extraordinarily useful and increasingly common.

Another library system in use at newspapers employs computer-accessed microfiche. Articles are indexed by key words and then called to a viewing screen for review. Copies of the articles may be printed from the microfiche if the user desires. The advantage of this system is that it allows the user to see the article as it appeared in the newspaper. Electronic data-base systems do not have that feature.

As a reporter you probably will have occasion to use portable VDTs. These permit you to transmit your story to the newspaper's computer system over telephone lines from almost any location. Some newspapers use terminals made specifically for newspapers, but others have found that portable personal computers are more useful; operators can use a variety of ready-made operating programs with them.

Personal computers are being used in newspaper offices, too. Some newspapers are using them to keep up with story assignments, and others are using them for news room budgeting. Still others are finding them useful to produce instant analyses of election results or to create maps and charts. The number of possibilities for using such devices in the news room is unlimited, and newspapers are just beginning to explore their potential.

Some reporters also have found themselves writing copy for various electronic publishing ventures in which their employers are involved. Many newspapers are now leasing cable television channels and programming local news on those channels.

Some publishers also are experimenting with videotex and teletext. Videotex refers to a form of two-way communication with a data base. A videotex consumer, for example, would be able to call to the television or computer screen the latest news and information such as theater listings and airline schedules. Videotex requires a connection with a central computer through cable television or telephone lines. Teletext uses an unused part of a television signal, called the vertical blanking interval, to transmit digital information that can be unscrambled by a decoder and called to the TV screen. The information can be left there as long as the viewer desires. Most teletext systems can contain only about 200 screenfuls of information, so their capacity is severely limited. Teletext's advantage is that, unlike videotex, it does not depend on a cable connection to a remote computer. Because of that, it is a promising system in areas such as the American and Canadian West, where great distances separate communities and cable television lines are prohibitively expensive to install.

Newspaper publishers are experimenting with such technologies because they represent new markets for news and information material they already have paid to gather. Some experts believe that such technologies eventually will replace newspapers and magazines, which rely upon costly distribution systems and consume vast amounts of expensive paper. Whether that prediction will come true is far from clear. It is clear that many publishers view reporters as information collectors and disseminators. If new methods of distributing information can be made profitable, reporters will be expected to adapt.

Suggested Readings

Editors of the Harvard Post. "How to Produce a Small Newspaper." Port Washington, N.Y.: Harvard Common Press, 1978. A good discussion of the modern newspaper production process.

Rucker, Frank W., and Herbert L. Williams. "Newspaper Organization and Management." 5th ed. Ames, Iowa: Iowa State University Press, 1978. This book details the structure of American newspapers and their operation.

Seybold, John W. "Fundamentals of Modern Photocomposition." Media, Pa.: Seybold Publications Inc., 1979. A thorough primer on newspaper production methods, past and present.

PART TWO

Basic Skills

3

Using a
Stylebook

A burro is an ass. A burrow is a hole in the ground. As a journalist you
are expected to know the difference.

That piece of advice can be found in The United Press International
Stylebook, a reference manual otherwise free of wit. If nothing else,
the passage serves to dispel the myth that style rules encourage
bland writing and conformity in newspapers.

Instead, style rules provide needed consistency throughout the
paper so that the reader can focus on content, not differences of little substance. Some readers, for example, are irritated to find *employee* in one story and *employe* in the next. Both spellings can be
found in dictionaries, but observing a style rule eliminates that
annoying inconsistency. Style rules help reporters and editors avoid
wasting time arguing about such details as the correct spelling of
OK (or okay). Even more important, style rules provide guidance in
the often troublesome areas of grammar, punctuation, capitalization, abbreviation and the like.

Despite that, editors are far from unanimous in their support of
style. Louis D. Boccardi of The Associated Press wrote that journalists approach style questions with varying degrees of passion:
"Some don't really think it's important. Some agree that basically
there should be uniformity for reading ease if nothing else. Still others are prepared to duel over a wayward lowercase." Boccardi's
comment appears in the foreword of The Associated Press Stylebook, a book designed as a reference manual as well as a stylebook.
It is almost identical to The United Press International Stylebook.

Indeed, the two services collaborated in writing them as a service to clients who subscribe to both.

Together, the AP and UPI stylebooks are the major source of American newspaper style. Many newspapers rely upon them as their only source of style. Some issue supplements listing deviations from wire service style and establishing local style rules. A few, mostly large newspapers, have their own stylebooks.

Because newspapers depend so heavily upon the AP and UPI stylebooks, this chapter focuses on the rules they establish. It is designed to point out the most common violations of style so that you, as a reporter, will learn to avoid them. It would be difficult, if not impossible, for you to commit to memory all 242 pages of style rules in the AP Stylebook. But you can learn to avoid the most common mistakes while developing the habit of referring to your stylebook when in doubt.

In this chapter you will learn:

1. How the AP and UPI style rules developed and how they serve reporters.
2. The most common errors in style and how to avoid them.

The Origin and Usefulness of Style Rules

It may seem odd that newspapers rely upon the wire services to establish style, but there is a practical reason for it. Before newspapers converted to computer-assisted editing, Teletypesetter tape often was used to set wire service copy. TTS tape is perforated paper tape coded to correspond to the text transmitted by a wire service. Newspapers were able to use this tape to operate automated, hot-metal linecasting machines and thus set wire service copy rapidly and economically. Tape-driven linecasters were faster than those operated manually, and one person could monitor several such machines, reducing the labor needed to set type.

It was an efficient process with one exception: Each time an editor made a correction on the copy, the correction had to be set manually. This was time-consuming and discouraged editing. Another complication was that the AP and UPI had no common style. A newspaper that subscribed to both was forced to make style corrections in one or the other to achieve consistency, which led to more costly corrections.

Prompted by complaints from clients and pressure from newspaper industry leaders, the two competitors agreed to discuss the problem. The result was a manual that resolved almost all differences in style between the two major wire services. Each service published its own version, but the key passages were identical.

These stylebooks found wide acceptance in the newspaper industry. Newspapers adopted the style as their own to minimize the number of changes in TTS-generated and locally produced copy. As a result the wire services became the arbiters of style.

The introduction of video display terminal systems in the 1970s made it easier for newspapers to make changes in wire service copy, but by then the style was entrenched. Most editors are happy with what has evolved, and few are inclined to devote time and effort to writing their own stylebooks. It is safe to say that wire service style is with us to stay.

In fact, newspaper editors warmly embraced revised versions of the AP and UPI stylebooks first issued in the 1970s. They were greatly expanded, and entries were alphabetized, making the stylebooks valuable reference works. In them are the correct spellings of hundreds of corporation names; information on religious beliefs; rules on punctuation, grammar and capitalization; and thousands of other useful items. The AP Stylebook even contains a useful section on libel law.

Those who have used the stylebooks know how helpful they can be. They realize that consistency is an important quality for a newspaper and that style helps provide that consistency. They also realize that consistency does not require writers to fall into a lock-step monotony, as critics of style have charged. There is ample room within the constraints of style rules for excellent styles of writing, including writing that carries the stamp of its author. Consider this example:

My little sister is dead of a heroin overdose.

She snorted almost a gram and her respiratory system couldn't handle the load. Her body was found in her convertible on a dead-end St. Louis County road.

Police found her curled as if asleep in the back seat, covered by my father's old Navy blanket. Her dog, Red, a sickly Irish setter she had raised from a pup, was with her in the car.

I was talking on the phone when the operator interrupted with a call from my older brother, Jerry.

"Tom." His voice made it clear that the news wasn't good. "Jodi's dead."

My mind jammed with images of the gangly, red-haired girl who emerged after 22 years as the sweetest and loveliest of young women.

Two days later, in bitter shock over the absurd events that caused my sister's death, I sat numbly in the funeral home and thought that Jodi would have loved the beautiful flowers being carried in.

After watching the mourners view her painted face, mumble rehearsed words of kindness and disappear, I knew what had killed my sister. . . .

That article by UPI's Tom Uhlenbrock is vivid and well-written. The reader feels the author's emotion and shares his sorrow. Yet within that brief example Uhlenbrock heeded a number of style rules, including the following:

- *Dead-end* is hyphenated when used as an adjective and is written as two words *(dead end)* when used as a noun.
- *County* is capitalized when it is an integral part of a name.
- *Navy* is capitalized when referring to the U.S. Navy.
- Non-restrictive or non-essential words or clauses are set off with commas. (Jodi had only one dog, Red, so the name is set off with commas. If she had more than one dog, the commas would be omitted because the name Red would be essential to the meaning. Likewise, the author has only one brother, Jerry. Since his name is not essential to the meaning of the sentence, or is non-restrictive, it is set off with a comma.)
- *Red-haired* is one acceptable way to refer to a person with red hair.
- The numbers *one* through *nine* are spelled out. Numerals are used for numbers of *10* or more, including *22*, Jodi's age.

Certainly Uhlenbrock's writing style was not limited by observing these and other style rules. Those rules did not interfere with the message he had to convey. Consistency is maintained because they are observed. Conformity is not required.

Common Style Errors

CAPITALIZATION

Newspapers conform to the basic rule of capitalization of the English language: Proper nouns — specific persons, places and things — are capitalized; common nouns are not. That rule is simple enough, but knowing when to capitalize words in other usages may not be as obvious.

When in doubt about whether to capitalize, refer to your stylebook. If that fails to satisfy you, refer to the primary supplemental reference established by the AP and UPI, Webster's New World Dictionary of the American Language, Second College Edition.

Trademarks. Almost every editor has received a letter that reads something like this:

```
Dear Editor:
   We were delighted to read your April 5 article about the
popularity of Frisbees in your community.
   Unfortunately, however, you failed to capitalize the
word Frisbee throughout the article. Since the word Fris-
bee is a trademark of our company, it should always be cap-
italized.
```

Such warnings of trademark infringements usually are nice enough. Businesses realize there are many trademarked words, and it is difficult for editors to keep up with them all. Only when violations repeatedly occur are threats of lawsuits tossed about.

Reporters and editors generally do try to ensure that they don't turn words that are trademarks into generic terms. Companies register such words to protect their rights to them and have every reason to expect that newspapers will honor those rights.

Newspapers, on the other hand, aren't eager to provide knowingly what amounts to free advertising for products in their news columns. Reporters and editors are encouraged to use generic words instead.

Some examples of substitution are:

- Use *real estate agent* or *salesperson* rather than *Realtor*, a trademark of the National Association of Real Estate Boards.
- Use *soft drink* or *cola* rather than *Coke*, a trademark of the Coca-Cola Co.
- Use *gelatin*, not *Jell-O*.
- Use *bleach*, not *Clorox*.
- Use *refrigerator*, not *Frigidaire*.

The list of such words is lengthy, and some may be real sources of confusion. It is permissible to use *jeep*, for example, when referring to an Army vehicle, but the similarly named civilian vehicle is a *Jeep*. When in doubt, refer to the AP or UPI stylebooks, which list many trademarked names.

Plurals of Proper Nouns.   More confusion can result when referring to plurals of proper nouns. You would write about the *Tennessee Legislature* and the *Colorado Legislature* when they are used in the singular form. The plural, however, would be *Tennessee and Colorado legislatures*. The same rule applies when referring to streets: *Ninth Street* and *Cherry Street*, but *Ninth and Cherry streets*.

Religious Terms.   References to a deity often cause confusion. Style provides for the capitalization of proper names referring to a monotheistic deity, such as *God, Buddha, Allah, the Son, the Father.* However, pronouns used to refer to a deity — *he, him, thee, thou* — are lowercase.

Titles. For the unwary reporter, titles are another source of trouble. Generally, formal titles used directly before an individual's name are capitalized: *President Ronald Reagan, Secretary of State George P. Shultz, Queen Elizabeth II.* Used after the name, they are lowercase: *Ronald Reagan, president of the United States; George P. Shultz, secretary of state; Elizabeth II, queen of England.*

Occupational titles — those more descriptive of a person's job than formal status — generally are not capitalized. Thus, you should lowercase references to *movie star Robert Redford, astronaut Neil Armstrong* or *outfielder Reggie Jackson.*

Direct Quotation. Perhaps the most abused rule of capitalization deals with the first word of a direct quotation. That word should be capitalized following the source only if:

1. It starts a complete sentence.
2. It is separated from the source by a comma.
3. It appears in direct quotation marks.

Thus, it is permissible to write:

Reagan said, "It was a tiring trip."

Reagan said "it was a tiring trip."

Reagan said it was a tiring trip.

These constructions are incorrect:

Reagan said "It was a tiring trip."

Reagan said, "it was a tiring trip."

Reagan said, it was a tiring trip.

ABBREVIATIONS

Abbreviations save much space for newspapers in a year's time but editors use them only when the reader will recognize them instantly. Newspapers are in the business of communicating to their readers. Saving space to the detriment of understanding is an intolerable offense.

There are many exceptions to the rules of abbreviation discussed below. They can be determined only by consulting a stylebook, and in each case the meaning of the abbreviation should be clear.

State Names. By the time of the last revision of the AP and UPI stylebooks, the U.S. Postal Service had begun using two-letter abbreviations for each state. They were rejected for newspaper use, however, because of the potential for confusion. *MS*, the post office abbreviation for *Mississippi*, could be mistaken for *Missouri* or the recently popularized courtesy title for a woman, *Ms.* Instead, AP and UPI editors chose to use the more familiar state abbreviations that had won general acceptance through the years.

State names are abbreviated only when they follow city names. All two-word states can be abbreviated, usually with the first letter of each word. In the following list only West Virginia is an exception:

New Hampshire (N.H.)   North Dakota (N.D.)
New Jersey (N.J.)   Rhode Island (R.I.)
New Mexico (N.M.)   South Carolina (S.C.)
New York (N.Y.)   South Dakota (S.D.)
North Carolina (N.C.)   West Virginia (W.Va.)

The names of eight states never are abbreviated by AP and UPI, although some newspapers make exceptions:

Alaska   Maine
Hawaii   Ohio
Idaho   Texas
Iowa   Utah

The others are recognized easily:

Alabama (Ala.)   Michigan (Mich.)
Arizona (Ariz.)   Minnesota (Minn.)
Arkansas (Ark.)   Mississippi (Miss.)
California (Calif.)   Missouri (Mo.)
Colorado (Colo.)   Montana (Mont.)
Connecticut (Conn.)   Nebraska (Neb.)
Delaware (Del.)   Nevada (Nev.)
Florida (Fla.)   Oklahoma (Okla.)
Georgia (Ga.)   Oregon (Ore.)
Illinois (Ill.)   Pennsylvania (Pa.)
Indiana (Ind.)   Tennessee (Tenn.)
Kansas (Kan.)   Vermont (Vt.)
Kentucky (Ky.)   Virginia (Va.)
Louisiana (La.)   Washington (Wash.)
Maryland (Md.)   Wisconsin (Wis.)
Massachusetts (Mass.)   Wyoming (Wyo.)

The most common mistakes are made when abbreviating *California* (*Calif.,* not *Cal.*) *Kansas* (*Kan.,* not *Kans.*), *Kentucky* (*Ky.,* not *Ken.*), *Nebraska* (*Neb.,* not *Nebr.*), *Pennsylvania* (*Pa.,* not *Penn.*) and *Wisconsin* (*Wis.,* not *Wisc.*).

Dates. Confusion can also arise in abbreviating dates. Months are abbreviated only when followed by the day of the month in constructions such as *Sept. 13*. Five months are never abbreviated: *March, April, May, June* and *July*. These are easy to remember since they begin with March and are consecutive. Therefore, write *Nov. 6*, but *March 16*. Days of the week are never abbreviated in newspapers, except in tabular matter such as stock market listings.

Addresses. Street names also are a source of confusion. The words *street, avenue* and *boulevard* can be abbreviated, but only when preceded by a street name and number:

He lives at 311 Ninth St.

He rode down Ninth Street.

The same rule applies in abbreviating direction with an address. Write *311 S. Ninth St.*, but *South Ninth Street*. Addresses with the directions northeast, southeast, southwest and northwest are abbreviated with periods:

He lives at 212 Westwinds Drive S.W. in Chicago.

Courtesy Titles. The most controversial abbreviations used by newspapers are those used for courtesy titles. In general, a person's name is used in full — including the preferred given name and initial — on first reference: *William B. Simon, H. Lamar Hunt*. On subsequent references, men are referred to by last name only. Women, however, are given courtesy titles — *Miss, Mrs.* or *Ms.* — on second and subsequent references.

This distinction rankles feminists, but for the present that is the style. Only in sports stories do the AP and UPI stylebooks permit the identification of a woman by surname on second and subsequent references. Perhaps when they are revised again, this distinction will be dropped. Indeed, many newspapers already have changed this practice by dropping courtesy titles altogether or by using courtesy titles for both men and women. There may be other exceptions. *Mr.* may be used on second and subsequent references to a man in an obituary and, at some newspapers, in editorials. The form *Mr. and Mrs. Roger Johnson* also is acceptable.

Other Abbreviations. Generally, abbreviations of one- and two-word terms take periods and abbreviations of terms consisting of three or more words do not. Thus, write *U.S.* and *U.N.*, but *FBI, CIA* and *mph*. An exception is made when an abbreviation without periods spells an unrelated word. Write *c.o.d.*, not *cod*, which is a kind of fish. Other exceptions are listed in your stylebook, the most common of which is *TV* (no periods).

PUNCTUATION

Without a doubt, the most abused style rules are those that deal with punctuation. Part of the reason is that style rules adopted by newspapers differ somewhat from the rules of punctuation most of us learned in grammar school. The major punctuation rules that should concern you as a reporter are discussed below.

Periods. In school you may have been taught that there are times when quotation marks are to be placed inside the period at the end of a sentence, as in the following example:

Stephen Crane wrote "The Red Badge of Courage".

In newspapers, however, the period always goes inside the quotation marks:

Stephen Crane wrote "The Red Badge of Courage."

On the other hand, a period can be placed inside or outside a closing parenthesis, depending on the usage. If the parenthetical phrase is a complete sentence, the period goes inside the parenthesis. If it is not a complete sentence, it goes outside:

John bought all the dogs at the kennel (except the German shepherd).

John bought all the dogs at the kennel. (The total cost was $239.)

Commas. Like periods, commas always are placed inside quotation marks.

Newspapers often omit commas before conjunctions in series of items unless the omission confuses the meaning:

The school's colors are black, gold and white.

I had orange juice, toast, and ham and eggs for breakfast.

Newspaper style also calls for the elimination of commas between words that relate closely: *Martin Luther King Jr.*, not *Martin Luther King, Jr.*

Commas are used with appositives, adjacent nouns with the same relationship to the rest of the sentence, even before a conjunction:

John Smith, a freshman, Ralph Jones, a sophomore, and Bill Keith, a senior, were elected.

Milwaukee, Wis., and Melbourne, Fla., were selected as sites for the tournament.

When referring to dates, do not use commas when only the month and year are mentioned:

President Reagan was inaugurated in January 1981 on the steps of the Capitol.

When the month and year are accompanied by an exact date, however, commas are used to set off the year:

President Reagan was inaugurated on Jan. 20, 1981, on the steps of the Capitol.

Notice that the comma is needed after the year as well as before.

Semicolons. Semicolons are used to indicate greater separation of thought and information than commas convey, but less than the separation a period implies:

Survivors include a son, James Jones of Chicago; two sisters, Jane Thompson of Chicago and Jill Revel of Milwaukee; and several grandchildren.

Note that the semicolon is used before the final *and* in such a series.

The semicolon is rarely used in newspapers to link independent clauses when a coordinating conjunction is missing:

His plane arrived at 10 p.m.; it was due at 9 a.m.

Despite the infrequent use of such a construction, it is permissible.

Dashes. To indicate an abrupt change, dashes are used:

We will win the game — if I can play.

They also can be used to set off a series within a phrase:

The flowers — white, yellow and red — adorned the flower box below the window.

Dashes should be used sparingly, though. When used to excess they make for difficult reading.

Hyphens. The abused or forgotten punctuation mark in almost all writing in this country is the hyphen. Unfortunately, newspapers are among the worst offenders. Hyphens are plentiful on sports pages:

The Tigers won 14-7.

Too often, however, newspaper reporters and editors omit the necessary hyphen when two or more words function as a compound adjective:

He is an out-of-state student.

A 30-yard field goal led to the last-minute victory.

Omit the hyphen, however, in compound modifiers when the adverb *very* or adverbs ending in *-ly* are involved: *a very cold morning, an easily remembered rule.*

Increasingly, hyphens are disappearing when two words are joined to function as a noun: *makeup*, not *make-up; layout*, not *lay-out*.

Suspensive hyphenation also creates trouble for reporters, who frequently omit the hyphens. Write *a 10- to 30-year prison term*, not *a 10 to 30 year prison term* or *a 10 to 30-year prison term*. In this usage the writer refers to a 10-year prison term and a 30-year prison term. By omitting the first *year*, space is saved, yet the meaning is clear. Completion of the phrase is suspended until after the second numeral, which accounts for the term suspensive hyphenation.

Apostrophes. Apostrophes are used most often in possessives. They also are used to indicate omitted letters *(I've, rock 'n' roll, ne'er-do-well)* or omitted figures *(Spirit of '76, class of '62, the '20s)*. They also are used for plurals of a single letter: *your p's and q's, the Oakland A's*.

The apostrophe is not used for plurals of numerals or multiple-letter combinations: *1920s, ABCs*.

In newspaper usage, the possessive of plural nouns and singular proper names ending with the letter *s* is formed with an apostrophe: *the girls' books, the horses' stables, Dickens' novels, Texas' schools*. The possessive of singular common nouns ending with *s* is formed with *'s*, unless the next word begins with *s*: *hostess's invitation, hostess' story*.

Generally, the possessive of singular nouns ending with *s* sounds such as *ce*, *x* and *z* should be followed by *'s*: *justice's verdict, Marx's theories, Butz's jokes*. There are exceptions in some cases when words not ending in *s* have an *s* sound and are followed by a word that begins with *s*. Thus, you should write *appearance' sake* or *conscience' sake*, but you must add the *'s* in the case of *appearance's cost* or *conscience's voice*. A common error is to use the apostrophe in the possessive *its. It's* is the contraction of *it is; its* is the possessive form.

Question Marks and Exclamation Points. Question marks often are placed improperly in relation to quotation marks. The meaning dictates how a question mark is used:

Who wrote "Gone with the Wind"?

He asked, "How long will it take?"

In the first example, the entire sentence, not just the quoted material, is the question posed. In the second example, only the quoted portion of the sentence is a question.

The question mark supersedes the comma normally used when supplying attribution for a quotation:

"Who is there?" she asked.

Similarly, an exclamation point replaces the comma in attributing a direct quotation:

"Halt!" the guard shouted.

NUMERALS

Whether a numeral is written out or shown in figures usually depends on usage. Because of that, reporters frequently are confused about which is correct.

The General Rule. Figures are used in address numbers, ages, dates, highway designations, monetary units, percentages, speeds, sports, temperatures and times. They also are used to identify aircraft and weapons by model number and following the abbreviation *No.*, as in *No. 1 man.*

Exceptions. There are exceptions to this rule. Amounts of less than 1 percent are written out *(four-tenths percent)* unless used in a series *(.04 percent, .05 percent and .06 percent).*

Casual references to temperatures, other than actual thermometer readings, also are written out:

The temperature at 9 p.m. was 8 degrees, a drop of four degrees since noon.

Casual numbers are written out when the numbers one through nine are used infrequently in a story:

The baker made eight pies last night.

The school will accept only three more students.

Suggested Readings

The Associated Press Stylebook. New York: The Associated Press, 1979. This manual is almost identical to The United Press International Stylebook but contains a useful section on libel law.

Copperud, Roy H. A Dictionary of Usage and Style. New York: Hawthorn Books, 1964. A useful reference work.

Jordan, Lewis, ed. The New York Times Manual of Style and Usage. New York: Times Books, 1976. A popular supplement to the wire service stylebooks.

The United Press International Stylebook. New York: United Press International, 1977. Almost identical to the AP stylebook, but without the section on libel.

The Washington Post Deskbook on Style. New York: McGraw-Hill, 1978. Another popular supplement to the wire service stylebooks.

Webster's New World Dictionary of the American Language, Second College Edition. New York: William Collins–World Publishing Co. Inc., 1976. The dictionary recommended by the wire services as a supplemental reference work.

4

The Inverted Pyramid

Many people were surprised that USA Today, the most innovative newspaper ever marketed, built its product around the *inverted pyramid*, a story form used by newspapers since the turn of the century. USA Today uses the inverted pyramid because it is the most space-efficient story form known. It permits writers to go on at great length, or, as is more often the case, to deliver the most important information in a paragraph or two. That attribute is what USA Today capitalizes on most; it is marketed as a paper you can read quickly. A national story that might be 10 paragraphs in your local newspaper will probably be five in USA Today. As the newspaper's soaring circulation figures demonstrate, there clearly is an audience for that approach to the news.

The king in "Alice in Wonderland" would never succeed as an editor at USA Today. Asked where to start, he replied, "Begin at the beginning and go on till you come to the end; then stop." Reporters often begin at the end.

Like the miner sifting through a million grains of sand for a speck of gold, the reporter pans the bits of information for the nugget that belongs in the lead. That information — the climax of the event, the theme statement of a speech, the result of an investigation — is presented as simply and clearly as possible in the first paragraph. It sets the tone. It advertises what is coming in the rest of the story. It conveys the most important information in the story.

The lead sits atop a news-writing formula called the inverted pyramid, in which information is arranged in descending order of importance. Newspapers developed this story formula for two important reasons:

Figure 4.1 Front Page of USA Today for July 20–22, 1984.

1. The reader may stop reading at any time, and thus it is necessary to provide the important news first. A person who reads as little as one paragraph gets the essential elements in the story.

2. Many newspaper stories are cut to fit a certain amount of space, and cutting is easier if information is presented in order of descending importance. The inverted pyramid format allows editors to cut stories from the bottom quickly without destroying the story.

The first is a necessary concession to a readership distracted by radio and television, by children and private concerns. Many subscribers read only a few paragraphs of most stories. If a reporter were to write an account of a car accident by starting when the driver got into the car to begin a trip, many readers would never stay with the story long enough to find out that the driver was killed.

By the turn of the century, the inverted pyramid was fairly common. Before then, reporters were less direct. In 1869 The New York Herald sent Henry Morton Stanley to Africa to find the famous explorer-missionary David Livingstone. Stanley's famous account of the meeting began:

> Only two months gone, and what a change in my feelings! But two months ago, what a peevish, fretful soul was mine! What a hopeless prospect presented itself before your correspondent!

After several similar sentences, the writer reports, "And the only answer to it all is [that] Livingstone, the hero traveler, is alongside of me."

Stanley reported the most important information so casually that unless the headline reported the news, today's subscriber probably would not have read far enough into the story to learn that Livingstone had been found. Today's reporter would probably begin the story like this:

```
Dr. David Livingstone, the missionary-explorer missing
for six years, is working with natives in an African vil-
lage on the shores of Lake Tanganyika.
```

The second function of the inverted pyramid — permitting editors to cut the story from the bottom — fulfills a mechanical requirement. If the story does not fit in the space allotted to it, an editor, working against a deadline, has to shorten the story quickly. If it is organized according to the inverted pyramid formula, the story can be shortened by eliminating paragraphs from the bottom. Because the most important information is contained in the first several paragraphs, the story will not be destroyed. But if an editor had cut Stanley's story from the bottom, we would never have had these now famous lines, which ended the story:

> "Dr. Livingstone, I presume?" And
> he says, "Yes."

In Part Three, where basic story types are discussed, we shall see some examples of stories that are more effectively written in less traditional forms than in the inverted pyramid form, and in Chapter 15 we will discuss other ways to organize a news story. It may be that in the next several years, the inverted pyramid will become less important to newspapers. But if there is a change, it will be through evolution, not revolution.

While the inverted pyramid delivers the important news first, it does not encourage subscribers to read the entire story. There is no suspense. Besides, broadcast journalists usually can get the news to consumers first, and they do it by using the inverted pyramid. Although readers consistently say in surveys that they want news from their newspapers, many editors believe readers want some of that news written in a form other than the traditional inverted pyramid.

The production advantage of the inverted pyramid also is becoming less important. On video display terminals stories can be edited quickly to fit a given space rather than just shortened from the bottom.

But the day when the inverted pyramid is relegated to journalism history books is not yet here and probably never will be. Perhaps 90 percent of the stories in today's newspapers are written in the style of the inverted pyramid. As long as newspapers continue to emphasize the quick, direct, simple approach to communications, and as long as millions of readers continue to accept it, the inverted pyramid will serve the journalist well, and every journalist should master its form. Those who do will be those who have mastered the art of making news judgments. The inverted pyramid forces the journalist to identify and rank the most newsworthy elements in each story. That is important work. No matter what kind of stories you deal with — whether obituaries, accidents, speeches, press conferences, fires or meetings — you will be required to use the skills you learn here.

In this chapter you will learn:

1. How to write leads.

2. How to organize a story using the inverted pyramid.

How to Write Leads

To write a lead, you first must recognize what goes into one. Journalists traditionally answer six questions. They are:

1. Who?
2. What?
3. When?
4. Where?
5. Why?
6. How?

The information from every event you witness and every story you hear can be reduced to answers to these six questions. Consider this example of an incoming call at fire headquarters:

"Fire department," the dispatcher answers.

"Hello. At about 10 o'clock, I was lying on my bed watching TV and smoking," the voice says. "I must have fallen asleep about 10:30 because that's when the football game was over. Anyway, I woke up just now and my bedroom is on fire...."

That dialogue isn't very informative or convincing. More likely our sleepy television viewer awoke in a smoke-filled room, crawled to the telephone and dialed frantically. The conversation at headquarters would more likely have gone like this:

"Fire department."

"FIRE!" a voice at the other end yells.

"Where?" the dispatcher asks.

"At 1705 West Haven Street."

When fire is licking at his heels, even a non-journalist knows the lead. How the fire started is not important to the dispatcher; that a house is burning — and where that house is located — is.

The journalist must go through essentially the same process to determine the lead. Whereas the caller served the fire department, the reporter must serve his or her readers. What is most important to them?

After the fire is over, there is much information a reporter must gather. Among the questions a reporter would routinely ask are these:

- When did it start?
- When was it reported?
- Who reported it?
- How was it reported?
- How long did it take the Fire Department to respond?
- How long did it take to extinguish the fire?
- How many fires have been attributed to careless smoking this year?
- How does that compare to figures in previous years?
- Were there any injuries or deaths?
- What was the damage?
- Did the smoker have insurance on his house?
- Will there be charges filed against the smoker?

With this information in hand, you can begin to write the story.

WRITING THE LEAD

Start looking over your notes.

The who? A smoker, Henry Smith, 29. The age is important. Along with other personal information, such as address and occupation, it differentiates him from other Henry Smiths in the readership area.

What? Fire caused damage estimated by the fire chief at $2,500.

Where? 1705 W. Haven St.

When? The call was received at 10:55 p.m., Tuesday. Firefighters from Station 19 arrived at the scene at 11:04. The fire was extinguished at 11:30.

Why? The fire was started by carelessness on the part of Smith, according to Fire Chief Bill Malone.

How? Smith said he fell asleep in bed while he was smoking a cigarette.

If you had asked other questions, you might have also learned from the fire department that it was only the third fire this year caused by smoking in bed. At this time last year, there had been four such fires. Smith said he had insurance. The fire chief said there will not be any charges filed against Smith. It was the first fire at this house. Smith was not injured.

Assume your city editor has suggested you hold it to about four

Figure 4.2 The Six Elements of a News Lead.

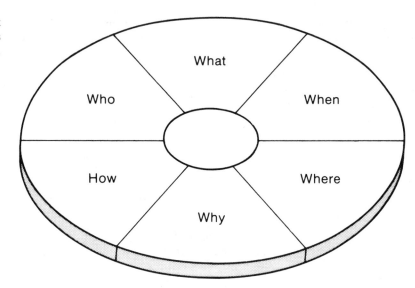

paragraphs. Your first step is to rank the information in descending order of importance. There are lots of fires in this town, but only three this year have been caused by smoking in bed. Perhaps that's the most important thing about this story. You begin to type:

```
    A fire started by a careless smoker caused an estimated
$2,500 in damage to a home.
```

Only 16 words. You should try to hold every lead to fewer than 35 words if possible. Maybe it's too brief, though. Have you left anything out? Maybe you should include the time element — to give the story a sense of immediacy. You rewrite:

```
    A Tuesday night fire started by a careless smoker caused
an estimated $2,500 in damage to a home at 1705 W. Haven
St.
```

The reader would also want to know "where." Is it near my house? Is it someone I know? Besides, you still have only 23 words.

Just then the city editor walks by and glances over your shoulder. "Who said it was a careless smoker?" the editor asks. "Stay out of the story."

You realize you have committed a basic error in news writing: You have allowed an unattributed opinion to slip into the story. You have two choices. You can attribute the "careless smoker" information to the fire chief in the lead or you can rewrite. You choose to rewrite by using the chief's exact words. You also realize that your sentence emphasizes the damage instead of the cause. You write:

```
    Fire that caused an estimated $2,500 in damage to a home
at 1705 W. Haven St. Tuesday night was caused by smoking in
bed, Fire Chief Bill Malone said.
```

Now 29 words have answered the question of "what" (a fire), "where" (1705 W. Haven St.), "when" (Tuesday night), and "how" (smoking in bed). And it is attributed. But you have not answered "who" and "why." You continue, still ranking the information in descending order of importance.

```
    The owner of the home, Henry Smith, 29, said he fell
asleep in bed while smoking a cigarette. When he awoke
about 30 minutes later, the room was filled with smoke.
    Firemen arrived nine minutes after receiving the call.
It took them 26 minutes to extinguish the fire, which was
confined to the bedroom of the one-story house.
    According to Chief Malone, this is the third fire this
year caused by careless smokers.
    Smith, who was not injured, said the house was insured.
```

You take the story to the city editor, who reads through the copy quickly. Then she checks the telephone book and the city directory.

As you watch, she crosses out "caused an estimated $2,500 in" and "to" and changes "damage" to "damaged." She also specifies who was smoking. The lead now reads:

```
    Fire that damaged a home at 1705 W. Haven St. Tuesday
night was caused when the occupant fell asleep while smok-
ing in bed, Fire Chief Bill Malone said.
```

She is eliminating the less important to emphasize the most important aspects of the story. Besides, $2,500 isn't much money when you are talking about a house fire. Put it lower in the story.

This time, though, you have an even more serious problem. Both the telephone book and the city directory list the gentleman who lives at 1705 W. Haven St. as Henry Smyth. S-m-y-t-h.

Never put a name in a story without checking the spelling, even when the source tells you his name is Smith.

There are several lessons you can learn from this experience. They are:

1. *Always* check names.
2. Keep the lead short.
3. Attribute opinion. (Smoking in bed is a fact. That it was careless is an opinion.)

4. Find out the who, what, where, when, why and how. However, if they have no bearing on the story, they might not have to be included.

5. Report information basic to the story even if it is routine. Not everything you learn is important enough to be reported, but you'll never know unless you gather the information.

ALTERNATE LEADS

In the lead reporting the fire, the "what" (fire) is of secondary importance to how it started. A slightly different set of facts would affect the news value of the elements and, consequently, your story. For instance, if Smyth turned out to have been a convicted arsonist, you probably would have emphasized that bizarre twist to the story:

> A convicted arsonist awoke Tuesday night to find that his bedroom was filled with smoke. He escaped and later said that he had fallen asleep while smoking.
> Henry Smyth, 29, who served a three-year term for . . .

If Smyth were the mayor, that would be newsworthy:

> Mayor Henry Smyth escaped injury Tuesday night when he awoke to find his bedroom filled with smoke. Smyth said he had fallen asleep while smoking in bed.

No journalist relies on formulas to write inverted pyramid leads, but you may find it useful, especially in the beginning, to learn some typical types of leads. The labels that follow are arbitrary, but the approaches are not. Here are some types of leads that can help you write once you have decided what is most important:

1. Immediate-identification leads.
2. Delayed-identification leads.
3. Summary leads.
4. Multiple-elements leads.
5. Leads with a twist.

The nature of the story dictates the kind of lead. The first fire story can be categorized as a summary lead that emphasized "how." The second lead was a delayed-identification lead that emphasized "what." And the third was an immediate-identification lead that emphasized "what." Let's look at each of the types of leads in more detail.

Immediate-Identification Leads

In the immediate-identification lead, one of the most important facts is "who." Reporters often use this approach when someone important or someone whose name is widely recognized is making news. Consider the following example:

> NEW YORK (UPI) — Richard Nixon predicted Friday that Republicans will be the first to nominate a woman as vice president, maybe in 1988.

If the writer had begun the story with the lead, "A former president predicted Friday that Republicans will be the first to nominate a woman as vice president," an important category of information — "who" — would have been delayed until the second paragraph. Well-known names catch the reader's eye and interest.

Any action by a person in the public eye can merit an immediate identification:

> Pop singer Michael Jackson was hospitalized in good condition with second-degree burns on his scalp last night after his hair caught fire while he was filming a commercial.

It would make no sense to delay the identification of someone as well-known as Jackson. Names, as People magazine has shown, make news.

In an accident, the "who" may be important because it is someone well known by name or position:

> MADISON, Wis. — Mayor John Jones was killed today in a two-car collision two blocks from his home.

In small communities the "who" in an accident may always be in the lead. In larger communities names are not as recognizable. As a rule, if the name is well-known, it would appear in the lead.

Delayed-Identification Leads

When a reporter uses a *delayed-identification lead*, usually it is because the person or persons involved have little name recognition among the readers. John Jones, the mayor, is well-known; John Jones, the carpenter, is not. Thus, in fairly large cities an accident is usually reported like this:

> MADISON, Wis. — A 39-year-old carpenter was killed today in a two-car collision two blocks from his home.
>
> Dead is William Domonske of 205 W. Oak St. Injured in the accident and taken to Mercy Hospital were Mary Craig of 204 Maple Ave., and Rebecca Roets, 12, of 207 Maple Ave.

There are two other occasions when the reporter may choose to delay identification of the person involved in the story until the second paragraph. They are:

1. When the person's name may not be well-known but his or her position, title or achievements are important or interesting.
2. When the lead is becoming too wordy.

In the following examples, the titles of those making news are well-known but the names are not:

> STUTTGART, West Germany — A 20-year-old American soldier assigned to a Pershing 2 nuclear-missile unit was kidnapped by "six German demonstrators" early Saturday, a West German police official reported.
>
> Hans-Peter Sturm, a senior police officer in Stuttgart, identified the missing soldier as Lane Fowler . . .

> WASHINGTON — A Senate subcommittee chairman angrily accused the Environmental Protection Agency of foot-dragging yesterday for failing to remove foods contaminated with the deadly pesticide ethyl dibromide from the marketplace.
>
> Sen. David Durenberger, R—Minn., said the public . . .

In both cases, the "what" — the kidnapping and the allegation — is more important than the "who." However, if you are writing for the soldier's home-town or even home-state newspaper or broadcast station, or if you are writing in Durenberger's home state, the "who" might be important enough to put in the lead.

Titles are often bulky. "Chairman of the Federal Communications Commission" assures you of clutter even before you finish writing the rest of the sentence. "United Nations ambassador" takes away many options from the writer. When dealing with these types of titles, writers often choose to use the title and delay introducing the name until the second or third paragraph. While the name often is shorter, it is more important that the title be introduced first. Many people would not recognize the name of the chairman of the FCC or the ambassador to the United Nations. Thus, stories about them might open:

WASHINGTON — The U.S. ambassador to the United Nations today accused three Arab states of refusing to negotiate for peace "in good faith."

WASHINGTON — The chairman of the Federal Communications Commission said today that networks must decrease the amount of sex and violence shown on television.

In both examples, "who" made the statements is more important than the name of the person holding the position.

Summary Leads

When a reporter deals with a story with several important elements, he or she may choose to sum up what happened in a *summary lead* rather than highlight a specific action. It is one of the few times that a general statement is preferable to specific action.

When the Occupational Safety and Health Administration announced it was revising many of the rules that had irritated employers for years, both wire services wrote a summary lead:

WASHINGTON (UPI) — The Labor Department Monday proposed to dump 1,100 outmoded, busybody regulations, governing such problems as the kinds of wood used in stepladders to construction requirements of privies on building sites.

WASHINGTON (AP) — The government guardian of safety and health in the workplace proposed on Monday to shed 1,100 rules and thereby lose some of its reputation as a nitpicker.

While UPI did refer to two specific rules to be changed, both wire services summarized the scope and reasons for the action rather than dwell on any of the 1,100 rules that were changed.

Likewise, if the city council rewrites the city ordinances, unless one of the changes is of overriding importance, most reporters will use a summary lead:

MOLINE, Ill. — The City Council replaced the city's 75-year-old municipal code with a revised version Tuesday night.

The basic question the reporter must answer is whether the whole of the action is more important than any of its parts. If the answer is yes, a summary lead is in order.

Multiple-Elements Leads

In some stories, choosing one theme for the lead is too restrictive. In such cases the reporter can choose a *multiple-elements lead* to work more information into the first paragraph. But such a lead must be written within the confines of a clear, simple sentence or sentences. Consider this example:

> PORTLAND, Wash. — The City Council Tuesday ordered three department heads fired, established an administrative review board, and said it would begin to monitor the work habits of administrators.

Notice that not only the actions but also the construction of the verb phrases within the sentence are parallel. Parallel structure also characterizes this news extract, which presents a visual picture of the scene of a tragedy:

> BAY CITY, Mich. — A flash fire that swept through a landmark downtown hotel Saturday killed at least 12 persons, injured 60 more and forced scores of residents to leap from windows and the roof in near-zero cold.

In the last example, we are told where it happened, what happened, how many were killed and injured.

Some multiple-elements leads actually consist of two paragraphs. This occurs when the reporter decides that there are several elements that need prominent display. For example:

> The Board of Education Tuesday night voted to lower the tax rate 12 cents per $100 valuation. Members then approved a budget $150,000 less than last year's and instructed the superintendent to decrease the staff by 25 people.
>
> The board also approved a set of student conduct rules, which include a provision that students with three or more unexcused absences a year will be suspended for a week.

Simpler leads are preferable. But a multiple-elements lead is one of the options to be used by a reporter. Use it sparingly.

Leads With a Twist

Although the inverted pyramid is designed to tell readers the news first and fast, not all stories begin with the most important statement. When the news is unusual, often the lead is, too.

When a group of suspected drug dealers was arrested at a wedding, the Associated Press account focused on the oddity:

> NARRAGANSETT, R.I. (AP) — The wedding guests included drug suspects, the social coordinator was a narcotics agent, the justice of the peace was a police chief, and 52 officers were party crashers.
>
> For the unsuspecting bride and groom, the ceremony Friday night was truly unforgettable — a sting operation set up by state and local police that led to 30 arrests.

Not exactly your traditional wedding or your traditional lead. Yet, the essential information is contained within the first two paragraphs. A less imaginative writer would have written something like this:

> Thirty suspected drug dealers, including a couple about to be married, were arrested at a wedding Friday night.

That approach is like slapping a generic label on a Mercedes-Benz. The inverted pyramid approach is not so rigid that there isn't room for fun and oddity.

Story Organization

Like the theater marquee, the lead is an attention getter. Sometimes the movie doesn't fulfill the promises of the marquee; sometimes the story doesn't fulfill the promises of the lead. In either case the customer is dissatisfied.

The inverted pyramid is designed to help reporters put information in logical order. It forces the reporter to rank, in order of importance, the information to be presented.

Just as there is a checklist for writing the lead, there is also a checklist for assembling the rest of the inverted pyramid. Included on that checklist are the following rules:

1. Introduce additional important information you were not able to include in the lead.
2. Elaborate on the information presented in the lead.
3. Continue introducing new information in the order in which you have ranked it by importance.

4. Develop the ideas in the same order in which you have introduced them.
5. Generally, use only one new idea in each paragraph.

Let's see how the pros do it.

ONE-SUBJECT STORIES

Many newspaper stories report on a single subject. The following UPI article on cross-ownership of newspapers and broadcast properties is typical of this type of newspaper story and is a professionally written example of inverted pyramid form:

1. The news: what the Justice Department said

WASHINGTON (UPI) — The Justice Department says a U.S. appeals court went too far last March in requiring the breakup of most jointly owned newspaper and broadcast combinations in the same market.

2. Details to support the lead and the time element

The government, in a brief filed late Tuesday with the Supreme Court, conceded the Federal Communications Commission erred in issuing rules in 1975 allowing most existing combinations to remain while barring future ones.

3. Elaboration on the Justice Department's reasoning for its conclusion

But it said the U.S. Appeals Court for the District of Columbia "should not . . . have entered an order effectively requiring divestiture of existing cross-ownerships operating in the same market."

4. More elaboration

"The court's function ended once it had exposed the error in the commission's reasoning," it said.

5. A new element, a call for action

The government brief urged the Supreme Court to set aside that portion of the ruling and send the case back to the FCC for drafting of new rules "based on a reasoned application of the governing legal principles."

6. Date for the hearing of the appealed case for which the brief was written

The Supreme Court plans to hear arguments Jan. 16 on appeals by the FCC, publishers and broadcasters from the lower-court decision, which if allowed to stand could lead to the breakup of more than 100 newspaper-broadcast combinations in 44 states.

7–9. Background information

The FCC rules barred future newspaper-broadcast cross-ownerships in the same market but required divestiture of existing combinations in only 16 cases where monopoly situations existed.

The appeals court, ruling on a public interest group's challenge to the rules, upheld the ban on future joint newspaper-broadcast ownership in the same city. But it said divestiture should be required of existing co-located combinations, "except in those cases where the evidence clearly discloses that cross-ownership is in the public interest."

Some publishers already have begun swapping stations to sidestep the ruling.

10–13. Less important details from the brief

The Justice Department, in its brief, disagreed in part with the FCC, which it normally would be representing before the high court.

The FCC says most existing combinations should be left in place to preserve local ownership and management, avoid economic dislocation and prevent disruption and instability of service.

But the Justice Department brief said the "grandfather clause" protecting incumbent licensees represents an arbitrary compromise of the FCC policy of promoting media ownership diversity.

It said most newspaper owners are not involved in management of common market broadcast stations, and "it strains credulity to assert that the transfer of several hundred million dollars of existing assets from one group of investors to another would have any discernible effect on the national economy."

The story meets the test of the inverted pyramid. The lead presents a simple, clear statement. Subsequent paragraphs explain and provide evidence to support the lead. There is only one idea to a paragraph. The reader is given all essential information in the first five paragraphs.

MULTIPLE-ELEMENTS STORY

Earlier in this chapter, we discussed multiple-elements leads. They occur most often when you are reporting on councils, boards, commissions, legislatures and even the U.S. Supreme Court. Any of those bodies act on numerous subjects in one sitting. Frequently, their actions are unrelated, and more than one action is often important enough to merit attention in the lead. You have three options:

1. You can write more than one story. That, of course, depends on permission from your editor. There may not be enough space.

2. You can write a summary box. It would be displayed along with the story. In it you would list the major actions taken by the council or decisions issued by the court.

3. You can write a multiple-elements lead and story. Let's go back to the one we used earlier when discussing leads:

The Board of Education Tuesday night voted to lower the tax rate 12 cents per $100 valuation. Members then approved a budget $150,000 less than last year's and instructed the superintendent to decrease the staff by 25 people.

The board also approved a set of student conduct rules, which include a provision that students with three or more unexcused absences a year will be suspended for a week.

There are four newsworthy actions in these two paragraphs: establishing a tax rate, approving a budget, cutting staff and adopting conduct rules. In this and all stories that deal with several important elements, the writer highlights the most important. Sometimes there are several that can be equated, as in the school board example. Most of the time, one action stands out above the rest. When it does, it is important to summarize other actions after the lead. For instance, if you and your editor judged that establishing the tax rate was more important than anything else that happened at the school board meeting, you would approach it like this:

Lead   The Board of Education Tuesday night voted to lower the tax rate 12 cents per $100 valuation.

Support for lead   The new rate is $1.18 per $100 valuation. That means that if your property is assessed at $30,000, your school tax will be $354 next year.

Summary of other action   The board also approved a budget that is $150,000 less than last year's, instructed the superintendent to cut the staff by 25 and approved a set of rules governing student conduct.

Notice that the lead is followed by a paragraph that supports and enlarges upon the information in it before the summary paragraph appears. Whether you need a support paragraph before summarizing other action depends upon how complete you are able to make the lead.

In all multiple-elements stories, the first two or three paragraphs determine the order of the rest of the story. To maintain coherence in your story, you must then provide the details of the actions in the order in which you have introduced them. In the school board story, that means that the next several paragraphs would look something like this:

Saying that "economic conditions require we give citizens tax relief," School Board President Harold Lister led the drive to cut the budget. The action passed with only member Morgan Ernest dissenting.

Superintendent Todd Russell said he would have to lay off 10 to 15 people to comply with the board directive. The rest of the positions will be vacated by those leaving voluntarily or retiring.

"I don't like it," Russell said. "I don't want to do it, but I will."

The $150,000 budget cut represents a decrease of 5 percent in the $3 million budget. The staff layoffs will save about $500,000, but the district will receive $200,000 less in state aid next year. Other costs, such as busing and hot lunch service, will increase about $150,000.

Faculty president Terrell Roberts said the teachers would meet Thursday to decide what, if any, action they would take. He added, however, that the teachers had not been consulted and that many of them were displeased.

There were also many displeased students. About 50 of them attended the meeting to present a petition with 352 signatures against the proposed rules of conduct. Despite that, the board voted 7–0 to adopt them. There are about 1,500 students in the school. . . .

The most important thing to remember about multiple-elements stories is to go back and explain the items in the same order in which they were introduced.

5
Interviewing

David Hacker of the Kansas City (Mo.) Times knew it was a long shot. Just four days earlier, a balcony in the Hyatt Regency Hotel had collapsed and killed 111 people. Kansas City was awash in grief. He wanted to talk to some of the relatives of the victims.

But how? And who?

He called a priest, whom he didn't even know. He described what he wanted, but told the priest that if he didn't think it would help the relatives and the community deal with the loss, he didn't want the priest to help. And he asked the priest not to answer then but to think about it and get back to him.

The priest not only got back to him but was able to convince a couple of the victims' wives to talk to Hacker. With this commitment, Hacker asked a rabbi for the same favor. The rabbi also helped.

That much savvy was needed just to get to the interviews. Once there, Hacker needed all the experience and skill he had acquired during his years as a journalist, but he knew that if he didn't get his foot in the door, he'd never have a chance to ask the questions.

Interviewing is the key to most stories you will write. Your ability to get people to talk to you is the difference between good and mediocre reporting.

Although you already have experience interviewing someone, you probably haven't thought much about how or why you've been doing it. And you probably haven't had much experience trying to get information from someone who wants to withhold it. Those few times you've tried, you probably have been frustrated:

"Professor, why did I get a B in your course?"
"Because you didn't deserve an A."
"Why not?"
"Because."

Sooner or later, you stomp out of the office. Now you are a reporter and confronted by a similar situation:

"Mr. Mayor, why did you fire the police chief?"
"I don't want to discuss that because it's a personnel matter."

Because journalists shouldn't go stomping out of the room when they are denied information, they must have other resources. The mayor may not want to discuss the firing; perhaps he never will. But a skillful questioner often can obtain information the source does not want to divulge or does not even realize he or she is giving. The reporter may ask, for instance, what qualities the mayor will be looking for in a new police chief. The answer may provide the clue to why he fired the last one.

Information is the merchandise of a journalist. While some of it is gathered from records and some from observation, most of it is gathered in person-to-person conversations. For that reason every journalist needs to develop interviewing skills.

Interviewing is an imperfect process. We can control some of the variables, but we cannot control the two that count the most: the interviewer and the source. Consequently, you must work hard to refine your skills. You simultaneously ask questions, digest responses, record answers, cajole the source, gauge reactions and look for details. This is no work for the unprepared.

In this chapter you will learn:

1. How to prepare for an interview.
2. How to phrase your questions.
3. How to establish rapport with a source.
4. How to ensure accuracy.

Preparing for the Interview

A reporter was assigned to interview Vivien Leigh, who was attending the premiere of the reissue of "Gone With the Wind." When he opened the interview by asking her what part she played in the film, Miss Leigh, whose portrayal of Scarlett O'Hara is a classic, indignantly ended the conversation — with good reason. A reporter who begins an interview without the proper preparation is like a pilot flying without a navigator. Both may make it, but flying blind is not the best way to get there.

The success of the interview depends as much on what you do before you ask the first question as it does on the questioning and writing. A. J. Liebling, a famous journalist, book author and press critic, didn't know much about horse racing, but his first question in an interview with jockey Eddie Arcaro was, "How many holes longer do you keep your left stirrup than your right?" Arcaro responded enthusiastically to the knowledgeable question. Liebling's research gave him the key to open the interview. A source who thinks the reporter is knowledgeable about the subject of the interview is more likely to speak frankly and fully than one who must explain everything as the conversation progresses.

Liebling was able to overcome Arcaro's skepticism with a single question. Syl Jones had considerably more difficulty with William Shockley, who won a Pulitzer Prize for his work developing the transistor. Jones, however, wanted to talk to him for Playboy magazine about much more volatile topics: Shockley's theory of black genetic inferiority and his revelation that he had participated in a Nobel-laureate sperm bank. Burned many times by the press, Shockley was exceedingly cautious.

Shockley often turned down reporters' requests to interview him because he believed they didn't know enough about genetics. By phone, Shockley quizzed Jones, a science and medical writer, about genetics. The quizzes involved complicated mathematical analyses of statistics designed by Shockley in support of his theories. After a few weeks of grilling, he agreed that Jones was competent enough to interview him.

But first Shockley wanted even more information. He asked for personal information, everything from where Jones was born to where he went to school. Jones told the rest of the story in Playboy:

> Long before this point in the process, most other reporters had written Shockley off as a kook and had given up. I was tempted to do the same. But something intrigued me: Never once did he ask my race or make any kind of racist remark, and he had no idea I was black. I didn't tell him, because I was hoping for a confrontation. . . .
>
> When a white photographer and I showed up at Stanford for the interview, Shockley instinctively reached to shake the photographer's hand with the greeting, "Hello, Mr. Jones." It was a wrong guess that seemed almost to stagger him. Obviously stunned by my blackness, he insisted that I submit to one final test, concocted on the spur of the moment, concerning the application of the Pythagorean theorem to some now long forgotten part of his dysgenic thesis. Somehow, I came up with a satisfactory explanation, and Shockley had no choice but to grant me the interview.

Let's hope you never have to overcome those kinds of barriers.

CONSIDERATION OF STORY TYPE

How you prepare for the interview depends in part on what kind of a story you intend to write. You may be doing a news story, a personality profile or an investigative piece. In each case you check the newspaper library and search the data bank, talk to other reporters and, if there's enough time, read magazine articles and books.

To prepare for a news story, you pay more attention to clips about the subject of the story than to those about the personality of the individual to be interviewed. To prepare for a profile, you look for personality quirks and the subject's interests, family, friends, travels and habits. To prepare for an investigative piece, you want to know both your subject matter and the person you are interviewing. Let's look at each of these three types of stories more closely.

The News Story

One day in August 1979, Paul Leavitt made a routine telephone call to a law enforcement source. Leavitt, the assistant city editor for the Des Moines (Iowa) Register, was working on a story. He knew the source from his days as a county government and courts reporter for the Register.

He expected the story, and the interview, to be routine. Polk County was building a new jail. Leavitt wanted to find out about the progress on the new building. The source begged ignorance. He said, "Oh, Leavitt, I don't know. I haven't had time to keep up on that, what with all these meetings on the pope's visit."

Leavitt didn't say anything right away. A less astute reporter might have let the source know he was surprised. The pope in Des Moines? Are you kidding? Instead, Leavitt remembered a story he had read about an Iowan who had extended an invitation for John Paul II to stop in Iowa during his American visit. Leavitt didn't think the Iowan had much of a chance. When the Vatican had announced the pope's visit, people from every state were bartering for a chance to bask in the worldwide limelight.

Still, the source's slip of the tongue seemed genuine. Leavitt finally replied, "Oh, yeah, that's right. When's he coming, anyway?"

"October 4," the source said.

As the conversation progressed, Leavitt waved frantically to the Register's managing editor. A major story was brewing.

"I started asking him some more questions," Leavitt recalls, "then it dawned on him that he probably wasn't supposed to be talking about this. But it was clear from what he said that the pope was definitely coming to Iowa. He even had the hours."

Before the conversation ended, Leavitt had learned of a meeting among the Secret Service, the Vatican, the U.S. State Department and Iowa law enforcement officials to discuss the trip. He also had learned when the pope would arrive, where he would arrive, where he would celebrate Mass and when he would leave.

As a result, the Register stunned its readers the next morning with a copyrighted story saying the pope would speak in Des Moines on Oct. 4. The story was printed three weeks before the Vatican released its official itinerary of the visit. Other area reporters scoffed at the story. One newspaper even printed a story poking fun at the thought of John Paul II hobnobbing in an Iowa cornfield.

Leavitt and the Register were vindicated. As scheduled, the pope arrived Oct. 4—and celebrated Mass in an Iowa cornfield.

Remembering his conversation with the source, and how a routine question turned into a bona fide scoop, Leavitt said, "I don't even remember what the original question was."

Leavitt probably would not have gotten the story had he not remembered the earlier story about the invitation and known something else about interviewing: When a source unwittingly gives you a scoop, sometimes it is best to act as if you already know it. That may encourage the source to give you more information.

The Profile

A reporter who was assigned to do a profile of the newly appointed chancellor of a local campus prepared for the interview differently. Because the newspaper library had nothing except the news story of the appointment, the reporter had to look elsewhere. He obtained a copy of her résumé. He read articles she had written and found a story about her in a national magazine. He asked search committee members their impressions of her. Since she had not yet assumed the office, only a few people on campus knew her at all. The reporter called former co-workers. By the time he arrived at the chancellor's office, he felt he knew what kind of person to expect.

And he was right. The conversation flowed easily. The reporter knew about her flying lessons, her dedication to physical fitness and her previous teaching experience. The chancellor-designate was at ease. The resulting story was full of detail and lively quotes:

NORMAN, Okla. — The University's next chancellor tolerates having the door opened for her. She enjoys a hand with her coat. But she would rather pull her own plane.

Before flight instructor Joe Estill can pull the red-striped two seater out of the hangar and begin the morning lesson, instructee Barbara Uehling steps between him and the tow handle.

In a falsetto imitation of some medieval gallant, she says, "Here, let me do that." The 45-year-old, 5-foot-2 provost of the University of Oklahoma at Norman nudges the 6-foot male aside, grabs the handle firmly with two fists and single-handedly pulls the Piper Cub 10 yards to the taxi strip.

Estill waits for his student to enter the plane and they begin practicing soft-field takeoffs and landings.

"Last summer I decided I work very hard and there ought to be a little time in life that's just for me," says Dr. Uehling, who was named chancellor of the University of Missouri's Columbia campus Feb. 24.

In flying she finds freedom. "There are no telephones, and when you're learning a skill like that which is so obviously a life-and-death matter, you don't have time to think of anything else. It completely absorbs me."

Dr. Uehling is three lessons away from her pilot's license. That may mean three weeks and that may mean more than three months. She is trying to land smoothly in her present post as chief academic officer at Oklahoma so she can take off as chancellor at Columbia before Aug. 1. As a result, she says she is lucky to be able to take one lesson every two weeks.

The Investigative Piece

The casual atmosphere of the Uehling interview is not always possible for the investigative reporter. Here, the adversary relationship determines both the preparation required and the atmosphere of the interview itself. An investigative reporter is like an attorney in a courtroom. Wise attorneys know what the answers to their questions will be. So do investigative reporters. Preparation is essential.

In the early stages of the investigation, you conduct some fishing expedition interviews: Because you don't know how much the source knows, you cast around. Start with persons on the fringes. Gather as much as you can from them. Study the records. Only after you have most of the evidence do you confront your central character. You start with a large circle and gradually draw it smaller.

When Glenn Bunting, a reporter for the San Jose (Calif.) Mercury News, heard complaints about the low caliber of workers turned out by a government-funded training agency, he quietly did a little checking. Before he had gone too far, he had a friendly interview with the administrator, who did not know the real purpose of Bunting's inquiries.

Then Bunting went to work. He tracked the trail of money. He examined bank statements and canceled checks, government audit reports, purchase orders and weekly time cards. He interviewed counselors and job-training instructors, law officers and others who did business with the agency. By the time he was ready to talk to the administrator again, he already had most of his story confirmed. This is how the story of the interview began:

> Robert Bernal was getting angry. Confronted with evidence of wrongdoing in Project DARE, his face turned red and his voice grew louder.
>
> "Why are you attacking me?" he asked. "You don't believe me, but everything I've told you is the truth. I haven't told you any barefaced lies."
>
> But he had.

Among other things, Bunting was able to show that Bernal had earned a "degree" not from Stanford as he claimed, but from San

Quentin Prison. Confronted with the evidence, Bernal told Bunting, "You never lose the stigma of being in prison. You have a tendency to build up a facade, a degree of phoniness — even saying that you have a college degree."

Bunting was able to pierce the deceptions because he had drawn the circle around Bernal tighter and tighter before he went into the interview.

OTHER PREPARATORY CONSIDERATIONS

All this homework is important, but it may be something as trifling as your appearance that determines whether you will have a successful interview. You would hardly wear cutoff shorts into a corporation president's suite, and you wouldn't wear a three-piece suit to talk to underground revolutionaries. It is your right to wear your hair however you wish and to wear whatever clothes you want, but it is the source's prerogative to refuse to talk to you. Most reporters choose to blend in with the environment.

You have now done the appropriate homework. You are properly attired. You have made an appointment and told the source how much time you need. Before you leave, you should write down a list of questions you want to ask. They will guide you through the interview and prevent you from missing important topics altogether. The best way to have a spontaneous conversation is to have questions prepared. You'll be more relaxed. The thinking you have to do to write the questions will help prepare you. Having questions prepared relieves you of the need to be mentally searching for the next question as the source is answering the last one. If you are trying to think of the next question, you will not be paying close attention to what is being said, and you might miss the most important part of the interview.

Having prepared questions does not mean you must use them. Sometimes the interview takes off in a richer direction than you anticipated. This happened, for example, when Saul Pett, an Associated Press special correspondent, interviewed Richard Nixon shortly after his landslide re-election victory.

> "I walked into the office and said, 'How are you?'" Pett says. President Nixon began talking. Pett tried to interrupt, but it finally occurred to him to let the president talk. "I said to myself, 'You damn fool, you're getting a good story. Let him talk.' He was full of confidence. People who feel confident in themselves have a way of revealing themselves."

Based on the information you have gathered already, you know *what* you want to ask. Now you must be careful about *how* you ask the questions.

Phrasing the Question

Listen to an accomplished courtroom lawyer ask questions. How the question is structured often determines whether the lawyer will win the case. Journalists face the same challenge. Reporters have missed many stories because they didn't know how to ask questions. Quantitative research has shown how just a slight wording change affects the results of a survey. If you want to know whether citizens favor a city plan to beautify the downtown area, you can ask the question in several ways:

- Do you favor the city council's plan to beautify the downtown area?
- The city council plans to spend $3 million beautifying the downtown area. Are you in favor of this?
- Do you think the downtown area needs physical changes?
- Which of the following actions do you favor?
    — Building a traffic loop around the downtown area.
    — Prohibiting all automobile traffic in an area bounded by Providence Road, Ash Street, College Avenue and Elm Street.
    — Having all the downtown store fronts remodeled to carry out a single theme and putting in brick streets, shrubbery and benches.
    — None of the above.

How you structure that question may affect the survey results by several percentage points. Similarly, how you ask questions in an interview may affect the response.

A reporter who was investigating possible job discrimination against blacks conducted several interviews before she told her city editor she didn't think the blacks with whom she talked were being frank with her. "When I ask them if they have ever been discriminated against, they always tell me no. But three times now during the course of the interviews, they have said things that indicate they have been. How do I get them to tell me about it?" she asks.

"Perhaps it's the way you are asking the question," the city editor replies. "When you ask someone whether they have ever been discriminated against, you are forcing them to answer yes or no. Don't be so blunt. Ask them if others with the same qualifications at work have been advanced faster than they have. Ask if they are paid the same amount as whites for the same work. Ask them what they think they would be doing today if they were white. Ask them if they know of any qualified blacks who were denied jobs." The city editor was giving the reporter examples of both closed- and open-ended questions. Each has its specific strengths.

OPEN-ENDED QUESTIONS

Open-ended questions allow the respondent some flexibility. Black persons may not respond frankly when asked whether they have ever been discriminated against. The question calls for a yes-no response. But an open-ended question such as "What would you be doing today if you were white?" is not so personal. It does not sound as threatening to the respondent. In response to an open-ended question, the source often reveals more than he or she realizes or intends to do.

A sports writer who was interviewing a pro scout at a college football game wanted to know who the scout was there to see. When the scout diplomatically declined to be specific, the reporter tried another approach. He asked a series of questions:

- "What kind of qualities does a pro scout look for in an athlete?"
- "Do you think any of the players here today have those talents?"
- "Who would you put into that category?"

The reporter worked from the general to the specific until he had the information he wanted. Open-ended questions are less direct and less threatening. They are more exploratory and more flexible.

CLOSED-ENDED QUESTIONS

Eventually the reporter needs to close in on a subject, to flush out the detail, to get the respondent to be specific. *Closed-ended questions* are designed to elicit specific responses.

Instead of asking the mayor, "What did you think of the conference in Washington, D.C.?" you ask, "What did you learn in the session 'Funds You May Not Know Are Available'?" Instead of asking a previous employee to appraise the chancellor-designate's managerial abilities, you ask, "How well does Uehling listen to the people who work for her?" "Do the people who work for her have specific jobs duties?" "Does she explain her decisions?"

Asking a vague question invites a vague answer. By asking a specific question, you are more likely to get a specific answer.

Knowing exactly when to ask a closed-ended question or when to be less specific is not something you can plan ahead of time. The type of information you are seeking and the chemistry between the interviewer and the source are the determining factors. You must make on-the-spot decisions.

Establishing a Rapport

The right chemistry produces an interview that is fun for both parties. When John Lindsay was mayor of New York, the AP's Pett opened an interview with the question, "Would you want your daughter to marry a mayor of New York?" Lindsay roared, and Pett had a great interview.

But he wasn't as successful when he interviewed President Jimmy Carter. "I made my little opening joke, and I found myself laughing harder than he was. Then he looked at his watch and said, 'OK, Saul, let's get on with it.'"

Pett had more success with President Ronald Reagan. The president noticed Pett adjusting his hearing aid. Reagan told him he had one bad ear, too, because blanks were fired from a gun too close to his head during his movie-making days. Reagan arranged the chairs so they were sitting good ear to good ear.

Rapport — the relationship between the reporter and the source — is crucial to the success of the interview. The relationship is sometimes relaxed, sometimes strained. Often it is somewhere in between. The type of relationship you try to establish with your source is determined by the kind of story you are doing. Several approaches are possible.

Figure 5.1 Establishing a Rapport. Saul Pett's interview with President Reagan went smoothly after they quickly established common ground—they both have a hearing problem.

INTERVIEW APPROACHES

For most news stories and personality profiles, the reporter has more to gain if the subject is at ease. Often that can be accomplished by starting off with small talk. Ask about a trophy, the plants or an engraved pen. Bring up something humorous you have found during your research. Ask about something you know the source will want to talk about. In other interviews, if you think the subject might be skeptical about your knowledge of the field, open with a question that shows you have done your homework.

Reporters who can show sources what they have in common also have more success getting information. When Janet Chusmir, now publisher of the Boulder (Colo.) Camera, was a reporter for the Miami Herald, she was assigned to interview the parents of Bernardine Dohrn. Dohrn was a suspect in an anti-war protest bombing and a fugitive. Many reporters, including some from the Herald, had tried to talk to the parents. None had succeeded.

Chusmir went to their home and knocked on the door. She identified herself and told them why she was there. They said they didn't want to talk. She said she understood because she was a parent, too. She told them she wasn't feeling well and asked for a glass of water.

Figure 5.2 Interview Approaches. Janet Chusmir's success as an interviewer is due in part to her ability to empathize with her subjects.

They complied with her request. She edged into the house and sat down to drink the water. While she sat there, they chatted about, among other things, why they didn't want to be interviewed. Before she left, she had enough information for a story. While the request for water bought her time, it was her ability to talk to them sympathetically parent to parent that made her successful.

On another occasion, Chusmir was among a group of reporters who showed up expecting to witness kidnappers return a mother's child. The kidnappers never showed up. The police slipped the mother into the back seat of a police car and edged through the crowd. As the car went by her, Chusmir tapped on the window. The mother rolled it down slightly. "I hope you find your child," Chusmir said. The woman told her to call. Chusmir did and got an exclusive story.

"One of the mistakes reporters make is that they are not human," Chusmir says. "I genuinely feel for these people. I think sources can sense that."

Rapport also depends upon where your conduct the interview. Many persons, especially those unaccustomed to being interviewed, feel more comfortable in their work place. Go to them. Talk to the businessperson in the office, to the athlete in the locker room, to the conductor in the music room. On the other hand, you may get a better interview elsewhere if the source can't relax there. Reporters

Figure 5.3 Interviewing in the Work Place. A reporter can sometimes establish a better rapport by going to the subject's work environment. Here Anna Quindlin, reporter for The New York Times, interviews a subway employee.

have talked to politicians during car rides between campaign appearances. They've gone sailing with businesspeople and hunting with athletes. One reporter doing a feature on a police chief spent a weekend with the chief, who was painting his home. To do a profile, you will want to have more than one interview. Vary the location. New surroundings can make a difference.

There are extremes, of course. To interview Cambodia's Prince Sihanouk, the AP's Peter Arnett once accompanied him to a rice paddy where the prince stripped to his underwear and dug with the peasants. "In looking back, he didn't say anything important," Arnett says, "but it was a fantastic situation."

In that instance, the fact that Arnett wasn't alone with Sihanouk didn't make any difference, but in most interviews it will. Get your source away from co-workers, friends or family. The source will either play to them as if they were an audience or be inhibited by them. Persons who are seldom interviewed are often nervous enough even without others besides the reporter listening.

There are times, however, when the reporter would rather have the source edgy, nervous or even scared. When you are doing an investigation, you may want the key characters to feel uneasy. You may pretend you know more than you actually do. You want them to know that the material you have is substantive and serious. Seymour Hersh, a Pulitzer Prize–winning investigative reporter, uses this tactic. Time magazine once quoted a government official commenting on Hersh: "He wheedles, cajoles, pleads, threatens, asks a leading question, uses little tidbits as if he knew the whole story. When he finishes you feel like a wet rag."

In some cases, however, it is better even in an investigation to take a low-key approach. Let the source relax. Talk around the subject but gradually bring the discussion to the key issues. The surprise element may work to your favor.

So may the sympathetic approach. When the source is speaking, you may nod or punctuate the source's responses with comments such as "That's interesting." Sources who think you are sympathetic are more likely to be forthcoming. That was the key to Chusmir's success. Researchers have found, for instance, that a simple "mm-hmmm" affects the length of the answer interviewers get.

OTHER PRACTICAL CONSIDERATIONS

Where you sit in relation to the person you are interviewing can be important. Unless you deliberately are trying to make those interviewed feel uncomfortable, do not sit directly in front of them. Permit your sources to establish eye contact if and when they wish.

Some persons are even more disturbed by the way a reporter

takes notes. A tape recorder ensures accuracy of quotes, but it makes many speakers self-conscious or nervous. Writing notes longhand interferes with your ability to digest what is being said. But not taking any notes at all is risky. Only a few reporters can leave an interview and accurately write down what was said. Certainly no one can do it and reproduce direct quotes verbatim. You should learn shorthand or develop a system of your own.

Techniques for Ensuring Accuracy

Accuracy is a major problem in all interviews. Both the question and the answer may be ambiguous. You may not understand what is said. You may record it incorrectly. You may not know the context of the remarks. Your biases may interfere with the message.

You have no control over some of the things that may affect the accuracy of the answers you receive in an interview. In 1946 two researchers conducted an experiment in which a group of people were asked, "Do you think there are too many Jews holding government offices and jobs?" The interviewers were divided into four groups: Jewish in appearance with a Jewish name; Jewish in appearance; non-Jewish in appearance; and non-Jewish in appearance with a non-Jewish name. Ten percent more people answered yes to the non-Jewish-appearing interviewer than they did to the Jewish-appearing interviewer with a Jewish name. Some respondents tailored their answer to what they believed the interviewer wanted to hear.

Some possibilities for making errors or introducing bias are unavoidable, but others are not. To ensure as accurate and complete reporting as possible, you should use all the techniques available to obtain a good interview, including observing, understanding what you hear and asking follow-up questions. Let's examine these and other techniques.

OBSERVING

Some reporters look but do not see. The detail they miss may be the difference between a routine story and one that is a delight to read. It wasn't delightful to read about the flood damage in Hattiesburg, Miss., but reporter Sharon Wertz's observations as she listened to one of the victims brought the agony home to the readers:

> "You know," Cheryl says, covering her anguished face with her hands, her shoulders shaking, "we canceled our flood insurance two

> months ago. The premiums went up.
> . . . Who would have thought this
> would happen?"
>   She wipes her reddened eyes.
>   "I'm sorry," she says, sniffing.
> "We're really lucky to be alive."

The reporter who interviewed chancellor-designate Uehling also was an observer:

> Don Quixote hangs on the wall.
> Across the room an executive-size
> desk is dwarfed by piles of memos,
> reports and correspondence. . . .
>   Professional journals replace over-
> sized picture books for browsing.
> And the bindings are wrinkled:
> Somebody is reading them.

These same powers of observation serve the investigative reporter. Is the subject nervous? What kinds of questions are striking home? The mayor may deny that he is going to fire the police chief, but the reporter who notices the chief's personnel file sitting on an adjacent work table may have reason to continue the investigation.

UNDERSTANDING

Understanding what you see is crucial to the news-gathering process. So is understanding what you hear. It is not enough merely to record what is being said; you must also digest it. The reporter who was investigating job discrimination was listening but not understanding. Her sources were telling her about incidents of discrimination, but all she heard were their denials.

In his interview with President Nixon, the AP's Pett was not listening at first. He wanted to ask his own questions, but he quickly realized that Nixon was revealing more about himself then he would answering Pett's questions. He let the president talk. The Miami Herald's Chusmir listens, too. Once when she was interviewing Joan Fontaine, the actress, Chusmir mentioned that she had a daughter about the same age as Fontaine's. Fontaine asked, "Is she jealous of you?" Listening closely, Chusmir correctly deduced that Fontaine was revealing a problem of jealousy in the family, and the interview took an unexpected turn.

Sometimes what you don't hear may be the message. The reporter who was trying to find out if the mayor was going to fire the police chief asked several questions about the chief's performance. What struck the reporter during the interview was the mayor's lack of enthusiasm for the chief. That unintentional tip kept the reporter working on the story until he confirmed it.

ASKING FOLLOW-UP QUESTIONS

If you understand what the source is saying, you can ask meaningful follow-up questions. There is nothing worse than briefing your city editor on the interview and having the editor ask you, "Well, did you ask . . ." Having to say no is embarrassing.

Even if you go into an interview armed with a list of questions, the most important probably will be the ones you ask in response to an answer. A reporter who was doing a story on bidding procedures was interviewing the mayor. The reporter asked how bid specifications were written. In the course of his reply, the mayor mentioned that the president of a construction firm had assured him the last bid specifications were adequate. The alert reporter picked up on the statement:

"When did you talk to him?"
"About three weeks ago," the mayor said.
"That's before the specifications were published, wasn't it?"
"Yes, we asked him to look them over for us."
"Did he find anything wrong with the way they were written?"
"Oh, he changed a few minor things. Nothing important."
"Did officials of any other construction firms see the bid specifications before they were advertised?"
"No, he was the only one."

Gradually, on the basis of one offhand comment by the mayor, the reporter was able to piece together a solid story on the questionable relationship between the city and the construction firm.

OTHER TECHNIQUES

While most questions are designed to get information, some are asked as a delaying tactic. A reporter who is taking notes may fall behind. An occasional, "Will you explain that?" or, "I didn't really understand that," will give the reporter time to catch up. Other questions are intended to encourage a longer response. "Go on with that," or, "Tell me more about that," encourage the speaker to add more detail.

You don't have to be stalling for time to say you don't understand. Don't be embarrassed to admit you haven't grasped something. It is better to admit to one person you don't understand than to advertise your ignorance on newsprint in front of thousands. Once you have written the story, check with your sources. Check the facts. Check the concepts. Catch your errors before publication. You'll look better to your editors, your readers will be served better, your newspaper will have more credibility, and your sources will be happy to talk to you the next time.

Another device for making the source talk on is not a question at all; it is a pause. You are signaling the source that you expect more. But the lack of a response from you is much more ambiguous than "Tell me more about that." It may indicate that you were skeptical of what was just said, that you didn't understand, that the answer was inadequate or several other possibilities. The source will be forced to react. The only problem with this, says the AP's Pett, "is that it invites the dull to be dull at greater length."

Many dull interviews become interesting after they end. There are two things you should always do when you finish your questions: Check key facts, figures and quotes and then put away your pen but keep your ears open. You are not breaching any ethical rule if you continue to ask questions after you have put away your pen or turned off the tape recorder. That's when some sources loosen up. Many reporters find they get their best material after the formal interview has ended and they are having a cup of coffee with the source.

Suggested Readings

Metzler, Ken. "Creative Interviewing." Englewood Cliffs, N.J.: Prentice-Hall, 1977. An invaluable in-depth look at problems of interviewing.

Rivers, William. "Finding Facts." Englewood Cliffs, N.J.: Prentice-Hall, 1975. Chapter 3 is particularly useful to someone trying to improve the phrasing of questions.

6

Quotes and Attribution

"And you can quote me on that."

Many people who say these words don't expect to be quoted. They mean only that they are sure of what they are saying and are not afraid or ashamed to say it. Nonetheless, these are sweet words to a reporter.

Direct quotes add color and credibility to your story. By using direct quotes, you are telling readers you are putting them directly in touch with the speaker. Like a letter, direct quotes are personal. Quotation marks signal the reader that something special is coming. Direct quotes provide a story with a change of pace, a breath of air. They also loosen up a clump of dense type.

Not everything people say should be put into direct quotes. You need to learn what to quote directly, when to use partial quotes and when to paraphrase. You also must learn how and how often to attribute quotations and other information. Like a researcher, you must know when information must be tied to a source. However, attributing a remark or some information does not excuse you from a possible libel suit. And, of course, you want to be fair.

Being fair sometimes is difficult when sources do not want to be quoted. For that reason you also must learn how to deal with off-the-record quotes and background information.

In this chapter you will learn:

1. What is worth quoting directly.
2. How and when to attribute direct and indirect quotes.
3. How to handle both on- and off-the-record information.

What to Quote Directly

Crisp, succinct, meaningful quotes spice up every story. But you can overdo a good thing. You need direct quotes in your stories, and you also need to develop your skill in recognizing what is worth quoting. Here are some guidelines:

1. Use direct quotes when someone says something unique.
2. Use direct quotes when someone says something uniquely.
3. Use direct quotes when someone important says something important.

Let's look at these guidelines further.

UNIQUE MATERIAL

When you can say, "Ah, I never heard that before," you can be quite sure your readers also would like to know exactly what the speaker said. Instead of quoting someone at length, look for the kernel. Sometimes it is something surprising, something neither you nor your readers would expect that person to say. For example, at the first Crosby Pro-Am Golf Tournament after Bing Crosby's death, his widow became upset over the mournful tones of sportscaster Jim McKay. Mrs. Crosby said she finally intervened because McKay "was so lugubrious, so breast-beating he made me want to throw up." And consider this unexpected statement by an 80-year-old man: "Dog food's not so bad when you're hungry."

Striking statements like these should be quoted, but there is no reason to place simple, factual material inside quotation marks. Here is a segment of copy from a story about the similarities in the careers of a father and his son that needed no quotes at all:

> "My son was born on campus," says the elder Denney, 208 Westridge Drive, a professor in regional and community affairs.
> "In fact, he was born in the same hospital that I met my wife," he says, explaining he was in Noyes Hospital with a fractured spine when she was a student nurse.
> Since that time, he has earned his bachelor's degree "technically in agriculture with a major in biological science and conservation."

Although the quoted material is informative, it contains nothing particularly interesting, surprising, disturbing, new or even different. It should be written:

Denney, of 208 Westridge Drive, is a professor in regional and community affairs. While hospitalized in Noyes Hospital with a fractured spine, he met a student nurse who became his wife. Twenty years later, his son was born at the same hospital.

The son has since earned a bachelor's degree in agriculture with a major in biological science and conservation.

The first version has 72 words; the second, with 58 words, is tighter and better.

Sometimes spoken material is unique not because of individual remarks that are surprising or new, but because of extended dialogue that can tell the story more effectively than writers can in their own words. The writer of the following story made excellent use of dialogue:

Lou Provancha pushed his wire-rimmed glasses up on his nose and leaned toward the man in the wheelchair.

"What is today, Jake?" he asked.

Jake twisted slightly and stared at the floor.

"Jake," Provancha said, "Jake, look up here."

A long silence filled the tiny, cluttered room on the sixth floor of the University Medical Center.

Provancha, a licensed practical nurse at the hospital, glanced at the reporter. "Jake was in a coma a week ago," he explained. "He couldn't talk."

Provancha pointed to a wooden board propped up on the table beside him.

"Jake, what is today? What does it say here? What is this word? I've got my finger pointed right at it."

Jake squinted at the word. With a sudden effort, like a man heaving a bag of cement mix onto a truck bed, he said:

"Tuesday."

Provancha grinned. It was a small victory for both of them.

The shaggy-haired nurse was coaxing his patient step-by-step back into the world he had known before a car accident pitched him into a two-month-long coma, with its resulting disorientation and memory loss.

THE UNIQUE EXPRESSION

When you as a listener can say, "Ah, I never heard it said *that* way before," you know you have something quotable. Be on the lookout for the clever, the colorful, the colloquial. For example, an old gentleman talking about his organic garden said, "It's hard to tell people to watch what they eat. You eat health, you know."

A professor lecturing on graphic design said, "When you think it looks like a mistake, it is." The same professor once was explaining that elements in a design should not call attention to themselves: "You don't walk up to a beautiful painting in someone's home and say, 'That's a beautiful frame.'"

Sometimes something said uniquely is a colloquialism. Colloquialisms can add color and life to your copy. For example, a person from Louisiana may say: "I was just fixing to leave when the phone rang." A person from an area in Pennsylvania "makes the light out" when turning off the lights. And people in and around Fort Wayne, Ind., "redd up" the dishes after a meal, meaning that they wash them and put them where they belong.

Capturing Dialect or Accent

Using colorful or colloquial expressions helps the writer capture a person in a particular environment. The same is true when you write the way people talk:

> "Are you gonna go?" he asked.
> "No, I ain't goin'," she replied.

In everyday speech hardly anyone enunciates perfectly. To do so would sound affected. In fiction, therefore, it is common to use spellings that match speech. But when conversation is written down in newspaper reporting, readers expect correct, full spellings. Not only is correct spelling easier to read, it is also less difficult to write. Capturing dialect is difficult, as these passages from a story about actress Roz Kelly, the girl with whom the Fonz fell in love on "Happy Days," illustrate:

> "Boy, it's hot out theah," she started, "I could sure use a nice cold beer. How about it, uh? Wanta go get a couple beers?"

It seems strange that if she says "theah," she wouldn't also say "beeah." Or perhaps she said, "How 'bout it, uh?" And if she said "wanta," maybe she also said "geta."

In another passage, the author has Ms. Kelly speaking "straight" English:

> "Would you believe I used to dress like that all the time? Dates didn't want to be seen with me. I was always being asked to change clothes before going out."

Then later in the story, she reverts to less formal speech:

> "I'm tired of pickin' up checks. I've never been ta college, so I'd like ta take a coupla classes. I wanta take law so I can find out who's stealing

> the country. And I wanta take geol-
> ogy. The San Andreas Fault is my
> hobby, y'know? I think man can beat
> out nature.''

First Ms. Kelly wanted "a couple beers." Then she wanted to take "a coupla classes." In the same passage she is tired of "pickin'" up checks, but she wants to find out who's "stealing" the country. It is unlikely Ms. Kelly is that inconsistent in her speech.

The writer of this story tried to show us something of the character of Roz Kelly. If he wanted to convey her speech patterns, he should either have been consistent or simply reported that she talked the same off the set as on it.

Sometimes when a newspaper attempts to quote someone saying something uniquely it betrays a bias. Years ago some Northern newspapers delighted in quoting Gov. George Wallace exactly, even trying to reproduce his Southern drawl. But some of these same newspapers did not try to reproduce the Boston accent of John F. Kennedy or of his brothers.

IMPORTANT QUOTES BY IMPORTANT PEOPLE

If citizen Joe Smith says, "Something must be done about this coal strike," you may or may not consider it worth quoting. But if the president of the United States says, "Something must be done about this coal strike," many papers would quote him. Generally reporters quote public officials or known personalities in their news stories (though not everything the famous say is worth quoting).

Quoting sources that readers are likely to know lends authority, credibility and interest to your story. Presumably, a meteorologist knows something about the weather, a doctor about health, a chemistry professor about chemicals. On the other hand, it is unlikely that a television star knows a great deal about cameras, even if he or she makes commercials about cameras.

Verification

When someone important says something important, but perhaps false, just putting the material in quotes does not relieve you of the responsibility for the inaccuracies. Citizens, officials and candidates for office often say things that may be partially true or altogether untrue and perhaps even libelous. Quotations, like any other information you gather, need verification.

During the time of Sen. Joseph McCarthy, many newspapers, in the interest of strict objectivity, day after day quoted the Wisconsin senator's charges and countercharges. (It should be pointed out that some publishers did this because they agreed with his stance and because his remarks sold newspapers.) Few papers thought it was their responsibility to quote others who were pointing out the obvious errors and inconsistencies in the demagogue's remarks. Today, however, in the interest of balance, fairness and objectivity, many papers leave out, correct or point out the errors in some quotations. This may be done in the article itself or in an accompanying story.

If candidate Billy Joe Harkness says that his opponent Jimbo McGown is a member of the Ku Klux Klan, you should check before you print the charge. Good reporters don't stop looking and checking just because someone gives them some information. Look for yourself. Prisoners may have an altogether different account of a riot from the one the prison officials give you. Your story will not be complete unless you talk to all sides.

Problems in Direct Quotation

PARAPHRASING QUOTES

While some quotations need verification, others need clarification. Do not quote someone unless you are sure of what that person means. The reason (or excuse), "But that's what the man said," is not a sufficient reason to use the quote. It is much better to skip a quotation altogether than to confuse the reader.

The best way to avoid confusing and unclear quotes or needlessly long and wordy quotes is to paraphrase. It is the meaning of the speaker that you must convey to the reader. As a reporter you must have confidence that at times you are able to convey that meaning in fewer words and in better language than the speaker did. You can save your editors a lot of work if you shorten quotes. Digesting, condensing and clarifying quotes take more effort than simply recording them word for word. You will not impress anyone with long quotations. On the contrary, you may be guilty of some lazy writing. Here is a quote that could be cut drastically:

```
"When I first started singing lessons I assumed I would be
a public school teacher and maybe, if I was good enough, a
voice teacher," he says. "When I graduated from the uni-
versity, I still thought I would be a teacher, and I wanted
to teach."
```

A rewrite says it more succinctly:

```
When he first started singing lessons, and even after he
graduated from the university, he wanted to be a public
school voice teacher.
```

PARTIAL QUOTES

It is also much better to paraphrase or to use full quotes than to use fragmentary or partial quotes. Some editors would have you avoid "orphan quotes" almost altogether. Here is an example of the overuse of partial quotes:

```
The mayor said citizens should "turn off" unnecessary
lights and "turn down" thermostats "to 65 degrees."
```

The sentence would be better with no quotation marks at all.

If it is a particular phrase that has special significance or meaning, a partial quote may be justifiable. For example, in President Nixon's speech announcing the end of the Vietnam War, he repeatedly used the words "peace with honor," a phrase he had used often in his efforts to bring the war to an end. A reporter covering this speech hardly could have used those words without putting them in quotes.

When you do use partial quotes, do not put quotation marks around something the speaker could not have said. Suppose a speaker told a student audience at a university, "I am pleased and thrilled with your attendance here tonight." It would be incorrect to write:

```
The speaker said she was "pleased and thrilled with the
students' attendance."
```

Partial quotes often contain an ellipsis inside them to tell the reader that some of the words of the quote are missing. For example:

```
"I have come here tonight . . . and I have crossed state
lines . . . to conspire against the government."
```

This practice at times may be justifiable. But you should not keep the reader guessing and wondering what is missing. Sometimes the actual meaning of the speaker can be distorted by dropping certain words. If a critic writes about a three-act play, "A great hit — except for the first three acts," an ad that picks up only the first part of that quote is guilty of misrepresentation.

CORRECTING QUOTES

Quoting people directly can raise problems when people speak ungrammatically or in sentence fragments — for example, at press conferences or during informal interviews. Although quotation marks mean you are capturing the exact language, it is accepted practice on many newspapers to correct grammar and to put a person's remarks into complete sentences. None of us regularly speaks in perfect, grammatical sentences. But if we were writing down our remarks, presumably we would write grammatically.

Even the best reporters differ on when or even whether to do this. To More magazine's question, "Do you fix quotes to make the person you're quoting sound grammatical?" columnist James Kilpatrick replied:

Sure. It's elementary courtesy, and everyone does it. You don't change the substance of your subject's thought, of course. You could make anyone in politics look ridiculous if you quoted him verbatim all the time with all the ands, ifs, buts, and ers.

Jack Newfield, then senior editor for The Village Voice, said:

No, I don't. New York political leader Meade Esposito's colorfulness comes from his lack of grammar.

Sally Quinn, reporter for The Washington Post, said:

If the person used bad grammar as a matter of course, I would never fix a quote. But if it's in the middle of a sentence — if he starts out using the plural and switches his train of thought and ends up using the singular — rather than put in the bad grammar, which really wouldn't be fair, I'll change it.

Finally, the AP Stylebook says:

Quotations normally should be corrected to avoid the errors in grammar and word usage that often occur unnoticed when someone is speaking but are embarrassing in print.

OBSCENITY

On most newspapers, *some* things people say are never permitted in print, even if they say it uniquely. Newspapers rarely print obscenities, profanities or even vulgarities unless they are essential to the story. In The Washington Post, for example, obscenities may be used only with the approval of a top editor. Even then, for "hard-core" obscenities referring to the body and sexual or excretory functions, the Post's stylebook calls for the use of the first letter followed by dashes.

Attributing Direct and Indirect Quotes

In composition and creative writing classes, you may have been told to avoid repeating the same word. You probably picked up your thesaurus to look for a synonym for the word "say," a colorless word. Without much research you may have found a hundred or more substitutes. None of them is wrong. Indeed, writers may search long for the exact word they need to convey a particular nuance of meaning. For example:

A presidential candidate *announces* the choice of a running mate.

An arrested man *divulges* the names of his accomplices.

A judge *pronounces* sentence.

At other times, in the interest of precise and lively writing you may write:

"I'll get you for that," she *whispered.*

"I object," he *shouted.*

Nevertheless, reporters and editors prefer forms of the verb "to say" in most instances, even if they are repeated throughout a story. They have good reasons for doing so. "Said" is unobtrusive. Rather than appearing tiresome and repetitious, it hides in the news columns and calls no attention to itself. "Said" is also neutral. It has no connotations. To use the word "said" is to be objective.

Some of the synonyms for "said" sound innocent enough — but be careful. If you report a city official "claimed," or "maintained" or "contended," you are implying that you do not quite believe what the official said. "Said" is the solution to your problem. If you have evidence that what the official is saying is incorrect, you should include the correct information or evidence in your story.

In some newspaper accounts of labor negotiations, company officials always "ask," while labor leaders always "demand." "Demanding" something sounds harsh and unreasonable, while "asking" for something is calm and reasonable. A reporter who uses these words in this context is taking an editorial stand — consciously or unconsciously.

Other words you may be tempted to use as a substitute for "say" are simply unacceptable because they represent improper usage. For example.

"You don't really mean that," he winked.
"Of course I do," she grinned.
"But what if someone heard you say that," he frowned.
"Oh, you are a fool," she laughed.

You cannot wink a word. It is difficult, if not impossible, to grin, frown or laugh words. But you may want to say this:

"Not again," he said, moaning.
"I'm afraid so," she said with a grin.

This usage is correct, but often it is not necessary or even helpful to add phrases like "with a grin." On the other hand, sometimes those three words are necessary to convey the meaning of the speaker.

Learning the correct words for attribution is the first step. Here are some other guidelines you should follow when attributing information:

1. *If a direct quote is more than one sentence long, place the attribution at the end of the first sentence.* For example:

> "The car overturned at least three times," the policeman said. "None of the four passengers was hurt. Luckily, the car did not explode into flames."

That one attribution is adequate. It would be redundant to write:

> "The car overturned at least three times," the policeman said. "None of the four passengers was hurt," he added. "Luckily, the car did not explode into flames," he continued.

Nor should you write:

> "The car overturned at least three times. None of the four passengers was hurt. Luckily, the car did not explode into flames," the policeman said.

Do not keep the reader wondering who is doing the talking. On the other hand, ordinarily you should not place the attribution at the beginning of a quote:

> The policeman said: "The car overturned at least three times. None of the four passengers was hurt. Luckily, the car did not explode into flames."

However, if direct quotes from two different speakers follow one another, you should start the second with the attribution to avoid confusion:

> "The driver must have not seen the curve," an eyewitness said. "Once the car left the road, all I saw was a cloud of dust."
> The policeman said: "The car overturned at least three times. None of the four passengers was hurt. Luckily, the car did not explode into flames."

Notice that when an attribution precedes a direct quotation that is more than one sentence long, wire service style requires that a colon follow the attribution.

2. *Do not follow a fragment of a quote with a continuing complete sentence of quotation.* Avoid this construction:

The mayor said the time had come "to turn off some lights. We all must do something to conserve electricity."

The correct form is to separate partial quotes and complete quotes:

The time has come "to turn off some lights," the mayor said. "We all must do something to conserve electricity."

3. *The first time you attribute a direct or indirect quote, identify the speaker fully.* How fully depends upon how well the speaker is known to the readers. In Springfield, Ill., it is sufficient to identify the mayor simply as Mayor John Johnston. But if a story in the Chicago Tribune referred to the mayor of Springfield, the first reference would have to be "John Johnston, mayor of Springfield" — unless, of course, the dateline for the story was Springfield.

4. *Don't attribute direct quotes to more than one person, as in the following:*

"Flames were shooting out everywhere. Then electrical wires began falling, and voices were heard screaming," witnesses said.

All you have to do is eliminate the quotation marks, if indeed any witness made the statements.

Whatever you do, do not make up a source. Never attribute a statement to "a witness" unless you have the witness. At times you may ask a witness to confirm what you have seen, but never invent quotes for anonymous witnesses. Inventing witnesses and making up quotes is dishonest, inaccurate and inexcusable.

5. *In stories covering past news events, use the past tense in attributions, and use it throughout the story.* However, stories that do not report on news events, such as features, may be more effective if the attributions are consistently in the present tense. In a feature story such as a personality profile, when it is safe to assume that what the person once said, he or she would still say, you may use the present tense. For example, when you write, "'I like being the mayor,' she says," you are indicating that she still enjoys it.

6. *Ordinarily, place the noun or pronoun before the verb in attributions.*

"Everything is under control," the sheriff said.

If you must identify a person by including a long title, it is better to begin the attribution with the verb:

"I enjoy the challenge," says Jack Berry, associate dean for graduate studies and research.

Handling Both On- and
Off-the-Record Information

USING A SOURCE WHO DOES NOT WISH TO BE NAMED

Sometimes a speaker or source may not want to be quoted at all — directly or indirectly. Diana Dawson, now a reporter with the Kansas City (Mo.) Star, tells this story of her experience in Memphis:

I had been investigating the Memphis, Tenn., mental health system for about a month with Mike Mansur, Press-Scimitar medical writer, when we stumbled upon two doctors who were fed up with the system. Both worked with the state hospital in Bolivar, Tenn., on a consultant basis. And both were appalled by what they'd observed.

"You can't use our names or identify us in any way whatsoever," said one of the doctors. "We have to maintain a working relationship with the staff there. It's important for the patients that we are able to go in, work with the docs and catch some of the things that are going wrong."

The consultants told stories of a state hospital that served all of western Tennessee but had no certified psychiatrists. Some doctors had been treated for drug and alcohol problems. The one considered the most skilled had killed himself. There were extremely few doctors for the number of patients.

With that, we checked the state hospital personnel files and found that there were, indeed, no certified doctors. We sat down with the medical chief and a staffing chart to determine the staff-patient ratios. We picked up a copy of the psychiatrist's autopsy report.

As our investigation continued, one of the sources led us to the records we needed to prove that the patients who were taken to the city hospital emergency room with mental problems were often released within a matter of hours. They were released even if they had proven themselves dangerous to the public.

The seven-part series that resulted won Tennessee's UPI grand prize for public service.

And well it should have. Here's how the first of that series began:

Human warehousing — the stashing away of society's insane stepchildren — theoretically ended in 1977.

But today, mental health professionals — including the superintendent of the Gothic asylum called Western Mental Health Institute in Bolivar — say the state psychiatric hospital's level of staffing remains suited only to human storage.

"This place is staffed for custodial care," said Dr. William Jennings, superintendent of Western.

Half the clinical staff consists of psychiatric technicians who have a high school education or less. As darkness falls on Bolivar, the technicians often become responsible for entire wards.

Western's more than 500 patients

are seen by a staff of only six licensed physicians, which includes the superintendent and one doctor who has been on sick leave for more than two months.

The six physicians, each responsible for care of between 25 and 93 patients, work as many as 96 hours a week. The licensed doctors also are responsible for every move made by the eight unlicensed doctors, who have medical degrees but have not passed their state board examinations.

That is the kind of reporting that often results from talking to sources who refused to be named. You must learn to use sound professional judgment in handling them. If you agree to accept their information, you must honor their requests to remain off the record. Breaching that confidence destroys trust and credibility. But it is your obligation to take that information elsewhere to confirm it and get it on the record.

GUIDELINES FOR CITING SOURCES

Bob Woodward and Carl Bernstein, who as Washington Post reporters helped uncover the Watergate scandal that eventually led to the resignation of President Richard M. Nixon, were criticized for citing "high-level sources" without identifying them. Even though Woodward and Bernstein say they did not use this technique unless two independent sources had given them the same information, anonymous sources should be used rarely.

Not naming sources is dangerous for two important reasons. First, such information lacks credibility and makes the reporter and the newspaper suspect. Second, the source may be lying. He or she may be out to discredit someone or may be floating a trial balloon to test public reaction on some issue or event. Skilled diplomats and politicians know how to use reporters to take the temperature of public opinion. If the public reacts negatively, the sources will not proceed with whatever plans they leaked to the press. The press has been used — and has become less credible.

Some reporters make these distinctions regarding sources and attribution:

1. *Off the record:* You may not use the information.
2. *Not for attribution:* You may use the information but may not attribute it.
3. *Background:* You may use it with a general title for a source (e.g., "a White House aide said").
4. *Deep background:* You may use the information, but you must say it on your own.

By no means is there agreement on these terms. When most people say off the record, they mean not for attribution. For Richard Reeves, political reporter for New York magazine, off the record means that you cannot use the information in any way. For James Kilpatrick, off the record is not for quotation, and not for attribution means the same thing. Kilpatrick also thinks there is no difference between background and deep background. Sally Quinn agrees and thinks the term deep background is just a joke. Seymour Hersh, author and former reporter for the New York Times, says the terms are different for everyone.

Miles Beller, a reporter for the Los Angeles Herald-Examiner, agrees. Writing in Editor & Publisher, Beller says:

> Universally misunderstood and misread by journalists of every stripe, "off the record" suffers from more crude interpretations than does John Cleland's "Fanny Hill." For some reporters, "don't quote me." Others take it to mean "use the information but peg it to a 'a high ranking official,' 'a government spokesman,' 'a well-placed Western diplomat' or any other such 'fill-in-the-blank sources.' " Still others believe that the phrase has lost even the slightest vestige of meaning and should be taken as seriously as Have-a-Nice-Day slogans emblazoned on T-shirts.

Because there is little agreement among journalists, sources may be equally vague about the terms. Your obligation is to make sure you and your sources understand each other. Set the ground rules ahead of time. Clarify your terms. And be sure you know the policy of your paper in these matters.

For example, many newspapers do not allow reporters to use unidentified sources unless an editor knows the source and approves the usage.

Smart reporters do not allow a speaker suddenly to claim something is off the record. Mike Feinsilber of the Associated Press tells this story:

> David Gergen — of all people — forgot the ground rules.
> Gergen is director of communications for President Reagan and an old White House hand. He wrote speeches for Richard Nixon and was Gerald Ford's director of communications.
> Tradition in Washington, and elsewhere, is that a public official cannot go off the record after he has said his piece. And that's the rule that Gergen forgot.
> One day last week, he was addressing 150 advertising executives attending the annual conference of the American Association of Advertising Agencies. It was late in the afternoon; the scene was a meeting room in a Washington hotel.
> In his half-hour speech, Gergen spoke with somewhat more candor than administration officials — especially those who brief reporters regularly — usually display.

Then during a question-and-answer session, one of the advertising executives asked about the administration's efforts to reverse anti-nuclear sentiment among college students in Europe. He started to answer, then interrupted himself.

"This is all off the record, isn't it?" he asked.

From the back of the room, I shouted, "No."

"Who are you with?"

"The Associated Press."

"Well, can we put this on background (not for attribution)?"

"Nope."

Gergen wound up his remarks quickly. . . .

The AP was the only news organization there. And it was on the record.

Nevertheless, if a city manager or the police chief wishes to have a background session with you, unless it is against newspaper policy, you should not refuse. Often these officials are trying to be as open as they can under certain circumstances. Without such background sessions the task of reporting complex issues intelligently is nearly impossible. But you must be aware that you are hearing only one point of view and that the information may be self-serving.

Miles Beller gives this example:

Several years ago a woman phoned this reporter and "wanted to go off the record" in regard to a Los Angeles official's "secret ownership of a Las Vegas radio station" and other questionable holdings tied to this public servant. Funny thing though, the caller plumb forgot to mention that she was working for another candidate. This bit of minutia probably just slipped her mind, what with her man trailing so badly and the election a few weeks away.

Some sources make a habit of saying everything off the record and of giving commonplace information in background sessions. Although you cannot use a source who asks to remain off the record, you may use information if one or more of the following is true:

1. It is a matter of public record.
2. It is generally known.
3. It is available from several sources.
4. You yourself are a witness.

If you are a witness to damages or injuries, do not include yourself in the story. Attribute this information to the police or to other authorities. But if you are on the scene of an accident and can see that three people were involved, you do not have to write: "'Three people were involved in the accident,' Officer Osbord said." If you are unsure of the information or if there are conclusions or generalities involved, your editor probably will want you to attribute it to an official or to a witness. At other times your editor may want you to write a first-person account.

Knowing when and how to attribute background information is an art you will have to give special care and attention to all your days as a reporter. Remember:

1. When possible, set the ground rules with your sources ahead of time.
2. Know your newspaper's policy in these matters.

Suggested Readings

Anderson, James. "The Background of Backgrounders." UPI Reporter, June 22, 1978. A defense and some warnings about background and off-the-record information.

Beller, Miles. "For and Off the Record." Editor & Publisher, Jan. 2, 1982, p. 56. Argues cogently against overuse of off-the-record information.

Callihan, E.L. "Grammar for Journalists." Rev. ed. Radnor, Pa.: Chilton Book Company, 1979. Good section on how to punctuate, attribute and handle quotations.

Krohe, James, Jr. "Fixing Quotes Cheats Public, Editor Says." Publisher's Auxiliary, April 30, 1979. Argues that quotes should never be changed.

"Using Sources." ASNE Bulletin, September 1983, pp. 17–22. An excellent discussion by various experts: "Sources and Principles," by Peter J. Bridge; "Sourcerers Are Bad People," by Richard Smyser; "We Have Helped Create the Monster," by James I. Houck; "How Really Protected Are We?" by Everette E. Dennis.

PART THREE

Basic Stories

7

Sources and Searches

"There's no such thing as an original story idea," a prize-winning editor told a group of journalists assembled for a workshop. "We all steal ideas from each other."

There's a certain amount of truth in that statement, although every good story must start somewhere. Good ideas are valued in journalism. The reporter or editor who regularly comes up with a good new story idea or a fresh angle for an old one quickly becomes a valued member of the news room staff.

How do reporters and editors come up with those ideas or find those fresh angles? The answer should be obvious: They are curious people who are aware of the world around them. They read their own publications and they read what others write. Many consider The Wall Street Journal, The New York Times, TIME magazine or some other publication "must" reading. They localize stories in those national publications, or perhaps a single sentence provides the spark for a story idea. They probably watch television and listen to radio, and they probably do a lot of talking with co-workers, friends, neighbors and even casual acquaintances. They take time to chat with the service station attendant, the grocer and the plumber. All can be good sources of story ideas. The good reporters and editors, it is said, have a "nose for news."

Those trained to sniff out stories know that good ideas abound. Every human has a story to tell; the good reporter finds the person with a story worth retelling.

There are other sources of ideas, too. Several companies publish tip sheets for editors. Successful ideas in one city are tried in another, frequently with a new twist.

Once the good idea is found, the work has just begun. Good reporters leave no stones unturned in developing the best possible stories. They are not satisfied with stories that rely on a single source; they seek out more. Good reporters check the library, they check reference materials, they check with more people, they check every verifiable fact. Reference materials are essential to the careful reporter, and the well-organized newspaper office has plenty of reference resources.

The best reporters of the 1980s are going one step farther: They are searching for more information and new angles in electronic data bases. The proliferation of such data bases is a boon of major proportion to reporters and editors. The amount of material available in data bases that can be used to supplement a story is staggering. Top-flight reporters are learning to tap this source of information with regularity.

In this chapter you will learn:

1. Where news people turn for sources of news.
2. How reference materials can be used to verify facts.
3. How computer data-base searches are improving reporting.

Finding the Story

Readers bring some story ideas to the newspaper office. Most story ideas, though, are the result of an active imagination, a lively curiosity and a little help from friends. Journalists soon learn to recognize how stories written for other publications can be written for their own. They get in the habit of carrying a little notebook to jot down ideas when something somebody says strikes a responsive chord.

But even for good journalists, the wellspring of ideas sometimes dries up. Bank these 10 sources of story ideas, good for any time and any place, for the day that happens to you.

1. *Other people.* As a journalist you meet many persons. What are they talking about when they aren't talking business? What have they heard lately? Journalists have to listen, even when it means eavesdropping while having a cup of coffee. What interests people? There is no better source of story ideas than the people you meet while you are off-duty. They are, after all, your readers.

2. *Other publications.* Stories are recycled across the country. Read other newspapers, magazines, books, pamphlets, the magazines and newsletters of businesses and organizations.

Not all stories will work in every community. You have to know your own readership. A story about urban renewal would attract more attention in New York than in Helena, Mont. The problems of water supply in the West could not be adapted to make a story on the East Coast. But a story about the federal government's hot-lunch program probably could be done in New York, Kansas and California.

When you are reading other publications for ideas, remember that you should not duplicate a story. You are looking for ideas. Think of a new angle.

3. *Press releases*. Some press releases from public relations people are used, but many of them are not. Yet they can be a valuable source of story ideas. News that one company has posted increased profits may be worth one or two paragraphs; news that several companies in your community are prospering may be a front-page story. A handout stating that an employee received a 40-year pin may be worth a follow-up.

4. *A social services directory*. Many cities and counties have a composite listing of all agencies providing social services. Look beyond the pages. There are stories of people serving — or not serving — people. Each of those agencies and their clients is a story.

5. *Government reports*. Flowing from Washington like flood waters are pages and pages of statistics. Behind every statistic, however, is a person. Every person can be a story. The census reports, for instance, list not only the number of people in a community, but also their income and education, how many cars they own, whether they rent or own a house. They tell much more, too. Find out what, and you have a treasure chest of stories.

6. *Stories in your own newspaper*. Many a stream has yielded gold nuggets after the first wave of miners has left. Newspapers sometimes play hit-and-run journalism. Ask yourself if the human-interest angle has been reported adequately. When your newspaper is concentrating on the election winners, maybe you can get an interesting story by talking to the losers and their supporters. After the story of the two-car accident has been written, perhaps there is a feature on the victims whose lives have been changed. And when the unemployment statistics are reported in your paper, remember that behind each of those numbers is a person without a job.

News stories are not the only source of ideas. Read the records column: Can you spot a trend developing in the police report or the births or divorce listings? Is the divorce rate up? Are several crimes committed in one neighborhood?

7. *Advertisements*. In the advertisements, particularly the classifieds, you may find everything from a come-on for an illegal massage parlor to an auction notice from a family losing its home. Look

through the Yellow Pages, too. Your fingers might walk right up to a story.

8. *Wire copy*. Browse through the copy from your wire services. Are there stories that can be localized? When a story comes across the wires describing the increase in the rate of inflation, you should ask how the people in your community will be affected. Or if a foundation reports that Johnny can't read, you should talk to your local education officials. Can the Johnnys in your community read any better than the national average?

9. *Local news briefs*. Usually reports of local happenings are phoned in; sometimes they are brought in, written longhand on a piece of scratch paper. News of an upcoming family reunion may or may not be printed, but the enterprising reporter who spots the information that there will be five generations present probably has a story that will receive substantial play in the paper. A note that the Westside Neighborhood Association is planning its annual fund-raiser may result in a feature on how the neighbors plan to raise funds to upgrade recreational facilities in their area. This source of stories often is overlooked. A city editor once received a call from a man who said he thought the paper might be interested in a story about his daughter coming to visit. The city editor tried to brush him off. Just before the man hung up, the editor heard, "I haven't seen her in 32 years. I thought she was dead."

10. *You*. In the final analysis you are the one who must be alert enough to look and listen to what is going on around you. Ask yourself why, as in, "Why do people act the way they do?" Ask yourself what, as in, "What are people thinking about? What are their fears, their anxieties?" Ask yourself when, as in, "When that happened, what else was going on?" And wonder about things, as in, "I wonder if that's true in my town."

Reporters who are attuned to people rather than institutions will find the world around them a rich source of human interest stories. Don't tune out.

Checking the Facts

A wealth of information is available for the thorough reporter who wants to develop the sound habit of checking every verifiable fact that goes into a story. Some of that information can be found in the reference manuals maintained in most news rooms or in newspaper libraries. A good reporter will learn quickly what materials are available.

Here is a list of 20 of the most commonly used references:

1. Local and area telephone directories. Used for verifying the spelling of names and addresses. Usually reliable but not infallible.
2. City directories. These can be found in most cities. They provide the same information as the telephone directory but also may provide information on the occupations of citizens and the owners or managers of businesses. Useful street indexes provide information on the names of next-door neighbors.
3. State manuals. Each state government publishes a directory that provides useful information on various government agencies. These directories sometimes list the salaries of all state employees.
4. Maps of the city, county, state, nation and world. Local maps usually are posted in the news room. Others may be found in atlases.
5. Bartlett's Familiar Quotations (Little, Brown).
6. Congressional Directory (Government Printing Service). Provides profiles of members of Congress.
7. Congressional Record (Government Printing Office). Complete proceedings of the U.S. House and Senate.
8. Current Biography (Wilson). Profiles of prominent persons, published monthly.
9. Dictionary of American Biography (Scribner's).
10. Facts on File (Facts on File Inc.). Weekly compilation of news from metropolitan newspapers.
11. Guinness Book of World Records (Guinness Superlatives). World records listed in countless categories.
12. National Trade and Professional Associations of the United States (Columbia Books, Washington, D.C.).
13. Readers' Guide to Periodical Literature (Wilson). Index to magazine articles on a host of subjects.
14. Statistical Abstract of the United States (Government Printing Office). Digest of data collected and published by all federal agencies.
15. Webster's Biographical Dictionary (Merriam).
16. Webster's New World Dictionary of the American Language, Second College Edition. Primary reference dictionary recommended by both The Associated Press and United Press International.
17. Webster's Third New International Dictionary. Unabridged dictionary recommended by AP and UPI.

18. Who's Who (St. Martin's, New York). World listings.
19. Who's Who in America (Marquis). Biennial publication.
20. World Almanac and Book of Facts (Newspaper Enterprise Association). Published annually.

These useful publications, and many others like them, enable reporters to verify data and to avoid the unnecessary embarrassment caused by recognizable errors.

DATA-BASE SEARCHES

Reporters increasingly are searching data bases in the process of collecting information. Many newspapers have made terminals available in their reference libraries to help reporters make such searches. If terminals are not available at your newspaper, try the local library; many libraries now have them. Most of the major data-base services also are available to individuals, and a home-computer user may be able to help. The information that follows is designed not to train you in the use of such services but to give you an idea of the kinds of invaluable material that may be just a computer connection away. This material was compiled with the assistance of Investigative Reporters and Editors Inc., P.O. Box 838, Columbia, Mo. 65205.

Figure 7.1 Data-Base Searches. Computer data bases provide reporters and editors with a wealth of information at the touch of a button.

SAMPLING OF AVAILABLE MATERIAL

Most data bases contain bibliographies annotated and cross-indexed by subject matter. The major vendor with the most data bases at this writing is Dialog, a Palo Alto, Calif., company owned by Lockheed. Dialog contains literally hundreds of data bases, each with a wealth of information. Users are charged for using the service according to the length of time their computer is connected to the data base. To give you an idea of what is available through Dialog, just one of many data-base services, here are descriptions of just a few of its data bases and the connect charges as of 1984:

ASI (American Statistics Index): From 1973 to present, 55,000 records, monthly updates (Congressional Information Service Inc., Washington, D.C.). ASI is a comprehensive index of the statistical publications from more than 400 central or regional issuing agencies of the U.S. government. ASI provides abstracts and indexing of all federal statistical publications, including non-Government Printing Office publications, which contain social, economic, demographic or natural resources data. It also covers a selection of publications with scientific and technical data. All types of publications are covered, including periodicals, as special, one-time reports; as items within a larger continuing report series; or as annual or biennial reports. Types of statistical data to be found in ASI include population and economic censuses; foreign trade data; Consumer Price Index reports; unemployment statistics; agricultural data on production, yield, prices, etc.; vital statistics; educational data and much more. Cost is $90 per online connect hour and 25 cents per full record printed offline.

Congressional Record Abstracts: From 1976 to present, 205,000 records, weekly updates (Capitol Services International, Washington, D.C.). This data base provides comprehensive abstracts covering each issue of the Congressional Record, the official journal of the proceedings of the U.S. Congress. Coverage includes congressional activities regarding bills and resolutions, committee and subcommittee reports, public laws, executive communications and speeches, and inserted materials. Records include data on bills, members of Congress, roll-call votes, reference to floor debates and specific issues. Abstracts are included. Cost is $75 per online connect hour and 15 cents per full record printed offline.

Foundations Grants Index: From 1973 to present, 105,600 records, bimonthly updates (The Foundation Center, New York, N.Y.). This data base contains information on grants awarded by more than 400 major American philanthropic foundations, representing all records from the Foundations Grants Index section of the bimonthly Foundation News. Information on grants given by foundations is useful in determining types and amounts of grants awarded because foundations seldom announce the availability of funds for specific purposes. Each foundation conforms to the description of a "nongovernmental nonprofit organization, with funds and program managed by its own trustees or directors, and established to maintain or aid social, common educational, charitable, religious or other activities serving the common welfare, primarily through the making of grants," as defined in the Foundation Directory, Edition 5. Approximately 20,000 grant records are added to the file each year. Grants are given primarily in the fields of education, health, welfare, sciences, international activities, humanities and religion, with education as the most-favored field for foundation giving. Grants to individuals and grants of less than $5,000 are not included. Cost is $60 per connect hour and 30 cents per full record printed offline.

Legal Resource Index: From 1980 to present, 53,000 records, monthly updates (Information Access Corp., Menlo Park, Calif.). This data base provides cover-to-cover indexing of more than 660 key law journals and five law newspapers plus legal monographs and government publications from the Library of Congress MARC data base. It comprehensively indexes articles, book reviews, case notes, president's pages, columns, letters to the editor, obituaries, transcripts, biographical pieces, and editorials providing access to valuable secondary information for the legal profession and others. Relevant articles from Magazine Index (File 47) and National Newspaper Index (File 111) are also included. Cost is $90 per online connect hour and 20 cents per full record printed offline.

Magazine Index: From 1976 to present, 588,500 citations, monthly updates (Information Access Corp., Menlo Park, Calif.). This data base is the first online data base to offer truly broad coverage of general magazines. It was created especially for general reference librarians who must handle a constant flow of diverse requests for information from the mundane to the scholarly to the lighthearted. It covers more than 370 popular magazines and provides extensive coverage of current affairs, leisure-time activities, home-centered arts, sports, recreation and travel, the performing arts, business, science and technology, consumer product evaluations, and other areas. In addition to being a valuable tool for the public and academic library information desks, it also will serve business and government libraries with information not available on any other online data base. In particular, libraries serving patrons in the fields of market research, public relations, government relations, journalism, food and nutrition, and the social sciences will find it to be a significant new resource. Cost is $75 per online connect hour and 20 cents per full record printed offline.

Newsearch: Current month only, daily updates (Information Access Corp., Los Altos, Calif.). This data base is a daily index of more than 2,000 news stories, information articles and book reviews from more than 1,400 of the most important newspapers, magazines and periodicals. Every working day the previous day's news stories are indexed and added to Newsearch to provide current information on product reviews; executive and corporation news; current events; book, record and theater reviews; and much more. At the end of each month, the magazine article data is transferred to the Magazine Index data base; the newspaper indexing data is transferred to the National Newspaper Index data base. Daily indexing from Legal Resource Index, Management Contents, and Trade and Industry Index is also transferred at the end of each month. Newsearch is available both publicly and on a special subscription basis. Cost is $95 per online connect hour and 20 cents per full record printed offline.

Standard and Poor's News: September 1979 to present, 234,000 records, weekly updates (Standard and Poor's Corp., New York, N.Y.). This data base offers both general news and financial information on more than 10,000 publicly owned U.S. corporations. It covers interim earnings, management changes, contract awards, mergers, acquisitions, bond descriptions and corporate background, including subsidiaries, litigation and officers. It is the most up-to-date and comprehensive online source of annual reports, interim earnings reports and statistical data of U.S. companies. It is a major source of financial information for competitive analysis and investing and is the equivalent of the printed Standard and Poor's Corp. Records Daily News and Cumulative News. Cost is $85 per online connect hour and 15 cents per full record printed offline.

Remember that these are merely a few of the hundreds of data bases available through just one source, Dialog. The information now available to reporters through such services is invaluable. Your college or local library may offer a class in data-base search techniques.

EXAMPLE OF A SEARCH

Let's say that the Environmental Protection Agency has just released information that it is concerned about a toxic waste dump in our area. Some of the chemicals detected there are in the form of deadly dioxin. As a reporter, you want to know what other stories have been written about toxic waste dumps and dioxin in particular. In consultation with your data-base search expert, you determine that three key words—"toxic," "waste" and "dioxin"—best describe the material for which you are searching. After a review of the available data bases, you decide that three, the Magazine Index, the Congressional Information Service and Enviroline, are the best sources. The computer searches those data bases and finds that the Magazine Index has 36 citations of interest, Congressional Information Service has more than 200 and Enviroline has 16. You choose 25 of the 200 possible citations from CIS and all those from the other data bases. Here is a sample of what you will receive:

DIALOG File 40: ENVIROLINE - 71-83/Jan (Copr. EIC Inc.) (Item 5 of 13) User 26025 11feb83 3706

136456   *79-003711
DEADLY LEGACY: DIOXIN AND THE VIETNAM VETERAN, THOMASSON W. A.
B ATOMIC SCIENTISTS, MAY 79, V35, N5, P15 (5)
FEATURE ARTICLE: IN 1961, THE U.S. ARMY IN CONJUNCTION WITH THE GOVERNMENT OF S. VIETNAM BEGAN A PROGRAM OF DEFOLIATION. AGENT ORANGE WITH ITS DIOXIN CONTAMINANT CEASED TO BE USED IN VIETNAM IN 1970, AND THE MATTER OF TERATOGENICITY WAS FORGOTTEN-UNTIL 1978, WHEN THE SUSPICION WAS RAISED THAT VETERANS EXPOSED TO AGENT ORANGE SUFFERED SYMPTOMS OF DIOXIN POISONING. OFFICIALS WHO ARE IN A POSITION TO FIND OUT HAVE SHOWN LITTLE INTEREST IN DOING SO. THE RISKS OF 2,4,5-T ARE DISCUSSED. (2 PHOTOS)
DESCRIPTORS: *DIOXINS ; *PATHOLOGY, HUMAN; *2, 4, 5-T HERBICIDE ; *HERBICIDE DAMAGE ; *VIETNAM ; CARCINOGENIC AGENTS ; *TERATOGENIC AGENTS ; *MUTAGENIC AGENTS ; DOW CHEMICAL CO ; HEALTH FACILITIES ; OREGON ; ITALY ; CHICAGO ; COMMONER, BARRY
REVIEW CLASSIFICATION: 02

These listings direct you to the newspapers, magazines and other publications you want. The data-base search will save many hours of time you may have spent in searching for such articles in the Readers' Guide to Periodical Literature and similar publications. Such a search also greatly reduces the chance that an important article will be overlooked. Data-base searches make simple the kind of searches that were seldom made in the past because they were too time-consuming or too non-productive. Data-base searches also help small newspapers that in the past have been unable to afford to give a reporter the time to conduct such searches in traditional ways.

Clearly, data-base searching techniques will be increasingly important to learn as newspapers and radio and television stations begin to go about the task of researching their stories more scientifically.

MAJOR DATA-BASE VENDORS

Here is a list of major data-base vendors of interest to journalists:

BRS/After Dark
1200 Route 7
Latham, N.Y. 12110
(518) 783-1161

CompuServe
P.O. Box 20212
5000 Arlington Centre Blvd.
Columbus, Ohio 43220
(800) 848-8199

Dialog
3460 Hillview Ave., Dept. 79
Palo Alto, Calif. 94304
(800) 227-1927

Dow Jones News Retrieval
P.O. Box 300
Princeton, N.J. 08540
(800) 345-8500

News Net
945 Haverford Rd.
Bryn Mawr, Pa. 19010
(215) 527-8030

The Source
P.O. Box 1305
McLean, Va. 22101
(703) 734-7523

8

Press Releases

Reporters don't go out and dig up all the stories they write. Many stories come to them. They are mailed, telephoned, telexed or hand-delivered by people who want to get something in the paper. They come from people or offices with different titles: public relations departments, public information offices, community relations bureaus, press agents, press secretaries and publicity offices. The people who write them call their stories *press releases*; other journalists are more apt to call them *handouts*.

Because good publicity is so important, private individuals, corporations and government agencies spend a great deal of money to obtain it. Much of the money goes for the salaries of skilled and experienced personnel, many of whom have worked in the news business. Part of their job is to write publicity releases that newspapers will use.

Press releases are both a help and a hindrance to a newspaper. They help because without them, newspapers would need many more reporters. They are a hindrance because they sometimes contain incomplete or even incorrect information. Wise editors do not discard press releases without reading them. Many are given to reporters (often the newest reporter) for checking out and for possible rewrite.

When your editor hands you a press release, you are expected to know what to do with it. You must be able to recognize the news in the release, applying all that you have learned about news values. The release may lead you to a good story. Your resourcefulness may improve your chances of being assigned to bigger things.

In this chapter you will learn:

1. What types of press releases there are.
2. How to handle the press release.

After you have read a number of press releases, you will notice that generally they fall into three categories:

1. Announcements of coming events or of personnel matters—hiring, promoting, retiring and the like.
2. Information regarding a cause.
3. Information that is meant to build someone's or some organization's image.

Recognizing the types and purposes of press releases (and that some are hybrids and serve more than one purpose) will help you know how to rewrite them.

ANNOUNCEMENTS

Organizations use the newspaper to tell their members and the public about coming events. For example:

> The Camera Club will have a special meeting at Wyatt's Cafeteria at 7 p.m. on Wednesday, March 22. Marvin Miller will present a slide program on ''Yellowstone in Winter.'' All interested persons are invited to attend.

Although the release promotes the Camera Club, it also serves as a public-service announcement. Newspapers that print such announcements are serving their readers. Here is another example:

> The first reception of the new season of the Springfield Art League will be on Sunday, Sept. 11, 3 to 5 p.m. in the Fine Arts Building.
> Included in the exhibition will be paintings, serigraphs, sculpture, batiks, weaving, pottery, jewelry, all created by Art League members, who throughout the summer have been preparing works for this opening exhibit of the season.
> The event also will feature local member-artists' State Fair entries, thus giving all who could not get to the fair the opportunity to see these works.
> The exhibition continues to Friday, Sept. 16. All gallery events and exhibitions are free.

Other press release announcements concern appointments, promotions, hiring and retiring. The announcement of an appointment may read like this:

James McAlester, internationally known rural sociolo-
gist at Mannheim University, has been appointed to the
board of directors of Bread for the World, according to
James Coburn, executive director of the humanitarian organization.

McAlester attended his first board meeting Jan. 22 in New
York City. He has been on the university faculty since
1974. Prior to that, he served as the Ford Foundation representative in India for 17 years.

The 19,000-member Bread for the World organization is a
"broad-based interdenominational movement of Christian
citizens who advocate government policies that address
the basic causes of hunger in the world," says Coburn.

The occasion for this release is the appointment of McAlester. But
the release also describes the purpose of the Bread for the World organization. By educating readers regarding the organization's purpose, the writer hoped to promote its cause.

Companies often send releases when an employee has been promoted. For example:

James B. Withers Jr. was named senior vice president in
charge of sales of the J. B. Withers Company, it was announced Tuesday.

Withers, who has been with the company in the sales division for two years, will head a sales force of 23 persons.

"We are sure Jim can do the job," James B. Withers Sr.,
company president, said. "He brings youth, intelligence
and enthusiasm to the job. We're pleased he has decided to
stay with the company."

Founded in 1936, the J. B. Withers Company is the country's second-largest manufacturer of dog and cat collars.

A release like this one is an attempt by the company to get its name
before the public and to create employee good will. Written in the
form of an announcement, it is an attempt at free publicity.

CAUSE-PROMOTING RELEASES

The second category of press releases seeks to further a cause.
Some of these releases come from worthwhile causes in need of
funds or of volunteers. For example, the letter reprinted below is
from a county chairman of the American Heart Association to the
editor of a newspaper. It is not written in the form of a release, but
its effect is meant to be the same:

The alumnae and collegiate members of the Alpha Phi Sorority have just completed their annual Alpha Phi "Help-

ing Hearts'' lollipop sale. This year Valerie Knight,
project chairman, led sorority members to achieve record-
breaking sales. The lollipop sale is a national project of
the Alpha Phi Sorority.

Sunday, March 5, Valerie Knight presented a check for
$1,800 to the American Heart Association, Shelby County
Unit. The contribution was presented during a reception at
the Alpha Phi house. This contribution is an important
part of the annual fund-raising campaign of the American
Heart Association.

I wish to extend special thanks to the members of Alpha
Phi and in particular to Valerie Knight for this outstanding project. In addition, I wish to thank the many merchants who participated in the project by selling lolli-
pops in their businesses.

Heads of organizations such as this attempt to alert the public to
their messages in any way they can. Any release, notice or letter they
can get printed without paying for it leaves money for the cause that
they represent. Sometimes the cause is a local private college:

Libbi Given, director of the Adelphos College community
campaign, has named 17 division chairpersons for the fund
drive that will begin Sept. 21.

The division heads met Sept. 9 to organize for the campaign, which has a $100,000 goal, an increase of $22,000
over last year's local gift support.

The college has developed a four-year gift support plan
to raise $8.5 million. Included in the amount is $4.5 million in Annual Fund gifts to provide assistance with the
operating expenses of the college, as it plans almost to
double its endowment base and renovate existing on- and
off-campus facilities.

Again, the cause is a good one. The college needs money, and to raise
money it must publicize its fund drive.

IMAGE-BUILDING RELEASES

Another kind of press release serves to build up someone's or
some organization's image. Politicians seek to be elected or to be re-
elected. They desire as much *free* publicity as they can get. For example:

James M. Merlin, honorary chairman of the board and director of Merlin Corporation, has been named honorary
chairman of the Finance Committee, which will seek statewide financial support for the campaign to elect William
C. Candace as U.S. senator from Maine.

>   Merlin, a nationally recognized civic leader and philan-
>   thropist, termed the election of Candace "one of the most
>   important and far-reaching decisions the voters of Maine
>   will ever make. The nation's financial crisis can only be
>   solved through the kind of economic leadership Candace has
>   demonstrated."

The appointment of Merlin as honorary chairman serves only to promote the image of the senator. The quote is self-serving.

Organizations and government agencies at all levels often try to build their public image. Many of them have local mayors proclaim a day or a week of recognition, as in the following:

>   Mayor James Lampert has proclaimed Saturday, May 6, as
>   Fire Service Recognition Day. The Springfield Fire De-
>   partment in conjunction with the University Fire Service
>   Training Division is sponsoring a demonstration of fire
>   apparatus and equipment at the Springfield Fire Training
>   Center. The displays are from 10 a.m. to 5 p.m. at 700 Bear
>   Blvd. All citizens are urged to attend the display or visit
>   their neighborhood fire station on May 6.
>   Our PRODUCT is your SAFETY.

If an editor hands you a release such as this, he or she probably has decided that it is worth using in some form. The rest is up to you.

Handling the Press Release

Regardless of the type of press release, be sure to read the information on the top. Here is an example:

```
NEWS FROM SUNSET              Office of Public Information
                             Sunset Community College
Contact: Sheila Gretchen     Springfield
                             Phone (315) 443-2231 Ext. 695

                             Betty S. Snead
                             Director of Public Informa-
                             tion

                             IMMEDIATE RELEASE
                             November 8, 1985
```

The top of the release usually tells you the following information:

1. The place or institution involved.
2. The address and phone number.

3. The name of the director of information.
4. The release date, or date on which the announcement should be printed, which is often "immediate."
5. The date on which the release was sent.
6. The name of the contact person from whom you may secure further information.

All of that information may be useful to you. Many news releases leave unanswered questions. You probably will want to contact people other than the director of information or even the contact person if you have serious doubts about some of the data given. But for routine accuracy checks, the persons listed on the release will do the job. They may lead you to other sources who may be helpful. Sometimes you may have sources of your own. And sometimes you will uncover the real story only from people not connected with or recommended by the director of information.

You may have to consult your editor regarding the release date. As a courtesy most newspapers honor release dates. However, sometimes a morning or evening paper will publish the release early because waiting until the following day would render the information useless. Also, once a release is public knowledge, editors feel justified in publishing whatever information it contains, even prior to the suggested release date. A release date is broken for all when it is broken by one.

REWRITING THE ANNOUNCEMENT RELEASE

Sometimes directors of information want nothing more than a listing on the record or calendar page of a newspaper. Here is an example:

```
FOR THE CALENDAR

  Elisabeth Bertke, quiltmaker and designer from Salem,
Massachusetts, will discuss her work at 7:00 o'clock P.M.
Tues., February 7, in Charters Auditorium, Hampton Col-
lege. Two quilts designed and constructed by Bertke are
included in the exhibit "The New American Quilt," cur-
rently on display at the Smith Art Gallery.
  "This is an exciting display," Betty Martin, president
of the Smith Art Gallery board of directors, said. "You
simply can't afford to miss it."
```

This simple release may go directly to the copy desk or to a special calendar editor. If given to you, rewrite it. Some newspapers insist that you rewrite every news release if for no other reason than to avoid the embarrassment of running the same story as a competing newspaper. For some it is a matter of integrity and professionalism.

First note all the violations of AP style:

- Massachusetts should be abbreviated.
- 7:00 o'clock P.M. should be 7 p.m.
- Tues. should be spelled out.
- February should be abbreviated.
- A hyphen should be inserted in quilt-maker.

Avoid relying on the copy desk to do your work if the rewrite is given to you.

You should check other points as well. First, determine the spelling of Bertke's name, and see if there is an apostrophe in Charters Auditorium. The Smith Art Gallery may or may not be on the Hampton campus. Ask how long the exhibit will be at the gallery. Are quilts made by local people included in the exhibit? Perhaps your questions will lead to a feature story on local quilt-making.

In your rewrite you will drop the quotation of Betty Martin. But you may insert better, less self-serving and less promotional quotes.

Here is another example:

Mr. Richard G. Henderson has been selected as the Outstanding Biology Teacher of Nevada of the year by the National Association of Biology Teachers. He was previously selected as Nevada Science Educator of the year.

As an outstanding representative of good high-school biology teaching Henderson will receive a certificate and a series 50 binocular microscope with an engraved citation. Henderson has been teaching at Hickman High School since 1963.

The story is far from earthshaking, but the honor is statewide. On large newspapers the release may not get much play. A small community newspaper, however, will use it and perhaps enlarge upon it.

A first reading of the release tells you it is wordy and that it leaves many questions unanswered. Henderson may be an interesting fellow, but the release tells us little about him. You should approach this release in the same way you approach any news release: Finish the reporting and then rewrite it. News style demands a new lead to the release:

A Hickman High School science teacher has been named Outstanding Biology Teacher of the year by the National Association of Biology Teachers.

Richard G. Henderson, a Hickson teacher since 1963, will receive a certificate and a series 50 binocular microscope with an engraved citation.
Previously selected as Nevada Science Educator of the year, Henderson . . .

Here the story runs out of information. You need to ask the following questions:

- Age?
- Degrees from where?
- Local address?
- Wife, family?
- Annual award? One teacher selected from each state?
- Any previous Hickman winners? Or from local high schools?
- Year he received Nevada Science Educator award?
- Nominated for the award by whom?
- Date and place of bestowal? Public ceremony?
- Value of series 50 binocular microscope?

Then call Henderson and find out how he feels about the award. Talk to the principal, to fellow teachers and to some of Henderson's students. Good quotations will spice up your story.

REWRITING THE CAUSE RELEASE

Newspapers generally cooperate with causes that are community-oriented. Press releases like the following get attention:

A free tax clinic for low-income persons and senior citizens will be held on Feb. 9 and 10 in Springfield.
The clinic is sponsored by the Central State Counties' Human Development Corporation in cooperation with the Mannheim University School of Accountancy.
Senior and graduate accounting students under the direct supervision of accounting faculty members will work with each taxpayer to help that taxpayer complete accurately his or her tax return.
The Human Development Corporation encourages persons especially to use the clinic who may be eligible for senior citizens' credits or other credits.
This is the fifth year the clinic has operated in Shelby County. Last year more than 275 persons in the eight counties served were assisted.
For information regarding location of the clinics and to

```
make an appointment, contact the Shelby County Human De-
velopment Corporation, 600 E. Broadway, Room 103,
Springfield, 449-8376.
```

Again, you need more information. To begin with, you need to know more about the Human Development Corporation. A background paragraph on its origins, where it gets its money and its other areas of concern will put the story into context.

The release is unclear about who is eligible. What must your income be? How old must you be? Also, you must find out the exact locations of the clinics.

Once you have all your questions answered, dig for some human interest. Talk to a participating faculty member and to students who have helped before and will help again. Then talk to some people who have been helped in the past and to some who will come for help. Obviously, you must talk to those in charge of the joint effort.

Since efforts like these are in the public interest, newspapers will give them space. They will be more critical with releases that are merely self-serving.

REWRITING THE IMAGE-BUILDING RELEASE

The following is a typical release from a politician:

```
Sen. John C. Smith said today that nearly $400,000 in
grants have been given final approval by two departments
of the federal government for interlocking improvements
in Springfield and Shelby County.
    Smith said, ''This is something I have been working for
this past year. It is a chance to show that federal agen-
cies are interested in communities. It also demonstrates
that two agencies can work together to produce a coordi-
nated, workable solution to improve a blighted area in
Springfield.''
    The grants, Smith said, come from the Federal Bureau of
Outdoor Recreation -- $247,000 for purchasing Baltimore
and Ohio railroad rights of way and developing a strip
park, and the Department of Housing and Urban Development
-- $150,000 for planning the Flat Branch area. The second
grant also stipulates that part of the money be used to co-
ordinate the two projects, the B&O strip park and the Flat
Branch redevelopment.
    ''I think residents of Springfield and Shelby County
will have a chance to help out in the planning of these two
facilities. I hope this means the entire community will
express opinions and come to a conclusion that will see
these projects become a reality in the next two years.''
```

The first four words of the release indicate who is being served by the release. A Springfield reporter might write the lead this way to serve the reader:

```
Springfield and Shelby County will receive nearly
$400,000 in federal grants to fund the B&O strip park and
the Flat Branch redevelopment project, Sen. John C. Smith
said today.
```

The second paragraph of the release is a long and newsless quote from the senator. Probably he did not say those words at all; they were written by his press agent. You should eliminate them, or if you want a quote from the senator, call him and talk to him yourself.

The second paragraph of the story should indicate the source of the funding:

```
The grants come from two federal agencies. The Federal
Bureau of Outdoor Recreation granted $247,000 for pur-
chasing the Baltimore & Ohio Railroad rights of way and for
developing a strip park, and the Department of Housing and
Urban Development granted $150,000 for planning the Flat
Branch area. The second grant also stipulates that part of
the money be used to coordinate the two projects.
```

Smith's last quote could be handled this way:

```
Smith said he hoped Springfield and Shelby County resi-
dents will have a chance to help plan the two facilities.
"I hope this means the entire community will express opin-
ions and come to a conclusion that will see these projects
become a reality in the next two years."
```

Like many news releases of this kind, this announcement would trigger other news stories in the local papers. This story would call for local reactions from city and county officials and from local residents. The editor might assign several stories on the matter.

Rewriting an Organization's Image-Building Release

Releases from organizations can also be self-serving—and sometimes misleading. Suppose you were given this press release to rewrite:

```
Springfield - Dogcatchers in Springfield make a higher
beginning salary than Springfield teachers, as discovered
in a recent survey by the Springfield Community Teachers
Association. According to their research, a beginning
```

teacher in the Springfield public school system makes $10,300 while a dogcatcher starts at $10,830, or $530 more than a beginning teacher. "This is a shameful situation for an educational community," said Tom Monnin, Springfield SCTA Salary Committee chairman.

The statistics gathered by the Springfield SCTA Salary Committee indicate that police with a bachelor's degree make $14,130, while a beginning teacher with a bachelor's degree makes $10,300. This is a $3,830 gap in beginning salaries for public employees with comparable education. Following is a comparison of beginning salaries of some Springfield city employees and of public school teachers for the school year:

Occupation	Beginning Salary
Police with B.S.	$14,130
Firefighter with B.S.	13,988
Meter Reader	10,830
Animal Control Officer	10,830
Bus Operator	10,387
Teacher with B.S.	10,300

"Springfield teachers do not think city employees are overpaid but that teachers are underpaid," Monnin said.

Even though teachers work under a 9¼-month contract, the workweek is not 40 hours. When the hours for preparing and grading, attending sports events, musical concerts, dances, other after-school activities, and PTA meetings are considered, a teacher's workweek is much longer than 40 hours. Summer break is used by many teachers for advanced preparation at the university, at their own expense.

The Springfield SCTA Salary Committee will present their salary proposal at the next meeting of the Springfield Board of Education.

The Springfield SCTA represents approximately 523 members in the public school system.

For additional information contact Tom Monnin, Springfield SCTA Salary Committee Chairman, at 552-6794 (Central High School) or 553-2975 (home).

Your first task is to read the release carefully. The lead cleverly suggests that dogcatchers make as much money as teachers do, although it speaks only of "beginning" salaries. The more you read the release, the more uncomfortable you should feel with it. No one can blame teachers for wanting more money, but there are other compensations to consider. What about working conditions? Teachers in Springfield's schools hardly have to put their lives on the line the way police officers and firefighters do. Most people don't want to spend their lives chasing stray dogs.

The fact that teachers work for a little more than nine months a year is down in the fourth paragraph. The release fails to mention a two-week break over Christmas and a week off in the spring semester. Most dogcatchers get two weeks off all year.

Was the release trying to suggest that because teachers actually spend more than 40 hours a week working, they should not have to work more than 9¼ months? Not all teachers spend all their lives going to summer school. You probably know several who have summer jobs.

The release compares the beginning salary of a teacher with that of a police officer who has a comparable degree. Before you turn in a rewrite of the release, you have a lot of checking to do.

One reporter began by calling Animal Control. He told Tom Merell, the officer who answered his call, that he had a press release saying that animal control officers start with higher salaries than Springfield's schoolteachers.

"Could be," Merell replied. "But I sure wish I got summers off like those teachers. I got nothing against teachers. But most of them make more money than I'll ever make."

The reporter asked him to explain.

"Look," Merell said, "the most money any animal control officer can make is $12,757, and it will take him quite a few years to make that. I know some teachers who are making more than $16,000. Besides, students don't bite many teachers."

The reporter knew he was on to something. Comparing beginning salaries was one thing. But how much could a person eventually earn in a position?

The reporter then called the city of Springfield's office of personnel. "Yes," the director of personnel said, "$14,130 is the beginning salary for a police officer with a B.S. degree."

The reporter then asked whether anyone could get hired at that salary if he or she had a B.S. degree.

"Most people wouldn't stand a chance of being hired," he said. "We have more than 100 applicants for every position, so we can be quite choosy. Unless a person has had some real experience as a police officer, I don't think he would make it."

Further questioning revealed that a top salary for a police officer was $17,125 after 4½ years of service. When asked about the $13,988 beginning salary of a firefighter, the personnel officer replied:

"You wouldn't begin at that salary. Everyone is hired at $11,944 for a trial period of at least six months. If you work out OK, you might jump up to $13,988. Again, there are a lot of other considerations besides the college degree."

Further checking revealed that the press release did indeed contain wrong information about the beginning salaries of firefighters. The reporter then called a high school teacher. He asked her if she had to put in more than 40 hours a week at her job.

"Oh, yes," she said. "I teach a section of English composition, and I have a lot of papers to grade. I used to spend a lot of evenings preparing for classes, but once you've taught a course, it gets easier. And then I have to go to all those football games and basketball games."

The reporter then found out that she was indeed required to attend, but only because she was in charge of the cheerleaders. When he expressed sympathy, the teacher replied, "No, I really don't mind. After all, I get $800 a year extra for being in charge of the cheerleaders."

The reporter then learned from someone at the Springfield School Board personnel office that quite a few teachers received compensation for after-school activities—coaching, directing plays, directing musical activities, chaperoning dances. Teachers sponsoring class and club activities could earn from $300 to $800; a sponsor of the pep squad could earn up to $1,000. The top teacher's salary without any of these extras was $17,272.

Now the reporter was ready to call Tom Monnin, the man whose name was on the release for additional information. He asked if it was fair to compare a beginning teacher's salary with a beginning dogcatcher's salary when the top pay for a dogcatcher was $12,757 and the top teacher's salary was $17,272. Monnin explained that it took 16 years for a teacher with a master's degree plus 60 hours to reach that top salary. A teacher with a bachelor's degree could make $13,620 after 11 years of teaching. When the reporter asked about the summer off and other vacations, Monnin replied, "I figure I work a 60-hour week. That means I work 51¾ 40-hour weeks a year."

Monnin acknowledged that many teachers got paid extra for extracurricular activities. "But not all of them do," he said. "And there are many activities we do feel the responsibility to attend."

When asked about the argument that teachers do not have to put their lives on the line the way police and fire officials and even dogcatchers do, Monnin replied:

"It's debatable who has to put their lives on the line. We're not as bad off as some schools, but we often have to restrain students physically."

Only now was the reporter ready to write the story. Here's what he wrote:

```
The Springfield Community Teachers Association said
Tuesday that beginning dogcatchers earn more than begin-
ning teachers.
```

What the teachers did not say was that a teacher eventually can earn nearly $5,000 more a year than a dogcatcher can earn.

The SCTA statement was included with a survey that lists starting teachers' salaries at $10,300 and a Springfield dogcatcher's starting salary at $10,830. Other figures listed as beginning salaries are: police with a bachelor's degree, $14,130; firefighters with a bachelor's degree, $13,988; meter reader, $10,830; bus operator, $10,387.

"This is a shameful situation for an educational community," said Tom Monnin, the Springfield SCTA Salary Committee chairman. "Springfield teachers do not think city employees are overpaid but that teachers are underpaid."

The association officers said that even though teachers work under a 9¼-month contract, extracurricular activities extend the work week beyond 40 hours. Summer break, they said, is used for advanced study at the teachers' own expense.

"I figure I work a 60-hour week," Monnin said in an interview. "That means I work 51¾ 40-hour weeks a year."

Some extracurricular activities such as coaching, directing plays and supervising cheerleaders earn extra compensation.

Teachers are not compelled to attend after-school functions, but "we do feel the responsibility to attend," Monnin said.

Teachers also feel compelled to continue their education. Top pay for a teacher with only a bachelor's degree is $13,620 after 11 years of teaching. A teacher with a master's degree plus 60 hours of classes can earn $17,272 after 16 years of teaching.

A police officer with a bachelor's degree can reach a top salary of $17,125 after 4½ years of police work. But a person with a bachelor's degree and no police work experience is not likely to be hired, said Phil James, the Springfield director of personnel. James also said all firefighters are hired at $11,944. If a person has a bachelor's degree and stays on, he or she could make $13,988 after a six-month trial period.

Top pay for a dogcatcher is $12,757. "I sure wish I got summers off like those teachers," Tom Merell, an animal control officer, said. "I got nothing against teachers. But most of them make more money than I'll ever make. . . . Besides, students don't bite many teachers."

The SCTA Salary Committee will present its salary proposal at the next meeting of the Springfield Board of Education.

The reporter did with this press release what should be done with many of them. He was not satisfied with the way it was written, nor with the information it contained. By asking some important questions, he was able to put together an informative and more accurate story. Without saying that the press release was dishonest or misleading, the reporter corrected or clarified some of the information contained in it. The plight of the teachers is told clearly and objectively, but it is placed in a much better perspective than was found in the press release.

Like many press releases, this one was the basis for a story the newspaper otherwise would not have had. That is why editors pay attention to them and why reporters look for the real story. Remember:

1. Read the information on the top of the release form.
2. Check the news style. Ask questions about missing information. Verify any spellings or information you have doubts about.
3. Take for granted you are to do a rewrite. Fill in missing information. Tighten the copy.
4. Watch for self-serving quotations and information. Look for news. Write the news.
5. Look for other news stories — local angles, reactions, and the like — triggered by the release.

Suggested Readings

Cutlip, Scott M. and Allen H. Center. "Effective Public Relations." 5th ed. revised. Englewood Cliffs, N.J.: Prentice-Hall, Inc., 1982. This has become the standard college text on the subject, treating all aspects of public relations.

Reeves, Richard. "Our National Flacks." Esquire, December 1977, pp. 68, 70. Reeves talked with 16 reporters and editors holding public relations jobs with the Carter administration, who said that press coverage was accurate generally, but that the press should work harder to ferret out governmental news.

9

Obituaries

Fortunately for The Associated Press, Mark Twain had a sense of humor about himself as well as the world around him. When the AP carried the news in 1897 that Twain had died, the author cabled the news agency from London. "The reports of my death," he observed dryly, "are greatly exaggerated."

The Associated Press was certainly not the first nor will it be the last to report someone's death mistakenly. Many newspapers ran Ernest Hemingway's obituary in 1953 when it was thought he had died in an airplane crash in Africa. Some, like Twain and Hemingway, are amused by these mistakes. Some sue. Most read the obituaries, or "obits" as they are known in the trade, with great interest. Friends, co-workers, neighbors, former classmates, creditors, casual acquaintances — all are interested. Everybody knows somebody.

And obituaries are read critically. If the deceased was an Odd Fellow, you'd better not say he was an Elk. If she belonged to the Shiloh Baptist Church, count on a phone call if you say it was Bethany Baptist. Michael Davies, then editor of the Kansas City (Mo.) Star and Times, once told of a call from an owner of a funeral home. The caller was complaining about inaccuracies in obituaries. Skeptical, Davies checked all the next day's obits. He was shocked to find an error of some kind in nearly every one. "If we can't get obits right, how can we expect readers to believe the Page 1 stories?" he asked. For many people an obituary is the only story the paper ever carries about them. You are summing up a life in five paragraphs. That's important work.

Despite this importance many newspapers do not publish a news obituary unless the person who dies is well-known. At those papers the advertising department handles obituaries as paid notices. Many metropolitan papers have adopted this policy because to publish obits on everyone who died in the area would require a substantial amount of space. At papers where obits are handled as advertising, the skill and creativity a reporter brings to the reporting and writing of the story are missing.

Still, there are many reporters who wish their papers would handle obits as advertising matter. These are the reporters who look at obits as a tedious exercise in formula writing. Often that attitude is fostered by editors who assign the obits only to new reporters.

Other papers have a completely different philosophy. They give the assignment to anyone and everyone in the news room. Deborah Howell, editor of the St. Paul (Minn.) Pioneer Press, says, "I constantly remind assignment editors to search for reasons to do an obit, rather than reasons not to write one." Some papers have reporters who specialize in writing this type of story. The New York Times has a reporter interview important public figures to write advance obits. The wire services and most large newspapers write obits in advance about famous people. When these people die, the newspaper or wire service can move quickly not only to report the death but also to provide complete biographical information on the individual. They understand that they are writing about life, not death.

Even if you work at a paper where most obituaries are run as paid notices, when a well-known person dies, the news department will want a story. Knowing how to report and write an obit is important

Figure 9.1 Assigning Obituaries. Deborah Howell and editors like her encourage their staffs to view obituaries as an opportunity rather than a chore.

to you because you may make your first impression on a city editor by the way you handle the assignment. The city editor will examine your work critically. Is the information correct? Is it complete? Did you check additional sources? Did you follow newspaper style? Did you follow newspaper policy? This chapter will examine such questions.

In this chapter you will learn:

1. How to write an obituary and what information you will need.
2. Where to get interesting material.
3. What policies newspapers may follow in printing obituary information.

Basic Obituary Information and Style

An obituary is a news story. You should apply the same standards of crafting a lead and building the body of an obituary as you do to other stories.

CRAFTING A LEAD

You begin by answering the same questions you would in any news story: who (Michael Kelly, 57, of 1234 West St.), what (died), where (at Regional Hospital), when (Tuesday night), why (heart attack) and how (suffered while jogging). With this information, you are ready to start the story.

The fact that Kelly died of a heart attack suffered while jogging may well be the lead, but the reporter does not know until the rest of the information essential to every obituary is gathered. You also must know survivors, funeral services, burial place, visitation, if any, achievements, occupation and memberships. Any of these items can yield the nugget that appears in the lead. Too often, reporters don't bother to look, and the result is an unimaginative formula lead such as the following:

```
Michael Kelly, 57, of 1234 West St., died Tuesday night
at Regional Hospital.
```

Another standard approach would be:

```
Funeral services for Michael Kelly, 57, of 1234 West St.,
will be at 2 p.m. Thursday at the First Baptist Church.
```

Those leads are found too often in newspapers. Some papers, though, ask their reporters to look for the distinguishing characteristics of a person's life. It may be volunteer service, a unique or important job, service in public office or even just having a name of historical significance. Whatever distinguishes a person can be the lead of the obituary:

> For 35 years, Michael Kelly, 57, of 1234 West St., served others by working as a volunteer for the United Way.
> On Thursday at 2 p.m. at the First Baptist Church, more than 100 of his fellow volunteers will attend funeral services for Mr. Kelly, who died Tuesday night of a heart attack suffered while jogging.

In the preceding example, most of the information traditionally placed in the lead paragraph is delayed until the second paragraph.

Writing approaches can be as varied for obituaries as for any other news story. For instance, the following story emphasizes the personal reactions of those who knew the deceased:

> Few persons knew her name, but nearly everyone knew her face.
> For 43 years, Mary Jones, the city's cheerful cashier, made paying your utility bills a little easier.
> Tuesday morning after she failed to report to work, two fellow employees found her dead in her home at 432 East St., where she died apparently of a heart attack. She was 63.
> By Tuesday afternoon, employees had placed a simple sign on the counter where Miss Jones had worked.
> "We regret to inform you that your favorite cashier, Mary Jones, died this morning. We all miss her."
> "She had a smile and a quip for everybody who came in here," said June Foster, a bookkeeper in the office.
> "She even made people who were mad about their bills go away laughing."

BUILDING THE STORY BODY

After deciding on an interesting lead, you should proceed by including the information basic to every obituary: funeral arrangements, survivors, date and place of birth, employment history, memberships and achievements. For Mary Jones, the rest of the obituary may read like this:

> The Rev. Roger Hotchkiss will celebrate the funeral Mass at 1:30 p.m. Friday at Sacred Heart Catholic Church, 209 Westbend Ave.

Burial will be in Resthaven Cemetery.

Friends may call at the Morgan Funeral Home from 6 to 9 p.m. Thursday.

Miss Jones was born on Oct. 6, 1921, in Ames, Iowa. She moved to Springfield in 1937 and worked for three years as a department store clerk before joining the city staff.

She was a member of the League of Women Voters, the Catholic Women's Club and the Downtown Civic League.

She is survived by one brother, Edward, of Milwaukee, and one sister, Gina Thompson, of Chicago.

Most of this information is provided by the mortuary on a standard form. Because this information normally is obtained directly from the family, it generally is accurate. But you still should check the spelling of all names.

CHOOSING YOUR WORDS

Avoid much of the language found on mortuary forms and in obituaries prepared by morticians. The phrasing often is more fitting for a eulogy than a newspaper story.

Because of the sensitivity of the subject matter, euphemisms have crept into the vocabulary of obituary writers. "Loved ones," "passed away," "our dearly beloved brother and father," "the departed" and "remains" may be fine for eulogies, but such terms are out of place in a news story.

Watch your language, too, when you report the cause and circumstances of a death. Unless the doctor is at fault, a person usually dies not "as a result of an operation" but "following" or "after" one. Also, a person dies "unexpectedly" but not "suddenly." All deaths are sudden. Note, too, that a person dies "apparently of a heart attack" but not of "an apparent heart attack." And a person dies of injuries "suffered," not "received."

Be careful with religious terms. Catholics "celebrate" Mass; some Jews worship in "temples," others in "synagogues." An Episcopal priest who heads a parish is a "rector," not a "pastor." Followers of Mohammed are called "Moslems," although there is an organization known as the "Black Muslims."

Consult your wire service stylebook when you have a question.

The stylebook prescribes usage in another instance, too. A man is survived by his wife, not his widow, and a woman is survived by her husband, not her widower. In fact, you will need to consult the stylebook often when you are writing an obit. Do you use titles such as Mr. and Mrs.? Do you identify pallbearers? Do you say when memorial contributions are requested?

Once you have checked the spelling and corrected the language, it is time to begin gathering additional information.

Sources of Information

MORTUARY FORMS

For many newspapers the standard form from the mortuary mentioned previously is the primary source of information. The mortuary can be of further help if more information is needed. Does your city editor want a picture of the deceased? Call the mortuary. It usually can obtain one quickly from the family. Is there some conflicting or unclear information on the form? Call the mortuary.

But writing obituaries from the mortuary's information alone is a clerk's work. As a reporter you should go beyond the form. Sometimes, what the obituary form doesn't tell you is as important as what it does say.

For the writer of the following obit, the first clue that the death notice was unusual was the age. The deceased was 12. That alone was enough for the reporter to start asking questions. The result was an obituary that moved from the records column to the front page:

Sherrill Ann Grimes, 12, lost her lifetime struggle against a mysterious muscle ailment Wednesday night. The day she died was the first day she had ever been admitted as a hospital inpatient.

Although they knew it was coming, the end came suddenly for Sherrill's family and school friends, said her father, Lester, of 1912 Jackson St.

Just last Friday, she attended special classes at the Parkade School. "She loved it there," Grimes said. "Like at recess, when the sixth graders would come in and read to her. She always wanted to be the center of attention."

"Bright as a silver dollar" was the way one of Sherrill's early teachers described her. In fact, no one will ever know. Sherrill couldn't talk.

"We didn't know what she knew or didn't know," her father said. Sherrill's only communication with the world around her came in the form of smiles and frowns — her symbols for yes and no.

"There were times when I'd come around the corner and kind of stick my head around and say 'boo,'" her father recalled. "She smiled. She liked that."

The care and attention Sherrill demanded makes the loss particularly hard for her family to accept, Grimes said. "I can't really put it into words. You cope with it the best you can, keep her comfortable and happy. We always took her with us."

Sherrill came down with bronchitis Friday. Complications forced her to be admitted Wednesday to Boone County Hospital, where she died later that night.

Sherrill's fight for life was uphill all the way. It started simply enough when she was four months old. Her mother, Bonnie, noticed she "wasn't holding up her head" like her other children.

Although her ailment was never nailed down, doctors found Sherrill's muscles held only half the tissues and fibers in a normal child's body. The diagnosis: a type of cerebral palsy. The prognosis: Sherrill had little chance to live past the age of two. Medical knowledge offered little help.

150

Sherrill was born in Columbia on Jan. 15, 1965. She is survived by her parents; one brother, Michael Eugene Grimes; one sister, Terrie Lynn Grimes, both of the home; and her grandparents, Gordon Grimes of Seale, Ala., and Mrs. Carrie Harris of Phoenix, Ariz.

Services will be at 3:30 p.m. today at the Memorial Funeral Chapel with the Rev. Jack Gleason conducting. Burial will follow at the Memorial Park Cemetery.

The family will receive friends at the Memorial Funeral Home until time for burial.

The reporter who wrote this obituary obviously did a great deal of research beyond what was on the mortuary form. Because the girl was not a public figure, the reporter could not consult a reference work such as *Who's Who in America* or a national publication. But the reporter did have access to the newspaper morgue and could interview the girl's family and friends. These are the sources that can help make interesting copy.

Another good source at some papers is the paid funeral notices. One that appeared in the St. Paul (Minn.) Pioneer Press mentioned that there would be a party after the funeral. With the permission of the family, the reporter attended. His story began:

> The ladies sat in a circle of lawn chairs in the neatly clipped backyard, between the pea patch on the right and the tomatoes and cucumbers on the left, sipping their gentle scotches and bourbons and beers, while the mosquitoes buzzed around their ears, and the evening slowly faded without pain into the night.

Whatever the source, verify the information. Too many newspapers have been victims of a hoax because a reporter took information by phone and failed to check with any other source.

THE NEWSPAPER LIBRARY

In the newspaper library, also called the newspaper morgue, you may find an interview with the deceased, an interesting feature story or clips indicating activities not included on the obituary form. In an interview or feature story the person may have made a statement about a philosophy of life that would be appropriate to include in the obituary. The subject also may have indicated his or her goals in life, against which later accomplishments can be measured. The names of friends and co-workers can be found in the clips as well. These persons are often the source of rich anecdotes and comments about the deceased.

A reporter assigned to do the obituary of a local man, Harold Ri-

Figure 9.2 Start at the Newspaper Library. Good reporting for obituaries and all other stories begins at the newspaper library, also called the morgue. The library, such as this one at the Boston Globe, contains newspaper clippings, photographs and reference materials.

back, hit pay dirt in the newspaper morgue. There he found the names of two associates, Pauline Yost and Viva Spiers, from whom he was able to secure some interesting details:

When Harold Riback was a student at the university, he drove a salvage truck to St. Louis at night for his father's business. He always took his books so he could study when he stopped to rest.

"Even when he was young, he was very ambitious," said Pauline Yost, the secretary for the Boone County

Democratic party, while reminiscing about Riback, 66, who died Monday morning at Boone County Hospital.

"When he agreed to a project, you didn't have just a name, you had a completely involved person," said Viva Spiers, the Sixth Ward Democratic committeewoman.

Those same files also yielded another interesting quote from Riback himself:

Mr. Riback once said, "I've always had a strong community commitment. My dad used to say,

'Whenever you've enjoyed the fruits of the harvest, you have to save a little bit of the seed for the next year's crop.' When you benefit from the community, you have to give it back. This philosophy has had a strong bearing on my life.''

That is the type of statement a newspaper obtains if it has a regular program of interviewing public figures for their obituaries in advance of their death. Because most newspapers do not, looking through the morgue is the next best thing.

INTERVIEWING FAMILY AND FRIENDS

Papers treat public figures in more detail not only because they are newsworthy but also because reporters know more about them. Even though private citizens usually are less newsworthy, many good stories about them are never written because the reporter did not — or was afraid to — do the reporting. The fear is usually unfounded. William Buchanan, who has written many obituaries for the Boston Globe, said his calls are almost always welcomed: "The person I called appreciated that someone cared enough to want to know more about a loved one."

That's true even in the worst of circumstances, such as a suicide. Karen Ball, a reporter for the Columbia Missourian, learned that lesson when she was assigned to do a story on Robert Somers, a university professor who had committed suicide. Karen didn't look forward to calling Mrs. Somers. First, Karen talked to students, Somers' colleagues and university staff members. She obtained a copy of his resume.

"By knowing a lot about him — where he'd studied, what his interests were and where he worked — I knew that I could go into an interview with a bereaved relative and at least have something to talk about," she says.

She approached Mrs. Somers in person and explained that her husband was respected and liked. Mrs. Somers agreed to talk. To get her to elaborate on his personality and what he was like away from school, Karen prodded her with questions about their children, where they had lived before and other family matters. She also talked to Somers' mother. Karen told her some of the positive things that students and faculty had said about her son. That helped the mother vent her sorrow and helped Karen write her story. It began:

Miko Somers sat at her kitchen table folding and unfolding her youngest daughter's bib as she talked about her husband.

"He could never do anything halfway," Mrs. Somers says. "He set such a high standard for himself. Whatever he did had to be the very best, and he pushed himself to make it that way."

Today Mrs. Somers buries her husband. Monday, Robert Somers, 40, her husband for 17 years, the father of their four daughters and an associate professor in the University's history department, took his life by driving his car head-on into a tree.

Not all calls to the family of the deceased go so smoothly. A reporter working for a Memphis paper during the Vietnam War had the assignment to call the parents of a soldier killed in action. The news of his death was reported by the Pentagon and had been distributed by the wire services. The news of the death, however, had not reached the mother. The reporter found himself in the position of unwittingly being the first to tell her; the Pentagon mistakenly had released the name before the family was notified.

The embarrassed reporter apologized. The shocked mother regained her composure enough to give the reporter the information he needed. And the newspaper angrily notified the Pentagon.

Newspaper Policy

Newspaper policy often dictates what will — and will not — be included in an obituary. Those newspapers that do have written policies may prescribe how to handle everything from addresses to suicides.

Some newspapers, for instance, prohibit a statement such as, "In lieu of flowers, the family requests donations be made to the county humane society." This prohibition is in response to lobbying from florists.

Because of threats to the safety of property and the individuals involved, in some cities even information essential to the obituary no longer appears in the paper. Some newspapers specifically tell reporters not to include the address.

Criminals have used information taken from the obituary columns to prey on widows. Knowing the time of the funeral and the address of the deceased makes it easy to plan a break-in at the empty residence during the services. Therefore, this information also may be withheld.

Two other kinds of information newspapers may have restrictive policies on are the cause of death and potentially embarrassing information.

CAUSE OF DEATH

If the person who dies is not a public figure and the family does not wish to divulge the cause of death, some newspapers will agree. That is questionable news judgment. The reader wants to know what caused the death. A reporter should call the mortuary, the family, the attending physician and the appropriate medical officer. Only if none of these sources will talk should the newspaper leave out the cause of death. The Des Moines (Iowa) Register and Tribune will refuse to run an obituary without the cause of death.

A death certificate must be filed for each death, but obtaining it often takes days. And even if the reporter has timely access to it, the cause of death listed on it is often vague.

If the death is caused by cancer or a heart attack or is the result of an accident, most families do not object to including the cause in the obituary. But if the cause is cirrhosis of the liver brought on by heavy drinking, many families do object, and most papers do not insist on printing the cause.

If the deceased was a public figure or was young, most newspapers insist on the cause of death.

If the death is the result of suicide or foul play, reporters can obtain the information from the police or the medical examiner. Some newspapers include suicide as a cause of death in the obituary; others print it in a separate news story, and still others ignore it altogether. This is one way to report it:

Services for Gary O'Neal, 34, a local carpenter's union officer, will be at 9 a.m. Thursday in the First Baptist Church.

Coroner Mike Pardee ruled that Mr. O'Neal died Tuesday of a self-inflicted gunshot wound.

EMBARRASSING INFORMATION

Another newspaper policy affecting obituaries concerns embarrassing information. If you discover that the person you are writing about was 77 and had served a short jail term for breaking and entering when he was 21, your editor probably would not include it in the obituary. It is a relatively minor offense committed years earlier. However, if you discover that your subject had served a term for child molestation and was well-known since then for having spent hundreds of hours as a volunteer with youth groups, the question would be much less clear-cut. Some editors would include it; most would not. In fact, many would not run the featurized version of the obituary at all because of that piece of information. But, if the deceased were an avowed homosexual and active in the gay rights movement, many newspapers would include participation in the movement in the obituary.

These examples involved information that is part of the public record — the first two from official court documents, the third from newspaper reports. But the reporter also may gather information that is not part of any record. If a reporter discovers that a person was an unannounced alcoholic, should that information be used?

In the case of a private citizen, the reporter probably would leave it out. When dealing with a public figure, the reporter probably would include it. Since you cannot libel a dead person, the question is not one of law but of taste and the public's need to know.

Buchanan, of the Boston Globe, said a man's grandson once called to complain because Buchanan had written that the deceased had been convicted of shaking down motorists when he was a high-ranking police official. Buchanan responded, "I cannot make the man something in death that he was not in life."

When author W. Somerset Maugham died, The New York Times reported that he was a homosexual even though the subject generally had not been discussed in public before. When public figures die, newspapers sometimes make the first public mention of drinking problems in their obituaries.

The crucial factor in determining the extent to which you should report details of an individual's private life is whether the deceased was a public or private person. A *public figure* is one who has been in the public eye. An officeholder, a participant in civic or social activities, a person who spoke out at public meetings or through the mass media, a performer, an author, a speaker — these all are public figures.

POLICY OPTIONS

Whether the subject is a public figure or private citizen, the decisions newspapers must make when dealing with the obituary are sensitive and complicated. These are the options your newspaper has:

1. Run an obituary that ignores any embarrassing information and, if necessary, leave out the cause of death. If circumstances surrounding the death warrant a news story, run it separate from the obituary.
2. Insist on including embarrassing details and the cause of death in the obituary.
3. Insist on including embarrassing details and the cause of death in the obituary only for public figures.
4. Put a limit on how far back in the person's life to use derogatory information such as a conviction.
5. Print everything newsworthy that is learned about a public figure but not about private figures.
6. Print everything thought newsworthy about public and private figures.
7. Decide each case as it comes up.

It is the reporter's obligation to be aware of the newspaper's policy. In the absence of a clear policy statement, the reporter should consult the city editor.

Suggested Readings

Hart, Jack and Janis Johnson. "A Clash Between the Public's Right to Know and a Family's Need for Privacy." The Quill, May 1979, pp. 19–24. An account of the backlash against a newspaper that printed a syndicated story of how the daughter of a locally prominent family had died a big-city prostitute.

Rambo, David C. "Obits: Newspapers' Eternal Draw for Readers." presstime, November 1983, pp. 30–32. A roundup of how various newspapers treat obituaries.

"Why Do We Handle Obits in Such Deadly Fashion?" The Bulletin, ASNE, July–August 1982, pp. 7–13. Various editors describe their attitudes toward obituaries and tell about their experiences handling obits.

10

Speeches, News Conferences and Meetings

You can be quite sure that in your first year or so of general-assignment reporting you will be assigned to cover many speeches, news conferences and meetings. They are sometimes routine, sometimes of great importance. Communities often elect and re-elect their leaders on the basis of their performance at these events. Communities are rallied to causes and nations to wars.

For example, before President Lyndon B. Johnson's televised address on the Gulf of Tonkin incident in 1964, a Harris Survey showed that less than half of the electorate approved of the president's Vietnam policy. After his address, a second poll indicated that 70 percent approved. Before President Richard M. Nixon addressed the nation to attempt to justify the invasion of Cambodia in 1970, a Harris Survey showed that only 7 percent of the public supported the decision. Following Nixon's TV address, more than 50 percent approved of the president's action.

Some have said that it was President Kennedy's display of intelligence and wit at news conferences that got him elected and earned him respect as president. On the other hand, President Nixon had little flair for give and take, and less love for reporters. Consequently, his performance at news conferences added little to his popularity.

Because speeches, news conferences and meetings are similar, all three will be treated in this chapter. But the distinguishing characteristics of these three forms should be kept in mind.

A speech is a public talk. Someone stands and speaks to an audience in person or on radio or television. Regardless of the medium the nature of a speech is the same: It is a one-way communication; the speaker speaks, and the audience listens.

Speakers usually are invited and sometimes paid to address an audience. That is not the case with those who hold a *news confer-ence*. Persons "call" a news conference. They do not send invitations to the general public, but they do alert members of the various news media. The media respond because of the importance of the person calling the news conference and because that person may have something newsworthy to say. The person holding the news confer-ence often begins with an opening statement and then usually ac-cepts questions from reporters. A news conference is meant to be a two-way communication.

Unlike speeches and news conferences, meetings are not held with an audience in mind, even though an audience may be present and allowed to participate. A meeting is primarily for communica-tion among the members of a group or organization, whether a local parent-teacher association or the Congress of the United States. If reporters are permitted to witness a meeting, they are there to re-port to the public what is of interest and importance. This task of the news media is especially important if the meeting is of a govern-mental body that deals with the public's money collected from taxes.

You can be sure that you will spend a great deal of your time as a reporter covering speeches, news conferences and meetings. For that reason you will want to learn all you can about covering them well.

In this chapter you will learn:

1. How to prepare to cover speeches, news conferences and meet-ings.
2. What is involved in covering speeches, news conferences and meetings.
3. How to structure and write the speech, news conference and meeting story.

Preparation

The professional reporter knows that preparation makes cover-ing a story much easier. In all cases reporters must do their home-work. Preparations for the speech, news conference and meeting story are much the same. Let's begin with a speech story.

PREPARING FOR THE SPEECH STORY

Not every speech you are assigned to cover will demand a great deal of research. Many speakers and speeches will be dry and routine. The person giving it will be someone you know or someone you have covered before. At other times you may be given an assignment on short notice and may be forced to find background information after you have heard the speech. But never take the speaker or the topic for granted. A failure to get enough background on the speaker and on the speech nearly guarantees failure at writing a comprehensive speech story.

When one reporter was assigned to cover a speech by Kenneth Clark, he presumed that this was the Kenneth Clark who had done so much on culture and civilization on public television. When he called the information service at the public library, he discovered two famous Kenneth Clarks. One, Kenneth Mackenzie Clark, was indeed an expert on civilization and the arts. The other, Kenneth Bancroft Clark, was a psychiatrist and author, most famous for writing "Dark Ghetto," the study of the effects of the ghetto upon Harlem children. It was the psychiatrist who was giving a speech.

The first step in your research is to get the right person. Middle initials are important; sometimes they are not enough. Sometimes checking the address is not enough. One reporter wrote about the wrong person because he did not know that a father and son shared the same name at the same address.

Before doing research on the speaker, contact the group sponsoring the speech and ask for the topic. When you learn that, you might need some reading to prepare you to understand it better. If you are lucky, you may get a copy of the speech ahead of time. Also check your newspaper library to see what your paper has done on the speaker. If you have access to a data bank, use it. If the assignment calls for it, visit your local library and check the references noted on pages 125–29 in Chapter 7.

If the speech is important enough, you might want to contact the speaker ahead of time for a brief interview. If he or she is from out of town, you might plan for a meeting at the airport. You might also arrange ahead of time to interview the speaker after the speech. You may have some questions and some points to clarify.

Again, not every speech will demand this much effort. But even the routine speech assignment needs preparation. It may seem obvious, for instance, that the reason Gene Martin, the director of the local library, is addressing the state Writer's Guild is to tell members how to use the library to write better stories. Not so. Gene Martin also is a successful "true confessions" writer. He has been published dozens of times in such magazines as True Confessions, True Romance and others. He may be addressing the guild on how he does it.

Sooner or later you may be called upon to cover speeches of major political candidates, perhaps even of the president of the United States. For this task, too, you need background — lots of it. It demands that you read the news and that you know what is going on. You *must* keep up with current events.

PREPARING FOR THE NEWS CONFERENCE STORY

Preparing for a news conference is like preparing for speeches. You need to know the up-to-date background of the person giving the news conference, and you must learn why the news conference is being held.

Often the person holding the news conference has an announcement or an opening statement. Unless that statement is leaked to the press, you will not know its content ahead of time. But you can do some educated guessing. Check out any rumors. Call the person's associates, friends, secretary. The more prepared you are, the better chance you have of coming away with a coherent, readable story.

A problem you will encounter at news conferences is that every reporter there has a line of questions to pursue. Your editor may want certain information, and other editors may want something else. You will not have time to think out your questions once you are there: The job of recording the responses to other reporters' questions will keep you too busy.

It may be impossible, as well, to arrange an interview before or after the news conference. If the person holding the news conference wanted to grant individual reporters interviews, he or she probably would not have called the news conference. But you can give it a try. You never know, and you may end up with some exclusive information.

PREPARING FOR THE MEETING STORY

You never know just what to expect at a meeting, either. But again, you must do your best to prepare for it. Who are the people holding the meeting? What kind of an organization is it? Who are the key figures? Again, the morgue is your first stop.

Contact some of the key figures. See if you can find out what the meeting is about. Perhaps the president or the secretary has a written agenda for the meeting. If you know the main subject to be discussed at the meeting, you will be able to study and investigate the issues before arriving. Knowing what to expect and being familiar with the issues will make covering the meeting much easier.

A reporter with a regular *beat*, or assigned area of responsibility, usually covers the meetings of more important organizations and of groups like the city council, the school board or the county board. (Beat reporting is discussed in Chapter 16.) A beat reporter has a continuing familiarity with the organization and with the issues involved. Often the meetings of important organizations are preceded by an *advance* — a report dealing with the subjects and issues to be dealt with in the upcoming meeting.

In summary, then, to cover speeches, news conferences and meetings well, you must arm yourself with information concerning the people involved and the issues to be discussed. Do your homework.

Covering Speeches, Meetings and News Conferences

The story is often told of the reporter who prepared well for a speech assignment, contacted the speaker, got a copy of the speech, wrote the story and spent the evening in a bar. He didn't know until after the speech story was handed in that the speech had been canceled.

And then there's the yarn about the reporter who was assigned to cover a meeting and came back to tell the city editor there was no story.

"Why not?" the city editor asked.

"Because the meeting was canceled."

"Why was that?"

"Well," replied the young reporter, "when the meeting started, some of the board members got in this big argument. Finally, three of them walked out. The president then canceled the meeting because there was no quorum."

The reporter had been sent to cover a meeting. But the canceled meeting and the circumstances surrounding its cancellation probably were of more interest to readers than the meeting itself would have been.

Preparing to cover events is only the beginning. Knowing what to do when you get there is the next step. Remember this: Covering the *content* of a speech, news conference, or meeting often is only half of the job — and sometimes the less important half. You must cover the entire *event* — the time, place, circumstances, number of people involved and possible consequences of what was said or of the actions taken.

To achieve total coverage, of content and event, you must remember to:

1. Get the content correct. Tape recorders can be helpful, but *always* take good notes. Quote people exactly and in context.
2. Note the background, personal characteristics and mannerisms of the main participants.
3. Cover the event. Look around the edges — at the audience (size, reactions), and sometimes at what is happening outside the building.
4. Get there early, position yourself and hang around afterward.

Let's take a closer look at each of these.

GETTING THE CONTENT CORRECT

You may find the tape recorder useful in covering the content of speeches, news conferences and meetings. Tape recorders often scare newspaper people, but they need not. As with anything else, you must practice using a tape recorder. You must use it again and again to become completely familiar with its idiosyncrasies. In other words, learning to operate tape recorders is not enough. You need to be comfortable with the one you are using. For example, you must be sure just how sensitive the microphone is. It is sound you want, and sound you must get.

The most frequent complaint you may hear about tape recorders is that it takes too long to listen to the entire recording. You may have to listen to a whole speech again just to find a certain quote that you want to check. But you may avoid this problem if you have a tape recorder with a digital counter. At any point in a speech or a meeting when something of importance is said, you need only to note the number on the counter. Finding it later will then be no problem.

But one thing you *must* do even if you are tape-recording an event: You must take notes in exactly the same way that you would if you were not tape-recording. The truth of the matter is, you may *not* be. Malfunctions can occur with the best machines at the most inopportune times.

So, with or without a tape recorder, you must become a proficient note taker. Many veteran reporters wish they had taken a shorthand or speed-writing course early in their careers. You may find it useful to buy a speed-writing manual and become used to certain symbols. Every reporter sooner or later adopts or creates some shortcuts in note taking. You will have to do the same.

You may be one of those fortunate people with a fantastic memory. Some reporters develop an incredible knack of re-creating whole conversations with complete accuracy without taking a note. But you may be one of those who takes reams of notes. If you are, take them as neatly as you can. Many of us sometimes cannot read our own handwriting — a nuisance, particularly when a proper name is involved.

Taking notes is most crucial when you wish to record direct quotes. Putting someone's words in quotation marks means only one thing: You are quoting the person word for word, exactly as the person spoke. Speeches, news conferences and meetings all demand that you be able to record direct quotes. Your stories will be lifeless and lack credibility without them. A speech story, for example, should contain many direct quotes.

Whether covering a speech, news conference or meeting, you must be careful to quote people in context. For example, if a speaker gives supportive evidence for an argument, you would be unfair not to report it. Quotes can be misleading if you carelessly or deliberately juxtapose them. Combining quotes with no indication that something was said in between them can lead to inaccuracies and to charges of unfairness. Suppose, for example, someone said:

> "Cutting down fuel costs can be an easy thing. If you have easy access to wood, you should invest in a good wood-burning stove. With little effort, you can cut your fuel bills in half."

If the reporter were to leave out the middle sentence of that quote, the speaker would be made to look ridiculous:

> "Cutting down fuel costs can be an easy thing. With little effort, you can cut your fuel bills in half."

But there is more to the speaker than the words he or she is saying. Quoting the speaker at length or printing a speech in its entirety may at times be justified. But when you quote a whole speech you are recording it, not reporting it. The overall content of the speech may or may not be news. Sometimes the news may be what a speaker left unsaid. You must decide what is newsworthy.

DESCRIBING THE PARTICIPANTS

In addition to listening to what a speaker says, you must watch for other things. A tape recording misses the facial expressions and the gestures of a speaker. These sometimes are more important than the words themselves.

For example, you may have heard the story of how Soviet Premier Nikita Khrushchev pounded the table with his shoe in the United Nations General Assembly on Sept. 20, 1960. But you probably are unsure about what he was saying or what he was protesting. Similarly, many remember the setting of President Franklin D. Roosevelt's fireside chats, but few remember the content.

Simply recording the words of a speaker (or of the person holding a news conference or participating at a meeting) does not indicate volume and tone of voice, inflections, pauses, emphases, and reactions to and from those in attendance. You may note that a speaker very deliberately winked while reading a sentence. Or you may notice an unmistakable sarcasm in the speaker's voice.

Regardless of who the speaker is or where the speech is taking place, you always must note the speaker's background. A person's words often must be measured against that individual's background. For example, if an ex-Communist is speaking on communism, this fact may have a bearing on what is said. If a former CIA agent speaks about corruption in the CIA, the message would not be adequately reported if the person's background were not mentioned.

Sometimes purely physical facts about the speaker are essential to the story. A blind man pleading for funds to educate the blind, a one-armed veteran speaking about the hell of war, a gray-haired woman speaking about care for the elderly — all must be described physically for the story to be accurate and understandable.

You also should note what the person who introduces a speaker says. This may help you understand the significance of the speaker and the importance of what he or she has to say.

COVERING THE EVENT

At all these events keep an eye on the audience and on what's happening around the edges. You need to measure the mood of the audience by noting the tone of the questions. Are they sharply worded? Is there much laughter or applause? Perhaps members of the audience boo. Does the speaker or the person holding the news conference or the person presiding over the meeting remain calm and in control at all times? Is there a casual bantering or joking with the audience? Is the audience stacked with supporters or detractors?

Sometimes the real action is taking place outside in the form of a picket line or protest of some kind. Sometimes it is right in front of you.

In the 1960s, civil rights and anti-war activists made many a speech and meeting interesting and newsworthy. When John Howard Griffin, author of "Black Like Me," spoke in a college auditorium in Milwaukee, the audience and reporters noted the number of police officers who were continually clearing the aisles of the crowded hall. Not too unusual — just enforcing the fire code, the officers said. But some were puzzled by the fact that Griffin left immediately after his speech without giving the audience any chance for questions and discussion. It was all the more surprising because Griffin is a warm and generous man, and he had an urgent anti-racist message he wished to share.

One enterprising reporter found out someone had threatened Griffin's life. Though Griffin insisted on delivering the speech, police whisked him away immediately after he finished. Obviously, this, not anything Griffin said that night, was the lead for the story.

Most speeches do not involve threats on the speaker's life. But don't overlook the obvious. For example, you always should note the size of the audience. Reporting a "full house" means little unless you indicate the house capacity. One way to estimate attendance is to count how many people are sitting in a row or in a typical section. Then you simply multiply that number by the number of rows or sections in the hall.

ARRIVING, POSITIONING YOURSELF AND STAYING ON

Most reporters arrive early. At some events they have special seating, but you should probably not count on it unless you know for sure. At a speech, for example, sitting in the first row is not necessarily the best thing to do. Perhaps you should be in a position that enables you to see the reaction of the audience. If there is a question-and-answer period, you may want to be able to see the questioner. And you certainly want to be in a good position to ask questions yourself.

At a news conference the position you're in may help you get the attention of the person holding the conference. You should have your questions prepared, but preparing them is not enough. You have seen presidential news conferences on television, and you know how difficult it is to get the president's attention. Though on a smaller scale, any news conference presents the reporter with the same difficulties. You have seen how difficult it is for reporters to follow up on their own questions. At some news conferences you will not be called upon twice.

But you must do more than try to get your own questions answered. You must listen to others' questions and be able to recognize the making of a good story. Too often a good question is dropped without follow-up because reporters are not listening carefully or are too intent upon pursuing their own questions. Listen for what is newsworthy and pursue it. Sticking with an important subject will make the job of writing the story easier. Remember, when the news conference is finished, you will have a story to write. Piecing together notes on dozens of unrelated topics can be difficult, if not impossible.

At a meeting you should be in a position to see and hear the main participants. Ordinarily, a board or council will sit facing the audience. Before the meeting starts you should know which members are sitting where. You may want to assign each participant a number so that you do not have to write the person's name each time he or she speaks. You also can draw a sketch of where they are sitting. In this way you will be able to quote someone by number, even if you do not know the name until later. Know who the officers are. The president or the secretary may have some handouts before the meeting. You may receive copies of resolutions up for consideration at the meeting. After a meeting, sometimes the secretary can help you fill in missing words or information.

As a general rule, when the speech, news conference or meeting is over, don't rush off. Hang around awhile. Some of the best stories happen afterward. You should have some questions to ask. You may want some clarifications, or you may arrange to interview a key

Figure 10.1 Covering News Conferences. Reporters at news conferences, especially those called by presidents, often have difficulty getting the speaker's attention.

spokesman. Listen for reactions from those in attendance. If you are covering a night meeting for an afternoon paper, you may be able to raise some questions and answer others that were not brought up or clarified at the meeting.

Structuring and Writing Your Story

Writing the lead for the speech, news conference or meeting story is no different from writing a lead for any story. All of the qualities of the lead discussed in Chapter 4 are important here.

You must be careful not to emphasize something about these events that is of great interest or curiosity but that does not lead into the rest of your story. It is tempting, for example, to lead with a striking quote. But rarely does a speaker or someone holding a press conference highlight the content or the main point in a single, quotable sentence. As always, there are exceptions. As a lead for one of Dr. Martin Luther King Jr.'s addresses, a good reporter might have begun with, "I have a dream."

Because of the nature of the inverted pyramid news story, rarely should you follow the chronology of the event you are covering. But the flow of your story may demand some attention to chronology. If you pay no attention to chronology, you may distort or cause the readers to misinterpret the meaning of the event.

WRITING THE SPEECH STORY

Let's look at how the pros reported President Ronald Reagan's 1984 State of the Union address. Here's part of the story as it appeared in the Commercial Appeal of Memphis, Tenn., under the byline of Associated Press writer James Gerstenzang:

WASHINGTON (AP) — President Reagan declared in an election-year State of the Union address last night that "America is back, standing tall," and he sought constitutional power to trim spending and pare the federal deficit — without raising taxes.

Reagan also told a joint session of Congress he is determined to keep American forces in Lebanon because the United States must never be turned away by "state-sponsored terrorism."

Reagan also asked congressional leaders to join him in developing a "down payment" on the federal deficit by enacting "some of the less contentious spending cuts" he already has proposed and by closing tax loopholes. But he rejected a major tax boost as a "Band-Aid solution to cure an illness that has been coming on for half a century."

The president proposed one costly new item himself — a permanently manned space station, costing $8 billion over eight years, "to develop our next frontier."

He asked for a constitutional

amendment to give him "line item" authority to veto selected congressional projects without killing entire money bills — a power long sought and always denied his predecessors. And he repeated his support for a so-called balanced budget amendment that would make it more difficult for Congress to approve red-ink spending. Reagan's own budget plan, due next week, is expected to carry a deficit of $180 billion.

Gerstenzang combined several important points in his first sentence and then went on in separate paragraphs to continue his summary (or umbrella) lead. Such a lead is common for a long, important speech such as this. Richard Bradee's lead in the Milwaukee Sentinel was similar:

WASHINGTON, D.C. — President Reagan called Wednesday night for a bipartisan panel to decide how to make a $100 billion, three-year down payment on reducing budget deficits.

In a speech to a joint session of Congress, Reagan gave the nation an upbeat view of the State of the Union and called for new efforts to build a manned space station and clean up the environment. His environmental proposals would require nearly 50% more money than he requested for the Environmental Protection Agency a year ago.

"There is renewed energy and optimism throughout the land. America is back — standing tall, looking to the '80s with courage, confidence and hope," Reagan said.

Another reporter, Thomas J. Brazaitis of the Cleveland Plain Dealer, also referred to the deficit in his lead, but his opening paragraphs were more interpretative:

WASHINGTON — At a time when Americans are worried about war abroad and frightened by the federal budget deficit at home, President Reagan last night assured his countrymen, "America is back — standing tall, looking to the '80s with courage, confidence and hope."

In his State of the Union address to Congress, Reagan, the eternal optimist who led the country into and out of the worst recession since the Great Depression, declared: "Tonight we can be proud of one of the best recoveries in decades. Send away the handwringers and doubting Thomases. Hope is reborn. . . ."

Because of a recent terrorist bombing at the Capitol, where the speech was delivered, security was tighter than any time ever, putting an ironic spin on Reagan's claim "the United States is safer, stronger and more secure in 1984 than before."

The election-year speech stuck to tried-and-true conservative themes. One surprise was a scheme to cut the budget deficit by $100 billion over the next three years.

To senators and congressmen waffling on whether to keep U.S. Marines in Lebanon, Reagan said, "We must not be driven from our objectives for peace by state-sponsored terrorism."

To members of Congress who have called for a tax increase to cut the deficit (a record $195.5 billion last year), Reagan said, "Increasing taxes is a Band-Aid solution which does nothing to cure an illness that has been coming on for half a century."

These leads show us that although there is likely to be some agreement among the professional reporters, there is no *one* way to begin a story. All three of these newspapers carried other stories about the address, particularly reactions of the Democrats. Some newspapers carried lists that summarized the president's main points. The St. Petersburg (Fla.) Times carried a wire story on the speech, but in a bright, colored box and in large type summarized Reagan's main points:

Reagan urges . . .

1. "A permanent, manned space station." Reagan told NASA to get the job done within a decade.
2. Leaders of both parties in Congress to join him in developing a "down payment" on the federal deficit.
3. Improved ties with the Soviets and continued diplomatic efforts in the Mideast, Latin America and Southern Africa.
4. Tuition tax credits and a constitutional amendment allowing voluntary prayer in schools.

But there is more to covering a speech than merely covering the content. Some reporters did not forget to cover the event as well. In the seventh paragraph of his story, Gerstenzang wrote:

Reagan was greeted by the traditional standing ovation upon his arrival in the House chamber at 8:01 p.m. CST. But Democrats sat on their hands until they punctuated with a cheer his statement that "we must bring federal deficits down." They roared even louder when he added: "How we do that makes all the difference."

Gerstenzang continued:

The President's visit to the Capitol was marked by the tightest security measures ever witnessed there. While Reagan spoke, his wife, Nancy, watched from the gallery. House and Senate members, the Cabinet and diplomats were seated in the chamber. The diplomatic corps arrived en masse aboard buses, as part of the security precautions.

Gerstenzang also included some interpretation and background:

Reagan, who has been unable to achieve half of the spending cuts he has sought, said that some adjustments in the tax laws, coupled with the "less contentious" reductions he wants in the budget, could cut the deficit by about $100 billion over three years.

Later, he wrote:

Reagan, whose administration has come under attack by environmentalists, said that he will request for the Environmental Protection Agency one of the largest percentage budget increases of any agency.

Toward the end of his report, Gerstenzang wrote:

> But mostly, the speech offered the nation a look at the president highlighting what he views as his accomplishments in three years and five days in office. And four days before he plans to tell the nation whether he will run for a second term, he offered a strong dose of optimism about the nation's future.

By giving us some reaction of the Democrats, by describing who was there and how some of them arrived there, by giving us some background and interpretation, Gerstenzang makes readers feel as if they are there. He covered the event as well as the content. You should try to do the same.

WRITING THE NEWS CONFERENCE STORY

Writing the news conference story may be a bit more of a challenge. And because you will come to the conference with different questions in mind than your fellow reporters, you may come away with a different story. At least your lead may be different from those of other reporters.

A news conference often covers a wide gamut of topics. Often it begins with a statement from the person who called the conference. On the night of Feb. 22, 1984, President Reagan began his news conference by noting the return of Congress from its recess. Reagan said he wanted to "highlight three matters at the top of the domestic agenda for the next 10 days." The first concerned an anti-crime bill; the second, a bill for prayer in schools; the third, negotiations on a down payment for projected budget deficits.

But the first question asked of Reagan that night concerned the withdrawal of Marines from Lebanon. Most reporters picked up their lead from that first question, not from the prepared statement of the president.

For example, Benjamin Taylor of the Boston Globe began his story:

> WASHINGTON — President Ronald Reagan last night said the decision to send U.S. Marines into Lebanon was his and that he had "no regret" about "trying to bring peace to that troubled country."
>
> Reagan, maintaining that the decision to pull back the Marines from the Beirut airport to U.S. Navy ships off shore was made because of possible future terrorist attacks, also said, "We're not bugging out; we're just going to a little more defensible position."

Now look at Taylor's third paragraph, which serves as the transition to the other topics covered in the news conference. Taylor makes the transition by referring to the event:

> In his 22nd nationally televised, prime-time news conference, and the first in more than two months, Reagan also:

Taylor then follows with a device commonly used in news conference stories. He summarizes what he considered the most important topics of the conference:

- Defended Secretary of State George P. Shultz, a prime proponent of the administration's Lebanon policy, contending that Shultz had done a "splendid job" and insisting that he had "every confidence in the world in" the secretary of state.
- Dismissed critics who contend that Reagan is not spending enough time at his job and is a disengaged president, saying, "They don't know what they're talking about."
- Reiterated his promise to keep the Straits of Hormuz from being closed by Iran as a result of the Iraq-Iran war, which is heating up again.
- Said the recent announcement by the Soviets that they are willing to agree to on-site inspection with regard to chemical warfare was a "good sign" in the prospect for easing East-West relations under Konstantin U. Chernenko, the new Soviet leader.

Taylor's next paragraph summarizes the president's opening statement. He then winds his way through the maze of topics more or less in the order in which they came up. It's an approach you would do well to imitate. What is most important is that you write a coherent, intelligible account. Transitions become extremely important: "On other subjects, the president said . . ." "Reagan was asked if . . ." "The president also defended his position . . ." "Again he stressed . . ." And don't forget: Making a summary of the topics covered will make your job easier for you and for the reader. You may place those summaries in a separate box or sidebar. You may even be asked to write several related stories. Regardless of how you do it, remember to cover the event as well as the content.

WRITING THE MEETING STORY

Readers also want you to take their place at the meeting you are covering. Let's look at a simple meeting story — in this case a meeting of a local school board:

The decision of three national corporations to protest a formula used to compute their property taxes is causing more than $264,000 to be withheld from the Walnut School District's operating budget for the 1985–86 school year.

Superintendent Ralph Thompson said at Monday's school board meeting that International Business Machines Corp., NCR Corp. and Xerox are protesting that the method used in computing their 1984 property taxes was no longer valid. Nine California counties are involved in similar disputes.

The taxes, totaling $264,688, are being held in escrow by the county until the matter is resolved. Part, if not all, of the money eventually may be returned to the district, but the administration cannot determine when or how much.

"If we take a quarter million dollars out of our program at this time, it could have a devastating effect," Thompson said. "Once you've built that money into your budget and you lose it, you've lost a major source of income."

Mike Harper, the county prosecuting attorney, and Larry Woods, the school district attorney, advised board members to take a "wait-and-see attitude," Thompson said. He said that one alternative would be to challenge the corporations in court. A final decision will be made later.

The board also delayed action on repayment of $80,000 to IBM in a separate tax dispute. The corporation claims the district owes it for overpaid 1976 property taxes. The county commission has ruled the claim is legitimate and must be repaid.

A possible source of additional income, however, could be House Bill 1002, Thompson said. If passed, this appropriations bill would provide an additional $46 million for state education, approximately $250,000 of which could go to the Walnut School District.

Charles Campbell, the district architect, said plans for the area's new vocational technical school to be built on the Rock Bridge High School campus will be given to contractors in February. Bids will be presented at the March 13 board meeting.

The board voted to have classes on Presidents Day, Feb. 20, to make up for time missed because of the teacher strike.

The issue of the meeting was money problems — a subject that concerns every taxpayer. The writer jumped right into the subject in the lead and then in the second paragraph gave us the who, when and where. The reporter then dealt with specifics, naming names and citing figures, and quoted the key person at the meeting. In the last two paragraphs the writer dealt with other matters discussed in the meeting.

Even meetings on complicated subjects need not begin with heavy, ponderous prose. Once a story about how cancer can be caused by enzymes that normally are supposed to repair cells, started with the lead, "Even enzymes make mistakes." Though the subject was heavy, the lead was great.

Remember, you are allowed to use your imagination. And you are expected to write well — even for an everyday event like a speech, news conference or meeting.

Suggested Readings

Rivers, William L. "Finding Facts." Englewood Cliffs, N.J.: Prentice-Hall Inc., 1975. Chapter 6, "Central Sources," is particularly helpful, but other chapters also are useful.

11

Accidents, Fires and Disasters

Stories about accidents, fires and disasters have been a principal ingredient of newspapers for many years. There's a good reason for that. In a nationwide survey prepared for the American Newspaper Publishers Association and the Newspaper Readership Council, news of crime and accidents ranked behind only government news and military news in reader interest. That study confirmed what editors have known for years: When people hear sirens, they want to know what happened and, perhaps more important, whether their friends or acquaintances were involved.

Newspapers also cover these events in their capacity as watchdog for the public over government agencies. If the police were slow in responding to an accident, is it because there are not enough officers or because they are poorly supervised? Did someone die needlessly because police, fire or ambulance personnel were slow, poorly trained or inefficient? To ask these questions on behalf of their readers, reporters must observe public officials as they perform their duties.

In news rooms and newspaper bureaus throughout the country, editors and reporters stay tuned to the police and fire radio frequencies on monitors provided for that purpose. When they hear something out of the ordinary, reporters and photographers are dispatched to the scene.

Editors have varying ideas about which stories about accidents, fires and disasters are worth reporting at all and which are worth developing into major articles. Perhaps the most important factor in that decision is the size of the city and its newspaper. An apartment

Figures 11.1–11.3 The Importance of Good Photographs. These Pulitzer Prize–winning photographs had tremendous impact on readers and served to attract them to the accompanying stories about a truck accident, a fire and an airplane crash. Good photographs always help communicate the drama of such events.

fire in which nobody was hurt may be routine in New York City and merit only one or two paragraphs, if any space at all. But in Cedar City, Utah, a similar fire may be unusual enough to warrant more extensive coverage.

As a beginning reporter you almost certainly will be assigned to cover an accident or fire. You even may become part of a team of reporters and photographers assigned to cover a disaster. Consequently, you need to know what to expect and how to get the information you need.

In many ways covering accidents, fires and disasters is the simplest form of reporting. The subject matter lends itself to the classic inverted pyramid writing style. But you also can produce far more interesting accounts of the pain and suffering — and often the remarkable strength — of people who have encountered crisis.

As a reporter assigned to cover an accident, fire or disaster, you must report the effects of the event on the victims. Only then can you write a story that tells the event in terms of the human experience. We will discuss the reporting of both the event and its personal aftermaths here.

In this chapter you will learn:

1. How to cover the scene of an accident, fire or disaster.
2. How to complete the reporting.

Covering the Scene

Whether you are assigned to cover an accident, fire or disaster, many of the facts and all of the color are gathered at the scene. By being there, you will have a better picture of what happened. Too many reporters, however, cover accidents and fires as purely passive observers. You must observe. But you also must actively solicit information from those who are there. Many of them, including those directly involved, you may never be able to find again. With that advice in mind, let us turn to the techniques you should employ to secure that information at each of the scenes you will cover.

THE SCENE OF AN ACCIDENT

When dispatched to the scene of an accident, you first must concentrate on gathering the facts. You should move as quickly as possible to collect this information:

1. The names, ages, addresses and conditions of the victims.
2. Accounts of witnesses or police reconstructions of what happened.
3. When the accident occurred.
4. Where it occurred.
5. Why it happened or who was at fault, as determined by officials in charge of the investigation.

If that list sounds familiar, it should. You could simplify it to read *who, what, when, where* and *why.* As in any news story, that information is essential. You must gather such information as quickly as possible after being assigned to the story. If the accident has just taken place, a visit to the scene is essential. Just as essential is knowing what to do when you get there. These suggestions will help:

1. *Question the person in charge of the investigation.* This individual will attempt to gather much of the same information you want. A police officer, for example, needs to know who was involved, what happened, when it happened and who was at fault. If you are able to establish a good relationship with the investigator, you may be able to secure much of the information you need from this one source.

Remember, though, that the spellings of names, addresses and similar facts must be verified later. Any veteran reporter can tell you that police officers and other public officials are notoriously bad spellers and often make errors in recording names of the victims. To avoid such errors, call relatives of the victims or consult the city directory, telephone book or other similar sources to check your information.

2. *Try to find and interview witnesses.* Police and other investigators may lead you directly to the best witnesses. The most accurate account of what happened usually comes from witnesses, and the investigators will try to find them. You should, too, and a good way to do that is to watch the investigators. Listen in as they interview a witness, or corner the witness after they are finished. If there is time, of course, try to find your own witnesses. You cannot always rely upon investigators to do your work for you, and you should not.

3. *Try to find friends or relatives of the victims.* These sources are helpful in piecing together information about the victims. Through them you often get tips about even better stories.

4. *If possible, interview the victims.* Survivors of an accident may be badly shaken, but if they are able to talk, they can provide first-hand detail that an official report never could. Make every attempt to interview those involved.

5. *Talk with others at the scene.* If someone has been killed, an ambulance paramedic or the medical examiner may be able to give you some indication of what caused the death. At least you can learn from them where the bodies or the injured will be taken. That may help, because later the mortician or hospital officials may be able to provide information you need for your story.

Of course, your deadline will have a major impact on the amount of information you are able to gather. If you must meet a deadline soon after arriving at the scene, you probably will be forced to stick to the basics of who, what, when, where, why and how. For that reason, it is important to gather that information first. Then, if you have time, you can concentrate on details and color information to make the story more readable.

This account of a tractor-trailer accident was produced in a race against the clock by the staff of an afternoon newspaper:

A truck driver was killed and a woman was injured this morning when a tractor-trailer believed to be hauling gasoline overturned and exploded on Interstate 70, turning the highway into a conflagration.

Both lanes of I-70 were backed up for miles after an eastbound car glanced off a pickup truck, hurdled the concrete median and collided with a tanker truck heading west.

The explosion was immediate, witnesses said. Residents along Texas Avenue reported the initial fireball reached the north side of the street, which is about 300 yards from the scene of the accident. A wooded area was scorched, but no houses were damaged.

Police evacuated the 600 block of Texas Avenue for fear that the fire would spread, but residents were returning to their homes at 12:35 p.m., about an hour after the collision. Authorities also unsuccessfully attempted to hold back the onlookers who gravitated to a nearby shopping center parking lot to view the blaze.

Police did not identify the driver of the truck, which was owned by a Tulsa, Okla., firm named Transport Delivery Co. "Apparently it was gasoline," said Steve Paulsell, chief of the County Fire Protection District. "That's what it smelled like." Other officials reported the truck may have been hauling fuel oil or diesel fuel. . . .

For an afternoon newspaper with an early afternoon deadline, such a story presents major problems, particularly when it occurs, as this one did, at about 11:30 a.m. Four reporters were dispatched to the scene; all of them called in information to a writer back at the office. There was little time to interview eyewitnesses. Because of the pressing deadline, the reporters were forced to gather most of their information from fire and police officials at the scene.

Writers for the morning newspaper, by comparison, had plenty of time to gather rich detail to tell the story in human terms. Much of the breaking news value was diminished by the next morning because of intense coverage by the afternoon newspaper, radio and television. It was time to tell the story of a hero:

Witnesses credited an off-duty fireman with saving a woman's life Monday following a spectacular four-vehicle collision on Interstate 70 just east of its intersection with Business Loop 70.

The driver of a gasoline truck involved in the fiery crash was not so lucky. Bill Borgmeyer, 62, of Jefferson City died in the cab of his rig, which jackknifed, overturned and exploded in flames when he swerved in a futile attempt to avoid hitting a car driven by Leta Hanes, 33, of Nelson, Mo.

Mrs. Hanes, who was thrown from her auto by the impact, was lying unconscious within 10 feet of the blazing fuel when firefighter Richard Walden arrived at the crash scene.

"I knew what was going on," Walden recalled, "and I knew I had to get her away from there." Despite the intense heat, Walden dragged the woman to safety.

"She had some scrapes, a cut on her knee and was beat around a little bit," Walden said. "Other than that, she was fine."

Mrs. Hanes was taken to Boone Hospital Center, where she was reported in satisfactory condition Monday night.

Smoke billowing from the accident scene reportedly was visible 30 miles away. Westbound interstate traffic was backed up as far as five miles. Several city streets became snarled for several hours when traffic was diverted to Business Loop 70. The eastbound lane of I-70 was reopened about 2 p.m.; the westbound lane was not reopened until 3 p.m. . . .

The story added detail and eyewitness accounts from several other people:

"It was a big red fireball," said Don Mongan of Clear Spring, Mo., who was driving about 100 yards behind the Borgmeyer rig when the crash occurred. "It exploded right away, as soon as it rolled over on its side."

Doug McConnell, 23, was in the kitchen of his nearby home at 606 Texas Ave. when the house shook.

"I heard a boom, and all of a sudden there was fire," he said. "It looked like a firecracker or something."

The richness of detail in the second account and the eyewitness descriptions of what happened make that story more interesting. The importance of adding such detail is apparent.

THE SCENE OF A FIRE

Accidents and fires present similar problems for the reporter, but at a fire of any size you can expect more confusion than at the scene of an accident. One major difference, then, is that the officer in charge will be busier. At the scene of an accident the damage has been done and the authorities usually are free to concentrate on their investigation. At a fire the officer in charge is busy directing firefighters and probably will be unable to talk with you. The investigation will not even begin until the fire is extinguished. In many cases the cause of the fire will not be known for hours, days or weeks. In fact, it may never be known. Seldom is that the case in an accident, except perhaps for air accidents.

Another problem is that you may not have access to the immediate area of the fire. Barriers often are erected to keep the public — and representatives of the news media — from coming close to a burning structure. The obvious reason is safety, but such barriers may hamper your reporting. You may not be able to come close enough to firefighters to learn about the problems they are having or to obtain the quotes you need to improve your story.

These problems probably will make covering a fire more difficult than covering an accident. Despite the difficulties, you cover the scene in much the same way, interviewing officials and witnesses at the scene. You also should try to interview the owner. Because the official investigation will not have begun, you must conduct your own. When covering any fire, you must learn:

1. The location of the fire.
2. The names, ages and addresses of those killed, injured or missing.
3. The name of the building's owner or, in the case of a grass fire or forest fire, the name of the landowner.
4. The value of the building and its contents or the value of the land.
5. Whether the building and contents were insured for fire damage. (Open land seldom is.)
6. The time the fire started, who reported it and how many firefighters and pieces of equipment were called to the scene.
7. What caused it, if known.

As in any story, the basics are who, what, when, where, why and how. But the nature of the fire will raise other questions that must be answered. Of primary importance is whether life is endangered. If not, the amount of property damage becomes the major emphasis of the story. Was arson involved? Was the building insured for its full value? Was there an earlier fire there? Were any rare or extremely valuable objects inside? Were there explosives inside that complicated fighting the fire and posed an even greater threat than the fire itself?

Your job is to answer these questions for the newspaper's readers. You will be able to obtain some of that information later on from the official fire reports if they are ready before your story deadline (see Figure 11.4). But most of it will come from interviews conducted at the scene with the best available sources. Finding your sources may not be easy, but you can start looking for the highest-ranking fire official.

Another important source in covering fire stories is the fire marshal, whose job is to determine the cause of the fire and, if arson is involved, to bring charges against the arsonist. You should make every effort to talk with the fire marshal at the scene, if he or she is available. But more likely the marshal will be the primary source of a second-day story.

As in covering any *spot news* story, in which news is breaking quickly, deadlines will determine how much you can do at the scene. If your deadline is hours away, you can concentrate on the event and those connected with it. You will have time to find the little boy whose puppy was killed in the fire or interview the firefighter who first entered the building. But if you have only minutes until your deadline, you may have to press the fire captain in charge for as much information as possible. You may have to coax from the captain every tidbit, even make a nuisance of yourself, to find the information you need. Through it all, you can expect confusion. There is little order to be found in the chaos of a fire.

THE SCENE OF A DISASTER

Disasters present special problems because investigators themselves may have difficulty determining where to begin. When, for example, tornadoes slice through cities, efforts may be concentrated on finding those trapped in the rubble of buildings. No one may know for certain who is trapped or where they are, or, in fact, whether anyone is trapped at all.

Such confusion makes your job more difficult. Officials often are caught up in the turmoil of the moment and overestimate the number of people killed or the amount of damage. In some instances you may find yourself in the unusual position of being ahead of the investigators. You may be in a better position to determine the death toll or estimate the damage. At least you will be able to make an informed judgment about the accuracy of what you are told. American newspaper history is filled with incidents of reporters' quoting inflated estimates of deaths and damage. Failure to make informed

DATE	TIME	ADDRESS	

PAGE   OF **CASUALTY REPORT**   FD-500

CHANGE 2 ☐ (74)
DELETE 3 ☐

INCIDENT NO.   EXP
8 0 9 0 5 1 3
1 2 3   7 8 9

NAME
S A N D O Z A   M A N U E L   R
LAST, FIRST MIDDLE   33 34 35 36

AGE 3 2   Time of Injury 0 9 4 5   MONTH 0 2   DAY 0 8   YEAR 8 4
39 40   45

HOME ADDRESS
307 Banning Ave., Apt. 3

TELEPHONE
487-9088

46 SEX
1 ☒ Male
2 ☐ Female

47 CASUALTY TYPE
1 ☒ Fire Casualty
2 ☐ Action Casualty
3 ☐ EMS Casualty

48 SEVERITY
1 ☒ Injury
2 ☐ Death

49 AFFILIATION
1 ☐ Fire Service
2 ☐ Other Emergency Personnel
3 ☒ Civilian

FAMILIARITY WITH STRUCTURE
Occupant   50

LOCATION AT IGNITION
Unknown   51

CONDITION BEFORE INJURY
Unknown   52

CONDITION PREVENTING ESCAPE
N/A   53

ACTIVITY AT TIME OF INJURY
Leaving building   54

CAUSE OF INJURY
Falling debris   55

NATURE OF INJURY
Broken leg   56

PART OF BODY INJURED
Leg   57

DISPOSITION
Hospitalized   58

REMARKS:
Occupant was leaving burning structure when burning eave fell and struck his leg.

By   #31   Ambulance   to   General   Hospital

NAME
LAST, FIRST MIDDLE   33 34 35 36

AGE   Time of Injury   MONTH   DAY   YEAR
39 40   45

HOME ADDRESS

TELEPHONE

46 SEX
1 ☐ Male
2 ☐ Female

47 CASUALTY TYPE
1 ☐ Fire Casualty
2 ☐ Action Casualty
3 ☐ EMS Casualty

48 SEVERITY
1 ☐ Injury
2 ☐ Death

49 AFFILIATION
1 ☐ Fire Service
2 ☐ Other Emergency Personnel
3 ☐ Civilian

FAMILIARITY WITH STRUCTURE   50

LOCATION AT IGNITION   51

CONDITION BEFORE INJURY   52

CONDITION PREVENTING ESCAPE   53

ACTIVITY AT TIME OF INJURY   54

CAUSE OF INJURY   55

NATURE OF INJURY   56

PART OF BODY INJURED   57

DISPOSITION   58

REMARKS:

By   Ambulance   to   Hospital

Nelson Riley
Supervisor*
*Injury reports for fire personnel,
Immediate supervisor to sign here.

SIGNATURE of person completing form/DATE
John R. Sanders

Printed in U.S.A.

Figure 11.4   Fire Report. This casualty report is typical of the types of reports available to reporters at most fire stations.

judgments about the accuracy of those estimates leaves your newspaper open to charges of irresponsibility.

In addition to confusion you may well encounter hazards to your personal safety as a reporter at the scene of a disaster. After a tornado, for example, electric wires may lie on the ground for hours until repair crews are able to reach them. At the scene of an earthquake you may be frighteningly close to a wall about to collapse. As you go about your work, you must avoid all such hazards; you will be of little value to your newspaper in a hospital bed. More importantly, what little information you can learn by being that close probably is not worth the risk. Nevertheless, there will be times when you will be forced into dangerous situations.

At the scene of a disaster, you can expect the unexpected. One beginning reporter for a Memphis, Tenn., newspaper learned this when dispatched to the scene of a tornado in Forrest City, Ark., about 60 miles from the office. He gathered information about the disaster for a few hours, then decided to call his editor for further instructions. He found that all the telephone lines to Memphis were down because of the storm. After a few minutes of indecision, he remembered having driven by a telephone company service office earlier in the evening. He went there, and when a few lines were re-established, his call to Memphis was one of the first out of Forrest City after the tornado. Presence of mind like that is important in such situations.

Fortunately, when disasters strike, you may not have to shoulder the entire reporting load. In such cases editors usually mobilize their reporting staffs to gather as much information as they can as quickly as possible. You probably will be assigned a specific responsibility, such as interviewing witnesses or survivors. You may then be asked to write a *sidebar*, a secondary story that runs with the major story and usually captures the personal side of an event. Other reporters may focus on the damage involved and compile lists of the dead and injured.

Completing the Reporting

In reporting almost any account of an accident, fire or disaster, your work at the scene will be merely the beginning. When you return to the office and sort through your notes, you probably will find that many questions remain unanswered. You must check with other sources.

SOURCES TO CHECK

An industrial accident will prompt calls to company executives or a corporate safety officer and may require you to check with local, state and federal regulatory agencies as well. If a worker is severely burned by a toxic chemical, you may have to call the federal government's Occupational Safety and Health Administration to learn what safety precautions are mandated for the use of the chemical. Only then will you be able to determine if there is reason to suspect the company — or the worker — of violating OSHA restrictions designed to ensure safety in the workplace.

Airplane crashes require a check with the Federal Aviation Administration, which investigates all of them, regardless of their severity. FAA investigators usually cooperate with reporters by revealing likely causes of crashes. Try to get such information because FAA investigations routinely last several months, and by then the cause of the crash may have little news value.

When you cover a drowning you may want to check with local authorities to find out if swimming is permitted where the drowning occurred. State water-patrol officials may help when you are reporting boating accidents.

In this well-regulated society there are government regulatory agencies at all levels that can provide details to help you focus on the problem. City agencies that deal with such matters can be found at city hall; similar county agencies probably will be located at the courthouse or county office building. State regulatory agencies are located in your state capital; regional offices of federal agencies usually are located in a nearby large city. Take advantage of their expertise.

This also is the time to call relatives of victims and to verify information gathered at the scene that can be checked with other sources. The nature and extent of such checks is dictated by the circumstances.

FOLLOW-UP STORIES

Most editors expect their reporters to initiate follows to major stories of accidents, fires and disasters. Sometimes, the follows are as good as or better than the original stories. Several months after a series of fires blamed on an arsonist resulted in the loss of several businesses and national attention, Jill Young Miller of the Columbia (Mo.) Daily Tribune decided to see what had become of the companies affected:

Anne Moore remembers all too well the call that shook her from her sleep last spring and summoned her to the corner of 10th Street and Broadway. A silver bowl and a faded floor plan are her only mementos of the D&M Sound Systems Inc. store that flames destroyed May 27.

D&M President Moore keeps both treasures in her new store at 700 Fay St. She and other local entrepreneurs have spent the past several months piecing together their businesses destroyed during the city's arson plague last spring.

No one has been charged with setting the Stephens Endowment Building fire that devastated D&M, the Columbia Art League, the French Room Hairdressing Salon, Spinning Wheel Realty, The Copy Center and Orlanco Financial Corp. Nor has the culprit been identified in the 10 other blazes investigators say were deliberately set last spring.

An intergovernmental arson task force folded in July after arson charges were filed against two men in unrelated fires — one in Rocheport and the other at the former Brown Derby Liquors, 120 S. Ninth St. Those two fires preceded the rash of blazes that struck fear into the busi-ness community for six weeks.

Orlanco, which owned the turn-of-the-century building housing the businesses, has not decided whether to rebuild or to sell the property. Orlanco President Chris Kelly, Moore's brother, says several people have offered to buy the property, which he declined to tag with a value.

"It's worth quite a bit," he says, considering the property is "right in the very core of the retail district."

Options for the land include retail stores, offices or a combination of both, Kelly says. "We think it can be made into the dominant corner in downtown Columbia."

In the meantime, all of the businesses but The Copy Center have found new quarters.

There was not nearly enough insurance to replace what was lost, says Mildred Grissum, who owned the business at 14 N. 10th St. for five years. Grissum, now a secretary in the U.S. Department of Commerce's local office, harbors no hope of reopening her business. "At my age, I wasn't ready to start again."

Columbia Fire Chief Girard Wren estimates damages from last spring's spate of fires at $5 million. . . .

Too often, reporters fail to produce such retrospective articles, perhaps because of the press of newer, more timely events. Those who avoid that temptation can find good articles that not only will please editors but also will interest readers.

THE STORY OF A CRASH AND ITS FOLLOW-UP

The importance of pursuing every angle of a major story is illustrated by reviewing coverage in the San Jose (Calif.) Mercury of a tragedy that almost became a disaster. A small airplane with four people aboard lost power after takeoff and crashed into an elementary school parking lot. First- and second-grade students on recess were on a playground only 50 feet from the crash site.

When editors at the Mercury learned of the crash, they sent reporters and photographers to the scene. One concentrated on the main news story, which was to become the *lead story* for the day — the one most prominently displayed on the front page. This was the result:

A light plane crashed into an elementary school parking lot near 150 children on noontime recess in East San Jose Wednesday, killing three of the four persons aboard.

No one on the ground was injured, although the plane exploded and burned within 50 feet of first and second graders on the playground at Katherine Smith School, 2025 Clarice Drive.

Among the dead was the plane's pilot, Francis K. Allen, who had 13 years of flying experience — but who never before had flown the type of plane that he died in Wednesday, his daughter, Debbie Schlict, said.

Allen, 51, lived at 1398 Cerro Verde Lane, San Jose.

He was being checked out in the plane, a single-engine Bellanca, by an 18-year-old licensed instructor, who also was killed. The instructor was identified as Ralph G. Anello, 1681 The Alameda, Apt. 31, San Jose, who also served as co-pilot.

A Federal Aviation Administration spokesman said it is not uncommon for an 18-year-old to be an instructor. "As long as you're certified, there are no restrictions," he said.

The third victim was Ila Diane Cooper, 32, of 390 Bluefield Drive, San Jose.

The survivor, who scrambled clear of the wreck, is Lawrence Allen Herbst, 32, of 5870 Christ Drive, also San Jose. He was in stable condition at Alexian Brothers Hospital Wednesday night with first- and second-degree burns on his face, hands and elbows.

The plane apparently lost power on takeoff at 12:13 p.m. from Reid-Hillview Airport, circled south and plunged into the parking lot at the front of the school after a flight of only one minute.

Alerted by two playground aides, the children saw the faltering aircraft heading for them and ran, screaming, for the shelter of a nearby classroom wing, a witness said.

The craft overturned one car, and it and four other vehicles were bathed in flames as the plane's gas tank exploded.

Witnesses said it appeared the pilot may have nosed the craft into the ground at the last moment to avoid hitting the playground, which was in direct line with the plane's final course.

The youngest victim, Anello, is the son of Superior Judge Peter Anello, who is on vacation in Italy.

Mrs. Cooper, an employee at IBM, is survived by her husband, Donald, and two children.

Allen also was an employee at IBM.

The victims died of extensive burns, not crash injuries, the coroner's office reported.

Authorities said the plane had been rented from Western Aviation Flight Center Inc. at Reid-Hillview.

One of the first on the scene and one who helped lead Herbst away from the burning craft was Trellis Walker of San Jose, a special investigator for the Department of Defense.

"I arrived about 30 seconds after the plane hit," said Walker. "The man was staggering away from the plane, screaming, 'Oh, my God! Oh, my God! There are three others in there. Get them out!'"

"The engine was making so much noise that everyone heard the plane coming," said David Bess, a custodian at the school who was walking on the sidewalk beside the parking lot when the plane hit. . . .

The reporter who wrote that story tells concisely what happened, reports the names, ages and addresses of the victims and quickly anticipates a question that readers are likely to ask: Isn't it unusual for an 18-year-old man to be a flight instructor? A spokesman for the FAA said it is not. The reporter then identifies the survivor of the crash, who understandably was not available for an interview, and tells the reader that the crash was caused by an apparent loss of power. He describes the scene, works in other details about those involved and quotes witnesses.

All the information except that from the FAA spokesman was gathered at the scene. The story is as complete as possible with the information available. There are other ways this story could have been written, but the plan chosen by this reporter worked well.

Colleagues, meanwhile, were working on related stories. Because the school was so near the airport, San Jose school officials had anticipated the possibility of something similar happening. This story emphasized that angle:

"Sure, we've thought something like this might happen someday," said James Smith. "But what could we possibly do to prepare for it?"

Smith, superintendent of the Evergreen School District, was at Katherine Smith School within half an hour Wednesday after a small airplane crashed into the parking lot.

"We have emergency procedures for things like this, and they were followed," he said. "In this case, they were the same procedures we would use for a fire drill. All the children were evacuated immediately to the back play yard, a great distance away from the crash."

The school staff responded immediately. As Principal Jennie Collett ordered the evacuation, custodian Dave Bess ran out to the flaming plane with a fire extinguisher.

"I saw the crash through the window (of the school office)," said school nurse Laura Everett. "I ran to the front door to see if I could help. But just as I got there, an aide came in and shouted for someone to call the Fire Department. I saw there was nobody else in the office, so I called for the Fire Department and an ambulance.

"Then I ran outside, but by that time the fire was great, and I didn't attempt to get near the plane."

The Evergreen District has only two school nurses. The other nurse rushed to Smith School as soon as she heard about the crash, Mrs. Everett said.

Editors of the Mercury knew that many of their readers have children of elementary school age. They knew that readers would cringe at the thought of their children playing within 50 feet of a plane crash site and would wonder if the school system's emergency procedures were adequate. The response of this school's staff could be indicative. In reporting this story the Mercury was fulfilling its responsibility of serving as a watchdog over a government agency — in this case the school system.

Other sidebars in the Mercury that day provided profiles of two of the victims, the pilot and his young instructor, and an overview of the airport from which the plane took off. That story answered questions readers may have had about traffic and previous crashes at the airport, and about what other facilities were nearby.

Reporters for the Mercury continued to work on the story and the next day this appeared:

Shortly after noon Wednesday, Mrs. Carmen Eros, a playground aide at Katherine Smith Elementary School, heard a loud grating noise, looked up and saw a plane heading straight for the kindergarten building where her grandson is a pupil.

At first, Mrs. Eros was so panicked she was unable to move and could think of nothing but her grandson, Adam. Then she heard the pupils, who were on their lunch recess, begin screaming.

"Without thinking I grabbed three little kids near me and covered their eyes so they wouldn't see," Mrs. Eros said. "Then I yelled to the other aide to get the kids to the building. The kids were crying and screaming, just like us."

Seconds later Mrs. Eros heard an explosion, stopped running and turned around.

"The plane now was heading right towards us and white smoke was coming from its tail," she said, motioning with her hands. "Then all of a sudden, the nose of the plane headed to the ground and it looked like the pilot crash-landed to avoid hitting us.

"I saw a man fly out of the plane, land on the sidewalk and roll over and over. Then I heard someone from the plane yell, 'Help the others! Help the others!' "

After hearing the explosion, the teachers ran outside and helped the aides gather the children inside the building. Mrs. Eros was dizzy and in shock, she said. As soon as the children were safe in the building, she went into the nurse's office and passed out.

Wednesday night she could not sleep at all, she said, and Thursday she was so nervous she made an appointment to see a doctor about getting some medication to relax. All day at work Thursday, when she was on the playground, she got chills whenever she glanced at the spot where the plane crashed.

Killed in the crash were Ralph Anello, 18; F. Kempton Allen, 51; and Ila Diane Cooper, 32.

"When you see something like that, it's hard to just forget about it. I'm still real shaken up. I wish I could sleep or at least relax. I hate to think how close all the children and my grandson came to disaster. Thank God nothing happened to the kids."

In an effort to determine the cause of the crash, federal inspectors tore down the engine of the Bellanca aircraft Thursday afternoon, but preliminary examination failed to disclose anything significant.

Jerry Jamison of the National Transportation Safety Board and Chuck Burns, coordinator of the Federal Aviation Administration, spent the day inspecting engine debris and the flight control system.

Burns said he did not think the plane ran out of fuel because of the fire that erupted after the crash.

It may be weeks before the final determination of why the plane crashed is made, the officials said.

In this story the writer looks at the crash through the eyes of a witness and follows up on the investigation of the crash.

That kind of reporting and writing makes stories of accidents, fires and disasters more readable and more meaningful. It allows the reader to know what it was like to be there. As in most good reporting, the human element is entwined with the news.

12
Crime and the Courts

Ever since Benjamin Day borrowed an idea from London newspapers and began publishing police court reports in his New York Sun, crime news has played an important role in American journalism. The Sun's humorous accounts of drunkenness, thefts and street-walking were a hit with the citizens of New York in 1838, and they soon made that newspaper New York's largest daily. Today's newspaper accounts of crime probably are less humorous and more responsible, and there can be little doubt that court reporting is more subdued. Now few editors seriously consider peddling crime news as a means of building circulation.

That does not mean, however, that crime and court reports are any less important to today's editors than they were in making the Sun an overnight success. Indeed, such reports are so common in American newspapers that a reporter's first assignment may well involve one or the other.

Why is there such an emphasis on crime? Editors answer in part that the public *needs* to know about it. A public not alerted to a series of murders, for example, may be easy prey for the murderer. Police officials reinforce this view by insisting that public awareness is the key to controlling the nation's soaring crime rate. Editors often add that the public *wants* to know about crime. Readers may not subscribe to newspapers because they contain crime news, but they still are fascinated by it and interested in it.

Because of the emphasis on crime, almost every reporter eventually is called upon to cover a crime or a court hearing. Such stories are not covered exclusively by reporters who have police and court beats. The general-assignment reporter often is dispatched to the

190

scene of a crime or to a courtroom when reporters with beats are occupied elsewhere.

The reporter who covers a crime or follows it through the courts walks squarely into the middle of the free press–fair trial controversy. Because of past abuses by the press, real or perceived, in recent years judges and trial lawyers have sought to prevent the publication of evidence or details of a crime that in their view may make it difficult to impanel an impartial jury. A judge's attempt to protect a defendant's Sixth Amendment right to an impartial jury seemingly may conflict with the reporter's responsibility to inform the public. But almost invariably that apparent conflict is resolved by the judge invoking the power to order a change of venue or to sequester the jury. A change of venue means that the trial is moved to a location where pretrial news coverage may have been less extensive. When a judge sequesters a jury, jurors are not allowed to go home, read newspapers, listen to radio or watch television during the trial.

The media are vital in transmitting crime and court news. The public wants to have such news, editors are eager to provide it, and judges and lawyers are determined to limit it. As a reporter who almost certainly will cover crime and the courts, you must know how to meet the expectations of the public and your editors without trampling on the rights of the accused.

In this chapter you will learn:

1. How crime news is covered and written.
2. How court news involving crime is covered and written.
3. How questions of taste and responsibility affect crime and court reporting.

Gathering and Writing Crime News

SOURCES OF INFORMATION

The last thing Tom Wicker expected to write on Nov. 22, 1963, was a crime story. Wicker, then White House correspondent for The New York Times, was accompanying President John F. Kennedy on a goodwill visit to Texas. Kennedy was trying to re-establish good relations with the southern wing of the Democratic Party, and Wicker expected little more than to cover a few speeches and to interview some of the key figures.

The rest is history. An assassin's bullet hit Kennedy as his motorcade passed through Dallas' Dealey Plaza. Soon afterward the president died at Parkland Hospital, and Wicker found himself asking some of the same questions any reporter who covers a murder must ask. How many times was the victim hit? From where were the shots fired? What kind of weapon was used? What is the name of the accused? The list of such questions was endless, and many of them still have not been answered to everyone's satisfaction. Wicker later wrote:

> At first no one knew what happened, or how, or where, much less why. Gradually, bits and pieces began to fall together and within two hours a reasonably coherent version of the story began to be possible. Even now, however, I know no reporter who was there who has a clear and orderly picture of that surrealistic afternoon; it is still a matter of bits and pieces thrown hastily into something like a whole.

The example, of course, is an extreme one. Few reporters are likely to cover a presidential assassination. But the incident illustrates how difficult it is to piece together an account of a crime, even when, as in this case, there are thousands of witnesses.

Most information comes from three major sources:

1. Police officials and their reports.
2. The victim or victims.
3. The witness or witnesses.

The circumstances of the crime may determine which of these three is most important, which should be checked first or whether they should be checked at all. If the victim is available, as a reporter you should make every effort to get an interview. But if the victim and witnesses are unavailable, the police and their report become primary sources.

When your editor assigns you to a crime story is important. If you are dispatched to the scene of the crime as it happens or soon afterward, you probably will interview the victim and witnesses first. The police report can wait. But if you are assigned to write about a crime that occurred the night before, the police report is the starting point.

Police and Police Reports

A police officer investigating a crime covers much of the same ground you do. The officer is interested in who was involved, what happened, when, where, why and how. Those details are needed to complete the official report of the incident, and you need them for your story.

When you write about crime, the police report always should be checked. It is often the source of such basic information as:

BURGLARY

1 OFFENSE		2 CASE #
Burglary		32701

3 OCCURRED AT (ADDRESS)	4 DATE/TIME OCCURRED	5 DATE/TIME REPORTED	6 DATE/TIME REPORT WRITTEN
308 Maple St.	0100 - 0800	0830	0945 - 11 March

7 PERSON REPORTING	RAC	SEX	DOB	ADDRESS	HOME PHONE	BUS PHONE
Linda L. Mellotti	W	F	9-11-45	308 Maple St.	372-1124	372-9988

8 OWNER OF BUILDING

ADDRESS	HOME PHONE	BUS PHONE

9 WITNESS   NONE

RAC	SEX	DOB	ADDRESS	HOME PHONE	BUS PHONE

10 VICTIM (FIRM OR INDIVIDUAL)

RAC	SEX	DOB	ADDRESS	HOME PHONE	BUS PHONE

11 RESIDENCE ☒ NONRESIDENCE ☐	12 FORCE ☒ NO FORCE ☐	13 DAY ☐ NIGHT ☒	14 TYPE OF BUSINESS UNKNOWN ☐	15 POINT OF ENTRY Back door	16 HOW WAS ENTRY GAINED Glass broken to unlock door

17 TYPE OF LOCK OR STRUCTURE DEFEATED Type A	18 DAMAGE CAUSED BY ENTRY Broken window glass	19 WHO SECURED BLDG Occupant

STOLEN PROP	20 QUAN	21 TYPE	22 BRAND	23 SERIAL #	24 PHYSICAL DESCRIPTION	25 VALUE	26 DATE ENTERED	BY	27 DATE CLEARED	TIME/DATE	BY
A	1	Console	GE	Unknown	TV set	$300					

28 SUSPECT NAME   NONE

HT	WT	EYES	HAIR	BUILD	FACIAL HAIR	RAC	SEX	DOB	HAT	COAT	SHIRT	TROUSERS	SHOES	ADDRESS	HOME PHONE	BUS PHONE

UNUSUAL IDENTIFIERS

MARKS SCARS & TATTOOS

SUSPECT VEHICLE COLOR	YEAR	MAKE	MODEL	STYLE	VIN	LIC YR	LIC STATE	LIC TYPE	LIC NUMBER

29 INVESTIGATING OFFICER	DEPT	30 APPROVED BY	31 EVIDENCE COLLECTED BY	32 PHOTOGRAPHY BY PHOTO OBTAINED	33 REASSIGNED TO	BY

34 NARRATIVE

Victim works night shift at Milan Hospital. Residence entered while she was working. TV set only item known missing.

Figure 12.1 Police Report. This burglary report is typical of the types of reports available to reporters at most police stations.

WORK SHEET

193

1. A description of what happened.
2. The location of the incident.
3. The name, age and address of the victim.
4. The name, age and address of the suspect, if any.
5. The exact offense with which the suspect is charged.
6. The extent of injuries, if any.
7. The names, ages and addresses of the witnesses.

The reporter who arrives at the scene of a crime as it takes place or immediately afterward has the advantage of being able to gather much of that information firsthand. When timely coverage is impossible, however, the police report allows the reporter to catch up quickly. The names of those with knowledge of the incident usually appear on the report, and the reporter uses that information to learn the story.

Crime stories often are written from the police report alone. In the case of routine stories, some editors view such reporting as sufficient. Good newspapers, however, demand much more because police reports frequently are inaccurate. Most experienced reporters have read reports in which the names of those involved are misspelled, ages are wrongly stated and other basic information is inaccurate. Sometimes such errors are a result of sloppy reporting by the investigating officer or mistakes in transcribing notes into a formal report. Occasionally the officer may lie in an attempt to cover up shortcomings in the investigation of misconduct at the scene of the crime. Whatever the reason, good reporters do their own reporting and do not depend solely upon a police officer's account.

Despite possible inadequacies, the investigating officer frequently can provide some quotes to make a story more readable. Rather than describe the sequence of events in the language of a police report, you should try to give it some life with interesting observations from that officer or a police official involved with the case.

The Victim

The difficulty of obtaining information about a crime often is caused by the confusion that accompanies such events. The victim may be unavailable for interviews. Even if the victim is available, the trauma of the event may have prompted enough hysteria to preclude reconstruction of the event.

That does not mean, however, that the victim's words necessarily are useless. One young reporter sent to cover a bank robbery returned to the office and announced to his editor, "I couldn't get a thing from the teller. As the cops took her away, she just kept mumbling, 'That big black gun! That big black gun!'" The editor smiled, leaned back in his chair and said, "That's your lead." He realized that the shocked teller's repetition of that phrase said more about the terror of the moment than the reporter could have conveyed in several paragraphs.

Not always, of course, is the victim's account of the story incoherent. One young reporter discovered that fact his first day on the job while filling in for the ailing police-beat reporter. In checking through a pile of offense reports, the reporter noticed that the police had captured a man armed with a rifle who had forced a cab driver to drive around town for an hour at gunpoint. The reporter called the cab driver, who by then was off duty, and produced an interesting story about a quick-thinking cabbie who worked his way out of a sticky situation.

"I just kept flippin' the button on the microphone (of the cab's two-way radio)," the driver said.

The cab company dispatcher grew curious and asked the driver if his cab was still occupied.

"I told him it was. He must have realized I was nervous and called the police."

Moments later, a police officer spotted the cab. The man with the rifle jumped from the back seat and fled, but the police officer caught him. The story itself was not important, but the account of the quick-witted cabbie made it interesting. In most cases the victim's account adds immeasurably to a crime story.

Witnesses

Frequently the account of a witness is more accurate and vivid than the account of the victim. And frequently a witness will be available for an interview when a victim is not. If the victim has been taken to a hospital or is huddled with the police giving them details of what happened, you are effectively cut off from a major source.

Witnesses, like police officers and the victim, can provide vivid detail and direct quotes to make the story more readable. In addition, witnesses can provide a new view of what happened. Only after interviewing them can you determine if that view will be a useful addition to your story.

Conflicting accounts of an incident sometimes surface when you interview several sources. Such conflicts may be difficult, if not impossible, to resolve. A victim, for example, may describe an incident one way and a witness another. Presumably the victim is in the best position to know what really happened, but, because of the stress the victim encountered, the account of the witness may be more accurate. On the other hand, a cool-headed victim is certainly more reliable than a distressed witness. Seldom can the reporter resolve conflicting reports, so the best answer to this puzzle may be to acknowledge the conflict and to publish both versions of the story.

Other Possible Sources

The major sources are important, but crime reporting does not depend solely on them. In most cases there are other sources, perhaps including relatives, friends and neighbors of the victim; the victim's doctor; the medical examiner; the prosecuting attorney; and the suspect's lawyer. A good reporter quickly pieces together an account of the crime and uses that information to determine what the sources of information are.

WRITING THE STORY

There is no magic formula for writing crime news. Solid reporting techniques pay off just as they do in other types of reporting. Then it is a matter of writing the story as the facts demand.

Sometimes the events of a crime are most effectively told in chronological order, particularly when the story is complex (this story approach is discussed in more detail in Chapter 15). More often a traditional inverted-pyramid style is best. How much time the reporter has to file the story also influences the approach. Let's take a look at how the newspaper accounts of two crimes were developed over time and why different writing styles seemed appropriate for each.

The Chronologically Ordered Story

Gathering facts from the many sources available and sorting through conflicting information can be time-consuming. Sometimes the reporter may have to write before all the facts are gathered. The result is a bare-bones story written to meet a deadline. Such circumstances often lead to crime stories written like this:

A Highway Patrol marksman shot and killed a Kansas man in a rural area south of Springfield this morning after the victim threatened to blow off the head of his apparent hostage.

A hitchhiker reportedly told police earlier this morning that his "ride" had plans to rob a service station on Interstate 70. That tip apparently followed an earlier report of a van leaving a station at the Millersburg exit of I-70 without paying for gasoline.

An ensuing hour-long chase ended at 9:30 a.m. in an isolated meadow in the Pierpont area when Capt. N. E. Tinnin fired a single shot into the stomach of the suspect, identified as Jim Phipps of Kansas City, Kan.

Phipps, armed with a sawed-off shotgun, and his "hostage," identified as Anthony Curtis Lilly, 17, also of Kansas City, Kan., eluded police by fleeing into a rugged, wooded area at the end of Bennett Lane, a dead-end gravel road off Route 163.

Tinnin said he fired the shot with a .253-caliber sniper rifle when it appeared Phipps was going to shoot Lilly. Two troopers' efforts to persuade Phipps to throw down his weapon and surrender were unsuccessful, Tinnin said.

Note that even in this bare-bones account, the available facts of this particular story seem to dictate a chronological approach.

The reporter who produced that story for an afternoon newspaper did a good job of collecting information following a puzzling incident. Still, several words and phrases (the *apparent* hostage, a hitchhiker *reportedly* told police, a tip *apparently* followed) provide tip-offs that the series of events was not entirely clear.

With more time to learn the full story, a reporter for the city's morning newspaper resolved many of those conflicts. As a result, readers got a more complete account of what occurred:

James Phipps and Anthony Lilly, a pair of 17-year-olds from Kansas City, Kan., were heading west on Interstate 70 at 7:30 a.m. Friday, returning from a trip to Arkansas.

Within the next hour and a half, Phipps had used a sawed-off shotgun stolen in Arkansas to take Lilly hostage, and, after holding that shotgun to Lilly's head, was shot and killed by a Highway Patrol captain on the edge of a rugged wooded area south of Springfield.

As the episode ended, local officials had only begun to piece together a bizarre tragedy that involved a high-speed chase, airplane and helicopter surveillance, a march through a wooded ravine and the evacuation of several frightened citizens from their country homes.

As police reconstructed the incident, Phipps and Lilly decided to stop for gas at the Millersburg exit east of Springfield at about 7:30 a.m. With them in the van was Robert Paul Hudson Jr., a San Francisco-bound hitchhiker.

Hudson was not present at the shooting. He had fled Lilly's van at the Millersburg exit after he first suspected trouble.

The trouble began when Lilly and Phipps openly plotted to steal some gasoline at Millersburg, Hudson told police. He said the pair had agreed to display the shotgun if trouble arose with station attendants.

Hudson said he persuaded Phipps to drop him off before they stopped for gas. He then caught a ride to Springfield and told his driver of the robbery plans he had overheard. After dropping Hudson off near the Providence Road exit, the driver called Springfield police, who picked up Hudson.

Meanwhile, Phipps and Lilly put $5.90 worth of gas in the van and drove off without paying. The station attendant notified authorities.

As he approached Springfield, Phipps turned onto U.S. 63 South, where he was spotted by Highway Patrol troopers Tom Halford and Greg Overfelt. They began a high-speed chase, which ended on a dead-end gravel road near Pierpont.

During the chase, which included a U-turn near Ashland, Phipps bumped the Highway Patrol car twice, forcing Halford to run into the highway's median.

Upon reaching the dead end, the suspects abandoned the van and ran into a nearby barn. At that point, Phipps, who Highway Patrol officers said was wanted in Kansas for escaping from a detention center, turned the shotgun on Lilly.

When Halford and Overfelt tried to talk with Phipps from outside the barn, they were met with obscenities. Phipps threatened to "blow (Lilly's) head off," and vowed not to be captured alive.

Phipps then left the barn and walked into a wooded area, pressing the gun against Lilly's head. Halford and Overfelt followed at a safe distance but were close enough to speak with Phipps.

While other officers from the Highway Patrol, the Boone County Sheriff's Department and Springfield police arrived at the scene, residents in the area were warned to evacuate their homes. A Highway Patrol plane and helicopter flew low over the woods, following the suspects and the troopers through the woods.

The four walked through a deep and densely wooded ravine. Upon seeing a partially constructed house in a nearby clearing, Phipps demanded of officers waiting in the clearing that his van be driven around to the house, at which time he would release his hostage.

Halford said, "They disappeared up over the ridge. I heard some shouting (Phipps' demands) and then I heard the shot."

After entering the clearing from the woods, Phipps apparently had been briefly confused by the officers on either side of him and had lowered his gun for a moment.

That was long enough for Highway Patrol Capt. N. E. Tinnin to shoot Phipps in the abdomen with a high-powered rifle. It was about 8:45 a.m. Phipps was taken to Boone County Hospital, where he soon died.

That story is as complete as possible under the circumstances. The reporter who wrote it decided to describe the chain of events in chronological order both because of the complexity of the story and because the drama of the actual events is most vividly communicated in a chronological story form.

The story is also made effective by its wealth of detail, including the names of the troopers involved, details of the chase and much, much more. The reporter had to talk with many witnesses to piece together this account. The hard work paid off, however, in the form of an informative, readable story.

Notice how the third paragraph sets the scene and provides a transition into the chronological account. Such attention to the details of good writing helps the reader understand the story with a minimum of effort. (Writing the chronologically ordered story is discussed further in Chapter 15.)

The Sidebar Story.   If a number of people witnessed or were affected by a crime, the main story may be supplemented by a sidebar story that deals with the personal impact of the crime. The writer of the chronological account above also decided to write a separate story on nearby residents, who had little to add to the main story but became a part of the situation nonetheless:

In the grass at the edge of a woods near Pierpont Friday afternoon, the only remaining signs of James Phipps were a six-inch circle of blood, a doctor's syringe, a blood-stained button and the imprints in the mud where Phipps fell after he was shot by a Highway Patrol officer.

Elsewhere in the area, it was a quiet, sunny, spring day in a country-side dotted by farms and houses. But inside some of those houses, dwellers still were shaken by the morning's events that had forced a police order for them to evacuate their homes.

Mrs. Janes G. Thorne lives on Cheavens Road across the clearing from where Phipps was shot. Mrs. Thorne had not heard the evacuation notice, so when she saw area officers crouching with guns at the end of her driveway, she decided to investigate.

"I was the surprise they weren't expecting," she told a Highway Patrol officer Friday afternoon. "I walked out just before the excitement."

When the officers saw Mrs. Thorne "they were obviously very upset and shouted for me to get out of here," she said. "I was here alone and asked them how I was supposed to leave. All they said was 'Just get out of here!' "

Down the road, Clarence Stallman had been warned of the situation by officers and noticed the circling airplane and helicopter. "I said, 'Are they headed this way soon?' and they said, 'They're here,' " said Stallman.

After Stallman notified his neighbors, he picked up Mrs. Thorne at her home and left the area just before the shooting.

On the next street over, Ronald Nichols had no intention of running.

"I didn't know what was happening," Nichols said. "The wife was scared to death and didn't know what to do. I grabbed my gun and looked for them."

Another neighbor, Mrs. Charles Emmons, first was alerted by the sound of the surveillance plane. "The plane was flying so low I thought it was going to come into the house," she said. "I was frightened. This is something you think will never happen to you."

Then Mrs. Emmons flashed a relieved smile. "It's been quite a morning," she said.

The Inverted Pyramid Account

The techniques of writing in chronological order and separating the accounts of witnesses from the main story worked well in the above case. More often, however, crime stories are written in the classic inverted pyramid style:

A masked robber took $1,056 from a clerk at Gibson's Liquor Store Friday night, then eluded police in a chase through nearby alleys.

The clerk, Robert Simpson, 42, of 206 Fourth St., said a man wearing a red ski mask entered the store at about 7:35 p.m. The man demanded that Simpson empty the contents of the cash register into a brown grocery bag.

Simpson obeyed but managed to trigger a silent alarm button under the counter.

The robber ordered Simpson into a storage room in the rear of the building at 411 Fourth St.

Officer J. O. Holton, responding to the alarm, arrived at the store as the suspect left the building and fled south on foot.

Holton chased the man south on

Fourth Street until he turned west into an alley near the corner of Olson Street. Holton said he followed the suspect for about four blocks until he lost sight of him.

Simpson said receipts showed that $1,056 was missing from the cash register. He described the robber as about 5 feet 11 with a bandage on his right thumb. He was wearing blue jeans and a black leather coat.

Police have no suspects.

Such an account is adequate but can be written directly from the police report. An enterprising reporter can add much to a story of this sort by taking the time to interview the clerk and police officer.

After filing this story for the first edition, a reporter found time to call the police officer. He had little to add. Then the reporter contacted the clerk, who had plenty to say. This was the result:

"I'm tired of being robbed and I'm afraid of being shot," says Robert Simpson. "So I told the owner I quit." Simpson, 42, of 206 Fourth St., quit his job as night clerk at Gibson's Liquor Store today after being robbed for the fourth time in three weeks Friday night.

Simpson said a man wearing a red ski mask entered the store at 411 Fourth St. at about 7:35 p.m. and demanded money. Simpson emptied $1,056 into a grocery bag the robber carried and was ordered into a storage room at the rear of the building.

"He said he'd blow off my head if I didn't cooperate, so I did exactly what he told me," Simpson said. "But I managed to set off the alarm button under the counter while I was emptying the cash register."

Officer J. O. Holton responded to the alarm and arrived as the robber left the store, but lost him as he fled through nearby alleys on foot.

"We keep asking the cops to set up a stakeout, but they don't do anything," Simpson said. "I know they've got a lot of problems, but that place is always getting hit."

Police records revealed that Gibson's was robbed of $502 Sept. 10, $732 Sept. 14 and $221 Sept. 24. Simpson was the clerk each time.

"This may have been the same guy who robbed me last time," Simpson said, "but I can't be sure because of that mask. Last time he had a different one."

Police Chief Ralph Marshall said he has ordered patrol cars to check the vicinity of the liquor store more often and is considering the owner's request for a stakeout.

"That's just great," Simpson said. "But they can let someone else be the goat. I quit."

Simpson described the robber as a heavyset man about 5 feet 11 inches tall. He was wearing blue jeans and a black leather jacket and had a bandage on his right thumb.

Police have no suspects.

The reporter took the time to get a good interview, and the direct quotes add to the readability of the story. The reporter also recognized and brought out the best angle: the personal fear and frustration experienced by persons in high-crime areas. The result is a much more imaginative use of the basic inverted pyramid formula and a much more interesting story.

The clerk, in the course of his remarks, supplied an important tip about repeated robberies at the store. Two weeks later, police arrested a man as he tried to rob the store during a stakeout. The earlier report was used for background, and a complete story resulted.

Court Organization and Procedure

When a suspect is apprehended and charged with a crime, the job is not finished. Indeed, it has only begun. Because the public wants and needs to know whether the suspect is guilty and, if so, what punishment is imposed, the media devote much time and space to court coverage of criminal charges.

At first glance reporting court news appears to be simple. You listen to the judicial proceeding, ask a few questions afterward and write a story. It may be that simple if you have a thorough knowledge of criminal law and court procedure. If not, it can be extremely confusing. No journalism textbook or class can prepare you to deal with all the intricacies of criminal law. That is a subject better suited for law schools. You should learn the basics of law, court organization and procedure, however. With this foundation you will be prepared to cover court proceedings with at least some understanding of what is happening. This knowledge can be supplemented by asking questions of the judge and attorneys involved.

COURT ORGANIZATION

In the United States there are two court systems, federal and state. Each state has a unique system, but there are many similarities. The average citizen has the most contact with the city or municipal courts. These courts have jurisdiction over traffic or other minor offenses involving city ordinances. News from these courts is handled as a matter of record in many newspapers.

Cases involving violations of state statutes usually are handled in the state trial courts that can be found in most counties. These courts of general jurisdiction (often called circuit or superior courts) handle cases ranging from domestic relations matters to murder. General jurisdiction is an important designation. It means these courts can and do try more cases of more varieties than any other court, including federal district (trial) courts.

Federal district courts have jurisdiction over cases involving interpretation of the U. S. Constitution, civil rights, election disputes, commerce and antitrust matters, postal regulations, federal tax laws and similar types of cases. Federal trial courts also have jurisdiction in actions between citizens of different states when the amount in controversy exceeds $10,000.

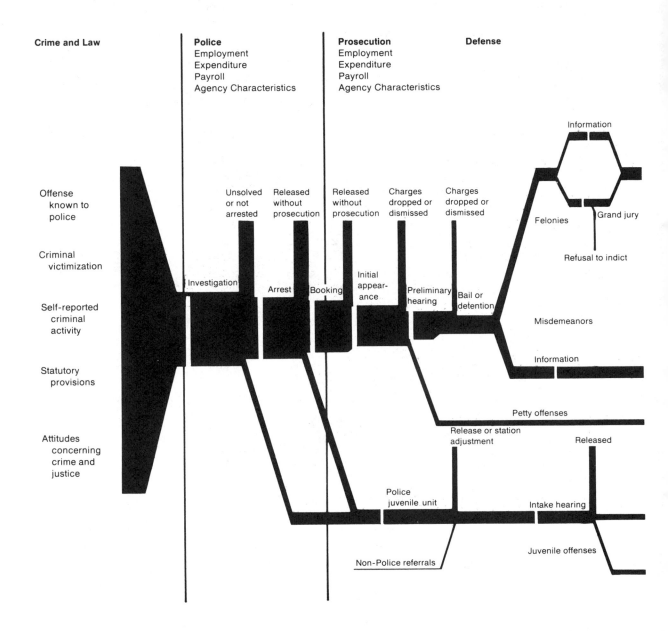

Figure 12.2 Criminal Justice System. This chart shows how cases proceed through the U.S. criminal justice system.

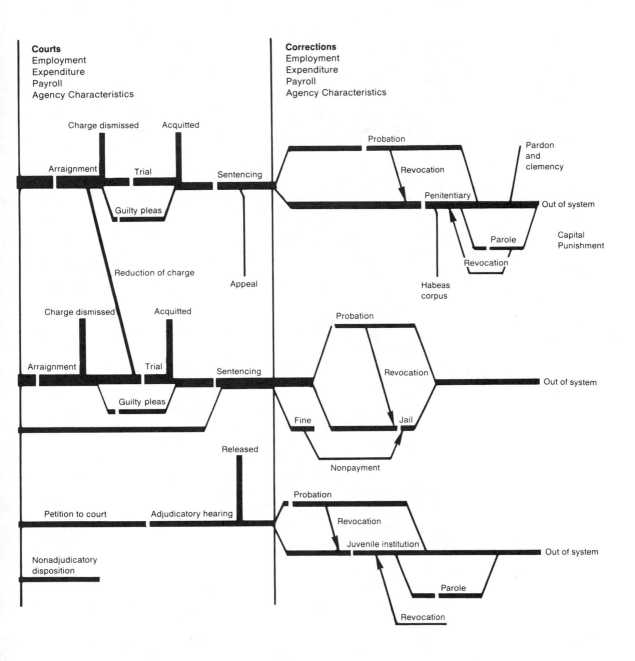

COURT PROCEDURE

Crimes are categorized under state statutes according to their seriousness. The two primary categories of crimes are *misdemeanors* and *felonies*. Under modern statutes, the distinction between felonies and misdemeanors involves whether the offense is punishable by imprisonment in a state penitentiary or the county jail. Thus, most state statutes describe a misdemeanor as an offense punishable by a fine or a county jail term not to exceed one year or both. Felonies are punishable by death, a fine or a prison sentence of more than one year.

Pretrial Proceedings in Criminal Cases

A person arrested in connection with a crime usually is taken to a police station for fingerprinting, photographing, and perhaps a sobriety test or a lineup. Statements may be taken and used in evidence only after the person arrested has been informed of and waives what police and lawyers call "*Miranda rights*," so named because the requirement was imposed in a Supreme Court case involving a defendant named Miranda. Usually within 24 hours a charge must be filed or the person must be released. The time limit may vary from state to state, but all have some limitation to prevent unreasonable detention.

Initial Appearance

If, after consulting with police and reviewing the evidence, the prosecuting (or state or circuit) attorney decides to file charges, the defendant usually is brought before a judge and is informed of the charges, the right to have an attorney (either hired by the defendant or appointed by the court if the defendant is indigent) and the right to remain silent. Bail usually is set at this time.

If the charge is a misdemeanor and the defendant pleads guilty, the case usually is disposed of immediately, and a sentence is imposed or a fine is levied. If the plea is not guilty, a trial date usually is set.

If the crime is a felony, the defendant does not enter a plea. The judge will set a date for a *preliminary hearing*, unless the defendant waives the right to such a hearing. If the defendant waives this hearing, he or she is bound over to the general jurisdiction trial court. The process of being bound over means simply that the records of the case will be sent to the trial court.

A preliminary hearing in felony cases usually is held before a magistrate or lower-level judge in state court systems. The prosecutor presents evidence to try to convince the judge there is *probable cause* to believe that a crime has been committed and probable cause that the defendant committed it.

The defendant has the right to cross-examine the state's witnesses and the accused may present evidence, but this normally is not done. Thus, stories about preliminary hearings often are one-sided. Because of that, care must be exercised in writing the story so it is well-balanced. If the judge does find that there is probable cause, the prosecuting attorney then must file what is called an *information* within a short period of time (usually 10 days) after the judge has ordered the defendant bound over for trial. This information must be based on the judge's findings of probable cause.

Under most state constitutions, it is possible to bring a person accused in a felony case to trial in one of two ways. One is the preliminary hearing; the other is a *grand jury indictment*. In federal courts, the U.S. Constitution requires indictment by a grand jury in felony cases instead of a preliminary hearing.

Grand jury hearings are secret. Jurors and witnesses are sworn not to reveal information about what takes place in the grand jury room, and potential defendants are not allowed to be present when testimony is given concerning them. The prosecuting attorney presents evidence to the jury, which must determine whether there is probable cause to prosecute. The prosecutor acts as adviser to the jury.

A grand jury returns a *true bill* when probable cause is found. A *no true bill* is returned if no probable cause is found. When a grand jury finds probable cause, an indictment is signed by the grand jury foreman and the prosecuting attorney. It then is presented in open court to a trial judge.

If the defendant is not already in custody, the judge orders an arrest warrant issued for the accused. *Arraignment* in the trial court follows. This is the first formal presentation of the information or the indictment to the defendant. The arraignment is conducted in open court, and the defendant enters a plea to the charge. Three pleas — guilty, not guilty and not guilty by reason of mental disease or defect — are possible.

A process known as *plea bargaining* sometimes is used at this point. Under this process, a defendant may change a plea from not guilty to guilty in return for a lighter sentence than may be imposed if a jury returns a guilty verdict. Typically, in such circumstances the defendant pleads guilty to a lesser charge than the one outstanding. A defendant charged with premeditated or first-degree murder, for example, may plead guilty to a reduced charge of manslaughter. The prosecutor often is willing to go along with such an arrangement if the time and expense of a trial can be saved and if justice is served.

If a guilty plea is entered, the judge may impose a sentence immediately, or a pre-sentencing investigation of the defendant's background may be ordered to help the judge set punishment. Many jurisdictions require pre-sentencing investigations, at least in felony cases. If sentencing is delayed for that purpose, a sentencing date usually is set to allow ample time for completion of the report. If a not-guilty plea is entered, the judge sets a trial date. Most jurisdictions have statutes or court rules requiring speedy trials in criminal cases and setting time limits from the date of the charge being filed to the date of the trial.

As the prosecutor and defense attorney prepare for trial, *motions* may be filed for disclosure of evidence, suppression of evidence and similar rulings. Journalists will have a special interest if a defense attorney files a motion for a change of venue, which allows the trial to be conducted in a county other than the one in which the crime occurred. Requests for venue changes often result from pretrial stories in the local media that may prejudice potential jurors.

The Trial

The trial starts as a jury, usually made up of 12 members and at least one alternate, is selected from a group of citizens called for jury duty. During the selection process (called *voir dire*) the prosecutor and defense attorney question the prospective jurors to identify jurors that each side hopes will be sympathetic to its position.

Each attorney is allowed to eliminate a certain number of individuals from consideration as jurors without having to state a reason. Thus, a prospective juror believed to be prejudiced against the attorney's view can be dismissed. Elimination of a prospective juror for cause (if, for example, he or she is related to the accused) also is permitted. An unlimited number of challenges for cause is allowed each attorney. Once 12 jurors and at least one alternate are chosen and sworn, the prosecutor makes an *opening statement*. The opening statement outlines how the prosecutor, acting on behalf of the state, expects to prove each of the elements of the crime. The defense attorney may follow with an outline of the defense or may wait until after the prosecution has introduced its evidence. The defense also may waive an opening statement.

To establish what happened and to link the defendant to the crime, witnesses for the state are called to the stand. During this procedure the prosecutor asks questions, and the witness responds. The defense attorney then has an opportunity to *cross-examine* the witness. Frequently, one attorney will object to questions posed by the other and the judge must arbitrate. When the defense attorney finishes cross-examination, the prosecutor conducts *re-direct examination* to try to clarify points for the jury that may have become confused during cross-examination and to bolster the credibility of a witness whose credibility may have been damaged on cross-examination. Then the defense attorney may conduct another cross-examination and the prosecutor may conduct a re-direct examination. This can continue until both sides have exhausted all questions they want to ask the witness. After all the prosecution witnesses have testified and the state rests its case, the defense almost always makes a *motion for acquittal* in which it argues that the state has failed to prove its case beyond a reasonable doubt. Almost as routinely as such motions are made, they are denied.

The defense then calls witnesses to support its case, and the prosecutor is allowed to cross-examine them. Finally, when all witnesses have testified, the defense rests. The prosecutor then calls *rebuttal witnesses* in an attempt to discredit testimony of the defense. The defense then has the right to present even more witnesses, called *surrebuttal witnesses*. After the various rebuttal witnesses have testified, the judge explains to the jury what verdicts it can return and outlines points of law that are key to the case in jury instructions. The prosecutor then makes his closing argument, usually an impassioned plea for a guilty verdict addressed directly to the jury. The defense attorney follows with a similar argument and the prosecutor is allowed a final rebuttal. The jury then retires to deliberate. Because unanimous verdicts are required for acquittal or conviction in a criminal trial, deliberations often are protracted. If the jury fails to reach a unanimous verdict (*a hung jury*) after a reasonable period of time, the judge may order a *mistrial*, in which event the entire case will be retried from the beginning of jury selection.

If a verdict is reached, the jury returns to the courtroom, where the verdict is read. In some states juries are permitted to recommend sentences when guilty verdicts are reached, but the final decision always is made by the judge unless a crime carries a mandatory sentence. Sentencing may be done immediately, but more likely a pre-sentencing report will be ordered and a sentencing date set.

The defense often files a motion asking that a guilty verdict be set aside. Such motions usually are denied. A motion for a new trial usually brings similar results. However, in most jurisdictions a motion for a new trial and a denial is a prerequisite to the filing of an appeal. Appeals often follow guilty verdicts, so a verdict seldom is final in that sense. Except in extreme circumstances involving serious crimes, judges often permit the defendant to be released on bail pending the outcome of appeals.

Writing Court Stories

Throughout the court procedure, a reporter has opportunities to write stories. The extent to which the reporter does so, of course, depends on the importance of the case and the amount of local interest in it. In a major case the filing of every motion may prompt a story; in other cases only the verdict may be important. As in any type of reporting, news value is the determining factor.

Also, as in any form of reporting, accuracy is important. Perhaps no other area of writing requires as much caution as the reporting of crime and court news. The potential for libel is great.

AVOIDING LIBELOUS STATEMENTS

Libel is damage to a person's reputation caused by a written statement that brings the person into hatred, contempt or ridicule, or injuries his or her business or occupational pursuits (see Chapter 22). Reporters must be extremely careful about what they write.

One of the greatest dangers is the possibility of writing that someone is charged with a crime more serious than is the case. After checking clippings in the newspaper library, for example, one reporter wrote:

> The rape trial of John L. Duncan, 25, of 3925 Oak St. has been set for Dec. 10 in Jefferson County Circuit Court.
>
> Duncan is charged in connection with the June 6 rape of a Melton High School girl near Fletcher Park.

Duncan had been charged with rape following his arrest, but the prosecutor later determined the evidence was insufficient to win a rape conviction. The charge had been reduced to assault, and the newspaper had to print a correction.

In any story involving arrests, caution flags must be raised. The reporter must have a sound working knowledge of libel law and what can and cannot be written about an incident. The reporter who writes this, for example, is asking for trouble:

```
John R. Milton, 35, of 206 East St., was arrested Monday
on a charge of assaulting a police officer.
```

Only a prosecutor, not a police officer, may file charges. In many cases, a police officer may arrest a person with the intent of asking the prosecutor to file a certain charge. Then, when the prosecutor examines the evidence, the evidence may warrant only a lesser charge. For that reason, most newspaper editors prefer to print the name of an arrested person only after the charge has been filed. Unfortunately, deadline constraints sometimes make that impossible, and many newspapers publish the names of those arrested before the charge is filed. A decision to publish a name in such circumstances requires extreme caution. If an individual were arrested in connection with a rape and the newspaper printed that information, only to learn later that the prosecutor had filed a charge of assault, a libel suit could result. Once the charge is filed, the lead should be written like this:

```
    John R. Milton, 35, of 206 East St. was charged Monday
with assaulting a police officer.
    Prosecutor Steve Scott said . . .
```

By writing the lead this way, the reporter shows that Milton not only has been arrested but also has been charged with a crime by the prosecutor. Carelessness leads not only to libel suits but also to attacks on a suspect's reputation. If the suspect is judged not guilty, both the newspaper and the suspect suffer.

Reporters who cover court news encounter many such pitfalls. They are not trained as attorneys, and it takes time to develop a sound working knowledge of legal proceedings. The only recourse is to ask as many questions as necessary when a point of law is not clear. It is far better to display ignorance of the law openly than to commit a serious error that harms the reputation of the accused and opens the newspaper to costly libel litigation.

On the other hand, it is important to know that anything said in open court is fair game for reporters. If, in an opening statement, a prosecutor says the defendant is "nothing but scum, a smut peddler bent on polluting the mind of every child in the city," then by all means report it in context in your story. But if a spectator makes that same statement in the hallway during a recess, you probably would not report it. Courts do not extend the qualified privilege to report court proceedings beyond the context of the official proceeding.

CONTINUING COVERAGE OF THE PROSECUTION

With the above points in mind, let's trace a criminal case from the time of arrest through the trial to show how a newspaper might report each step. Here is a typical first story:

An unemployed carpenter was arrested today and charged with the Aug. 6 murder of Springfield socialite Anne Compton.

Lester L. Rivers, 32, of 209 E. Dillow Lane, was charged with first-degree murder, Prosecuting Attorney Mel Singleton said.

Chief of Detectives E. L. Hall said Rivers was arrested on a warrant after a three-month investigation by a team of three detectives. He declined to comment on what led investigators to Rivers.

Miss Compton's body was found in the Peabody River by two fishermen on the morning of Aug. 7. She had been beaten to death with a blunt instrument, according to Dr. Ronald R. Miller, the county medical examiner.

This straightforward account of the arrest was filed on deadline. Later, the reporter would interview neighbors about Rivers' personality and write an improved story for other editions. This bare-bones story, however, provides a glimpse of several key points in covering arrest stories.

Notice that the reporter carefully chose the words "arrested and charged with" rather than "arrested for," a phrase that may carry a connotation of guilt.

Another important element of all crime and court coverage is the tie-back sentence. This relates a story to events covered in a previous story — in this case, the report of the crime itself. It is important to state clearly — and near the beginning of the story — which crime is involved and to provide enough information about it so that the reader recognizes it. Clarification of the crime is important even in major stories with ready identification in the community. This story does that by recounting when and where Miss Compton's body was found and by whom. It also tells that she died after being hit with a blunt instrument.

The following morning the suspect was taken to Magistrate Court for his initial court appearance. Here is a part of the story that resulted:

Lester L. Rivers appeared in Magistrate Court today charged with first-degree murder in connection with the Aug. 6 beating death of Springfield socialite Anne Compton.

Judge Harold L. Robbins scheduled a preliminary hearing for Nov. 10 and set bail at $10,000.

Robbins assigned Public Defender Ogden Ball to represent Rivers, 32, of 209 E. Dillow Lane.

Rivers said nothing during the 10-minute session as the judge informed him of his right to remain silent and his right to an attorney. Ball asked Robbins to set the bail at a "reasonable amount for a man who is unemployed." Rivers is a carpenter who was fired from his last job in June.

Despite the seriousness of the charge, it is essential that Rivers be free to help prepare his defense, Ball said.

Police have said nothing about a possible connection between Rivers and Miss Compton, whose body was found in the Peabody River by two fishermen on the morning of Aug. 7. She had been beaten to death.

The reporter clearly outlined the exact charge and reported on key points of the brief hearing. Again, the link to the crime is important to inform the reader of which murder is involved.

Next came the preliminary hearing, where the first evidence linking the defendant to the crime was revealed:

Lester L. Rivers will be tried in Jefferson County Circuit Court for the Aug. 6 murder of Springfield socialite Anne Compton.

Magistrate Judge Harold L. Robbins ruled today that there is probable cause that a crime was committed and probable cause that Rivers did it. Rivers was bound over for trial in Circuit Court.

Rivers, 32, of 209 E. Dillow Lane, is being held in Jefferson County Jail. He has been unable to post bail of $10,000.

At today's preliminary hearing, Medical Examiner Ronald L. Miller testified that a tire tool recovered from Rivers' car at the time of his arrest "could have been used in the beating death of Miss Compton." Her body was found floating in the Peabody River Aug. 7.

James L. Mullaney, a lab technician for the FBI crime laboratory in Washington, D.C., testified that "traces of blood on the tire tool matched Miss Compton's blood type."

In reporting such testimony, the reporter was careful to use direct quotes and not overstate the facts. The medical examiner testified that the tire tool *could have been used* in the murder. If he had said it *was used*, a stronger lead would have been needed.

Defense attorneys usually use such hearings to learn about the evidence against their clients and do not present any witnesses. This apparently was the motive here, because neither the police nor the prosecutor had made a public statement on evidence in the case. They probably were being careful not to release prejudicial information that could be grounds for reversal of a verdict.

The prosecutor then filed an *information*, as state law allowed. The defendant was arraigned in Circuit Court, and the result was a routine story that began as follows:

Circuit Judge John L. Lee refused today to reduce the bail of Lester L. Rivers, who is charged with first-degree murder in the Aug. 6 death of socialite Anne Compton.

Rivers pleaded not guilty.

Repeating a request he made earlier in Magistrate Court, Public Defender Ogden Ball urged that Rivers' bail be reduced from $10,000 so he could be freed to assist in preparing his defense.

The not guilty plea was expected, so the reporter concentrated on a more interesting aspect of the hearing, the renewed request for reduced bail. Finally, after a series of motions was reported routinely, the trial began:

Jury selection began today in the first-degree murder trial of Lester L. Rivers, who is charged with the Aug. 6 beating death of socialite Anne Compton.

Public Defender Ogden Ball, Rivers' attorney, and Prosecuting Attorney Mel Singleton both expect jury selection to be complete by 5 p.m.

The selection process started after court convened at 10 a.m. The only incident occurred just before the lunch break as Singleton was questioning prospective juror Jerome L. Tinker, 33, of 408 Woodland Terrace.

"I went to school with that guy," said Tinker, pointing to Rivers, who was seated in the courtroom. "He wouldn't hurt nobody."

Singleton immediately asked that Tinker be removed from the jury panel, and Circuit Judge John L. Lee agreed.

Rivers smiled as Tinker made his statement, but otherwise sat quietly, occasionally conferring with Ball.

The testimony is about to begin, so the reporter set the stage here, describing the courtroom scene. Jury selection often is routine and becomes newsworthy only in important or interesting cases.

Trial coverage can be tedious, but when the case is an interesting one, the stories are easy to write. The reporter picks the most interesting testimony for leads as the trial progresses:

A service station owner testified today that Lester L. Rivers offered a ride to socialite Anne Compton less than an hour before she was beaten to death Aug. 6.

Ralph R. Eagle, the station owner, was a witness at the first-degree murder trial of Rivers in Jefferson County Circuit Court.

"I told her I'd call a cab," Eagle testified, "but Rivers offered her a ride to her boyfriend's house." Miss Compton had gone to the service station after her car broke down nearby.

Under cross-examination, Public Defender Ogden Ball, Rivers' attorney, questioned whether Rivers was the man who offered the ride.

"If it wasn't him, it was his twin brother," Eagle said.

"Then you're not really sure it was Mr. Rivers, are you?" Ball asked.

"I sure am," Eagle replied.

"You think you're sure, Mr. Eagle, but you really didn't get a good look at him, did you?"

"I sold him some gas and got a good look at him when I took the money."

"But it was night, wasn't it, Mr. Eagle?" Ball asked.

"That place doesn't have the best lighting in the world, but I saw him all right."

The reporter focused on the key testimony of the trial by capturing it in the words of the participants. Good note-taking ability becomes important here, because trial coverage is greatly enhanced with direct quotation of key exchanges. Long exchanges may necessitate the use of the question-and-answer format:

Ball: In fact, a lot of the lights above those gas pumps are out, aren't they, Mr. Eagle?

Eagle: Yes, but I stood right by him.

Q. I have no doubt you thought

you saw Mr. Rivers, but there's always the possibility it could have been someone else. Isn't that true?

A. No, it looked just like him.

Q. It appeared to be him, but it may not have been because you really couldn't see him that well, could you?

A. Well, it was kind of dark out there.

Finally, there is the verdict story, which usually is one of the easiest to write:

Lester L. Rivers was found guilty of first-degree murder today in the Aug. 6 beating death of socialite Anne Compton.

Rivers stood motionless in Jefferson County Circuit Court as the jury foreman returned the verdict. Judge John L. Lee set sentencing for Dec. 10.

Rivers, 32, of 209 E. Dillow Lane, could be sentenced to death in the electric chair or life imprisonment in the State Penitentiary.

Public Defender Ogden Ball, Rivers' attorney, said he will appeal.

After the verdict was announced, Mr. and Mrs. Lilborn L. Compton, the victim's parents, were escorted from the courtroom by friends. Both refused to talk with reporters.

Many other types of stories could have been written about such a trial. Lengthy jury deliberations, for example, might prompt stories about the anxiety of the defendant and attorneys and their speculation about the cause of the delay.

Covering court news requires care and good reporting. As in any kind of reporting, you must be well-prepared. If you understand the language of the courts and how they are organized, your job is simplified.

Taste and Responsibility

Some of the darkest moments in the history of the American press have involved coverage of crime and the courts. Certainly the sensational treatment of crime news was a hallmark of the Yellow Journalism era at the turn of the century. In the late 1890s, for example, William Randolph Hearst's New York Journal scored a major success in building circulation with its reports of the "Guldensuppe mystery." The headless, legless, armless torso of a man was found in the East River, and Hearst's Journal printed every gory detail as one part of the body after another was found in various boroughs of New York. Few would charge that the press of today is that tasteless, but much of the criticism newspapers receive still is centered on crime reporting.

THE FREE PRESS–FAIR TRIAL CONTROVERSY

Criticism of the press and its coverage of crime often is traced to the 1954 murder trial of Dr. Samuel Sheppard in Cleveland. Sheppard, an osteopath, was accused of murdering his wife. News coverage in the Cleveland newspapers, which included front-page editorials, was intense. The Supreme Court said the trial judge did not fulfill his duty to protect the jury from the news coverage that saturated the community and to control disruptive influences in the courtroom.

That case more than any other ignited what is known as the free press–fair trial controversy. It continued throughout the 1960s. Lawyers charged that the press ignored the Sixth Amendment right of the accused to an impartial jury, and the press countered with charges that lawyers ignored the First Amendment.

Editors realize that coverage of a crime can make it difficult to impanel an impartial jury, but they argue that courts have available many remedies other than restricting the flow of information. In the Sheppard case, for example, the Supreme Court justices said a change of venue, which moves the trial to a location where publicity is not as intense, could have been ordered. Other remedies suggested by the court in such cases are to continue (delay) the trial, to grant a new trial or to head off possible outside influences during the trial by sequestering the jury. Editors also argue that acquittals have been won in some of the most publicized cases in recent years. Among these are the trial of black activist Angela Davis and the first trial of former U.S. Attorney General John Mitchell.

Despite the remedies the Supreme Court offered in the Sheppard case, trial judges continued to be concerned about impaneling impartial juries. Beginning in 1972, when a federal district judge in Baton Rouge, La., ordered two reporters not to report on a pretrial hearing they had attended, the problem of gag orders arose. Finally, in 1976, in the landmark case of *Nebraska Press Association* v. *Stuart*, the Supreme Court ruled that a gag order was an unconstitutional prior restraint that violated the First Amendment to the Constitution. The justices did not go so far as to rule that all gag orders are invalid. But in each case, the trial judge has to prove that an order restraining publication would protect the rights of the accused.

That, of course, did not end the concerns of trial judges. Rather than issue gag orders restricting the press from reporting court proceedings, some attempted to close their courtrooms. In the first such case to reach the Supreme Court, *Gannett* v. *DePasquale*, the press and public suffered a severe blow. On July 2, 1979, in a highly controversial decision, the justices said, "We hold that members of the public have no constitutional right under the Sixth and Fourteenth amendments to attend criminal trials."

As a result of this decision and the confusion that followed, the Supreme Court of Virginia sanctioned the closing of an entire criminal trial. The accused was acquitted during the second day of the secret trial. The U.S. Supreme Court agreed to hear the appeal of the trial judge's action in a case known as *Richmond Newspapers* v. *Virginia*. On July 2, 1980, the court said "the trial of a criminal case must be open to the public." Only a court finding of an "overriding interest," which was not defined, would be grounds for closing a criminal trial.

In Massachusetts, a judge excluded the public and press from the entire trial of a man accused of raping three teenagers. A Massachusetts law provided for the mandatory closing of rape trials. The state argued that cases involving sex offenses against minors should be excluded from open-trial requirements. The U.S. Supreme Court held in 1982 in *Boston Newspapers* v. *Superior Court* that the mandatory closure law violated the First Amendment right of access to

Figure 12.3 The Free Press–Fair Trial Controversy. The Sam Sheppard murder trial in 1954 raised questions about how much reporters should be allowed to write during judicial proceedings. The carnival atmosphere of the trial fostered sensationalism, and reporters covering it rushed to the courthouse press room, shown here, to report every detail to their editors.

criminal trials established in the *Richmond Newspapers* case. The justices ruled that when a state attempts to deny the right of access in an effort to inhibit the disclosure of sensitive information, it must show that the denial "is necessitated by a compelling governmental interest." The court indicated in the opinion that in some cases *in camera* proceedings for youthful witnesses may be appropriate. In camera proceedings are those that take place in a judge's chambers outside the view of the press and public.

Finally, in *Press-Enterprise* v. *Riverside County Superior Court*, the Supreme Court ruled that a court order closing the jury selection process in a rape-murder case was invalid. The court ruled that jury selection has been a public process with exceptions only for good cause.

These cases appeared to uphold the right of the press and public to have access to criminal proceedings. Judges, however, have a duty to protect the rights of the accused, and similar situations may arise in the future. The Supreme Court of the State of Washington, in *Federated Publications* v. *Swedberg*, held in 1981 that press access to pretrial hearings may be conditioned on the agreement of reporters to abide by voluntary press-bar guidelines that exist in some states. The decision involved a preliminary hearing in a Bellingham, Wash., murder case tied to the "Hillside strangler" murders in the Los Angeles area. The state Supreme Court ruled that the lower court order was "a good-faith attempt to accommodate the interest of both defendant and press." The lower court had required reporters covering the hearing to sign a document in which the reporters agreed to abide by press-bar guidelines. The state Supreme Court said the document should be taken as a moral commitment on the part of the reporters, not as a legally enforceable document.

The U.S. Supreme Court in 1982 refused to hear an appeal of that case. Fortunately, many states have statutes to the effect that "the setting of every court shall be public and every person may freely attend the same." When such statutes are in place, the closed courtroom controversy appears to be moot. When states have no such statute, the result seems to be:

1. That a criminal trial must be open unless there is an "overriding interest" that requires some part of it to be closed.
2. That judges must find some overriding interest before closing pretrial hearings.

One effect of the Washington decision is that many media groups are withdrawing from state press-bar agreements in the few states that have such guidelines. Their reasoning is that the voluntary guidelines in effect can become mandatory.

The fact remains that there are many ways for judges to protect the rights of the accused without trampling on the rights of the press and public to attend trials and pretrial hearings. Indeed, most editors are sensitive to the rights of the accused. Most exercise self-restraint when publishing information about a crime. Many have attempted to establish written policy on such matters, though others insist that individual cases must be judged on their merits.

DISPUTED ISSUES

Some of the major issues involving taste and responsibility in crime and court reporting are these:

1. When should the newspaper publish details of how a murder or another crime was committed?
2. When should the newspaper publish details about sex crimes or print the names of sex-crime victims?
3. When should newspapers publish a suspect's confession or even the fact that the suspect has confessed?
4. When should newspapers write about a defendant's prior criminal record?
5. When should newspapers print the names of juveniles charged with crimes?

None of these questions can be answered to everyone's satisfaction, and it is doubtful whether rules can be established to apply in all such situations. There have been charges that when newspapers print details of a murder, some people employ the techniques outlined to commit more murders. This charge is directed more frequently at television, but newspapers have not been immune.

The reporting of sex crimes also causes controversy. Most editors think of their publications as family newspapers and are properly hesitant about reporting the lurid details of sex crimes. What began as an interesting murder case in one college town turned into grist for the scandal mill. A college professor murdered one of his students who had asked for after-hours tutoring. When police unraveled the morbid tale of the professor, a homosexual necrophiliac, knowing what to write for the family newspaper became a major problem for the reporter. The newspaper provided information to the public on what had happened but deliberately avoiding the sensationalism that could have resulted. Even during the trial, specifics were avoided in favor of testimony that revealed the nature of the case in general terms:

> "He lived in a world of fantasies,"
> the doctor said. "He spent much of
> his time daydreaming about homo-
> sexual, necrophilic, homicidal, sui-
> cidal and cannibalistic fantasies."

To have been more specific would have been revolting to many of the newspaper's readers.

A related problem is the question of how to handle rape reports. Too often, rapes are not reported to police because victims are unwilling to appear in court to testify against the suspects. Defense attorneys sometimes use such occasions to attack the victim's morals and imply that she consented to sexual relations. Many victims decline to press charges because of fear that their names will be made public in newspapers and on radio and television. There is, after all, still a lingering tendency to attach a social stigma to the rape victim, despite increasing public awareness of the nature of the crime.

In some states "rape shield" statutes have been passed to prohibit a defendant from delving into the rape victim's prior sexual activity unless some connection can be shown with the circumstances of the rape charged.

Many editors will not publish details of a suspect's confession in an effort to protect an accused person's rights. Publication of such information blocks the way for a fair trial perhaps more easily than anything a newspaper can do. Some newspapers, however, continue to publish assertions by police or prosecutors that a confession has been signed. Many question whether such information isn't just as prejudicial as the confession statement itself.

Occasionally, the question arises of whether to publish or to suppress an unsolicited confession. After a youth was charged with a series of robberies and was certified to stand trial as an adult, a newspaper reporter called the defendant, who was free on bail, for an interview. The result was interesting:

> Ricketts said he and two others
> took money from the service station
> "because we was broke at the time
> and needed the money, and we was
> ignorant."
> He said they had "no idea we'd
> ever get caught. It wasn't worth it."

The defendant went on to admit to two other robberies in what amounted to a confession to the newspaper and its readers. The editor, who would not have printed a simple statement by police that the defendant had confessed to the crime, printed this one. Why?

The editor reasoned that information about a confession to police amounts to secondhand, hearsay information. The confession to a reporter, however, was firsthand information obtained by the newspaper directly from the accused.

Lawyers also view as prejudicial the publication of a defendant's prior criminal record. Even if authorities refuse to divulge that information, much of it may be in the newspaper morgue. Should it be published? Most editors believe it should, particularly if a prior conviction was for a similar offense. Most attorneys disagree.

Whether to use the names of juveniles charged with crimes is a troublesome issue as well. Most states prohibit law enforcement officers and court officials from releasing the names of juveniles. The reasoning of those who oppose releasing juveniles' names is that the publicity marks them for life as criminals. Those who hold this view argue that there is ample opportunity for these individuals to change their ways and become good citizens — if the newspaper does not stamp them as criminals. Others argue that juveniles who commit serious offenses, such as rape and armed robbery, should be treated as adults.

Questions such as these elicit divergent views from editors. Little guidance for the reporter can be offered here. Because the decision to publish or not to publish is the editor's, not the reporter's, consultation is necessary. Each case must be decided on its merits.

Suggested Readings

Franklin, Marc A. "The First Amendment and the Fourth Estate." Mineola, N.Y.: The Foundation Press, 1977. A good explanation of the law of the press.

Nelson, Harold L., and Dwight L. Teeter, Jr. "Law of Mass Communication." Mineola, N.Y.: The Foundation Press, 1973. An excellent compilation of law as it affects the working reporter.

Newsman's Guide to Legalese. Harrisburg, Pa.: Pennsylvania Bar Association, 1973. Handy reference work for the reporter working on a crime or court story.

13

Follows

Details of the first Watergate story were phoned in by Alfred E. Lewis, a Washington Post police reporter for 35 years. The first front-page Watergate story carried his byline. It was the work of eight reporters, one named Bob Woodward. The same paper carried a story about the suspects by Carl Bernstein. As Woodward and Bernstein wrote later in "All the President's Men," city editor Barry Sussman asked them to return to the office that Sunday morning to "follow up." Thus began one of the most intensely followed events in the history of newspapers. By reporting it, Woodward and Bernstein led The Washington Post to a Pulitzer Prize and became million-aires.

After the National Guard shot and killed four students at Kent State University in Ohio in 1970, the Akron Beacon Journal sent a team of reporters to the campus to try to re-create the events. The result was a massive report that challenged the official version of the tragedy. For following up a story, the Akron Beacon Journal group, like The Washington Post, won a Pulitzer Prize.

What follows a news story may be as important or interesting as the original story. After people ask what happened, they usually ask, what happened next? Because newspapers cannot wait to go to press until a story is complete, follow-up stories (or, simply, follows) are common.

A *follow* may tell the readers what happened next, or it may catch up or complete a story broken by another paper. It may keep readers posted about a story that is breaking or continuing. Or a follow may deal with something that happened months ago and report developments since then.

Follows are part of every newspaper and the major portion of news magazines. Some papers and magazines offer regular columns or sections of follows. Sometimes they are the most looked for and the most read items a publication has to offer.

Because you will be assigned follow stories, you must learn the proper techniques for writing them.

In this chapter you will learn:

1. How to create a second-cycle story.
2. What kinds of developing stories you can report and write on.
3. How to write an update.

Creating the Second-Cycle Story

Even the best newspapers sometimes get scooped on a story. The same is true of broadcast news operations, radio or television. Competition is not a thing of the past. Newspapers try to get stories before they appear on television and vice versa. Also competing are vigorous suburban dailies and weeklies, weekly news magazines, and newspapers from other areas, including the national newspapers The New York Times, The Wall Street Journal and USA Today.

Sometimes one medium gets the story first because of when the news breaks. In rare cities that still have competing morning and afternoon papers, an afternoon paper will have news that occurred after the morning paper has gone to press and vice versa. A news me-

Figure 13.1 Follows Make the News.
Watergate has come to mean all the events that led to the resignation of Pres. Richard M. Nixon. The Watergate story was a series of follows, and the persons who wrote most of them were Bob Woodward (right) and Carl Bernstein.

dium should never give exactly the same story as its competitor, but neither can it ignore a story that is newsworthy.

A *second-cycle story* provides a fresh slant. By writing such a story, reporters allow readers and listeners to catch up with or follow a story that has already broken. To give a fresh slant to second-cycle stories, reporters can:

1. Supply information not available when the first story was written.
2. Use enterprise to uncover information not contained in the original.
3. Supply fresh details, color and background, even when nothing of substance is new.
4. Respond to the news of the first story with analysis, possible developments or the reactions of people whom the news would affect.
5. Gather local reactions to a national or international story.

Let's look at each of these approaches.

SUPPLYING PREVIOUSLY UNAVAILABLE INFORMATION

When you are asked to do a rewrite of a story appearing in a competing newspaper, you are expected to make your story as dissimilar as possible without distorting the facts. Read the story carefully. Verify all the information yourself. Then discover whether you can add any new information or report any developments since your competitor wrote the story. For example, here is part of a morning newspaper's story:

Police called to a northside residence Wednesday found the body of a teen-age boy lying between a toolshed and a garage.

Police said the victim had been tentatively identified as a 14-year-old Springfield youth. However, authorities withheld his name until relatives could make a positive identification.

Lt. Richard Moses and Dr. Erwin Busiek, the medical examiner, said the victim had received several large wounds, one in his head and another on his chest. Authorities said a large rock was found near the body, but they had not determined if he had been beaten, stabbed or shot to death.

An autopsy was scheduled for later Wednesday at St. John's Hospital.

A reporter rewriting the story for the afternoon paper called the police station and found that more information had become available. His story began:

> A 14-year-old boy, whose body was found Wednesday near a northside residence, has been identified as Maurice Comstock of Springfield, police said.
>
> Dr. Erwin Busiek, the medical examiner, said Comstock died from a skull fracture. A large rock near the body could have been the murder weapon, police said.

The second reporter was able to identify the victim and to give the cause of death. In this case the new information was readily available from routine sources.

UNCOVERING NEW INFORMATION

Many times you may have to do some digging to find additional information. An enterprising reporter sometimes wins bigger play with a recycled story than with the original. For example, when one newspaper reported that a man, James Wiley, had been arrested on a driving-while-intoxicated charge, a reporter from the competing newspaper asked the police a few questions and looked at police records. What was at first a routine item on the records page became a front-page story, which began this way:

> For the third time in the last six months, James Wiley, of 403 W. Third St., has been arrested on a driving-while-intoxicated charge.
>
> Springfield police said Wiley, whose driver's license had been suspended, was using his brother-in-law's license last night.

You show enterprise when, through your own initiative, you uncover previously unknown information or add up known information to come up with a new result.

SUPPLYING DETAILS, COLOR AND BACKGROUND

When a story appears to cover all bases and no new developments have occurred, you still can dig for more details. Here is an example of how a reporter who followed a story made it worth reading a second time. The story first appeared like this:

A 20-year-old Mercer County man drowned while swimming with friends yesterday afternoon at Finger Lakes State Park.

Arthur James Frazier, of 164 Crescent Meadows Trailer Court, drowned at about 5:10 p.m., said Maj. Jim White of the Mercer County Sheriff's Department.

Frazier's body was recovered about seven hours later by divers and a rescue squad from the Mercer County Volunteer Fire Protection District.

White said Frazier swam across the lake with Stanley Shenski, 20, of Springsdale, and apparently tired on his way back.

Shenski said he attempted to carry the youth after he became tired but said Frazier struggled away from him and went under about 15 feet from shore. Shenski and other friends dived for Frazier but could not find him.

Here is the second-cycle story:

Just 20 feet from life.

"I got him within 20 feet of shore. Then he said he could make it. But he couldn't. When I got back to him, he pulled me under."

A dejected Stanley Shenski, 20, of Springsdale, was on the verge of tears. Perhaps it was anger, frustration — how could it happen that a good, strong swimmer could not swim just 20 more feet?

Yet, his friend Arthur James Frazier, 20, of 164 Crescent Meadows Trailer Park, had drowned at Finger Lakes State Park. His body was recovered early this morning.

"He told me he was tired, so we rested a while before swimming back. It was only 50 feet across," Shenski said.

Shenski was also angry about something else. Other swimmers, as many as 10 or 12 of them, were enjoying the lake that sunny Thursday afternoon. Shenski said he and Frazier did a lot of shouting for help.

But apparently no one heard them.

By interviewing the survivor and digging for details, the reporter was able to keep the story on the front page. The more-engaging lead sets the scene before telling the story.

Here is another example of how a reporter recycled a news story into a news feature. The morning paper's account began like this:

Charles W. Moreland of Jacksonville, Fla., has been appointed administrator of Myron Barnes State Cancer Hospital by Dr. Whitney Cole, director of the State Division of Health.

Moreland, 54, succeeds Warren Mills, who retired last week after nine years as director. At a news conference, Cole praised Mills for "outstanding leadership" and cited the multimillion dollar building program completed during Mills' tenure as an example of his achievements.

A reporter for the competing afternoon paper wrote it this way:

At 5:30 this morning, employees at Myron Barnes State Cancer Hospital caught their first bleary-eyed glimpse of the hospital's new administrator— he was roaming the halls.

But Charles W. Moreland's motive for the early morning stroll wasn't secret. He didn't expect to find someone taking one too many coffee breaks. Instead, he says, "I just wanted to meet the people who work here.''

The 54-year-old Moreland will meet a host of people in the next few days. He was named administrator of Myron Barnes by Dr. Whitney Cole, health director in the State Department of Social Services.

Moreland succeeds Warren Mills, 67, who retired after nine years as administrator.

The writer of the second story chose to tell us something more than the news of the naming of a new administrator. We learn something *about* the new administrator. By doing this, the reporter tempted even those who had read the morning paper's version to look at the story again.

Here's another example. First, the morning paper's version:

Susan Teller, Fourth Ward Councilwoman since 1971, announced her resignation, effective Sept. 1, at Monday night's City Council meeting.

Ms. Teller will move with her three daughters, Melanie, Betty and Diana, to Ann Arbor, Mich., to work for the University of Michigan as an instructor in city planning. She said she would remain with the council through August to help choose a new city manager and to formulate the new city budget.

"I'd like to stay with the city manager search, since I've been through it before," she said.

Ms. Teller was a council member when George Billing was chosen in 1973 as Springfield's city manager.

The story of the same resignation appeared this way in the city's afternoon competing newspaper:

Fourth Ward Councilwoman Susan Teller, in her characteristically quiet way, waited her turn when it came time for general comments by Springfield City Council members at the end of last night's meeting.

Then she said, "At the end of the summer, I will be moving to Ann Arbor, Mich., to become an instructor in city planning at the University of Michigan."

Just like that. No dramatics. Teller was resigning the council seat she had been elected to three times and had held 7½ years.

She had kept her decision to herself. Even Sam Jaspers, the Sixth Ward representative who is her closest friend on the council, learned the news only last weekend.

Mayor James Burd, clearly unprepared, said, "This is a surprise," and then mustered his wits for a short tribute to Teller, although he noted there would be time for more comments later.

"Susan has demonstrated an outstanding ability to take care of her constituents' needs," Burd said.

Teller said she would continue to serve on the council through August, giving her a hand in the selection of the new city manager and in the preparation of next year's city budget.

The morning newspaper carried a straight news lead. The writer of the follow wrote a more reflective feature lead. Then he allowed the councilwoman herself to tell the news by means of a direct quote. The third paragraph continues the feature style with its use of sentence fragments. The reporter had nothing new to report, but he recycled the story in an entertaining and informative manner.

RESPONDING WITH ANALYSIS, POSSIBLE DEVELOPMENTS AND REACTIONS

Though an afternoon paper can choose to recycle the same information as its morning competitor, it has several other choices, some of them better.

1. Lead with an analytical approach:

The resignation of Councilwoman Susan Teller gives the conservatives an opportunity for the first time in six years to control the City Council.

2. Lead with possible developments:

John James, the conservative candidate defeated by Susan Teller in the 1978 elections, appears to be the favorite to replace her.

3. Lead with reaction:

Mayor James Burd said he was stunned to learn that Councilwoman Susan Teller would be leaving the council in August.

Sometimes newspapers follow or recycle their own stories in the three ways mentioned above. For example, after a story appeared saying that supporters of a proposed right-to-work state constitutional amendment had obtained enough signatures to put their measure on the next ballot, the newspaper followed with this reaction story:

An opponent of the right-to-work amendment, Democratic auditor candidate Warren Hearnes, says the proposal to prohibit mandatory union membership would pass if the vote were taken now.

The amendment was certified for the Nov. 7 ballot Friday by Secretary of State James Kirkpatrick. The proposal received sufficient signatures in eight of the 10 congressional districts.

Having the measure on the November ballot, Hearnes said, also will divert money away from himself and other candidates.

Both Hearnes and his opponent — Republican James Antonio — doubted the right-to-work issue would directly affect the auditor's race, the only statewide office on the ballot.

"The only bearing — the only question I have is how many votes is it going to bring out," Hearnes said. "Without it, you would have around a million. With it, I have no idea."

The story gives readers a different perspective on the news that the right-to-work issue would be on the ballot. Note the second paragraph. Its first sentence ties the lead to a previous story announcing that the amendment would be on the ballot. The second sentence reports spot news. Then the third paragraph picks up on the lead and discusses the issue's relevance to the election of the next state auditor.

GATHERING LOCAL REACTIONS TO A NON-LOCAL STORY

Often a newspaper follows a national or international story by seeking local reactions. How has a declining or low inflation rate affected the buying habits of local consumers? How have cuts in Medicare affected a local nursing home?

When customers were concerned about telephone rates after the breakup of AT&T, a newspaper kept readers informed with this story:

Your phone bill won't be going up. At least not for now.

The U.S. Senate is now pondering a bill that would block proposed access fees for residential customers and small businesses and force phone companies to continue relying on revenue from inflated long distance rates to subsidize local service.

All this resulting from the federally ordered breakup of telecommunications giant AT&T.

"As of Jan. 1, 1985," says GTE public affairs director Ron Hopwood, "nothing has changed for GTE customers."

The local-reaction follow brings the story home. It shows the community how local people are affected by an event.

Writing the Developing Story

As events unfold, a newspaper reports the latest developments to its readers. Often there is a story on the following day, and sometimes a story continues to develop over weeks or months.

The *developing story* begins with the new information in the lead. In the second or third paragraph you write a tie-back to the previous story. A tie-back, you may recall, is a brief review of the previous story. Remember, some readers may not have read the previous story. But be careful not to become bogged down in too many details in the tie-back paragraph. If you spend too much time on it, the reader is likely to forget what the present story is about. After this background, you need a good transition back to the new information. The usual organization of the developing story, then, is:

1. New lead.
2. Tie-back.

3. Transition.
4. Return to the story.

For example, when an American citizen was killed in El Salvador, a developing story that appeared the next day began this way:

Lead   SAN SALVADOR, El Salvador (UPI) — The U.S. Embassy knew of combat on the highway where an American woman was killed and could have informed her family if they had asked before traveling the route, a U.S. official said Friday.

Tie-back   Linda Louise Cancel, 23, a native of Culver City, Calif., was killed Thursday by gunfire from the hills along the Military Route highway, about 70 miles east of San Salvador, the U.S. Embassy said.

Transition   Arrangements were pending for transporting her body back to the United States, said Gregory Lagana, embassy spokesman.

Back to story   When guerrillas set up a roadblock as they did Thursday, they usually put riflemen in nearby hills to protect those on the road and to ensure that all vehicles stop.

Most developing stories are of three kinds. They may:

1. Follow the natural course of events.
2. Affect the course of events through enterprising reporting.
3. Both follow and affect the course of events.

FOLLOWING THE COURSE OF EVENTS

Some follows result from events taking their natural course. In stories of trials or a weather disaster, for example, all the reporter has to do is keep up with them.

In the following sequence of stories a community was about to lose its city manager. Its newspaper kept its citizens informed about the developments. Note especially the leads and tie-backs in the stories following the initial story. The initial story began:

Springfield City Manager Jim Thompson has applied for a job as city manager of Peoria, Ill.

The Peoria Chronicle said Thursday Thompson is among 12 finalists for the city manager's job there.

Peoria's Mayor Ron Myer declined to say whether that's so. Myer did say, however, that there were 87 applicants for the job.

Two weeks later:

Lead   Springfield City Manager Jim Thompson still is in the running for the job of city manager in Peoria, Ill.

Tie-back   Thompson, city manager here for 5½ years, was one of 87 applicants for the job in Peoria. City officials there and Thompson here refuse to discuss the matter.

Transition	But the Peoria Chronicle has reported that Thompson is now among five finalists for the position.
Back to story	The finalists were asked to submit names of references by today. The council may narrow the field further before flying candidates to Peoria for interviews later this month.

Three weeks later:

Lead	Though not the front-runner, Springfield City Manager Jim Thompson has survived another screening for the city manager's job in Peoria, Ill.
Tie-back	The Peoria City Council, in a closed session Thursday, named Thompson as one of three finalists for the position. One of 87 initial applicants, Thompson earlier survived two other screening steps. He should learn within a month whether the job is his.
Transition	But Thompson is not first in line. The Peoria Chronicle said that Thompson's remaining rivals are Glen Yale, 56, Peoria's acting city manager, and Gerald R. Dale, 45, city manager of Vallejo, Calif.
Back to story	Yale is considered the front-runner.

Three weeks later:

Lead	In a surprising turnabout, Springfield City Manager Jim Thompson reportedly has emerged the front-runner for the city manager's job in Peoria, Ill.
Tie-back	Thompson, now one of two finalists, was considered second choice after Glen Yale, Peoria's acting city manager. The Peoria City Council eliminated Gerald R. Dale as a contender.
Transition	The job may now go to Thompson.
Back to story	At a closed meeting Thursday night, the council's consensus was 4 to 3 in favor of Thompson, according to the Peoria Chronicle. The final selection should come within two or three days.

Three days later:

Lead	Weeks of speculation ended last night when Springfield City Manager Jim Thompson announced he has resigned to take the city manager's job in Peoria, Ill.
Tie-back	Thompson, Springfield's city manager for the past 5½ years, was chosen from among 87 applicants for the job. His top contender was Glen Yale, Peoria's acting city manager, who until recent days was considered the front-runner.
Transition	Thompson's announcement came in the middle of the Springfield City Council meeting.
Back to story	His resignation is effective July 1, and he will begin work in Peoria July 5. The job will mean an $8,150 raise for Thompson.

In each instance the lead gives the new information, the tie-back puts the story into context, and the transition moves the story back to support the lead.

To write the developing story, you must establish reliable sources and consult with them regularly. Don't count on the persons involved to keep you informed. Look for others with a stake in the story. In this case the reporter needed sources in Springfield and in Peoria. No source should be ignored, even if it is another newspaper. It is better, though, to do your own reporting in order to be sure your story is right.

ENTERPRISE

Good reporters do more than keep up with events as they happen. Some stories would die unless reporters found information on their own initiative that otherwise would not be known. Reporters sometimes make the story happen.

When the city of Wichita, Kan., became involved with the Panhandle Eastern Pipeline Co. in a $1.25 billion coal gasification project, the Eagle-Beacon became interested in the project. In a long series of articles the newspaper exposed the city's secret dealing. For example, reporters discovered that members of the city's project team were so anxious to avoid detection that they made certain they did not fly on the same plane to meetings with Panhandle Eastern officials. The newspaper then detailed the significant risks the city would be taking if it continued to become involved in this massive, unproven technology.

Because of the newness and complexity of the subject, reporters had to study and learn from the few experts around the country who could discuss the technology involved. Because of their diligence and persistence, the citizens of Wichita were told what city officials were not telling them. As a result, citizens voted down a multimillion dollar bond issue that was to fund the coal gasification plant, and the Eagle-Beacon won numerous awards for its coverage.

Good reporters are enterprising; they are full of energy and initiative. They are curious, inquisitive and skeptical. They ask the readers' questions: Why? What next? How does this affect me? What is this going to cost me? Virtually every news event has unanswered questions. Answer them.

FOLLOWING AND AFFECTING THE COURSE OF EVENTS

Many times a developing story will do both: keep up with events as they happen, and affect the course of events through enterprising reporting. Such was the case, for example, in The Louisville (Ky.) Courier-Journal's Pulitizer Prize–winning coverage of the Beverly Hills Supper Club fire in Southgate, Ky. Here are excerpts from that continuing coverage:

May 30:

Course of events

Firemen continued to search for bodies in the burnt-out rubble of the Beverly Hills Supper Club yesterday after what Gov. Julian Carroll called "the worst tragedy in Kentucky's history."

Meanwhile, officials began looking into the cause of the blaze that left at least 200 people dead — and possibly as many as 400 — and considering ways to prevent future tragedies.

June 10:

Course of events

The electrical engineer who headed a private company's investigation that pinpointed the cause of a fire at the Beverly Hills Supper Club said yesterday that he is now being kept out of the building by irate state officials.

Jim Donnelly, an engineer with Systems Engineering Associates (SEA), which conducted the investigation for Travelers Insurance Co., said that state police Commissioner Ken Bradenburgh apparently is angry because the result of the company's investigation was leaked to the press.

June 12:

Enterprise

The black smoke that filled the Beverly Hills Supper Club minutes after the May 28 fire was discovered may have contained deadly cyanide gases, The Courier-Journal has learned.

Laboratory tests performed for The Courier-Journal show that cyanides were present in smoke produced by burning foam-rubber padding in chairs identical to those at the supper club.

June 13:

Enterprise

The Beverly Hills Supper Club was built in violation of a 30-year-old building code that requires automatic sprinkler systems and other fire-prevention measures, The Courier-Journal has learned.

The plush nightclub, which burned May 28 killing 164 people, had no sprinkler system.

July 20:

Enterprise

The Beverly Hills Supper Club was opened to the public in 1971 in violation of several fire laws despite warnings from state fire officials and a grand jury investigation.

Plans for the club, which was to be "the showplace of the nation," were not submitted to the state until two months before it was judged ready for occupancy, according to records in the state fire marshal's office.

And those plans list 10 major design flaws, which apparently were never corrected before the May 28 fire that killed 164 people.

Sept. 19:

Course of events

The report of the state's investigation into last May's fire at the Beverly Hills Supper Club outlines many violations of state and federal fire safety standards, terming some of them intentional.

"Surely the most culpable acts that created and contributed to maintenance of fire hazards were intentional violations of known safety standards," the report said.

Sept. 20:

Enterprise

The state's investigation of the fire at the Beverly Hills Supper Club, which has already caused a major shake-up in the state fire marshall's office, may produce other bombshells.

The investigation is far from complete, said Ovid Lewis, the law school professor who wrote much of the report about the May 28 fire at the Southgate, Ky., club that killed 164 people.

Lewis pointed out three critical areas for further investigation during an exclusive interview with The Courier-Journal following his testimony before a congressional subcommittee yesterday.

Sept. 24:

Enterprise

Two of the three employees of the Kentucky fire marshal's office who were suspended in the wake of the Beverly Hills fire investigation admitted knowledge of violations at the supper club but took no action.

Oct. 24:

Enterprise

State fire officials, who have denied any knowledge of fire code violations at the Beverly Hills Supper Club before the May 28 fire, were informed of violations by one of their inspectors in 1973 or 1974.

The Courier-Journal has learned that Deputy Fire Marshal John Bramiage reported the violations after inspecting the club in one of those years.

The violations, listed in a report found recently in the basement of the Capital Plaza Building in Frankfort, were never corrected. The fire at the Southgate, Ky., club killed 164 people.

Jan. 1, 1978:

Course of events

Spurred by disaster and new federal laws, the 1978 General Assembly is expected to consider several public safety measures.

High on the priority list of both the administration and the legislators are bills that would revamp and strengthen the state fire marshal's office.

Concern about enforcement of the state fire codes grew out of a fire at Beverly Hills Supper Club. The club in Southgate, Ky., burned May 28, killing 164 people.

An exhaustive state investigation revealed numerous violations of the fire code at the club, haphazard record keeping by the fire marshal's office and confusion among state and local officials over who was responsible for enforcing the code.

When the embers of the supper club fire had cooled, reporter Richard Whitt of The Courier-Journal did not leave. He kept looking, asking questions. Dissatisfied with official reports, he conducted his own investigations and even undertook some tests of his own. The follows that he produced are classic examples of a combination of developing stories and enterprise.

Writing an Update

A third type of follow is the *update*. After a story about a person or a situation has been published, a later look may result in another story, possibly of major significance. Newspapers often have been criticized for hit-and-run reporting, for arousing the curiosity or the ire of citizens and then dropping the matter. Because of that criticism and because of reader interest, some newspapers have begun regular sections of update stories.

A good example of a simple update began with this routine story:

The Springfield police will continue spot-checks, which have helped reduce the number of Springfield vehicles without city license stickers.

The spot-checks, like Tuesday's of 300 vehicles, 17 of which were cited for failure to possess a city sticker, have helped enforce the city's vehicle tax law, Police Maj. Bill Smith said. The checks are not aimed at catching any particular violation but are general inspections of the car and its driver.

At about the time of the spot-checks "the lines seem to start forming" at the city cashier's window, said W. J. McGee of the city business license office, but there are still many vehicle owners who neglect the vehicle tax law because "it's still too hard to enforce."

McGee said about 16,000 stickers were sold in September 1985, but that now there may be 5,000 vehicles in the city without stickers. The permits are valid for a year, from October to October, and can be bought at any time.

A week later a check on the sale of city stickers resulted in the following update story:

If the response to last week's vehicle spot-checks by Springfield police is any indication, the average Springfield citizen's sense of civic responsibility may need an occasional nudge.

The nudge this time came in the form of news that motorists without their required city-tax stickers were prime targets of vehicle inspectors. That bit of information brought a deluge of sticker buyers to the city cashier's office.

Police Maj. Bill Smith said the spot-checks were not directed specifically against any particular violation. Still, their effect on sticker purchases has been marked. Seventeen drivers were cited for sticker violation in last Tuesday's check of 300 cars.

"When it came out in the paper, we had them lined up" to buy stickers, a city cashier said Monday. "All three (cashiers) sell maybe 10 to 20 stickers on a normal day," she said, "but last Thursday and Friday definitely were not normal. I would guess I alone had at least 100 the first day."

The lead of the update story refers immediately to the news of the week before. The quote in the fourth paragraph talks about the effects of the newspaper story. An enterprising reporter suspected that the first story might cause some motorists to buy stickers. He was right.

If the story has not come to the readers' attention for a long period of time, you must help by giving more background information on the original story. Nearly a year after a series of articles about a missing girl, for example, a reporter wrote this update:

Mary Dorset never arrived at work that Saturday, Aug. 7, 1983.

Her sister Betty found her apartment open, her unfed cat outside the front door. All her clothing was there. Even her shoes were in the apartment. Betty said she must have left barefooted.

Mary Dorset, who was 23 when she disappeared, was living in Springfield after dropping out as an education major at the university.

In the 13 months since her disappearance, police have traced dozens of separate leads in trying to locate her. Nothing has been successful.

Maj. Will Jones of the Springfield police, the man who led the search for Mary Dorset, says the case has been a puzzling one from the start.

"It's peculiar we couldn't trace her movements better than we did," Jones says. "People who should have known something didn't know at all. It was just strange."

The story then reviewed the leads police had followed in trying to find Mary Dorset. The piece concluded:

Yet Jones says he is not ready to give up. "I haven't closed the case out yet. I'm still hunting her. I'm not going to quit on her yet.

"It gnaws at you," he says. "Her picture is still hanging in there on the bulletin board."

Although the story is not a happy one, readers have had a question answered that may have bothered them from time to time: Did they ever find Mary Dorset?

Other good examples of updates are stories measuring a politician's campaign promises against his or her performance one or two years later, or those checking whether a law has been effective in correcting the abuses the legislators intended it to correct. Sometimes an update has nostalgic appeal: Whatever happened to . . . ?

If a story is worth writing in the first place, it probably is worth following — a day, a week, a month, a year later. Readers are interested. It's up to you to satisfy that interest.

PART FOUR

Effective Writing

14

The Importance of Good Writing

Surveying news rooms full of reporters, many editors are asking: Where are the writers? The editor who picks up the paper and reads this lead has reason to ask.

> The Planning and Zoning Commission Thursday approved a petition to downzone land in the east-campus area from multifamily to two-family use.

But the editor who finds this account of the same meeting knows there is at least one writer on the staff:

> There is "a time to be born, a time to die, a time to rezone," Mark Stevenson reminded the Planning and Zoning Commission Thursday night. And this is not the time, he argued, to rezone the neighborhood east of the university.
> The commission, while not addressing the first two points, decided that the time to rezone, at least, had come.

The time also has come to re-emphasize the importance of good writing. Editors are demanding it. Whenever organizations such as

Figure 14.1 Encouraging Good Writing. Syndicated columnist James Kilpatrick urges writers to take greater care in practicing their craft.

the Associate Press Managing Editors convene, there is talk of the need to stress writing skills. The editors once heard syndicated columnist James Kilpatrick, himself an expert writer, challenge them:

> If 99 percent of what we write is instantly blown away with the wind, well that is how the world is. I would suggest to you . . . if we write upon the sand, let us write as well as we can upon the sand before the waves come in.

If Kilpatrick's challenge to your pride is not enough, then the demands of the editors who are doing the hiring and of the readers who are doing the buying should be. One journalist whose prose is not being washed away with the sand is Saul Pett, special correspondent for The Associated Press. Consider this excerpt about New York Mayor Ed Koch, in which Pett matches his writing cadence to his subject:

> He is the freshest thing to blossom in New York since chopped liver, a mixed metaphor of a politician, the antithesis of the packaged leader, irrepressible, candid, impolitic, spontaneous, funny, feisty, independent, uncowed by voter blocs, unsexy, unhandsome, unfashionable and altogether charismatic, a man oddly at

peace with himself in an unpeaceful place, a mayor who presides over the country's largest Babel with unseemly joy.

The writer — and the mayor — set a breathless pace. Washington Post writer Henry Mitchell brings dry wit to an account of a genteel sport:

> Up rose the sun, and up rose 100 of the nation's most energetic basset hounds to streak through the woods of Loudoun County, Va., in search of their quarry at 6:30 a.m. yesterday morning.
>
> The rabbit was seen many times in the ensuing hours, though not often by the bassets.

Good writing such as this is seen frequently these days, though not often enough by newspaper readers. Too much of what we put on newsprint is dull, awkward and pedestrian. As a result, many editors feel they need to improve the writing in their papers. Editors are searching their staffs for writers and are finding many of them in the lifestyle sections, where they have fled during the past 10 years. Some of these writers are returning now to news. Others who never left have been stimulated by the lifestyle writers' attention to writing quality. Many papers have writing coaches; others sponsor clinics on writing. One result of this emphasis on quality of writing is that when an editor assigns an otherwise routine story, instead of a pedestrian piece, today's reporter may give it a twist. Reporters did just that in the following leads:

> Warm comes in varying degrees:
> The warm that came to Des Moines Thursday was 32 degrees — but that was cause for rejoicing as the city's record cold spell came to an end.

> NEW YORK — The friendly skies looked distinctly gray Wednesday as the British-American dogfight over trans-Atlantic air fares heated up again.

> For people faced with things so bad they wouldn't touch them with a 10-foot pole, Neiman-Marcus' Christmas gift catalogue has the perfect gift — an 11-foot pole.

Because dull writing is more common than writing that has vitality, editors are looking for those unusual people who can combine reporting and writing talents. The journalist whose prose jerks around the page like a mouse trapped in a room with a cat has no future in the business. The days when a reporter could hide behind the talents of a rewrite desk are over. To emphasize that point, in 1979 the American Society of Newspaper Editors made improved writing one of its principal long-range goals. Each year, in cooperation with the Poynter Institute of St. Petersburg, Fla., it awards $1,000 to the winners in several categories of the writing competition it sponsors. The winning entries are published by the institute in a book series entitled, "Best Newspaper Writing."

Many well-known writers — among them, Daniel Defoe, Stephen Crane, Mark Twain and Ernest Hemingway — began their careers as journalists. A more recent list would include the names John Hersey, Tom Wolfe and Gay Talese as well. Two of the recent Pulitzer Prize winners — Saul Pett of The Associated Press and Teresa Carpenter, a contract writer for The Village Voice — won as much for their writing as for their reporting. On newspapers around the country today, small but growing numbers of journalists are producing literature daily as they deal with everything from accidents to affairs of state. If you have the craftsman's respect for the language, the artist's imagination and the dedication to learn how to combine them, you too may produce literature. We cannot teach you how to write, but we can offer some guidelines to help you learn how.

We should all attempt to bring quality writing, wit and knowledge to our work. If we succeed, newspapers will be not only informative, but also enjoyable; not only educational, but also entertaining; and not only bought, but also read.

In this chapter you will learn:

1. Five characteristics of all good writing.
2. How the skills of reporting make good writing possible.

Elements of Good Writing

Good writing has five characteristics:

1. It is precise.
2. It is clear.
3. It has a pace appropriate to the content.

**Figures 14.2–14.3
Early Newspaperman.**
Mark Twain, known today to most people as a book author, began his career as a newspaper reporter and editor. He first gained national fame with his letters sent to newspapers while on a cruise in 1867.

TERRITORIAL-Enterprise
Mark Twain, Editor 1863
Virginia City, Nevada.

4. It uses transitional devices that lead the reader from one thought to the next.
5. It appeals to the reader's senses.

Let's look at each of these characteristics.

PRECISION

Precisely — that is the way words should be used. They should mean exactly what you intend them to mean. You should never use "uninterested" when you mean "disinterested." Nor should you use "allude" for "refer," "presume" for "assume," "endeavor" for "try," "fewer" for "less," "farther" for "further." If you report that fire has destroyed a house, you mean it must be rebuilt, not repaired. If you say firefighters donned oxygen masks to enter a burning building, you are impugning either their intelligence or yours. Oxygen is dangerous around fire; firefighters use air tanks. You can make the mayor "say," "declare," "claim" or "growl" — but only one is accurate.

Words are the tools of your trade. Like the mechanic who uses a three-sixteenth-inch wrench for a specific nut, the writer can use only certain words in certain situations. Unlike the mechanic, who can choose only that one wrench, the writer has many words from which to choose. That freedom can be both exhilarating and dangerous.

Freedom in word choice is exhilarating when the result is a well-turned phrase. Consider this description of Lexington, Kentucky's, caste system written by Sally Quinn of The Washington Post:

> One's social situation is more or less defined by one's horse situation: i.e., whether you've got 'em or you don't.

But freedom is dangerous when it results in nouns masquerading as verbs (prioritize, impact, maximize) or jargon masquerading as respectable English (input, output and throughput). Kilpatrick has a cure for this ailment:

> When your reporters feel the innovative impulse, suggest that they lie down until it goes away.

Precision, however, means more than knowing the etymology of a word; it means knowing precisely what you want to say. Instead of saying, "The City Council wants to locate the landfill three blocks from downtown," to be precise, you say, "Some members of the City Council . . ." Or better yet, "Five members of the City Council . . ."

Precision means writing in the conditional when discussing proposals:

Incorrect: The bill *will* make it illegal . . .

Correct: The bill *would* make it illegal . . .

The use of "will" is imprecise because the legislation has not been passed. By using "would," you are saying, "If the legislature passes the bill, it would . . ."

CLARITY

Before typing a single word, reporters should remind themselves of three simple rules:

1. Rely on simple sentences.
2. Use correct grammar.
3. Think clearly.

The result will be clear writing.

Simple Sentences

The readers of one newspaper once confronted the following one-sentence paragraph:

> "Paradoxically, cancer-causing mutations often result from the repair of a cell by error-prone enzymes and not the 'carcinogenic' substance's damage to the cell," Abe Eisenstark, director of biological sciences at the university, said at a meeting of the Ad Hoc Council of Environmental Carcinogenesis Wednesday night at the Cancer Research Center.

If there is a message in those 53 words, it would take a copy editor, a lexicologist and a Nobel Prize–winning scientist to decipher it. The message simply is not clear. Although the sentence is not typical of newspaper writing, it is not unusual either. Too much of what is written is mumbo jumbo. For instance:

> Approximately two billion tons of sediment from land erosion enter our nation's waters every year. While industrial waste and sewage treatment plants receive a great deal of attention, according to the Department of Agriculture the number one polluter of our waterways is "non-point" pollution.

The writer of that lead contributed some linguistic pollution of his own. The message may have been clear in his mind, but it became trapped in a maze of complex sentences, ambiguous phrases and misplaced modifiers.

One remedy for unclear writing is the simple sentence. The following has impact because the message is stated clearly in a simple sentence:

> NEW YORK — The moon may still be wobbling from a colossal meteorite impact 800 years ago.

Contrast that lead with this complex sentence on the same subject:

> NEW YORK — From measurements with high-precision laser beams bounced off reflectors left at three lunar sites by Apollo astronauts, plus one atop an unmanned Soviet lunar vehicle, scientists believe that the moon is still wobbling from a colossal meteorite impact 800 years ago.

The reader probably is wobbling, too.

Grammatical Usage

Errors in grammar are far too common in newspaper writing, and because of them, meaning is obscured. Consider this example:

> The Senate Tuesday rejected another attempt to block adoption of a tax increase proposal by weighing it down with complicating amendments.

Because of the loose sentence structure, the reader cannot be sure whether the proponents or the opponents of the measure tried to defeat the tax increase by attaching the amendments. The phrase "by weighing it down with complicating amendments" incorrectly modifies the Senate. Because of its placement, some readers may assume it refers to the tax increase proposal, which is also incorrect. The phrase is supposed to modify "opponents," but that term does not even make an appearance in the sentence. The sentence could have been rewritten this way:

```
The Senate Tuesday rejected another attempt to stop
adoption of legislation to raise taxes. Opponents had
tried to block the increase by adding amendments.
```

No one who aspires to be a writer will succeed without knowing the rules of grammar. Dangling participles, split infinitives, noun-verb disagreements, pronoun-antecedent disagreements and misplaced modifiers are like enemy troops: They attack your sentences and destroy the meaning. The best defense is to construct tight, strong sentences. Here are some typical errors and ways to correct them:

Incorrect antecedent:	Each of the boys brought their sleeping bags.
Correct:	Each of the boys brought his sleeping bag.
Dangling participle:	The mayor told the taxpayer to submit a claim to the clerk, bringing it to her before noon.
Correct:	The mayor told the taxpayer to submit a claim to the clerk before noon.
Split infinitive:	The mayor agreed to soon submit his resignation.
Correct:	The mayor agreed to submit his resignation soon.
Misplaced modifier:	Despite his size, the coach said Jones would play forward.
Correct:	The coach said that Jones, despite his size, would play forward.

Clear Thinking

A story must have a beginning, middle and end. Put in a maze, rats make many mistakes before they find their way out. So do writers who start a sentence, a paragraph or a story without knowing where it will end. The problem is most obvious when the reporter is unsure of the lead. The result usually is a story that jumps from one idea to another without transitions and without supporting evidence for each idea introduced. When you are sure of your lead, the rest of the story often will fall in place.

If you cover a meeting at which the city council votes on five ordinances, lead with the most important one. If the other votes are important enough to merit early mention, summarize them in the second paragraph. Support your lead, then pick up the rest of the action. For example:

Lead	The Springfield City Council voted Tuesday to make four streets in the downtown area one-way.
Summarize other action:	The council also raised parking fines to $5, voted to buy two snowplows, ordered a study of downtown parking facilities and hired a firm to audit the city.
Support lead:	Effective March 1, the four streets that will be one-way are . . .

Too many reporters would try to work several of the council actions into the lead and then would not know where to go in the second and third paragraphs.

You must guide your readers through the story. If you do not know the trail, both you and your readers will get lost.

PACING

The untrained observer looking at a new car may see the glossy finish, flashy chrome and stylish lines. An engineer may see the hundreds of complicated working parts under the hood.

Like the untrained observer, the reader enjoys a story because of the message. Another writer will recognize the author's skillful use of techniques that make the story readable.

One of those rarely noticed but important techniques is pacing. Sentences, as much as the words themselves, give a story mood. Short sentences convey action, tension, movement. A series of long sentences conveys a more relaxed mood; long sentences slow down the reader.

Between these two extremes are sentences of varying lengths, and good writers use them all. Not all sentences should be long. Or short. Nor should they all be of medium length. An abrupt change in sentence length draws attention to the sentence. Try it sometime.

Giving the precisely selected words the proper pace is a skill of the creative writer. Describing the assassination of President Kennedy, some writers used short, clipped sentences to convey the frantic atmosphere. The cadence of the sentences describing the funeral was slow, reflecting the rhythmic pace of the lone black horse as it led the slain president's bier down Pennsylvania Avenue.

The pace also was appropriately slow when Greta Tilley described her visit to the home of a 16-year-old high school girl who had committed suicide. Tilley, a reporter for the Greensboro (N.C.) News and Record, relied on moderate to long sentences to describe the scene:

On this cold January morning, the bed is covered with school homework papers, letters, a directory of colleges, a family photo album and high school and junior high yearbooks, which Douglas Oxendine eagerly has taken from his daughter's closet and drawers to help open her life to a stranger.

Near the spot where the rifle once was lodged is a large cardboard box. Inside are nine manila envelopes, each tagged with a Greensboro Police Department label.

In the hours after Tonja's death, Detective Ken Brady was particularly interested in the single sheet of notebook paper marked "Evidence No. 12." In uneven, penciled script, lines of poetry are listed along with corresponding page numbers that show where the poems can be found in the 11th-grade literature book, "Encounters." Each poem is about death.

Although the sentences are long, there is variety. They range from five to 49 words. Rhythm does not mean sameness.

Some writers read their copy aloud to themselves. Their ear tells them if the story has the proper pace and variety. The beginning writer should count the number of words in each sentence.

Variety not only in length of consecutive sentences but from one part of the story to another is what UPI's George Frank wrote into his account of the attempted assassination of Gerald Ford. Notice that in the opening section, the pace is leisurely, as is the peaceful and relaxed scene in the park. When the would-be assassin lunges forward, the sentences become staccato:

22	SACRAMENTO, Calif. (UPI) — The day was sunny and beautiful, and the tiny woman in red waited with other spectators for President Ford to walk by.
10	Most of the well-wishers wanted to shake Ford's hand.
7	The woman in red had a gun.
31	Lynette Alice Fromme, 27, known as "Squeaky" in the terrorist Charles Manson family to which she belongs, stood quietly behind the spectators on the grounds of the state capitol, eyewitnesses said.
15	"Oh, what a beautiful day," she told a girl in the crowd, Karen Skelton, 14.
8	"She looked like a gypsy," Karen said later.
15	Squeaky wore a long red gown and red turban, and carried a large, red
5	purse. They matched her red hair.
25	On her forehead was a red "X" carved during the 1971 Los Angeles trial in which Manson and three women followers were convicted of murder.
22	Squeaky, who had moved to Sacramento in northern California to be closer to the imprisoned Manson, 41, waited patiently for President Ford.
9	In her purse was a loaded .45 caliber automatic.
4/9	The sun beat down. The spectators squirmed in the 90-plus-degree heat.
6	Then, suddenly, the crowd perked up. Ford had emerged from the Senator
20	Hotel and was coming up a sidewalk through the park of the capitol grounds.
5	Secret Service agents accompanied him.
8	He stopped to return greetings from the crowd.
11	The spectators, restrained by a rope, pressed forward to say hello.
12	He faced to his left and reached out for the extended hands.

11   "Good morning," he said to the well-wishers, one after another.

4   Squeaky made her move.

14   She lunged forward from the rear of spectators, splitting them away on both sides.

17   Now she was only two feet from the president and, said police, aimed the gun at him.

15   Ford saw the revolver and "the color went out of his face," said Karen Skelton.

14   He looked "alarmed, frightened, and he hunched over," said another spectator, Roy Miller, 50.

18   At that moment, Secret Service Agent Larry Buendorf took the action that may have saved the president's life. Risking his own life, he lunged forward
14   and threw himself between Squeaky and Ford.

12   He wrestled Squeaky to the ground, and he and police disarmed her.

6   Squeaky screamed, "He's not your servant."

9   Then she told police, "Easy, guys, don't batter me. The gun didn't go off."

5   Four or five agents threw themselves around the president and pushed him
16   away from the crowd.

14   Ford's knees, troubled in the past, buckled in the crush, and he almost
5   stumbled. But he stood up quickly.

12   "The country is in a mess," shouted Squeaky as officers handcuffed her.
6   "The man is not your president."

20   Moments later, as a police car drove her away, she had a faint smile on her face and appeared calm.

Before Frank reports that Fromme was carrying a gun in her purse, the average sentence length is 16 words. From that point, where the tension begins to build, until the last line, the average sentence length is only 10 words.

TRANSITIONS

Besides being well-paced, good writing also uses transitions to lead the reader imperceptibly from one thought to the next. Transitions assure the reader that the writer has a sense of direction. A transition is a bridge. It can be a word, a phrase, a sentence or a paragraph. The reference to "memory" transports us from the first to the second paragraph in this example:

> Mr. and Mrs. Lester Einbender are using their memory to project life as it might have been.
>
> That memory centers around a son named Michael, a rheumatic disease called lupus and a desire to honor one while conquering the other.

The word "That" in "That memory" is a demonstrative adjective. Its use is subtle, but its impact is dramatic. If you write "A memory," you are not linking the reader to the memory already mentioned; if you write "The memory," you are being more specific; if you write "That memory," you are pointing directly at the memory in the preceding paragraph. Because it is good only for general references, "a" is called an indefinite modifier; because it is more specific, "the" is called a definite modifier; because it is most specific, "that" is called a demonstrative. It demonstrates precisely the word or phrase to which you are referring.

These linkages help you achieve coherence, the logical connection of ideas. The linkages transfer you from one sentence to the next, from one paragraph to the next. The different types of linkages are called transitions. Writers unfamiliar with transitions merely stack paragraphs, like wood, atop one another. Transitions keep the story, if not the woodpile, from falling apart.

Repeating a word or phrase is one way to keep the story from falling apart. In the example above, the writer used both a demonstrative adjective (others include "this," "these" and "those") and repeated a word. Another way is to use the demonstrative as a pronoun. Reporting on an interview with Idi Amin, then president of Uganda, a writer used "that" as a pronoun to create a smooth transition:

> "I am protected by God," Amin, a Moslem, said recently. "I am not afraid of any man because I know when I am going to die."
>
> That, apparently, will not be soon. He told Ugandans in January that he planned to guide their fortunes indefinitely.

Repetition of a phrase or of sentence construction, called parallelism, is another way to guide readers through a story. Writers frequently use parallelism to achieve coherence.

Writing about the complicated subject of nuclear-waste disposal in America, Donald Barlett and James Steele of The Philadelphia Inquirer relied on parallelism for coherence and emphasis:

> This assessment may prove overly optimistic. For perhaps in no other area of modern technology have so many experts in the government, industry and science been so wrong so many times over so many years as have those involved in radioactive waste.
>
> They said, repeatedly, that radioactive waste could be handled like any other industrial refuse. It cannot.
>
> They said that science had most of the answers, and was on the verge of getting the few it did not have, for dealing with radioactive waste permanently. It did not, and it does not.

They said that some of it could be buried in the ground, like garbage in a landfill, and that it would pose no health hazard because it would never move. It moved.

They said that liquid radioactive waste could be put in storage tanks, and that rigorous safety systems would immediately detect any leaks. The tanks leaked for weeks and no one noticed.

Chronology and references to time are other ways to tie a story together. Words and phrases such as "now," "since then," and "two days later," are invaluable in helping readers understand where they have been and where they are going. Chronology is important in everything from reports of automobile accidents (which car entered the intersection first?) to recaps of events that occurred over months or even years. For instance, Barlett and Steele's stories covered 35 years of efforts to store nuclear waste.

Transitions include but are not limited to "and," "but" and "however." A word, a phrase, a thought, like a road sign, leads the reader from one paragraph to the next. The linkages that make the following story coherent are shown by the connecting lines.

WASHINGTON — The invitation read: "Carolyn Deaver, Fred J. Hayman and Marvin S. Traub invite you . . ."

In Washington, the names of Hayman and Traub would normally draw little attention. They are presidents of high-priced emporiums — Giorgio's of Rodeo Drive in Beverly Hills and Bloomingdale's — but they are not everyday names in this town of name-droppers.

On the other hand, the name Deaver is another matter. Just ask Carolyn Deaver, the wife of Michael K. Deaver, the deputy chief of staff at the White House.

"It's a plus," she conceded with a smile as she discussed plans for a luncheon and fashion show she was organizing to introduce "Giorgio," a perfume to be carried by Bloomingdale's here.

"But," she added, wise to Washington ways, "I have a feeling that when you are out of power, it can fade just as quickly."

Mrs. Deaver is a consultant with Mary Pettus & Associates, a public relations company that specializes in organizing events such as the perfume luncheon. How does she go about her work?

"Fred Hayman is a friend who has done some very nice things for us in the past," said Mrs. Deaver. "He telephoned and said he'd like it very much if I could help him out in introducing his new fragrance line in Washington. Since we also represent the Hay Adams Hotel, we thought we'd have the luncheon at the hotel and show the Washington ladies what was going on there in terms of renovation as well."

The Washington ladies turned out in force. Ambassadorial and congressional wives, as well as administration figures and well-known faces from the social scene, gathered at yellow and white tables decorated with freesia to dine on salmon as the scent of Giorgio wafted across the room.

SENSORY APPEAL

As you chauffeur the reader through the scenes in your story, you can drive down the road or over the green-laced, rolling hills of Kentucky. You can report that a car hit a skunk, or you can convey the nauseating smell. A word here, a phrase there and you hear the plane ripping the tin roof off the house; smell the acrid tires burning on a flaming car; feel the boxing glove's leather rasp against the skin. Good writing appeals to one or more of our five senses: sight, hearing, smell, taste and touch.

Whether he was reporting or writing a novel, Ernest Hemingway appealed to the reader's senses. Reporting for The New York Times from Madrid during the Spanish Civil War, he wrote:

> There is a rifle fire all night long. The rifles go "tacrong, carong, craang, tacrong," and then a machine gun opens up. It has a bigger caliber and is much louder — "rong, cararibg, rong, rong."

Moving to another war and another writer, we get the same sense of detail. Reporting for the Chicago Daily News, Keyes Beech described his flight from Saigon during the panic of the American evacuation from that city in 1975:

> We were only men fighting for our lives, scratching, clawing, pushing ever closer to that wall. We were like animals. . . .
> I lay on a tin roof gasping for breath like a landed fish, then dropped to the ground. God bless the Marines; I was one myself in the last of the just wars.

Through Hemingway's ears, we listen not just to gunfire, but "rong, cararibg, rong, rong." Through Beech's fingers we feel not just a roof, but a tin roof.

Knowing when a detail enhances the story rather than just making it wordy is the skill of an accomplished writer. Some details are as out of place as white tennis shoes with a black business suit. If Beech had written, "Wearing blue denim jeans, white sneakers and a torn blue shirt, I lay on a tin roof gasping for breath like a landed fish . . ." we would laugh instead of marvel at the description. What he was wearing was not important.

But what country music singer Tammy Wynette was wearing was important in a profile of her, and reporter Leola Floren captured the scene this way:

On stage, she is surrounded by musicians in green suits and cowboy boots. Stuck there in the middle, Tammy looks like one smooth pearl in a bucket of peas. Her wavy blond hair tumbles over bare shoulders to the middle of her back. Her black, strapless gown is of the kind the slightly bad girls wore to the senior prom: slit up past the knees in the back, cut so low in front there isn't any decent place to pin a corsage. When she picks up her guitar, you think it ought to be a champagne glass, she looks so elegant.

Another writer gives the reader a visual picture of Johnny Cash on stage: "He moves with the grace of a little boy who has to go to the bathroom." Physical description like this can be helpful in establishing the tone of a piece — in this case, a humorous tone. In other cases, though, it is distracting.

Assigned to cover a dress-up day at a local elementary school, a reporter produced a story that began this way:

Denita Perrigo, 10, went to her fifth-grade class at New Bloomfield Elementary School Wednesday. Dressed as a hillbilly, she wore a *floppy straw hat* and her father's *oversized flannel shirt*, and she sported *Magic-marker freckles*.

That might have been enough to prompt any self-respecting teacher to send Denita to the principal's office — except that the principal was wearing a *sheriff's uniform, circa 1910*, complete with a *tinfoil badge* on his chest.

The writing is better because the reporter wrote not just about what she was told but also about what she observed. The words in italics identify the reporting she did with her eyes.

A reporter once wrote of a landlord and "his pregnant wife" who testified at a city council meeting against a proposed ordinance to license rental units. Because the fact that the landlord's wife was pregnant had no bearing on the story, it was deleted by the editor. If, while testifying, the landlord's wife had fainted, reporting her pregnancy would have been appropriate. The good writer must know when detail is appropriate.

USING ANALOGIES

Good writers also know how to use another literary device called analogy. Analogies permit writers to show similarities and contrasts. Similes show similarities by using "like" or "as": "Tammy looks like one smooth pearl in a bucket of peas." Describing a long-distance runner, another writer used this simile: "Her legs, so rubbery they wobbled like jelly, shook and then surrendered."

The metaphor is the first cousin of the simile. Where the simile compares one thing to another, a metaphor says one thing is another: "Tammy is one smooth pearl in a bucket of peas." A metaphor is a stronger analogy than a simile. Sports columnist Jim Murray once described football coach John Robinson in metaphorical language: "He's the world's biggest Easter rabbit, a marshmallow sundae."

With similes and metaphors, writers draw word pictures. Reading about Tammy Wynette, you see white and green. You picture Robinson as pudgy, friendly, smiling. The techniques set the pages of a scrapbook of images turning in each reader's mind.

The technique of analogy is also important to every journalist trying to make dimensions and numbers meaningful. That's important whether you are writing about the national debt or the size of the offensive guard. You make numbers meaningful by translating them. Writing about the national debt, one college reporter pointed out it was enough to operate the university for decades. No number means much unless it is compared to something else.

Instead of writing that 75 percent of the people in the United States do not know that you are innocent until proven guilty, say that three of four people do not know. Trying to show how far a marathoner runs in a single race, one writer pointed out that it is farther than Jim Brown and Franco Harris, professional football's all-time leading runners, gained together in their entire careers.

Analogies are your film; use them to take word pictures.

Good Writing Begins with Good Reporting

Without the proper ingredients, the best chef is no better than a short-order cook. Without the proper use of participant accounts, personal observation, and detail, the best writer writes dull stories. Good writing begins with good reporting.

INTERVIEWING PARTICIPANTS

A car-truck accident: Is it routine? That depends on the reporting. The writer of the story below gathered information only from lifeless police reports:

A 39-year-old St. Louis man whose car was run over this morning by a truck walked out of Columbia Regional Hospital in good condition and was transferred to a St. Louis hospital.

Wheel marks from a tractor-trailer hauling 25,000 pounds of meat could be seen from the rear of Frank Cramer's 1975 Cadillac along the roof to the front. The car was a total wreck, but Cramer walked away with only minor injuries, according to police reports.

The driver of the truck, Alan Charles Floyd, 24, of Dallas, Texas, was issued a summons for following Cramer's car too closely.

Floyd told police he was attempting to pass Cramer on Interstate 70 near the Business Loop 70 exit when he lost control of his truck. Floyd told police he didn't remember what happened after that.

A witness told police he saw Cramer's car disappear beneath the tractor-trailer.

Cramer said he was headed east in the right lane of I-70 when he saw headlights approaching him from behind. Then he felt a collision. Cramer's vehicle was pushed into a guardrail, then rolled into a ditch. The truck turned on its side.

Floyd was treated for injuries at the University of Missouri-Columbia Medical Center and was released, according to police reports.

Two passengers in the truck, Terry Grider from Rockwell City, Iowa, and Tom Garner from Dallas, Texas, received minor injuries.

A 42-year-old Chesterfield, Mo., man was a passenger in Cramer's vehicle. He also received minor injuries.

The details of an apparently remarkable accident are lost in this dull account.

Another reporter recognized the story's potential. Not only did he use the police report, he talked to both of the passengers in the car and obtained a comment from a police officer. Good reporting permitted the writer to insert the human angle into a terrifying human experience:

Frank Cramer of St. Louis slowed his Cadillac Coupe de Ville late Tuesday night as he entered the construction area along Interstate 70, one-quarter mile west of the Business Loop 70 overpass.

In his rear-view mirror he saw two large headlights bearing down on him, the light reflecting off the rain-slick pavement. Then his car was hit.

Bruce Bynum of Chesterville was a passenger in the car. "I looked behind us, and all I saw was one huge headlight shining in the rear window," he said. "Then it started up over the car and smashed in the glass."

"I can't get the guy off the top of the car!" Cramer yelled.

"Frank," Bynum said, "I think we've had it."

The story is true, and Columbia police say they are surprised that Cramer, 39, and Bynum, 42, lived to

tell it. Cramer's car was run over by a truck hauling 25,000 pounds of frozen meat and driven by Alan Floyd, 24, of Dallas, Texas.

The truck drove over the left side of the car, Bynum said, pinning it against the guardrail and sliding down the highway on top of it.

"I could hear the engine going over us," Bynum said. "It seemed to go on for ever and ever."

At the end of the guardrail the car flew off the road. Bynum said he remembers telling Cramer, "It's all over."

"Yeah," Cramer replied, "things aren't going too well."

The car came to rest in a field 50 feet from the highway.

"I busted my door open and pulled him out," Bynum said. "He was pinned under the roof — it was smashed to the seat." Bynum said that was when he saw the two tire tracks running over the car from trunk to hood.

Cramer and Bynum were taken to Columbia Regional Hospital. Bynum was treated and released, and Cramer transferred in good condition to a St. Louis hospital early Wednesday.

Floyd, 24, and his passenger, Tom Garner, also of Dallas, were treated at the University Medical Center and released.

"It's lucky for all of them that they got out of that one alive," said Columbia police Capt. Carl Antimi. "They shouldn't have."

Bynum, reached Wednesday afternoon at his home, agreed. "It's amazing. I don't know how we got out of it," he said. "I figure we had the 'Force' with us."

Floyd was summoned for careless and imprudent driving, and is scheduled to appear in Magistrate Court Nov. 22.

This version tells the story through the eyes of two of the participants. The detail — the view in the mirror, the reference to the rain-slicked pavement and the effective use of dialogue — puts the reader in the car with the victims.

DIGGING FOR THE TELLING DETAIL

Specific detail gathered by observant and questioning reporters always wins out over general description. A young reporter for the Columbia Missourian learned that the hard way. His assignment began when the city desk heard that an elderly victim of crime committed a week earlier had died in the hospital that evening. The reporter was sent to interview the victim's neighbors, one of whom had seen a man carrying a television out of the victim's house the night she was injured. Suspicious, the neighbor had summoned police, who arrived in time to make the arrest. They found the beaten victim inside the house.

The reporter's first draft was a dry, straightforward account of the neighbor's reactions to the woman's death and the burglary. The story obviously deserved much more.

Did the victim live alone? What is the neighborhood like? Were there many break-ins in that area? Were the neighbors friendly to her? What was her house like? Nearly every question directed at the reporter required him to return to the scene. He had failed to do his reporting.

He wrote a second draft that the city editor was moments from approving. "By the way," the reporter mentioned, "did you know the television set that guy tried to steal didn't even work?" That's when he started writing this third version:

When 11-year-old Tracy Britt visited her neighbor Rose Shock in the small, one-story house just two doors off Providence Road, they just talked, mostly, because the television set was broken.

One week ago tonight, another neighbor, Al Zacher of 300 Wilkes Blvd., heard suspicious noises. Looking outside, he saw a man carrying the television set that didn't work from Mrs. Shock's home. As the man set the television down and headed for a green station wagon, Zacher called the police.

Inside lay Mrs. Shock, battered about the face.

Sunday in Boone County Hospital, where she worked as a dietitian for many years before she retired in 1955, 85-year-old Rose Shock died.

If Mrs. Shock's relatives had their way, she would not have been living in the house with aluminum siding and paint peeling from its window frames at 302 Wilkes Blvd. After her house was burglarized last summer, her family tried to convince her to move.

"She didn't seem to be too alarmed to be living by herself," her sister, Ruth Tremaine of 306 Hartley Court, said Monday: "She'd been living there 18 or 19 years and she was happier there than she would have been anywhere else. We wanted her to go, but she just wanted to stay in her own home."

Widowed since 1948, Mrs. Shock, cane in hand, would walk around the yard and talk to her neighbors. Gladys and Paul Ray of 410 Wilkes Blvd. lived near her for several years. To them, she was a "nice, gentle, kind person."

Ruth Britt, who lived around the corner at 804 N. Fourth St., had been to Mrs. Shock's home a few times with her children.

"I didn't even know her last name," she said. "We just always called her Rosie."

"My children loved her, and, as old as she was, she was always glad to see them."

Mrs. Shock's home is located in a neighborhood caught between a spreading downtown commercial district and Business Loop 70. Before and after school, the unkempt city streets and sidewalks teem with students from Jefferson Junior High School and Hickman High School. When Mrs. Shock bought the house, Columbia had a population of about 30,000 and Providence Road was just being expanded from two lanes to four lanes. In those postwar baby boom years, the seeds for a changing neighborhood were being planted.

Now residents of the neighborhood are afraid.

"When something like this happens close to you, you think about it more," said Mrs. Ray.

Some residents spoke bluntly about their fear of burglary and refused to give their names because they believed it increased their chances of being victimized. A woman who lives down the street from the Shock home says, "They ought to string a few of them up down at the courthouse. That might teach them a lesson."

Another neighbor also criticized the system.

"They're letting them get by too easy," said Dorothy Mustain of 304 Wilkes Blvd. "If they'd punish them more so they'd have to suffer like the ladies they're beating up, maybe that would put a stop to it."

David Herron, 45, of 207 Providence Walkway, is being held in lieu of $100,000 bond in connection with the incident. He is charged with assault with intent to kill, carrying a concealed weapon and first-degree robbery.

Prosecuting Attorney Milt Harper said Monday he will meet with the medical examiner Thursday before deciding whether to file additional charges. He is waiting for results of autopsy tests to be returned from Jefferson City.

Monday night, flashing red lights atop Columbia police cars once again lit up the Wilkes Boulevard neighborhood. Police were investigating a report of a burglary at Zacher's house.

We see dirty streets, hear crowds of students walking down the sidewalk in front of Rose Shock's house, see the aluminum siding and feel the peeling paint. We learn that Mrs. Shock died in the hospital where she worked for many years. We know, too, the sad irony that she was killed over a broken television set.

Good writing does not require the talent of a Dickens or a Hemingway. Good reporting makes good writing possible.

Suggested Readings

Barzun, Jacques. "Simple & Direct." New York: Harper & Row, 1975. An excellent rhetoric book that explains many of the details of sentence construction.

Bernstein, Theodore. "The Careful Writer." Boston: Atheneum, 1975. An excellent desk book for people concerned with both grammar and the precision of their language.

The Missouri Group. "The Writing Book." Englewood Cliffs, N.J.: Prentice-Hall Inc., 1984. Book-length treatment of chapters 14 and 15 in "News Reporting and Writing."

Strunk, William, and E.B. White. "The Elements of Style." 3rd ed. New York: Macmillan, 1979. This little book practices what it preaches. For the beginner it is a good primer; for the pro it is a good review of writing rules and the meaning of words.

15

Alternatives to the Inverted Pyramid

For all its strengths, the inverted pyramid has a telling weakness: It cannot maintain, let alone build, reader interest as the story progresses. After the first three paragraphs, it is not going to get any better. It doesn't have to be that way all the time. Good writing and alternative story forms have always been available to journalists to tell stories. Whether it is spot news or a personality profile, the information can be handled in a variety of ways that will meet readers' needs. Some writers recognize that already. As a result, occasionally readers are treated to the exception:

> Friday night they had double-dated to the movies in Independence. Saturday they had driven to a friend's party in Sibley. Sunday they were all dead.
>
> Four Independence teen-agers, two still in high school and two friends since kindergarten, were killed late Saturday night.

Even though these two paragraphs open a spot news story, the traditional who, what, when, where, why and how don't come until after the first paragraph.

Alternative approaches such as this have been used for some time for other kinds of stories. These include:

1. *Backgrounders*, which explain and update the news.
2. *Investigative pieces*, which reveal information and make news.
3. *Profiles*, which explain people and organizations.
4. *Human-interest* stories, which describe people.
5. *Brighteners*, which bring a smile to the reader.

Profiles, human-interest pieces and brighteners traditionally are lumped under the heading "features." What they have in common is the lack of a hard news event. The stories are not event-oriented.

Many textbooks have chapters on feature writing. This one doesn't because the authors believe that the literary techniques of good writing belong in any story, and that any story, event-oriented or not, can be told in a form other than the inverted pyramid. Alternative story structures are not used as often on spot news because deadline pressure sometimes prevents the reporter from gathering anything beyond the basic facts. Space, too, is a consideration. The inverted pyramid requires the fewest words because the most important information comes first. The narrative story form takes longer to get to the point. Detail, and the literary devices used to weave it in, also take precious space.

But when the time and space are available, take advantage of them. Whether you are writing about a car accident, the Boy Scouts, the health-care system, corruption in government or the 8-year-old running the corner lemonade stand, writing the story will be easier if you know some of the alternatives to the inverted pyramid. None of the alternative story forms has attained the widespread use or recognition of the inverted pyramid, and none is as detailed a formula as the inverted pyramid. All, however, help you organize your story and attract readership. And attracting the reader's attention is, after all, part of our job.

In this chapter you will learn:

1. How to structure a story using the focus structure.
2. Two variations of the focus structure.
3. How to write a story using extended dialogue.
4. How to write a story that is organized chronologically.
5. When to use first-person accounts and how to do so effectively.

The Focus Structure

For centuries, writers have used the literary device of telling a story through the eyes of one person or by examining part of the whole. The device makes large institutions, complex issues and seven-digit numbers meaningful. Few of us can comprehend the size of the U.S. budget, but we can understand the numbers on our own paycheck. Not many of us can explain the marketing system for wheat, but we could if we followed a bushel of wheat from the time it was planted until a consumer picked up a loaf of bread in the supermarket.

Even though Joseph Stalin was hardly talking about literary approaches, he summed up the impact of focusing on a part of the whole when he said, "Ten million deaths are a statistic; one death is a tragedy."

Individual newspaper journalists have used the technique often, but no newspaper has seized upon it like The Wall Street Journal. In its daily column-one feature examining national and international issues, the Journal routinely and expertly puts a literary magnifying glass on the individual involved in an issue or institution. Readers who find little to interest them in a story about IBM may read about it if it is told through the eyes of a rising young executive. Those to whom unemployment rates are meaningless may eagerly follow a story about the jobless if it is told through the eyes of a factory worker who has been laid off because the company shut down rather than comply with anti-pollution standards.

This alternative approach, which combines the best of the in-

Figure 15.1 Making It Readable. In its daily column-one story, The Wall Street Journal perfected an organizational formula that permits the reporter to describe large institutions and complex issues in understandable terms.

verted pyramid and the narrative forms, is now used often in newspapers and magazines throughout the country. Robert Reinhold used it for a story in The New York Times about women trying to compete in the electronics industry in Silicon Valley. Rather than talk in general terms about women, he focused on one:

> PALO ALTO, Calif. — Delicate northern lights filtered through the blinds, painting the office with soft colors. Behind the wooden desk, topped with a vase of fresh carnations, sat Carolyn J. Morris, a 39-year-old Texan who was trained as a girl to sit quietly with hands in lap and not argue.
>
> But nothing of what Miss Morris is up to these days is very quiet. At her desk, cluttered with computer printouts and a bottle of aspirin, she is doing what comes naturally in this capital of the American computer and electronics industry: founding her own company.

With a specific example planted in readers' minds, the writer then moved to the larger issue:

> As such, she represents an assertive breed of women who are taking advantage of the free-wheeling entrepreneurial spirit that marks Silicon Valley . . .

The writer has used Carolyn Morris to represent all women entrepreneurs in Silicon Valley. Readers can empathize with her; they can't empathize with issues or institutions. Journalists too often overlook this literary technique.

When they do, the story is usually cold. When there is no one for readers to reach out and touch, they may not read at all. One newspaper mistakenly separated the human touch from the main story, which began this way:

> Roots — they become more important with each passing decade. They are the ties to family, friends, home and community. Roots make the past tangible, the present understandable, and the uncertainty of the future bearable.
>
> But in our increasingly mobile society, families tend to scatter. Senior citizens, often widowed, find it financially or physically difficult to maintain their homes. Many of their friends are in the same situation. Reluctantly, they sell their homes and move to communities where housing and transportation are more affordable.
>
> So the roots get severed.
>
> But not always. Through a shared housing program now offered by the Eden Council of Hope and Opportunity . . .

The sidebar, a second story dealing with the same topic, began this way:

> If you ask Helen Velasques and Es-
> ther Stobeck what they value most
> about the new lives they have built
> for themselves, ''independence''
> would be the response.
> They are two senior citizens who
> have benefited from a concept
> known as ''shared housing.''
> Through the Fremont office of the
> Eden Council of Hope and Opportu-
> nity . . .

The writer would have used less space and gotten better results if she had combined the stories and put the women in the opening.

Reporters working on local stories have just as many opportunities to apply this approach as those writing national and international stories. Instead of being preoccupied with the thousands of dollars your United Way is raising or its campaign organization, for example, you can focus on the people who benefit — or fail to benefit — from the campaign. If the streets in your city are bad, write about the problem from the point of view of a driver. Or if Dutch elm disease is killing the trees in your city, concentrate on a homeowner who has lost several. The focus structure offers the writer a powerful method of reducing institutions, statistics and cosmic issues to a level readers can relate to and appreciate.

Advertising agencies use the technique, too. That's why instead of being solicited for money to help the poor and starving in a foreign country, you are asked to support one child or one family for only pennies a day. The advertising gives poverty and hunger a face. Millions starving are a statistic; one child starving is a tragedy.

STEPS IN APPLYING THE STRUCTURE

The focus structure is applied through an established sequence of steps (see Figure 15.3). Focusing on the individual is the first and most important. Three more steps follow:

1. Providing a transition to the larger issue.
2. Reporting on the issue or institution.
3. Providing a strong finish that returns to the subject of your focus or carries a summary statement.

Let's look at each of these steps.

The Transition

Transitions ease the reader from the personalized openings to the issues being reported. In the article about Silicon Valley, discussed

Put your love to the test.

How much love do you have to give?
Answer these simple questions and find out.

If I saw a lost, frightened child on my street, I would immediately stop and help.
☐ YES ☐ NO

I often feel frustrated and helpless when I see a news story about desperately poor or sick children.
☐ YES ☐ NO

I believe that no child should ever have to do without nourishing food, decent housing, medical care, or schooling.
☐ YES ☐ NO

I think that the best way to help children is not through handouts—but rather, by teaching families to help themselves.
☐ YES ☐ NO

I believe that impoverished children should receive help within their *own* families.
☐ YES ☐ NO

I especially wish there were an effective way I could personally help just *one* desperately poor child and family.
☐ YES ☐ NO

If I could be assured that my money was being spent effectively, I would definitely consider helping.
☐ YES ☐ NO

If I could help a child for as little as 72¢ a day, I would.
☐ YES ☐ NO

If you answered "YES" to these questions, you are the kind of person who *can* help a desperately poor child overseas… through *Foster Parents Plan*. In fact, for just 72¢ a day, you can make it possible for the child you sponsor to have nourishing food, medical care, decent housing, schooling…and hope. Imagine. Your spare change could change a child's life.

Foster Parents Plan lets you help your Foster Child within the child's own family. And more, the small amount you give goes toward teaching families to work together—by growing more food, digging wells, and building schools. You'll see the results for *yourself*. Through pictures. Detailed progress reports. And letters written in your Foster Child's own words.

How can you sponsor a child now and pass the test of love? Just answer "YES" to the rest of these questions, mail this entire application, or call toll-free 1-800-556-7918 today.

To start helping even faster, call toll-free:

1-800-556-7918

In RI call 401-738-5600

Detach and mail this entire application or call toll-free today.

Foster Parents Plan was founded in 1937 and this year will aid over 223,000 Foster Children and their families in more than 20 countries. We are non-profit, non-sectarian, non-political, and respect the culture and religion of the families we assist. Of course, your sponsorship is 100% tax-deductible, and a detailed annual report and financial statement are available on request.

☐ YES. I want to give $22 a month—just 72¢ a day—to sponsor *one* desperately poor child through *Foster Parents Plan* —making it possible for the child and family to have a better life, both now and in the future.

☐ YES. I want to help a: ☐ Boy ☐ Girl ☐ Either
☐ **Wherever the need is greatest,** or as indicated below:
☐ Africa ☐ El Salvador ☐ Indonesia
☐ Bolivia ☐ Guatemala ☐ Nepal
☐ Colombia ☐ Honduras ☐ The Philippines
☐ Egypt ☐ India ☐ Thailand

☐ YES. I want to sponsor a child of about this age:
☐ 3-6 ☐ 7-10 ☐ 11-14 ☐ Any age 3-14.

☐ YES. I have enclosed a check for $22 for my first month's support of my Foster Child. Please send me a photograph, case history, and complete Foster Parent Sponsorship Kit.

☐ NO. I'm not ready to become a Foster Parent yet. But please send me information about the child I would be sponsoring. Within 10 days I'll make my decision. E308

☐ Mr. ☐ Mrs.
☐ Miss ☐ Ms. _____

Address _____ Apt. #

City _____ State _____ Zip
Mail to: Kenneth H. Phillips, National Executive Director
Foster Parents Plan, 157 Plan Way, Warwick, RI 02887

Foster Parents Plan.
Your love *does* make the difference.

Figure 15.2 The Focus Structure. This advertisement for the Foster Parents Plan arouses interest and sympathy in the reader by showing pictures of two potential foster children.

Figure 15.3 Steps in applying the Wall Street Journal Formula.

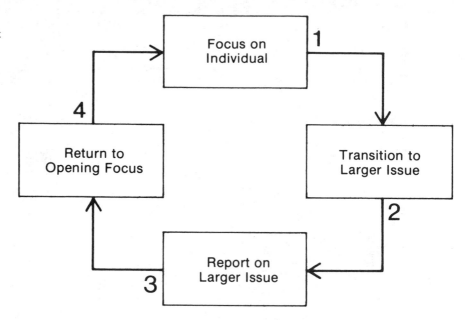

earlier, the transitional paragraph connects Carolyn Morris to all women entrepreneurs. We call it the theme paragraph.

Some writers call this transition the "nut" paragraph. Here the reader learns the reason for the story. The paragraph usually includes most of the information found in the lead of an inverted pyramid story. When The Wall Street Journal reported on changes in bidding procedures at the Pentagon, for three paragraphs it discussed how money could be saved by changing the bid requirements for Worcestershire sauce. The theme paragraph put the relatively unimportant Worcestershire sauce in context:

> The savings of less than four cents a bottle is pint-sized next to the $49 billion the Defense Department will spend this year to arm and supply the military. But Pentagon officials hope to realize more savings on vast numbers of other purchases by dropping specifications for thousands of products and purchasing commercial items instead.

Here the transitional sentence begins with the sauce and ends with the $49 billion projected savings if the bid revision program is successful. This transition from the specific to the general comes in the fourth paragraph. In other stories, it might be in the second, third or fifth. The transition always should come near the top of the story.

Exposition of the Larger Issue

After the transition you begin the exposition of your story. Reporting on this larger issue or institution is your reason for writing. You have left Carolyn Morris in her office. You have left the Worcestershire sauce at the Pentagon. Now you must construct the body of your story. In the story about Silicon Valley, the reporter chose to begin by providing explanation:

The women who work here say Silicon Valley is both the best and the worst place in the country for women to work. On the one hand, they say, the fierce competition and frantic pace of innovation put a high premium on competence, regardless of sex or other factors. On the other hand, they say, because the field of electronics has long been dominated by men, women must adapt to a "chauvinistic" engineering mentality and culture to survive.

Constructing the body of the focus structure is similar to writing the inverted pyramid story. Until the ending, you arrange the material in descending order of importance. Whether you are able to maintain the interest of the reader throughout the story depends on your writing skills.

One way to maintain interest is to refer to the spotlighted individual or subject in the body of the story. Another is to lace the informational material with anecdotes and colorful description. For example, in the story about Pentagon bidding procedures, we find this anecdote deep in the story:

Federal purchase specifications have long been a symbol of bureaucratic bedlam. Several years ago Sen. Lawton Chiles disclosed that someone trying to sell mousetraps to the military would have to comply with about 500 pages of specifications. The requirements included one for "wire, steel, carbon (high carbon, round, for mechanical springs, general purpose)." The Florida Democrat concluded that the detailed standards were so stultifying that "if you build a better mousetrap, don't try to sell it to the federal government."

Embarrassed, the government trimmed its mousetrap standard to less than a page.

Anecdotes help, but the most important elements of all are focus, detail and transitions. These three elements are important whether you are writing a human-interest feature about a former teacher on her 100th birthday or a profile of a professional athlete. Nearly any story can be told using the focus structure. But they all need to have focus, detail and transitions.

Focus requires that you be clear about your objectives from the beginning. For example, if you have decided the most interesting aspect of the athlete is his personality, focus on the traits that make him the way he is. What and who influenced him? What is his philosophy? If he happens to hunt deer for recreation, don't include that fact unless it is germane to the story. It might, for instance, be an example of how competitive he is.

Focus requires a goal not only when you write but also when you ask questions. Sometimes you can identify the focus when you are preparing yourself for the interview. Other times you will not know until during the interview what your focus will be.

Look for detail. Don't tell; show. Instead of reporting simply that Mark Goldberg, corporate president, is a competitive, combative, single-minded individual, provide concrete examples. How does he treat his secretary? His vice presidents? Can people who work for him — and who used to work for him — give you anecdotes about how he treats them? Maybe the person who sold him his last car has the same impression of him as one of the corporate officers. Detail combined with focus makes the story easier to write and more interesting for others to read.

Interest, of course, depends not just on detail but also on the care you've taken to construct the story so that it flows from one thought to the next. The transitions you build into your story often will determine whether readers move on to something else in the paper or continue reading your story.

This focus-detail-transition test is crucial to good writing. Pass this test, and your story will evoke a reaction from your readers: humor, anger, frustration, sympathy. When you win that kind of commitment from your reader, you have successfully written the story.

The Finish

One characteristic of a well-written story is a strong finish, the fourth step in the focus structure. Unlike the inverted pyramid in which the importance of the material diminishes as the story concludes, this story structure requires a strong finish.

The best technique is to return to the person or thing introduced at the beginning. The technique is called a tie-back, and it is one of the significant differences between the inverted pyramid and the focus structure. The inverted pyramid story diminishes in importance and interest so that it can be cut from the end. The focus structure has an ending. When San Francisco spent its first day under an ordinance that says nonsmokers must be given smoke-free rooms to work in, The New York Times opened its report this way:

The Victorian mansion where Linda Servis works has about as many nooks and crannies as an English muffin, and so, when she and the rest of the staff of Evans Pacific Realty reported for work today, they already had it worked out.

Smokers here, nonsmokers there, nonsmokers here, smokers there. It was the first day of San Francisco's strict new ordinance on smoking . . .

Miss Servis, who does not smoke, chose to work in the smoking room at her office because her business partner is a smoker, and it was more important for her to be in the same room with him. But she said he had promised to quit smoking and had signed up with a hypnotist . . .

The story went on to discuss other aspects of life under the smoking ordinance. It concluded by returning to Miss Servis:

> Miss Servis's business partner was not the only smoker who thought of the hypnotist. She said he could not get an appointment until March 20.

The snappy ending not only provides a tie-back but also provides evidence that one effect of the ordinance is that many people were trying to stop smoking. The appointment was three weeks later.

Variations of the Focus Structure

The focus structure allows you to tell the general story by focusing on an individual or smaller part of the story and delaying the traditional "lead" information. That is the primary alternative to the inverted pyramid. There are two variations of this alternative approach. We see them in stories that use:

1. Scenic leads.
2. Anecdotal leads.

In both the scenic and anecdotal approaches only the openings differ from the basic formula. The rest of the story's structure — transition, account of an issue or institution and close — is the same.

SCENIC LEADS

Using a *scenic lead* is an effective way to attract the reader's attention. In this approach the writer re-creates a scene, with or without the leading characters, that is relevant to the point of the story. In an article about the Amish preparing for winter, a writer for the Columbia (Mo.) Daily Tribune opened with this scene:

The countryside was in pause, between days of bountiful harvest and those that would be stern, stingy and cold.

Cornstalks, tied together by hand, pointed to a sky laden with low gray clouds pushing in from the west. Brown leaves clung stubbornly to tall trees that looked gaunt and stark as, in undress, they girthed for the winter. Tawny grasses waved stiffly in the chilly wind.

Most of the land looked drab. But in some fields winter wheat was getting a toehold, and its green beginnings hinted at yet another genesis in the spring.

Overhead, no power or telephone lines cluttered the scenery. Along gravel lanes, riders with horses and buggies traveled unhurriedly. Numerous signs told of homemade candies, sorghum and peanut brittle for sale.

This is a country where Amish people live. And if the land was preparing to rest, the people living on it and from it were not. On every farm, in barnyard and in field, people labored. It is their way to work hard, and most of the work is done by horse or by hand. "It's been that way a long time, and God made it that way, and we feel to keep it," one farmer explained.

The opening scene slips into the transition in the last paragraph of the excerpt. From there, the writer describes how the Amish go about the fall harvest.

In the scenic approach writers can take any of several directions after the opening, but generally they continue to use detailed descriptions to back up the general points they are making. The important characteristic of the story throughout is focus on relevant descriptive scenes.

ANECDOTAL LEADS

A second variation of the formula is the anecdotal lead. An anecdote, a short recreation of an event or narrative of an incident that is interesting or amusing, attracts readership. Rick Atkinson, national correspondent for The Kansas City (Mo.) Times, recreated an event when he wrote an advance about a trial of a man accused of passing secrets to the enemy. The story begins as if it were a spy novel:

It was cool and hazy on May 2 when 2nd Lt. Christopher Michael Cooke strolled out of Washington's National Airport at 5:25 p.m. after a flight from Wichita. The lanky missile launch officer, dressed in civilian brown shoes and a dark pinstripe suit, seemed too preoccupied to notice the Air Force counterespionage agents shadowing him through the TWA terminal.

The agents had one standing order from Strategic Air Command headquarters in Omaha, Neb.: Keep your distance unless he heads for the Soviet Embassy. Arrest him if he tries to enter the embassy.

Bypassing the baggage area, Cooke hopped into Diamond Cab N. 800 and gave his destination to driver Nestor Bouzas: "Russian embassy."

The taxi eased onto George Washington Parkway, steering north through traffic across the 14th Street Bridge before eventually turning onto 16th Street toward the embassy. Cooke, who initially struck the driver as wearing "a sad look on his face," suddenly turned gabby and asked Bouzas if he were Greek.

No, Bouzas replied, "I'm a Spaniard." That set the lieutenant to chattering about Spanish wine and food and the weather.

Cooke climbed out of the cab in front of the embassy as dusk began sifting over the capital. He paid the $7 fare plus a dollar tip with a $20 bill. Then he turned on his heel and strolled to the gate. No one stopped him. The agents had lost their quarry in the snarled airport traffic.

That is an unusually long opening, but it works because it is narrative and it builds tension. After we learn that Cooke walked unimpeded into the Russian embassy, the writer quickly turns to the transition, the theme paragraph:

Charged with passing secrets to the enemy and making unauthorized visits to the Soviet Embassy, Cooke faces a possible 52 years at hard labor in prison and a dishonorable discharge.

Yet the case has lurched beyond questions of crime and punishment into realms that are highly embarrassing to the Air Force. At issue is the Air Force's disputed promise of immunity granted Cooke in exchange for his confession. The bungled investigation is filled with enough enticing legal conundrums to lure famed barrister F. Lee Bailey into the case as Cooke's co-counsel.

Your job is to tell a story. Oftentimes you can do it best by telling little stories within larger ones. Anecdotes make the readers' journey through your story so much easier and more pleasant.

Extended Dialogue Stories

Occasionally, the reporter comes upon a person so quotable or a story so overwhelming that it is better to step aside and let the subjects speak for themselves at length. When either of these conditions is met, you may disregard the rules of when to quote people as detailed in Chapter 6.

You still must provide an opening, a close and transitions within the body of the story. In the opening you may use any of the approaches discussed thus far in this chapter — or even a more traditional opening that contains the standard "lead" information. But the emphasis thereafter is on the speech of the persons involved. It is nearly impossible to do this type of story if you have failed to tape-record the interviews.

When Margo Huston of The Milwaukee Journal wrote a series about the elderly entitled, "I'll Never Leave My Home. Would You?" her opening article described the plight of Bertha. She began like this:

> This is the house that Bertha built: Shabby bungalow, shades drawn, dark. You've seen this house, somewhere. When you were a kid, you called it haunted and raced past, screaming.
>
> This is the woman who lived in the house that Bertha built: Urine soaks through her wheelchair, trickles down her swollen legs, into the open sores, over her bleeding bare feet and lands in a pool in the warped wood floor.

Not far into the story, the writer lets the reader eavesdrop as Bertha's husband expresses his frustrations.

"When you get married, you take a vow for better, for worse, in sickness and in health. So I try to live up to the vow as good as I can."

He speaks in raspy spurts, politely, gentlemanly and, but for his filthy T-shirt and urine-soaked trousers, has the classy demeanor of Chief Ironside.

"I was dead in love with her when I married her, and I'm still dead in love with her," he almost shouts. "But I made up my mind, this nagging can't go on. What's the use of her sitting in that chair all night, all day, all night?"

He holds out his sad arms and laments, "They've lost their strength. I can't lift her anymore.

"When the police were here last, she said I deliberately pushed her off the chair."

His wife coughs, sputters, purses her lips, then she shouts, "There you go. Are you going to shut up? Are you going to let me talk to the lady?"

This time, he doesn't let her.

"You know yourself," he explains, "when you're wet, it smarts and burns. She can't stand it, so she wiggles and wiggles and gets on the edge of her chair and then she goes over. That's the God's truth as I swear on a stack of Bibles."

Silence, a rare moment.

His wife looks up with all the dignity she can muster. "I have been all my life a self-standing person."

"And that's the trouble," concludes her husband.

But for the fact that the reporter was there to witness the exchange, this script could have been taken from a novel. It was not, and the reporting and writing earned Margo Huston a Pulitzer Prize.

Extended dialogue also is effective when you want to capture an interesting speech pattern. When a reporter did a feature on an itinerant painter, she captured this bit of color, which would have been lost in a tighter paraphrase:

Figure 15.4   Prize-winning Writing. In her Pulitzer Prize-winning series on the plight of the elderly, The Milwaukee Journal's Margo Huston attracted readers with her excellent writing.

"Well, I'll tell you, sweetheart," Widick says, "I was bummin' in California with a guy by the name of Archie Duckett. We was on the road, sweetheart, and we was in this park when somebody said something about a flagpole. We said, 'We'll paint your pole,' Archie and me. So they offered us $8 for a 50-foot pole. We went down to the paint store because we had to supply our own paintbrushes, and that was that. I'd never done it before, but I'd seen it done."

Remember this about extended dialogue:

1. Don't try writing it unless you have used a tape recorder. You are being less than honest if you think you can reproduce large blocks of dialogue verbatim with no aid. An expert at shorthand might be able to reproduce dialogue but not dialect.

2. Don't use the approach as an excuse for emptying your notebook — or tape recorder — into the newspaper's columns. That is laziness.

3. Do use it sparingly.

The Chronological Approach

Besides the focus structure, variations of that structure and the extended dialogue story, journalists have another alternative to the inverted pyramid — the chronological approach. Oddly enough, it is not necessary to begin at the beginning to use this approach. Often writers will open with a scene from the story they are reporting, provide a paragraph or two to put the scene in context, and then pick up the chronological report at the beginning.

Alice Hartmann of the Kansas City (Mo.) Times used this approach when she returned to the scene of a hotel fire two months later:

Setting the scene

It is just after 3 o'clock on a bitterly cold Saturday morning in January. The sky is clear. A west wind blows haltingly, pumping more cold on deserted downtown streets.

For firefighters it is four more hours before quitting time. . . .

And at 1005 Broadway, the place tenants call "the House" is, in its noisy way, quiet. Some residents sleep in the rooms lining five floors of the long, wide hallways. Others lie sleepless, waiting for dawn.

In the lobby of the massive hotel, Carl Kendall, the night desk clerk, bickers with Mrs. Martha Donovan over change for a dollar. . . .

On the third floor, Mrs. Margaret Nichols has almost dropped off to sleep when the racket begins over her head. It sounds like a fight. . . .

Transition and theme paragraph

Different people, playing different roles in different parts of the sleeping city . . . But that Jan. 28 morning they will be thrown together in a nightmare they will never forget: The Coates House fire. The worst fire in Kansas City history.

Chronological approach

3:50 a.m. — Working the night shift at the Estille Hotel at 1018 Broadway, Joseph Patrick Hoyle sits behind the front desk making out occupancy reports. He hears a scream outside. From the street Hoyle sees smoke coming from the top floor of the Coates House.

Her minute-by-minute report that follows covers the next critical two hours of the fire. The news of the fire or the deaths certainly was not new to Kansas City residents. But her reporting uncovered many anecdotes and ironies. The chronological approach permitted her to bring together people from all over the city in a cohesive and compelling account.

Even when writers do begin at the beginning, they usually provide a transition to the background paragraphs and then return to the narrative. This alternate approach differs only in the lead. The writer starts the clock ticking in the opening scene, then provides a context for the story before continuing with the narrative. Here, for example, is the story of a kidnapping:

274

Beginning at the beginning   Banker Henry Venski kissed his wife, Margaret, and his 3-year-old daughter, Kathy, and climbed into his Lincoln Continental for the 20-minute drive to work Tuesday. In his mind, he already was going over some of the problems he would encounter that day.

Transition   As he swung the car out on the business loop, Venski had no idea that business problems would be of no importance that day, for 10 minutes after he arrived at work, he would receive a call telling him that his daughter had been kidnapped. For the next five hours, the bank was the furthest thing from his mind. Forty-eight hours after the ordeal was over, Venski and his wife reconstructed the minute-by-minute events that saw their daughter returned safely. Two men were charged with the kidnapping. This is the Venskis' story:

Picking up chronological approach   8:10 a.m. Venski had just reached his desk when his secretary told him his wife was calling.

Sometimes, however, the essential information is so important that even delaying it until the third or fourth paragraph is too late. Yet a straight inverted pyramid approach is not the most effective way to maintain readership beyond the first several paragraphs.

One solution, proposed by Roy Peter Clark, director of The Writing Center at the Poynter Institute for Modern Media Studies, is to use the inverted pyramid opening and then switch to chronology. The structure lends itself primarily to events that have inherent drama, such as crimes, fires, rescues, sporting events and some trials. Using this approach, the Venski kidnapping could be handled this way:

Police today rescued a banker's 3-year-old daughter after she had been held captive for five hours by kidnappers.

Two men, John H. Johnson, 25, and Andrew McKinney, 36, both of 221 W. Cornell St., are being held without bond in Springfield County Jail. Police recovered the $50,000 ransom that Henry Venski, president of First National Bank, offered for his daughter, Kathy. She was unharmed.

Police and the Venskis said this is what happened:

Ten minutes after he arrived at work, Venski received a call from the kidnappers . . .

The structure has two important advantages: It permits the writer to give the most important information first, and it permits the writer to tell the rest of the story in chronological order. That should encourage some of the readers to stay with the story longer without irritating others who want to know what happened quickly.

An anecdotal lead works well on chronological stories, too. When the Kansas City (Mo.) Star received a story about a man who killed a pet deer, the paper could have written the traditional news lead:

August John Scherer, 28, Brownwood, was fined $400 Wednesday after he was found guilty of killing a pet fawn.

Instead, the Star chose an anecdotal approach and left the punch until the end.

AQUILLA, Mo. — Three years ago Harold Merick, who runs Angus cattle on a 240-acre farm near this southeast Missouri community, found a fawn tangled in his wire fence.

The fawn, a doe, had struggled in the wire. She was bloody, half-crazed with fear and, most of all, alone. So Merick, his wife, Mary, and their daughter, Sandra, who was then 8, adopted the doe. They managed to dress the wounds and in time, with softness and tenderness, to wipe the film of fear from the doe's eyes.

The fawn survived, and they named her Joanie.

Joanie grew. She grazed with the Mericks' cattle, occasionally being bossed around by a calfless cow in need of company — no matter how odd-looking.

Mrs. Merick remembers Joanie was a joy.

"We'd get school buses filled with kids who came to look," she said. "So did people just driving by, fascinated at this deer in among the cattle. Everybody around here knew her. Most people knew her name, too."

Although Joanie grew to be a fine, strong doe, she never went near the Mericks' fences, which she could have bounded over easily. She apparently was content being a deer in a herd of cattle.

On April 13 an early-rising neighbor heard three shots, looked out and saw Joanie staggering around the pasture. Down near a gravel road was a man with a rifle. The neighbor called the Mericks.

Merick arrived in time to confront a man by the road with a small, yellow pickup truck. He remembered later there was a farm strike sticker in the rear window. Asked what he was doing, the man said he was just "watching the deer."

Merick went off to see whether he could help Joanie. He couldn't. A veterinary report later said the animal was hit by two bullets, one piercing the heart.

By the time Merick returned, the man was gone. But Merick remembered the truck.

Don May, a Missouri Conservation Commission agent, found 14 trucks fitting the same general description within a five-mile area. None belonged to the man Merick described.

But just as he was about to give up, May saw the 15th. In it was a man who two hours after he was arrested made a statement about killing the deer.

And in Stoddard County Magistrate Court here Wednesday, 28-year-old August John Scherer, a Brownwood, Mo., liquor store owner, was found guilty of discharging a firearm from a public highway and for hunting out of season. Scherer was fined $400 — the largest fine ever levied in the county for such an offense.

Asked why he shot Joanie, Scherer replied:

"Just for fun."

When the question "what happened?" is not answered until the end, as in the preceding example, the story is commonly called a suspended-interest account. The only difference between it and the approach in the kidnap story is that instead of providing a transition into the news near the top, the writer structures the entire story chronologically.

First-Person Stories

In all its variations, the focus structure is also appropriate for first-person stories. Some follow the basic structure. Some rely on dialogue; some are chronological.

While the organization is flexible, the subject matter is not. Such stories are most effective when the personal, first-person viewpoint adds a special dimension to the story that no other writing approach could capture. A daughter describing her father's battle with terminal cancer would be remiss not to use "I." Readers can empathize with the special father-daughter relationship.

One of the most effective uses of a first-person story is when the reporter is involved in an unusual event. For instance, when an off-duty reporter for the Columbia Missourian became a participant in a suicide, the situation clearly called for a first-person story:

It looks so easy on "Kojak," and it always works. Someone teeters on a ledge. A cop says, "Let's talk about it." There are a few minutes of tense silence, portentous music, and the person staggers in through the window. Case closed; problem solved.

It isn't like that in real life.

If I hadn't wrecked my car Sunday night, I wouldn't have been walking along Broadway at College Avenue Monday morning when a young man ended his life from the Stephens College overpass at Broadway and College. But I was, and I tried to help. I did all the right things — I had someone call campus security, followed the man, kept a few feet away from him, asked if he wanted to "talk about it."

He jumped anyhow.

So infrequently would a reporter ever be involved in a suicide that the first-person approach is warranted. The account permits the reader to share not only the event, but also the emotions of the participant who tried to stop the suicide.

Most first-person stories involve participatory journalism (see pp. 373–375). Reporters take the reader on the court with the athletes, backstage with the stars, into the fields with the migrants, into the mental hospital with the inmates. When the reporter participates rather than watching others do something, there may be a first-person story worth writing. But use the approach sparingly. It too easily becomes an ego trip or a subterfuge for lazy reporters.

Putting It Together

We have talked about alternative openings, transitions, theme paragraphs, anecdotes and tie-backs. When a columnist for the Des

Moines (Iowa) Register killed his wife, their retarded daughter and himself, the newspaper felt obliged to tell the story in depth. The task fell to Ken Fuson, who used all the devices described in this chapter, and used them with sensitivity. The story is reproduced here in its entirety because it is an example of the impact of good reporting, good writing and an alternate story structure.

On what might have been the proudest day of his professional life, when he was in New York City to accept one of the nation's most cherished newspaper writing awards, Robert Hullihan shared a piece of his tormented life with a friend.

For some five hours on a beautiful spring day in 1975, Hullihan and his boss, Michael Gartner, walked along the streets of Greenwich Village. Hullihan did most of the talking, which was out of character for the normally shy reporter.

He described the tragedies that had marked his life — the birth of a severely retarded daughter who didn't recognize him, the drowning of a son whose body was never found, deaths of close friends, and seemingly endless health problems for him and his wife, Thelma.

"It was one terrible thing after another," Gartner, now president of the Des Moines Register and Tribune Company, recalled. "Finally, he looked at me and he said, 'You know, if God only kept a scorecard, He'd leave me alone by now.'"

The statement reflected Hullihan at his wry, ironic, despairing and witty best.

Like a bewildered character in a Greek play, Hullihan wore the dramatic masks of comedy and tragedy at all times. When the smiling mask emerged, he was a warm, caring, gentle man who could write like a poet and find a smile in what he considered the absurdity of everyday life.

But Hullihan could never mask his pain for long. As the mask of comedy slipped, the tragic one prevailed, revealing a deeply troubled, brooding man who could, as he did last Sun-day, pull out a .38-caliber revolver and kill his 57-year-old wife and 32-year-old retarded daughter, Julia Ann, before turning the gun on himself.

The incongruities and contradictions that marked Robert Hullihan's 61-year life stood out most sharply in his death. As they attended funeral services for the family Wednesday in Des Moines, Hullihan's friends tried to connect the disparities.

They remembered the genial Hullihan, the witty, brilliant writer. They remembered the morose Hullihan, the puzzling, suicidal friend. Few had known the violent Hullihan, the shocking, plotting murderer.

Each sought to understand.

While recalling his friend with fondness and admiration, Gartner emphasized that the calculated way Hullihan planned and executed the slayings of his wife and daughter "was the ultimate vicious, cruel deed, and you can't lose sight of that."

•

Death preoccupied Hullihan. He talked, wrote, joked and fretted about it, often whimsically, but so much so that friends accepted his frequent musings as an essential element of his personality.

Time after time, death reverberated as a central theme through his stories. A profile on Clarence Hall, an 83-year-old Minburn man, focused on what one-liners Hall would use to ward off Death. "I thought he was coming to talk about my woodworking," Hall recalled Tuesday.

Last April, in what ostensibly was a correction to tell readers he had misspelled a name, Hullihan took readers on a tour of the cemetery plot where he would be buried some six months later. Pondering his profession and his eventual fate, he noted, "The writer believes that clever writing earns him credits with death."

Half-jokingly, half-seriously, Hullihan instructed friends and colleagues what he expected when he died. Reporter Gary Heinlein, he said, would write the obituary. The first paragraph would say, "He never got it quite right." The picture would show him, with the bemused look of a man who should know better, interviewing Lamar, the dog of QuikTrip fame. Indeed, Register staffers found Sunday that all pictures of Hullihan were missing from the newspaper's library, except a basic mug shot and the photo with Lamar.

In the story about his trip to the cemetery, Hullihan noted, "You know, there's room on that stone for a really clever epitaph." And he provided one in a note to Gartner: "He wrote like a silkworm — and with about the same intellectual content."

If someone reacted to his mournful musings with worry, Hullihan left himself a way out, often by cracking an only-kidding grin.

Lifelong friend Wayne DeMouth said Hullihan had made death a part of his life since the two men grew up together in Boone. "He always was kind of despairing, with a sense of hopelessness and a feeling of remorse," he said.

Friends say Hullihan wasn't ghoulish. "His view was a very fatalistic, sort of ironic certitude that, in the end, the world was going to deal you dirt," said Register Editor James P. Gannon.

While often light-hearted about his mortality, Hullihan candidly exposed his darker side, outlining to friends the events that might lead to his suicide. That, too, was accepted as a part of who he was.

Not one of those friends, for example, expressed surprise at Hullihan's suicide Sunday. They were shocked by the violence of it, and in particular the slaying of his wife, but Hullihan had broached suicide so often that no one could predict when, how or even whether it would happen.

"Because he talked about it so often to so many people, it wasn't as if you felt, 'Oh, my God, here's a signal and I have to go and find this man some help,'" said Register reporter Susan Caba, whom Hullihan described in his suicide note as his closest colleague. "We didn't realize how fragile he really was."

Many friends insisted Hullihan would not have been helped by counseling, and would have rejected the notion.

DeMouth compared his friend to a record: "When you played Hullihan, you got a dirge on one side and a sprightly minuet on the other. That was Bob Hullihan. On one side he would talk about the everlasting pity of it all. On the other, he would say, 'Humor, humor, inexhaustible humor.'"

●

In 1973, the year he started work on the Des Moines Tribune, Hullihan quickly revealed to readers a hint of his preoccupation with death, analyzing the best buys in cemetery plots. He also revealed his whimsical side, posing as a stranger to the city and directing a cabbie to show him the sights, suggesting Iowans could stay warm during the winter by practicing Tumo, "a kind of fiery meditation favored by Tibetan hermits" and keeping track of the jokes used by kids at Halloween.

This, his readers learned, was a reporter who chased people, not police cars, who panned for nuggets of gold in what looked like mountains of dirt, and who found the extraordinary in the ordinary.

He even looked like a humorist, a cross between Merlin and a college professor, whose angular face was awash in white — as in wise — whiskers. He had the slender fingers of a pianist and the slightly cautious walk of a man greatly concerned (which he was) about reaching the 10-year requirement for a pension he would never use.

His path to newspaper writing did not follow the normal course. A veteran of World War II and the Korean War, he earned his stripes in civilian life as a word merchant in the advertising business.

Tom Stoner, chairman of the board of Stoner Broadcasting System, said Hullihan was unmatched as a billboard designer for Stoner Systems Inc.

Even today, his billboards are legendary, such as the well-meaning hoax to keep bullfighting out of Des Moines. Or the one that showed a small boy in pajamas looking warily at a bathtub as the message said, "Let Him Skip His Bath Tonight — a Public Service for Little Boys."

Drake Mabry, then managing editor of the Tribune, persuaded Hullihan to try newspaper work, which he always wanted to do but wasn't sure he was good enough.

His stories carried his unmistakable stamp. His fans could tell a Hullihan story without a byline, something the reserved writer would have preferred. After he was transferred to The Register, editors referred to his stories as "Hullihan pieces" because they broke all other molds. There is no file in the Register library under the heading of "Off the Beaten Track." You have to look under H.

For a while, his writing ran as a column called "The Edge of the Crowd," which was where he operated, sizing up those who passed and sidetracking the most usual and unusual so he could pose a few questions to them.

He interviewed dogs, talking elevators, the Penthouse Pets of the Year, a man "seeking to redeem an anonymous life by becoming the world's champion bus rider" and the man whose voice gives the time and temperature. He wrote short stories, essays, commentaries and a multi-part fantasy on the life of a toad named Chester A. Nimitz.

Hullihan often would focus on "foremost authorities" in fields you might have thought were devoid of experts — sewer pipes, guanacos, roadrunners, bugs. Especially bugs. He had a fascination for all animals, particularly the tiny, crawling kind, and invariably informed his readers how they reproduced.

Through it all, he displayed an uncanny knack at being able to link two or more seemingly unrelated items, such as pigeons and starting a stalled car, or sensuality and driving through an automatic car wash.

"He looked at the world sideways," said John Karras, a Register editor and close friend of Hullihan's. "He always found some weird connection."

In 1975, only two years after he rented an electric typewriter because he didn't know how to use the Tribune's old, manual machines, Hullihan won the Ernie Pyle Memorial Award, generally considered the most prestigious honor for a newspaper feature writer. The judges noted his "talent for turning everyday occurrences into uncommonly readable prose."

But Hullihan rarely accepted praise. He didn't believe himself worthy. He was an insecure writer, often wondering after he turned in a piece whether he would ever write another one.

"I think with any major talent, the person has some kind of standard that is beyond anything that the rest of us can conceive of," Karras said. "He's always falling short of his standard, whereas the rest of the world isn't even aware of it.

"So, by such a definition, he is always a failure."

●

When Julia Ann Hullihan was born in 1951, the umbilical cord choked off oxygen to her brain. She was sent in 1958 to the Woodward

State Hospital-School. Every Sunday, Hullihan and his wife, who remained fiercely devoted to her "Sissy," drove to Woodward to visit the child.

Friends say Hullihan began to detest the trips. "He told me 10 or 11 years ago that he had given up on his daughter and he never mentioned it again," said Wilbur Rose, Hullihan's accountant.

But still he went. When asked why, friends say Hullihan would respond that he went for Thelma and she went for Julia, who apparently gave indications she recognized her mother.

Thelma Hullihan worked the last 10 years at the Polk County Association for Retarded Citizens. Tom Doidge, executive director of the association, said the couple donated from $300 to $500 every year toward a scholarship fund for a client.

Thelma, he said, "looked at her work as a commitment to her daughter."

Friends say Robert Hullihan was very close to the couple's other child, Michael. When the youth was attending the University of Iowa, the father and son read selections from "Death of a Salesman" to each other.

In January 1969, Michael drowned in Iowa City. The body was never found. In many ways, friends say, neither Robert nor Thelma recovered.

DeMouth said the fate of his children didn't form Robert Hullihan's bleak outlook on life, but reaffirmed it. Said Stoner: "His son had an optimistic outlook on life that Bob always wanted to have. When his son died, any trace of that hopeful side of Bob died, too."

The masks stayed on for good.

"He was an accomplished actor about himself," Gartner said. "He

Figure 15.5
Photographs Complement a Story.
This photograph, which accompanied Ken Fuson's story about Robert Hullihan's death, captures Hullihan in a whimsical mood.

was living through one tragedy after another and yet going out and writing these droll, funny pieces, these lovely pieces. That was just all a mask."

Always, friends say, Hullihan turned his family responsibilities into burdens. He told several people that he felt Thelma couldn't survive without him and that he was worried about Julia's fate should he die. Those concerns were exacerbated in 1978 when Hullihan underwent multiple-bypass surgery for heart troubles.

Hullihan used to say that if he hadn't married his wife, he would have made a pass at her. Most of their friends say the couple was devoted to one another, despite strains that might have snapped most marriages. Dr. Donald McBride, the family's physician, said both suffered from mild bouts of chronic depression.

●

On Friday, Hullihan turned in an expense account sheet for a trip he had taken to Ames, where he had written his last story, a front-page feature on the man who invented the electronic digital computer.

Register columnist Patrick Lackey visited the Hullihans Saturday night, later recalling that Hullihan was "his normal, thoughtful, slightly depressed self."

All the time, a suicide note was locked in his desk. It was a matter-of-fact laundry list of what his brother, William, should do, written as if he had planned a vacation. "Sorry for the trouble and cost," he wrote. "View this as an attempt to bring some efficiency to the matter of terminations — a kind of pain-control clinic."

Sometime early Sunday, Hullihan and his wife started on the trip to Woodward. First they stopped at the Crestview Acres Retirement Home, where Hullihan's mother, Alta, is a resident. She usually makes the trip, but didn't feel like going Sunday.

Patricia Olson, the home's administrator, said Hullihan called twice to see if his mother would join the trip. He then came over. "He told her she was the best mother in the world and started crying and got back in the car. That's what she told me," Olson said.

"I think she's very realistic about what might have happened" had she gone, Olson said.

Sometime after 11 a.m., the Hullihans pulled in front of the Linden Court Building, where Julia Ann lived at the Woodward Hospital-School. As they left, Thelma took the wheel, with Julia in the front seat next to her. Robert sat in the back.

The bodies were found in the car, only a few hundred feet from the building.

"The only loss here is Thelma," the suicide note said. "A marvelous woman of heart-breaking charm. She is at a high point of happiness right now. She loves her new house and thinks this place, Green Meadows, is 'heaven.'

"What better time?"

●

His friends searched for clues to what could have triggered the outburst of violence from someone considered so gentle. A medical problem? McBride didn't know of any. The move to a new house? Perhaps. One friend said Hullihan said he felt like he had "lost his history" in the move and even made an attempt to buy back his former home.

"Maybe there was no triggering event," Gannon said. "He may have just run out of the will or the energy to cope with it all."

His friends were stunned by Hullihan's use of a gun. They also were varied in their reactions.

There was anger. "He did this supremely vicious and arrogant thing," Gartner said. "And I'm sure this will be an extraordinarily unpopular thing to say, but you can't forget that, either. He not only killed his own self, but his wife, who by his own note was at the height of her happiness.''

There was bitterness. "A lot of people are angry at Bob for terminating Thelma's life,'' Doidge said, "because she had so much to give. . . . He made that choice for her. It's too bad she couldn't have made that choice for herself.''

There was forgiveness. "I don't consider it violent and cold. I consider it a desperate effort,'' said Phyllis Conway, described in the suicide note as one of the Hullihans' closest friends. "He couldn't go on and he was afraid that Thelma couldn't go on without him.''

There was compassion. "Right or wrong,'' Karras said, "I think he felt that those people depended on him totally for any support that they had and, when he was gone, they were going to be set adrift in what he knew as an extremely cruel world.''

There was an attempt at understanding. "A lot of us are mad at him,'' Caba said, "but we're judging him from the standpoint of our own hurt and not taking into consideration his hurt. . . .

"He created a scene in which you are forced to participate, while he is standing on the side somewhere chortling, observing and defining. He's put us all in a position of trying to define who he was.''

●

In some respects, the incident last Sunday was the ultimate "Hullihan piece,'' with two disparate elements — the happy mask of a warm, creative genius and the tragic mask of, however well-meaning, a cold-blooded killer.

But this story will not, as Hullihan's always did, end in a neat, witty, amusing little package, because the one man who could, as usual, tie the contradictions together was the man who pulled the trigger.

Suggested Readings

Clark, Roy Peter. "A New Shape for the News,'' Washington Journalism Review, March 1984, pp. 46–47. Clark describes how to combine the inverted pyramid and the narrative story forms.

Griffin, Dick, and Rob Warden, eds. "Done in a Day.'' Chicago: Swallow Press, 1977. On the occasion of its centennial, The Chicago Daily News produced this book of reprints, which allows the student of writing to observe some outstanding examples of the craft.

Snyder, Louis L., and Richard B. Morris, eds. "A Treasury of Great Reporting.'' 2nd ed. New York: Simon & Schuster, 1971. The reader can trace the evolution of several writing styles in American journalism.

Washington Post Writers Group. "Writing in Style.'' Edited by Laura Longley Babb. Boston: Houghton Mifflin, 1975. Writers for the Post lifestyle section expanded the boundaries of writing style, and this book has several outstanding examples of the new journalism.

16
Covering a Beat

Meet Jeff Leen, a young reporter for the Miami Herald. He had been covering the police beat in Palm Beach County for about four months when his investment of time and effort paid off in a front-page story. Let him tell you how:

I was still visiting every day, talking as often about a sergeant's new white German shepherd puppy or a corporal's unpublished police novel as I was about the latest breaking and entering or the upcoming drug sweeps.

One day, over the phone, a tip came.

"You may be interested in this," an officer said. "The State Attorney's office dropped the charges on a guy we arrested for rape last fall."

A 72-year-old senile woman, a tourist from Ohio who thought she was in California, had wandered 15 blocks into a ghetto bar. She was the only white woman there, and when she met and danced with a 36-year-old ex-convict, no one interceded. He took her to the back seat of a car and had sex with her. The police caught them in the act, but the prosecutors said the woman's senility prevented her from testifying, so the charges had to be dropped. The felon walked.

"I just thought it might be something that you'd be interested in," the officer said.

Some time after the story ran, I was sitting in the police station, making my rounds. The sergeant chatted amiably about the lack of news and the trouble he was having house-training his puppy. His phone rang. It was my competition calling.

"I don't know how Jeff Leen always gets these stories," the sergeant said, smiling at me. "No, we don't favor any one newspaper. Well, you see, Jeff drops in here every day and . . ."

Beat reporting is the backbone of any newspaper's coverage of its community. The reporter who covers a beat keeps the paper's read-

Figure 16.1 Be There.
Miami Herald reporter
Jeff Leen was successful
on the police beat largely
due to his frequent visits
to the police station.

ers abreast of what government, business or some other powerful
institution is doing, what it is about to do and what the effects are of
what it has done in the past.

Many young reporters start their careers covering a local beat,
such as the police, the courts, local government or the schools.
Those with specialized training or some experience may be assigned
beats such as business, medicine, science or the arts. A successful
career may take a reporter on to the state capital or to Washington,
where the beats include Congress, the executive agencies, the Supreme Court and the White House.

On small papers or broadcast stations with limited staffs, one reporter may be responsible for several beats. On big papers, such as
the Herald, several reporters may be assigned to an important beat,
such as education or county government.

In this chapter you will learn:

1. Some basic principles for covering a beat.
2. How to apply those principles in covering the most common
   beats.

Principles for Reporters on a Beat

Whether the beat you cover is the public library or the Pentagon,
the county courthouse or the White House, the principles of covering it are the same. If you want to succeed as a reporter on that beat,
you must:

1. Be prepared.
2. Be alert.
3. Be persistent.
4. Be there.
5. Be wary.

That checklist will help you win the trust of your sources, keep up with important developments on your beat and avoid the trap of writing for your sources instead of your readers. Let's take a closer look at what each of those rules means in practice.

BE PREPARED

Where should preparation begin? For you, it has already begun. To work effectively, any journalist needs a basic understanding of the workings of society and its various governments. You need to know at least the rudiments of psychology, economics and history. That is why the best education for a journalist is a broad-based one, providing exposure to the widest possible sampling of human knowledge. But that exposure will not be enough when you face an important source on your first beat. You will need more specific information, which you can acquire by familiarizing yourself with written accounts or records or by talking to sources.

Reading for Background

In preparing to cover a beat, any beat, your first stop is the newspaper library. Read the clips. Make notes of what appear to be continuing issues, questions left dangling in previous stories or possible ideas for stories to come. Go back three or four years in your research. History may not repeat itself, but a knowledge of it helps you assess the significance of current events and provides clues to what you can expect in the future.

The morgue is only the start of your preparation, however. You must become familiar with the laws governing the institution you cover. Find the state statutes or the city charter that created the agencies you will be covering. Learn what the powers, the duties, the limitations are of each official. You may be surprised to discover that somebody is failing to do all the law requires. Somebody else may be doing more than the law allows.

In one Missouri town a reporter discovered that the county auditor was supposed to be checking the books of every agency every year. He wasn't doing it. After dozens of stories and two grand jury investigations, two members of the county court and the county clerk pleaded guilty to misconduct in office. The auditor resigned. The books now are checked regularly.

Look at your state's open meetings and open records laws, too. Every state has such laws, though they vary widely in scope and effectiveness. Knowing what is open to the public by law can be a valuable tool for a reporter dealing with officials who may find it more convenient to govern privately.

Talking to Sources

Now you're ready to start talking to people. Your first interviews should be conducted in the news room, with your predecessor on the beat, your city editor and any veterans who can shed some light on the kinds of things that rarely appear in statute books or even newspaper stories. Who have been good sources in the past? Who will lie to you? Who drinks to excess? Who seems to be living extravagantly? Whose friends are big land developers? Who wants to run for national office? Remember that you are hearing gossip, filtered through the biases of those relating it. Be a little skeptical.

Some understanding of the workings of your own news room won't hurt, either. Has your predecessor on the beat been promoted, or transferred because he or she was unsatisfactory? Will an introduction from your predecessor help you or hurt you with your sources? And what are your city editor's expectations? Is yours a paper of record, trying to report virtually every activity of government, or will you have time to do some investigative work and analysis? Trying to live up to your boss's expectations is easier if you know in advance what they are.

Only after gaining as much background as possible are you ready to face the people you will be covering. A quick handshake and a superficial question or two may be all you have time for in the first encounter, but within a week you should arrange for sit-down conversations with your most important sources. These are get-acquainted sessions. You are trying to get to know the sources, but don't forget that they need to know you, too, if they are going to respect and trust you.

You may have noticed that the preparation for covering a beat is similar to the preparation for an interview or for a single-story assignment. The difference is that preparing for a beat is more detailed and requires more time and work. Instead of just preparing for a short-term task, you are laying the foundation for an important part of your career. A beat assignment nearly always lasts at least six months and often two years or more. That understanding helps shape your first round of meetings with sources.

A story may emerge from those first interviews, but their purpose is much broader. You are trying to establish a relationship, trying to convert strangers into helpful partners in news gathering. To do that, you demonstrate an interest in the sources as people as well as officials. Ask about their families, their interests, their philosophy, their goals. Make clear with your questions that you are interested rather than ignorant. (Don't ask if the source is married. You should already know that. Say, "I understand your daughter is in law school. Is she going into politics, too?" Similarly, don't ask if your source has any hobbies. Find that out beforehand. Say, "So you collect pornographic comic books. Sure takes your mind off the budget, doesn't it?")

And be prepared to give something of yourself. If you both like to fish, or you both went to Vassar, or you both have children about the same age, seize on those ties. All of us feel more comfortable with people who have something in common with us. This is the time, too, to let the source know that you know something about the office and that you're interested in it.

Was she elected as a reformer? Ask about the opposition she is encountering. Is it budget time? Let him know you're aware of the problems with last year's budget. Has he complained that he lacks the statutory power to do a satisfactory job? Ask if he's lobbying to change the law. Nothing does so much to create a warm reporter-source relationship as the reporter's demonstrated knowledge of and interest in the beat.

Solid preparation will help you avoid asking stupid questions. More important, it will help you make sure you ask the right questions. And because you have taken the trouble to get to know your sources, you are more likely to come away with responsive answers to the questions you ask.

BE ALERT

The germ of a good story is hidden in many a routine one. Consider these possibilities:

• A veteran detective who is also president of the police officers' association is being transferred to the patrol division. It's a routine transfer, says a spokesman for the chief of police, a normal part of the detective's career pattern. The managing editor of the paper knows better. A former police reporter who has kept up her contacts, she knows a bitter struggle for control of the department is being waged behind the scenes. The new police chief is on one side, and the detective leads the opposition. The chief won't talk, but the detective and his colleagues are eager to tell their side. The public is let in on at least one version of a significant development in city affairs.

• The United Fund, the nonprofit organization that solicits money to support all sorts of voluntary agencies, announces with regret that, once again, it has not met its fund-raising goal. One paper in town prints the announcement. The reporter who covers the beat for the other paper, however, has heard rumblings that all is not well within the organization. He visits a trusted source on the board of directors. Yes, he is told, there is a problem — the executive director. He just isn't competent. That's off the record, of course. The reporter talks with several other board members, who tell the same story. All are worried about the agency's image and hope the reporter won't use the information. The reporter goes outside the board to other community leaders and the heads of funded organizations. He finds a few who are fed up enough to talk on the record and others who refuse to have their names used. The story runs. The executive director retires. Under a new director, the fund reaches its goal for the first time in years.

• On the list of rezoning requests up for approval by the city council, the city hall reporter spots one that looks odd. It is for a change from agricultural to apartment zoning at an address she hasn't heard of. The planning department recommends approval. The reporter drops in on a friend in the assessor's office whose job requires him to be familiar with land deals, since he has to keep the property tax roll up to date. "Oh, yeah," he says. "That land's way out. Those streets aren't built yet." He lowers his voice. "It might be interesting to see who holds the mortgage." After a visit to the recorder of deeds' office, a call to the state capital to find out the names of the officers of two corporations, and an interview with a real estate agent, the reporter uncovers an interesting fact. The newly elected mayor, formerly chairman of the planning commission, sold that land to a developer and held the mortgage himself. The real estate salesman, thinking he is about to be featured in a business-page piece on the planned development, recalls that the mayor had assured the buyer that rezoning is no problem. The problem has turned out to be the mayor's.

Important stories are seldom labeled as such. In many cases the people involved may not realize the significance of what they are doing. Probably more often they realize it but hope nobody else will. The motivation for secrecy may be dishonesty, the desire to protect an image or a conviction that the public will misunderstand.

As a reporter on a beat you will find that many public officials and public employees think they know more about what is good for the public than the public does. The theory of democratic government is that an informed citizenry can make decisions, or elect representatives to make decisions, in its own best interests. If you are the reporter assigned to city hall, the school board or the courthouse, you carry a heavy responsibility for helping your readers put that theory into practice. To discharge that responsibility, you must probe beneath the surface of events in search of the "why's" and "how's" that lead to understanding.

When you are presented with a press release or hear an announcement or cover a vote, ask yourself these questions before passing the event off in a few paragraphs:

1. *Who will benefit from this, and who will be hurt?* If the tentative answer to the first part suggests private interests, or the answer to the second part is the public, some digging is in order.

2. *How important is this?* In the zoning example cited earlier the importance lay in the possibility of wrongdoing. In the United Fund example the importance lay in the fund's role as collector of several hundred thousand dollars and as supporter of widely used social agencies. An event that is likely to affect many people for good or ill usually deserves more explanation than one affecting only a handful.

3. *Who is for this, and who is against it?* Answers to these questions often are obvious or at least easy to figure out. When you know them, the answers to the first two questions usually become clearer.

4. *How much will this activity cost, and who pays?* An architect's design for renovating downtown may look less attractive when the price tag is attached. The chamber of commerce's drive to lure new industry may require taxpayers to pay for new roads, sewers, fire protection, even schools and other services for an increased population.

Once you have asked the questions and gotten answers, the story may turn out to be about no more than it appeared to be on the surface. But if you don't ask them, you — and your readers — may find out too late that more was there than met the eye.

BE PERSISTENT

Persistence means two things to a reporter on a beat. First, it means that when you ask a question, you cannot give up until you get an answer. Second, it means that you must keep track of slow-developing projects or problems.

Insisting on a Responsive Answer

One of the most common faults of beginning reporters is that they give up too easily. They settle for answers that are unresponsive to their questions, or they come back to the news room not sure they understand what they were told. In either case the result is an incomplete, confusing story.

Figure 16.2 Be Persistent. Reporters on a beat, such as these people interviewing New York mayor Edward Koch on a bus, sometimes must go to unusual lengths to make contact with their subjects.

"Why is it that our fourth-graders score below average on these reading tests?" you ask the school superintendent.

He may reply, "Let me first conceptualize the parameters of the socio-economic context for you."

The real answer probably is, "I only wish I knew."

Your job is to cut through the jargon and the evasions in search of substance. Often, that is not an easy task. Many experts, or people who want to be regarded as experts, are so caught up in the technical language of their special field that they find it almost impossible to communicate clearly. Many others seek refuge in gobbledygook or resort to evasion when they don't know an answer or find the answer embarrassing. Educators and lawyers are particularly adept at such tactics.

Listen politely for a few minutes while the superintendent conceptualizes his parameters. Then, when he finishes or pauses for breath, lead him back toward where you want to go. One way is to say, "It sounds to me as if you're saying . . ." and rephrase what he has told you in simple language. At those times when you simply are in the dark — and that may be often — just confess your puzzlement and ask for a translation. And keep coming back to the point: "But how does all that affect reading scores?" "How can the problem be solved?" "What are you doing about it?"

The techniques you have learned for preparing for interviews and conducting them will help you. Your preparation for the beat will help, too. Probably most helpful, though, are the questions you keep asking yourself rather than your source: "Does that make sense to me?" "Can I make it make sense to my readers?" Don't quit until the answer is yes. You should not be obnoxious, but you do have to persist.

Following Up Slow Developments

You have to persist as well in following the course of slow-developing events. No gardener sits and watches a seed germinate. His eyes would glaze over long before any change was apparent. He does, however, check every few days, looking for the green shoots that tell him the process is taking place as it should. If the shoots are late, he digs in to investigate.

Beat reporting is the same way. A downtown redevelopment plan, say, or a revision in a school's curriculum is announced. The story is on the plans and the hoped-for benefits. The seed is planted. If it is planted on your beat, make a note to yourself to check on it in a week or two. And a week or two after that. And a month after that. Start a file of reminders so you won't forget. Such a file often is called a "tickler" because it serves to tickle your memory.

Like seeds, important projects of government or business take time to develop. Often what happens during that long, out-of-public-view development is more important than the announcements at the occasional news conferences or the promises of the promotional brochures. Compromises are made. Original plans turn out to be impractical or politically unpalatable. Consultants are hired. Contracts are signed. Public money is spent. The public interest may be served, or it may not.

Sometimes the story is that nothing is happening. At other times the story may be that the wrong things are happening. Consulting contracts may go to cronies of the mayor. Redevelopment may enhance the property values of big downtown landowners. Curriculum revisions may be shaped by some influential pressure group.

Even if nothing improper is taking place, the persistent reporter will give the readers an occasional update. At stake, after all, is the public's money and welfare.

BE THERE

In beat reporting as in lovemaking, there is no substitute for personal contact. Trying to do either by telephone just won't work. The only way to cover a beat is to be there — every day, if possible. Joking with the secretaries, talking politics with council members and lawyers, worrying over the budget or trading gossip with the professional staff, you must make yourself seem to be a part of the community you are covering.

Lisa Hoffman prefers to think of her beat as a sort of extended family. She says:

> To become part of the family, you must convince your sources that you're a human being and that you're interested in them as people, too. I take them out to lunch or for drinks. I ask about their spouses and children and tell them about the fight I had with my boyfriend and the movie I saw Saturday night. I bitch about my editors and grumble about the play of a story. Many have only a "Front Page" perspective of the news business, and most are fascinated by how the process really works.

Assigned to cover federal courts for the Miami Herald, she cultivates her sources diligently. She tells how:

> I check each morning with the secretaries who answer the phones, open the mail, prepare the dockets. Like most mothers, they're the ones who keep the household running. They also know first what's going on.

Figure 16.3 Cultivate Sources. Miami Herald reporter Lisa Hoffman contacted people at many levels of the criminal justice system while covering the court beat.

Then I check in with the law clerks to the various judges. These folks, usually young, opinionated, bright and swelled with ego, have the ear of the judge, do their research and often write decisions for them.

I pay my respects a few times a week to the judges themselves, father figures if ever there were any.

I've found that U.S. marshals, like bailiffs in state courts, can be the nosy, neglected aunts. They know who the good lawyers and judges are, but no one ever asks. They know when the grand jury meets and usually can identify the prominent folks who come to testify.

One of my best sources now is the guy who runs the courthouse coffee shop.

Remember that the sources who are most important to you probably are in great demand by others, too. They have jobs to do. Maneuver to get as much of their time as you need, but don't demand too much. Do your homework first. Don't expect a school superintendent to explain basic concepts of education. You can learn that information from an aide or from reading. What you need to learn from the superintendent is how he or she intends to apply those concepts, or why they seem to be inapplicable here. Find out what a "Class I felony" is before asking the police chief why they are increasing. You will get the time you need more readily if busy sources know their time will not be wasted.

There are other simple techniques you can use to build and maintain good relationships with the people on your beat. Here are some of them:

1. *Do a favor when you can.* As a reporter you spend much of your time asking other people to do favors for you — giving you their time, sharing information they need not share, looking up records and figures. If a source needs a favor in return, don't refuse unless it would be unethical. The favors asked usually are small things, such as getting a daughter's engagement picture or a club announcement in the paper, procuring a print of a picture taken with the governor to decorate the official's wall, bringing in a few copies of a favorable feature you wrote.

2. *Don't shun good news.* One ill-founded but common complaint is that newspapers print nothing but bad news. Admittedly, there is usually no story when people are doing what they are supposed to do. Sometimes there should be, if they do their duty uncommonly well or have done it for a very long time or do it under the burden of some handicap. Sources like these "good news" stories and so do readers.

3. *Protect your sources.* Many people in government, politicians and bureaucrats alike, are willing to tell a reporter things they are

not willing to have their names attached to in print or otherwise. Some of the time, such would-be anonymous sources are trying to use you to enhance their own positions. You have to protect yourself and your readers against that possibility. Confer with an editor if you have doubts. Most papers are properly wary of relying on unnamed sources. Sometimes, though, the requests for anonymity are valid, necessary to protect the source's career. Once you have agreed to protect a source, you must do it. Don't tell anyone but your editor. An inability to keep your mouth shut can cost you more than a source. It can cost you your reputation.

4. *Above all, be accurate.* An inaccurate reporter is worse than useless. Inaccurate reporting leads first to loss of respect from sources, then to loss of the sources themselves, and finally to loss of the job. If you are a good, tough reporter, not everybody on your beat will love you. But if you are an accurate reporter, they will have to respect you.

The best way to assure accuracy is to check and double-check. Many of the stories you will write are complicated. You will be expected to digest budgets, master plans, legal opinions, and complicated discussions, and to translate these into language your readers can understand. When in doubt, ask somebody. If you are unclear about the city manager's explanation of the budget before the council, arrange a meeting afterward and go over it. If the school board's brief in a legal case has you confused, call the lawyer who wrote it. If the new master land-use plan strikes you as vague, go to the planner. If you are writing a story on a subject you feel tentative about, arrange to read it back to the sources when it is complete. Not all experts relish being asked to translate their jargon into English, so in some cases you will have to insist, politely. The best persuader is the assurance that it is far better for them to take a few minutes to explain now than to see themselves misrepresented in print.

Remember, beat reporting is a lot like gardening. Both require you to be in the field every day, cultivating. And in both the amount of the harvest is directly proportional to the amount of labor invested.

BE WARY

The point of all this effort — this preparation, perceptiveness, persistence and personal contact — is to keep your readers informed. That is an obvious statement, but it needs to be made because every reporter on a beat is under pressures that can obscure the readers' importance. You must be wary of this problem.

You will have little to do with 99.9 percent of your readers. They will not write you notes when you have done a story they like or call you when they dislike what you have written. They will not offer to buy you a cup of coffee or lunch, or stop you in the hall to urge you to see things their way. But your sources will.

The Source Trap

If you write that city council members are thinking about raising the property tax rate, you probably will hear complaints from council members about premature disclosure. If you write that the police department is wracked by dissension, expect a less-than-friendly reaction from the chief. If you write that the school superintendent is looking for a new job, the chances are that he or she will deny it even though the story is true.

All sources have points of view, programs to sell, careers to advance, opponents to undercut. It is likely and legitimate that they will try to persuade you of the merit of their viewpoint, try to sell their programs through the columns of your newspaper, try to shape the news to help their careers.

Be wary of sources' efforts to use you. You can lose the critical distance a reporter must maintain from those being covered. When that happens, you start thinking like a participant rather than an observer. You begin writing for your sources rather than your audience. This is a real danger. No one can spend as much time as a reporter on a beat does with sources or devote as much effort to understanding them without becoming sympathetic. You may forget you are writing for the outsiders when you associate so closely with the insiders.

Many veteran police reporters, for example, begin thinking like those they cover, some of them even adopting the common police officer's suspicion of journalists. The police reporter for one big-city radio station first took to carrying a gun, then quit reporting altogether to do public relations work for the sheriff's department.

One eastern newspaper had a veteran reporter covering the courts for years. A tall, dignified man with an impressive potbelly, he was called "Judge" by many of his sources, including some who were judges. He knew more law than some prosecutors and more about courthouse politics than many politicians. The trouble was that he thought, and wrote, more like a lawyer than a reporter. When he used the first-person plural pronoun in conversation, he often was referring to the attorney general's office instead of to himself and his colleagues on the paper. His writing was full of writs, dicta and other untranslated language of the law. It had become his language. Like too many diligent reporters assigned a beat, he had become part of the beat rather than an observer of it.

Writing for Readers

What does it mean to write for your readers instead of your sources? It means that you must follow these important guidelines:

1. *Translate.* The language of bureaucrats, educators and lawyers is not the same language most people speak. You need to learn the jargon of your sources, but you also need to translate it into standard English for your readers. The city planning consultant might say, "Preliminarily, the concept appeared to permit attainment of all our criteria; but, when we cost it out, we have to question its economic viability." Your lead could translate that to:

```
The proposed plan for downtown redevelopment looks good
on paper, but it may cost too much, the city's planning
consultant said today.
```

2. *Make your writing human.* In big government and big business, humanity often gets lost in numbers. Your readers want and need to know the impact of those numbers on real people. How many people will be displaced by a new highway? And who are they? Who will be affected by a school closing or a welfare cut? When a police report announced that burglaries were up by 35 percent in the last two months, an enterprising reporter told the story through the eyes of a victim. It began this way:

> Viola Patterson picked her way through the shattered glass from her front door, passed the table where her television used to sit, and stopped before the cabinet that had held her family silver.
> She wept.
> Mrs. Patterson, 72, is one of the more than 75 people victimized by burglars in the last two months.

3. *Think of the public pocketbook.* If the tax rate is going up 14 cents, how much will it cost the average homeowner? If city employees are seeking a 10 percent raise, how much will that cost in all? And what do they make now? If garbage collection fees are about to be increased, how do they compare to fees in comparable cities?

The city manager proposed "adjusting" the price of electricity to lower the cost to industrial customers and raise rates to private homes. The city hall reporter did a quick survey of comparable cities around the state. Then she wrote:

City residents, who already pay more for their electricity than residents of eight similar-sized cities around the state, would be charged an average of $4 per month more under a proposal announced Tuesday by City Manager Barry Kovac.

Industrial users, whose rate now is about average among the nine cities, would enjoy the second-lowest rate under Kovac's proposal.

Kovac defended his plan as "equitable and necessary to ensure continued economic growth for the city."

4. *Get out of the office.* City council votes are important, but far more people will have personal contact with government in the form of a police officer, a clerk, or a bus driver than they will with a council member. Go to where government meets its constituents. Ride a bus. Visit a classroom. Patrol with a police officer. Not only will you get a reader's-eye view of your beat, but you may also find some unexpected stories.

5. *Ask the reader's questions.* Why? How much will it cost me? What will I get out of it? You are the public's ombudsman.

Remember, a good beat reporter has to be prepared, be alert, be persistent and be there. If you keep in mind, too, who you are writing for, you'll keep the customers — and the editors — satisfied.

Covering the Most Important Local Beats

Your political science courses will introduce you to the structure of government, but from a reporter's viewpoint, function is usually even more important than structure. You must learn who holds the real power, who has the most influence on the power holders and who are the most likely sources of accurate information. The specifics vary from city to city, but there are some general principles that will help you in covering any form of state or local institution.

1. *Information is power.* The holder of information may be a professional administrator — the city manager, school superintendent, police chief, or court clerk — or it may be an elected official — the mayor, chairman of the county commission, or chairman of the school board. The job title is unimportant. Find the person who knows in detail how any organization really works, where the money goes and how decisions are made. Get to know that person because he (or, increasingly, she) will be the most important person on your beat.

2. *The budget is the blueprint.* This principle is a corollary of the first. Just as detailed knowledge of how an organization works is the key to controlling it, an understanding of the organization's budget

is the key to knowing how that organization works. A budget is the blueprint for the organization's activities. The budget tells where the money comes from and where it goes. It tells how many people are on the payroll and how much they are paid. It tells what programs are planned for the year and how much they will cost. Over several years' time, the budget tells where the budget makers' priorities are, what they see as their organization's role in the community.

So, find copies of the last two or three years' budgets for your beat. Try to decipher them. Learn all you can from your predecessor and from newspaper clips. Then, find the architect who drew up this blueprint — the budget director or the clerk or the assistant superintendent — and get a translation. Ask all the questions you can think of. Write down the answers.

When budget-making time arrives, follow every step. Attend every public hearing and every private discussion session you can. In those dollar figures are some of the most important stories you will write — stories of how much your readers will be paying for schools and roads and garbage pickup, stories of what they will get for their money. You'll find a guide to understanding budgets at the end of this chapter.

3. *Distributing power and money is politics.* While looking for your beat's power centers and unraveling its budget mysteries, you will be absorbing as well the most interesting part of beat reporting — politics.

At any organizational level, in any form, power and money go hand-in-hand with politics. Politics provides the mechanisms through which limited resources are allocated among many competing groups. Neither elections nor political parties are necessary for politics. You will have to learn to spot more subtle forms of political maneuvering.

If you are covering city hall, for example, pay close attention as the city budget is being drafted. You may find the major's pet project being written in by the city manager. Nobody elects the city manager, but it is good politics for him or her to keep the mayor happy. Are the builders influential in town? If so, you will probably find plenty of road and sewer projects in the budget. Are the city employees unionized? Look for healthy wage and benefit increases if they are. Is there a vocal retirees' organization? That may account for the proposed senior citizens' center. None of those projects is necessarily bad just because every one of them is political. But you and your readers ought to know who is getting what and why.

Now suppose an election is coming up, and the builders' campaign contributions will be heavy. A councilman who is running for mayor switches his vote from money for parks to money for new roads. Has a deal been made? Has a vote been sold? That's politics, too. Some digging is in order.

Power, money and politics are the crucial factors to watch in any beat reporting. With this in mind, let's take a closer look at the most important local beats.

CITY AND COUNTY GOVERNMENT

Most medium-sized cities have council-manager governments. The mayor and council members hire a professional administrator to manage the day-to-day affairs of the city. The manager, in turn, hires the police and fire chiefs, the public works director and the other department heads. Under the city charter the council is supposed to make policy and leave its implementation to the manager. Council members usually are forbidden to meddle in the affairs of any department.

Some small towns and a decreasing number of big cities have governments in which the mayor serves as chief administrator. Chicago under the late boss Richard Daley was probably the best-known example. Whatever the structure, you will have a range of good sources to draw on.

Subordinate Administrators. They know details of budgets, planning and zoning, and personnel matters. They are seldom in the spotlight, so many of them welcome a reporter's attention so long as the reporter does not get them into trouble. Many are bright and ambitious, willing to second-guess their superiors and gossip about politics, again providing you can assure them the risk is low.

Council Members. Politicians, as a rule, love to talk. What they say is not always believable, and you have to be wary of their attempts to use you, but they will talk. Like most of us, they are more likely to tell someone else's secret or expose the other guy's deal. So, ask one council member about the political forces behind another member's pet project while asking the other about the first's mayoral ambitions. That way you probably will learn all there is to know.

Pressure Groups. You can get an expert view of the city's land-use policies from land developers and a different view from conservationists. The manager or the personnel director will tell one side of the labor-management story. The head of the employees' union tells the other. How about the school board's record in hiring minorities? Get to know the head of the NAACP or of the Urban League chapter. Public officials respond to pressure. As a reporter you need to understand those pressures and who applies them.

Public Citizens. Consumer advocate Ralph Nader made the term popular, but every town has people — lawyers, housewives, business executives, retirees — who serve on charter commissions, head bond campaigns, work in elections and advise behind the scenes. Such people can be sources of sound background information and of useful assessments of officeholders.

Opponents. The best way to find out the weaknesses of any person or program is to talk with an opponent. Seek out the board member who wants to fire the school superintendent. Look up the police captain demoted by the new chief. Chat with the leader of the opposition to the new hospital. There are at least two sides to every public question and every public figure. Your job is to explore them all.

Once you have found the sources, keep looking, listening and asking for tips, for explanations, for reactions, for stories. The fun is just starting.

Covering a city is very much like covering a county government. In both cases you deal with politicians, with administrators, with budgets, with problems. The similarities may be obscured by differences in structure and style, however.

Cities are more likely to have professional administrators, for example. The administration of county governments is more likely to be in the hands of elected commissioners, supervisors or judges. Counties, too, are more likely to have a multitude of elected officials, from the sheriff to the recorder of deeds. City governments are more likely to be bureaucratized. One way to generalize about the differences is to say that city governments often are more efficient and county governments are more responsive.

These differences frequently mean, for a reporter, that county government is easier to cover. More elected officials mean more politicians. That, in turn, can mean more talkative sources, more open conflict, more points at which constituents and reporters alike can gain access to the governmental structure.

The principles and the problems of reporting are the same. The budget remains the blueprint whether it is drafted by a professional administrator or an elected officeholder. Knowledge is power whether it is the city manager or the elected county clerk who knows where the money goes. Politics is politics.

THE SCHOOLS

No institution is more important to any community than its schools. None is worse covered. And none is more demanding of or rewarding to a reporter. The issues that arise on the school beat are among the most important in our society. If it is your beat, be prepared to write about racial tensions, drug abuse, obscenity versus free speech, religious conflict, crime, labor-management disputes, politics, sex — and, yes, education.

The process of learning and teaching can be obscured by the furor arising from the more dramatic issues. Even when everyone else seems to have forgotten, though, you must not forget that all those are only side issues. The most important part of the school beat is what goes on in the classroom.

The classroom is not an easy place to cover. You may have trouble getting into one. Administrators frequently turn down such requests on the ground that a reporter's presence would be disruptive. It would, at first. But a good teacher and an unobtrusive reporter can overcome that drawback in minutes. Many papers every fall assign a reporter to an elementary school classroom. He or she visits frequently, gets to know teacher and pupils, becomes part of the furniture. And that reporter captures for readers much of the sight and sound and feeling of education.

There are other ways, too, of letting readers in on how well — or how badly — the schools are doing their job. Every school system administers some kind of standard tests designed to measure how well its students compare either to a set standard or to other students. The results of such tests are or ought to be public information. Insist on learning about them. Test scores are an inadequate measure of school quality, but they are good indicators. When you base a story on them, be sure you understand what is really being compared and what factors outside the schools may affect the scores.

Be alert to other indicators of school quality. You can find out how many graduates of your school system go to college, how many win scholarships and to what colleges. You can find out how your school system measures up to the standards of the state department of education. Does it hold the highest classification?. If not, why not? National organizations of teachers, librarians and administrators also publish standards they think schools should meet. How close do your schools come?

In education, as in anything, you get what you pay for. How does the pay of teachers in your district compare to similar-sized districts? How does the tax rate compare? What is the turnover among teachers?

You also should get to know as many teachers, administrators and students as possible. You can learn to pick out the teachers who really care about children and learning. One way to do that is to encourage them to talk about their jobs. A good teacher's warmth will come through.

One reason schools are covered poorly is that the beat often does not produce the obvious, easy stories of politics, personalities and conflict that the city hall or police beats yield. School board meetings usually produce a spark only when a side issue intrudes. Most school board members are more comfortable talking about issues other than education itself, which often is left to the professionals.

As a reporter dealing with professional educators, seeking to learn the substance of their work, your skills of translation will be tested as seldom before. The jargon of education can be virtually unintelligible. Reading, writing and arithmetic are no more. You may encounter "conceptualizing, verbal expression and computational skills." A person who is certified to teach is "certificated." The school library has become the "learning resource center." English may be "language arts."

Educators sometimes resist, but your job demands that their language be translated into that of your readers. Don't be dazzled by it. Much of the jargon is a disguise for the fact that teaching remains an art rather than the science many educators would like it to be.

The politics and the budgets of schools are very much like those of other institutions. The uniquely important things about the school are the classroom and what happens inside it. Your reporting will suffer if you forget that fact. So will your readers.

THE POLICE BEAT

The police beat probably produces more good, readable stories per hour of reporter time than any other beat. It also produces some of the worst, laziest reporting and generates many of our most serious legal and ethical problems. It is the beat many cub reporters start on and the beat many veterans stay on until they have become almost part of the force. It offers great frustration and great opportunity. All these contradictions arise from the nature of police work and of reporting.

If you are going to be a police reporter — and nearly every reporter is, at least briefly — the first thing you have to understand is what police officers are and what they do. We hire police officers to protect us from each other. We require them to deal every day with the dregs of society. Abuse and danger are parts of the job, as is boredom. We pay police officers mediocre wages and accord them little status. We ask them to be brave but compassionate, stern but tolerant. What we get very often is less what we ask for than what we should expect. Police work seldom attracts saints. Police officers are frequently cynical, often prejudiced, occasionally dishonest.

When you walk into the station for the first time as a reporter, expect to be met with some suspicion, even hostility. Young reporters often are perceived by police as being radical, unkempt, anti-authority. How closely does that description fit you or your classmates? And how many of you are pro-cop?

Police departments are quasi-military organizations, with strict chains of command and strong discipline. Their members are sworn to uphold the status quo. The reasons that police and young reporters are mutually suspicious should be clear by now.

Then how do you cover these people? You do so by using the same tricks of the trade you ply at city hall or in the schools. You should:

1. *Prepare yourself.* Take a course in law enforcement, if you can, or take a course in constitutional law. You also might read Joseph Wambaugh's novels for a realistic portrait of the police.

2. *Try to fit in.* Get a haircut, dress conservatively and learn the language. Remember that police officers, like the rest of us, usually are quicker to trust people who look and act like they do.

3. *Lend a sympathetic ear.* You enjoy talking about yourself to somebody who seems to be interested; so do most police officers. They know they have a tough job, and they like to be appreciated. Open your mind, and try to understand points of view with which you may disagree strongly.

4. *Encourage gossip.* Police officers may gossip even more than reporters do. Encourage such talk over a cup of coffee at the station, while tagging along in a patrol car or over a beer after the shift. The stories will be one-sided and exaggerated, but you may learn a lot. Those war stories are fascinating, besides.

5. *Talk with other police-watchers.* Lawyers can be good sources, especially the prosecutors and public defenders who associate every day with the police. Other law enforcement sources are good, too. Sheriff's deputies, for example, may be eager to talk about dishonesty or inefficiency in the city police department, and city police may be eager to reciprocate.

One important reason for all this work is that little of the information you need and want as a police reporter is material you are entitled to under public records laws. By law you are entitled to see only the arrest sheet (also called the arrest log, or the blotter). This record tells you only the identity of the person arrested, the charge and when the arrest took place. You are *not* entitled by law to see the arrest report or to interview the officers involved.

Writing a story depends on securing more than the bare-bones information. Finding out details depends on the good will you have generated with the desk sergeant, the shift commander and the officers on the case. The dangers — of being unfair, of damaging your and your paper's reputation — are ever-present. Good reporting requires that you know what the dangers are and how to try to avoid them.

The greatest danger arises from the one-sidedness and frequent inaccuracy of police reports. At best, the reports represent the officer's viewpoint. Particularly in cases involving violence, danger, confusion or possible repercussions, there may be plausible viewpoints different from that of the police officer. Conflicting interpretations of the same situation lead many times to the dropping of charges.

To protect yourself, and to be fair to the accused, be skeptical. Attribute any accusatory statement to the officer who made it. If the room for doubt is great enough, talk to the accused, his or her relatives or lawyer, and any witnesses you can find. The result is almost sure to be a fairer, more complete story.

Sometimes, a police officer lies. A Miami patrolman killed a fleeing suspect. The officer reported that he had pursued the victim, a robbery suspect, into a blind alley. There, he said, the man reached for his belt as though he had a gun. The patrolman claimed to have fired in self-defense.

Jim Buchanan, a reporter for the Miami Herald, had his doubts. He found witnesses, read the medical examiner's report and talked to other police officers. The witnesses said the dead youth had not offered a threat and had not even been armed. The medical examiner's report showed that the shot had come from behind, not in front of, the victim. The bullet's path showed that it had been fired from below its target. Other policemen said the officer who did the shooting was known to carry a "throwdown" gun. A "throwdown" is a weapon some police officers carry so that, if they shoot an unarmed person, the gun can be dropped near the victim as if it had been his. Investigators are likely to be harder on an officer who shoots somebody who is unarmed than they are if the victim had a weapon.

Buchanan's story demonstrated that the youth had been killed while climbing a high fence at the end of the alley, not while threatening the officer. He was able to show that the officer and others could have captured instead of killing. The youth's parents sued the city and were awarded $300,000. Buchanan won no prizes for his work. It was just the kind of probing that good reporters are supposed to do.

Reporters from The Philadelphia Inquirer spent months looking behind police reports, investigating charges of brutality and cover-ups by Philadelphia detectives. For their work in finding a pattern of confessions extracted by beatings, of fabricated evidence and other abuses, they won a Pulitzer Prize.

You may not win the Pulitzer, but you will win the respect of your peers and your readers if you remember that seeking the truth is the heart of your craft.

THE COURTS

One way to begin trying to understand the American judicial system is to think of it as a kind of game. The opposing players in a criminal case are the state, which is the accuser, and the defendant, who is the accused. In a civil case the opponents are the plaintiff and the defendant. Each player is represented by a lawyer, who does everything possible to win for his or her client. The judge referees the contest, insisting that all players abide by the rules. At the end, the judge (sometimes with a jury) decides who won.

Such an irreverent description grossly oversimplifies a system that, because of its independence and usual honesty, stands second only to a free press in protecting the liberty of Americans. But it may help in demystifying a system that also can overawe a beginning reporter.

There is a great deal in courts and the law to inspire awe. Black-robed judges and learned attorneys speak a language full of Latin phrases and highly specialized terms. Written motions, arguments and decisions are laden with convoluted sentences and references unintelligible to the uninitiated. A court can deprive you of your money or your freedom.

You can hardly cover the courts aggressively while standing awestruck, though, so here are some tips that may help restore your working skepticism:

1. *Never trust a lawyer unless you know him or her very well.* Although most lawyers are honest, every lawyer is an advocate. Consequently, everything he or she writes or says must be interpreted as being designed to help a client and hurt the opponent. That is true whether the lawyer represents the defense or prosecution in a criminal case or represents either side in a civil lawsuit. Bar association codes of ethics forbid it, but many lawyers will try to use reporters to win some advantage. Be suspicious.

2. *A judge's word may be law, but it isn't gospel.* Not every judge is a legal scholar. Most judges are, or have been, politicians. All judges are human. They are subject to error, capable of prejudice. Some are even dishonest. Otto Kerner was a judge of a federal appeals court when he was convicted of corruption that occurred while he

was governor of Illinois. Abe Fortas was a justice of the U.S. Supreme Court, a close adviser of President Lyndon B. Johnson, and Johnson's nominee for chief justice when a reporter disclosed he was receiving regular payments from a man convicted of violating federal law. Fortas resigned from the court.

3. *Truth and justice do not always prevail.* Prosecutors sometimes conceal evidence favorable to the defense. Defense lawyers sometimes seize on technicalities or rely on witnesses they know to be unreliable in order to win acquittals. Judges sometimes misinterpret the rules or ignore them. Innocent people do go to jail, and guilty ones go free. Courts are no more perfect than are newspapers. The two combined can produce frightening scenes, such as the one in Cleveland in 1954 when the newspapers screamed for blood and a political judge denied Dr. Sam Sheppard the most basic rights before convicting him of murdering his wife. The Supreme Court decision overturning that conviction became a landmark in spelling out proper trial procedures. In other cases, the press has helped correct miscarriages of justice. Reporter Gene Miller has won two Pulitzer Prizes for winning freedom for persons wrongfully imprisoned after unjust murder convictions.

The judicial system is not exempt from honest and critical reporting. And the sources of that reporting — just as in city hall or the police station — are records and people. First, a few words about court records, where to find them and how to use them.

Court Records

Whenever a case is filed in court — whether it is a criminal charge or a civil lawsuit — the court clerk assigns it a number. It also has a title. In the case of a criminal charge, the title will be *State* v. *Joe Doakes*, or something similar. (The "v." is short for "versus," the Latin word meaning "against.") A civil case — a lawsuit seeking damages, for example — could be *Joe Doakes* v. *John Doe*. Doakes would be the plaintiff, the party filing the suit. Doe would be the defendant. In order to secure the records from the clerk, you must know the case number or its title, which lawyers also call the "style" of the case.

We saw in the chapter on crime and the courts how criminal cases work their way through the court system. You can follow those cases, of course, by checking the file. At least in the more important criminal cases, however, you usually keep track by checking with the prosecutor and defense lawyers.

Once a civil suit has been filed, the defense files a reply. The plaintiff may file a motion seeking information. The defense may file a motion to dismiss the suit, which the plaintiff will answer. The judge rules on each motion. You can follow it all by checking the file regularly. Except in rare cases, all motions and information filed with the court become public records. Often, information from lawsuits can provide you with interesting insights into the otherwise private affairs of prominent persons or businesses.

Many lawsuits never go to trial before judge or jury. It is common procedure for lawyers to struggle for advantage over a period of months, filing motions and countermotions to gain the best position or to sound out the other side's strength. Then, after a trial date has been set, one side or the other will propose a settlement, which is negotiated. The case is dropped. One reason for that course of action is that the details of an out-of-court settlement need not be made public, unlike the outcome of a trial.

Human Sources

If a case goes to trial, you cover civil and criminal proceedings in much the same way. You must listen to testimony and, during breaks, corner lawyers for both sides to seek explanation and elaboration, while filling in the background from court records and your morgue. Your personal contacts are important sources of information during this process.

Lawyers. The best sources on the court beat are likely to be lawyers. Every courthouse reporter needs to win the confidence and good will of the prosecutor and his or her staff. Not only can they keep you abreast of developments in criminal prosecution, they often can — because assistant prosecutors generally are young, political and ambitious — keep you tuned in to all sorts of interesting and useful courthouse gossip. They are good sources for tips on who the best and worst judges are, which local officials may be on the take, which defense lawyers are less than upright. Like all gossip, such tips need careful handling and thorough checking. But the raw material is often there.

Lawyers in private practice can be grouped, from a reporter's viewpoint, into two classes — those who will talk and those who won't. The former class usually includes young lawyers, politically ambitious lawyers and criminal defense lawyers, all of whom often find publicity helpful. Cultivate them. Lawyers have egos only slightly smaller than those of reporters. Feed those egos. Encourage them to talk about themselves, their triumphs, their ambitions. You will reap story possibilities, background information and gossip to trade with other sources.

Judges. Don't ignore judges as sources, either. Some are so conscious of their dignity and their images that they have no time for reporters. Remember, though, that most judges in most states are elected to their jobs. That makes them politicians, and it is a rare politician who slams the door on a friendly reporter. Even many federal judges, who are appointed by the president, have done a stint in politics and still have their taste for newspaper ink. Judges' egos may be even bigger than reporters'. Treat every judge accordingly.

Other Court Sources. Many other court functionaries can be helpful sources. Police officers and sheriff's deputies or U.S. marshals assigned to court duty often are underworked and glad of a chance to talk about whatever they know, which may turn out to be good backstage stuff. The bailiffs who shout for order in court and help the judge on with a robe may be retired police officers or small-time politicians and also talkative. And secretaries, as everywhere, are good to know and even better to have know you.

You cover the courts, then, as you cover any other beat. You learn the language, figure out the records and develop your sources.

RELIGION

National surveys show that Americans in the 1980s take religion seriously. Two-thirds say they are members of a church or synagogue; three-quarters consider themselves religious. That is far more than the number who take part in politics or organized sports. Yet religion attracts far less attention from journalists. A Los Angeles Times study found that fewer than 200 newspapers even have religion reporters.

There are signs that journalism is catching up. The number of papers devoting more than 100 column inches a week to news of religion doubled between the early 1970s and the early 1980s. It's not hard to see why. Just consider some of the continuing stories in which religion plays a central or at least a major part: The rise of the New Right and the Moral Majority; the issues of abortion, euthanasia and capital punishment; the drive for a constitutional amendment to allow prayer in schools; the anti-nuclear-weapons movement; civil war in Northern Ireland, India and the Middle East; the election of two consecutive U.S. presidents who were self-proclaimed born-again Christians.

Like any other beat, religion has a variety of specialized sources and specialized problems. Read as widely as you can. The best coverage of religion and related issues can be found in such magazines as Christianity Today, the National Catholic Reporter, Christian Century, Cross Currents, Worldview, U.S. Catholic, Commonweal and Commentary. Don't overlook the denominational publications that may serve your area.

For theological expertise and local comment on major stories about religion, look up theology professors at the nearest university or seminary. But beware of their possible bias. Knowing the local religious activists, both in the clergy and outside it, may be useful, too. Who are the rebels criticizing their co-religionists for lack of concern about civil rights, poverty or other social issues? Who are the powers behind the pulpit quietly raising money, directing its spending and guiding the institution?

Because churches are also businesses, public records can be useful sources. Records in the tax assessor's office can tell you how much property the church or synagogue owns and give you at least some idea of its worth. Many churches own business buildings, parking lots, rental housing. They pay no income taxes, but their economic impact is great. Another source for checking on that economic impact can be Form 990, which churches must file with the Internal Revenue Service to maintain their tax-exempt status. Those forms are public records. A check of such sources led the Kansas City (Mo.) Times to this church-as-business story, which ran on the front page:

Millions of tax dollars are going unpaid every year because many church-operated schools quietly launder tuition payments through church collection plates and deduct them as charitable contributions.

With 17,000 students in the Roman Catholic schools of the Kansas City–St. Joseph Diocese alone, no one knows exactly how much tax money slips through the collection plate loophole. Certainly not all churches or the schools they operate offer a tuition laundry, but a survey by the Times reveals the practice is widespread throughout the country and apparently growing in popularity.

Other stories are waiting to be found. One reason that more are not found is that religious institutions and individuals too often escape the critical scrutiny that politicians and businesspeople must undergo. Religious leaders are human. They are often good, sometimes devious, occasionally rascally. Be respectful, but remember that a member of the clergy who demands deferential treatment just might be hiding something behind that ecclesiastical smile.

Another special problem in covering religion is the emotional intensity with which many people hold to their beliefs. If you do serious reporting, you will not be able to avoid arousing somebody's wrath. You can avoid arousing it needlessly, however, by doing your homework.

Do not confuse a Southern Baptist with an American Baptist, or a Lutheran of the Missouri Synod with a Lutheran of the American Lutheran Church. You will not get very far interviewing a Jesuit if you ask him what denomination he belongs to. But not every Roman Catholic priest is a Jesuit. Don't attribute the same beliefs to Orthodox and Reform Jews. And remember that Jews and Christians, though they dominate America's religious life, are only a fraction of the world's religious believers.

Some stories about religion are uplifting. They tell of selfless service to the poor, the sick, the forgotten and abandoned. They illustrate values other than money or power. They describe the courage of people who put lives and property on the line for human rights or in opposition to war. Others are not so uplifting. Parishes run up huge debts. Parochial schools hire badly trained, poorly paid teachers. Blacks are refused admission. Women are refused ordination.

Stained-glass windows are no barrier to politics. Religious issues, such as abortion, homosexuality and capital punishment, are often also political issues. Churches may use their economic clout to combat injustice or to support it. Belief can be blind.

Whatever side of religion it explores, a good story about religion will wind up on the front page along with the best of the city hall or medical stories. The techniques for getting those stories are no different, either.

SCIENCE, MEDICINE AND THE ENVIRONMENT

If you start work on a small or medium-sized newspaper, you may find that nobody is assigned full time to cover science, medicine or environmental issues. You may have a chance to stake out one or more of these interesting and important areas for yourself. On big papers such beats usually are covered by specialists, perhaps with some academic training in the area and certainly with several years of experience. Big paper or small, you will need some basic courses in the physical and biological sciences. And you will need an introduction to the special problems and sources encountered in this area.

On these beats there will be fewer meetings to attend or offices to visit than on a city hall or school beat. More of the stories here are likely to be generated by your own enterprise or by applying the local touch to a national story. You can find out what a new pesticide ban will mean to local farmers, for instance. Or you can determine whether local doctors are using a new arthritis treatment, or what a researcher at the state university is learning about the effects of alcohol on rats.

Where can you look for story ideas? Specialized publications are good places to start. Read the Journal of the American Medical Association, the New England Journal of Medicine, and Medical World. New developments and issues in medicine are covered in news stories. Scientific American and Science News are informed but readable sources of ideas in all the sciences. For environmental issues, read Natural History magazine. Your state's conservation department may put out a publication. Get on the mailing lists of the National Wildlife Federation, the Sierra Club, the Audubon Society and Friends of the Earth.

Nearly every community has human sources, too. In medicine these include members of the local medical association, the administrator of the hospital and public health officials. In the sciences, look for local school or college faculty, employees of government agencies such as extension or research centers, even interested amateurs such as those in astronomy societies. In the area of environment there usually is no shortage of advocacy groups or of industries that want to defend their interests. State and federal regulatory and research agencies are helpful, too.

The special problems posed by scientific beats begin with the language your sources use. It is a language full of Latin phrases, technical terms and numbers. You will have to learn enough of it both to ask intelligent questions and to translate the answers for your readers. A good medical dictionary and science dictionary are invaluable. Use them, and continue asking for explanations until you are sure you understand.

Another problem may be convincing scientists and physicians to talk to you in any language. Many of them have had little contact with reporters. Much of the contact they have had probably has been unpleasant, either because it arose from some controversy or because the reporter was unprepared. Reluctant sources are much more likely to cooperate if you demonstrate that you have done your homework, so you have at least some idea of what they are talking about. Promise to check your story with the sources. Accuracy is as much your goal as theirs.

In medicine a concern for privacy may deter some sources from talking freely. A physician's allegiance is, and should be, to the patient. As a reporter you have no legal right to know a patient's condition or ailment. That is true even if the patient is a public official. In fact, most information about a person's medical history and condition is protected by law from disclosure by governmental record keepers. When the mayor goes to the hospital, then, and you want to know why, your only tools are your persuasiveness and the good will you have built up with hospital officials, the attending physician or the mayor's family.

Sources also may be guarded in comments about their work. Most researchers in medicine and science are cautious in making any claims about the significance or certainty of their work. Some are not so cautious. You must be. Check and double-check, with the researcher involved and others knowledgeable in the field, before describing any development as "important" or "dramatic" or "frightening." Overstatement will damage your credibility with sources and readers.

Sometimes a researcher will be reluctant to discuss his or her work until it has been published in a professional journal or reported at a convention. Such presentation may be more important to the scientist than any newspaper publicity. An agreement to give you first notice when he or she is ready to go public may be the best you can do in those circumstances.

Despite difficulties, the coverage of science, medicine or the environment offers great challenges and rewards. The challenge is discovering and explaining developments and issues that are important to your readers. The rewards, as in all other areas of reporting, can be prizes, pay raises or — most important — recognition by your sources and your peers of a job well done. The key to success in covering these beats is the same as for any other beat: be prepared, be alert, be persistent, be there and be wary.

Making Sense of Budgets

Because the budget is the blueprint that guides the operation of any governmental agency, a reporter must learn to read it, just as a carpenter must learn to read an architect's blueprint. In either case, that isn't as difficult as it appears at first glance.

Every budget, whether it's your personal budget or the budget of the U.S. government, has two basic parts — revenues (income) and expenditures (outgo). Government revenues come from such sources as taxes, fees and service charges, and payments from other agencies (such as state aid to schools). The budget usually shows, in dollar figures and percentages, the sources of the agency's money. Expenditures go for such things as staff salaries, purchase of supplies, payment of utility bills, construction and maintenance of facilities, and insurance. Expenditures usually are listed either by line or by program. The difference is this: A "line item" budget shows a separate line for each expenditure, such as "Salary of police chief — $50,000." A "program" budget provides less detail but shows more clearly what each activity of the agency costs; for example, "Burglary prevention program — $25,000."

Now let's see what kinds of stories budgets may yield and where to look for those stories. Take a minute to scan Figure 16.4. This is the summary page from the annual budget of a small city.

The most important budget stories usually deal with changes, trends and comparisons. Budget figures change, of course, every year. At costs increase, so do budgets. But look in our sample budget

Figure 16.4 Summary Page of a Typical City Budget.

GENERAL FUND — SUMMARY

PURPOSE

The General Fund is used to finance and account for a large portion of the current operation expenditures and capital outlays of City Government. The General Fund is one of the largest and most important of the City's funds because most governmental programs (Police, Fire, Public Works, Parks and Recreation, etc.) are generally financed wholly or partially from it. The General Fund has a greater number and variety of revenue sources than any other fund, and its resources normally finance a wider range of activities.

APPROPRIATIONS

	Actual Fiscal Year 1983	Budget Fiscal Year 1984	Revised Fiscal Year 1984	Adopted Fiscal Year 1985
Personnel Services	$ 9,500,353	$11,306,619	$11,245,394	$12,212,336
Materials and Supplies	1,490,573	1,787,220	1,794,362	1,986,551
Training and Schools	93,942	150,517	170,475	219,455
Utilities	606,125	649,606	652,094	722,785
Services	1,618,525	1,865,283	1,933,300	2,254,983
Insurance and Miscellaneous	1,792,366	1,556,911	1,783,700	1,614,265
Total Operating	15,101,884	17,316,156	17,579,325	19,010,375
Capital Additions	561,145	1,123,543	875,238	460,143
Total Operating and Capital	15,663,029	18,439,699	18,454,563	19,470,518
Contingency	——	200,000	200,000	100,000
Total	$15,663,029	$18,639,699	$18,654,563	$19,570,518

at the line for the Parks and Recreation Department. There's a decrease between Fiscal Year (FY) 1984 and 1985. Why? The summary page doesn't tell you, so you'll have to look behind it, at the detail pages. There, you'll discover that the drop results from a proposal by the city staff to halt funding of a summer employment program for teenagers. That's a story.

Another change that may be newsworthy is the sharp increase in the Police Department budget. You'd better find out the reasons for that, too. In this case, the detail pages of the budget show that most of the increase is going to pay for an administrative reorganization that is adding several new positions at the top of the department. The patrol division is actually being reduced. Another story.

Look again at that Police Department line. Follow it back to FY 1983 and you'll see that the increase last year was even bigger. In two years, the budget for police has increased by nearly one-third. That's an interesting trend. The same pattern holds for the Fire De-

GENERAL FUND — SUMMARY   Figure 16.4 (continued)

DEPARTMENT EXPENDITURES

	Actual Fiscal Year 1983	Budget Fiscal Year 1984	Revised Fiscal Year 1984	Adopted Fiscal Year 1985
City Council	$ 75,144	$ 105,207	$ 90,457	$ 84,235
City Clerk	61,281	70,778	74,444	91,867
City Manager	155,992	181,219	179,125	192,900
Municipal Court	164,631	196,389	175,019	181,462
Personnel	143,366	197,844	186,247	203,020
Law Department	198,296	266,819	248,170	288,550
Planning & Community Development	295,509	377,126	360,272	405,870
Finance Department	893,344	940,450	983,342	1,212,234
Fire Department	2,837,744	3,421,112	3,257,356	3,694,333
Police Department	3,300,472	4,007,593	4,139,085	4,375,336
Health	1,033,188	1,179,243	1,157,607	1,293,362
Community Services	50,882	74,952	74,758	78,673
Energy Management	——	——	54,925	66,191
Public Works	2,838,605	3,374,152	3,381,044	3,509,979
Parks and Recreation	1,218,221	1,367,143	1,400,334	1,337,682
Communications & Info. Services	532,153	730,129	742,835	715,324
City General	1,864,200	1,949,543	1,949,543	1,739,500
Total Department Expenditures	15,663,028	18,439,699	18,454,563	19,470,518
Contingency	——	200,000	200,000	100,000
Total	$15,663,028	$18,639,699	$18,654,563	$19,570,518

partment. Some more checking is in order. With copies of previous budgets, you can see how far back the growth trend runs. You can also get from the departments the statistics on crimes and fires. Are the budget-makers responding to a demonstrated need for more protection, or is something else at work behind the scenes?

More generally, you can trace patterns in the growth of city services and city taxes, and you can compare those with changes in population. Are the rates of change comparable? Is population growth outstripping growth in services? Are residents paying more per capita for city services than five or 10 years ago? More good story possibilities.

Another kind of comparison can be useful to your readers, too. How does your city government compare in cost and services to the governments of comparable cities? A few phone calls can add perspective to budget figures. Some professional organizations have recommended levels of service, such as number of police or firefighters per 1,000 inhabitants, that can help you help your readers assess how well they're being governed.

The same guidelines can be applied to the analysis of any budget. The numbers will be different, as will the department names, but the structures will be much the same. Whether you're covering the school board or the statehouse, look for changes, trends and comparisons.

Another document that is vital to understanding the finances of local government is the annual financial report. The financial report may be a few pages or it may be a book. In any case, its purpose is relatively simple. As the name suggests, this is the explanation of the organization's financial status at the end of its fiscal year, which often is not the same as the end of the calendar year. Here you will find an accounting of all the income the organization received during the year from taxes, fees, state and federal grants, etc. You'll also find status reports on all the organization's operating funds, such as its capital improvement fund, its debt-service fund and its general fund.

Making sense of the financial report, like the budget, isn't as hard as it probably looks. For one thing, usually the financial officer includes a narrative that highlights the most important points, at least from his or her viewpoint. But you should dig behind the narrative to examine the numbers for yourself. The single most important section of the report is called the statement of revenues, expenditures and changes in fund balance, which provides important measures of the organization's financial health. Depending on the comprehensiveness of the statement, you may have to refer to the budget document as well. You can check:

1. Revenues actually received compared to budgeted revenues.
2. Actual spending compared to budgeted spending.
3. Actual spending compared to actual revenue.
4. Changes in fund balances available for spending in years to come.

Look, for example, at Figure 16.5. This combined statement gives a picture of a city in good financial health. How can you tell? Look first at the bottom line. All of the end-of-year fund balances are positive. (Negative balances, or deficits, are shown in parentheses.) Now look at the totals in the far right-hand columns. They show an increase of more than $5 million in total funds available at the end of Fiscal Year 1984 as compared to 1983. That seems a phenomenal increase, more than 50 percent. Better look more closely.

Run your eyes up those "total" columns. The explanation for the increase is about halfway up. In 1984, you see, the city sold general obligation bonds and received $6.8 million in extra income. Those bonds, of course, will have to be repaid over a period of years. In fact, then, the city has taken on a major new obligation rather than having reaped a windfall. If that hasn't already been reported, it should be now.

This statement also shows you what is happening from one year to the next in each of the city's major revenue sources. Sales tax revenue is up dramatically, while property tax revenue is down. That's good news for owners of homes and businesses. It suggests that the tax rate on real estate has been reduced. It also suggests that economic activity has picked up significantly. With a little more reporting, you may be onto another good story or two.

There are other clues that may lead to other stories. As in these examples, they'll require more reporting and more explanation than any reporter can pull from the numbers by themselves. Document in hand, head for the budget officer. The guidelines offered here should help you shape your questions and understand the answers. With financial statements, as with budgets, look for changes, trends and comparisons. And always look hard at those numbers in parentheses.

The national accounting firm of Price Waterhouse publishes a simply written guide that provides more detail than is possible here. It is called "Understanding Local Government Financial Statements." You can get a copy for the asking.

Suggested Readings

Hayes, Frederick O'Reilly. "How to Read a Budget." Columbia Journalism Review, January/February 1976, p. 21. Useful hints for budget analysis of any public agency, with a list of sources of more budgetary and policy information.

Royko, Mike. "Boss." New York: New American Library, 1971. A classic, brilliantly written study of urban machine politics.

Ullmann, John, and Steve Honeyman, editors. "The Reporter's Handbook." New York, St. Martin's Press, 1983. The first comprehensive guide to using public records and documents, written by members of Investigative Reporters and Editors. A must for serious reporters. See also the readings after the Investigative Reporting chapter. They'll be useful in beat reporting, too.

ALL GOVERNMENTAL FUND TYPES AND EXPENDABLE TRUST FUNDS FOR THE YEAR ENDED SEPTEMBER 30, 1984

	GOVERNMENTAL FUND TYPES		
	General Fund	Special Revenue Funds	Debt Service Funds
REVENUES			
General property taxes	$ 663,932	$ 530,713	$192,104
Sales tax	3,967,138	3,367,510	——
Other local taxes	3,138,904	228,718	——
Licenses and permits	253,287	5,146	——
Fines	378,207	——	——
Fees and service charges	244,356	——	——
Special assessments authorized	——	——	——
Intragovernmental	4,139,690	——	——
Revenue from other governmental units	796,292	1,164,482	——
Building rentals	——	——	——
Interest	1,314,130	196,612	6,228
Miscellaneous	53,548	——	——
TOTAL REVENUES	14,949,484	5,493,181	198,332
EXPENDITURES:			
Current:			
Policy development and administration	2,328,546	291,493	——
Public safety	8,403,851	——	——
Transportation	2,387,534	——	——
Health and environment	1,617,146	——	——
Personal development	1,915,376	622,065	——
Public buildings	——	——	——
Miscellaneous non-programmed activities:			
Interest expense	273,195	——	——
Other	34,975	——	——
Capital outlay	——	——	——
Debt service:			
Redemption of serial bonds	——	——	175,000
Interest	——	——	278,488
Fiscal agent fees	——	——	758
TOTAL EXPENDITURES	16,960,623	913,558	454,246
EXCESS (DEFICIENCY) OF REVENUES OVER EXPENDITURES	(2,011,139)	4,579,623	(255,914)

Figure 16.5 (continued)

GOVERNMENTAL FUND TYPES		FIDUCIARY FUND TYPE	TOTAL (MEMORANDUM ONLY)	
Capital Projects Fund	Special Assessment Funds	Expendable Trust Funds	1984	1983
$ ——	$ ——	$ ——	$ 1,386,749	$ 1,961,851
——	——	——	7,334,648	4,967,691
——	——	——	3,367,622	2,923,775
——	——	——	258,433	247,608
——	——	——	378,207	346,224
——	——	1,129,784	1,374,140	328,185
——	490,159	——	490,159	359,862
——	——	——	4,139,690	3,911,418
154,919	——	901,815	3,017,508	3,087,431
——	——	172,766	172,766	175,479
23,282	——	88,428	1,628,680	1,869,874
29,226	——	——	82,774	97,593
207,427	490,159	2,292,793	23,631,376	20,276,991
——	——	3,338	2,623,377	2,285,509
——	——	——	8,403,851	6,998,232
——	——	——	2,387,534	1,996,520
——	——	1,080,811	2,697,957	1,652,809
——	——	——	2,537,441	2,084,648
——	——	371,942	371,942	336,204
——	——	——	273,195	486,031
——	——	——	34,975	4,296
1,287,520	2,357,784	——	3,645,304	1,990,648
——	——	——	175,000	155,000
——	——	——	278,488	32,435
——	——	——	758	285
1,287,520	2,357,784	1,456,091	23,429,822	18,022,617
(1,080,093)	(1,867,625)	836,702	201,554	2,254,374

Figure 16.5 (continued)

	GOVERNMENTAL FUND TYPES		
	General Fund	Special Revenue Funds	Debt Service Funds
OTHER FINANCING SOURCES (USES):			
Proceeds of general obligation bonds	——	——	——
Operating transfers from other funds	3,011,358	62,974	266,711
Operating transfers to other funds	(1,292,723)	(3,348,303)	——
TOTAL OTHER FINANCING SOURCES (USES)	1,718,635	(3,285,329)	266,711
EXCESS (DEFICIENCY) OF REVENUES AND OTHER FINANCING SOURCES OVER EXPENDITURES AND OTHER FINANCING USES	(292,504)	1,294,294	10,797
FUND BALANCES, BEGINNING OF YEAR	4,195,912	3,004,533	43,645
Equity transfer to Recreation Services Fund	——	——	——
Contribution to Water & Electric Utility Fund	——	——	——
Contribution to Sanitary Sewer Utility Fund	——	——	——
Contribution to Regional Airport Fund	(200,000)	——	——
Contribution to Public Transportation Fund	——	——	——
Contribution to Parking Facilities Fund	——	——	——
Contribution to Recreation Services Fund	——	(152,000)	——
FUND BALANCES, END OF YEAR	$ 3,703,408	$4,146,827	$ 54,442

Figure 16.5 (continued)

GOVERNMENTAL FUND TYPES		FIDUCIARY FUND TYPE	TOTAL (MEMORANDUM ONLY)	
Capital Projects Fund	Special Assessment Funds	Expendable Trust Funds	1984	1983
5,681,633	1,134,261	——	6,815,894	——
415,038	469,865	——	4,225,946	3,466,261
——	(99,667)	(527,506)	(5,268,199)	(4,401,847)
6,096,671	1,504,459	(527,506)	5,773,641	(935,586)
5,016,578	(363,166)	309,196	5,975,195	1,318,788
628,856	781,248	514,378	9,168,572	8,489,184
——	——	(1,532)	(1,532)	(292,958)
——	——	——	——	(30,395)
——	——	——	——	(71,367)
——	——	——	(200,000)	(160,191)
——	——	——	——	(4,000)
——	——	——	——	(15,489)
——	——	——	(152,000)	(65,000)
$5,645,434	$ 418,082	$ 822,042	$14,790,235	$ 9,168,572

17

Business and Consumer News

Not so long ago, business news was regarded by many reporters and editors as that dreary stuff full of numbers and unfathomable terms that separated the stock market tables from the ads somewhere in the back of the paper. Those days are gone. Business has become big news. Newspapers in the past few years have expanded both the quantity and the quality of their coverage of economic activities. Investigative and analytical stories, reports on community efforts to lure new industries or bolster old ones, and profiles of corporate decision makers now turn up on the front page as well as the business page.

Likewise, newspapers today devote much more attention to stories aimed at the consumers of what business sells. In front-page stories and feature-page columns, newspapers are telling readers how to do everything from buying insurance to reducing energy use. Other consumer stories may expose frauds or report on the efforts of lobbying groups.

The surge in popularity — among journalists and readers alike — of these two closely related types of stories reflects a growing awareness of how economics, politics and everyday life are linked. Inflation affects tax policies, which affect paychecks. International alliances affect tariff rates, which in turn affect imports, prices and jobs, and even election outcomes. Virtually any story can be a business story. And nearly any business story can be a consumer story.

Business news and consumer news are among the major beats of

322

many newspapers. Increasingly, the reporters who cover these beats are emerging from business journalism programs at such schools of journalism as the University of Missouri, Columbia University and American University. Many other business reporters have had their skills sharpened at mid-career programs offered by Missouri, Columbia and the Wharton School at the University of Pennsylvania. But you don't have to be a specialist to do good work in either field. You do need an understanding of basic economics, a working knowledge of the language of business, and the skills of any reporter on a beat. You also need an awareness of the special sources and special problems of these beats, which we will examine here.

In this chapter you will learn:

1. How to prepare to cover business news.
2. Where to find it.
3. How to understand the numbers of business.
4. How to find and report consumer news.

Preparing to Cover Business News

The range of business stories can be as broad as the range of business itself. A business story may be about promotions and retirements. It may concentrate on a company's potential profits, of interest to investors and potential investors in that company. It can be a story about a new kind of instant camera that would interest not just shareholders of the company but potential buyers as well. It may deal with a drought in Kansas that affects the price farmers in Michigan will get for their wheat and the price homemakers in Florida may pay for English muffins. It can be a personality profile of a corporate executive that gives some insight into the way business is conducted. It may be about a new industrial plant that could affect persons looking for jobs, or owners of stores that sell goods to people with jobs. Or it can focus on the style of dress in New York offices — trends that may indicate how readers elsewhere may soon dress.

These stories have obvious local angles. Sometimes, though, the local angle is not that obvious. The story about a decision by the Federal Reserve Board's Open Market Committee to expand or tighten the money supply may seem esoteric. But it can affect your readers' ability to get a loan for a new car or house and the rate they pay for that loan. Or it can affect them in how it adds to or subtracts from inflation. News of a sizable trade deficit for the United States may weaken the value of the dollar and increase the price of a Sony TV, a Volkswagen or a bottle of Cutty Sark Scotch whisky.

Although most major corporate and economic decisions that affect us all are made in Washington, New York, Chicago and a few other major metropolitan centers, those cities do not have a monopoly on the creation and coverage of business news. Even in towns of a few thousand residents, businesses will be opening or closing, manufacturing plants will be increasing or decreasing production, hiring or firing employees. And those residents will be spending money for houses or cars, ski trips or Harris tweeds, or socking it away in the town's banks or savings and loan associations. There is a business story in every such development.

Business stories can be as bright and as interesting as any story in any other section of the paper. That is demonstrated every day in such publications as The Wall Street Journal, The New York Times, the Chicago Tribune, Business Week and Fortune magazine. Here, for example, is the beginning of a Boston Globe story about fraud in the commodity futures trading business:

> The town of Vina, Ala. (pop. 366), will never be the same.
>
> Chuck LeMieux went down there in the spring of 1973 and they're still talking about him. And looking for him.
>
> It started when he bought the Vina Packing Co. Just walked in, courted the bankers, got some cash and bought it. Bought it with 10 years of unpaid debt behind him, his pingpong ball company — Tennex — going bust in Connecticut, his two radio stations — WELM and WKOP — on the brink of receivership in New York, City National Bank of Bridgeport about to foreclose on his mortgages, and dunning letters coming from all over the world.
>
> But the hundreds of thousands of dollars owed up North didn't stop him from acting like a Rockefeller down South.

You don't have to be from Vina to want to read on.

HOW TO REPORT BUSINESS STORIES

What separates a business story from a soccer story — or, for that matter, a soccer story from a story about atomic particles — is the knowledge and language required to ask the right questions, to recognize the newsworthy answers and to write the story in a way that the reader without specialized knowledge will understand. A reporter who understands the subject can explain what the jargon means.

For example, the term "prime rate" by itself may be meaningless to a majority of newspaper readers. If the reporter explains that the prime rate is a benchmark interest rate banks quote to their customers and that it is a somewhat negotiable figure, readers can see that an increase of one percentage point in the prime rate probably will result in a higher rate of interest on a car loan or home mortgage.

But beware of writing in such simplistic terms that you tell your readers nothing useful. Besides failing your readers, you will lose respect for your newspaper in the business community. The Wall Street Journal avoids both traps by shunning jargon as much as possible and explaining any technical terms essential to the story. In one story, for example, the Journal explained the terms Federal Open Market Committee, federal funds rate, M1, M2 and free-reserve position. The sophisticated reader might know what those terms mean, but no doubt many of the paper's readers wouldn't. The Boston Globe series mentioned earlier on the highly complicated problem of commodity options included a glossary of terms and an explanation of the mechanics of the business.

Former presidential economic adviser Gardner Ackley once said he would like to see two things in people covering economics and business news: first, that they had taken a course in economics, and second, that they had passed it. Financial journalist Louis Rukeyser urges newspapers to enlarge their "coverage of the nation's economic scene: reporting, analysis and commentary of the highest order, adequately and prominently displayed. . . . We need more bright young journalists educated and trained, able and willing to operate on that broad frontier where politics and economics meet — and confuse each other."

Most journalism schools and departments require students to take at least one course in economics, but too often that course is regarded in the same light as dental surgery or a hangover: If we hold our breath and dull our senses, time will take care of the pain.

Much of the animosity — and there is real animosity — between the press and business arises because too many practitioners of each neither understand nor want to understand what the other is trying to accomplish. Many reporters regard profits as some kind of social disease. Reporters and editors often see their own work as a noble demonstration of the freedom guaranteed by the Constitution but look upon business and business people as, at best, necessary evils. Many business managers view reporters and editors with a similar lack of respect or understanding.

You need not approve of everything business does, but to condemn it for trying to do what it is supposed to do — earn a profit — is like complaining about apples because they don't taste like oranges. Even Jane Fonda, activist and actress turned entrepreneur, says her exposure to business has changed her attitudes. "I am much more sensitive to the bottom line, and I must live with the tensions and contradictions that that brings," she told Fortune magazine. Business executives must realize that it is not the job of the press to make them look good and that reporters who ask tough questions or refuse to swallow every press release are not attacking the foundations of the free enterprise system.

The mistrust that many businesspeople have of the press can make it difficult to cover stories adequately, even when it would be in their interest to see that the story is told. Or, if executives are willing to talk, they may become angry if the reporter quotes an opposing point of view or points out a wart on the corporate visage.

The best antidote a reporter can use against this congenital animosity is to report fairly and accurately what a business is doing and saying. By always being fair, you usually can win the trust and confidence of businesspeople, even if the latter reserve admiration for someone who can squeeze a few more cents of per-share profits out of the third quarter.

As in covering any other beat, the main precaution to take in covering the business beat is to guard against becoming so close to your sources that you start to think more like them than like a reporter. Being conscious of that danger usually is enough to prevent its happening, but another way is to switch beats occasionally so you can deal with new people and new sets of circumstances.

Since business executives tend to be cautious when it comes to talking with reporters, it may help you to dress more like a business manager than a guru. That does not mean that you have to think like a manager, but appearances do count, and businesspeople, like reporters, plumbers, generals and linebackers, feel more comfortable with their own kind.

The more you can demonstrate that you understand their business, the more likely you are to generate the trust that will draw out the information you seek. "Understanding" is not synonymous with "sympathy," but ignorance usually means a reporter is apt to misinterpret what is said. When the Columbia Missourian put together a package on "Who Owns Main Street?" sources spent hours talking with the reporters because they felt comfortable with the reporters' extensive knowledge of the complicated subject.

Although public relations people often are helpful in providing background information and directing you to the executives who can provide other comment and information, you should try to get to know as many company officials as you can. Sometimes you can do this best through a "harmless" interview, one not generated by a crisis but intended simply to learn about what the company is doing. Perhaps you can arrange to have lunch, to see what the officials are thinking about and to give them a chance to see you are probably not the demon they may have thought you to be.

Always remember that a company, government agency or pressure group may be trying to use you to plant stories that serve some special interest. Companies want a story to make them look favorable to investors with the hope of driving up the price of the stock or to make them attractive merger partners. If you are suspicious, do some more digging; talk to competitors and analysts, and ask detailed questions. Just because a company or some other group is pushing a story does not mean you have to write it. The best place for some interview notes is the wastebasket.

In short, a business reporter should be all the things a good reporter is — honest, fair, alert to possible new stories and to new angles on old stories. Business writing can be rewarding, both financially (because specialists usually earn premium pay) and intellectually.

WHERE TO FIND BUSINESS NEWS

The starting point in writing a business story is similar to that of any story — understanding the subject you're writing about. For the business reporter, that almost always means some basic research into the subject. For openers, check your paper's library to learn what's been written locally about your topic or company.

Then move on to other secondary sources. The good business reporter knows how to use the Readers' Guide to Periodical Literature, the Business Periodicals Index, The New York Times Index, The Wall Street Journal Index and perhaps the National Newspaper Index (which indexes the Times, the Journal, The Los Angeles Times, The Washington Post and the Christian Science Monitor). These indexes will tell you where to find stories about your business or industry.

Another valuable secondary source for business reporters is Predicasts' F & S Index of Corporations and Industries, considered by many the best index for company and industry information. Predicasts indexes a broad range of business, financial and industrial periodicals, plus a few reports by brokerage houses. For information on foreign companies, see Predicasts' F & S Index International. The Public Affairs Information Service Bulletin is a less inclusive index from the areas of economics, social conditions, public administration and international relations.

Of growing importance are computer searches of data bases that provide lists and summaries of stories published on a broad range of subjects. Typical companies providing data are Newsearch, Standard & Poor's, Predicasts, Dow Jones and Disclosure Inc.

Records and Reports

Here are some good sources of information that you will find invaluable when writing business stories.

1. Corporate data. Basic information on corporations can be found in three directories published annually. Each usually is in your university or public library. Dun & Bradstreet's Million Dollar Directory includes almost 40,000 U.S. companies worth $1 million or more. It lists officers and directors, products or services, sales, number of employees and address and telephone number. The Middle Market Directory profiles companies worth $500,000 to $999,999. The three-volume Standard & Poor's Register of Corporations, Directors and Executives provides similar information for some 36,000 U.S. and Canadian companies. Volume 2 lists executives and directors with brief biographies. The third directory is the Thomas Register of American Manufacturers and Thomas Register Catalog File. The 11 volumes are more comprehensive than the other two directories.

2. Investment data. To get specific information about the financial performance of a company or an industry, check reports prepared by Standard & Poor's (especially valuable is S&P's Compustat Services Inc.), Moody's, Dun & Bradstreet or Value Line Investment Survey. These reports also discuss company prospects and major trends. Also helpful are annual corporate scoreboards prepared by Fortune, Business Week and Forbes magazines. You would be wise to purchase and file these issues for future reference.

3. Financial ratios. To assess a company's financial picture and management, you should compare your subject's financial ratios with the averages for other firms in the same industry. Industry ratios and averages can be found in reports prepared by Dun & Bradstreet, Moody's, S&P's Compustat and in a number of trade journals.

4. Company filings. For years the Securities and Exchange Commission operated under the guiding principle that companies should make available a maximum amount of information so that stockholders could make the most informed decision regarding management's performance. The SEC preferred to keep out of corporate affairs and let the stockholders provide necessary discipline. Much of that information was made public through SEC filings. In recent years, the SEC has required less information, but corporate filings remain a valuable source of information for reporters. The novice should start with the annual report, the 10-K and the proxy statement, all of which generally can be obtained from the company simply by asking. The annual report and 10-K give you an overview of the company's operations and finances. The proxy statement, which goes to shareholders before the annual meeting or other important meetings, provides an outline of issues to be voted on. It also can contain genuine news nuggets about the company's dealings. When Seafirst Corp. asked shareholders to approve its merger with a subsidiary of BankAmerica Corp. in May 1983, the company disclosed on Page 35 of the 244-page document that the SEC was conducting an informal investigation into whether Seafirst had violated federal laws on financial disclosure. The 1982 CBS proxy statement noted that former anchorman Walter Cronkite had a contract that would pay him $1 million annually for seven years for acting as special correspondent and consultant and for various "special assignments."

Another valuable SEC document is the prospectus, which is filed when new stock is being offered. The prospectus gives an overview of the company's operation and finances, what it owns and controls, and how it plans to use the proceeds of the stock sale. Also worth noting are the 8-K, the 10-Q and the 13-D. The 8-K, or current update, must be filed within 15 days after any significant changes occur, including changed control of the company, major purchases or the hiring of new auditors. The 10-Q is the unaudited quarterly update of the 10-K. The 13-D must be filed by persons or companies buying more than 5 percent of most publicly held companies.

Many companies are quite willing to send you their annual report, 10-K and proxy statement. They may even send you the other documents outlined above. To keep up with SEC filings, you may want to follow the SEC News Digest at your local library. To obtain specific filings, you can contact Disclosure Inc. or Charles E. Simon and Co., both of which, for a fee, will provide copies of reports filed with the SEC by public companies.

5. Trade press. Beyond the newspapers and magazines you all know and read is another segment of journalism known as the trade press. In these journals and house organs you will find grocers talking with grocers, undertakers talking with undertakers and bankers talking with bankers. You will learn the important issues in a field, how an industry markets its products and services, and what legislation it fears and favors. Interested in health care and physicians? Try Medical Economics, where investigative reporter Jessica Mitford predicts you will find "many a crass and wonderfully quotable appeal to the avarice of the practitioners of the healing arts." When Chris Welles wrote a piece on the health hazards of modern cosmetics, much of his best information came from trade magazines. He found the specific periodicals by looking in the Drug & Cosmetics Periodicals Index and the F & S Index of Corporations and Industries.

A number of trade publications are independent and objective. Among them are Advertising Age, Aviation Week & Space Technology, Institutional Investor, Oil & Gas Journal, American Banker,

Medical World News and Variety. Many more, however, are virtual industry public relations organs. Even these can be valuable for learning about current issues, marketing and lobbying strategies, and even market shares. To find trade publications, consult the Standard Periodical Directory, Ulrich's International Periodicals Directory, Standard Rate & Data Service: Business Publication Rates and Data, and Ayer Directory of Publications.

6. Newsletters.   Newsletters have become an important source of inside information in recent years. Some are purely ideological, but others can be valuable. Among the best are Energy Daily, Nucleonics Week, Education Daily, Higher Education Daily and the Washington Report on Medicine. To find newsletters, consult The Newsletter Yearbook Directory.

7. Associations.   Although trade associations clearly represent the interests of their members, they can provide expert commentary on current issues or give explanations from the perspective of the industry. When The New York Times reported on the revival of the moving industry, the Household Goods Carriers Bureau, a major trade group, proved to be an important source. The Wall Street Journal found the National Association of Realtors a valuable source for a story on housing costs. To find trade associations, look in the Encyclopedia of Associations or the National Trade and Professional Associations of the United States and Canada and Labor Unions.

8. Directories.   Directories can be an invaluable tool in seeking information on companies, organizations or individuals. You can use them to learn who makes a certain product, to identify company officers or directors, or to find an expert source for an interview. Basic directories include Who's Who, Directory of Directories, Guide to American Directories, Consultants and Consulting Organizations Directory, Directory of Special Libraries & Information Centers, Research Centers Directory, Consumer Sourcebook, Statistical Sources and Directory of Industrial Data Sources. To contact companies by phone or mail, look in the National Directory of Addresses and Telephone Numbers, published by Concord Reference Books Inc.

9. Court records.   Most companies disclose only information required by the SEC. But when a corporation sues or is sued, an extensive amount of material becomes available. In preparing her story on Jim Walter Corp. for the Jackson (Miss.) Clarion-Ledger, Maria Halkias found court records of great value. "A complicated lawsuit filed by consumers, subcontractors or former employees can tell a lot about a company's personality that doesn't always come out of the interviews," she said. "The discovery period often makes public exhibits that would be difficult for a reporter to get his hands on, such as contracts, memos, correspondence, working papers, etc. Also, depositions can reveal company practices or intentions that would probably be denied in an interview." Check courts of all levels, including bankruptcy court.

10. Others.　The preceding items are certainly not exhaustive. Other relevant materials may be found at local tax and record-keeping offices, as well as in filings with the Federal Trade Commission, the Federal Communications Commission, the Food and Drug Administration, the Interstate Commerce Commission, the Labor Department and various state agencies. Crain's Chicago Business used Census Bureau figures as the basis of a story on retail sales trends. The U.S. Government Manual lists and describes government agencies, including their functions and programs. And a number of private firms specialize in economic analysis, such as the Wharton Economic Forecasting Associates and Chase Econometrics. In writing about the benefits OPEC could reap from the oil company mergers of early 1984, The Wall Street Journal cited figures generated by the Wharton firm.

Don't overlook documents and testimony from congressional hearings. Chris Welles drew much of the best material for his book on the ending of fixed brokerage commissions, "The Last Days of the Club," from the 29 volumes of hearings and reports that came out of several years of investigations by two congressional subcommittees. The best indication of the vast array of materials available is found in the preface to "Empire," the extensive examination of the Howard Hughes empire by Donald L. Barlett and James B. Steele. They cite as their sources:

> thousands of Hughes' handwritten and dictated memoranda, family letters, CIA memoranda, FBI reports, contracts with nearly a dozen departments and agencies of the federal government, loan agreements, corporate charters, census reports, college records, federal income-tax returns, Oral History transcripts, partnership agreements, autopsy reports, birth and death records, marriage license applications, divorce records, naturalization petitions, bankruptcy records, corporation annual reports, stock offering circulars, real estate assessment records, notary public commissions, applications for pilot certificates, powers of attorney, minutes of board meetings of Hughes' companies, police records, transcripts of Securities and Exchange Commission proceedings, annual assessment work affidavits, transcripts of Civil Aeronautics Board proceedings, the daily logs of Hughes' activities, hearings and reports of committees of the House of Representatives and Senate, transcripts of Federal Communications Commission proceedings, wills, estates records, grand jury testimony, trial transcripts, civil and criminal court records.

For guidance through the maze of documents, directories and other source books, several sources are particularly valuable. They are "Business Information Sources," by Lorna M. Daniells, published by University of California Press; "The Reporter's Handbook: An Investigator's Guide to Documents and Techniques," edited by John Ullmann and Steve Honeyman, published by St. Martin's Press; "Manual of Corporate Investigation," published by the AFL-CIO; "Building Corporate Profiles: Sources & Strategies for Investigative Reporters," by Alan Guggenheim, published by Salem Press; "Where to Find Business Information," by David M. Brownstone and Gorton Carruth, published by John Wiley & Sons; and "The Encyclopedia of Business Information Sources," published by Gale Research Co.

Human Sources

Who are the people you should talk to on the business beat? Here are some who are important sources of information.

1. Company officials. Although many public relations people can be helpful, the most valuable information probably will come from the head of the corporation or its divisions. Chief executive officers are powerful people, either out front or behind the scenes, in your community. They are often interesting, usually well-informed. Not all of them will be glad to see you, but you need to make every effort to see them. Don't automatically assume the public relations person is trying to block your path. Many people working in corporate communications are truly professional and can be of assistance.

2. Analysts. To learn what the experts think about specific companies, many business reporters contact securities analysts. Analysts can be valuable if they are not overused and if you get information on the company from other sources as well. When it wrote about the possibility that broadcasting and entertainment companies could become takeover targets, The Wall Street Journal strengthened its story with a quote from an analyst with Donaldson Lufkin & Jenrette Securities. To find the appropriate analyst, consult Nelson's Directory of Wall Street Research or the Financial Analysts Federation membership directory.

Other analysts and researchers, frequently economists, are employed by banks, trade groups, Chambers of Commerce and local businesses. They often are willing to talk because the exposure is good for their organizations. In its story on the oil mergers, the Journal also spoke with former Energy Secretary James R. Schlesinger, senior adviser to the investment firm of Lehman Brothers Kuhn Loeb Inc.

3. Academic experts.   Your college or university will have faculty members with training and experience in varying areas of business and economics. Often they are good sources of local reaction to national developments or analysis of economic trends. They are usually happy to cooperate. Many university public information offices prepare lists of their nationally or regionally known experts and their phone numbers. The lists are available for the asking.

4. Chamber of Commerce officials.   Their bias is clearly pro-business, and they will seldom make an on-the-record negative comment about business, but they usually know who is who and what is what in the business community. The chamber may be involved in such projects as downtown revitalization and industry recruiting.

5. Former employees.   The best business reporters say that frequently their most valuable sources are former employees of the company they're profiling. Writes Welles, "Nobody knows more about a corporation than someone who has actually worked there." He warns, "Many, probably most, have axes to grind, especially if they were fired; indeed, the more willing they are to talk, the more biased they are likely to be." The good reporter will show care in using materials thus gained.

6. Labor leaders.   For the other side of many business stories and for pieces on working conditions, upcoming contracts and politics, get to know local union officials. The workings, legal and otherwise, of unions make good stories, too.

7. Others.   Don't overlook the value of a company's customers, suppliers and competitors. You also may want to consult with local bankers, legislators, legislative staff members, law enforcement agencies and regulators, board members, oversight committee members, and the like.

Announcements and Meetings

The source of much business news, and the *starting point* for many good stories, is the announcement by a company of a new product or the firm's reaction to some action by a government agency. Such announcements should be treated like any press release. The same standards apply to judging newsworthiness, and the same reporting techniques come into play.

The news may come in a news conference, which may be called to respond to a general situation such as a strike or oil shortage. Or it may be called to try to add some glitter to a corporate announcement the company feels will be ignored if done by press releases alone. You can almost tell how newsworthy something is going to be by the amount of paraphernalia on hand in the press conference room. The more charts, graphs, enlarged photos, projectors and screens in the room, the more likely you are to be dazzled instead of enlightened. They should not be ignored, however, because you can never be sure in advance that something newsworthy will *not* be said.

If you work in a city where one or more corporations are based, you will have the opportunity to cover an annual meeting, which invariably produces some news. Although some are more lively and more newsworthy than others, all say something about the state of the company's business and provide an opportunity for shareholders to ask management questions about the company's performance. A typical story on an annual meeting might begin:

> Executives of Condor Airlines assured stockholders Monday that, despite last year's loss of $1.8 million, the company is in no danger of collapse or takeover.
>
> Company president Fred Sherman told the annual meeting that passenger numbers are climbing and so is revenue.
>
> "If the government would just lift some of its silly and unneeded so-called safety requirements, we would be in the black in no time," he said.
>
> In answer to a question from the floor, Sherman defended the 10 percent salary raises given the company's top executives.
>
> "If you want top people, you've got to pay top salaries," he said. Sherman's salary went up last year from $100,000 to $110,000.

Reporter Enterprise

As in other areas of journalism, often the best business news stories are generated by a reporter's own initiative, sparked by a hunch or a tip passed along by an editor, a shareholder, or a disgruntled employee or customer. Sometimes, a self-promoting source can lead to a good story. When the president of a commodity options firm called the Boston Globe to suggest a story on her company, reporter Susan Trausch was dispatched. It was a new company and headed by a woman. But the reporter quickly became suspicious of some things she saw and was told. The investigation that followed produced a series on abuses in an unregulated industry and won several national prizes. The original caller got her name in the paper, all right, but hardly as she had expected.

In other cases a press release may raise questions that turn into stories. For example, a routine announcement of an executive appointment may lead a curious reporter to a story about the financial problems that produced the changes in leadership. A stockholder's question may result in a story about a new trend in corporate financing or a shift in emphasis on operations within the company. Sometimes, an offhand comment at lunch about what one executive has heard about another company will lead to a front-page story after you do some digging. Or a former employee's call that a company is quietly laying off workers may produce a story about the firm's declining fortunes.

A discussion by Chicago Tribune writers and editors about how to explain the impact of world trade on Illinois residents led to a six-part series that won the University of Missouri's business journalism award. The series began by focusing on one worker's plight (a writing technique we discussed in Chapter 15):

"You work for a joint 22 years. Then they tell you one day that it's all over. Where do you go? For me, it's all over. I'll sell my excess junk and go on welfare. If that's what they want, that's what they'll get."

Steve Soltis is 47. Last September, his job as a steel shearer vanished when Youngstown Sheet & Tube Co. closed part of its ancient mill beside the Mahoning River in Youngstown, Ohio, and laid off 5,000 workers. . . .

Steve Soltis is a casualty in one of the battles in a threatening world trade war.

This and most other major business stories are developed by using a combination of human and documentary sources. The techniques are no different from those of covering city hall, sports or science.

LOOKING AT THE NUMBERS

Although most reporters find accounting about as appealing as quantum physics or microbiology, an understanding of the numbers business generates is essential to any intelligent analysis of a company or industry. The most complete summary of the financial picture of a business is found in the annual report.

An annual report may be viewed as a statement of the image a company wants to project. Some companies print their reports on the highest quality paper and fill them with big, bright color pictures; others try to project an image of dignity. Occasionally an annual report's presentation will reflect the financial health or illness of a company. The 1980 Chrysler Corp. report is a classic; the company reported a net loss of $1.7 billion in a black-and-white report that was 32 pages long, on plain paper stock and without a single photograph. The next year it reported a loss of "only" $475 million in a report on heavier paper, and with 16 color pictures of its best-selling products. In 1982 Chrysler touted a profit of $170 million in a splashy, multi-colored report that included a color portrait of Chairman Lee Iacocca.

More than 100 million copies of annual reports are pumped out each year at a cost of $1 to $5 each. Before its breakup, AT&T printed more than 4.5 million copies annually. Reports are sent to shareholders, investment analysts, employees, customers, public affairs officers, corporate sales divisions, journalists and professors.

Annual reports can be a valuable tool, but you should realize that they are not written to be read like a magazine. Rather, annual reports should be approached by sections with specific goals in mind. Accountants suggest that readers skim sections and move from point to point. They note that it is less like reading than a process of digging out information.

Most veterans start with the auditor's report, which is generally located near the back between the explanations of the footnotes and the supplemental financial information. A two-paragraph report is standard; it states that the material conforms to generally accepted auditing standards and that it fairly represents the financial condition of the company. Anything longer than two paragraphs usually indicates problems. The 1980 Braniff International Corp. annual report, an anemic 20 pages, contained a four-paragraph report that warned, "There are conditions which indicate that the company may be unable to continue as a going concern." The Wall Street Journal story on the report said it spelled out the extent of the company's financial troubles. Of course, such a harsh statement came as no surprise to reporters covering Braniff regularly because they had seen the quarterly results and other indications of financial difficulties. But it is unusual for accountants to be so forthright; that in itself made the event newsworthy.

Next, move to the footnotes. The first note usually deals with the accounting policies used in preparing the report. Look for techniques that could affect earnings. For example, if the company changed its method of calculating inventories, profits would be affected. First-in, first-out (FIFO) inventory valuation uses the assumption that the goods that are sold are those that have been in inventory the longest; last-in, first-out (LIFO) valuation assumes that the goods sold have been in inventory the shortest. Movement from FIFO inventory valuation to LIFO would tend to decrease reported profits in a period of rising prices. So before you come to a conclusion about earnings, determine if the figure is being produced by accounting techniques or management decisions. Another footnote will deal with pension policies. Determine the size of the firm's unfunded pension liabilities. Then see if the company has changed its assumptions on the rate of return for invested pension funds. Both could be the basis for stories.

Now flip back to the front and find the report from the chairman. It is usually addressed "To our shareholders" and should give an overview of company performance. It also should tell why the firm performed as it did and what it sees for the years ahead. In the 1982 Warner Communications Inc. report, Chairman Stephen J. Ross told how that year had been a disappointment despite record earnings because Warner knew 1983 would be a bad year. Ross then discussed the Atari unit's plummeting earnings and the prospects for a rebound. The comments reflected the more forthright approach the SEC in recent years has urged corporate management to take in the chairman's letter.

Next take a few minutes to look over the company's operating divisions to get an idea of its different products. You should look for areas that will help the company in the future. Perhaps a new product has been developed or another company has been acquired that will boost profits.

After that you're ready to look at the numbers. These financial statements tell you if the company's earnings are increasing or decreasing, if sales are up or down, if the company's financial ratios are in line with its industry or not. The balance sheet should be considered a snapshot of the company on one day, generally the last day of the fiscal year. The left side of the balance sheet lists the assets, or what the company owns. On the right side are the liabilities, or what the company owes, and the shareholders' equity, or the dollar value of what stockholders own. The two sides must balance, so the balance sheet can be summarized as assets equal liabilities plus shareholders' equity. Current assets are what the company could convert into cash quickly; current liabilities are due in a year and are paid out of current assets. The difference between the two is an important figure called working capital. Management and stockholders want this number to grow each year. If it doesn't, problems may be looming. On the Foremost-McKesson balance sheets (see Figure 17.1), you can determine that the company's working capital for 1983 was $307,273,000, an increase from the $279,910,000 of the previous year.

The second major report is the income statement, which also is referred to as an earnings report or a statement of profit and loss. It answers the key question: How much money did the company make for the year? Look first at net sales or operating revenues and determine if they are going up or down. If they are going up, are they going up faster than last year and faster than the rate of inflation? If sales are rising slower than inflation, the company could have serious problems. At Panhandle Eastern Corp., a natural gas supplier, operating revenues have risen slowly over the last three years. (See Figure 17.2)

The income statement also shows how much it cost to sell the company's products and arrives at an operating profit or net income or net profit figure for the year. Again, determine its trend and factor in inflation. Keep in mind that these numbers may be affected by things other than ongoing operations. A company might have sold

CONSOLIDATED BALANCE SHEETS
Foremost-McKesson, Inc.
(In thousands)

ASSETS

March 31	1983	1982	1981
CURRENT ASSETS			
Cash	$ 46,748	$ 43,108	$ 34,615
Receivables (Note 2)	369,259	335,447	314,540
Inventories (Notes 1 and 3)	418,993	388,393	387,401
Prepaid expenses (Note 13)	13,677	12,066	12,075
Total	848,677	779,014	748,631
PROPERTY, PLANT AND EQUIPMENT (Notes 1 and 10)			
Land	16,927	18,551	12,180
Buildings	111,892	116,308	99,895
Machinery and equipment	271,930	245,523	200,938
Total	400,749	380,382	313,013
Accumulated depreciation	150,531	141,678	119,915
Net	250,218	238,704	193,098
INVESTMENTS			
Foreign companies (Notes 1 and 4)	34,634	36,219	36,984
Other (Notes 1 and 5)	59,853	29,024	8,085
Total	94,487	65,243	45,069
OTHER ASSETS			
Goodwill and other intangibles	93,000	91,312	91,090
Net assets of discontinued operations (Note 6)	41,730	112,574	108,131
Notes receivable	30,784	30,963	24,300
Other	13,916	10,785	5,114
Total	179,430	245,634	228,635
Total	$1,372,812	$1,328,595	$1,215,433

See Financial Notes.

Figure 17.1   A Typical Corporate Balance Sheet.

off a losing division, which would increase the net profit for one year. For Panhandle Eastern, net income has been declining for the last three years, reflecting general problems in the natural gas industry and specific problems with Panhandle Eastern's liquefied natural gas contracts with Algeria.

If looked at with the same cautious eye, earnings per share also

CONSOLIDATED BALANCE SHEETS
Foremost-McKesson, Inc.
(In thousands)

LIABILITIES AND EQUITY	Figure 17.1 (continued)		
March 31	1983	1982	1981
CURRENT LIABILITIES			
Accounts and drafts payable	$ 429,633	$ 395,068	$ 355,700
Current portion of long-term debt (Notes 8 and 10)	14,138	15,762	32,130
Salaries and wages	35,036	35,307	33,631
Taxes	15,398	15,853	26,572
Interest and dividends	16,930	15,800	14,485
Other	30,269	21,314	22,927
Total	541,404	499,104	485,445
LONG-TERM DEBT			
Nonconvertible debt (Note 8)	156,056	189,062	164,728
Convertible debt (Note 9)	87,960	92,684	29,068
Capital lease obligations (Note 10)	19,269	23,077	26,944
Total	263,285	304,823	220,740
DEFERRED TAXES ON INCOME (Note 13)	57,840	43,129	29,031
REDEEMABLE PREFERRED STOCK— SERIES B (Note 11)	191	196	4,220
NONREDEEMABLE PREFERRED STOCK— SERIES A (Note 11)	14,371	16,670	22,009
COMMON STOCKHOLDER EQUITY (Note 12)			
Common stock	37,707	36,165	33,054
Other capital	117,029	96,922	67,420
Retained earnings	422,172	405,971	364,776
Accumulated translation adjustment (Note 1)	(5,805)	(3,024)	
Treasury shares, at cost	(75,382)	(71,361)	(11,262)
Net	495,721	464,673	453,988
Total	$1,372,812	$1,328,595	$1,215,433

can be helpful. Earnings per share is determined by dividing net earnings, minus preferred stock dividends, by the average number of common shares outstanding during the year. Investors often focus inordinately on EPS without considering the varied factors that

CONSOLIDATED STATEMENT OF INCOME
Panhandle Eastern Corporation and Subsidiaries
(In thousands)

Years Ended December 31		1983	1982	1981
OPERATING REVENUES	Gas *Note 3*	$3,019,659	$2,864,735	$2,669,537
	Crude oil and liquids	184,214	211,322	216,322
	Drilling contracts	113,126	209,642	227,768
	Other	88,246	98,574	147,915
	Total	3,405,245	3,384,273	3,261,542
COSTS AND EXPENSES	Gas purchased	1,962,285	2,166,299	2,011,075
	General and administrative	127,633	142,389	120,657
	Operating	490,709	375,874	326,432
	Maintenance	58,679	70,123	67,654
	Depreciation, depletion and amortization *Note 2*	226,346	198,531	187,280
	State, local and miscellaneous Federal taxes *Note 9*	57,643	48,173	87,376
		2,923,295	3,001,389	2,800,474
	Provisions for helium royalty, gas royalty, Alaskan project and coal gasification *Notes 10, 17 and 19*	47,017	51,534	36,961
	Total	2,970,312	3,052,923	2,837,435
	Operating Income	434,933	331,350	424,107
OTHER INCOME	Equity in earnings of unconsolidated affiliates *Note 10*	57,870	30,850	33,983
	Allowance for equity funds charged to construction	——	19,722	17,198
	Dividends—National Distillers and Chemical Corp.	6,600	6,600	6,600
	Interest and miscellaneous	37,081	20,512	23,859
	Total	101,551	77,684	81,640
	Gross income	536,484	409,034	505,747
INTEREST EXPENSE	Interest and other charges	250,255	223,174	203,669
	Interest on borrowed funds charged to construction	(26,294)	(75,109)	(82,104)
	Total	223,961	148,065	121,565
	Income before income taxes	312,523	260,969	384,182
TAXES ON INCOME	Provision for income taxes	168,696	116,347	178,177
	Investment tax credit	(8,611)	(75,254)	(55,599)
	Total *Note 4*	160,085	41,093	122,578
NET INCOME		$ 152,438	$ 219,876	$ 261,604
	Average shares outstanding (Thousands)	41,866	40,997	40,115
	Earnings per common share	$3.64	$5.36	$6.52

See accompanying notes to consolidated financial statements

Figure 17.2 **A Typical Corporate Income Statement.**

could affect it. You also might find the net retained earnings at the bottom of the page. While investors want to see EPS rising, management likes to see retained earnings increase because it means the firm has more funds to put back into business activity to spur growth.

The third important report you will find is variously called the statement of sources and applications of funds, the sources and uses of funds or the statement of changes in financial position. This statement adds net income and depreciation to produce total cash flow. It shows what the company did with its cash. The key figure here is increase or decrease in working capital. The Wendy's statement shows that working capital decreased in 1983, rose in 1982 and decreased in '81. (See Figure 17.3) The alert reporter would ask questions about those fluctuations.

Company management and financial analysts calculate a number of ratios to gain better insights into the financial health of an organization. One important test of earnings is the relation of net income to sales — also called net profit ratio or return on sales — which is obtained through dividing net income by sales. This will tell you how much of profit after taxes was produced by each dollar of sales. This figure will vary by industry, but the 1983 Business Week all-industry (1,200 largest corporations in 39 industries) composite return on sales was 4.5 percent, a solid rebound from the 3.6 percent in recession-plagued 1982. One ratio that investors find particularly interesting is return on equity, which shows how hard the shareholders' investment is working. To find it, divide net income minus preferred dividends by the common stockholders' equity for the previous year. The 1983 Business Week all-industry composite return on equity was 11.5 percent, a bit better than the 11 percent of 1982.

Because of the recession and high interest rates of the early 1980s, many companies borrowed substantial sums at high rates. To determine if your company is too heavily in debt, divide the long-term liabilities by the stockholders' equity, which will give you the debt-to-equity ratio. A high ratio shows that the company has borrowed extensively, which by itself isn't bad. If sales are growing and cash is coming in, the debt may present no problem. But if sales slow, watch for problems. Some industries — like utilities — have higher ratios than others.

To determine how easily your company can meet its obligations, divide the current assets by the current liabilities to yield the current or working capital ratio. Nonfinancial companies should have on hand twice as much in assets as liabilities; a ratio of 4 or 5 to 1 is generally excessive.

Investors will be particularly interested in the price-earnings (P/E) ratio and the dividend payout. The P/E ratio is calculated by dividing the company's price per share in the stock market by its earn-

CONSOLIDATED STATEMENT OF CHANGES IN FINANCIAL POSITION
Wendy's International, Inc. and Subsidiaries
(In thousands)

Years Ended December 31	1983	1982	1981
SOURCES OF WORKING CAPITAL			
Operations:			
Net income	$ 55,220	$ 44,102	$ 36,852
Items not involving working capital:			
Depreciation and amortization	26,276	22,151	16,291
Deferred income taxes	7,678	6,157	3,948
Total from operations	89,174	72,410	57,091
Property and equipment dispositions, net	5,562	4,376	2,649
Additional long-term obligations	6,132	23,401	34,145
Purchase of franchises—long-term obligations	3,986		41,522
Issuances of common stock	486	29,085	46,040
Unexpended construction funds	5,434	1,094	(7,067)
Net decrease (increase) in other assets	1,719	(8,426)	(9,688)
Total sources of working capital	112,493	121,940	164,692
DISPOSITIONS OF WORKING CAPITAL			
Property and equipment additions	80,227	70,620	68,749
Payments on long-term obligations,			
including conversions to current	25,593	18,063	20,129
Cash dividends	10,597	7,810	6,722
Investment in and advances to equity subsidiaries, net	6,019	7,884	4,587
Purchase of franchises and Sisters International, Inc.:			
Property and equipment, net	3,251		52,782
Cost in excess of net assets acquired	2,520		11,436
Other	1,290		4,282
Other changes, net	(65)	4,109	3,438
Total dispositions of working capital	129,432	108,486	172,125
EFFECTS OF FOREIGN CURRENCY TRANSLATION			
Reduction in property and equipment	2,555	3,145	
Reduction in term debt	(924)	(731)	
Reduction in shareholders' equity	(1,460)	(2,335)	
Net effect of foreign currency translation	171	79	
(DECREASE) INCREASE IN WORKING CAPITAL	$ (16,768)	$ 13,533	$ (7,433)

Figure 17.3 A Typical Corporate Statement of Changes in Financial Position.

CONSOLIDATED STATEMENT OF CHANGES IN FINANCIAL POSITION

Wendy's International, Inc. and Subsidiaries

Figure 17.3 (continued)

(In thousands)

Years Ended December 31	1983	1982	1981
CHANGE IN COMPONENTS OF WORKING CAPITAL			
Increase (decrease) in Current assets:			
Cash and Short-term investments	$ (6,074)	$ 16,421	$ 9,199
Accounts and Notes receivable	1,565	(1,348)	5,040
Advances to equity subsidiaries	4,833		
Inventories and other	1,067	2,614	(338)
	1,391	17,687	13,901
Increase (decrease) in Current liabilities:			
Accounts and drafts payable and Accrued expenses	17,295	(2,997)	18,021
Income taxes	(3,035)	9,885	(2,183)
Current portion of long-term obligations	3,899	(2,734)	5,496
	18,159	4,154	21,334
(DECREASE) INCREASE IN WORKING CAPITAL	$ (16,768)	$13,533	$ (7,433)

The accompanying notes beginning on page 32 are an integral part of the consolidated financial statements.

ings per share. So if the stock is selling for $50 per share and earnings are $3, the P/E would be about 17 to 1, or the stock would be selling for about 17 times earnings. Generally, the P/E will be higher for a company that is growing, is doing well and apparently will continue to perform well. Over the past 40 years, the P/E for industrial stocks followed by Standard & Poor's has ranged from 5.9 to 22.4.

Dividends are declared quarterly and generally are prominently noted in the annual report. Dividends are an inducement to shareholders to invest in a company. Because companies want to see dividends rise each quarter, they sometimes go so far as to change their accounting or pension assumptions so enough funds will be available to increase dividends.

Now that you have taken a quick look at an annual report and its numbers, it is time for some important words of caution. First, the numbers in an annual report, although certified by an auditor and presented in accordance with Securities and Exchange Commission regulations, are not definitive because they are a function of the accounting assumptions used in their preparation. That leads to the second and third points: A company's numbers should be looked at in the context of both its industry and several years' performance.

To understand how well a firm is performing, the numbers must be examined along with those of other firms in the same industry. For example, the debt-equity ratios of utilities are much higher than those of most manufacturing companies, such as auto manufacturers. Look at how the company has performed for the last five to 10 years. Then you will discern trends, instead of basing your conclusions on a year's performance, which may be atypical.

The next caution: Don't think reading this section or passing an accounting course makes you qualified to analyze a company's finances. Rather, use the knowledge gained in this chapter to reach some preliminary conclusions that you should pursue with the experts and then with company officials. Only the best reporters are qualified to draw conclusions from company financial data and only after years of study and practice.

To develop a better understanding of company finances, many reporters attend mid-career workshops on accounting and financial analysis held at universities. You can develop a better understanding of this complex subject by reading several books. Among the best are: "Understanding Wall Street," published by the New York Stock Exchange; "How to Read a Financial Report," published by Merrill Lynch; "Accounting: The Language of Business," by Sidney Davidson, Clyde P. Stickney and Roman L. Weil, published by Thomas Horton and Daughters Inc.; "Understanding Financial Statements," by John N. Myer, published by Mentor Books; and "Techniques of Financial Analysis," by Erich A. Helfert, published by Richard D. Irwin, Inc.

Business Week, Fortune and Forbes compile annual corporate scoreboards that contain a wealth of information. The wise reporter purchases and files these issues for future reference. A number of companies prepare supplements to their annual reports to make them easier to understand, including International Paper Co., Phillips Petroleum Co. and Armstrong World Industries. Figgie International Inc. even prepares an annual report for children called "Ump's Fwat."

Consumer News

The phrase "consumer news" is in its broadest sense arbitrary and redundant. All news is, directly or indirectly, about consumers. And many business stories could just as easily be called consumer stories. A story about the stock market may affect or be of interest to "consumers" of stocks and bonds even though those items aren't "consumed" in the same sense as corn flakes. A story about OPEC raising the price of crude oil affects consumers of gasoline and many other products refined from crude oil. A story about a drought that may drive up the price of wheat has an impact on consumers of hamburger buns. And a story that beef prices are increasing affects the consumer of the hamburger that goes with the bun. The person who has purchased the newspaper in which your stories run is a consumer of newspapers.

Consumer news deals with events or ideas that affect readers in their role as buyers of goods and services in the marketplace. Although news of that kind has existed for as long as there have been newspapers and was spread by word of mouth long before that, its development as a conscious area of coverage generally began in the mid-1960s with the development of vocal consumer groups. The consumer movement was helped along immeasurably by Ralph Nader's book "Unsafe at Any Speed," an attack on the Chevrolet Corvair. General Motors Corp.'s subsequent attempts to spy on him and the ensuing publicity when the matter went before Congress also generated interest.

Figure 17.4   Consumer Advocacy. Ralph Nader popularized the role of the "public citizen" as a force for change and as a source for consumer reporters.

In many ways consumerism is as much a political as an economic movement. The wave of federal, state and local regulations promulgated in the 1960s and '70s attests to that fact. Such legislation has affected producers of goods not only in the area of safety, but also in the realms of finance, labeling and pricing.

The media have played such a major role in publicizing crusaders such as Nader and their causes that in many respects the consumer movement is a creature of the media. Those who espouse consumer causes recognize the power public exposure can bring them. This means to you as a reporter that, while consumer groups may be friendlier than businesspeople, they too will try to use you to their advantage.

WHERE TO FIND CONSUMER NEWS

Sources of consumer news fall into three general categories: government agencies, quasi-public consumer groups, and private businesses. Let's consider each of these groups.

Government Agencies

Many municipalities, especially large cities, have a public consumer advocate who reports to the mayor and calls public attention to problems that affect consumers. Most county prosecuting attorneys' offices also have someone — or even a whole department — to challenge business practices of questionable legality. Cases of consumer fraud — cases where people pay for something they do not receive or pay for something of one quality and receive something less — are handled by these offices.

At the state level most states have a consumer affairs office to investigate consumer problems and to order or recommend solutions. In addition, state attorneys general investigate and prosecute cases of consumer fraud. Most states also have regulatory commissions that represent the public in a variety of areas. The most common commissions regulate insurance rates and practices, rates and levels of service of utilities and transportation companies, and practices of banks and savings and loan associations.

At the federal level, the government regulatory agencies involved in consumer affairs have the power to make rules and the power to enforce them. Among these are:

- The Federal Trade Commission, which oversees matters related to advertising and product safety.
- The Food and Drug Administration, which watches over prices and safety rules for drugs, foods and a variety of other health-related items.

- The Securities and Exchange Commission, which oversees the registration of securities in corporations and regulates the exchange, or trading, of those securities.
- The Interstate Commerce Commission, which regulates prices and levels of service provided by surface-transportation companies in interstate commerce.
- The Federal Power Commission, which regulates the rates and levels of service provided by interstate energy companies.

Virtually every other federal cabinet office or agency deals with some form of consumer protection, ranging from banking and finance to education to housing to highway and vehicle safety. These agencies are useful to reporters in several ways. First, they are good sources of background information and data of almost every conceivable form. Second, they are good sources of "hard" information such as the results of investigations, cautionary orders, and the status of legislation affecting their area of expertise. Also, public information officers of these offices, regulatory agencies and even congressmen and senators usually are accessible and helpful in ferreting out information for reporters. You may have to make several calls to Washington to get plugged into the right office, but that can be done easily and quite quickly. Many federal agencies have regional offices in major cities.

Quasi-Public Consumer Groups

Quasi-public consumer groups are composed of private citizens who say they represent the consumer's interest. They, too, are often good sources of background information or comment.

Consumers Union, which publishes the popular Consumer Reports, and Common Cause, which lobbies for federal and state legislation, are general in nature. Others are specialists, such as the Sierra Club, which concentrates on environmental matters. Still other groups may be more local in scope. They may try to enact such legislation as returnable-bottle ordinances or to fight what they perceive as discrimination in the way housing loans are made by banks and savings and loan associations. The Better Business Bureau monitors local business practices.

These groups, through their ability to attract the attention of the media and to find sympathetic ears in Washington and the state capitals, have a greater impact on legislation and news coverage than their numbers would suggest. It is always a good idea to try to determine just who a particular group represents and how broad its support is, especially in cases where the group has not already established its legitimacy. The group may be an association with many members or merely a self-appointed committee with little or no gen-

Figure 17.5   Consumer Reporting. Consumer Reports is a good source of story ideas and information on product quality and other issues important to nearly every reader.

eral support. One person, under the guise of an association or committee, can rent a hotel meeting room and call a news conference to say almost anything. Such is the nature of the media that in most cases at least one reporter will attend the news conference and write something about it. The broader a group's support, the greater the impact of its statement. If Consumer Reports says an auto model is dangerous, that judgment is national news. If an individual says the same thing, nobody pays any attention.

Businesses

Virtually all large corporations and many smaller ones have public relations departments. They function to try to present their company in the most favorable light and to mask the scars as well as possible when the company is attacked from the outside, whether by the press, the government or a consumer group.

Because of the successes of the consumer movement, a number of companies have taken the offensive and have instituted programs they deem to be in the public interest. We see oil companies telling drivers how to economize on gasoline, the electric utility telling homeowners how to keep their electric bills at a minimum, banks suggesting ways to manage money better, and the telephone company pointing out the times it is least expensive to make long-distance calls.

Corporate public relations people can be valuable sources for a variety of stories by providing background information or comments and reactions to events affecting their company. Also, they may help a reporter place an event in some sort of perspective as it affects a company or industry. Sometimes they are good primary sources for feature stories about products or personalities.

HOW TO REPORT CONSUMER STORIES

Consumer stories may be "exposés," bringing to light a practice relating to consumers that is dangerous or that increases the price of a product or service. Research for such stories can be simple and inexpensive to conduct and the findings may arouse intense reader interest. The project can be something as simple as buying hamburger at every supermarket in town to see if all purchases weigh what they are marked. Or it may be something that takes more time and work, such as surveying auto repair shops to see how much unnecessary repair work is done or how much necessary repair work is not diagnosed. The St. Petersburg (Fla.) Times, for example, has a feature called "Watch This Space," in which the claims of advertising are put to the test. Sometimes the claims prove exaggerated, and sometimes they are accurate. The story is readable either way. Thomas P. Lee of the Tucson (Ariz.) Citizen explored how consumers paid $5 million more for natural gas than necessary, demonstrating that stories can be both business- and consumer-oriented.

Consumer stories also may be informational, intended to help readers make wiser or less expensive purchases. For example, if beef prices are rising, you may suggest protein substitutes that will be as healthful and less expensive. Or you may want to discuss the advantages and disadvantages of buying a late-model used car instead of a new one. Or you can point out the advantages and disadvantages of buying term life insurance instead of ordinary life insurance.

Other consumer stories may be cautionary, warning readers of impending price increases for products, quality problems with products or questionable practices of business or consumer groups. Such stories can have great impact. The Knight-Ridder chain's revelation that the Firestone radial tires suspected of repeated failures had not passed some of the company's own quality tests helped force a recall that cost the company millions of dollars. Ralph Nader's exposé of the Corvair led to the discontinuance of the model.

Sometimes the newspaper can act as a surrogate for consumers. The best example of this is the "Action Line" kind of question-and-answer column published in many newspapers. A column like this has the power of the paper behind questions to companies and thus often is more successful than an individual in reaching satisfactory settlements on questions of refunds, undelivered purchases and other reader complaints.

Consumer and business news stories can provide valuable services not only to readers who are consumers but to readers who are producers and financiers and regulators as well. But they must be carefully reported and compellingly written.

One especially valuable source of information for consumer stories is the Consumer Sourcebook, published by Gale Research Co. The two volumes describe more than 135 federal and 800 state and local agencies and bureaus that provide aid or information dealing with consumers.

Suggested Readings

Barlett, Donald L., and James B. Steele. "Empire: The Life, Legend and Madness of Howard Hughes." New York: Norton Press, 1979. Massive study of Hughes' empire showing diversity of documentary sources authors used in their research.

Bonafede, Dom. "We're the Good, Rich Guys." Washington Journalism Review, January/February 1979, p. 26. A critique of the public relations efforts by big business.

MacDougall, A. Kent. "Ninety Seconds to Tell It All: Big Business and the News Media." Homewood, Ill.: Dow Jones–Irwin, 1981. Examination of the business-press relationship.

Mitford, Jessica. "Poison Penmanship: The Gentle Art of Muckraking." New York: Vintage Books, 1957. Valuable introduction on sources, especially the trade press, and then 17 investigative pieces with commentary on the reporting techniques.

Morgan, Dan. "Merchants of Grain." New York: The Viking Press, 1979. Excellent use of sources in analysis of the international grain trade. Especially impressive because the companies are privately held.

Rukeyser, Louis. "What's Ahead for the Economy: The Challenge and the Chance." New York: Simon and Schuster, 1983. Overview and commentary on major economic issues of the 1980s from a free-market perspective.

18

Sports

This may be the most famous lead ever written for a newspaper story:

Outlined against a blue-gray October sky, the Four Horsemen rode again. In dramatic lore, they are known as Famine, Pestilence, Destruction and Death. These are only aliases. Their real names are Stuhldreher, Miller, Crowley and Layden. They formed the crest of the South Bend cyclone before which another fighting Army football team was swept over the precipice at the Polo Grounds yesterday afternoon as 55,000 spectators peered down on the bewildering panorama spread on the green plain below.

Sportswriting, like the rest of the world, has changed since Grantland Rice crafted those flowery phrases to begin his account of the 1924 Notre Dame–Army game. Styles are less ornate. Subject matter is more diverse. Some reporters, at least, have begun to explore the business and sociology of sports.

In many ways, though, Grantland Rice would feel at home in today's sports departments. Most sports reporters still are sports fans. Critical, probing reporting still is the exception rather than the rule. Writers trying to be colorful still spew out copy that is full of clichés instead.

Readers deserve better. Even if sports were only the toy department of life, sportswriting — like toys — should be entertaining and educational. But sports in America is more than that. The heroes and the language of sports are woven into our politics and our literature. Sports itself is big business. Any institution so pervasive and influential demands solid coverage. Sports offers a reporter all the elements of which good stories are made — triumph, heartbreak, courage, skullduggery, comedy, artistry, even love and hate.

352

Some of America's best-known writers and journalists began as sportswriters. Ernest Hemingway, Damon Runyon, Heywood Broun, Paul Gallico and Ring Lardner were among them. New York Times columnist James Reston not only wrote sports, but spent some time as traveling secretary for the Cincinnati Reds baseball team before turning to political reporting. The late Red Smith never left the sports pages but won the Pulitzer Prize for his columns.

In this chapter you will learn:

1. How to apply the techniques of beat reporting to the special challenges of sports.
2. How to cover a sports event.
3. How to avoid the trap of clichés in writing sports.

Covering the Sports Beat

A sportswriter for The Washington Post once wrote a column describing a typical colleague. He concluded:

> He lives in a beautiful world where it's always game time and yesterday's tragedies fade like the ripples on a lake. He's the eternal juvenile who would not change places with a king. He's Pagliacci, the Pied Piper, Walter Mitty, Peter Pan, and Jack Armstrong, the All-American Boy.

That description hardly fits a good reporter. Can you imagine an aggressive city hall reporter "living in a beautiful world where it's always council meeting time"?

Another writer, Leonard Schecter, was even harsher. He characterized most sports reporters as "so droolingly grateful for the opportunity to make their living as nonpaying fans at sporting events that they devoted much of their energy to stepping on no toes."

Few reporters in other areas are fans of the subjects they cover. Reporters who cover education don't go to school board meetings for fun. Medical writers don't spend their days off watching operations. Many sports reporters, though, were sports fans first. The sports editor of one Florida newspaper so worshiped the New York Yankees that he named his firstborn son after Mickey Mantle.

Many sports reporters, of course, do not fit Schecter's description. The best — and those who are trying to emulate the best —

bring to their work the same critical eyes and probing questions that good reporters on any other beat do. They have to. You will have to, as well, if you want to do more than the "consistently bland and hero worshipful" coverage Schecter sees from too many of his colleagues.

In Chapter 16, we discussed the techniques employed by successful reporters. Review them. They apply to coverage of sports as well as to politics or education or science. Now we will see how they can help you meet the special challenges of reporting sports.

BEING PREPARED

Before you even thought about sports reporting, the chances are that you were reading, watching, playing sports. In that sense, at least, preparing to be a sports reporter is easier than preparing to cover city hall. Nobody grows up reading budgets. But there is more to preparation than immersing yourself in sports. Competition pushes people to their limits, bringing out their best and worst. So you need to know some psychology. Sports has played a major role in the struggles of blacks and women for equality. So you need to know some sociology and history. Sports, professional and amateur, is big business. So you need a background in economics. Some of our greatest writers have portrayed life through sports. So you need to explore literature.

Grantland Rice, the most famous American sportswriter in the first half of this century, graduated Phi Beta Kappa from Vanderbilt University. He majored in Latin and Greek. His prose may have been overblown by our standards, but he wrote some memorable poetry, too. And he knew who the Four Horsemen of the Apocalypse were.

BEING ALERT AND PERSISTENT

Not long after the University of Texas coach complained that Oklahoma was spying on his team before their game, a reporter for the Oklahoma City Times spotted a helicopter landing near the Oklahoma stadium. Curious, he learned that its passenger was the oilman identified as the employer of the "spy." More digging revealed that the oilman was a heavy gambler and a business associate of the Oklahoma coach. Reporters learned that the "spy" had lived in the home of an Oklahoma assistant coach.

Then, as sports reporter Frank Boggs and investigative reporter Jack Taylor were checking some leads on the gambling angle, they encountered an investigator from the National Collegiate Athletic Association. Perhaps Oklahoma, which had been placed on probation for violating NCAA rules three times in the last 21 years, was being investigated again. The reporters checked NCAA and university sources. They confirmed that the NCAA was investigating allegations that football players were being helped by coaches to resell tickets at inflated prices.

The story was played at the top of Page One. University officials issued misleading denials. Fans in the football-mad state reacted bitterly — not against the university for cheating or lying but against the newspaper and its reporters for telling the truth. Hundreds of subscriptions were canceled. Boggs was given police protection after receiving threats against his life. Even Taylor's father questioned the mid-season timing of the stories.

The reporters persisted, and further details of the investigation were published. Boggs devoted a column to defending himself and explaining sportswriting. He wrote:

> Maybe sportswriters are gullible, perhaps naive. We exist in a world of excitement and Sousa music and beautiful cheerleading girls who surely will wind up in tears whether their team won or lost. We often become good friends of the coaches and of their wives, and when a coach is under attack, we feel doubly saddened. . . .
>
> But sportswriters are also newspapermen, and they must be newspapermen first and sportswriters second.

If more sports reporters displayed the alertness and persistence of the Oklahoma City reporters, no room would be left for distinctions between "sportswriters" and "newspapermen." There should be no difference.

The thrill of the contest and the roar of the crowd can obscure the real story. Long Island's Newsday, for example, looked behind the victory of a championship high school swimming team and found that three team members had used fake addresses to enroll in the school. Sports editor John Steadman of the Baltimore News American found a great story in a sport most sports pages ignore — slow-pitch softball. He wrote:

> There was a throw from the outfield, the runner was coming to the plate and catcher Paul Rasinski turned to make the tag. That's when it happened. . . .
>
> Tomorrow, it'll be one year. An anniversary.
>
> Now Paul Rasinski is trying to learn to walk again. It hasn't been easy.

Steadman went on to tell a story of rare courage — the story of a young athlete who had become a quadriplegic. It was more than just a sports story.

Here are a few tips to help you find stories that are different from — and better than — the ones everyone else is writing:

1. *Look for the losers.* Losing may not — as football coaches and other philosophers like to assert — build character, but it certainly bares character. Winners are likely to be full of confidence, champagne and clichés. Losers are likely to be full of self-doubt, second-guessing and surliness. Winners' dressing rooms are magnets for sportswriters, but you usually can tell your readers more about the game and those who play it by seeking out the losers.

2. *Look for the bench warmers.* If you follow the reporting crowd, you'll end up in front of your local version of Joe Thiesman or Chris Evert-Lloyd every time. Head in the other direction. Talk to the would-be football player who has spent four years practicing but never gets into a game. Talk to the woman who dreams of being a professional golfer but is not yet good enough. Talk to the baseball player who is growing old in the minor leagues. If you do, you may find people who both love their sport more and understand it better than do the stars. You may find less press agentry and more humanity.

3. *Look beyond the crowds.* Some of the best, and most important, sports stories draw neither crowds of reporters nor crowds of fans. The recent and rapid growth of women's sports is one example. Under the pressure of federal law — the "Title IX" you read and hear about — the traditional male dominance of facilities and money in school and college athletics is giving way slowly to equal treatment for women. From junior high schools to major universities, women's teams now compete in virtually every sport except football. With better coaching and more incentive, the quality of performance is increasing, too. The results of this revolution are likely to be felt far beyond the playing fields, just as the earlier admission of blacks to athletic equality advanced blacks' standing in other areas. Male-run sports departments, like male-run athletic departments, can no longer overlook women athletes.

The so-called "minor" sports and "participant" sports are other largely untapped sources of good stories. More Americans watch birds than play football. More hunt or fish than play basketball. More watch stock car races that watch track meets. But those and similar sports are usually covered — if at all — by the newest or least talented reporter on the staff. Get out of the press box. Drop by a bowling alley, a skeet-shooting range, the local college's Frisbee-throwing tournament. Anywhere you find people competing — against each other, against nature, against their own limits — you can find good stories. Once you have found them, persist with follow-up questions and close observation until you have enough to satisfy your readers' desire to know the hows and whys.

Figure 18.1 Being There. Covering a game from the press box, as Al Harvin of The New York Times is doing, is one part of what it takes to be a good sports reporter.

BEING THERE AND DEVELOPING CONTACTS

Being there, of course, is half the fun of sports reporting. You're there at the big games, matches and meets. You're there in the locker rooms, on team buses and planes, with an inside view of athletics and athletes that few fans ever get. And you should be there, most of the time. If you are to answer your readers' questions, if you are to provide insight and anecdote, you must be there, most of the time.

Sometimes you should try being where the fans are. Plunk down $10 (of the newspaper's money) for an end-zone seat and write about a football game from the average fan's point of view. Cover a baseball game from the bleachers. Cold hot dogs and warm beer are as much a part of the event as is a double play. Watch one of those weekend sports shows on television and compare the way a track meet or a fishing trip is presented to the way it is in person. Join a city league softball team or a bowling league for a different kind of inside view.

A sports reporter must develop and cherish sources just as a city hall reporter must. You look for the same kinds of sources on both beats. Players, coaches and administrators — like city council members and city managers — are obvious sources. Go beyond them. Trainers and equipment managers have insiders' views and sometimes lack the fierce protectiveness that often keeps players, for example, from talking candidly. Alumni can be excellent sources for high school and college sports stories. If a coach is about to be fired or a new fund drive is being planned, important alumni are sure to be involved. You can find out who they are by checking with the alumni association or by examining the list of major contributors

Figure 18.2 Locker Room Interview. A Federal court ruling enabled women to interview in a professional baseball locker room for the first time. Most professional sports teams now either permit women in the locker rooms or set up separate interview rooms. But "being there" to conduct postgame interviews is still not always easy for women reporters.

that every college proudly compiles. The business managers and secretaries who handle the money can be invaluable for much-needed but seldom-done stories about the finances of sport at all levels. Former players sometimes will talk more candidly than those who are still involved in a program. As on any beat, look for people who may be disgruntled — a fired assistant coach, a benched star, a big contributor to a losing team. And when you find good sources, cherish them. Keep in contact, flatter them, protect them. They are your lifeline.

BEING WARY AND DIGGING FOR THE REAL STORY

It is even harder for a sports reporter than it is for a political or police reporter to maintain a critical distance from the beat. The most obvious reason is that most of the people who become sports reporters do so because they are sports fans. To be a fan is precisely the opposite of being a dispassionate, critical observer. In addition, athletics — especially big-time athletics — is glamorous and exciting. The sports reporter associates daily with the stars and the coaches whom others, including cynical city hall reporters and hard-bitten managing editors, pay to admire at a distance. Finally, sports figures ranging from high school coaches to owners of professional baseball teams deliberately and persistently seek to buy the favor of the reporters who cover their sports.

We are taught from childhood that it is disgraceful to bite the hand that feeds you. Professional, and many college, teams routinely feed reporters. (One Missouri newspaper created a minor furor when it disclosed that a lobbyist in the state capital took political reporters to St. Louis for baseball games. But it creates no furor at all for the same baseball team to give free admission, free food and free beer to the reporters covering those games.) Major-league baseball teams even pay reporters to serve as official scorers for the game. In one embarrassing incident the reporter-scorer made a controversial decision that preserved a no-hit game for a hometown pitcher. His story of the game made little mention of his official role. The reporter for the opposition paper wrote that if it had been *his* turn to be scorer, he would have ruled the other way.

Sports journalism used to be even more parasitic on the teams it covered than is the case now. At one time reporters routinely traveled with a team at the team's expense. Good newspapers pay their own way today.

Even today, however, many reporters find it rewarding monetarily as well as psychologically to stay in favor with the teams and athletes they cover. Many teams pay reporters to write promotional pieces for game programs. And writing personality profiles or "inside" accounts for the dozens of sports magazines can be a profitable sideline.

Most sports reporters, and the editors who permit such activities, argue that they are not corrupted by what they are given. Most surely are not. But temptation is there for those who would succumb. Beyond that, any writer who takes more than information from those he or she covers is also likely to receive pressure, however subtle, from the givers.

Every sports reporter is given a great deal by high school and college coaches or publicity agents, who feed reporters sheets of statistics, arrange interviews, provide space on the team bus or plane, and allow access to practice fields and locker rooms. And what do they want in return? They expect nothing more than an unbroken series of favorable stories. Too often, they get just that. Only the names have been changed in this excerpt from a metropolitan newspaper:

The State U. troops reported today to begin three weeks' tune-up before the Fighting Beagles invade Western State.

Offensive commander Pug Stanley had some thoughts available Thursday before some 90-odd players arrived.

"We really made some strides this year," Stanley declared. . . . Charlie Walker, he said, is no longer feeling his way around at quarterback. The Beagle pass catchers are hardly old men, but the top four targets are two juniors and two sophomores rather than two sophomores and two freshmen.

State U.'s heaviest artillery is located behind Charlie Walker. Beagle runners ranged from good to outstanding a year ago. Most are back, with a season's more experience.

"Our runners keep on getting better," commented their attack boss. "Our backfield has to be our biggest plus. We're going to burn some people with it this year."

The story did not mention that State U., which had managed only a 6–5 record the previous year against weak opposition, was universally picked to finish in the second division of its second-rate conference. That's not only bad writing, but bad reporting.

Anywhere athletics is taken seriously, from the high schools of Texas to the stadiums of the National Football League, athletes and coaches are used to being given special treatment. Many think of themselves as being somehow different from and better than ordinary people. Many fans agree. Good reporters, though, regard sports as a beat, not a love affair. Tom Tuley, executive sports editor of the Cincinnati Post, wrote:

> Slowly, but ever so surely, is vanishing the notion that the sports department's job is to cover the games and perpetuate the image that sports are pure, its participants are All-American boys, and its pages places simply to report the game and what was said after it was over.
>
> And who knows, maybe someday we'll even achieve equal status in job title. Through the years, it has always been ''reporter'' on the news side, sports ''writer'' in my world.
>
> I'm beginning to discover more sports reporters.

Those sports reporters maintain their distance from the people they cover, just as reporters on other beats do, by keeping their readers in mind. Readers want to know who won, and how. But they also want to know about other sides of sports, sides that may require some digging to expose. Readers' questions about sports financing and the story behind the story too often go unanswered.

Money.   Accountants have become as essential to sports as are athletes and trainers. Readers have a legitimate interest in everything from ticket prices to the impact of money on the actual contests.

The Real ''Why.''   When a key player is traded, as much as when a city manager is fired, readers want to know why. When athletes leave school without graduating, find out why. When the public is asked to pay for expansion of a stadium, tell the public why. One of the attractions of sports is that when the contest is over, the spectators can see who won and how. Often that is not true of struggles in government or business. The ''whys'' of sports, however, frequently are as hard to discover as they are in any other area.

The Real ''Who.''   Sports figures often appear to their fans, and sometimes to reporters, to be larger than life. In fact, athletics is an intensely human activity. Its participants have greater physical skills, and larger bank accounts, than most other people, but they are people. Probably the best two descriptions of what it is really like to be a major-league athlete were written by athletes — ''Ball Four'' by Jim Bouton and the novel ''North Dallas Forty'' by Pete Gent. Still, some of the best sportswriting results from the continuing effort by reporters to capture the humanity of games. Roger

Kahn, in perhaps the finest baseball book ever written, "The Boys of Summer," needed only two inches of type to reveal Carl Erskine, the old Dodger pitcher, in this scene with his wife and mongoloid son:

> Jimmy Erskine, nine, came forward at Betty's tug. He had the flat features and pinched nostrils of Mongolism.
> "Say, 'Hello, Roger,'" Betty said.
> Jimmy shook his head and sniffed.
> "Come on," Carl said.
> "Hosh-uh," Jimmy said. "Hosh-uh. Hosh-uh."
> "He's proud," Carl said, beaming. "He's been practicing to say your name all week, and he's proud as he can be." The father's strong right hand found Jimmy's neck. He hugged the little boy against his hip.

As Tom Tuley observed, sports reporting is much more than covering the contests and perpetuating the myths.

Covering the Contests

A major part of any sports reporter's job, however, is covering the games, matches or meets. That task is harder than it might seem. You have the same problems you would have in covering any event, from a city council meeting to a riot. You must decide what to put in your lead, capture the most interesting and significant developments, find some good quotes, answer as many of your readers' probable questions as you can, and meet your deadline. But a reporter covering a football game, for instance, has a major concern that a reporter writing about a council meeting does not have. Most of the readers of your football story already know a great deal about the game. Many were there. Others saw it on television or listened on radio. They know *what* happened. They expect you to tell them *why* and *how*.

A story like this one, though it may be easy to produce, falls far short of meeting that demand:

> Jefferson High turned two fumble recoveries into touchdowns and shut out Oakland High, 16–0, Monday night at Hickley Field.
>
> The Cyclones, who held Oakland to minus 32 yards rushing in the game, scored their points on consecutive possessions in the second quarter.
>
> The scoring started when Jefferson recovered a fumble at the Eagle 42-yard line and marched in for the score.

The reporter is adding little to what most fans already know. The only two quotes in the story, just two paragraphs from the end, could have been pulled from a list of coaches' stock comments, suitable for all occasions:

> "We didn't make the mistakes we did last week against West," said Cyclones Coach David Carlson.
> Oakland Coach Lyle Wheeler praised his defense after the game. "I thought they played real well. They were on the field the whole game."

Too many games are reported just as that one was, without probing the hows and whys. The reporter sits in the press box, has three-quarters of a story written before the game is over, breezes through each dressing room just long enough to ask, "Any comment, Coach?" and applies the finishing touches to the story on the way to the telephone or back to the office. But that is recording, not reporting.

Suppose, instead, that the reporter had done a little homework. Some digging would have revealed that this was Oakland's third loss of the season, with no victories. It would have shown that Coach Wheeler had predicted before the season a winning record, possibly a conference championship. And it would have shown that the player counted on to be the star of the team had been dropped from the squad just before the first game for "disciplinary reasons."

Suppose the reporter had gotten to know the players and supporters of the team. He or she would have learned that the black athletes and many of their parents believed the suspension of the star, who was black, was a case of racial discrimination by the white coach. And if he or she had gotten out of the press box, there might have been more revealing comments from players and fans, some explanation of what was seen on the field. The story might have read:

From the top row of the Hickley Field Stadium, Gary Thomas watched in agony as his former teammates at Oakland High lost their third game of the season, 16–0, to archrival Jefferson High.

He groaned each time an Oakland ball carrier was dropped for a loss. He cursed each of Oakland's four lost fumbles.

"Cut left," he muttered as halfback David Oldham ran head-on into four Jefferson tacklers. "Hold the ball, damn it," as Oldham fumbled.

The outcome of Friday's game would have been different, Thomas believes, if he had been on the field displaying the skills that made him the leading rusher in the conference last year as a junior.

But he is spending his senior season in the stands, suspended from the team for what Coach Lyle Wheeler calls "disciplinary reasons" after a fight with a white student in a school rest room. Thomas thinks he was discriminated against.

"The dude just don't like blacks," he said of Wheeler.

Black and white teammates agreed as they wearily dressed after the game that they want Thomas back in uniform.

"We ain't got a prayer without him," said Oldham, who is white.

Linebacker Chris Pannell, who is black, added, "He's the heart of this team. Without him, we got no heart."

Coach Wheeler, asked about the effect of Thomas' absence, responded by praising his defense. "I thought they played real well. They were on the field the whole game."

Jefferson ran 62 offensive plays to only 42 for Oakland. But, had it not been for the fumbles, which put Jefferson in easy scoring range three times, Oakland might have escaped with a scoreless tie.

That story tells its readers not only what happened, but how it happened and at least part of why it happened. It combines solid reporting with deft writing to add something that was new and interesting even for those who had seen or heard the game.

Notice first the form of the story. In sportswriting, as elsewhere in journalism, the inverted pyramid structure has given way in many cases to an alternate approach. You learned more about these alternatives in Chapter 15. In this story the reporter starts by setting the scene and introducing the most important character, while also providing essential information about the game. Your goals for the opening of any story about a sports event should be twofold:

1. *Focus on the unique element.* No sporting event is quite like any other. A perceptive reporter picks out what made this game different and shares it with the reader. The unique element may be a single play, a questionable ruling by an official, an untimely injury. Or it may be, as in this case, the missing player. Find that unique element and you have found the key to your story. Your lead may be a quote, the description of a scene, an analysis by some expert observer or your own summary of the contest's high point. Whatever opening device you choose, be sure the facts support it. A summary or analysis based on fact is permissible in a news story. Reliance on your own opinion is not.

2. *Tell the reader who won.* No description is so compelling and no analysis so astute that a reader will forgive you if you forget to say at the start what the outcome of the event was. The basic who, what and where must never be left out or buried in the body of your story. The story is, after all, about the contest.

As in the story on Oakland High, the body of your story should develop the unique angle brought out in the lead. This writing technique gives a unified focus and maintains the reader's interest. In the course of the story, you should also meet three other objectives:

1. *Describe what happened.* In addition to knowing the outcome, your audience will want to read at least the highlights of *how* it was reached, if only to savor them again. Analysis and background are hollow without the solid descriptive core of what happened. In the Oakland High story, that description begins in the second and third paragraphs and resumes in the last paragraph of the excerpt.

2. *Answer the reader's questions.* The story should supply the explanation — or part of it, at least — of *why* the game turned out as it did. It should tell its readers something they could not have discovered easily for themselves. The reporter of the Oakland High story accomplished that by taking the trouble to learn the background of the event, and then by seeking out the right sources. Rarely should you have to rely on your own expertise to answer the questions of why and how. Experts abound at virtually every sports event. Assistant coaches or scouts sit in the press box. The coaches and players directly involved are available after the game. Alumni, supporters, former players can be found if you will just go looking. The most important question for you to ask as a reporter is what your readers will want to know. Then try to find the answers for them.

3. *Get the competitors into the story by using good quotes.* Readers usually want to know what the competitors think about what they have done. When winners exult, when losers cry, put your readers in the scene. That is part of the attraction of sports. The hours spent getting to know them pay off when the athletes share with you — and your readers — what the contest was really like.

The preparation and techniques of interviewing are essentially the same in a locker room as in a politician's office, though you seldom have occasion to interview a mayor who is dressing or undressing. The reward for a good job in either situation is the same, too. You get, as in the story above, lively quotes that provide some insight.

Remember, you produce a good game story by:

1. Doing your homework before the game.
2. Spotting the unique element and building the story on it.
3. Telling your readers who won and how.
4. Answering the readers' questions.
5. Getting the participants into the story.

Those guidelines will serve you and your readers well, whether the event is a professional football game or the semifinals of the Sunday night bowling league.

Many sports journalists think of themselves more as "writers" than "reporters." This chapter is intended to help you become a sports reporter. But good writing is an important part of any top reporter's skills, and sports offers abundant material for good writing. Careless writers, however, can become trapped in sports clichés. Let's take a look at some examples of atrocious writing from the sports pages. Learning to recognize bad writing is the first step toward appreciating and producing the kinds of stories that win praise and lure readers.

RECOGNIZING AND AVOIDING SPORTS CLICHÉS

A managing editor who had read more sports stories than he could stand wrote a satirical essay on — and with — clichés for The Associated Press Managing Editors News. Here are a few sample lines:

> The rifle-armed field general succeeds because his team is quicker off the ball. When he isn't in the pocket or scrambling on the option, he operates out of the shotgun — firing bullets to his glue-fingered tight end and unloading bombs to the deep threat who works on the rookie corner back and finally burns him. Deep threats do not run, they fly.
>
> There's no more tomorrow. Scrappy knows that. And you have to respect him for it. That's why he plays them one game at a time. That's why he holds back nothing down the stretch.

You probably have read every cliché in those paragraphs on a sports page somewhere. They are ludicrous when they are strung together. But real stories that are only slightly less ludicrous often appear. Consider these examples:

Sandra Post ran a ragged pattern but recovered in sudden-death overtime yesterday.
— the Detroit News

Tall and talented Fred Warington parlayed his long, arching swing with a blazing putter here Tuesday. . . . He went 3-4-2-3-2 and appeared to be ready to blow the lid off the ancient Bedford layout when he finally came back to earth on the sixth hole.
— the Manchester (N.H.) Union Leader

Pete Rose . . . smacks out answers to questions with the same aggressiveness that earned him a 44-game hitting streak and 3,000 career hits.

Rose took BP (batting practice) before the Houston Sports Writers and Sportscasters Association "pitchers" Tuesday and didn't "take" a pitch. . . .

Rose also had several other hits (observations) during the session.
— The Associated Press

Let's look again to see just what makes that writing so bad. The principal problems are misused metaphors and out-of-place adjectives.

"Sandra Post ran a ragged pattern" is a pun, a weak attempt to play on the golfer's name with a phrase — "post pattern" — that is itself a football cliché. Puns should be avoided. Even worse is the failed attempt to transplant the jargon of one sport to another. The writer would have done better to stick to golf and tell readers something in the lead:

> Sandra Post played erratically for 18 holes, losing her lead in the Lady Stroh's Open, before winning the championship with a birdie on the second playoff hole.

The Union Leader writer substituted lazy generalities for precise description. To call a tournament winner "talented" is to belabor the obvious. The head of a golf club describes an arc, no matter who swings it. And if the putter was on fire, the story is badly underplayed. A better lead would have been:

> Fred Warington, a 17-year-old with an awkward-looking swing, putted brilliantly as he birdied the first five holes Tuesday on his way to a five-shot victory in the New England Golf Association Junior Championship.

Now you have told your readers something specific, while also conveying at least part of the scene. The sentence beginning "He went . . ." can be dropped. The only information in it has now been fitted into the lead.

The Pete Rose story is a misguided use of baseball terminology in a news conference setting. Nobody "smacks out" answers unless he is using a bongo drum for communication. Sportswriters aren't pitchers and questions aren't baseballs. In any case, when you use one word — such as "pitchers" — to stand for another — such as "questioners" — you should never put quotation marks or parentheses around it. If your substitute is so weak that you must call attention to it, find another word. Better yet, find another literary device. The lead could have been written:

> Pete Rose showed the Houston Sports Writers and Sportscasters Association Tuesday that his wit is as quick as his bat.

Good writing is precise, saying what the author means and nothing else. It is descriptive, re-creating for the reader the sights, the sounds, the smells of the event. It is suited in pace and in tone to the story, lively for an exciting game, somber for the reflections of a loser.

EFFECTIVE SPORTS WRITING

Much of the best sports writing, as well as the best reporting, is printed in Sports Illustrated magazine, where talented people who know their craft are given space and time to display their skills. Here is a paragraph from a story by Gilbert Rogin about an ocean-sailing race:

This is a catalog of all the living things we saw during our 12 days' passage. One whale blowing dispiritedly, its spout a feeble, windy fountain in its old, soft gray head. Flying fish. One came aboard; it was only an inch long but perfectly formed, its back as blue and shining as the sea it flew wildly out of, its eyes immense, round, blind in its dying, its wings, when we spread them, no larger than a bee's. A narrow,' silver fish that washed into the cockpit at night; we shone the flashlight on it, held it speculatively and then threw it back, but it was already dead. A squid. It came in over the weather rail. I fished with it from the stern when the sun rose, but it was quickly torn from the hook. Three bugs; one on the underside of a hatch cover, another vanishing down a cockpit drain, the last in the fo'c's'le. Albatrosses with white faces like clowns. Shearwaters. Little petrellike birds. Bo's'n birds. Spots of phosphorescence in the wake betraying anatomies. And one white bird searching like prudent Noah's dove. Many days we saw nothing.

Note the precision, the scene setting, the rhythm of the sentences. The writer could have said, "We saw fish, birds and bugs, but not many." Instead, he told his readers a good deal of what it is like to be at sea in a small, slow boat.

This is the climax of Sports Illustrated's story of the classic race between Roger Bannister and John Landy, who already had become the first two men to run a mile in less than four minutes:

Two hundred yards from home, Landy made his bid for decision and victory. But Bannister refused to be shaken, and with 90 yards to go he lengthened his plunging stride. He came up shoulder to shoulder, fought for momentum, pulled away to a four-yard lead and ran steadily and stylishly through a deafening clamor to the tape. He fell, arms flapping, legs buckling, into the arms of the English team manager a split second after the race was done.

No bad metaphors, no plays on words, no extravagant adverbs and adjectives are to be found here — just an account that gives readers a sense of being viewers.

Figure 18.3 Sports Reporting at Its Best. Much of the best sports coverage—reporting and writing—appears in the pages of Sports Illustrated.

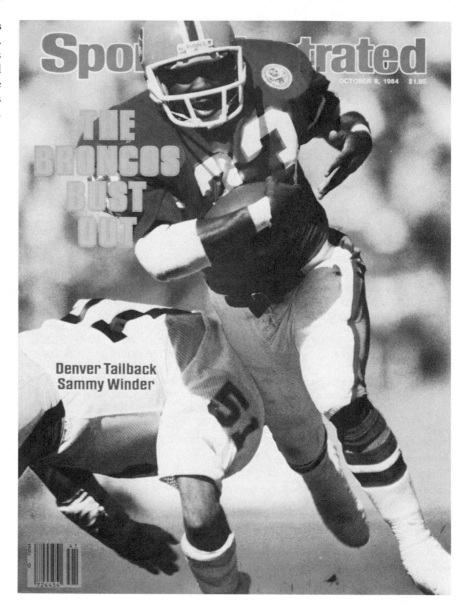

Perhaps the best contemporary sports reporter and writer is Thomas Boswell of The Washington Post. He has won the Best Newspaper Writing award of the American Society of Newspaper Editors. His work regularly heads the list of best sports stories published annually by the Sporting News. Here are a few samples. First, the opening of a story about aging baseball players:

The cleanup crews come at midnight, creeping into the ghostly quarter-light of empty ballparks with their slow-sweeping brooms and languorous, sluicing hoses. All season, they remove the inanimate refuse of a game. Now, in the dwindling days of September and October, they come to collect baseball souls.

Age is the sweeper, injury his broom.

Mixed among the burst beer cups and the mustard-smeared wrappers headed for the trash heap, we find old friends who are being consigned to the dust bin of baseball's history. If a night breeze blows a back page of the Sporting News down the stadium aisle, pick it up and squint at the one-time headline names now just fine print at the very bottom of a column of averages.

Notice the imagery, as gloomy as the subject matter. Notice the pacing, with long, complex sentences slowing the eye to match the mood of sadness. Notice the metaphor, age as the sweeper, injury the broom. But notice, too, the sharp-eyed description that must ring true to anyone who has ever seen or thought about the debris cast aside by a baseball crowd.

A little later in the same story:

"I like a look of Agony," wrote Emily Dickinson, "because I know it's true." For those with a taste for a true look, a glimpse beneath the mask, even if it be a glimpse of agony, then this is the proper time of year. Spring training is for hope; autumn is for reality. At every stop on the late-season baseball trail, we see that look of agony, although it hides behind many expressions.

Figure 18.4   Craftsman at Work. Thomas Boswell of The Washington Post sets a high standard for excellence in sports reporting and writing.

Familiarity with the classics of literature did not die with Grantland Rice. Boswell not only can find the line, he can make it work.

From another story, this one about a championship boxing match, comes a short paragraph that is equally powerful but sharply different in tone:

> Boxing is about pain. It is a night out for the carnivore in us, the hidden beast who is hungry.

Later in that story, Boswell returns to the theme:

> But boxing never changes. One central truth lies at its heart and it never alters: Pain is the most powerful and tangible force in life.
>
> The threat of torture, for instance, is stronger than the threat of death. Execution can be faced, but pain is corrosive, like an acid eating at the personality.
>
> Pain, as anyone with a toothache knows, drives out all other emotions and sensations before it. Pain is priority. It may even be man's strongest and most undeniable reality.
>
> And that is why the fight game stirs us, even as it repels us.

From the poetry of aging to the brutality of pain, a great writer matches his images, his pace, his word choice to his subject matter. The principles of careful observation and clear writing cover all occasions.

There is one other thing that sets a Boswell apart from many lesser writers. It is his attitude toward his readers. That may be worth copying, too. After winning the ASNE award, he told an interviewer:

> We vastly underestimate our audience in newspapers. In 11 years I have never had one letter from anybody saying, "What's all this high-falutin talk?" I get the most touching letters from people who seem semi-literate but who really appreciate what you're doing. I think the fact that people are capable of understanding the Bible, or sensing the emotion in Shakespeare, just proves how far they are above our expectations.

Suggested Readings

"Best Sports Stories." Published annually by The Sporting News, St. Louis, Mo.

Flood, Curt. "The Way It Is." New York: Trident Press, 1971. The first-person story of the baseball player whose challenge to the reserve clause revolutionized professional sports in America. Also noteworthy are the caustic comments on sportswriters.

Kahn, Roger. "The Boys of Summer." New York: New American Library, 1973. One of the best sports books ever.

Sports Illustrated. Features the best continuing examples of how sports should be reported.

19
Social Science Reporting Techniques

Even though most colleges group journalism or mass communication among the social sciences, most journalists undoubtedly regard their work as a craft or an art rather than as a science. Increasingly, however, reporters are turning to the techniques of the social sciences to help them tell stories that would be difficult or impossible to do in other ways.

The St. Louis Post-Dispatch wanted to find out whether a new, supposedly tougher, drunk-driving law was living up to expectations. Traditionally, reporters would have interviewed prosecutors and judges to come up with some impressions. The Post-Dispatch instead analyzed systematically all 3,306 cases handled under the new law. The story revealed that more than one-quarter of those arrested were continuing to drive. Both readers and some public officials were surprised.

Associated Press reporter Michael Graczyk didn't just interview or observe Houston, Texas, police officers as they practiced when to use — and when not to use — their pistols. He went through the course himself. It was a harrowing experience. His lead was, "A New York Times photographer is dead because I shot him by mistake. So is at least one Houston police officer." The deaths were faked, of course, but the emotion was not.

Other AP reporters checked on the efficiency of the U.S. Postal Service by mailing dozens of letters between AP bureaus.

Cooperating in an intensely competitive business, The Washington Post and ABC conduct national public-opinion polls jointly. So do The New York Times and CBS. Dozens of newspapers do their own local polling.

All these examples show the tools of the social sciences in the hands of journalists. In all these cases, the tools were used responsibly. There can be problems, though, even when proper care is taken. When pseudo-science creeps in, the problems for audiences and practitioners become greater.

What is a news organization to do, for example, when its public-opinion poll shows sharply different results from another, taken from the same population and covering the same topics? During the 1984 presidential campaign, such conflicts occurred between the Washington Post–ABC poll and the New York Times–CBS poll. The Post wrote a detailed story in which were explained the factors — including timing, question wording and order, and sheer chance — that could account for the differences. It would be hard to know whether readers felt better informed or just confused by the whole affair.

ABC's "Nightline" has been attacked by other journalists and professional pollsters alike for its repeated use of listener call-ins as a guide to public opinion. Experts pointed out that the callers were not at all representative of the population as a whole. "Nightline" continued the feature, with only an occasional disclaimer that the results weren't really scientific. Is that responsible journalism or a misleading gimmick?

In this chapter you will learn:

1. When and how to use four popular social-science techniques.
2. What to look out for when using or writing about any of them.
3. Detailed guidelines for the most common technique — public-opinion polling.

Participant Observation

When Al Pagel walked into the state mental hospital, he carried neither a notebook nor a tape recorder. He did not identify himself as a reporter. As far as officials or inmates knew, he was just another attendant. Eight hours a day for two weeks, he participated in the life of the people he was observing. He was verbally abused, physically attacked, smeared with human excrement. He was over-

Figure 19.1 Participant Observation. These two reporters for the Pottstown (Pa.) Mercury dressed in authentic Amish attire and went to Philadelphia to gain first-hand experience of how city residents would receive them. Here they are "helped" by a city policeman and a passerby.

worked, underpaid and untrained. His experiences, coupled with interviewing and background reading, helped him compile for The Miami Herald a story that probably could not have been told if he had relied on conventional reporting alone.

Pagel, like AP reporter Graczyk, was engaging in *participant observation*, a technique in which reporters disguise themselves to obtain inside stories. Subjects ranging from school teaching to vegetable picking have been explored using this technique. Sociologists and psychologists also use participant observation in their research, for the same reasons reporters do. Participant observers get first-hand, close-up pictures of their subjects not obtainable by studying statistics or by formal interviewing. Facts and feelings can be captured that otherwise would remain unknown.

Along with its unique advantages, participant observation also poses some unique problems. These are problems that may have no clear solutions, but you and your editors need at least to consider them before you set out to become an ambulance attendant or a migrant worker.

The Problem of Invasion of Privacy. Unless you identify yourself as a reporter, you are, in effect, spying on the lives of people who are not aware they are being observed — an ethically questionable activity. But if you do identify yourself, the advantages of the technique can be lost. Sensitivity is essential, especially when the people you write about may be embarrassed or have their jobs placed in jeopardy.

The Problem of Involvement.   There are two things to watch out for here. First, do not become so involved that you change the course of the events you are observing. You may be on stage, but you are not a star performer. Second, do not assume that the people you are observing feel the same way you do. No matter how hard you work at fitting in, you remain an outsider, a visitor. The view from inside a migrant workers' camp or a mental hospital is different when you know you will be there two weeks instead of two years or a lifetime.

The Problem of Generalizing.   Scientists know the danger of generalizing on the basis of limited observation. Reporters don't always know or sometimes forget. Keep in mind that while participant observation yields a detailed picture of a specific situation, it tells you nothing reliable about any other situation. Pagel could not assume that what he found in one ward of one hospital would be true of other wards in other hospitals. Participant observation is a good tool, but it is a limited one. It usually works best as a supplement to the standard techniques of interviewing and examining documents.

Systematic Study of Records

James Steele and Donald Barlett of the Philadelphia Inquirer spent months sifting through thousands of court records, noting information on defendants, victims, judges and sentences. They then fed their information into a computer. From their work Inquirer readers learned, for example, that blacks were more likely to be sentenced to jail than whites convicted of similar crimes. They also learned that harsher sentences were more frequent in cases with black defendants and white victims than in cases where defendant and victim were of the same race.

Political scientists, historians and other scholars long have used such systematic study of records in their research. Its use by reporters is still limited but growing. The advantage of detailed analysis of court records, budgets, voting records and other documents is that it permits reporters and readers to draw conclusions based on solid information. No amount of interviewing or courtroom observation could have produced the indisputable facts that Barlett and Steele turned up or that E. S. Evans of the Post-Dispatch found in his analysis of the drunk-driving law. Studies like theirs would have been nearly impossible without the use of a computer, but nearly every newspaper now has a computer or access to one. The programs needed for this kind of study are relatively simple. So the systematic study of records is within the reach of many newspapers.

The main obstacles to such study are shortages of time and money. The Philadelphia project took seven months of two reporters' time. On small papers, especially, you may have trouble freeing yourself for even seven days. And reporters' time and computer time both cost money. Editors and publishers must be convinced that the return will be worth the investment before they will approve. You probably should have at least some clues that wrongdoing, injustice or inefficiency exists before launching a systematic study.

Once you have launched a study, you should make sure that it is in fact systematic. You must either examine all the pertinent records or choose the ones you examine in such a way that they will be truly representative of the rest. Be sure you are asking the right questions and recording the information necessary to answer them. A computer can perform complicated analyses very quickly, but it cannot analyze facts that have not been fed into it. People who use computers have a word for that problem: GIGO. It is the acronym for "*Garbage In, Garbage Out.*"

Don't set out on a systematic study without assurances of time and money, a clear idea of what you're looking for and expert technical advice. If the expertise is unavailable at your newspaper, look to the nearest college.

Field Experiments

Instead of just asking questions about mail service, The Associated Press tested it. Letters were mailed from one bureau to another, some with ZIP codes and some without, some by air mail and some by regular first-class mail. A scientist conducting the same kind of test would call it a *field experiment*. In all such experiments researchers take some action in order to observe the effects.

Reporters rarely think of themselves as scientists, but they conduct a great many experiments. The mailing experiment is a common one. Another frequent test is to examine the honesty of auto mechanics by taking a car in perfect condition to several shops and reporting what each finds "wrong" with it. Consumer reporters also commonly check weights and measures: Does a "pound" of hamburger really weigh a pound? Or they test for discrimination by having a male and a female reporter apply for insurance policies or mortgages.

If they are to be successful, reporters' field experiments must follow the same guidelines — and avoid the same pitfalls — that scientists' experiments must. A little scientific jargon is necessary here. It is fairly straightforward, though, and it will be useful if you ever have the opportunity to set up an experiment.

BASIC EXPERIMENTAL METHODS AND TERMINOLOGY

Your field experiment must have a *hypothesis*, a statement of what you expect to find. Your hypothesis must be stated clearly and simply. When it is, it will help focus your attention on the two elements of the experiment — the independent variable and the dependent variable. The *variables*, just as their name implies, are the things that change during the experiment. The independent variable is what you think may be a cause. You change it and observe what happens to the dependent variable, the effect.

Let's take an example. Suppose you think bankers in your town are discriminating against women by demanding more collateral for loans from them than from men. Form a hypothesis: "Women are forced to put up more collateral to secure loans than men are." The variables are the sex of the borrower and the amount of collateral demanded. Sex is the independent variable, the suspected cause. For your experiment, then, you will have applicants of each sex seek a bank loan. You will be looking for any change in the dependent variable — the collateral demanded.

There are two other steps you must take to assure a successful experiment. First you must *control* the experiment. Every aspect of the experiment must be carefully structured to make sure that any change you observe is caused only by the independent variable you want to test. For example, your male and female loan applicants must be as much alike as possible in the financial details they provide, the way they dress, their race and their age. Otherwise, any differences in the responses by the loan officer might be due to something other than sex, the variable you are interested in. Also, the applicants should visit the same bank or banks and speak to the same officials. Without careful control of the experiment, you may end up unable to say with certainty that you have proved or disproved your hypothesis. Then you've got no story.

The other step is called *randomization*, or random selection. In a small town you could run your experiment at every bank. But in a big city that would be impossible. So, if you want to be sure that the results of the experiment apply to all the banks in town, you must choose at random the ones to approach. Randomization allows you to assume that what you select — 10 banks, for instance — is representative of the whole — the total number of banks in the city.

Choosing a bank or anything else, such as a name, at random simply means that you employ a method for choosing that gives every bank or every name an equal chance of being picked. The procedure for making a random selection is beyond the scope of an introductory reporting text. At the end of the chapter, several books will be listed in which you can find that and other material relating to the concepts introduced here. Much of that other material deals with statistics. Many experiments require statistical analysis to ensure that what you have found is significant. Most polls and surveys require some statistical analysis, too. Explanations of the fairly simple math involved also can be found in the books listed at the end of the chapter.

Public Opinion Polls

The Louisville (Ky.) Courier-Journal wanted to find out how the people who actually live where coal is mined feel about strip mining. So it asked them. Not every one of them was questioned, of course, since that would have been impractical. Instead the newspaper took a *poll* of about 600 persons, selected at random to be representative of the adult population of 10 coal-producing counties. They were interviewed by a professional polling firm. The results were tabulated, analyzed and printed.

In much the same way, newspapers, television networks and independent pollsters measure public opinion about everything from preferred breakfast cereals to favorite presidential candidates. Many newspapers regularly report the findings of reputable national polls conducted by such survey experts as the George Gallup and Louis Harris organizations.

When polls are conducted properly and reported carefully, they can be both interesting and useful, telling people something they could not know otherwise and perhaps even helping to produce wiser public policies. But when they are badly done or sloppily reported, polls can be bad news for journalists and readers alike.

The chances are good that sometime in your reporting career you will want to conduct an opinion poll or at least help with one your newspaper is conducting. The books listed at the end of the chapter will tell you much of what you need to know for that. Even if you never work on one, you almost certainly will be called on to write about the results of polls. What follows will help you understand what you are given and help you make sure your readers understand it, too.

REQUIREMENTS FOR SOUND POLLING

The Associated Press Managing Editors Association prepared a checklist of the information you should have and should share with your readers about any poll on which you are reporting. Included on that list were the following:

1. The identity of the sponsor of the survey.
2. The exact wording of the questions asked.
3. A definition of the population sampled.
4. The sample size and, where the survey design makes it relevant, the response rate.
5. Some indication of the allowance that should be made for sampling error.
6. Which results are based on only part of the sample (for example, probable voters, those who have heard of the candidate, or other subdivisions).
7. How the interviews were collected — in person, in homes, by phone, by mail, on street corners, or wherever.
8. When the interviews were collected.

Several of those points require some explanation.

The identity of the survey's sponsor is important to you and your readers because it gives some clues to possible bias. Most people would put more trust in a Gallup or Harris poll's report that, for instance, Smith is far ahead of Jones in the presidential campaign than they would in a poll sponsored by the Smith for President organization.

The exact wording of the questions is important because the answer received often depends at least in part on how the question was asked. (See Chapter 5 on interviewing for more detail.) The answer might well be different, for example, if a pollster asked, "Who do you favor for president, Jones or Smith?" rather than "Wouldn't Jones make a better president than Smith?"

In the third point on the checklist, the word "population" is another bit of jargon. Most of us use the word to mean the number of people living in the town, state or country. In science, however, *population* means the total number of people — or documents or milkweed plants or giraffes — in the group being studied. For an opinion survey the population might be all registered voters in the state, black males under 25 or female cigarette smokers. To understand what the results of a poll mean, you must know what population was studied. The word "sampled" simply refers to the procedure discussed earlier in which a small number — or *sample* — of persons is picked at random so as to be representative of the population.

The sample size is important because — all other things being equal — the larger the sample, the more reliable the survey results should be. The response rate is important especially in surveys conducted by mail, in which a low rate of response may invalidate the poll.

The *sampling error* of any survey is the allowance that must be made for the possibility that the opinion of the sample may not be exactly the same as the opinion of the whole population. A simpler name for it is "margin of error." The margin of error depends mainly on the size of the sample. For instance, all other things being equal, a sample of 400 would have a margin of error of 5 percent while a sample of 1,500 would have a margin of error of 3 percent. If, with a sample of 1,500, the poll shows Jones with 60 percent and Smith with 40 percent, you can be confident that Jones actually has between 57 and 63 percent while Smith actually has between 37 and 43 percent. The laws of probability say that the chances are 19 to 1 that the actual percentages fall in that range. Those odds make the information good enough to publish.

The existence of sampling error helps explain why it is important to know which results may be based on only part of the sample. The smaller that part, the greater the margin of error. In political polls it is always important to know whether the results include all eligible voters or just those likely to vote. The opinions of the likely voters are more important than the others.

When the interviews were collected may be of critical importance in interpreting the poll, especially during campaigns when the candidates themselves and other events may cause preferences to change significantly within a few days. A week-old poll may be meaningless if something dramatic has happened since it was taken. Candidates have been known to use such outdated results to make themselves look better than they really do, or their opponents worse. Be on guard.

When the poll is your newspaper's, the obligation remains to let your readers know how it was taken. It is also incumbent on the paper to reveal how reliable the poll is.

THE NEED FOR CAUTION IN INTERPRETING POLLS

Whether you are helping conduct a survey or just reporting on one produced by someone else, you must exercise caution. You should be on guard for a number of things:

1. *The people interviewed must be picked in a truly random fashion if you want to generalize from their responses to the whole population.* If they are not, you have no assurance that the interview subjects are really representative. The old-fashioned "man in the street" interview is practically worthless as an indicator of public opinion for this reason. The man or woman in the street probably differs in important ways from all those men and women who are not in the street when the questioner is.

Also invalid are such "polls" as the questionnaires congressmen mail to their constituents. Only strongly opinionated — and therefore unrepresentative — people are likely to return them. For the same reason the "question of the day" feature some newspapers and broadcast stations carry tells you nothing about the opinions of the great mass of people who do not respond. ABC's "Nightline" call-in had the same flaws.

2. *The closer the results, the harder it is to say anything definitive.* Look again at the example of the Smith-Jones campaign. Suppose the poll showed Smith with 52 and Jones with 48 percent. Smith may or may not be ahead. With the 3 percent margin of error, Smith could actually have only 49 percent, and Jones could have 51 percent. All that you can report safely about those results is that the race is too close to call. Many reporters — and pollsters — are simply not careful enough when the outcome is unclear.

3. *Beware of polls that claim to measure opinion on sensitive, complicated issues.* Many questions of morality, or social issues such as race relations, do not lend themselves to simple answers. Opinions on such matters can be measured, but only by highly skilled researchers using carefully designed questions. Anything less can be dangerously oversimplified and misleading.

Surveying, like field experiments, systematic analysis and participant observation, can help you as a reporter solve problems you could not handle as well by other techniques. But these are only tools. How effectively they are used — or how clumsily they are misused — depends on you.

Suggested Readings

Associated Press Managing Editors. "Watching the Polls." APME, 1975. Includes, in addition to the checklist mentioned in the text, simplified explanations of survey techniques and terms.

Campbell, Donald, and Julian Stanley. "Experimental and Quasi-Experimental Designs for Research." Skokie, Ill.: Rand McNally, 1966. A guide to field experimentation that is also useful in providing a better understanding of scientific research.

McCombs, Maxwell; Shaw, Donald L.; and David Grey. "Handbook of Reporting Methods." Boston: Houghton Mifflin, 1976. Offers examples of real-life uses of social science methods in journalism, but does not provide enough on statistics to serve as a guide in employing the methods.

Meyer, Philip. "Precision Journalism." Bloomington, Ind.: Indiana University Press, 1979. A detailed introduction to surveying, conducting field experiments and using statistics to analyze the results by a reporter who pioneered the use of these methods in journalism. The theoretical justification of the techniques is included as well.

Williams, Frederick. "Reasoning with Statistics." New York: Holt, Rinehart and Winston, 1979. A non-intimidating but sufficiently complex guide to using mathematical tools.

PART FIVE

Specialized Reporting

20

Investigative Reporting

From the outside, investigative reporting appears to be the glamorous side of journalism. That's not surprising. Investigative reporters are more likely than their colleagues to become famous. Who hasn't heard of Bob Woodward, Carl Bernstein, Seymour Hersh, Jack Anderson? "60 Minutes," the CBS news program that features investigative reporting, has a weekly audience matched by few programs. And the stories that attract attention, that affect the course of history, are likely to be investigative. Woodward and Bernstein helped topple a president with their digging into the Watergate scandal. Hersh's story of the My Lai massacre by American soldiers during the Vietnam War probably contributed to the public opposition that eventually ended the war.

From the inside, investigative reporting looks more like hard, frustrating, often dull, sometimes risky work. Days may be spent tracking down leads that prove fruitless. Weeks of effort may yield a story that goes unnoticed, or may yield no story at all. Pressures and even threats are common.

Still, most journalists would agree that nothing in the business is more important than the detailed, analytical examination of important issues and important people that is investigative reporting. Often, the best public service is performed with stories that attract little national attention but that expose to local readers injustices that should be rectified, corruption that should be punished or social problems that should be solved.

For example, months of work by two reporters for the Fort Wayne (Ind.) News-Sentinel showed how a growing religious cult's ban on medical treatment was condemning to death not only believers but sometimes children too young to make decisions for themselves or spouses unable to seek outside help. The stories also revealed weak laws and other failures by society to protect its young and helpless.

In Knoxville, Tenn., complaints of police brutality, mainly from the black community, had gone ignored for years by both the press and the power structure. Finally, the Knoxville Journal launched an investigation. Reporters were met with hostility, suspicion, closed records and frightened witnesses. Months of work finally produced a series of stories and editorials that forced an official investigation, identified the officers most often accused and led to changes at the top of the police department.

Such stories, and hundreds like them, are the payoff for the long hours, the frustrations and the expense. They make the investment in investigative reporting worthwhile for journalists and readers alike.

Investigative reporting has a rich tradition in the history of American journalism. The fiercely partisan editors of the Revolutionary era dug for facts as well as the mud they hurled at their opponents. At the turn of this century investigative reporting flowered with the

Figure 20.1 Original Muckraker. Ida Tarbell's early-twentieth-century work in examining Standard Oil helped set the pattern for modern investigative reporters.

"muckrakers," a title bestowed with anger by Theodore Roosevelt and worn with pride by the reporters. Lincoln Steffens dissected America's cities, one by one, laying bare the corrupt combinations of businessmen and politicians that ran them. Ida Tarbell exposed the economic stranglehold of the oil monopoly. Theodore Dreiser, Upton Sinclair and Frank Norris revealed the horrors of working life in factories and packing plants.

The complexities of big government, big business and big society will require even more widespread — and more sophisticated — investigative reporting if the press is to fulfill its role of keeping a free people fully informed.

Few editors assign beginning reporters to investigative work. It is the most demanding kind of reporting. Still, you need to know what it is and how to do it so that you will be ready when your chance comes. Many of the techniques can be used as well to produce good stories from what would otherwise be routine assignments.

In this chapter you will learn:

1. The process of investigative reporting.
2. How to find and use sources and records.
3. What kinds of obstacles you will face in doing investigative reporting.

The Process

BEGINNING AN INVESTIGATION

Most investigations start with a hunch or a *tip* that something or someone deserves a close look. No good reporter sets out on an investigation unless there is some basis for suspicion. That basis may be a grand jury report that leaves something untold or a tip that some public official is on the take. It may be a sudden upsurge in drug overdoses or it may be long-festering problems in the schools. Without some idea of what you're looking for, investigation is too likely to turn into wild goose chasing.

Based on the tip or suspicion together with whatever background material you have, you form a hypothesis. Reporters hardly ever use that term, but it is a useful one, because it shows the similarity between the processes of investigative reporting and scientific investigation. In both, the hypothesis is the statement of what you think is true. Your hypothesis may be, "The mayor is a crook," or, "The school system is being run incompetently." It is a good idea to state clearly your hypothesis when you start an investigation. By doing so, you focus on the heart of the problem and cut down on the possibility of any misunderstanding with your editor or other reporters who may be working with you.

Once the hypothesis is stated, the reporter — like the scientist — sets out to prove or disprove it. You should be open to the possibility of disproof. Reporters — like scientists — are not advocates. They are seekers of truth. No good reporter ignores or downplays evidence just because it contradicts his or her assumptions. In journalism as in science, the truth about a situation is often sharply different from what is expected. An open mind is an essential quality of a good investigative reporter. Remember, too, that you may have a good story even if your hypothesis is disproved.

CARRYING OUT THE INVESTIGATION

The actual investigative work usually proceeds in two stages. The first is what Robert W. Greene, Pulitzer Prize–winning reporter and editor for Newsday of Long Island, N.Y., calls the *sniff*. You sniff around in search of a trail worth following. If you find one, the second stage, the serious investigation, begins.

The preliminary checking should take no more than a day or two. Its purpose is not to prove the hypothesis but to find out the chances of proving it. You make that effort by talking with the most promising source or sources, skimming the most available records, consulting knowledgeable people in your news room. The two questions

Figure 20.2 Planning the Investigation. Bob Greene of Newsday takes a "sniff" to find out if a story is there before launching a major investigation.

you are trying to answer at this stage are, "Is there a story here?" and, "Am I going to be able to get it?" If the answer to either questions is no, there is little point in pursuing the investigation.

When the answer to both questions is yes, the real work begins. It begins with organization. Your hypothesis tells you where you want to go. Now you must figure out how to get there. Careful organization will keep you on the right track and will prevent you from overlooking anything important as you go. Many reporters take a kind of perverse pride in their illegible notebooks and cluttered desks. As an investigative reporter you may have a messy desk, but you should arrange your files of information clearly and coherently. Begin organizing by asking yourself these questions:

1. Who are my most promising sources? Who am I going to have trouble with? Who should I go to first? Second? Last?
2. What records do I need? Where are they? Which are public? How can I get to the ones that are not readily accessible?
3. What is the most I can hope to prove? What is the least that will still yield a story? How long should the investigation take?

Now draw up a plan of action. Experienced reporters often do this mentally. But when you are a beginner, it's a good idea to write out a plan and then to go over it with your editor. The editor may spot some holes in your planning or have something to add. And an editor is more likely to give you enough time if he or she has a clear idea of what has to be done.

Carry out your plan, allowing flexibility for the unexpected twists most investigations take. During your first round of interviews, keep asking who else you should talk to. While you are checking records, look for references to other files or other persons.

Be methodical. Many investigative reporters spend an hour or so at the end of every day adding up the score, going through their notes and searching their memories to analyze what they have learned and what they need next. Some develop elaborate, cross-indexed files of names, organizations, incidents. Others are less formal. Virtually all, however, use a code to disguise names of confidential sources so that those sources will remain secret even if the files are subpoenaed. The method you use isn't important, as long as you understand it. What is vitally important is that you have a method and use it. If you fail to keep careful track of where you're going, you may go in the wrong direction, or in circles.

An Example

Steve Woodward was less than a year out of journalism school when, as a reporter in a suburban bureau of the Kansas City (Mo.)

Star, he first heard the name of Frank Morgan. Over the next few months, the name kept popping up. Morgan, it appeared, owned a great deal of land. He was rumored to have an interest in several banks and to be the behind-the-scenes financier of important business developments. He won concessions from the zoning board and the tax assessor. He associated with important politicians. But despite all the activity, little was known about the man himself. He refused to be interviewed and forbade his associates to talk to reporters.

Woodward, intrigued, decided to investigate. In months of part-time work, while he kept up with his regular assignments, Woodward was able to put together from public records and interviews a word portrait of one of the city's most important but least-known businessmen. He traced Morgan's holdings in shopping centers, banks and apartment buildings into five states and showed them to be worth nearly half a billion dollars. He also produced a biographical sketch of Morgan, an account of his political connections and a look at Morgan's use of a "straw party" — a person apparently unconnected to him — to conceal ownership of real estate.

In a modest summary of his work, Woodward said, "No laws were broken by the persons named in the stories, and no one went to jail because of them. The stories were meant only to demonstrate how power really works."

Here's how he did it:

He began with the clippings in the newspaper morgue. He double-checked every name he could come up with that had a possible Morgan connection. Some seemingly unrelated individuals and corporations were linked by material from other records.

Then he went to the courthouse. There, depositions taken in the divorce case of a Morgan associate revealed numerous land transactions and yielded other names to check. The indexes showed a great number of lawsuits filed against Morgan and associates. These contained still more names of corporations and business properties.

Corporation records kept by the secretaries of state of Kansas and Missouri showed names and addresses of officers and directors and when the corporations were formed. For business partnerships that were not incorporated, much the same information came from the fictitious name files, also called "d.b.a." (for "doing business as") files, also in the secretary of state's office. A pattern of connections was beginning to emerge.

Most banking records are secret, but Woodward put to good use a federal form (FFIEC 003) that has been required since 1979 and that details the principal owners of the bank and any loans the bank has made to its owners. Depending on whether the bank has a national or state charter, the form can be obtained from the U.S. Comptroller of the Currency, the Federal Reserve Bank or the Federal Deposit Insurance Corporation.

City planning commission records included minutes of meetings, staff reports and other details of developments such as shopping centers. County collectors' records showed who paid the property taxes on various parcels. County recorders' offices produced details of land ownership and of the financing of purchases.

City directories, birth certificates, school and military records, all public, helped Woodward trace his subject's life from the beginning. Marriage records in the county courthouse showed not only his wife's maiden name but even which synagogue he attended.

Campaign finance reports — local, state and federal — revealed support for some politicians whose later actions benefited Morgan.

Even some of Morgan's federal income-tax records, closed by law, were opened to inspection when they were entered as evidence in a suit in the U.S. Tax Court. Woodward got them with a request under the Freedom of Information Act.

Finally, Woodward said, "I talked with dozens of real estate developers, city planners, politicians, bankers, appraisers — you name it. Many of their names I got from the clips. Others I got from lawsuits. Records gave me a start in tracking down the people who could fill in the gaps in my stories and demonstrated how documents and human sources can complement each other."

The result was a series of stories rich in detail that told Kansas Citians a great deal about a man who had been secretly shaping their city.

The importance of accuracy cannot be overstated. It is the most essential element in good journalism of any kind. In investigative reporting especially, inaccuracy leads to embarrassment, to ruined reputations and, sometimes, to lawsuits. The reputations ruined often are those of the careless reporter and newspaper. Most investigative stories have the effect of accusing somebody of wrongdoing or incompetence. Even if the target is a public official whose chances of suing successfully for libel are slim, fairness and decency require that you be sure of your facts before you put them in print.

The Washington Post, during its famous Watergate investigation, followed the policy of requiring verification from two independent sources before an allegation could be published. That is a good rule to follow. People make mistakes. They lie. Their memories fail. Documents can be misleading or confusing. Check and double-check. There is no good excuse for an error.

WRITING THE STORY

Most investigative stories require consultation with the newspaper's lawyer before publication. As a reporter you will have little or nothing to say about the choice of your paper's lawyer. That lawyer, though, will be an important part of your investigative career. The lawyer advises on what you can print safely and what you cannot.

Most editors heed their lawyers' advice. If you are lucky, your paper's lawyer will understand and sympathize with good, aggressive journalism. If he or she does not, you may find yourself forced to argue for your story. You will be better equipped for such an argument — and few reporters go through a career without several — if you understand at least the basics of the laws of libel and privacy. Chapter 22 outlines them. Several good books on law for journalists are available, too.

The last step before your investigation goes public is the writing and rewriting. After days or weeks of intense reporting effort, the writing strikes some investigative reporters as a chore — necessary but unimportant. That attitude is disastrous. The best reporting in the world is wasted unless it is read. Your hard-won exposé or painstaking analysis will disappear without a trace unless the writing attracts readers and maintains their interest. Most reporters and newspapers that are serious about investigative reporting recognize this. They stress good writing almost as much as solid reporting. The Chicago Tribune, for example, assigns an especially skilled writer to its Pulitzer Prize–winning investigative task force as it nears the completion of each project. The writer's sole job is to present months of reporting work as clearly and dramatically as possible. Other newspapers prefer to let their reporters do their own writing.

How do you write the results of a complicated investigation? The general answer is, as simply as you can. One approach is to use a *hard lead*, displaying your key findings in the first few paragraphs. Another approach, often used, is to adopt one of the alternative story structures discussed in Chapter 15.

For three months six Miami Herald reporters examined every aspect of two counties' failing school systems. Their findings ran in an eight-part series, which began by focusing on a single student:

> At 17, Frank Smith seems more harried than a high school student ought to be.
>
> Up at 6 a.m., due in class by 7, he endures five hours of lessons with less than 18 minutes for lunch. Building a romance, holding down a full-time job, he rushes from one responsibility to another in a car that is both his burden and his pride.
>
> Frank Smith, an 11th grader at Miami Killian High, is typical of thousands of youngsters in today's public schools.
>
> Shaken by his parents' divorce when he was 9, forced to fend for himself when his mother and stepfather were busy at work, Frank turned out like so many other kids: sometimes mischievous, usually affable, rarely diligent, but always on the move.
>
> Described by his teachers as an ''average'' student, Frank fits neatly into an educational system plagued by problems.

A big, complicated story is introduced in simple, human terms. Readers who might have been put off by the mass of evidence the reporters had assembled were lured in by the plight of one real person.

Instead of a single blockbuster story, the material was presented in a series of shorter, less-complex pieces. There were stories on incompetent teachers and principals, a story on the money shortage, another on the politics of school finance, stories on curriculum, one on bureaucracy and several sidebars on schools and individuals doing something right.

The Philadelphia Inquirer spent six months investigating the scandalous nursing home business in New Jersey. Here is the beginning of one of the resulting series of stories:

> For most of her 98 years, Alberta Senior was an inconspicuous domestic worker who earned little money, never married and had only a few friends.
>
> Her death on March 22 was equally anonymous. Her funeral and burial in a pauper's grave were paid for by the Monmouth County Welfare Department.
>
> Only in the last few weeks of her life, when she was finally taken to a hospital from a boarding home, did Miss Senior attract the attention of some of the influential persons who had overlooked her, and others like her, for so long. By then, the plodding bureaucracy had proved itself incapable of acting swiftly enough to help this woman who had spent nearly a century in society's shadows.

The writing here is of a quality not matched in many stories. The combination of good writing with careful, extensive reporting produced a story that was read widely.

Writing an investigative story so that it will be read takes the same attention to organization and to detail that any good writing does. Here are a few tips that apply even more to investigative than to other stories:

1. *Get people into the story.* Any investigation worth doing involves people in some way. Make them come alive with descriptive detail, the kind we learned of in Frank Smith's and Alberta Senior's cases.

2. *Keep it simple.* Look for ways to clarify and explain complicated situations. When you have a mass of information, consider spreading it over more than one story — in a series or in a main story with a sidebar. Think about how charts, graphs or lists can be used to present key facts clearly. Don't try to print everything you know. Enough to support your conclusions is sufficient; more than that is too much.

3. *Tell the reader what your research means.* A great temptation in investigative reporting is to "lay out the facts and let the reader draw the conclusions." That is unfair to you and your reader. Lay out the facts, of course, but tell the reader what they add up to. A re-

porter who had spent weeks investigating the deplorable conditions in his state's juvenile corrections facilities wrote this lead:

> Florida treats her delinquent children as if she hated them.

If the facts are there, drawing the obvious conclusions is not editorializing. It is good and helpful writing.

4. *Organize.* Careful organization is as important in writing the investigative story as in reporting it. The job will be easier if you have been organized all along. When you are ready to write, examine your notes again. Make an outline. Pick out your best quotes and anecdotes. Some reporters, if they are writing more than one story, separate their material into individual folders, one for each story. However you do it, know what you are going to say before you start to write.

Think of writing as the climax of a process that begins with a hypothesis, tests that hypothesis through careful investigation, checks and double-checks every fact, and satisfies the concerns of editors and the lawyer. Every step in that process is vital to success.

The Sources

Investigative reporters — like any other reporters — get their information from people or documents. The perfect source would be a person who had the pertinent documents and was eager to tell you what they meant. Don't count on finding the perfect source. Instead, count on having to piece together the information you need from a variety of people and records — some of the people not at all eager to talk to you and some of the records difficult to understand. Let's consider human sources first.

HUMAN SOURCES

Suppose you get a tip that the mayor received campaign contributions under the table from the engineering firm that just got a big city contract. Who might talk?

Enemies. A person's enemies usually are the best sources when you are trying to find out anything bad about him or her. More often than not, the enemies of a prominent person will have made it their business to find out as much as possible about that person's misdeeds and shortcomings. Frequently, they will share what they know with a friendly reporter.

Friends. Surprisingly, friends are sometimes nearly as revealing as enemies. In trying to explain and defend a friend's actions, they may tell you more than you knew before. Occasionally you may find that someone your target regards as a friend is not much of a friend after all.

Losers. Like enemies, losers often carry a grudge. Seek out the loser in the last election, the losing contender for the contract, the loser in a power struggle. Bad losers make good sources.

Victims. If you are investigating a failing school system, talk with its students and their parents. If your story is about nursing home abuses, talk with some patients and their relatives. The honest and hard-working employees caught in a corrupt or incompetent system are victims, too. They can give you specific examples and anecdotes. Their case histories can help you write the story.

Experts. Early in many investigations, there will be a great deal you may not understand. You may need someone to explain how the campaign finance laws could be circumvented, someone to interpret a contract, or someone to decipher a set of bid specifications. Lawyers, accountants, engineers or professors can help you figure out technical jargon or complicated transactions. If they refuse to comment on your specific case, fit the facts you have into a hypothetical situation.

Police. Investigative reporters and law enforcement agents often work the same territory. If you are wise, you will make friends with carefully selected agents. They can — and frequently will — be of great help. Their files may not be gold mines, but they have investigative tools and contacts you lack. When they get to know and trust you, they will share. Most police like seeing their and their organization's names in the paper. They know, too, that you can do some things they cannot. It takes less proof for you to be able to print that the mayor is a crook than it may take to convince a jury. Most police investigators want to corner wrongdoers any way they can. You can use that attitude to your advantage.

People in Trouble. Police use this source and so can you, although you cannot promise immunity or a lesser charge, as the police can. A classic case was the Watergate affair. Once the Nixon administration started to come unraveled, officials trying to save their careers and images began falling all over each other to give their self-serving versions of events. People will react similarly in lesser cases.

Managing Human Sources

As an investigative reporter, you cultivate sources in the same ways a reporter on a beat does. You just do it more quickly. One excellent tactic is to play on their self-interest. Losers and enemies want to get the so-and-so, and thus you have a common aim. (But don't go overboard. Your words could come back to haunt you.) Friends want their buddy's side of the story to be explained. So do you. If you keep in mind that, no matter how corrupt your target may be, he or she is still a human being, it may be easier to deal sympathetically with that person's friends. That attitude may help ensure that you treat the target fairly, as well.

Experts just want to explain the problem as you present it. And you just want to understand. People in trouble want sympathy and some assurance that they still merit respect. No reporter should have trouble conveying either attitude.

Another way to win and keep sources is to protect them. Occasionally, a reporter faces jail unless he or she reveals a source. Even jail is not too great a price to pay in order to keep a promise of confidentiality. More often, the threats to confidentiality are less dramatic. Other sources, or the target of the investigation, may casually ask, "Where'd you hear that?" Other reporters, over coffee or a beer, may ask the same question. Hold your tongue. The only person to whom a confidential source should ever be revealed is your editor.

Human sources pose problems as well as solving them. They may lie to you. To get at an enemy or protect a friend, to make themselves look better or someone else look worse — and sometimes just for fun — people lie to reporters. No reporter is safe and no source is above suspicion. They may use you, too, just as you are using them. The only reason most people involved on any side of a suspicious situation will talk about it is to enhance their own position. That is neither illegal nor immoral, but it can trip up a reporter who fails to take every self-serving statement with the appropriate grain of salt.

Sources may change their stories as well. People forget. Recollections and situations change. Pressures can be applied. Fear or love or ambition or greed can intrude. A source may deny tomorrow — or in court — what he or she told you today.

Finally, sources will seldom want to be identified. Even the enemies of a powerful person often are reluctant to see their names attached to their criticisms in print. So are friends. Experts, while willing to provide background information, often cite their codes of ethics when you ask them to go on the record. Police usually will cooperate fully only if you promise them anonymity — since they are not supposed to prosecute people in the newspapers. Stories without identifiable sources have less credibility with readers, with editors, even with colleagues.

WRITTEN SOURCES

Fortunately, not all sources are human. Records and documents neither lie nor change their stories, they have no axes to grind at your expense and they can be identified in print. Many useful documents are public records, available to you or any other citizen upon request. Others are non-public but still may be available through your human sources.

Public Records

As Steve Woodward's work shows, a great deal can be learned about individuals and organizations through records that are available for the asking, if you know where to ask. Let's take a look at some of the most valuable public records and where they can be found.

Property Records. Many investigations center on land — who owns it, who buys it, how it is zoned, how it is taxed. You can find out all those things from public records. Your county recorder's office (or its equivalent) has on file the ownership of every piece of land in the county and the history of past owners as well. Most such offices have their files cross-indexed so that you can find out the owner of the land if you know its location or the location and size of the property if you know the owner. Those files also will tell you who holds a mortgage on the land. The city or county tax assessor's office has on file the assessed valuation of the land, the basis for property taxes. Either the assessor or the local zoning agency can tell you for what use the property is zoned. All requests for rezoning are public information, too.

Corporation Records. Every corporation must file with the secretary of state a document showing the officers and principal agent of the company. The document must be filed with every state in which the company does business. The officers listed may be only "dummies," stand-ins for the real owners. Even if that is the case, you can find out at least who the stand-ins are. But that is only the beginning. Publicly held corporations must file annual reports with the Securities and Exchange Commission in Washington. The reports list officers, major stockholders, financial statements and any business dealing with other companies owned by the corporation. Non-profit corporations — such as foundations and charities — must file with the Internal Revenue Service an even more revealing statement, Form 990, showing how much money came in and where it went. Similar statements must be filed with the attorneys general of many states. Corporations often are regulated by state or federal agencies as well. They file regular reports with the regulating agency. Insurance companies, for instance, are regulated by state insurance commissioners. Nursing homes are regulated by various state agencies. Broadcasters are overseen by the Federal Communications Commission, truckers by the Interstate Commerce Commission. Labor unions must file detailed statements showing assets, officers' salaries, loans and other financial information with the U.S. Department of Labor. Those statements are called "5500 Forms."

Form **990**	**Return of Organization Exempt from Income Tax**	OMB No. 1545-0047
Department of the Treasury Internal Revenue Service	Under section 501(c) (except black lung benefit trust or private foundation), of the Internal Revenue Code or section 4947(a)(1) trust	19**83**

For the calendar year 1983, or fiscal year beginning , 1983, and ending , 19

Use IRS label. Otherwise, please print or type.	Name of organization	A Employer identification number (see instruction L)
	Address (number and street)	B State registration number (see instruction D)
	City or town, State, and ZIP code	C If address changed, check here ▶

D Check applicable box—Exempt under section ▶ ☐ 501(c) ( ) (insert number), OR ▶ ☐ section 4947(a)(1) trust
E Accounting method: ☐ Cash ☐ Accrual ☐ Other (specify) ▶
F Section 4947(a)(1) trusts filing this form in lieu of Form 1041, check here ▶ ☐ (see instruction C10).
G Is this a group return (see instruction J) filed for affiliates? . . . . ☐ Yes ☐ No   If "Yes" to either, give four-digit group exemption number
 Is this a separate return filed by a group affiliate? . . . . ☐ Yes ☐ No   (GEN) ▶

Note: *You may be required to use a copy of this return to satisfy State reporting requirements. See instruction D.*
☐ Check here if gross receipts are normally not more than $25,000. (See instruction B11.) You are not required to complete and file this return with IRS but may have to file it with one or more States.
☐ Check here if gross receipts are normally more than $25,000 and line 12 is $25,000 or less. Complete Parts I (except lines 13-15), III, IV, VI, and VII and only the indicated items in Parts II and V (see instruction I). If line 12 is more than $25,000, complete the entire return.

501(c)(3) organizations and 4947(a)(1) trusts must also complete and attach Schedule A (Form 990). (See instructions.)

PART I.—Statement of Support, Revenue, and Expenses and Changes in Fund Balances		(A) Total	These columns are optional—see instructions	
			(B) Unrestricted/ Expendable	(C) Restricted/ Nonexpendable
1 Contributions, gifts, grants, and similar amounts received:				
(a) Direct public support				
(b) Indirect public support				
(c) Government grants				
(d) Total (add lines 1(a) through 1(c)) (attach schedule—see instructions)				
2 Program service revenue (from Part IV, line (f))				
3 Membership dues and assessments				
4 Interest on savings and temporary cash investments				
5 Dividends and interest from securities				
6 (a) Gross rents				
(b) Minus: Rental expenses				
(c) Net rental income (loss)				
7 Other investment income (Describe ▶)				
8 (a) Gross amount from sale of Securities Other assets other than inventory .				
(b) Minus: cost or other basis and sales expenses . .				
(c) Gain (loss) (attach schedule)				
9 Special fundraising events and activities (attach schedule—see instructions):				
(a) Gross revenue (not including $ of contributions reported on line 1(a)) . . .				
(b) Minus: direct expenses				
(c) Net income (line 9(a) minus line 9(b))				
10 (a) Gross sales minus returns and allowances . .				
(b) Minus: Cost of goods sold (attach schedule) . .				
(c) Gross profit (loss)				
11 Other revenue (from Part IV, line (g))				
12 Total revenue (add lines 1(d), 2, 3, 4, 5, 6(c), 7, 8(c), 9(c), 10(c), and 11) .				
13 Program services (from line 44(B)) (see instructions)				
14 Management and general (from line 44(C)) (see instructions) . . .				
15 Fundraising (from line 44(D)) (see instructions)				
16 Payments to affiliates (attach schedule—see instructions)				
17 Total expenses (add lines 16 and 44(A))				
18 Excess (deficit) for the year (subtract line 17 from line 12) . . .				
19 Fund balances or net worth at beginning of year (from line 74(A)) . .				
20 Other changes in fund balances or net worth (attach explanation) . .				
21 Fund balances or net worth at end of year (add lines 18, 19, and 20) . .				

Labels down left side: Support and Revenue; Expenses; Fund Balances

For Paperwork Reduction Act Notice, see page 1 of the instructions.   Form **990** (1983)

Figure 20.3   Copy of an IRS Form 990.

Once you have such corporation records, you must interpret them. Your public library has books that tell you how. Or your newspaper's own business experts may be willing to help.

Court Records. Few people active in politics or business go through life without some involvement in court actions. Check the offices of the state and federal court clerk for records of lawsuits. The written arguments, sworn statements and answers to questions (interrogatories) may contain valuable details or provide leads to follow. Has your target been divorced? Legal struggles over assets can be revealing. Probate court files of your target's deceased associates may tell you something you need to know.

Campaign and Conflict-of-Interest Reports. Federal — and most state — campaign laws now require political candidates to disclose, during and after each campaign, lists of who gave what to whom. Those filings can yield stories on who is supporting the candidates. They also can be used later for comparing who gets what from which officeholder. Many states require officeholders to file statements of their business and stock holdings. These can be checked for possible conflicts of interest or used as background for profile stories.

Loan Records. Commercial lenders usually file statements showing property that has been used as security for loans. Known as Uniform Commercial Code filings, these can be found in the offices of state secretaries of state and, sometimes, in local recorders' offices.

Minutes and Transcripts. Most elected and appointed governing bodies, ranging from local planning and zoning commissions to the U.S. Congress, are required by law to keep minutes or transcripts of their meetings.

Using and Securing Public Records

The states and the federal government have laws designed to assure access to public records. Many of those laws — including the federal *Freedom of Information Act*, which was passed to improve access to government records — have gaping loopholes and time-consuming review procedures. Still, they have been and can be useful tools when all else fails. Learn the details of the law in your state. You can get information on access laws and their interpretations by contacting the Freedom of Information Center at the University of Missouri, Box 838, Columbia, Mo. 65205.

Non-Public Records

Non-public records are more difficult, but often not impossible, to obtain. To get them, you must know that they exist, where they are and how to gain access. Finding out about those things requires good human sources. You should know about a few of the most valuable non-public records.

Investigative Files. The investigative files of law enforcement agencies can be rich in information. You are likely to see them only if you have a good source in that, or an affiliated, agency. If you do obtain such files, treat them cautiously. They will be full of unsubstantiated allegations, rumor and misinformation. Be wary of accepting as fact anything you have not confirmed yourself.

Past Arrests and Convictions. Records of past arrests and convictions increasingly are being removed from public scrutiny. Usually these are easier to obtain from a friendly police or prosecuting official. And usually they are more trustworthy than raw investigative files.

Bank Records. Bank records would be helpful in many investigations, but they are among the most difficult to get. Bankers are trained to keep secrets. The government agencies that regulate banks are secretive as well. A friend in a bank is an investigative reporter's friend indeed.

Tax Records. Except for those made public by officeholders, tax records are guarded carefully by their custodians, and properly so. Leaks are rare.

Credit Checks. Sometimes, you can get otherwise unavailable information on a target's financial arrangements by arranging through your newspaper's business office for a credit check. Credit reports may reveal outstanding debts, a big bank account, major assets and business affiliations. Use that information with care. It is unofficial, and the companies that provide it intend it to be confidential.

Problems with Written Sources

Even when you can obtain them, records present problems. They are usually dull. Records give you names and numbers, not anecdotes or sparkling quotes. They are bare bones, not flesh and blood. They can be misleading and confusing. Many highly skilled lawyers and accountants spend careers interpreting the kinds of records you may find yourself attacking without their training. Misinterpreting a document is no less serious an error than misquoting a person. And it's easier to do.

Documents usually describe without explaining. You need to know the "why" of a land transaction or a loan. Records tell you only the "what."

Most investigative reporters use both human and documentary sources. People can explain what records cannot. Documents prove what good quotes cannot. You need people to lead you to documents and people to interpret what the documents mean. And you need records to substantiate what people tell you. The best investigative stories have both.

The Obstacles

You have seen now why investigative reporting is important and how it can be done. The picture would not be complete, though, without a brief look at the reasons why not every newspaper does investigative reporting. As a reporter you will face certain obstacles. You and your editors will have to overcome them if you are to do real investigative reporting. Good newspapers do overcome such obstacles.

The first obstacle is money. Investigative reporting is the most expensive kind of reporting. It takes time, and time is money. Steve Woodward spent months on his Frank Morgan story. Newsday's investigative team spent nine months on a series about heroin traffic. Two Miami Herald reporters spent most of their time for more than two years on an investigation of corruption in a federal housing program. Usually, the reporters doing investigations are the paper's best and highest-paid. Frequently, fees for experts are involved. Lawyers charge for looking over a story and much, much more if a suit is filed. Space to publish the results costs money, too.

The second obstacle is staffing. Most newspapers, large or small, are understaffed. When a reporter is devoting time to an investigation, somebody else must be found to fill the gap. Many editors are unable or unwilling to adjust for prolonged absences by a key reporter. You may be able to get around that obstacle by doing your investigating in bits and pieces, keeping up with routine assignments all the while. That kind of part-time probing requires a high level of dedication on your part and your editor's. Such commitment is hard to sustain over long stretches of time.

The third obstacle is a lack of courage. This is the greatest inhibitor. Investigative reporting *means* disturbing the status quo. It means poking into dark corners, asking hard questions about controversial, sensitive affairs. Investigative reporting upsets people. If you are looking into the right things, the people who get upset are likely to be important.

Violence or the threat of violence directed toward reporters and newspapers is rare. The 1975 murder of investigative reporter Don

Bolles in Phoenix was shocking partly because such things hardly ever happen. But pressure, usually applied to your editor or publisher, is common enough. It takes courage to stand up to such pressure.

The Nixon administration threatened the lucrative television licenses of the Washington Post Co. during the Watergate investigation. The federal government sued the New York Times, Boston Globe and St. Louis Post-Dispatch to prevent publication of the Pentagon Papers. FBI and CIA agents investigated newspapers and harassed reporters during the era of Vietnam and Watergate. Those were dramatic cases. The papers involved were big and rich, and they resisted.

Other pressures are directly economic. A newspaper's survival can be threatened. The financially weak Miami News ran a series of stories on grocery pricing, and grocery chains — whose ads are the life's blood of any paper — pulled out their advertising. The Philadelphia Inquirer, then also unprofitable, published exposés of police corruption. The wives of police officers picketed the paper, and sympathetic unions of mailers and deliverymen refused to distribute the paper. The cost was in the hundreds of thousands of dollars.

More common and less visible are the social pressures and social influence of editors' and publishers' peers. It is very common for the top executive of a newspaper to associate socially with the political and business leaders who may be the targets of investigative reporting. It is also common for the reporters who work for those executives to be pulled off such stories.

If you find yourself on a paper lacking money or staff, you can still find ways to do investigative reporting, at least part-time, if you want to badly enough. But if you find yourself on a paper lacking courage, you have only two choices — give up or leave.

Fortunately, investigative reporting is so important and its rewards are so substantial that more reporters than ever are finding the support to do it. You can, too.

Suggested Readings

Downie, Leonard, Jr. ''The New Muckrakers.'' New York: New Republic Book Co., 1976. Personality sketches and descriptions of how some of the best contemporary investigative reporters work.

The IRE Journal. Publication of Investigative Reporters and Editors Inc. Walter Williams Hall, University of Missouri, Columbia, Mo. 65205. Every issue has articles on investigations, guides to sources and documents, and a roundup of legal developments. Edited transcripts of IRE conferences also are available at the same address.

Rose, Louis J. "How to Investigate Your Friends and Enemies." St. Louis, Albion Press, 1981. Very good for nuts and bolts of investigating.

Ullmann, John, and Steve Honeyman, editors. "The Reporter's Handbook." New York: St. Martin's Press, 1983. Tells you how to get and how to use the most important records and documents.

Weinberg, Steve. "Trade Secrets of Washington Journalists." Washington, D.C.: Acropolis Press, 1981. Excellent guide to Washington sources, written and human.

Williams, Paul. "Investigative Reporting and Editing." Englewood Cliffs, N.J.: Prentice-Hall, Inc., 1978. Good on both how and why to investigate.

21
Broadcast News

You didn't even have to know who Buck Rogers was!

The date was Feb. 7, 1984. Millions, young and old and from nations all over the world, watched Navy Capt. Bruce McCandless flying through space at 17,500 miles per hour, free of any connecting lifelines to the space shuttle.

Television had done it again. And if people did not see or hear the live broadcast, they were able to see or hear a rebroadcast. The broadcast media had done what they do best: They had made it possible for the world to witness a historic event — while it happened and exactly as it happened.

Of course, the broadcast media are not always present to record the news while it is happening. Much of the time broadcast journalists must write and report the news after it has occurred. Writing for broadcast news is a relatively new profession. Few people heard the first radio newscasts in 1920, and few watched the first news items broadcast over experimental television in the 1920s. But according to a 1983 report by The Roper Organization Inc., when people were asked where they got most of their news, they said television, by the widest margin ever. Sixty-five percent said from television; 44 percent said newspapers. Moreover, television has been the most believable news medium since 1961, now enjoying a better than two-to-one advantage over newspapers.

Whereas the number of daily newspapers had decreased from 1,800 to 1,711 in the past 30 years (19 dailies ceased publication in 1982 alone), as of Jan. 1, 1983, there were 4,685 AM stations, 4,505 FM stations, and 1,090 television stations on the air. The 1983 Broadcasting/Cablecasting Yearbook also reported that the United

States had 5,000 operating cable systems serving 14,200 communities. Another 2,500 franchises had been approved but not built.

Many, if not most, of these broadcast media provide at least some news that is written for them by journalists working for the wire services or by journalists employed by them.

Selecting and writing news for television and radio is slightly different from selecting and writing news for newspapers. The differences arise primarily from the technology involved in print and in the electronic media. We will explore those differences here as we discuss news reporting and writing for the broadcast media.

In this chapter you will learn:

1. How the selection of broadcast news differs from that of printed news.
2. How to write broadcast news.
3. How to prepare broadcast copy.

Criteria for Selecting Broadcast News

In Chapter 1, you learned the most important criteria of news value: audience, impact, proximity, timeliness, prominence, unusualness and conflict. All of these criteria apply to the selection of broadcast news. But there are three major differences between print and broadcast news selection. Broadcast news writers emphasize:

1. Timeliness above all other news values.
2. Information more than explanation.
3. News that has audio or visual impact.

Let's consider each of these points.

TIMELINESS

The broadcast news writer emphasizes one criterion of news value — timeliness — more than the others. "When" something happens often determines whether a news item will be used in a newscast. The breaking story receives top priority.

Broadcast news "goes to press" many times a day. If an event is significant enough, regular programming can be interrupted. The broadcast media are the "now" media. This sense of immediacy influences everything in broadcast news, from what is reported to how it is reported. Even when television and radio air documentaries or in-depth segments, they try to infuse a sense of urgency, a strong feeling of the present, an emphasis on what's happening now.

INFORMATION

Timeliness often determines *why* a news item is broadcast; time, or lack of it, determines *how* it is reported. Because air time is so precious, broadcast news emphasizes the what and the where more than the why or the how. In other words, broadcasters are generally more concerned with information than with explanation. Most stories must be told in 20 to 30 seconds; rarely does a story run longer than two minutes. A minute of news read aloud is only 15 lines of copy, or about 150 words. After commercial time is subtracted, a half-hour newscast has only 22 minutes of news, which amounts to about one-half of a front page of a newspaper. Although broadcast news writers may never assume that their audience knows anything about a story, they may often have to assume that listeners or viewers will turn to their newspapers for further background and details.

AUDIO OR VISUAL IMPACT

A third difference between broadcast and print news results from the technology involved. Some news is selected for radio because a

Figure 21.1 TV Newswoman. In recent decades women have made gains in career opportunities as news reporters and editors.

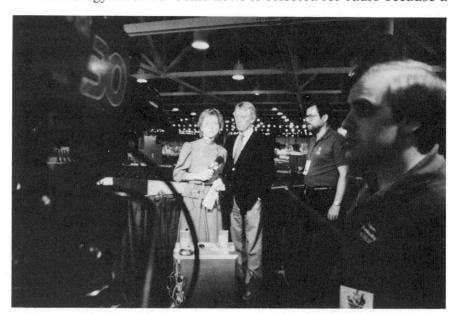

reporter has recorded an on-the-scene audio report. Some news is selected for television because it is visually appealing. For this reason news of accidents or of fires that may get attention only in the records column of the newspaper may get important play on a television newscast. If a television crew returns with good pictures of an event, that event may be part of the next newscast, regardless of its significance. Of course, this is not always the case.

Writing Broadcast News

Good writing is good writing, and most of what you have learned in Chapter 14 about writing applies also to broadcast news. However, the differences between broadcast news and print news affect how stories are written. Broadcast writing emphasizes certain characteristics that newspaper writing does not, and story structure may also vary.

CHARACTERISTICS OF BROADCAST WRITING

Because of the emphasis on timeliness in broadcast media, news writers must alter their style somewhat. They emphasize immediacy, aim for a conversational style, and try to write very tightly and clearly. When preparing news for radio or television, you should do the same.

Immediacy

Avoid the past tense as often as you can. In this United Press International wire service story, the present tense verbs are italicized:

> The country's largest conservation group *says* its research *shows* air and water quality in the United States improved significantly in the last 15 years. But it *says* the condition of wildlife, soil and living space *is* clearly worse. As a result, the National Wildlife Federation *says* the environment as a whole has deteriorated or barely held ground. The federation's environmental quality index *draws* on scientific research and interviews with experts from government, business and research institutions.

Notice that the verb "say" is in the present tense. That is accepted practice in broadcast writing. Of course, to be accurate, the past tense is sometimes necessary, as it is in the clause "air and water quality in the United States improved significantly in the last 15 years." If you must use the past tense, though, you should try whenever possible to use the present perfect tense because it points up immediacy. The clause "the environment as a whole has deterio-

Figure 21.2 No Substitute for Good Writing. The best broadcast news announcers are also the best broadcast news writers. Dan Rather helps to select and write all the news he broadcasts.

rated,'' written in the present perfect tense, also has the advantage of sounding natural and conversational.

Sometimes the sense of immediacy is underscored by adding the time element. You might say, ''just minutes ago,'' or on a morning newscast, ''this morning.'' If there is no danger of inaccuracy or of deceit, though, reference to time can be omitted. For example, if something happened yesterday, it may be reported today like this:

    The last of four strikes by East Coast longshoremen is
    over.

There is no need in this case to point out that the strike ended the day before. But if the past tense is used in a lead, the time element should be included:

    Negotiators for the trucking industry and the Teamsters
    union bargained in Washington until almost midnight last
    night, came ''very close'' on money issues, and agreed to
    go back at it this morning.

The best way to avoid the past tense is to avoid yesterday's story. You can do that by bringing yesterday's story up to date. By leading with a new development or a new fact, you may be able to use the present tense. Broadcast writers need to be especially aware of the techniques of follow-up stories described in Chapter 13.

Remember, radio and television are "live." Your copy must sound that way.

Conversational Style

"Write the way you talk" is good advice for most kinds of writing; it is imperative for broadcast writing. "Read your copy aloud" is good advice for most kinds of writing; for broadcast writing, that's what it's all about.

Conversational style is simple and informal. The key is to remember that you are talking to people. Tell them what just happened. Tell them what you just saw or heard. Imagine yourself going up to a friend and saying, "Guess what I just heard!"

Write so that your copy *sounds* good. Use simple, short sentences, written with transitive verbs in the active voice. People rarely use verbs in the passive voice when they talk; it usually sounds cumbersome and awkward. You don't go around saying, "Guess what I was just told by somebody."

Because casual speech contains contractions, they belong in your broadcast copy, too. For example:

```
    Palestinian sources say a cease-fire arranged by the
United Nations won't end all guerrilla operations.
```

Conversational style also permits the use of sentence fragments and of truncated sentences. Sentences are sometimes strung together loosely and sometimes begin with the conjunction "and," as in the following:

```
    The Electric Circus made the scene in the Big Apple last
night. No, it's not a plug-in version of Barnum and Bailey.
It's New York's newest disco, complete with fun-house mir-
rors and a carousel . . . along with three dance floors.
And it opened last night to an invitation-only crowd.
```

Writing in conversational style does not mean that you may use slang or colloquialism or that you should write ungrammatically. Nor should you use vulgar or off-color expressions. Remember that your audience is composed of people of all ages and sensitivities. The broadcast media have been given credit for raising the level of properly spoken English. Make your contribution.

Tight Phrasing

Although actual conversational English tends to be wordy, you must learn to write in a conversational style without being wordy. That means you must condense. Cut down on adjectives and adverbs. Eliminate the passive voice. Use strong active verbs. Make every word count.

Keeping it short means selecting facts carefully. Often you don't have time for the whole story. You need to tell the story understandably and briefly. To understand how to condense copy, let's first look at a wire story written for newspapers and then look at the same story written for broadcast. Here's the UPI newspaper story:

The Kansas Supreme Court Saturday said officials cannot prosecute the news media for publishing confidential information if the information was obtained from public records.

The justices said the First Amendment to the Constitution and Section 11 of the Kansas Bill of Rights forbid punishment of the news media for truthful reporting of facts gleaned from public records, even though those facts include the confidential name of the subject of an arrest warrant.

One justice, Robert Miller, issued an accompanying opinion expressing regret that the court's ruling would cause public officials to take greater pains to keep information from reporters.

The decision overturned the conviction of Stauffer Communications Inc., owner of the Topeka Daily Capital, for publishing the names of suspects being sought in a Lawrence murder case.

In December 1977, Sherry Pigg, Lawrence correspondent for the Capital, learned the occupants of a stolen car were being sought in connection with the killing of Samuel Norwood of Lawrence.

Ms. Pigg obtained the names of the suspects at the Douglas County District Court Clerk's office from a criminal appearance docket, which is a public record that was open to reporters' view.

The county attorney advised her it was against the law to disclose, or publish, the names in the arrest warrant before the suspects were apprehended. However, the newspaper published the names, sparking legal actions and a subsequent conviction in Douglas County.

The Supreme Court threw out the convictions.

The wire story then goes on to quote extensively from the decision written by Justice Alex Fromme. The same story appeared this way on AP Broadcast wire copy:

The State Supreme Court ruled unanimously today that truthful reporting of facts obtained from the public record cannot expose Kansas news media to criminal penalties. In deciding the case, the High Court upheld the right of news media to publish information contained in arrest or search warrants that were obtained from open court records before those warrants were actually served, despite provisions of a Kansas criminal law forbidding such disclosure by anyone. The court did not declare the law unconstitutional. It simply stated the statute could not be applied to the news media when the information is obtained from public documents.

In a later news summary the broadcast wire story appeared like this:

> The State Supreme Court ruled unanimously today that truthful reporting of facts obtained from the public record cannot expose Kansas news media to criminal penalties.

In the broadcast version the background is missing. For example, nothing is said about the origins of the case. Listeners or viewers must turn to their newspapers to learn the details. Researchers have found that those who watch television news generally spend more time reading their newspaper. They may be reading, in part, to get the background.

In broadcast news, tight writing is important even when there is more time. Broadcast writers waste no words, even in *documentaries*, which provide in-depth coverage of events. Here's how the famous CBS correspondent, Edward R. Murrow, introduced the well-known documentary on the state of migrant workers in this country:

> This is an American story that begins in Florida and ends in New Jersey and New York State with the harvest. It is a 1960 "Grapes of Wrath" that begins at the Mexican border in California and ends in Oregon and Washington. It is the story of men and women and children who work 136 days of the year and average 900 dollars a year. They travel in buses. They ride trucks. They follow the sun.

His style consists of simple, declarative sentences, written in the present tense, tightly, carefully, dramatically. It is casual and conversational; most of the words have one or two syllables. It is simple but not oversimplified. It is vivid and clear.

Clarity

Unlike the reader, viewers and listeners can't go back over the copy. They see or hear it only once, and their attention waxes and wanes. So, you must try harder to be clear and precise. All of the emphasis on condensing and writing tightly is useless if the message is not understood. Better not to report at all than to fill air time with messages that have no meaning.

Clarity demands that you write simply, in short sentences filled with nickel-and-dime words. Don't look for synonyms. Don't be afraid to repeat words or phrases. Oral communication needs reinforcement. Avoid foreign words and phrases; do not use Latin words (sine qua non) or Latinisms (somnambulist for sleepwalker). Avoid phrases like "the former" and "the latter." Repeat the proper names in the story rather than using pronouns. The listener can easily forget the name of the person to whom the pronoun refers.

When you are tempted to write a dependent clause in a sentence, make it an independent clause instead. Keep the subject close to the verb. Close the gap between the doer and the activity. Look at this news item:

> A man flagged down a Highway Patrol officer near Braden, Tennessee, today and told him a convict was hiding in his house. The prisoner, one of five who escaped from the Fort Pillow Prison on Saturday, surrendered peacefully.

The second sentence contains 12 words between the subject, "prisoner," and the verb, "surrendered." By the time the broadcaster reaches the verb, many listeners will have forgotten what the subject was. The story is easier to understand this way:

> A man flagged down a Highway Patrol officer near Braden, Tennessee, today and told him a convict was hiding in his house. The prisoner surrendered peacefully. He's one of five who escaped from the Fort Pillow Prison on Saturday.

The third sentence is still a complex sentence, but it is easily understood. The complex sentence is often just that — complex — only more so in oral communication.

Clarity also requires that you resist a clever turn of phrase. Although viewers and listeners probably are intelligent enough to understand it, they simply will not have the time. A good figure of speech takes time to savor. If listeners pause to savor it (presuming they grasped it in the first place), they will not hear what follows. Clever columnists often fail as radio commentators. Too often the listener asks, "What did he say?"

Of course, there are exceptions. The twist of a truism may convey a point with clarity and impact. In documentaries or commentaries the writer has more license. Even a literary allusion may be illuminating, as it was when Eric Sevareid concluded his remarks about the nation's farewell to Martin Luther King Jr.:

> So the label on his life must not be
> a long day's journey into night. It
> must be a long night's journey into
> day.

Generally, though, literary speech is undesirable. Even more dangerous than figures of speech are numerical figures. Don't barrage the listener with a series of numbers. If you must use statistics, break them down so that they are understandable. It is better to say, for example, that one out of every four Americans smokes than to say there are 54 million smokers in the United States. You may have to say how many billion dollars a federal program will cost, but you will help listeners understand if you say that it will cost the average wage earner $73 for each of the next five years.

Remember that you are writing for the benefit of your listeners. You serve them best by emphasizing immediacy and by writing conversationally, tightly and clearly.

STORY STRUCTURE

Now that we know the characteristics of broadcast writing, let's examine the story structure. Writers must craft broadcast leads somewhat differently from print leads. They must also construct special introductions and conclusions to filmed or recorded segments and synchronize their words with taped segments.

Writing the Broadcast Lead

Both newspaper and broadcast reporters must attract the attention of their audience. Much of what you learned in Chapter 15 applies to broadcast leads. But when you write for broadcast, you may need to attract attention differently.

One way to do this is by preparing your audience for what is to come. You cue the listeners to make sure they are tuned in. In effect, you are saying, "Now listen to this." You introduce the story with a general statement, something that will pique the interest of the audience, and then go to the specific. For example:

General   `Things are far from settled for Springfield's teacher`
Statement `strike.`
Specifics   `School officials and union representatives reached no`
               `agreement yesterday. They will not meet again for at least`
               `a week.`

Sometimes the lead, or setup, will be a simple phrase:

Setup   A tornado in Braddyville, Iowa.
Specifics   A tornado swept through the farming village of Braddyville, Iowa, this evening. And authorities report at
least half the town was leveled. They said four persons required hospitalization.

Sometimes the opening sentence will cover a number of news items:

There were several accidents in the Springfield vicinity
today.

"Cuing in" is only one method of opening a broadcast story. Other
leads go immediately into the what and the who, the where and the
when. In broadcast news the what is most important, followed by
who did the what. The time and the place may be included in the
lead, but seldom is the why or the how. If time permits, the why and
the how may come later in the story, but often they are omitted.

The first words of the leads are most important. Don't keep the
listener guessing as to what the story is about. Don't begin with a dependent clause as in this example:

Despite continued objections from Governor Carlin, a
second state spending-limit bill is scheduled for final
Senate action today.

The opening words are meaningless without what comes later. The
listener may not know what you are talking about. A better way to
introduce this story is:

The senate will vote today to limit state spending --
despite continued objections from Governor Carlin.

As you do in a lead for a newspaper story, be sure to "tee up," or
identify, an unfamiliar name. By introducing a person, you prepare
listeners for the name that they otherwise may miss. Do it this way:

Veteran Kansas City, Kansas, businessman and civic
leader Ivar Larson died yesterday in a nursing home at
age 83.

Don't mislead. The opening words must set the proper tone and
mood for the story. Attract attention but don't tease. Answer questions, but don't ask them. Question leads are for commercials. Lead
the listener into your story.

Writing Lead-ins and Wrap-ups

Broadcast journalists must learn how to write a different kind of lead, called the *lead-in*, that introduces a filmed or recorded excerpt from a news source or from another reporter. The functions of a lead-in are to set the scene by briefly telling the where, the when and sometimes the what, and to identify the source or reporter. Here's an example:

```
In Korea today, the mood was jubilant and hopeful. Bob
Smith reports.
```

Lead-ins should generate interest. Sometimes several sentences are used to provide background, as in the following:

```
We'll all be getting the official word this morning on
how much less our dollars bought last month. The consumer
price index for March is expected to show another sharp
rise in retail prices. The rate of inflation was one per-
cent in January and one-point-two percent in February.
Here's more on our inflation woes from Bill McKinney.
```

Be careful not to include in the lead-in what is in the story. Just as a headline should not be stolen from a lead of a newspaper story, the lead-in should not use the opening words of the correspondent. The writer must know the contents of the taped report in order to write a proper lead-in.

After the recorded report, you may want to wrap up the story before going on to the next item. This is especially important in radio copy since there are no visuals to identify the person just heard. If the story reported by Evelyn Turner was about a meeting to settle a strike, you might wrap up her report by adding information:

```
Turner reports negotiations will resume tomorrow.
```

A wrap-up such as this gives your story an ending and clearly separates it from the next story.

Writing for Videotape

Writing for a videotaped report really begins with the selection of the subject and how it is to be videotaped. The writing continues through the editing and selection process. And always, it is done with the pictures clearly in mind.

Words and pictures must be complementary, never interfering with each other. Neither should the words and pictures ignore each other. Your first responsibility is to relate the words to the pictures. If you do not, viewers will not get the message because they will be spending their time wondering what the pictures are about.

You can, however, stick too closely to the pictures by pointing out the obvious in a blow-by-blow account. You need to avoid both extremes and use what Russ Bensley of CBS News calls the "hit and run" technique. This means that at the beginning of a scene or when a scene changes you must tell the viewer where you are or what is happening. Once you are into the scene, the script may be more general and less closely tied to the pictures. For example, if the report concerns the continuation of a steel strike and the opening scene shows picketers outside the plant, you can explain the film by saying:

> Union members are still picketing Inland Steel today as the steel strike enters its third week.

Viewers now know two things that are not obvious in the film: who is picketing and where. If the scene should switch to people sitting around a table negotiating, you must again set the scene:

> Meanwhile, company officials and union leaders are continuing their meetings -- apparently without success.

Once you have related the words to the pictures, you may go on to tell other details of the strike. You are expected to provide information not contained in the pictures themselves. In other words, you must not only comment on the film, but complete it. Part of completing it is to give the report a wrap-up or a strong ending. Don't be cute and don't be obvious, but give the story an ending. The ending for the steel strike story might be:

> Experts agree on one sure result of the strike -- steel prices will rise again.

Now that you have learned some principles of writing broadcast news, you must learn how to prepare the copy.

Preparing Broadcast Copy

Preparing copy to be read by a newscaster is different from preparing it for a typesetter. Your goal is to make the copy easy for the newscaster to read and easy for the audience to understand. What follows will help you accomplish those two goals.

Figure 21.3 Sample of
Radio Copy.

```
west broadway

12-30

5-11-79

flanagan



     Members of Citizens for the Preservation of West Broadway

plan to gear up their petition drive again this weekend.  The group

began circulating petitions last weekend.

     The petitions request the City Council to repeal all previous

ordinances and resolutions on the widening.  Many residents of the

West Broadway area complain that the proposed widening project will

damage its residential nature.

     Petition-drive coordinator Vera Hanson says the group is pleased

with the show of support from residents all over Springfield . . .

but it won't know exactly how many signatures it has until next week.
```

Key for Figure 21.3:

"west broadway" is the slug for the story.
"12-30" is the time of the newscast.
"5-11-79" is the date of the broadcast.
"flanagan" is the name of the reporter.

Format. Most broadcast news editors want triple-spaced copy. Leave two to three inches on the top of the page and one to two inches on the bottom.

For radio copy, set your typewriter so that you have 70 characters to a line. Each line will average about 10 words and the newscaster will average 15 lines per minute. Some stations require you to start each story on a separate piece of paper. That way, the order of the stories can be rearranged, or stories can be added or dropped easily. If a story goes more than one page, write "MORE" in parentheses at the bottom of the page.

Television copy is written on the right half of the page in a 40-

character line. Each line will average about six words, and the newscaster will average about 25 lines per minute. The left side of the copy is used for audio or video information. This information, which is not to be read by the newscaster, is usually typed in all caps. The copy that is read is generally upper and lower case. In television copy the stories are numbered, and each story is on a separate page. If a story goes more than one page, write "MORE" in parenthesis at the bottom of the page.

Do not hyphenate words, and be sure to end a page with a complete sentence, or if possible, with a complete paragraph. If the next page should be missing in the middle of a broadcast, the newscaster can end, at least, with a complete sentence or paragraph.

At many stations copy is prepared for a *videoprompter*, a mechanical or electronic device that projects the copy next to the lens so that newscasters can read it while appearing to look straight into the lens. Copy for the videoprompter is often typed down a column in the middle of the page.

Date the first page of your script and type your last name in the upper left-hand corner of every page. Stations vary regarding these directions. The local news director determines the slug for a story and its placement. Some directors insist that the slug contain the time of the broadcast. If a story continues to a second page, write under the slug first add, or second add, or page 2, page 3, and so forth.

Names and Titles. Unlike in newspaper writing, well-known names, even on first reference, are not given in full. You may say Senator Proxmire of Wisconsin or Governor Gallen of New Hampshire. Middle initials should not be used unless they are a natural part of someone's name (Joe E. Brown) or unless they are necessary to distinguish two people with the same first and last names.

Titles should always precede names so that listeners are better prepared to hear the name. When you use titles, the first name and middle initial may be omitted. For example, broadcasters would say Vice President Bush and Secretary of Labor Donovan. Newspapers write out names like Thomas "Tip" O'Neill. In broadcast, use either the first name or the nickname, but not both.

Pronunciation. The writer's job is to help the person who reads the news pronounce the names of people and places correctly. To do this, you should write out difficult names phonetically in parentheses. NBC, for example, has its own reference list, and many individual stations have handbooks of their own. You may have to look up difficult names in unabridged dictionaries. If you don't find the name there, use your telephone. Call the person's office, or the consulate or embassy. If the name is of a U.S. town, try calling an operator in that town. There is no rhyme or reason to the way some people

Figure 21.4 Sample of
Television Copy.

```
       six              6-17              art              jorgenson


   MOC: JORGENSON                    A lesson in art and architecture paid

                                off for some Buchanan High School students

   SOF    :27                   today.  Ribbons were the prizes for winning
   NAT SND UNDER
   VOICE OVER
                                entries in a sketch exhibit of scenery and
   KEY: BUCHANAN HIGH SCHOOL
         :00-:05                buildings in the capital city area.

                                    The Springfield art club sponsored the

                                show and called in Springfield College art

                                professor Bill Ruess to jedge the artwork.

                                    Ruess says he was impressed by the

                                students' skills, especially those who tried

                                their hand at the different art media for

                                the first time.
```

Key for Figure 21.4

"six" is the time of the newscast.
"6-17" is the date of the broadcast.
"art" is the slug for the story.
"jorgenson" is the name of the reporter.

"MOC:" means the person is live on camera with audio from his microphone.
"SOF :27" means there is sound on the film lasting 27 seconds.
"NAT SND UNDER" means the film sound should be kept at a low level.
"VOICE OVER" means the voice is from the anchor person in the studio speaking over the film
    that is being shown
"KEY: BUCHANAN HIGH SCHOOL" indicates the title that should be shown over the film.
"00-05" indicates that the title should be shown five seconds after the report of this news item
    begins.

pronounce their names or to the way some names of places are pronounced. Never assume. Never try to figure it out. Find out. Here's
an example of how you should write out difficult names:

```
    For the second time in as many days, a former Argentine
junta (HOON-tah) leader has been detained in connection
with the 1982 Falklands war. Argentina lost that conflict
```

to Britain. A military tribunal ordered Admiral Jorge
Anaya (HOHR-hay ah-NIGH-yah) held after questioning him
for five-and-a-half hours today. Former military President Leopoldo Galtieri (lay-oh-POHL-doh gahl-tee-EH-ree)
was arrested yesterday.

Perhaps everyone knows how to pronounce Lima, Peru, but not
everyone can pronounce Lima (LIGH-mah), Ohio. You must note the
difference between NEW-erk, N.J., and new-ARK, Del., both spelled
Newark. And who would guess that Pago Pago is pronounced
PAHNG-oh PAHNG-oh?

Abbreviations. Generally, you should *not* use abbreviations in
broadcast copy. It is easier to read a word written out than to read
its abbreviation. Do not abbreviate the names of states, countries,
months, days of the week or military titles. There are exceptions,
and when you use them, use hyphens instead of periods because the
final period in the abbreviation may be misread as the end of a sentence.

You may abbreviate U-S when used as an adjective, and the U-S-S-
R; Dr., Mr., Mrs. and Ms.; a.m. and p.m. If initials are well known —
U-N, G-O-P, F-B-I — you may use them. Hyphens are not used for ac-
ronyms such as NATO and HUD, which are pronounced as one word.

Symbols and Numbers. Do *not* use symbols in broadcast copy
because a broadcaster can read a word more easily than he or she
can remember a symbol. Such symbols as the dollar sign ($) and the
percent sign (%) are never used. Don't even use the abbreviation for
number (no.).

Numbers can be a problem for both the announcer and the listener. As in newspaper style, write out numbers one through nine.
But write out eleven, too, because 11 might not be easily recognized
as a number. Use figures for 10, and from 12 to 999. The eye can easily take in a three-digit number, but write out the words thousand,
million and billion. Hence, 3,800,000 becomes three million, 800
thousand. Write out fractions (two-and-a-half million dollars) and
decimal points (three-point-two percent).

Some stations have exceptions. Figures often are used when giving the time (3:20 a.m.), sports scores and statistics (The score was
5 to 2), market reports (The Dow Jones industrial index was up
2-point-8 points) and addresses (30-0-2 Grand Street). In common
speech no one would give an address as three thousand two.

Ordinarily, you may round off big numbers. Thus 48-point-3 percent should be written "nearly half." But don't say "more than one
hundred" if 104 people died in an earthquake.

Use st, nd, rd, and th after dates: August 1st, September 2nd, October 3rd and November 4th. Make the year easy to pronounce: June 9th, 19-73.

Quotations and Attributions. Most broadcast news writers rarely use quotation marks. Because it is difficult and awkward to indicate to the listeners which words are being quoted, use indirect quotes or a paraphrase instead.

If it is important that listeners know the exact words of a quotation (as when the quoted words are startling, uncomplimentary or possibly libelous), the quote may be introduced by saying "in his own words," "with these words," "what she called," or "she put it this way." Most writers prefer to avoid the formal "quote" and "unquote," though "quote" is used more than "unquote." Note the following example:

```
In Hollings's words, quote, "There is no way to sell
Fritz Mondale toe to toe against Ronald Reagan."
```

If you must use a direct quotation, the attribution always should precede the quotation. Because listeners cannot see the quotation marks, they would have no way of knowing the words are a direct quote. If by chance the words were recognized as a quote, listeners would have no idea who is saying them. For the same reason, the attribution must always precede the indirect quote.

And if you must use a direct quotation, keep it short. If the quote is long and it is important to use it, you should use a tape of the person saying it. However, if you are compelled to use a quote of more than a sentence in your copy, break it up with phrases like, "Smith went on to say" or "and still quoting the senator."

Punctuation. In broadcast copy, less punctuation is good punctuation. The one exception is the comma. Commas help the reader pause at appropriate places. Use commas, for example, after introductory phrases referring to time and place, as in the following:

```
In Paris, three Americans on holiday met their death to-
day when their car overturned and caught fire.

Last August, beef prices had reached an all-time high.
```

Sometimes three periods are used in place of the comma. Periods also take the place of the parenthesis and of the semicolon. They indicate a pause and are more easily visible. The same is true of the dash — typed as two hyphens. Note the dash in the following example:

```
     Government sources say a study due out today will show
that the number of teen-agers who smoke is decreasing --
for the first time since 1968.
```

The only punctuation marks you need are the period, comma, question mark, dash, hyphen and, rarely, quotation marks. To make the words easier to read, use the hyphen in some words, even when the dictionary does not have it: anti-discrimination, co-equal, non-aggression.

Correcting Copy.   Do *not* use the copy-editing marks you learned for editing newspaper copy. If a word has an error in it, cross out the word and write the corrected word above it.

Note this sentence with newspaper copy editing:

```
                                   ℓ
The Stag Brewery at Belleville, (illinois), soon will be

hpased out of operation, and it's 230 workers already are

looking for new jbos.
```

Here's how you correct it for broadcasting:

```
                              Belleville, Illinois
     The Stag Brewery at Beleville, illinois, soon will be
phased                           its
hpased out of operation, and it's 230 workers already are
looking           jobs
lo-oking for new jbos.
```

Once again, your function is to make the copy easier to read. Avoid making the reader go up and down to find the right words, as in the following:

```
        price    gold    London
The pirce of glod in london at the afternoon fixing was

240 dollars.
```

Better to correct it this way:

```
         price of gold in London
The pirce-of-glod-in-london at the afternoon fixing was

240 dollars.
```

And, of course, always make your corrections neatly and clearly. Stations may vary in the writing style and in the preparation of copy. But if you learn what is presented here, you will be well-prepared. Differences will be small, and you will adapt to them easily.

Suggested Readings

Bliss, Edward, Jr. and John M. Patterson. "Writing News for Broadcast." 2nd ed. New York: Columbia University Press, 1978. Easily the best book on all aspects of broadcast news writing.

Fang, Irving E. "Television News, Radio News." 3rd Revised ed. Champlin, Minn.: Rada Press, 1980.

White, Ted, Adrian J. Meppen and Steve Young. "Broadcast News Writing, Reporting, and Production." New York: Macmillan Publishing Company, 1984. The best book on all aspects of broadcast news writing.

Williams, Jack. "All News All the Time." Quill, March 1978, pp. 21–26. Discusses the latest techniques and problems of all-news broadcast stations.

JUSTICE IS THE FIRST
OF THE VIRTUES
AGESILAUS II

FIRST ROW FOR LAWYERS
POLICE AND PRESS ONLY

PART SIX

Rights and Responsibilities

22

Press Law

"If you write that, I'll sue."

That threat can be intimidating to the young reporter who hears it for the first time. For those with a bit more experience, the situation will have been encountered many times. In either case, such a threat should not be taken lightly. It is at least possible that the person making it is both serious about the threat and accurate in insisting that your information is incorrect. If you are wrong, both you and your newspaper could suffer.

Reporters who know their stories are accurate are never intimidated by such threats. If what you write is true, and you can prove it, you have little to fear when threats of lawsuits are tossed about. The laws that pertain to libel, invasion of privacy and protection of sources are among the many you should know about. In an era when people increasingly turn to the courts to solve their problems, it makes sense to have an understanding of your rights as a journalist to gather and write the news. In recent years, the courts have chipped away at those rights in instances ranging from investigating prisons to covering divorce actions.

In one particularly threatening case that almost resulted in the closing of the Alton (Ill.) Telegraph, the libel judgment was for $9.2 million. The case ended in bankruptcy court, where the award was reduced to $2.1 million, still a major loss. Despite those setbacks, the press has ample opportunity to report the news as long as those reports are fair and accurate. It is important that you learn the essentials of libel and privacy and understand the basics of contempt of court.

In this chapter you will learn:

1. What rights you have as a journalist and the source of those rights.
2. How to spot potentially libelous situations and what to do about them.

3. When you might be invading someone's privacy.
4. What kinds of problems you may face in protecting confidential sources.

Your Rights

The Constitution signed in Philadelphia in 1787 did not contain explicit protections of freedom of speech and of the press. Those protections were added two years later, in the First Amendment, which states:

Congress shall make no law respecting an establishment of religion, or prohibiting the free exercise thereof; or abridging the freedom of speech, or of the press; or the right of the people peaceably to assemble, and to petition the Government for a redress of grievances.

Read that again: "Congress shall make no law . . . abridging the freedom of . . . the press." No other business in the United States enjoys that specific constitutional protection.

Why should there be such protection for the press? The Supreme Court gave an eloquent answer to that question in a 1957 obscenity decision. The press is protected, the court ruled, to assure the "unfettered interchange of ideas for bringing about the political and social changes desired by the people."

The free flow of ideas is necessary in a democracy because people who govern themselves need to know about their government and those who run it, as well as about the social and economic institutions that greatly affect their day-to-day lives. Most people get that information through newspapers, radio and television.

In 1966 Congress passed the *Freedom of Information Act* to assist anyone in finding out what is happening in our federal agencies. This act, which was amended in 1974 to improve access to government records, makes it easier for you to know about government business. All 50 states have similar *open-records laws*. Though of great assistance to the press, the laws also are used by individuals and businesses to gain information previously kept secret by the government. There are other laws assuring access to government transactions. The federal government and all the states have *open-meetings laws* — often called *sunshine laws* — requiring that the public's business be conducted in public.

The First Amendment, the Freedom of Information Act and sunshine laws demonstrate America's basic concern for citizen access to information needed for the "unfettered interchange of ideas." However, there are laws that reduce the scope of freedom of the press.

Libel

Traditionally, most of the laws limiting the absolute principle of freedom of the press have dealt with libel. These laws result from the desire of legislatures and courts to help individuals protect their reputations. This was explained by U.S. Supreme Court Justice Potter Stewart in a libel case:

> The right of a man to the protection of his own reputation from unjustified invasion and wrongful hurt reflects no more than our basic concept of the essential dignity and worth of every human being — a concept at the root of any decent system of ordered liberty.

Protection for reputations dates back centuries. In 17th-century England individuals were imprisoned for making libelous statements. One objective was to prevent criticism of the government. Another was to maintain the peace by avoiding duels. Duels are rare today, and government is freely criticized, but the desire to protect an individual's reputation is just as strong.

Libel is damage to a person's reputation caused by bringing him or her into hatred, contempt or ridicule in the eyes of a substantial and respectable group. That hatred, contempt or ridicule must be more than something that is unpleasant to the individual. Three areas are particularly sensitive:

1. Accusing someone of a crime.
2. Damaging a person in his or her public office or occupation. For example, if you reported that a kosher butcher sells bacon, not everyone would think less of the butcher. But it would be damaging to his reputation in some Jewish communities.
3. Accusing a woman of being unchaste. Many states have statutes that make an accusation of unchasteness a cause of action in a libel suit.

This characterization of libel does not mean you never can say a person committed a crime, was unethical in business or was adulterous. It does mean you must be sure that what you write is true.

LIBEL SUIT DEFENSES

There are three traditional defenses against libel: truth, privilege and fair comment and criticism. Two other constitutional defenses — the actual malice and negligence tests — are commonly used in more limited circumstances.

Truth

Truth is the best defense against libel. But knowing the truth is one thing; proving it is another. It will be difficult for you to know, for example, whether a person charged with arson actually started the fire. What can you do as a responsible reporter?

The law requires that you try to learn the truth in every way possible. Who told you that Joe Jones started the fire? The first source to check is the police or fire report. If a police officer or fire marshal says that Jones started a fire, you can report not that he did it but that he has been accused of doing it. You should go no further than the report unless you have information you would be willing to present in court.

Be sure you report no more than you know is true. You might, for instance, learn that Helen Greer has not paid any of her bills for two years, and the only way she can get merchandise is to pay cash when goods are delivered. Who gave you this information? If the truth is that a former employee of Ms. Greer told you, that is all the truth you have. The truth, then, is not that Helen Greer has not paid any of her bills for two years and has a bad credit rating. The only truth is that a former employee said it. Without supporting evidence for charges such as these, careful newspapers will not print them.

If you do and your newspaper is sued for damaging Helen Greer's reputation, you would have to try to convince the court that the charge was true because the former employee told you. But what if Ms. Greer presents canceled checks and calls suppliers, who deny that she owes them any money? You would lose the libel suit. You must be able to prove that Helen Greer is a credit risk before you print it, not just that she was accused of bad business practices by a former employee.

When a newspaper in Oklahoma reported that a wrestling coach had been accused of requiring a sixth-grader, who wanted to rejoin the team, to submit to a whipping by his fellow students while crawling naked through the legs of team members, the coach sued. He claimed damage to his reputation.

In cases like this, the reporter has to prove not just that one or more participants told of the incident but that the statements were true. This could result in some participants testifying to an occurrence and others testifying the incident never took place. A jury would have to decide on the credibility of the participants as they testified during a trial.

While you must always strive for absolute truth in all of your stories, the courts will settle for what is known as *substantial truth* in most cases. This means that you must be able to prove the essential elements of all you write.

Privilege

In addition to truth, the courts traditionally have allowed another defense against libel: privilege. This defense applies when you are covering any of the three branches of government. The courts allow legislators, judges and government executives the *absolute privilege* to say anything — true or false — when acting in their official capacities. The rationale is that the public interest is served when an official is allowed to speak freely and fearlessly about making laws, carrying them out or punishing those who do not obey them. Similarly, a party in a judicial proceeding, such as an attorney, court clerk or judge, is absolutely privileged to say or publish false and even defamatory information about another person during that proceeding.

In the executive branch it isn't always clear whose statements are privileged and when. The head of state and the major officers of executive departments of the federal and state governments are covered. But one court has held that "minor officials, such as a postmaster . . . are entitled only to a qualified privilege."

As a reporter you do have a *conditional privilege* to report what public officials say. Your privilege is conditional upon your report's being full, fair and accurate coverage of the court session, the legislative session or the president's press conference even if any one of those includes defamatory statements.

You can quote anything the president of the United States says without fear of losing a libel suit. But there are many other levels of executives in federal, state and local government. Mayors of small towns, for instance, often hold part-time positions. They are absolutely protected from libel suits, and you are conditionally privileged to report on what those officials say when they are acting in their official capacities. The problem arises when the mayor says something defamatory when not acting in an official capacity.

Fair Comment and Criticism

In some cases you may not be reporting but commenting and criticizing. The courts have protected writers who comment on and criticize the public offerings of anyone in the public eye. Included in this category are actors and actresses, sports figures, public officials and other newsworthy persons. Most often, such writing occurs in reviews of plays, books or movies, or commentary on service in hotels and restaurants.

The courts call this *fair comment and criticism*. You are protected as long as you do not misstate any of the facts on which you base your comments or criticism.

The Actual Malice Test

It was a small but momentous step from fair comment and criticism to the case of *New York Times* v. *Sullivan*. In 1964 the U.S. Supreme Court decided that First Amendment protection was broader than just the traditional defenses of truth and privilege and that the press needed even greater freedom in coverage of public officials.

The case started with an advertisement for funds in The New York Times of March 29, 1960, by the Committee to Defend Martin Luther King Jr. and the Struggle for Freedom in the South. The advertisement contained factual errors concerning the police, according to Montgomery, Ala., Commissioner L. B. Sullivan. He thought the errors damaged his reputation, and he won a half-million-dollar judgment against The New York Times in the Alabama trial court.

The Supreme Court said it was considering the case against the background of a profound national commitment to the principle that debate on public issues should be uninhibited, robust and wide open. Thus Justice William Brennan wrote that the Constitution requires a federal rule prohibiting a public official from recovering damages from the press for a defamatory falsehood relating to his or her official conduct. However, if a public official can prove that the press had knowledge that what was printed was false or that the story was printed with reckless disregard of whether it was false or not, he or she may recover damages.

The justices thereby gave you protection to write virtually anything about officeholders or candidates unless you know that what you are writing is false or you recklessly disregard the truth of what you write. They called this the *actual malice* test.

The actual malice test was applied later in a case involving a story on CBS's "60 Minutes" about a retired Army officer. Col. Anthony Herbert contended the broadcast falsely portrayed him as a liar. He tried to prove that producer Barry Lando recklessly disregarded whether it was a false broadcast or not. Herbert asked some questions that Lando claimed were protected by the First Amendment because they inquired into his state of mind and into the editorial processes during the production of the program.

The Supreme Court said on April 18, 1979, that the "thoughts and editorial processes of the alleged defamer would be open to examination." The court pointed out that protecting the editorial process "would constitute a substantial interference with the ability of a defamation plaintiff to establish . . . malice" as required by the New York Times case. The press greeted the ruling with displeasure, though some attorneys noted that the inquiry into the editorial process could help newspapers as much as hurt them. It could help by permitting journalists and their attorneys to demonstrate how careful they were in gathering and selecting the information printed.

Assume you were told that years ago your town's mayor had been involved in a bootlegging operation. Your source was a friend of the mayor who knew him 30 years ago in Idaho. You print the story. After it is published, you find it was not the mayor but his brother who was the bootlegger. The mayor sues. You are in trouble. You must try to convince the court that you should have been able to trust your source and that you did not act with "actual malice." If the source had given you many valid stories in the past, you might be able to convince the court that you had good reason to believe what you were told. You also would have to show what else you did or failed to do before you printed the story. Did you call anyone in Idaho to check? Did you talk to the mayor? Did you try other ways to verify the information? All these questions will be asked as the court tries to decide whether you recklessly disregarded the truth.

Usually a reporter who has tried diligently to do all possible research for a story will be able to meet the actual malice test and win a libel action. The key is verification: checking the information with as many sources as possible.

STANDARDS APPLICABLE TO PUBLIC FIGURES

This "actual malice" protection was expanded in two cases in 1967 to include not only public officials but also *public figures* — persons in the public eye but not in public office.

The first case stemmed from a Saturday Evening Post article that accused Coach Wally Butts of conspiring to fix a 1962 football game between Georgia and Alabama. At the time of the article, Butts was the athletic director of the University of Georgia. The article, entitled "The Story of a College Football Fix," was prefaced by a note from the editors of the Post stating:

> Not since the Chicago White Sox threw the 1919 World Series has there been a sports story as shocking as this one. . . . Before the University of Georgia played the University of Alabama . . . Wally Butts . . . gave (to Alabama's coach) . . . Georgia's plays, defensive patterns, all the significant secrets Georgia's football team possessed.

The Post reported that because of an electronic error about a week before the game, George Burnett, an Atlanta insurance salesman, accidentally had overheard a telephone conversation between Butts and the head coach of Alabama, Paul Bryant.

Coach Butts sued the Curtis Publishing Co., publishers of the Post, and won a verdict for $60,000 in general damages and $3 million in punitive damages. The Curtis Co. appealed the case to the Supreme Court and lost, although the amount of damages was reduced.

The second case was decided the same day. The Associated Press was sued by Gen. Edwin Walker for the distribution of a news dispatch giving an eyewitness account by an AP staffer on the campus of the University of Mississippi in the fall of 1962. The AP reported that Gen. Walker personally had led a student charge against federal marshals during a riot on the Mississippi campus as federal efforts were being made to enforce a court decree ordering the enrollment of a black student.

Walker was a retired general — a private citizen — at the time of the publication. He had won a $2 million libel suit in a trial court. The Supreme Court, however, ruled against him.

In both cases the stories were wrong. In both, the actual malice test was applied. What was the difference between the Butts and Walker cases? The justices said the football story was in no sense "hot news." They noted that the person who said he had heard the conversation was on probation in connection with bad-check charges and that the notes he had made were not even viewed by Post personnel before publication. The court also said, as evidence of actual malice on the part of the Post, that no one looked at the game films to see if the information was accurate; that a regular staffer, instead of a football expert, was assigned to the story; and that no check was made with someone knowledgeable in the sport. In short, the Post had not done an adequate job of reporting.

The evidence in the Walker case was considerably different. The court said the news in the Walker case required immediate dissemination because of the riot on campus. The justices noted that the AP received the information from a correspondent who was present on the campus and gave every indication of being trustworthy and competent.

In an earlier case the Supreme Court had defined a public official as a government employee who has, or appears to the public to have, substantial responsibility for or control over the conduct of governmental affairs. In the Butts and Walker cases the court used two definitions of a public figure. The first, like Butts, is a person who has assumed a role of special prominence in the affairs of society — someone who has pervasive power and influence in a community. The second, like Walker, is a person who has thrust himself into the forefront of a particular public controversy in order to influence the resolution of the issues involved.

There are other examples of "public figures." A college professor who has become involved with any public controversy ranging from grading practices to gay rights may have made himself or herself a public figure. A police officer who is the leader of the Police Association may be a public figure because of his or her power and influence.

In 1979, the Supreme Court decided three cases that help us determine who is a public figure and who is not. The first involved Mrs. Russell A. Firestone, who sued for libel after Time magazine reported that her husband's divorce petition had been granted on grounds of extreme cruelty and adultery. Mrs. Firestone, who had married into the Firestone Tire and Rubber Co. family, claimed that those were not the grounds for the divorce. She also insisted that she was not a public figure with the burden of proving actual malice. The Supreme Court agreed. It ruled that she had not thrust herself into the forefront of a public controversy in an attempt to influence the resolution of the issues involved. The court admitted that marital difficulties of extremely wealthy individuals may be of some interest to some portion of the reading public but added that Mrs. Firestone had not freely chosen to publicize private matters about her married life. The justices said she was compelled to go to court to "obtain legal release from the bonds of matrimony." They said she assumed no "special prominence in the resolution of public questions." The case was sent back to Florida for a finding of fault, and a new trial was ordered. Mrs. Firestone remarried, and the case was settled out of court.

The second of the 1979 cases involved Sen. William Proxmire of Wisconsin, who had started what he called the Golden Fleece Award. Each month he announced a winner who, in his opinion, had wasted government money. One such winner was Ronald Hutchinson, a behavioral scientist who had received federal funding for research designed to determine why animals clench their teeth. Hutchinson had published articles about his research in professional publications. In deciding that Hutchinson was not a public figure, the court ruled that he "did not thrust himself or his views into public controversy to influence others." The court admitted there may have been legitimate concerns about the way public funds were being spent, but said this was not enough to make Hutchinson a public figure.

The third 1979 case concerned an individual found guilty of contempt of court in 1958 for his failure to appear before a grand jury investigating Soviet espionage in the United States. Ilya Wolston's name had been included in a list of people indicted for serving as Soviet agents in a 1974 book published by the Reader's Digest Association. Wolston had not been indicted, and he sued. The Supreme Court, in deciding that he was not a public figure, found that Wolston had played only a minor role in whatever public controversy there may have been concerning the investigation of Soviet espionage. The court added that a private individual is not automatically transformed into a public figure merely by becoming involved in or being associated with a matter that attracts public attention.

Lower courts have ruled that in other situations individuals have become public figures by the nature of their activities. These include an attorney in local practice for 32 years who had been involved in major disputes and social activities, a newspaper publisher who regularly had taken strong public stands on controversial issues, and a college dean who had attempted to influence the proposed abolition of his position.

Assume you are covering a proposal to fluoridate the water of your town. Among those you may write about are:

- The mayor, who obviously is a public official.
- A doctor who has a private medical practice but is so concerned about the effects of fluoridation that he has made many public speeches. He has become a public figure because he has thrust himself to the forefront of the fluoridation controversy.
- A former state senator who now owns a radio station and is well-known in the community. She, too, is a public figure because of her prominence in the affairs of the city.

But how about the attorney who is handling the litigation for the individuals opposed to fluoridation? If he also is a spokesman for this group, he may be treated as a public figure. However, if he does no more than file the legal papers with the courts and leaves the press conferences and public appearances to others, he has not thrust himself to the forefront of the controversy. Do you have the same protection from a libel action when you write about him as you do with the persons you are certain are public figures or public officials?

In 1974 the Supreme Court said the answer usually is no. The justices said states may give more protection to private individuals if a newspaper or radio or television station damages their reputations than either public officials or public figures. The important phrase "may give more protection" is found in the landmark *Gertz* v. *Welch* case.

STANDARDS APPLICABLE TO PRIVATE CITIZENS

Private citizens who sue for punitive, or punishment, damages must meet the same actual malice test as public officials and public figures do. Because of the *Gertz* case, states have been allowed to set their own standards for libel cases involving private citizens who sue only for actual damages. Twenty states and the District of Columbia have adopted a *negligence test*. This test requires you to use the same care in gathering facts and writing your story as any reasonable reporter would use under the same or similar circumstances. If you make every effort to be fair and answer all the questions a reasonable person may ask, you probably would pass the negligence test.

One state, New York, has adopted a *gross negligence test*. Four states have established a more stringent standard that requires private citizens to prove actual malice. In the remaining states the matter is pending in courts and therefore unsettled, or there have been no cases to resolve the issue. Here is a state-by-state listing of the tests applicable in the 50 states and the District of Columbia:

Alabama	Unsettled
Alaska	Actual Malice
Arizona	Negligence
Arkansas	Negligence
California	Unsettled
Colorado	Actual Malice
Connecticut	Unsettled
Delaware	No Cases
District of Columbia	Negligence
Florida	Unsettled
Georgia	Unsettled
Hawaii	Negligence
Idaho	No Cases
Illinois	Negligence
Indiana	Actual Malice
Iowa	Unsettled
Kansas	Negligence
Kentucky	Negligence
Louisiana	Negligence
Maine	No Cases
Maryland	Negligence
Massachusetts	Negligence
Michigan	Actual Malice
Minnesota	No Cases
Mississippi	No Cases
Missouri	No Cases
Montana	Unsettled
Nebraska	No Cases
Nevada	No Cases
New Hampshire	Negligence
New Jersey	Unsettled
New Mexico	Negligence
New York	Gross Negligence
North Carolina	Unsettled
North Dakota	No Cases
Ohio	Negligence
Oklahoma	Negligence
Oregon	Unsettled

Pennsylvania	Unsettled
Rhode Island	No Cases
South Carolina	Negligence
South Dakota	No Cases
Tennessee	Negligence
Texas	Negligence
Utah	Negligence
Vermont	No Cases
Virginia	Unsettled
Washington	Negligence
West Virginia	Negligence
Wisconsin	Negligence
Wyoming	No Cases

Invasion of Privacy

Libel is damage to an individual's reputation. *Invasion of privacy* is a violation of a person's right to be left alone.

As a reporter you may be risking a successful invasion of privacy suit under the following circumstances:

1. You physically intrude into a private area to get a story or picture, an act closely related to trespass.
2. You publish a story or photograph about someone that is false but not defamatory.
3. You disclose something about an individual's private affairs that is true but also is offensive to individuals of ordinary sensibilities.
4. You use someone's name or picture in an advertisement or for similar purposes of trade. This is called "appropriation" and does not affect you when you are performing your reporting duties.

Your basic defense in an invasion of privacy suit is that you are a reporter covering a newsworthy situation. The courts usually protect the press against invasion of privacy suits when it is reporting matters of legitimate public interest. There are exceptions.

One arises when you invade someone's privacy by entering private property to get a story. You cannot trespass on private property to get a story or take a picture even if it is newsworthy. The courts will not protect you when you are a trespasser. Two Life magazine staffers lost an invasion of privacy suit because, posing as patients, they went into a man's home to get a story about a faith healer. You may enter private property only if you are invited by the owner or renter.

The court also will not protect you if you invade someone's privacy out of carelessness. For example, if a story or picture of a pedestrian struck by a careless driver is used again, a legal problem arises if the picture or part of the facts is used in a story, say, about careless pedestrians. The pedestrian who was hit could file a lawsuit charging either libel or invasion of privacy because the case may involve some damage to reputation. If it were the driver rather than the pedestrian who was careless, your later story also is false.

The Supreme Court has decided two cases in this area, known as "false light." The first concerned a play review in which Life magazine attempted to connect fictionalized material in "Desperate Hours" to the real-life experiences of a family. The justices ruled that the First Amendment precluded any reward of damages for false reports in matters of public interest without proof that the material was published with knowledge that it was false or with reckless disregard of truth. The press lost the other such case when the justices ruled that a direct quote from a person the reporter had not interviewed amounted to knowing or reckless publication of an untruth.

The third category of invasion of privacy that the courts recognize — unwanted publicity — concerns stories about incidents that, because they are true, cannot be defamatory but can be offensive to a person of ordinary sensibilities. An example is a picture published by Sports Illustrated in which a football fan's pants zipper was open. The fan sued for invasion of privacy but lost. Also in the area of unwanted publicity, the Supreme Court held in 1975 that truthfully reporting the name of a rape victim is permitted. In 1976 and again in 1979 the justices upheld the right of the press to publish the names of juveniles involved with the law because the information was truthful and of public significance.

The courts say that in order for privacy to be invaded, there must be a morbid and sensational prying into private lives. Merely being the subject of an unflattering and embarrassing article is not enough.

Protection of Sources and Notes

The final area you must know about is your ability — or inability — to protect your sources and notes. The problem may arise in various situations. A grand jury that is investigating a murder may ask you to reveal the source of a story you wrote about the murder. You may be asked to testify at a criminal or a civil trial. Or the police may obtain a warrant to search the news room, including your desk.

The conflict here is between a reporter's need to protect sources of information and the duty of every citizen to testify to help the courts determine justice. By the nature of your work as a reporter, you will usually be at the scene of events that are important and newsworthy. Anyone wanting the facts about an event can subpoena you to bring in all the details. Journalists usually resist. They work for their newspaper, radio or television station, not a law enforcement agency. Their ability to gather information would be compromised if the sources knew that their identities or their information would go to the police.

By 1984 some protection against testifying — *shield laws* — had been adopted by the legislatures in 26 states. The states are:

Alabama	Louisiana	New York
Alaska	Maryland	North Dakota
Arizona	Michigan	Ohio
Arkansas	Minnesota	Oklahoma
California	Montana	Oregon
Delaware	Nebraska	Pennsylvania
Illinois	Nevada	Rhode Island
Indiana	New Jersey	Tennessee
Kentucky	New Mexico	

Congress had not acted in this area, however, at least in part because journalists themselves were divided about the desirability of such legislation.

Even in states with shield laws, judges in most criminal cases involving grand juries will not allow you to keep your sources secret. In civil litigation you may be allowed to keep sources confidential in most cases unless the court finds that the information sought is:

1. Unavailable from other sources.
2. Relevant to the underlying litigation.
3. Of such critical importance to the lawsuit that it goes to the heart of the plaintiff's claim.

There has been only one Supreme Court decision to guide us. This case, in 1972, was one in which the sole issue, the justices said, was the obligation of reporters to respond to grand jury subpoenas as other citizens do and answer questions relevant to an investigation into a crime. According to the court, you cannot protect your source before a grand jury or in a criminal trial. William Farr, now a Los Angeles Times reporter, spent 46 days in virtual solitary confinement in a Los Angeles jail in 1971 for refusing to disclose to a judge his source for a newspaper article about the trial of Charles Manson, the mass murderer. Myron Farber spent 40 days in a New Jersey jail and his paper, The New York Times, was fined more than

$250,000 in 1978 for failure to comply with subpoenas directing them to produce documents and materials during a murder trial.

Despite the publicity, the Farber case is of limited legal importance outside New Jersey. The precedent-setting case is *U.S.* v. *Nixon.* The Nixon case requires a showing in court of the need for tapes, documents or other materials before people not directly involved in a court case can be ordered to comply with subpoenas.

That principle is relevancy, and it extends back to the Marie Torre case in 1958. Torre spent 10 days in jail in New York for refusing to disclose a confidential source the court said was relevant in a libel action by Judy Garland against CBS. Others have been jailed or threatened with jail by judges since John Peter Zenger, editor of the New York Weekly Journal, refused to reveal the name of the author of a letter in the Journal in 1735.

The only way to avoid such confrontation with the courts is not to promise a source you will keep his or her name confidential. Only for the most compelling reason should you get yourself into this judicial conflict between the First and Sixth amendments.

Suggested Readings

Media Law Reporter. Vol. 1. Washington, D.C.: Bureau of National Affairs, 1978.

Sanford, Bruce. "Synopsis of the Law of Libel and the Right of Privacy." New York: World Almanac Publications, 1981.

Schmidt, Benno C., Jr. "Freedom of the Press vs. Public Access." New York: Praeger, 1976.

Spencer, Dale R. "Law for the Newsman." 5th ed. Columbia, Mo.: Lucas Brothers, 1980.

23
Ethics

- A doctor who prescribes medicine for a patient without a proper examination would be violating a code of ethics. He could lose the right to practice.
- A lawyer who deliberately misleads a client would be guilty of violating a code of ethics. He could lose the right to practice.
- A certified public accountant who knowingly signs a statement misrepresenting a company's financial position would be violating a code of ethics. He could lose the right to practice.
- A journalist who accepts a stolen document and poses as a police investigator to get private telephone records might be violating a code of ethics. He could win a Pulitzer Prize.

The doctor, the lawyer and the accountant all have mandatory codes of ethics, prescribed by their professions. Because it would be contrary to the idea of a free press, journalists have not established such a code. To be effective, a mandatory code requires an enforcement mechanism. That means some form of licensing, and licensing is a denial of freedom of the press. The power to license is the power to censor. So far, none of the proposals to license journalists has been approved. And none will be as long as most journalists act responsibly.

Without an industrywide code of conduct, we must pick our way through the maze of ethical and unethical practices to distinguish the good from the bad. In this chapter we will establish some guideposts to help you through the maze. Although we will pose many questions, we will provide answers only to some. The answers to the rest will have to come from the ethical code you have developed from teachings at home, in church and school, and even in the streets.

444

You have a set of principles that guide your conduct. Some of the same principles that tell you when and if you should report someone in your class who cheats on an exam will help you to decide ethical questions you will encounter as a journalist. Other principles you will learn in this chapter, in other classes and on the job.

We begin with a definition of ethics as a system of principles that guides your conduct and helps you to distinguish between right and wrong or, in some cases, between two wrongs. Conduct is based on either motives or concern about the consequences of your acts, or both. Ethics also implies an obligation — to yourself or to someone else.

Simply stated, ethics is a standard of behavior. These days, it is especially important that journalists observe a high standard of behavior. The media, which have focused the public spotlight on unethical practices in so many of society's institutions, can afford to do no less for themselves. Some of the rocks the press has flung have ricocheted and cracked the glass.

The press has held up for scrutiny everyone from the captains of industry to the president of the United States, and many of them have been found wanting. Now many of those who have felt the sting of the press — along with others who have not — are asking about our practices.

If it is wrong for the government to lie, why is it all right for the press to do it? If it is wrong for the Justice Department to obtain someone's long-distance telephone records clandestinely, why is it all right for the press to do it? If there is no other way to expose serious government wrongdoing than by having someone steal a document, do you do it?

The questions pile up at our door while we search for the answers. Some may never be found. Others will.

In this chapter you will learn:

1. Three philosophical approaches that can provide answers to ethical questions.
2. Six categories of ethical questions.
3. How journalists have answered ethical questions without binding codes.

Three Ethical Philosophies

Joseph Fletcher, author of the book "Situation Ethics," tells a story about the time a friend arrived in St. Louis just before election day. His cab driver started talking about the campaign:

"I and my father and grandfather before me, and their fathers, have always been straight-ticket Republicans," the cabbie said.

"Ah," said the friend, himself a Republican, "I take it that means you will vote for Senator So-and-so."

"No," said the driver, "There are times when a man has to push his principles aside and do the right thing."

In his own way the cabbie was defining situation ethics, one of the three broad categories of ethical philosophies. The other two are absolutism and antinomianism. Let's look at each of the three.

ABSOLUTIST ETHICS

Absolutism holds that there is a fixed set of principles or laws, from which there should be no deviation. Principles become rules that, in turn, are treated like laws. That is why some refer to this kind of ethical philosophy as "legalism." If it is wrong to lie, it always is wrong to lie. If a murderer asks where his intended victim is, the absolutist could not lie to save a life. If the action is right, it does not matter whether a friend is killed. The consequences are irrelevant.

An absolutist or legalistic ethical philosophy could spawn a conscientious objector who not only would refuse to take up arms but who would refuse even to go to war as a medic. If war is absolutely wrong, it is absolutely wrong to participate in war in any way.

The absolutist journalist is concerned only with whether an event is newsworthy. If it is interesting, timely, significant or important, it is to be reported, regardless of the consequences. That is the rationale some publications used for printing instructions for making bombs, for printing the names of undercover agents and for identifying rape victims. That some persons might make bombs, that the lives of the undercover agents might be endangered or that the rape victims may suffer public degradation is of no concern to the absolutist.

The philosophy is attractive to some journalists because it assumes the need for full disclosure. Nothing newsworthy ever is withheld from the public. In the end, these journalists believe, publishing without fear of the consequences or without favor for one group's interests over another is the highest ethical principle.

ANTINOMIAN ETHICS

At the other end of the spectrum is *antinomianism*, which rejects all rules and, in effect, all ethics. The term *antinomian* means against law. The antinomian has neither a predetermined standard of conduct nor moral rules. Actions in any situation are spontaneous and unpredictable.

Antinomian journalists are not concerned with motives, consequences or obligations. That does not mean that they would always lie, cheat or steal. Antinomian journalists might pose as someone other than a journalist in an attempt to gather information on some occasions, and they would not be bothered by doing it. To them every situation is different. There are no principles that can guide decision-making. Antinomians have faith in their ability to extemporize in any situation. No premeditation or preparation is required.

While the concept of absolutism is attractive to many journalists, few choose antinomianism. Most mainstream journalists reject it because it is not only antithetical to their upbringing but also inconsistent with a responsible press. The principle that the press has a responsibility to the reader implies a concern for the consequences that antinomians do not have.

SITUATION ETHICS

Between the two extremes of antinomianism and absolutism is a third philosophy: situation ethics.

Unlike antinomianism, situationism does not hold that everything is relative. The situationist knows, understands and accepts the ethical maxims of the community and its heritage and weighs them carefully before making a decision. However, unlike the absolutist, the situationist is prepared to compromise them or to set them aside completely if unselfish love for one's neighbor demands it.

For example, a situationist most likely believes that lying is unethical. But if a murderer asks where his intended victim is, a situationist would lie to save a life.

Hence, for the situationist, everything is relative to one absolute: unselfish love of one's neighbor. The Christian bases this ethic on the teaching of the New Testament: You shall love your neighbor as yourself. Others would base it on various versions of the Golden Rule, found in Hebrew writing before the time of Christ. The book of Tobias states: What you hate, do not do to anyone. Hillel, a contemporary of Jesus, taught: What is hateful to yourself, do not do to your fellow men. Many religions profess love of neighbor as the highest good. The secular humanist, without an act of faith or promise of an afterlife, also professes human life, human values as the highest good.

In the broad sense then, for the person holding to situation ethics, people always come first. In every ethical dilemma, they always do what is best for people. Sometimes this takes the form of utilitarianism: they act in such a way that is good for the largest number of people. Sometimes this means that they must act to benefit the most number of people in the long run. Unlike the absolutist, the situationist is always concerned with the human consequences.

Making an ethical decision is often not an easy matter for the situationist. Yet, most situationists hold that what is clearly unethical is not to decide; not to decide is to make a decision.

The nature of the news business demands dozens of decisions daily: to print or not to print. When The New York Times discovered that President Kennedy had approved an undercover invasion of Cuba in 1961, the editors had to decide whether the interests of the government or the need of the people to know was more important. The editors knew the consequences of printing the story: Knowledge of the pending invasion would have stopped it. They decided not to print the story. The invasion was a disaster for the United States. Later, President Kennedy and the Times' editors agreed the story should have been printed.

The Times case illustrates the problem situation ethicists have. Where the rules are not absolute, there is opportunity for human error. On the other hand, where the rules are absolute, they also may be absolutely wrong.

Among the factors that the Times' editors used to make their on-the-spot decision was a concern for the nation's security as defined by the government. Fidel Castro had installed a Communist government in Cuba, and Kennedy argued that it was in the nation's interest to prevent the Soviet Union from gaining a strategic stronghold just 90 miles off our coast.

The absolutist would have printed the news without regard to the consequences. The Times' editors assessed the consequences and decided that the government's interest in national security was superior to the public's need to know. Ten years later when the Times obtained a copy of the classified "Pentagon Papers" that traced the course of this country's involvement in Vietnam, the Times had to weigh again what the government described as its national security interest against the people's need to know. This time, the editors decided to publish. The editors are situation ethicists. In two similar situations they chose different actions.

In some situations the consequences are easily assessed and a decision is reached quickly. In other cases the consequences are troubling. What would you do, for instance, if you had a story about a politician who kept his mistress on the public payroll? Most journalists would print it. What would you do if the distraught politician told you he would commit suicide if the story were published? Reporters who use situation ethics would examine their motives for wanting to publish the story. They would balance the consequences — the public's need to know and the possible death of a person — and decide whether to publish.

Most journalists today are situation ethicists. But unlike Fletcher and others whose philosophies of ethics have been developed against a theological background, a journalist's sense of ethics is more likely to come from a variety of influences. One of the most important is the profession itself. The journalistic ethic — the set of values governing conduct — asks its practitioners to be honest, independent of special interests, dedicated to the best truth obtainable, committed to open government and protective of the readers' interests. While the first four characteristics of the ethic are constant, journalists interpret the last one differently.

The Wall Street Journal perceives its readers' interests differently from the New York Times; The Miami Herald differently from The Los Angeles Times. When Joseph Pulitzer retired in 1907, he wrote a statement that serves yet today as the platform for the St. Louis Post-Dispatch. The paper, Pulitzer wrote, "will always fight for progress and reform, never tolerate injustice or corruption, always fight demagogues of all parties, never belong to any party, always oppose privileged classes and public plunderers, never lack sympathy with the poor, always remain devoted to the public welfare, never be satisfied with merely printing news, always be drastically independent, never be afraid to attack wrong, whether by predatory plutocracy or predatory poverty."

Pulitzer may have expressed it more strongly than most journalists, especially publishers, would, but that strong populist philosophy runs through much of journalism. Most journalists identify their readers as The Common Man. Their answers to a question such as whether to print the information about the crooked politician would be weighed, not just against the interests of the publisher, not just against the interests of the captains of industry, but against the interests of all people. It would be weighed, not just against the immediate impact, good or bad, but against the long-term impact. The prevailing ethic in journalism today is what John Stuart Mill called utilitarianism: the greatest good for the greatest number. For instance, a story about a person convicted of drunken driving would embarrass the driver and the family. But most journalists would argue that society needs to know about that driver and about how the courts are handling cases dealing with drunken drivers. It may have a deleterious immediate impact upon the family, but it will have a positive long-term impact upon the community.

Ethical Problems

Most ethical problems the reporter is likely to encounter fall into one of six categories. They are:

1. Payola.
2. Conflict of interest.

3. Withholding information.
4. Deceit.
5. Invasion of privacy.
6. Participation in the news.

Let's look at each of the six.

PAYOLA

- When sports reporters gather for the Kentucky Derby, they are treated to lavish parties with free drinks, expensive hors d'oeuvres and an orchestra. The scene is not much different the week preceding the Super Bowl and other major sporting events.
- Airlines inaugurating flights often invite media representatives to take the first flight free. Sometimes the destinations are attractive — such as Hawaii — and there is a stopover of at least a day.
- Television critics are invited to a whirlwind series of premiere showings, interviews and parties with the stars. The networks offer to pay all expenses of the reporters.
- The mayor remembers a reporter on the city hall beat on each holiday and birthday with a gift. It may range from a bottle of liquor to an honorary key to the city.

The *payola*, or money and gifts such as those described above, is usually given in expectation of favorable coverage. Sports promoters attract reporters from around the country to their events. Reporters justify the trip by writing stories.

Airlines usually get stories in the travel or business sections announcing new flights. And if the reporter has taken the flight, there may be another story extolling the virtues of visiting Hawaii or Japan or Katmandu — all serviced, incidentally, by the host airlines.

Networks would prefer reviews to be favorable, but mainly they want publicity. Their preview week for the critics guarantees stories in papers around the nation.

The mayor may not be looking for a specific favorable story, either. Instead he may be cultivating a relationship with the reporter. Eventually, however, the mayor may expect something in return.

Gifts, sometimes even outright cash payments, used to be common in the news business. At Christmas time some news rooms looked like department stores. Now many newspapers forbid reporters to accept gifts. If they are offered, they either are returned to the sender or donated to charity. Says Andrew Barnes, editor of the St. Petersburg (Fla.) Times, "We take nothing free from anybody."

Are reporters who don't pay their own way being bought? A good many persons inside and outside the press think that either they are being bought or they may give readers the impression they are. The appearance of impropriety may be as damaging as actual impropriety.

Standards Within the Industry

In many cases the decisions about whether to accept gifts, tickets or trips is taken out of the reporter's hands. Nearly 75 percent of the newspaper and broadcast stations responding to a 1983 survey for the Society of Professional Journalists/Sigma Delta Chi, said they had policies regarding acceptance of gifts. Policies vary widely. Some papers, like the St. Petersburg (Fla.) Times, prohibit reporters from accepting anything. The Charlotte (N.C.) News prohibits acceptance of anything valued above $5. At Charleston, W. Va., the limit is $10. At the Beaver Falls (Pa.) News-Tribune, a bottle of liquor is acceptable, but a case would be returned. Many newspapers have given their travel editors larger budgets instead of permitting them to accept free trips from airlines and travel agencies.

The issues involved are these:

1. Do reporters who accept free tickets or accommodations write more favorably about a subject than they would if the newspaper paid the expenses?
2. When promoters are paying the way, are stories written that otherwise would not be?
3. Does the public believe that a reporter is compromised by accepting free gifts or travel?

These issues are among the most easily addressed by the industry.

While it is by no means unanimous in its opinion, the industry is in general agreement that the press should avoid gifts and free travel. The issue that remains unresolved is whether there is a cutoff point. Is credibility impaired by a cup of coffee, a free meal or a free trip? Can journalists dashing about to cover a national political convention stop at a booth run by a special interest group, such as a railroad association, to grab a free snack? In 1983, 4,000 journalists from around the world were in Williamsburg, Va., to cover an economic summit conference. The U.S. government served free meals and did not have a system to bill journalists even if they had requested it. The Washington Post and The New York Times, among many others, permitted their reporters to accept the free food. Seymour Topping, the Times' managing editor, said, "We have quite strict rules requiring us to pay for transportation, hotels and so forth. Of course, if we are invited to dinner, for example, we don't want to be rude. If we did accept free food in Williamsburg, we did so through courtesy or choice."

Some of the companies that donated food said they did so for promotional payoffs. Topping said he couldn't conceive of any papers being guilty of promotional favoritism.

That sort of pressure is easier to avoid if you are one of 4,000 journalists in Williamsburg than if you are the only reporter from the only newspaper or station in town covering the local fair and are being provided free tickets, food or gifts. Some news organizations will estimate the cost of meals or travel and reimburse the host organization.

CONFLICT OF INTEREST

The second category of ethical questions is closely related to the first. With payola a reporter actually receives some material benefits. In the conflict-of-interest category the benefit often is intangible. This category differs from journalist as participant in that here the action is voluntary and outside the job. In the other category, which is discussed last, the journalist participates to get a story.

Some Questions

Reporters have the opportunity to forward the causes of organizations to which they belong, and that intangible benefit raises many questions. Do reporters' allegiances interfere with their ability to be objective? Can a member of either the Democratic or Republican party cover the political beat? Can religion editors objectively report on developments in their own churches? Can a reporter be a member of a city commission and report on city politics? Can a reporter objectively cover the school board if another reporter, an editor or a publisher is a member?

Some of the conflicts do involve material benefits. Can a financial reporter objectively report on a company in which he or she owns stock? Should a financial or business writer use inside knowledge to buy stocks, bonds or commodities? Can a sports reporter who is given four extra 50-yard-line tickets to sell or distribute to friends objectively report on a team? The Chicago Tribune requires members of its news staff to file annual financial disclosure statements.

Not even annual financial disclosure would have helped The Wall Street Journal detect that a reporter for its sensitive "Heard on the Street" column was leaking information about upcoming stories and that he and others were profiting by trading stock based on the information that would be printed. Favorable mention in the column often sent the value of a stock up several dollars a share.

The Journal fired the reporter after he conceded to the Securities and Exchange Commission that he had leaked the information. The Journal then reported on the case to its readers.

Sometimes the conflict arises because the reporters are serving themselves or the paper instead of the readers. This occurs when a reporter elects to do a story or a series that may have little interest or importance for readers but that would be a good entry for a journalism contest. Many trade associations give substantial cash awards for stories about their special interests, ranging from food and furniture to cigars and cars.

A conflict can arise, too, because the journalist holds a second job. Most papers now have written policies on the subject, and few allow reporters to work for a competitor or to do work that conflicts with their primary jobs. Writing press releases for a political candidate, for instance, would not be permitted.

A more troublesome conflict arises over a reporter's or editor's spouse working or volunteering for certain activities. The Seattle Times announced it would move its managing editor out of the news room when his wife was named press secretary to the Seattle mayor. The managing editor's wife gave up her job so her husband could keep his. The Times does not permit its editorial employees to make editorial decisions about people they are related to by blood or marriage.

The conflict may arise, finally, because of newspaper or management entanglements in the community. What is the newspaper's position with respect to the Chamber of Commerce if the publisher is the chamber's president? How does the paper treat the United Way when the editor is a member of the board of directors? If the newspaper corporation is involved in the creation of a special downtown taxing district, can the news room cover the issue objectively? Would the public perceive the coverage to be unbiased?

Some Answers

To most of the questions raised above, the answers, even to a situationist, are rather clear-cut. Sports reporters should accept no more than the press box seat they need to cover the game. No stories should be written purely as journalism contest entries. Some newspapers even forbid entry into trade association contests, some of which exist only to encourage publication of stories about a certain topic such as fashions or wine.

Many newspapers, in fact, prohibit their reporters from engaging in activities that they might be assigned to cover. This means that reporters, like civil service employees, forfeit some rights of citizenship: They may not participate in political campaigns or be stockholders in companies they may have to cover. They may not hold memberships even in nonpolitical governmental bodies such as city commissions. As of 1983, of 115 Newspaper Guild contracts covering news room employees, 66 required permission from the employer to do outside work, 87 prohibited employees from working for a competitive enterprise, 81 prohibited employees from outside work or activity that would embarrass or exploit their position with the company and 10 prohibited employees from being paid for working in public relations for any political group or candidate without the consent of the publisher.

The Guild contracts raise another complication. Publishers cannot simply impose codes upon employees; the National Labor Relations Board has often ruled that many ethical concerns, such as the acceptance of freebies or what employees can do in their spare time, is subject to negotiation. A Knoxville, Tenn., reporter who won a seat on a suburban school board was given the choice of resigning from the board or being fired from her job. Her grievance was taken to binding arbitration. Among other things, she pointed out that her employer's statement prohibiting such elective office was not part of the Guild contract.

Some newspapers allow reporters to participate in activities if they are not involved with the coverage. This kind of severance is not clear enough, however. A reporter covering a commission on which a fellow employee is a member has at least the appearance of a conflict of interest. And any leaks coming from that commission are likely to be blamed on the newspaper member.

Many publishers argue vigorously that the newspaper and its management need to be good citizens of their community. The newspaper, like other businesses, should use some of its money and talent to improve the community.

That issue was debated emotionally and publicly in Florida when several newspapers contributed money to an organization campaigning against legalized gambling. The newspapers' involvement was debated nearly as much as the gambling proposal. Reporters bought advertising space to criticize their executives' decisions to become involved financially in the campaign. One reporter filed a complaint with the National News Council, an independent body that monitors press performance, which responded: "Plainly, all involved in the Florida dispute . . . put at risk public belief in the integrity of independent news coverage and editorial expression."

The Gannett newspapers in Florida did not contribute. Gannett's president and chief executive officer, Allen H. Neuharth, said, "It seems to me if newspaper ownership gets financially involved on one side of a controversial public issue, it makes it much more difficult for the paper to do a totally fair and objective job covering the news aspects of that issue."

The publisher of the St. Petersburg papers, which did contribute to the anti-gambling forces, said it was part of being a good citizen. And one of the editors said, "In a superperfect world it would be better for non-newspaper sources to carry this fight, but there just aren't that many big corporations in Florida."

While some activities obviously must be proscribed, the newspaper can maintain its independence and be a good citizen. It has to be careful how it supports the causes and activities.

A publisher cannot serve on a school board or with the Chamber of Commerce without causing problems for reporters and damaging the newspaper's credibility. But the paper can serve the taxpayers of the school district in many other ways: by providing in-depth, expert coverage; by encouraging good candidates to run for the board; and by supporting tax issues editorially when the newspaper feels they are deserving.

The newspaper also can serve the Chamber of Commerce in many ways without having the publisher on the board. The newspaper is a dues-paying member, as are most other businesses in the community. It can invite promotion experts, advertising experts or downtown development experts to present free seminars to the merchants. Or, it can donate time from its art and graphics departments to design pamphlets and booklets. The paper might do the same for the United Way.

In none of these activities is it necessary for the news department to become involved. And while the absolutist would frown, the involvement is no more serious than accepting a cup of coffee from a news source.

Deeper involvement does cause problems. Ray Spangler, retired publisher of the Redwood City (Calif.) Tribune, recalled the time he served on an "unidentified committee of five" to advise the school district on a bond issue. "At our first meeting, one of the five, a subscriber, turned to me and said, 'I'd rather see my publisher on the sidelines than here.'" Spangler added, "He was wiser than I."

WITHHOLDING INFORMATION

A third category of ethical questions involves both reporters and editors, who must make decisions about withholding information. As a reporter you will make daily decisions about what will and will not be included in a story. Most of the decisions you make will be based on criteria of news value; if the news is timely, interesting and important, it should be reported. But there are times when other factors will influence your decision.

To what extent does the public have a need to know about an individual's private life? Does the public need to know details of the sexual entanglements of public officials? Is the inclusion of the addresses of elderly robbery victims who live alone an inducement for others to victimize them? Do you print the addresses of relatives in obituaries despite protests from police officials that publication is an invitation to criminals to enter the houses during the funeral services? When a private person commits suicide out of the public's view, should you report suicide as the cause of death? If the mayor is killed in a car accident and a dozen girlie magazines are found in his car, would you report that? These days, more journalists are thinking before acting, even in competitive situations.

Despite extensive efforts by some people in the campaign, newspapers and stations covering the 1983 gubernatorial contest in Mississippi declined to disseminate evidence that one of the candidates was a homosexual. The evidence, affidavits from male prostitutes who claimed to have had relations with one of the candidates, was offered to several journalists. Finally, the candidate's opponents held a press conference to make the charges public themselves. The press covered the conference. Asked why he wanted to publicize the case, the spokesman for the other candidate said, "We simply seek the truth, which, I thought, was a common trait I shared with the media." The accused candidate won the election, and on the day he was inaugurated, the Jackson Clarion-Ledger reported that the prostitutes said they had been paid for their statements and recanted.

A commonly accepted practice among both print and broadcast journalists is to withhold the names of sexual-assault victims because there is a perceived social stigma attached to being a rape victim. Two-thirds of the 375 editors who responded to a survey taken by Carol E. Oukrop of Kansas State University in 1983 said they would not print the name of a rape victim. Of those who thought it should be printed, nine out of 10 would wait until the trial to identify the victim.

Those who argue that the names should be printed say that the female can unjustly accuse a male without suffering the consequences of public scrutiny, that the social stigma of being a rape victim will never fade until the media start handling it as they do other crime news and that withholding those names makes the media vulnerable to pressure to withhold names in other news. For the moment, at least, those who withhold the names are clearly in the majority.

Even during the intensive national coverage of the trial of six men accused of raping a woman in a bar in Massachusetts, it was not until halfway through the trial that any news medium broke the self-imposed embargo against naming the victim. Even when the name was printed and broadcast, most others still did not use it. This, despite the fact that the trial was broadcast over cable television. Viewers knew the victim's name and face. That conduct is a long way from the anything-goes days that prevailed in the industry until the 1960s.

But the courts have given some signs of turning voluntary actions into mandatory practices. In 1981 a Washington state Superior Court judge ordered reporters to abide by voluntary bench-bar-press guidelines as a condition of attending a criminal pretrial hearing. In 1980 the U.S. Court of Appeals for the Western District of Missouri cited a newspaper policy not to print names of rape victims as evidence the editors were aware of the consequences of printing the information. The court ruled that a women who had been kidnapped briefly but not sexually assaulted could pursue a lawsuit against the newspaper for lawfully and accurately printing her name.

Cases such as these may slow or even reverse the growing number of media codes providing for the voluntary withholding of information.

Photography is another area of information that is being scrutinized more carefully these days. The most dramatic shots of tragedies, fires, rescues, crimes and accidents are no longer published routinely. That is because more and more, readers are saying that they find them offensive.

Because pictures are so powerful, they have impact beyond words. Some of the most offensive pictures ever taken are among the most widely praised and honored: the Saigon police chief shooting a Viet Cong soldier in the head at point-blank range; bodies stacked on each other in Guyana after the Rev. Jim Jones convinced his followers to poison themselves; a woman and child falling from a fire escape as helpless firefighters watch in Boston. Newspapers and television stations face the problem frequently on the local level. Do you show the face of a dead person? Do you show grieving relatives? Do you show death?

A small newspaper in Ohio once ran a three-picture sequence of a firefighter being pulled out of a harness by the swift undertow of a dam. He drowned. The community reacted bitterly to the photos that were run large on the front page. The editors thought they were glorifying a hero; the firefighter had saved two children first. The community thought the newspaper was tasteless.

Editors have found that proximity is an important consideration. Readers are more apt to accept pictures that show the faces of dead people if the people are not local. The pictures of the Ohio firefighter would not have elicited nearly as much response in Nebraska. A picture of a body under a blanket is much less offensive than one not covered, even if readers can't see the face. The larger that dramatic pictures are displayed, the more likely it is that some readers are going to believe the newspaper is sensationalizing the story.

Despite all this, few editors withhold pictures or film merely because some readers or viewers might object. The important thing is to know when and why they will object. Then if the decision is to print or broadcast, the editors can be prepared to answer the criticism with arguments considered before the decision was made rather than in hindsight.

Several surveys' results indicate that most editors are situationists. They are concerned about the consequences of their acts. While this concern helps them decide when and if to withhold information, in the industry there still is a tradition of fierce independence and loyalty to the reader.

David Lipman, managing editor of the St. Louis Post-Dispatch, summed it up for situationists: "If we sin, we should sin on the side of disclosures and not concealment."

DECEIT

A fourth category of ethical questions involves reporting techniques that might deceive readers, sources or those under investigation. Some of these practices are anathema to nearly everyone, others are more debatable, and still others may be illegal and yet be ethical. The question of deceit is perhaps the hardest one journalists must face.

Generally Disapproved Practices

Some journalistic techniques can deceive readers into thinking a story is accurate and fair. One such practice involves picking up quotes from newspaper clippings and recycling them as if they were timely and presented in the right context. Another involves reporting charges against an individual without giving adequate opportunity for reply in the same article. A third is the subtle use of words to color a story, such as "claims" for "says" and "demands" for "asks." And still another involves the subtle practice of ignoring news when it might be considered damaging to a newspaper's editorial or advertising interests.

No surveys are needed on these points. No ethical system can excuse these practices; no journalists brag of them. But a few do use them.

Debatable Practices

The undesirability of some other techniques is not so clear-cut. Lying, surprisingly enough, is one. If it is wrong to lie, then the absolutists never would conceal their identity to gather information. If the only way to attend a meeting of the Ku Klux Klan were to go as someone interested in joining, the absolutists never would get in. The situationist, however, would balance the information to be gained against the deceit involved.

Reporters who would never conceal their identity while gathering information for other news stories would seriously consider going undercover to report on the Ku Klux Klan and other clandestine groups. The Chicago Sun-Times bought and operated The Mirage tavern to gather information on corruption and bribe taking by city inspectors. The use of deceit may have cost them a Pulitzer Prize, though. Two members of the Pulitzer Prize board said after the awards were announced that they opposed journalists' participating in undercover activities.

Frequently, reporters are requested to conceal not their own identities but those of their sources. News columns and broadcasts are sprinkled with references such as "highly placed sources," "government officials," and "sources close to the president." In stories involving the federal government, these descriptions are often code

Figure 23.1 Use of Deception. The Chicago Sun Times set up a team of undercover reporters in a bar in order to document a system of bribery involving city inspectors. While the expose was successful, the paper may have lost a Pulitzer Prize because of the way it gathered the information.

words understood by other journalists but usually not known to the reader.

Widespread use of anonymous sources may be necessary when covering volatile diplomatic issues and exposing mismanagement or crime in public offices. But it is not necessary in all of these instances, and the practice is subject to abuse. Politicians and private parties alike use anonymity to destroy other persons' reputations, to test public opinion on new programs and to advance special interests. Reporters who allow themselves to be used by sources who have no legitimate reason for anonymity damage the credibility of their publications.

Even when the reporters decide that the requests are legitimate, they are obligated to double-check the accuracy of the information given. Verification is absolutely necessary.

Reporters use many techniques they would consider unethical in and of themselves, but that, in a given situation, may be justifiable. Reporters have looked through garbage cans for information. They have asked clerks and secretaries for copies of private or classified documents. They have led sources to believe they knew more than they really did in order to force more information into the open.

Much of consumer reporting involves the reporter acting in the role of the consumer. A typical example is taking a car to repair shops to see if customers are being overcharged. Such a story would be impossible to get if reporters identified themselves.

Lawbreaking Practices

Breaking into offices and receiving stolen documents are violations of the law. But laws do not make something ethical or unethical; they only make something legal or illegal. People who break the law must pay the penalty and suffer society's disapproval. Persons who say they have to break the law because obeying it would violate their principles risk being charged with setting themselves above the law.

Yet at times, journalists, among others, must consider breaking the laws for ethical principles. Publication of the "Pentagon Papers" is an example. The editors of The New York Times knew that accepting the stolen papers could have been interpreted as a violation of the law. They had to balance that against the service they would provide to citizens by publishing the documents. Their ethical responsibility to the citizens apparently overrode what could have been a violation of the law. As it turned out, the courts never decided the legality of the Times' act.

The courts did get involved when a reporter for the Potomac

News of Woodbridge, Va., was given a sergeant's badge for a day by the regional jail superintendent so the reporter could get into a state prison. He wanted to interview a prisoner there who said he had been raped by other prisoners. When the reporter told his superiors after he returned, they decided not to run the story because they could not condone his use of deception.

That would have been the end of it except that the regional jailer was suspended for his part in the incident. The paper then published a story explaining the reporter's role in it. Later, it published the interview with the prisoner under the headline, "LeVasseur the murderer now the victim." State corrections officials charged the reporter with impersonating a law officer and falsifying an official document.

Nearly all journalists agree that the story was a significant one: It showed that the prison system was unwilling or unable to protect prisoners from each other. But was the price worth it?

Many journalists would say the price was worth it if there were no other way to get the information. Louis Hodges, director of Studies in Applied Ethics at Washington & Lee University, adds another consideration: "No one was put at risk by the deception in the way people might be at risk if the reporter posed, for example, as a doctor or fireman."

On the other hand, many journalists believe that no deception is acceptable because the First Amendment does not protect that behavior. Many journalists are bothered by the contradictory position that it places journalists in: criticizing law officers for impersonating the media while they themselves are impersonating law officers. And finally, while the prisoner knew he was talking to a reporter, most of the time when reporters are undercover, the people do not know that their words may be printed or broadcast.

Laws complicate already complicated ethical questions for journalists. You cannot always assume that what is legal is the ethical thing to do; sometimes what is illegal is more ethical and, because it is illegal, even more difficult to do.

The Rationale for Certain Kinds of Deceit

It would be a much simpler life for reporters if gathering information were a matter of asking questions and obtaining responses. But the complexities of today's society make information gathering extremely difficult.

And the information reporters are trying to secure often is more technical, more valuable and more protected than ever. The records that reporters need to investigate government officials are locked in safes or stored in computers. Persons who fear for their jobs are afraid to talk to reporters. Some documents are shredded to destroy evidence, while others are classified to avoid embarrassment rather than to protect national security. Newspapers have begun to look at white-collar crime, which even law enforcement agencies with subpoena power have difficulty investigating.

Many journalists believe that these extraordinary problems require extraordinary measures. That is why some journalists are willing to deceive people *in some situations*. That is why some journalists are willing to accept stolen documents *in some situations*. But just as most journalists believe that if they must err, they should err on the side of publication rather than suppression, most also believe that journalists must try every legal and unquestionable means of gathering information before considering more dubious techniques.

Absolutist reporters cannot operate successfully in today's society. The information they need often is not available by conventional means. Situationists are more successful because they balance the good to be gained against the transgression to be committed.

It is a fine line that situationists must draw. Journalists not deeply committed to a set of ethical principles will too easily and too often forget those principles in the heat of the hunt for information. As a journalist you must be prepared to defend the ethical against the unethical, sometimes against your own employer. And you must be prepared ultimately to give up your job to defend your principles.

Invasion of Privacy

Sometimes even a thundering fullback chooses to run around, rather than over, a defender. The American public thinks that journalists too often simply run over people's private lives. For that reason and others, public confidence and respect for the press is relatively low. The perception that journalists peek in windows, crowd around private citizens who have been thrust into the public limelight and intrude into private spaces in pursuit of a story is based partly on fact and partly on fiction. Movies and television shows often portray the press as uncaring, insensitive, unthinking members of a pack whose only concern is to get the story. Journalists have questioned children of public figures to get information about their parents. People in the news have had journalists park in front of their houses 24 hours a day.

In some instances, that type of aggressive reporting is necessary. Elected or appointed officials who are ducking the press should be pursued. Waiting on a public street for them to come out of their houses is one thing; stopping their children or standing on their doorsteps is another.

But particularly when the press is dealing with people who are not public figures, most journalists now are willing to respect the source's wishes. A major test of this developing ethic was the bombing that killed 241 servicemen in Lebanon in 1983. Journalists rushed to interview the victims' families. Television cameras were pointed at the front doors of private citizens. Reporters asked to sit with families to record their anguish as they awaited word on whether their sons were among the dead. One television crew arrived at the home of a victim's family to be greeted by neighbors shouting, "Here come the ghouls." One TV cameraman shot film through a glass door as Marine officers delivered the news that the family's son had been a casualty.

Despite instances of atrocious lack of judgment, overall, the press acquitted itself quite well on the story. Many of the families who did not want to talk to the press were not bothered. A Marine Corps public relations officer in Washington, D.C., said that 75 percent of the families who were assisted by Marine Corps officials agreed to talk to the press. Many of the families who were asked later about their reactions to press coverage said it helped them deal with their grief. One father of a Marine who was killed said, "You hear a lot of criticism of the press. But in my case, they conducted themselves very well. With no exceptions, at the end of the conversations I had with reporters, they all set their jobs aside, and we talked as people. I really appreciated that."

All the families had a right to their privacy. The press invaded it only when the families did not want them around. The press and the public may have had a *need* to know the impact of the deaths on the families, but they did not have a *right* to know. Courts give us a legal definition of invasion of privacy; journalists must supply their own ethical definition.

The definition of privacy was extended by journalists to include the last name of the family whose son, born with severe immunological deficiency, had become a worldwide news story. The boy lived in a sterile bubble for 12 years. Many journalists knew the boy's name; no one printed it or broadcast it even when the boy died. Although the local community knew who the boy was, he went to his grave known only as David, the "bubble-boy," to most of the world.

If the press continues to exhibit such responsibility, public trust and confidence in it may grow. However, decisions to withhold information to protect someone's privacy are not made without cost. Every time it is done, the media get requests from others who want to be treated the same way. The extreme result of that type of policy is a nameless and faceless news report.

Participation in the News

At best, a journalist is a dispassionate observer. But it is hard to remain dispassionate when a man you are photographing is threatening to jump off the bridge and you might be able to grab him. It is hard to remain dispassionate when you are shooting TV film of someone rescuing a child from icy waters and you could be helping. It is hard to remain dispassionate if you are on the front lines during a war and a soldier next to you is wounded. It is hard to remain dispassionate when you are observing police brutality.

Reporters have faced all of those situations, and they have reacted as most human beings would. They reached out to help. Should they?

In each instance, the journalist becomes part of the news rather than just a reporter of it. Yet, you must weigh the consequences of a man committing suicide and a child drowning against your obligation to remain a reporter and represent your readers. Most journalists elect to act rather than watch.

But there are some not-so-clear-cut instances where a journalist becomes a participant. A Dallas Times Herald reporter was arrested for aiding illegal aliens because he was found in the car with them as they drove across Texas. He said he was observing how a church group smuggled refugees from war-torn Central America into the

Figure 23.2 Participation in the News. A reporter at the scene of a suicide attempt or other crisis situation must decide whether to record the event or to act.

country. The legal question is whether he had a right to be at the scene of a crime. Authorities didn't press the issue; they decided not to file charges. The ethical question is whether he ought to have participated, even if only by riding in the car with them once they were in Texas.

The television networks have found themselves at the eye of a storm because they are accused of being participants, rather than just reporters, of the electoral process. They have become participants, critics charge, by projecting election results before polls close. Critics are afraid that people will not vote if they believe the presidential race has already been decided. By staying away from the polls, non-voters affect other races. The networks argue that it is their constitutional right to report the news when they have it. It is now an ethical question; if enough politicians become aroused, it may become a legal one, too.

Members of a television crew from Anniston, Ala., became participants to a story when they filmed a man setting fire to himself. Oddly enough, the crew members became participants by not stopping him. The man had called the station several times to ask for coverage of his action, which he said was a protest over unemployment. The crew notified the police and then showed up at the park where the man said he would be. The police, however, did not find them. In the meantime, the cameraman filmed as the man doused himself with lighter fluid and tried to ignite himself. After 15 agonizing seconds, the first match went out. He poured more lighter fluid on and lit a second. This time, the fire quickly spread over his body. Not until the man was completely engulfed in flames did one of the journalists try to help him put it out.

The man survived. The journalists would not have become participants if they had not accepted the invitation to watch a self-immolation. The event may not have occurred if the TV crew did not show up.

Journalists have often been participants, sometimes trying to save lives, sometimes trying to get stories. When the action is taken to save a life, it is understandable. When the action is taken to get a story, it is questionable at best, despicable at worst. Yet, it is easy to criticize. Sometimes you become part of a story by covering it. Would you pick up a phone and call a hostage held captive in a house surrounded by the police if you could get an exclusive interview?

The Media Response

Journalists' commitment to ethical practices is not a new one. For generations, journalism has been practiced by honorable persons who have gone to jail, lost their jobs and suffered numerous other hardships in defense of their principles.

Journalism requires a commitment to truth, a sympathy for the public interest and a willingness to shun personal aggrandizement. But the journalist's ethical code is voluntary. As such, it has to be accepted on a personal, intellectual and moral basis. There are no licenses to be withdrawn, as in the case of the medical, legal and accounting professions. And that's as it should be, not only because a free press requires freedom from licensing, but also because ethical behavior cannot be legislated.

Even the existence of voluntary codes can be dangerous. As we indicated earlier, some judges have used them against journalists. In the one instance, a judge ordered all journalists who wanted to cover a trial to adhere to the voluntary press-bar guidelines in the state of Washington. His order was appealed but not overturned. In another case, a judge in a federal appeals court used a newspaper's policy to withhold the names of sexual assault victims against the newspaper when it printed the name of a female who had been kidnapped briefly. The judge ruled that the woman had a right to sue the newspaper for printing her name, even though it had been obtained lawfully.

The logical end of this type of judicial reasoning is that journalists are responsible for the consequences of everything they print. In Spain, a journalist was convicted of "professional negligence" because two people he named as government informers in a story were later killed. He was convicted despite the fact that the court never knew who the murderers were or why they killed the two men.

Although these are isolated examples, they are ominous warnings that, ironically, if a news medium has a voluntary code of ethics and does not adhere to it strictly, a court somewhere, sometime may use it against the medium. In those situations, a newspaper without a code may be better off legally.

The ethical codes for journalists are general statements of principles. The major ones — those of the Society of Professional Journalists/Sigma Delta Chi, the American Society of Newspaper Editors and the Associated Press Managing Editors — agree on the salient points: The press exists to serve reader interests and has a responsibility to do it fairly and accurately without fear or favor. Most of the ethical questions that we have addressed in this chapter are acknowledged in all three codes.

On payola and conflict of interest, the ASNE code says:

> The right of a newspaper to attract and hold readers is restricted by nothing but considerations of public welfare. . . . A journalist who uses his power for any selfish or otherwise unworthy purpose is faithless to a high trust.

On the same subject, the APME code states:

> The newspaper should report the news independent of its own interests. It should not give favored news treatment to advertisers or special interest groups. . . . Concern for community or business interests should not cause a newspaper to distort or misrepresent the facts. . . .
>
> The newspaper and its staff should make every effort to be free of obligations to news sources and special interests. . . . The newspaper should avoid even the appearance of obligation or conflict of interest.
>
> Newspapers should accept nothing of value from news sources or other outsiders. . . .
>
> Active involvement in such things as politics, community affairs, demonstrations on social causes may compromise the ability to report and edit without prejudice. . . .
>
> Outside employment that conflicts with news interests should be avoided. . . .
>
> Investments by staff members . . . that could conflict with the newspaper's ability to report the news or that would create the impression of conflict should be avoided.
>
> Stories should not be written or edited primarily for the purpose of winning awards and prizes.

The guidelines are less specific when dealing with the question of deceit. The general principle stated by the SPJ/SDX is: "The public's right to know of events of public importance and interest is the overriding mission of the mass media." The SPJ/SDX code also states: "Journalists will seek news that serves the public interest, despite the obstacles. They will make constant efforts to assure that the public's business is conducted in public and that public records are open to public inspection." And, according to the APME code, the newspaper "should vigorously expose wrongdoing or misuse of power, public or private. It should oppose selfish interests regardless of their power, size or influence." Some journalists take these statements to be acknowledgments of the occasional need to balance two wrongs: the wrong being committed by someone in public office and the wrong that may be committed by a journalist trying to report on that official.

There also are general guidelines that acknowledge invasion of privacy. The ASNE code says this:

> A newspaper should not invade private rights or feelings without sure warrant of public right as distinguished from public curiosity. . . .
>
> A newspaper cannot escape conviction of insincerity if while professing high moral purpose it supplies incentives to base conduct, such as are to be found in details of crime and vice, publication of which is not demonstrably for the general good.

The SPJ code addresses itself to the same problem in these words:

Journalists at all times will show respect for the dignity, privacy, rights and well-being of people encountered in the course of gathering and presenting the news. . . .

The news media must guard against invading a person's right to privacy.

The media should not pander to morbid curiosity about details of vice and crime.

No codes, whether mandatory or voluntary, can anticipate all situations. Even laws are constantly revised to accommodate omissions and changing social norms.

Taken as standards of behavior, the codes are adequate guidelines. Journalists must draw upon their own moral codes to provide specific answers to the complex questions faced in their daily work. The basic principle is stated in the SPJ code:

Journalists must be free of obligation to any interest other than the people's right to know.

Suggested Readings

Christians, Clifford, Kim Rotzoll and Mark Fackler. "Media Ethics." New York: Longman, 1984. Step-by-step analyses of 75 situations where ethical questions were raised in news, advertising and entertainment.

Goodwin, H. Eugene. "Groping for Ethics in Journalism." Ames: Iowa State University Press, 1984. Not only raises ethical questions but suggests means to answer them. Has case histories and anecdotes.

Langer, Ralph, Dallas Morning News, editor. "Professional Standards," APME 1977. A discussion of freebies and credibility, and a follow-up survey on editors' attitudes toward accepting freebies.

Langer, Ralph, Dallas Morning News, editor. "Professional Standards," APME 1983. A look at case studies of how editors handle the broad range of ethical questions. Also contains results of surveys of editors.

McCulloch, Frank, ed. "Drawing the Line." St. Petersburg, Fla.: The Poynter Institute, 1984. Thirty-one newspaper editors describe the toughest ethical decisions they ever had to make.

Merrill, John. "The Imperative of Freedom: A Philosophy of Journalistic Autonomy." New York: Hastings House, 1974. A good look at press ethics from a philosopher's point of view.

Tate, Cassandra. "Conflict of Interest: A Newspaper's Report on Itself." Columbia Journalism Review, July/August 1978, pp. 44–48. A reprint of the account from the Lewiston (Idaho) Morning Tribune, in which the paper examines the involvement of its management and staff in the community.

APPENDIX
Wire Service Style

The stylebooks of The Associated Press and United Press International serve as handy, alphabetized references to newspaper style. Unfortunately, that format makes learning the basics of style difficult because key rules are not categorized. In this appendix we have categorized style rules under the headings of Capitalization; Abbreviations and Acronyms; Punctuation; Numerals; and Grammar, Spelling and Word Usage. This should serve as an excellent reference for beginning reporters, but it should not be considered a substitute for the far more comprehensive stylebooks. The authors thank AP and UPI for granting permission to use excerpts from their stylebooks.

Capitalization

In general, avoid unnecessary capitals. Use a capital letter only if you can justify it by one of the principles listed here.

Many words and phrases, including special cases, are listed separately in the complete stylebooks. Entries that are capitalized without further comment should be capitalized in all uses.

If there is no relevant listing in the stylebooks for a particular word or phrase, consult Webster's New World Dictionary. Use lowercase if the dictionary lists it as an acceptable form for the sense in which the word is being used.

As used in the stylebooks, *capitalize* means to use uppercase for the first letter of a word. If additional capital letters are needed, they are called for by an example or a phrase such as *use all caps*.

Some basic principles:

PROPER NOUNS: Capitalize nouns that constitute the unique identification for a specific person, place or thing: *John, Mary, America, Boston, England.*

Some words, such as the examples just given, are always proper nouns. Some common nouns receive proper noun status when they are used as the name of a particular entity: *General Electric, Gulf Oil.*

PROPER NAMES: Capitalize common nouns such as *party, river, street,* and *west* when they are an integral part of the full name for a person, place or thing: *Democratic Party, Mississippi River, Fleet Street, West Virginia.*

Lowercase these common nouns when they stand alone in subsequent references: *the party, the river, the street.*

Lowercase the common noun elements of names in all plural uses: *the Democratic and Republican parties, Main and State streets, lakes Erie and Ontario.*

POPULAR NAMES: Some places and events lack officially designated proper names but have popular names that are the effective equivalent: *the Combat Zone* (a section of downtown Boston), *the Main Line* (a group of Philadelphia suburbs), *the South Side* (of Chicago), *the Badlands* (of North Dakota), *the Street* (the financial community in the Wall Street area of New York).

The principle applies also to shortened versions of the proper names for one-of-a-kind events: *the Series* (for the World Series), *the Derby* (for the Kentucky Derby). This practice should not, however, be interpreted as a license to ignore the general practice of lowercasing the common noun elements of a name when they stand alone.

DERIVATIVES: Capitalize words that are derived from a proper noun and still depend on it for their meaning: *American, Christian, Christianity, English, French, Marxism, Shakespearean.*

Lowercase words that are derived from a proper noun but no longer depend on it for their meaning: *french fries, herculean, manhattan cocktail, malapropism, pasteurize, quixotic, venetian blind.*

What follows is an alphabetical listing of other key points of capitalization.

academic departments   Use lowercase except for words that are proper nouns or adjectives: *the department of history, the history department, the department of English, the English department.*

administration   Lowercase: *the administration, the president's administration, the governor's administration, the Reagan administration.*

air force   Capitalize when referring to U.S. forces: *the U.S. Air Force, the Air Force, Air Force regulations. . . .*
Use lowercase for the forces of other nations: *the Israeli air force.*

animals   Capitalize the name of a specific animal, and use Roman numerals to show sequence: *Bowser, Whirlaway II.*
For breed names, follow the spelling and capitalization in Webster's New World Dictionary. For breeds not listed in the dictionary, capitalize words derived from proper nouns; use lowercase elsewhere: *basset hound, Boston terrier.*

army   Capitalize when referring to U.S. forces: *the U.S. Army, the Army, Army regulations.*
Use lowercase for the forces of other nations: *the French army.*

Bible   Capitalize, without quotation marks, when referring to the Scriptures of the Old Testament or the New Testament. Capitalize also related terms such as *the Gospels, Gospel of St. Mark, the Scriptures, the Holy Scriptures.*
Lowercase *biblical* in all uses.
Lowercase *bible* as a non-religious term: *My dictionary is my bible.*

brand names   When they are used, capitalize them.
Brand names normally should be used only if they are essential to a story.
Sometimes, however, the use of a brand name may not be essential but is acceptable because it lends an air of reality to a story: *He fished a Camel from his shirt pocket* may be preferable to the less specific *cigarette.*

building   . . . Capitalize the proper names of buildings, including the word *building* if it is an integral part of the proper name: *the Empire State Building.*

bureau   Capitalize when part of the formal name for an organization or agency: *the Bureau of Labor Statistics, the Newspaper Advertising Bureau.*
Lowercase when used alone or to designate a corporate subdivision: *the Washington bureau of The Associated Press.*

cabinet Capitalize references to a specific body of advisers heading executive departments for a president, king, governor, etc.: *The president-elect said he has not made his Cabinet selections.*

The capital letter distinguishes the word from the common noun meaning cupboard, which is lowercase.

Cabinet titles Capitalize the full title when used before a name; lowercase in other uses: *Secretary of State George P. Shultz,* but *Caspar W. Weinberger, secretary of defense.*

century Lowercase, spelling out numbers less than 10: *the first century, the 20th century.*

For proper names, follow the organization's practice: *20th Century Fox, Twentieth Century Fund, Twentieth Century Limited.*

chairman, chairwoman Capitalize as a formal title before a name: *company Chairman Henry Ford, committee Chairwoman Anne Roberts.*

Do not capitalize as a casual, temporary position: *meeting chairman Robert Jones.*

Do not use *chairperson* unless it is an organization's formal title for an office.

chief Capitalize as a formal title before a name: *He spoke to Police Chief Michael Codd. He spoke to Chief Michael Codd of the New York police.*

Lowercase when it is not a formal title: *union chief Walter Reuther.*

church Capitalize as part of the formal name of a building, a congregation or a denomination; lowercase in other uses: *St. Mary's Church, the Roman Catholic Church, the Catholic and Episcopal churches, a Roman Catholic church, a church.*

Lowercase in phrases where *the church* is used in an institutional sense: *He believes in separation of church and state. The pope said the church opposes abortion.*

city council Capitalize when part of a proper name: *the Boston City Council.*

Retain capitalization if the reference is to a specific council but the context does not require the city name:

BOSTON (AP)—The City Council ...

Lowercase in other uses: *the council, the Boston and New York city councils, a city council.*

committee   ... Capitalize when part of a formal name: *the House Appropriations Committee.*

Do not capitalize *committee* in shortened versions of long committee names: the Special Senate Select Committee to Investigate Improper Labor-Management Practices, for example, became the *rackets committee.*

congress   Capitalize *U.S. Congress* and *Congress* when referring to the U.S. Senate and House of Representatives. Although *Congress* sometimes is used as a substitute for the House, it properly is reserved for reference to both the Senate and House.

Capitalize *Congress* also if referring to a foreign body that uses the term, or its equivalent in a foreign language, as part of its formal name: *the Argentine Congress, the Congress.*

Lowercase when used as a synonym for *convention* or in second reference to an organization that uses the word as part of its formal name: *the Congress of Racial Equality, the congress.*

constitution   Capitalize references to the U.S. Constitution, with or without the *U.S.* modifier: *The president said he supports the Constitution.*

When referring to constitutions of other nations or of states, capitalize only with the name of a nation or a state: *the French Constitution, the Massachusetts Constitution, the nation's constitution, the state constitution, the constitution.*

Lowercase in other uses: *the organization's constitution.*

Lowercase *constitutional* in all uses.

courthouse   Capitalize with the name of a jurisdiction: *the Cook County Courthouse, the U.S. Courthouse.* Lowercase in other uses: *the county courthouse, the courthouse, the federal courthouse.*

Court House (two words) is used in the proper names of some communities: *Appomattox Court House, Va.*

court names   Capitalize the full proper names of courts at all levels.

Retain capitalization if *U.S.* or a state name is dropped: *the U.S. Supreme Court, the Supreme Court; the Massachusetts Superior Court, the state Superior Court, the Superior Court, Superior Court.*

For courts identified by a numeral: *2nd District Court, 8th U.S. Circuit Court of Appeals.*

directions and regions   In general, lowercase *north, south, northeast, northern,* etc. when they indicate compass direction; capitalize these words when they designate regions.

federal Use a capital letter for the architectural style and for corporate or governmental bodies that use the word as part of their formal names: *Federal Express, the Federal Trade Commission.* (See separate entries for governmental agencies.)

Lowercase when used as an adjective to distinguish something from state, county, city, town or private entities: *federal assistance, federal court, the federal government, a federal judge.*

Also: *federal District Court* (but *U.S. District Court* is preferred) and *federal Judge John Sirica* (but *U.S. District Judge John Sirica* is preferred).

federal court Always lowercase. The preferred form for first reference is to use the proper name of the court.

Do not create nonexistent entities such as *Manhattan Federal Court.* Instead, use *a federal court in Manhattan.*

food Most food names are lowercase: *apples, cheese, peanut butter.*

Capitalize brand names and trademarks: *Roquefort cheese, Tabasco sauce, Smithfield ham.*

Most proper nouns or adjectives are capitalized when they occur in a food name: *Boston brown bread, Russian dressing, Swiss cheese, Waldorf salad.*

Lowercase is used, however, when the food does not depend on the proper noun or adjective for its meaning: *french fries, graham crackers, manhattan cocktail.*

former Always lowercase. But retain capitalization for a formal title used immediately before a name: *former President Carter.*

fraternal organizations and service clubs Capitalize the proper names: *American Legion, Lions Club, Independent Order of Odd Fellows, Rotary Club.*

Capitalize also words describing membership: *He is a Legionnaire, a Lion, an Odd Fellow, an Optimist and a Rotarian.*

geographic names Capitalize common nouns when they form an integral part of a proper name, but lowercase them when they stand alone: *Pennsylvania Avenue, the avenue; the Philippine Islands, the islands; the Mississippi River, the river.*

Lowercase common nouns that are not part of a specific proper name: *the Pacific islands, the Swiss mountains, Chekiang province.*

government Always lowercase: *the federal government, the state government, the U.S. government.*

governmental bodies   Follow these guidelines:

FULL NAME: Capitalize the full proper names of governmental agencies, departments, and offices; *the U.S. Department of State, the Georgia Department of Human Resources, the Boston City Council, the Chicago Fire Department.*

WITHOUT JURISDICTION: Retain capitalization in referring to a specific body if the dateline or context makes the name of the nation, state, county, city, etc. unnecessary: *the Department of State* (in a story from Washington), *the Department of Human Resources* or *the state Department of Human Resources* (in a story from Georgia), *the City Council* (in a story from Boston), *the Fire Department* or *the city Fire Department* (in a story from Chicago).

Lowercase further condensations of the name: *the department, the council,* etc.

FLIP-FLOPPED NAMES: Retain capital letters for the name of a governmental body if its formal name is flopped to delete the word *of: the State Department, the Human Resources Department.*

GENERIC EQUIVALENTS: If a generic term has become the equivalent of a proper name in popular use, treat it as a proper name: *Walpole State Prison,* for example, even though the proper name is the *Massachusetts Correctional Institution-Walpole.*

PLURALS, NON-SPECIFIC REFERENCES: All words that are capitalized when part of a proper name should be lowercased when they are used in the plural or do not refer to a specific existing body. Some examples:

All states except Nebraska have a state senate. The town does not have a fire department. The bill requires city councils to provide matching funds. The president will address the lower houses of the New York and New Jersey legislatures.

heavenly bodies   Capitalize the proper names of planets, stars, constellations, etc.: *Mars, Arcturus, the Big Dipper, Aries.*

For comets, capitalize only the proper noun element of the name: *Halley's comet.*

Lowercase *sun* and *moon,* but if their Greek names are used, capitalize them: *Helios* and *Luna.*

historical periods and events   Capitalize the names of widely recognized epochs in anthropology, archaeology, geology and history: *the Bronze Age, the Dark Ages, the Middle Ages, the Pliocene Epoch.*

Capitalize also widely recognized popular names for periods and events: *the Atomic Age, the Boston Tea Party, the Civil War, the Exo-*

dus (of the Israelites from Egypt), *the Great Depression, Prohibition.*
Lowercase *century: the 18th century.*

Capitalize only the proper nouns or adjectives in general descriptions of a period: *ancient Greece, classical Rome, the Victorian era, the fall of Rome.*

holidays and holy days   Capitalize them: *New Year's Eve, New Year's Day, Groundhog Day, Easter, Hanukkah,* etc.

house of representatives   Capitalize when referring to a specific governmental body: *the U.S. House of Representatives, the Massachusetts House of Representatives.*

Capitalize shortened references that delete the words *of Representatives: the U.S. House, the Massachusetts House.*

Retain capitalization if *U.S.* or the name of a state is dropped but the reference is to a specific body:

BOSTON (AP) — The House has adjourned for the year.

Lowercase plural uses: *the Massachusetts and Rhode Island houses.*

Apply the same principles to similar legislative bodies such as *the Virginia House of Delegates.*

judge   Capitalize before a name when it is the formal title for an individual who presides in a court of law. Do not continue to use the title in second reference.

Do not use *court* as part of the title unless confusion would result without it:

— No *court* in the title: *U.S. District Judge John Sirica, District Judge John Sirica, federal Judge John Sirica, Judge John Sirica, U.S. Circuit Judge Homer Thornberry, appellate Judge John Blair.*

— *Court* needed in the title: *Juvenile Court Judge John Jones, Criminal Court Judge John Jones, Superior Court Judge Robert Harrison, state Supreme Court Judge William Cushing.*

When the formal title *chief judge* is relevant, put the court name after the judge's name: *Chief Judge John Sirica of the U.S. District Court in Washington, D.C.; Chief Judge Clement F. Haynsworth Jr. of the 4th U.S. Circuit Court of Appeals.*

Do not pile up long court names before the name of a judge. Make it *Judge John Smith of Allegheny County Common Pleas Court.* Not: *Allegheny County Common Pleas Court Judge John Smith.*

Lowercase *judge* as an occupational designation in phrases such as *beauty contest judge Bert Parks.*

legislature   Capitalize when preceded by the name of a state: *the Kansas Legislature.*

Retain capitalization when the state name is dropped but the reference is specifically to that state's legislature:

TOPEKA, Kan. (AP) — Both houses of the Legislature adjourned today.

Capitalize *legislature* in subsequent specific references and in such constructions as: *the 100th Legislature, the state Legislature.*

Lowercase *legislature* when used generically: *No legislature has approved the amendment.*

Use *legislature* in lowercase for all plural references: *The Arkansas and Colorado legislatures are considering the amendment.*

magazine names Capitalize the name but do not place it in quotes. Lowercase *magazine* unless it is part of the publication's formal title: *Harper's Magazine, Newsweek magazine, Time magazine.*

Check the masthead if in doubt.

monuments Capitalize the popular names of monuments and similar public attractions: *Lincoln Memorial, Statue of Liberty, Washington Monument, Leaning Tower of Pisa,* etc.

mountains Capitalize as part of a proper name: *Appalachian Mountains, Ozark Mountains, Rocky Mountains.*

Or simply: *the Appalachians, the Ozarks, the Rockies.*

nationalities and races Capitalize the proper names of nationalities, peoples, races, tribes, etc: *Arab, Arabic, African, Afro-American, American, Caucasian, Cherokee, Chinese* (both singular and plural), *Eskimo* (plural *Eskimos*), *French Canadian Gypsy (Gypsies), Japanese* (singular and plural), *Jew, Jewish, Latin, Negro (Negroes), Nordic, Oriental, Sioux, Swede,* etc.

Lowercase *black* (noun or adjective), *white, red, mulatto,* etc. . . .

Lowercase derogatory terms such as *honky* and *nigger.* Use them only in direct quotes when essential to the story.

navy Capitalize when referring to U.S. forces: *the U.S. Navy, the Navy, Navy policy.* . . .

Lowercase when referring to the naval forces of other nations: *the British navy.*

newspaper names Capitalize *the* in a newspaper's name if that is the way the publication prefers to be known.

Lowercase *the* before the newspaper names if a story mentions several papers, some of which use *the* as part of the name and some of which do not.

organizations and institutions Capitalize the full names of organizations and institutions: *the American Medical Association; First Presbyterian Church; General Motors Corp.; Harvard University; Harvard University Medical School; the Procrastinators Club; the Society of Professional Journalists/Sigma Delta Chi.*

Retain capitalization if *Co., Corp.* or a similar word is deleted from the full proper name: *General Motors.*

FLIP-FLOPPED NAMES: Retain capital letters when commonly accepted practice flops a name to delete the word *of: College of the Holy Cross, Holy Cross College; Harvard School of Dental Medicine, Harvard Dental School.*

Do not, however, flop formal names that are known to the public with the word *of: Massachusetts Institute of Technology,* for example, not *Massachusetts Technology Institute.*

planets Capitalize the proper names of planets: *Jupiter, Mars, Mercury, Neptune, Pluto, Saturn, Uranus, Venus.*

Capitalize *earth* when used as the proper name of our planet: *The astronauts returned to Earth.*

Lowercase nouns and adjectives derived from the proper names of planets and other heavenly bodies: *martian, jovian, lunar, solar, venusian.*

plants In general, lowercase the names of plants, but capitalize proper nouns or adjectives that occur in a name.

Some examples: *tree, fir, white fir, Douglas fir; Dutch elm, Scotch pine; clover, white clover, white Dutch clover.*

police department In communities where this is the formal name, capitalize *police department* with or without the name of the community: *the Los Angeles Police Department, the Police Department.*

If a police agency has some other formal name such as *Division of Police,* use that name if it is the way the department is known to the public. If the story uses *police department* as a generic term for such an agency, put *police department* in lowercase.

If a police agency with an unusual formal name is known to the public as a *police department,* treat *police department* as the name, capitalizing it with or without the name of the community. Use the formal name only if there is a special reason in the story.

If the proper name cannot be determined for some reason, such as the need to write about a police agency from a distance, treat *police department* as the proper name, capitalizing it with or without the name of the community.

Lowercase *police department* in plural uses: *the Los Angeles and San Francisco police departments.*

Lowercase *the department* whenever it stands alone.

political parties and philosophies Capitalize both the name of the party and the word *party* if it is customarily used as part of the organization's proper name: *the Democratic Party, the Republican Party.*

Capitalize *Communist, Conservative, Democrat, Liberal, Republican, Socialist,* etc. when they refer to the activities of a specific party or to individuals who are members of it. Lowercase these words when they refer to political philosophy. . . .

Lowercase the name of a philosophy in noun and adjective forms unless it is the derivative of a proper name: *communism, communist; fascism, fascist.* But: *Marxism, Marxist; Nazism, Nazi.*

pontiff Not a formal title. Always lowercase.

pope Capitalize when used as a formal title before a name; lowercase in all other uses: *Pope John Paul II spoke to the crowd. At the close of his address, the pope gave his blessing.*

presidency Always lowercase.

president Capitalize *president* only as a formal title before one or more names: *President Reagan, Presidents Ford and Carter.*

Lowercase in all other uses: *The president said today. He is running for president. Lincoln was president during the Civil War.*

religious references The basic guidelines:

DEITIES: Capitalize the proper names of monotheistic deities: *God, Allah, the Father, the Son, Jesus Christ, the Son of God, the Redeemer, the Holy Spirit,* etc.

Lowercase pronouns referring to the deity: *he, him, his, thee, thou, who, whose, thy,* etc.

Lowercase *gods* in referring to the deities of polytheistic religions.

Capitalize the proper names of pagan and mythological gods and goddesses: *Neptune, Thor, Venus,* etc.

Lowercase such words as *god-awful, goddamn, godlike, godliness, godsend.*

LIFE OF CHRIST: Capitalize the names of major events in the life of Jesus Christ in references that do not use his name: *The doctrines of the Last Supper, the Crucifixion, the Resurrection and the Ascension are central to Christian belief.*

But use lowercase when the words are used with his name: *The ascension of Jesus into heaven took place 40 days after his resurrection from the dead.*

Apply the principle also to events in the life of his mother: *He cited the doctrine of the Immaculate Conception and the Assumption.* But: *She referred to the assumption of Mary into heaven.*

RITES: Capitalize proper names for rites that commemorate the Last Supper or signify a belief in Christ's presence: *the Lord's Supper, Holy Communion, Holy Eucharist.*

Lowercase the names of other sacraments.

Capitalize *Benediction* and the *Mass.* But: *a high Mass, a low Mass, a requiem Mass.*

OTHER WORDS: Lowercase *heaven, hell, devil, angel, cherub, an apostle, a priest,* etc.

Capitalize *Hades* and *Satan.*

seasons Lowercase *spring, summer, fall, winter* and derivatives such as *springtime* unless part of a formal name: *Dartmouth Winter Carnival, Winter Olympics, Summer Olympics.*

senate Capitalize all specific references to governmental legislative bodies, regardless of whether the name of the nation or state is used: *the U.S. Senate, the Senate; the Virginia Senate, the state Senate, the Senate.*

Lowercase plural uses: *the Virginia and North Carolina senates.*

The same principles apply to foreign bodies.

Lowercase references to non-governmental bodies: *The student senate at Yale.*

sentences Capitalize the first word of every sentence, including quoted statements and direct questions:

Patrick Henry said, "I know not what course others may take, but as for me, give me liberty or give me death."

Capitalize the first word of a quoted statement if it constitutes a sentence, even if it was part of a larger sentence in the original: *Patrick Henry said, "Give me liberty or give me death."*

In direct questions, even without quotation marks: *The story answers the question, Where does true happiness really lie?*

Social Security Capitalize all references to the U.S. system.

Lowercase generic uses such as: *Is there a social security program in Sweden?*

state lowercase in all *state of* constructions: *the state of Maine, the states of Maine and Vermont.*

Do not capitalize *state* when used simply as an adjective to specify a level of jurisdiction: *state Rep. William Smith, the state Transportation Department, state funds.*

Apply the same principle to phrases such as *the city of Chicago, the town of Auburn,* etc.

statehouse Capitalize all references to a specific statehouse, with or without the name of the state: *The Massachusetts Statehouse is in Boston. The governor will visit the Statehouse today.*

Lowercase plural uses: *the Massachusetts and Rhode Island statehouses.*

subcommittee Lowercase when used with the name of a legislative body's full committee: *a Ways and Means subcommittee.*

Capitalize when a subcommittee has a proper name of its own: *the Senate Permanent Subcommittee on Investigations.*

titles In general, confine capitalization to formal titles used directly before an individual's name. . . . Lowercase and spell out titles when they are not used with an individual's name: *The president issued a statement. The pope gave his blessing.*

Lowercase and spell out titles in constructions that set them off from a name by commas: *The vice president, Nelson Rockefeller, declined to run again. John Paul II, the current pope, does not plan to retire.*

ABBREVIATED TITLES: The following formal titles are capitalized and abbreviated as shown when used before a name outside quotations: *Dr., Gov., Lt. Gov., Rep., Sen.* and certain military ranks. . . . Spell out all except *Dr.* when they are used in quotations.

All other formal titles are spelled out in all uses.

ACADEMIC TITLES: Capitalize and spell out formal titles such as *professor, dean, president, chancellor, chairman,* etc., when they precede a name. Lowercase elsewhere.

Lowercase modifiers such as *history* in *history Professor Oscar Handlin* or *department* in *department Chairman Jerome Wiesner.*

FORMAL TITLES: Capitalize formal titles when they are used immediately before one or more names: *Pope John Paul II, President Washington, Vice Presidents John Jones and William Smith.*

LEGISLATIVE TITLES: Use *Rep., Reps., Sen.* and *Sens.* as formal titles before one or more names in regular text. Spell out and capitalize these titles before one or more names in a direct quotation. Spell out and lowercase *representative* and *senator* in other uses.

Spell out other legislative titles in all uses. Capitalize formal titles such as *assemblyman, assemblywoman, city councilor, delegate,* etc., when they are used before a name. Lowercase in other uses.

Add *U.S.* or *state* before a title only if necessary to avoid confusion: *U.S. Sen. Gary Hart spoke with state Sen. Joseph Carter.*

First Reference Practice. The use of a title such as *Rep.* or *Sen.* in first reference is normal in most stories. It is not mandatory, however, provided an individual's title is given later in the story.

Deletion of the title on first reference is frequently appropriate, for example, when an individual has become well-known: *Barry Goldwater endorsed President Reagan today. The Arizona senator said he believes the president deserves another term.*

Second Reference. Do not use legislative titles before a name on second reference unless they are part of a direct quotation.

Congressman, Congresswoman, Rep. and *U.S. Rep.* are the preferred first-reference forms when a formal title is used before the name of a U.S. House member. The words *congressman* or *congresswoman,* in lowercase, may be used in subsequent references that do not use an individual's name, just as *senator* is used in references to members of the Senate.

Congressman and *congresswoman* should appear as capitalized formal titles before a name only in direct quotation.

Organizational Titles. Capitalize titles for formal, organizational offices within a legislative body when they are used before a name: *Speaker Thomas P. O'Neill, Majority Leader James C. Wright, Minority Leader Robert H. Michel, Democratic Whip Thomas S. Foley, Chairman Barry Goldwater of the Senate Intelligence Committee, President Pro Tem Strom Thurmond.*

MILITARY TITLES: Capitalize a military rank when used as a formal title before an individual's name.

Spell out and lowercase a title when it is substituted for a name: *Gen. John J. Pershing arrived today. An aide said the general would review the troops.*

ROYAL TITLES: Capitalize *king, queen,* etc., when used directly before a name.

trademark   A trademark is a brand, symbol, word, etc., used by a manufacturer or dealer and protected by law to prevent a competitor from using it: *Astroturf,* for a type of artificial grass, for example.

In general, use a generic equivalent unless the trademark name is essential to the story.

When a trademark is used, capitalize it.

union names The formal names of unions may be condensed to conventionally accepted short forms that capitalize characteristic words from the full name followed by *union* in lowercase.

Abbreviations and Acronyms

The notation *abbrev.* is used in the stylebooks to identify the abbreviated form that may be used for a word in some contexts.

A few universally recognized abbreviations are required in some circumstances. Some others are acceptable depending on the context. But in general, avoid alphabet soup.

The same principle applies to acronyms — pronounceable words formed from the initial letters in a series of words: *ALCOA, NATO, radar, scuba,* etc.

Guidance on how to use a particular abbreviation or acronym is provided in entries alphabetized according to the sequence of letters in the word or phrase.

Some general principles:

BEFORE A NAME: Abbreviate the following titles when used before a full name outside direct quotations: *Dr., Gov., Lt. Gov., Mr., Mrs., Rep., the Rev., Sen.* and certain military designations. . . . Spell out all except *Dr., Mr.* and *Mrs.* when they are used before a name in direct quotations.

AFTER A NAME: Abbreviate *junior* or *senior* after an individual's name. Abbreviate *company, corporation, incorporated* and *limited* when used after the name of a corporate entity.

In some cases, an academic degree may be abbreviated after an individual's name.

WITH DATES OR NUMERALS: Use the abbreviation *A.D., B.C., a.m., p.m., No.* and abbreviate certain months when used with the day of the month.

IN NUMBERED ADDRESSES: Abbreviate *avenue, boulevard* and *street* in numbered addresses: *He lives on Pennsylvania Avenue. He lives at 1600 Pennsylvania Ave.*

STATES AND NATIONS: The names of certain states, the *United States* and the *Union of Soviet Socialist Republics* (but not of other nations) are abbreviated with periods in some circumstances.

ACCEPTABLE BUT NOT REQUIRED: Some organizations and government agencies are widely recognized by their initials: *CIA, FBI, GOP.*

If the entry for such an organization notes that an abbreviation is acceptable in all references or on second reference, that does not mean that its use should be automatic. Let the context determine, for example, whether to use *Federal Bureau of Investigation* or *FBI*.

AVOID AWKWARD CONSTRUCTIONS: Do not follow an organization's full name with an abbreviation or acronym in parentheses or set off by dashes. If an abbreviation or acronym would not be clear on second reference without this arrangement, do not use it.

Names not commonly before the public should not be reduced to acronyms solely to save a few words.

SPECIAL CASES: Many abbreviations are desirable in tabulations and certain types of technical writing. See individual entries.

CAPS, PERIODS: Use capital letters and periods according to the listings in the stylebooks. For words not in the books, use the first-listed abbreviation in Webster's New World Dictionary.

If an abbreviation not listed in the books or in the dictionary achieves widespread acceptance, use capital letters. Omit periods unless the result would spell an unrelated word.

What follows is an alphabetical listing of other key points involving abbreviations and acronyms.

academic degrees   If mention of degrees is necessary to establish someone's credentials, the preferred form is to avoid an abbreviation and use instead a phrase such as: *John Jones, who has a doctorate in psychology.*

Use an apostrophe in *bachelor's degree, a master's,* etc.

Use such abbreviations as *B.A., M.A., LL.D.* and *Ph.D.* only when the need to identify many individuals by degree on first reference would make the preferred form cumbersome. Use these abbreviations only after a full name — never after just a last name.

When used after a name, an academic abbreviation is set off by commas: *Daniel Moynihan, Ph.D., spoke.*

Do not precede a name with a courtesy title for an academic degree and follow it with the abbreviation for the degree in the same reference.

addresses   Use the abbreviations *Ave., Blvd.* and *St.* only with a numbered address: *1600 Pennsylvania Ave.* Spell them out and capitalize when part of a formal street name without a number: *Pennsylvania Avenue.* Lowercase and spell out when used alone or with more than one street name: *Massachusetts and Pennsylvania avenues.*

All similar words (*alley, drive, road, terrace,* etc.) always are spelled out. Capitalize them when part of a formal name without a number; lowercase when used alone or with two or more names.

Always use figures for an address number: *9 Morningside Circle.*
Spell out and capitalize *First* through *Ninth* when used as street names; use figures with two letters for *10th* and above: *7 Fifth Ave., 100 21st St.*

AFL-CIO   Acceptable in all references for the *American Federation of Labor and Congress of Industrial Organizations.*

aircraft names   Use a hyphen when changing from letters to figures; no hyphen when adding a letter after figures.

AM   Acceptable in all references for the *amplitude modulation* system of radio transmission.

a.m., p.m.   Lowercase, with periods. Avoid the redundant *10 a.m. this morning.*

Amtrak   This acronym, drawn from the words *American travel by track,* may be used in all references to the *National Railroad Passenger Corp.* Do not use *AMTRAK.*

armed services   Do not use the abbreviations *USA, USAF* and *USN.*

assistant   Do not abbreviate. Capitalize only when part of a formal title before a name: *Assistant Secretary of State Thomas M. Tracy.* Wherever practical, however, an appositional construction should be used: *Thomas M. Tracy, assistant secretary of state.*

association   Do not abbreviate. Capitalize as part of a proper name: *American Medical Association.*

attorney general, attorneys general   Never abbreviate. Capitalize only when used as a title before a name: *Attorney General William French Smith.*

Bible   Do not abbreviate individual books of the Bible.
Citations listing the number of chapter(s) and verse(s) use this form: *Matthew 3:16, Luke 21:1–13, 1 Peter 2:1.*

brothers   Abbreviate as *Bros.* in formal company names: *Warner Bros.*
For possessives: *Warner Bros.' profits.*

Christmas   ... Never abbreviate *Christmas* to *Xmas* or any other form.

CIA   Acceptable in all references for *Central Intelligence Agency.*

c.o.d.   Acceptable in all references for *cash on delivery* or *collect on delivery.* (The use of lowercase is an exception to the first listing in Webster's New World.)

company, companies   Use *Co.* or *Cos.* when a business uses either word at the end of its proper name: *Ford Motor Co., American Broadcasting Cos.* But: *Aluminum Company of America.*

If *company* or *companies* appears alone in second reference, spell the word out.

The forms for possessives: *Ford Motor Co.'s profits, American Broadcasting Cos.' profits.*

Conrail   This acronym is acceptable in all references to *Consolidated Rail Corp.* (The corporation originally used *ConRail,* but later changed to *Conrail.*)

corporation   . . . Abbreviate as *Corp.* when a company or government agency uses the word at the end of its name: *Gulf Oil Corp., the Federal Deposit Insurance Corp.*

Spell out *corporation* when it occurs elsewhere in a name: *the Corporation for Public Broadcasting.*

Spell out and lowercase *corporation* whenever it stands alone.

The form for possessives: *Gulf Oil Corp.'s profits.*

detective   Do not abbreviate.

district attorney   Do not abbreviate.

doctor   Use *Dr.* in first reference as a formal title before the name of an individual who holds a doctor of medicine degree: *Dr. Jonas Salk.*

The form *Dr.,* or *Drs.* in a plural construction, applies to all first-reference uses before a name, including direct quotations.

If appropriate in the context, *Dr.* also may be used on first reference before the names of individuals who hold other types of doctoral degrees. However, because the public frequently identifies *Dr.* only with physicians, care should be taken to assure that the individual's specialty is stated in first or second reference. The only exception would be a story in which the context left no doubt that the person was a dentist, psychologist, chemist, historian, etc.

In some instances it also is necessary to specify that an individual identified as *Dr.* is a physician. One frequent case is a story reporting on joint research by physicians, biologists, etc.

Do not use *Dr.* before the names of individuals who hold only honorary doctorates.

Do not continue the use of *Dr.* in subsequent references.

ERA Acceptable in all references to baseball's *earned run average.*

Acceptable on second reference for *Equal Rights Amendment.*

FBI Acceptable in all references for *Federal Bureau of Investigation.*

FM Acceptable in all references for the *frequency modulation* system of radio transmission.

ICBM, ICBMs Acceptable on first reference for *intercontinental ballistic missile(s),* but the term should be defined in the body of a story.

Avoid the redundant *ICBM missiles.*

incorporated Abbreviate and capitalize as *Inc.* when used as part of a corporate name. It usually is not needed, but when it is used, do not set off with commas: *J.C. Penney Co. Inc. announced . . .*

IQ Acceptable in all references for *intelligence quotient.*

junior, senior Abbreviate as *Jr.* and *Sr.* only with full names of persons or animals. Do not precede by a comma: *Joseph P. Kennedy Jr.*

The notation *II* or *2nd* may be used if it is the individual's preference. Note, however, that *II* and *2nd* are not necessarily the equivalent of *junior* — they often are used by a grandson or nephew.

If necessary to distinguish between father and son in second reference, use the *elder Smith* or the *younger Smith.*

mount Spell out in all uses, including the names of communities and of mountains: *Mount Clemens, Mich.; Mount Everest.*

mph Acceptable in all references for *miles per hour* or *miles an hour.*

No. Use as the abbreviation for *number* in conjunction with a figure to indicate position or rank: *No. 1 man, No. 3 choice.*

Do not use in street addresses, with this exception: *No. 10 Downing St.,* the residence of Britain's prime minister.

Do not use in the names of schools: *Public School 19.*

point   Do not abbreviate. Capitalize as part of a proper name: *Point Pleasant.*

saint   Abbreviate as *St.* in the names of saints, cities and other places: *St. Jude; St. Paul, Minn.; St. John's, Newfoundland; St. Lawrence Seaway.*

Saint John   The spelling for the city in New Brunswick. To distinguish it from *St. John's, Newfoundland.*

Sault Ste. Marie, Mich., Sault Ste. Marie, Ontario   The abbreviation is *Ste.* instead of *St.* because the full name is *Sault Sainte Marie.*

state names   Follow these guidelines:

STANDING ALONE: Spell out the names of the 50 U.S. states when they stand alone in textual material. Any state name may be condensed, however, to fit typographical requirements for tabular materials.

EIGHT NOT ABBREVIATED: The names of eight states are never abbreviated in datelines or text: *Alaska, Hawaii, Idaho, Iowa, Maine, Ohio, Texas* and *Utah.*

ABBREVIATIONS REQUIRED: Use the state abbreviations listed at the end of this section:
— In conjunction with the name of a city, town, village or military base in most datelines.
— In conjunction with the name of a city, county, town, village or military base in text. See examples in punctuation section below.
— In short-form listings of party affiliation: *D-Ala., R-Mont.*
The abbreviations are:

Ala.	Md.	N.D.
Ariz.	Mass.	Okla.
Ark.	Mich.	Ore.
Calif.	Minn.	Pa.
Colo.	Miss.	R.I.
Conn.	Mo.	S.C.
Del.	Mont.	S.D.
Fla.	Neb.	Tenn.
Ga.	Nev.	Vt.
Ill.	N.H.	Va.
Ind.	N.J.	Wash.
Kan.	N.M.	W.Va.
Ky.	N.Y.	Wis.
La.	N.C.	Wyo.

TV Acceptable as an adjective or in such constructions as *cable TV*. But do not normally use as a noun unless part of a quotation.

UFO, UFOs Acceptable in all references for *unidentified flying object(s)*.

U.N. Used as an adjective, but not as a noun, for *United Nations*.

U.S. Used as an adjective, but not as a noun, for *United States*.

Punctuation and Hyphenation

Think of punctuation and hyphenation as a courtesy to your readers, designed to help them understand a story.

Inevitably, a mandate of this scope involves gray areas. For this reason, the punctuation entries in the stylebooks refer to guidelines rather than rules. Guidelines should not be treated casually, however.

ampersand (&) Use the ampersand when it is part of a company's formal name: *Baltimore & Ohio Railroad, Newport News Shipbuilding & Dry Dock Co.*

The ampersand should not otherwise be used in place of *and*.

all- Use a hyphen:

all-around (not all-round)	all-out
all-clear	all-star

anti- Hyphenate all except the following words, which have specific meanings of their own:

antibiotic	antiknock	antiphony
antibody	antimatter	antiseptic
anticlimax	antimony	antiserum
antidote	antiparticle*	antithesis
antifreeze	antipasto	antitoxin
antigen	antiperspirant	antitrust
antihistamine	antiphon	antitussive

*And similar terms in physics such as *antiproton*.

This approach has been adopted in the interests of readability and easily remembered consistency.

apostrophe (') Follow these guidelines:

POSSESSIVES: See the **possessives** entry.

OMITTED LETTERS: *I've, it's, don't, rock 'n' roll. 'Tis the season to be jolly. He is a ne'er-do-well.*

OMITTED FIGURES: *The class of '62. The Spirit of '76. The '20s.*

PLURALS OF A SINGLE LETTER: *Mind your p's and q's. He learned the three R's and brought home a report card with four A's and two B's. The Oakland A's won the pennant.*

DO NOT USE: For plurals of numerals or multiple-letter combinations.

by . . . In general, no hyphen. Some examples:

byline	byproduct
bypass	bystreet

By-election is an exception.

co- Retain the hyphen when forming nouns, adjectives and verbs that indicate occupation or status:

co-author	co-owner	co-signer
co-chairman	co-partner	co-star
co-defendant	co-pilot	co-worker
co-host	co-respondent (in a divorce suit)	

(Several are exceptions to Webster's New World in the interests of consistency.)
Use no hyphen in other combinations:

coed	coexist	cooperative
coeducation	coexistence	coordinate
coequal	cooperate	coordination

Cooperate, coordinate and related words are exceptions to the rule that a hyphen is used if a prefix ends in a vowel and the word that follows begins with the same vowel.

colon The most frequent use of a colon is at the end of a sentence to introduce lists, tabulations, texts, etc.
Capitalize the first word after a colon only if it is a proper noun or the start of a complete sentence: *He promised this: The company will make good all the losses.* But: *There were three considerations: expense, time and feasibility.*

INTRODUCING QUOTATIONS: Use a comma to introduce a direct quotation of one sentence that remains within a paragraph. Use a colon to introduce longer quotations within a paragraph and to end all paragraphs that introduce a paragraph of quoted material.

PLACEMENT WITH QUOTATION MARKS: Colons go outside quotation marks unless they are part of the quotation itself.

comma The following guidelines treat some of the most frequent questions about the use of commas. Additional guidelines on specialized uses are provided in separate entries. . . .

For more detailed guidance, consult "The Comma" and "Misused and Unnecessary Commas" in the Guide to Punctuation section in the back of Webster's New World Dictionary.

IN A SERIES: Use commas to separate elements in a series, but do not put a comma before the conjunction in a simple series: *The flag is red, white and blue. He would nominate Tom, Dick or Harry.*

Put a comma before the concluding conjunction in a series, however, if an integral element of the series requires a conjunction: *I had orange juice, toast, and ham and eggs for breakfast.*

Use a comma also before the concluding conjunction in a complex series of phrases: *The main points to consider are whether the athletes are skillful enough to compete, whether they have the stamina to endure the training, and whether they have the proper mental attitude.*

WITH EQUAL ADJECTIVES: Use commas to separate a series of adjectives equal in rank. If the commas could be replaced by the word *and* without changing the sense, the adjectives are equal: *a thoughtful, precise manner; a dark, dangerous street.*

Use no comma when the last adjective before a noun outranks its predecessors because it is an integral element of a noun phrase, which is the equivalent of a single noun: *a cheap fur coat* (the noun phrase is *fur coat*); *the old oaken bucket; a new, blue spring bonnet.*

WITH INTRODUCTORY CLAUSES AND PHRASES: A comma normally is used to separate an introductory clause or phrase from a main clause: *When he had tired of the mad pace of New York, he moved to Dubuque.*

The comma may be omitted after short introductory phrases if no ambiguity would result: *During the night he heard many noises.*

But use the comma if its omission would slow comprehension: *On the street below, the curious gathered.*

WITH CONJUNCTIONS: When a conjunction such as *and, but* or *for* links two clauses that could stand alone as separate sentences, use a comma before the conjunction in most cases: *She was glad she had looked, for a man was approaching the house.*

As a rule of thumb, use a comma if the subject of each clause is expressly stated: *We are visiting Washington, and we also plan a side trip to Williamsburg. We visited Washington, and our senator greeted us personally.* But no comma when the subject of the two clauses is the same and is not repeated in the second: *We are visiting Washington and plan to see the White House.*

The comma may be dropped if two clauses with expressly stated subjects are short. In general, however, favor use of a comma unless a particular literary effect is desired or it would distort the sense of a sentence.

INTRODUCING DIRECT QUOTES: Use a comma to introduce a complete, one-sentence quotation within a paragraph: *Wallace said, "She spent six months in Argentina and came back speaking English with a Spanish accent."* But use a colon to introduce quotations of more than one sentence.

Do not use a comma at the start of an indirect or partial quotation: *He said his victory put him "firmly on the road to a first-ballot nomination."*

BEFORE ATTRIBUTION: Use a comma instead of a period at the end of a quote that is followed by attribution: *"Rub my shoulders," Miss Cawley suggested.*

Do not use a comma, however, if the quoted statement ends with a question mark or exclamation point: *"Why should I?" he asked.*

WITH HOMETOWNS AND AGES: Use a comma to set off an individual's hometown when it is placed in apposition to a name: *Mary Richards, Minneapolis, and Maude Findlay, Tuckahoe, N.Y., were there.* However, the use of the word *of* without a comma between the individual's name and the city name generally is preferable: *Mary Richards of Minneapolis and Maude Findlay of Tuckahoe, N.Y., were there.*

If an individual's age is used, set it off by commas: *Maude Findlay, 48, Tuckahoe, N.Y., was present.* The use of the word *of* eliminates the need for a comma after the hometown if a state name is not needed: *Mary Richards, 36, of Minneapolis and Maude Findlay, 48, of Tuckahoe, N.Y., attended the party.*

IN LARGE FIGURES: Use a comma for most figures higher than 999. The major exceptions are: street addresses (*1234 Main St.*), broadcast frequencies (*1460 kilohertz*), room numbers, serial numbers, telephone numbers, and years (*1976*).

PLACEMENT WITH QUOTES: Commas always go inside quotation marks.

dash Follow these guidelines:

ABRUPT CHANGE: Use dashes to denote an abrupt change in thought in a sentence or an emphatic pause: *We will fly to Paris in June — if I get a raise. Smith offered a plan — it was unprecedented — to raise revenues.*

SERIES WITHIN A PHRASE: When a phrase that otherwise would be set off by commas contains a series of words that must be separated by commas, use dashes to set off the full phrase: *He listed the qualities — intelligence, charm, beauty, independence — that he liked in women.*

ATTRIBUTION: Use a dash before an author's or composer's name at the end of a quotation: *"Who steals my purse steals trash." — Shakespeare.*

IN DATELINES:

NEW YORK (UPI) — The city is broke.

IN LISTS: Dashes should be used to introduce individual sections of a list. Capitalize the first word following the dash. Use periods, not semicolons, at the end of each section. Example:

Jones gave the following reasons:
— He never ordered the package.
— If he did, it didn't come.
— If it did, he sent it back.

WITH SPACES: Put a space on both sides of a dash in all uses except the start of a paragraph and sports agate summaries.

ellipsis (. . .)   In general, treat an ellipsis as a three-letter word, constructed with three periods and two spaces, as shown here.

Use an ellipsis to indicate the deletion of one or more words in condensing quotes, texts and documents. Be especially careful to avoid deletions that would distort the meaning.

ex-   Use no hyphen for words that use *ex-* in the sense of *out of:*

excommunicate   expropriate

Hyphenate when using *ex-* in the sense of *former:*

ex-convict   ex-president

Do not capitalize *ex-* when attached to a formal title before a name: *ex-President Carter.* The prefix modifies the entire term: *ex-New York Gov. Nelson Rockefeller;* not *New York ex Gov.*

Usually *former* is better.

exclamation point (!)   Follow these guidelines:

EMPHATIC EXPRESSIONS: Use the mark to express a high degree of surprise, incredulity or other strong emotion.

AVOID OVERUSE: Use a comma after mild interjections. End mildly exclamatory sentences with a period.

PLACEMENT WITH QUOTES: Place the mark inside quotation marks when it is part of the quoted material: *"How wonderful!" he exclaimed. "Never!" she shouted.*

Place the mark outside quotation marks when it is not part of the quoted material: *I hated reading Spenser's "Faerie Queene"!*

extra- Do not use a hyphen when *extra-* means *outside of* unless the prefix is followed by a word beginning with *a* or a capitalized word:

extralegal	extraterrestrial
extramarital	extraterritorial

But:

extra-alimentary	extra-Britannic

Follow *extra-* with a hyphen when it is part of a compound modifier describing a condition beyond the usual size, extent or degree:

extra-base hit	extra-large book
extra-dry drink	extra-mild taste

fore- . . . In general, no hyphen. Some examples:

forebrain	foregoing
forefather	foretooth

There are three nautical exceptions, based on long-standing practice:

fore-topgallant	fore-topsail
fore-topmast	

full- Hyphenate when used to form compound modifiers:

full-dress	full-page
full-fledged	full-scale
full-length	

See the listings that follow and Webster's New World Dictionary for the spelling of other combinations.

great- Hyphenate *great-grandfather, great-great-grandmother,* etc.

Use *great grandfather* only if the intended meaning is that the grandfather was a great man.

hyphen Hyphens are joiners. Use them to avoid ambiguity or to form a single idea from two or more words.
Some guidelines:

AVOID AMBIGUITY: Use a hyphen whenever ambiguity would result if it were omitted: *The president will speak to small-business men.* (*Businessmen* normally is one word. But *The president will speak to small businessmen* is unclear.)

COMPOUND MODIFIERS: When a compound modifier — two or more words that express a single concept — precedes a noun, use hyphens to link all the words in the compound except the adverb *very* and all adverbs that end in *ly: a first-quarter touchdown, a bluish-green dress, a full-time job, a well-known man, a better-qualified woman, a know-it-all attitude, a very good time, an easily remembered rule.*

Many combinations that are hyphenated before a noun are not hyphenated when they occur after a noun: *The team scored in the first quarter. The dress, a bluish green, was attractive on her. She works full time. His attitude suggested that he knew it all.*

But when a modifier that would be hyphenated before a noun occurs instead after a form of the verb *to be*, the hyphen usually must be retained to avoid confusion: *The man is well-known. The woman is quick-witted. The children are soft-spoken. The play is second-rate.*

The principle of using a hyphen to avoid confusion explains why no hyphen is required with *very* and *ly* words. Readers can expect them to modify the word that follows. But if a combination such as *little-known man* were not hyphenated, the reader could logically be expecting *little* to be followed by a noun, as in *little man*. Instead, the reader encountering *little known* would have to back up mentally and make the compound connection on his own.

TWO-THOUGHT COMPOUNDS: *serio-comic, socio-economic.*

COMPOUND PROPER NOUNS AND ADJECTIVES: Use a hyphen to designate dual heritage: *Italian-American, Mexican-American.*
No hyphen, however, for *French Canadian* or *Latin American.*

AVOID DUPLICATED VOWELS, TRIPLED CONSONANTS: Examples:

anti-intellectual   shell-like
pre-empt

WITH NUMERALS: Use a hyphen to separate figures in odds, ratios, scores, some fractions and some vote tabulations. See examples in entries under these headings.

When large numbers must be spelled out, use a hyphen to connect a word ending in *y* to another word: *twenty-one, fifty-five,* etc.

SUSPENSIVE HYPHENATION: The form: *He received a 10- to 20-year sentence in prison.*

in- No hyphen when it means *not:*

inaccurate	insufferable

Often solid in other cases:

inbound	infighting
indoor	inpatient (n., adj.)
infield	

A few combinations take a hyphen, however:

in-depth	in-house
in-group	in-law

Follow Webster's New World when in doubt.

-in Precede with a hyphen:

break-in	walk-in
cave-in	write-in

parentheses In general, use parentheses around logos, as shown in the **datelines** entry, but otherwise be sparing with them.

Parentheses are jarring to the reader. Because they do not appear on many news service printers, there is also the danger that material inside them may be misinterpreted.

The temptation to use parentheses is a clue that a sentence is becoming contorted. Try to write it another way. If a sentence must contain incidental material, then commas or two dashes are frequently more effective. Use these alternatives whenever possible.

There are occasions, however, when parentheses are the only effective means of inserting necessary background or reference information. The stylebooks offer guidelines.

periods Follow these guidelines:

END OF DECLARATIVE SENTENCE: *The stylebook is finished.*

END OF A MILDLY IMPERATIVE SENTENCE: *Shut the door.*

Use an exclamation point if greater emphases is desired: *Be careful!*

END OF SOME RHETORICAL QUESTIONS: A period is preferable if a statement is more a suggestion than a question: *Why don't we go.*

END OF AN INDIRECT QUESTION: *He asked what the score was.*

INITIALS: *John F. Kennedy, T.S. Eliot.* (No space between *T.* and *S.*, to prevent them from being placed on two lines in typesetting.)

Abbreviations using only the initials of a name do not take periods: *JFK, LBJ.*

ENUMERATIONS: After numbers or letters in enumerating elements of a summary: *1. Wash the car. 2. Clean the basement.* Or: *A. Punctuate properly. B. Write simply.*

possessives   Follow these guidelines:

PLURAL NOUNS NOT ENDING IN S: Add *'s: the alumni's contributions, women's rights.*

PLURAL NOUNS ENDING IN S: Add only an apostrophe: *the churches' needs, the girls' toys, the horses' food, the ships' wake, states' rights, the VIPs' entrance.*

NOUNS PLURAL IN FORM, SINGULAR IN MEANING: Add only an apostrophe: *mathematics' rules, measles' effects.* (But see INANIMATE OBJECTIVES below.)

Apply the same principle when a plural word occurs in the formal name of a singular entity: *General Motors' profits, the United States' wealth.*

NOUNS THE SAME IN SINGULAR AND PLURAL: Treat them the same as plurals, even if the meaning is singular: *one corps' location, the two deer's tracks, the lone moose's antlers.*

SINGULAR NOUNS NOT ENDING IN S: Add *'s: the church's needs, the girl's toys, the horse's food, the ship's route, the VIP's seat.*

Some style guides say that singular nouns ending in *s* sounds such as *ce, x,* and *z* may take either the apostrophe alone or *'s.* See SPECIAL EXPRESSIONS below, but otherwise, for consistency and ease in remembering a rule, always use *'s* if the word does not end in the letter *s: Butz's policies, the fox's den, the justice's verdict, Marx's theories, the prince's life, Xerox's profits.*

SINGULAR COMMON NOUNS ENDING IN S: Add *'s* unless the next word begins with *s: the hostess's invitation, the hostess' seat; the witness's answer, the witness' story.*

SINGULAR PROPER NAMES ENDING IN S: Use only an apostrophe: *Achilles' heel, Agnes' book, Ceres' rites, Descartes' theories, Dickens' novels, Euripides' dramas, Hercules' labors, Jesus' life, Jules' seat, Kansas' schools, Moses' law, Socrates' life, Tennessee Williams' plays, Xerxes' armies.*

SPECIAL EXPRESSIONS: The following exceptions to the general rule for words not ending in *s* apply to words that end in an *s* sound and are followed by a word that begins with *s: for appearance' sake, for conscience' sake, for goodness' sake.* Use *'s* otherwise: *the appearance's cost, my conscience's voice.*

PRONOUNS: Personal, interrogative and relative pronouns have separate forms for the possessive. None involves an apostrophe: *mine, ours, your, yours, his, hers, its, theirs, whose.*

Caution: If you are using an apostrophe with a pronoun, always double-check to be sure that the meaning calls for a contraction; *you're, it's, there's, who's.*

Follow the rules listed above in forming the possessives of other pronouns: *another's idea, others' plans, someone's guess.*

COMPOUND WORDS: Applying the rules above, add an apostrophe or *'s* to the word closest to the object possessed: *the major general's decision, the major generals' decisions, the attorney general's request, the attorneys general's request.* See the **plurals** entry for guidelines on forming the plurals of these words.

Also: *anyone else's attitude, John Adams Jr.'s father, Benjamin Franklin of Pennsylvania's motion.* Whenever practical, however, recast the phrase to avoid ambiguity: *the motion by Benjamin Franklin of Pennsylvania.*

JOINT POSSESSION, INDIVIDUAL POSSESSION: Use a possessive form after only the last word if ownership is joint: *Fred and Sylvia's apartment, Fred and Sylvia's stocks.*

Use a possessive form after both words if the objects are individually owned: *Fred's and Sylvia's books.*

DESCRIPTIVE PHRASES: Do not add an apostrophe to a word ending in *s* when it is used primarily in a descriptive sense: *citizens band radio, a Cincinnati Reds infielder, a teachers college, a Teamsters request, a writers guide.*

Memory Aid: The apostrophe usually is not used if *for* or *by* rather than *of* would be appropriate in the longer form: *a radio band for citizens, a college for teachers, a guide for writers, a request by the Teamsters.*

An *'s* is required, however, when a term involves a plural word that does not end in *s: a children's hospital, a people's republic, the Young Men's Christian Association.*

DESCRIPTIVE NAMES: Some governmental, corporate and institutional organizations with a descriptive word in their names use an apostrophe; some do not. Follow the user's practice: *Actors Equity, Diners Club, the Ladies' Home Journal, the National Governors' Conference, the Veterans Administration.* See separate entries for these and similar names frequently in the news.

QUASI POSSESSIVES: Follow the rules above in composing the possessive form of words that occur in such phrases as *a day's pay, two weeks' vacation, three days' work, your money's worth*.

Frequently, however, a hyphenated form is clearer: *a two-week vacation, a three-day job*.

DOUBLE POSSESSIVE: Two conditions must apply for a double possessive — a phrase such as *a friend of John's* — to occur: 1. The word after *of* must refer to an animate object, and 2. The word before *of* must involve only a portion of the animate object's possessions.

Otherwise, do not use the possessive form on the word after *of: The friends of John Adams mourned his death*. (All the friends were involved.) *He is a friend of the college*. (Not *college's*, because college is inanimate).

Memory Aid: This construction occurs most often, and quite naturally, with the possessive forms of personal pronouns: *He is a friend of mine*.

INANIMATE OBJECTS: There is no blanket rule against creating a possessive form for an inanimate object, particularly if the object is treated in a personified sense. See some of the earlier examples, and note these: *death's call, the wind's murmur*.

In general, however, avoid excessive personalization of inanimate objects, and give preference to an *of* construction when it fits the makeup of the sentence. For example, the earlier references to *mathematics' rules* and *measles' effects* would better be phrased: *the rules of mathematics, the effects of measles*.

post- Follow Webster's New World. Hyphenate if not listed there.

Some words without a hyphen:

postdate	postgraduate	postscript
postdoctoral	postnuptial	postwar
postelection	postoperative	

Some words that use a hyphen:

post-bellum	post-mortem

prefixes See separate listings for commonly used prefixes.

Three rules are constant, although they yield some exceptions to first-listed spellings in Webster's New World Dictionary:

— Except for *cooperate* and *coordinate*, use a hyphen if the prefix ends in a vowel and the word that follows begins with the same vowel.

— Use a hyphen if the word that follows is capitalized.

— Use a hyphen to joint doubled prefixes: *sub-subparagraph*.

pro- Use a hyphen when coining words that denote support for something. Some examples:

pro-business   pro-life
pro-labor   pro-war

No hyphen when *pro* is used in other senses:

produce
pronoun
profile

question mark Follow these guidelines:

END OF A DIRECT QUESTION: *Who started the riot?*
Did he ask who started the riot? (The sentence as a whole is a direct question despite the indirect question at the end.)
You started the riot? (A question in the form of a declarative statement.)

INTERPOLATED QUESTION: *You told me — Did I hear you correctly? — that you started the riot.*

MULTIPLE QUESTIONS: Use a single question mark at the end of the full sentence:

Did you hear him say, "What right have you to ask about the riot?"
Did he plan the riot, employ assistants, and give the signal to begin?

Or, to cause full stops and throw emphasis on each element, break into separate sentence: *Did he plan the riot? Employ assistants? Give the signal to begin?*

CAUTION: Do not use question marks to indicate the end of indirect questions:

He asked who started the riot. To ask why the riot started is unnecessary. I want to know what the cause of the riot was. How foolish it is to ask what caused the riot.

QUESTION-AND-ANSWER FORMAT: Do not use quotation marks. Paragraph each speaker's words:

Q. Where did you keep it?
A. In a little tin box.

PLACEMENT WITH QUOTATION MARKS: Inside or outside, depending on the meaning:

Who wrote "Gone With the Wind"?
He asked, "How long will it take?"

MISCELLANEOUS: The question mark supersedes the comma that normally is used when supplying attribution for a quotation: *"Who is there?" she asked.*

quotation marks   The basic guidelines for open-quote marks (") and close-quote marks ("):

FOR DIRECT QUOTATIONS: To surround the exact words of a speaker or writer when reported in a story:

"I have no intention of staying," he replied.
"I do not object," he said, "to the tenor of the report."
Franklin said, "A penny saved is a penny earned."
A speculator said the practice is "too conservative for inflationary times."

RUNNING QUOTATIONS: If a full paragraph of quoted material is followed by a paragraph that continues the quotation, do not put close-quote marks at the end of the first paragraph. Do, however, put open-quote marks at the start of the second paragraph. Continue in this fashion for any succeeding paragraphs, using close-quote marks only at the end of the quoted material.

If a paragraph does not start with quotation marks but ends with a quotation that is continued in the next paragraph, do not use close-quote marks at the end of the introductory paragraph if the quoted material constitutes a full sentence. Use close-quote marks, however, if the quoted material does not constitute a full sentence.

DIALOGUE OR CONVERSATION: Each person's words, no matter how brief, are placed in a separate paragraph with quotation marks at the beginning and the end of each person's speech:

"Will you go?"
"Yes."
"When?"
"Thursday."

NOT IN Q-AND-A: Quotation marks are not required in formats that identify questions and answers by *Q.* and *A.*

NOT IN TEXTS: Quotation marks are not required in full texts, condensed texts or textual excerpts.

IRONY: Put quotation marks around a word or words used in an ironical sense: *The "debate" turned into a free-for-all.*

UNFAMILIAR TERMS: A word or words being introduced to readers may be placed in quotation marks on first reference:

Broadcast frequencies are measured in "kilohertz."

Do not put subsequent references to *kilohertz* in quotation marks.

AVOID UNNECESSARY FRAGMENTS: Do not use quotation marks to report a few ordinary words that a speaker or writer has used:

Wrong: *The senator said he would "go home to Michigan" if he lost the election.*

Right: *The senator said he would go home to Michigan if he lost the election.*

PARTIAL QUOTES: When a partial quote is used, do not put quotation marks around words that the speaker could not have used.

Suppose the individual said, *"I am horrified at your slovenly manners."*

Wrong: *She said she "was horrified at their slovenly manners."*

Right: *She said she was horrified at their "slovenly manners."*

Better when practical: Use the full quote.

QUOTES WITHIN QUOTES: Alternate between double quotation marks ("or") and single marks ('or'):

She said, *"I quote from his letter, 'I agree with Kipling that "the female of the species is more deadly than the male," but the phenomenon is not an unchangeable law of nature,' a remark he did not explain."*

Use three marks together if two quoted elements end at the same time: *She said, "He told me, 'I love you.'"*

PLACEMENT WITH OTHER PUNCTUATION: Follow these long-established printers' rules:

— The period and the comma always go within the quotation marks.

— The dash, the semicolon, the question mark and the exclamation point go within the quotation marks when they apply to the quoted matter only. They go outside when they apply to the whole sentence.

re- The rules in **prefixes** apply. The following examples of exceptions to first-listed spellings in Webster's New World are based on the general rule that a hyphen is used if a prefix ends in a vowel and the word that follows begins with the same vowel:

re-elect	re-enact	re-entry
re-election	re-engage	re-equip
re-emerge	re-enlist	re-establish
re-employ	re-enter	re-examine

For many other words, the sense is the governing factor:

recover (regain)	resign (quit)	reform (improve)
re-cover (cover again)	re-sign (sign again)	re-form (form again)

Otherwise, follow Webster's New World. Use a hyphen for words not listed there unless the hyphen would distort the sense.

semicolon In general, use the semicolon to indicate a greater separation of thought and information than a comma can convey but less than the separation that a period implies. The stylebooks offer guidelines.

suffixes See separate listings for commonly used suffixes.
Follow Webster's New World Dictionary for words not in this book.

If a word combination is not listed in Webster's New World, use two words for the verb form; hyphenate any noun or adjective forms.

suspensive hyphenation The form: *The 5- and 6-year-olds attend morning classes.*

Numerals

A numeral is a figure, letter, word or group of words expressing a number.

Roman numerals use the letters *I, V, X, L, C, D* and *M.* Use Roman numerals for wars and to show personal sequence for animals and people: *World War II, Native Dancer II, King George VI, Pope John XXIII.*

Arabic numerals use the figures *1, 2, 3, 4, 5, 6, 7, 8, 9* and *0.* Use Arabic forms unless Roman numerals are specifically required.

The figures *1, 2, 10, 101,* etc. and the corresponding words — *one, two, ten, one hundred one,* etc. — are called **cardinal numbers.** The term **ordinal number** applies to *1st, 2nd, 10th, 101st, first, second, tenth, one hundred first,* etc.

Follow these guidelines in using numerals:

LARGE NUMBERS: When large numbers must be spelled out, use a hyphen to connect a word ending in *y* to another word; do not use commas between other separate words that are part of one number: *twenty; thirty; twenty-one; thirty-one; one hundred forty-three; one thousand one hundred fifty-five; one million two hundred seventy-six thousand five hundred eighty-seven.*

SENTENCE START: Spell out a numeral at the beginning of a sentence. If necessary, recast the sentence. There is one exception — a numeral that identifies a calendar year.

Wrong: *993 freshmen entered the college last year.*
Right: *Last year 993 freshmen entered the college.*
Right: *1976 was a very good year.*

CASUAL USES: Spell out casual expressions:

A thousand times no! Thanks a million. He walked a quarter of a mile.

PROPER NAMES: Use words or numerals according to an organization's practice: *Colgate-Palmolive, Twentieth Century Fund, Big Ten.*

FIGURES OR WORDS? For ordinals:

— Spell out *first* through *ninth* when they indicate sequence in time or location — *first base, the First Amendment, he was first in line.* Starting with *10th*, use figures.

— Use *1st, 2nd, 3rd, 4th*, etc. when the sequence has been assigned in forming names. The principal examples are geographic, military and political designations such as *1st Ward, 7th Fleet* and *1st Sgt.*

OTHER USES: For uses not covered by these listings: Spell out whole numbers below 10, use figures for *10* and above. Typical examples: *The woman has three sons and two daughters. He has a fleet of 10 station wagons and two buses.*

IN A SERIES: Apply the appropriate guidelines: *They had 10 dogs, six cats and 97 hamsters. They had four four-room houses, 10 three-room houses and 12 10-room houses.*

What follows is an alphabetical listing of the other key points of using numerals.

act numbers   Use Arabic figures and capitalize *act: Act 1; Act 2, Scene 2.* But: *the first act, the second act.*

addresses   Always use figures for an address number: *9 Morningside Circle.*

Spell out and capitalize *First* through *Ninth* when used as street names; use figures with two letters for *10th* and above: *7 Fifth Ave., 100 21st St.*

ages   Always use figures. When the context does not require *years* or *years old*, the figure is presumed to be years.

aircraft names   Use a hyphen when changing from letters to figures; no hyphen when adding a letter after figures.

Some examples for aircraft often in the news: *B-1, BAC-111, C-5A, DC-10, FH-227, F-4, Phantom II, F-86 Sabre, L-1011, MiG-21, Tu-144, 727-100C, 747, 747B, VC-10.*

amendments to the Constitution Use *First Amendment, 10th Amendment,* etc.
Colloquial references to the Fifth Amendment's protection against self-incrimination are best avoided, but where appropriate: *He took the Fifth seven times.*

Arabic numerals The numerical figures *1, 2, 3, 4, 5, 6, 7, 8, 9, 10.*
In general, use Arabic forms unless denoting the sequence of wars or establishing a personal sequence for people and animals.

betting odds Use figures and a hyphen: *The odds were 5-4, he won despite 3-2 odds against him.*
The word *to* seldom is necessary, but when it appears it should be hyphenated in all constructions: *3-to-2 odds, odds of 3-to-2, the odds were 3-to-2.*

Celsius Use this term rather than *centigrade* for the temperature scale that is part of the metric system.
When giving a Celsius temperature, use these forms: *40 degrees Celsius* or *40° C* (Note the space and no period after the capital *C*) if degrees and Celsius are clear from the context.

cents Spell out the word *cents* and lowercase, using numerals for amounts less than a dollar: *5 cents, 12 cents.* Use the $ sign and decimal system for larger amounts: *$1.01, $2.50.*
Numerals alone, with or without a decimal point as appropriate, may be used in tabular matter.

congressional districts Use figures and capitalize *district* when joined with a figure: *the 1st Congressional District, the 1st District.*
Lowercase *district* whenever it stands alone.

court decisions Use figures and a hyphen: *The Supreme Court ruled 5-4, a 5-4 decision.* The word *to* is not needed, but use hyphens if it appears in quoted matter: *"the court ruled 5-to-4, the 5-to-4 decision."*

court names ... For courts identified by a numeral: *2nd District Court, 8th U.S. Circuit Court of Appeals.*

dates Always use Arabic figures, without *st, nd, rd* or *th*. See **months** for examples and punctuation guidelines.

decades Use Arabic figures to indicate decades of history. Use an apostrophe to indicate numerals that are left out; show plural by adding the letter *s: the 1890s, the '90s, the Gay '90s, the 1920s, the mid-1930s.*

decimal units Use a period and numerals to indicate decimal amounts. Decimalization should not exceed two places in textual material unless there are special circumstances.

dimensions Use figures and spell out *inches, feet, yards,* etc., to indicate depth, height, length and width. Hyphenate adjectival forms before nouns.

Use an apostrophe to indicate feet and quote marks to indicate inches (*5'6'*) only in very technical contexts.

distances Use figures for *10* and above, spell out *one* through *nine: He walked four miles.*

district . . . Use a figure and capitalize *district* when forming a proper name: *the 2nd District.*

dollars . . . Use figures and the $ sign in all except casual references or amounts without a figure: *The book cost $4. Dad, please give me a dollar. Dollars are flowing overseas.*

For specified amounts, the word takes a singular verb: *He said $500,000 is what they want.*

For amounts of more than $1 million, use the $ and numerals up to two decimal places. Do not link the numerals and the word by a hyphen: *He is worth $4.35 million. He is worth exactly $4,351,242. He proposed a $300 billion budget.*

The form for amounts less than $1 million: *$4, $25, $500, $1,000, $650,000.*

election returns Use figures, with commas every three digits starting at the right and counting left. Use the word *to* (not a hyphen) in separating different totals listed together: *Ronald Reagan defeated Jimmy Carter 43,899,248 to 35,481,435 in 1980* (this is the actual final figure).

Use the word *votes* if there is any possibility that the figures could be confused with a ratio: *Reagan defeated Carter 16 votes to 3 votes in Dixville Notch.*

Do not attempt to create adjectival forms such as *the 43,899,248-35,481,435 vote.*

fractions   Spell out amounts less than *1* in stories, using hyphens between the words: *two-thirds, four-fifths, seven-sixteenths,* etc.

Use figures for precise amounts larger than *1*, converting to decimals whenever practical.

Fractions are preferred, however, in stories about stocks. . . .

When using fractional characters, remember that most newspaper type fonts can set only ⅛, ¼, ⅜, ½, ⅝, ¾ and ⅞ as one unit; use 1½, 2⅝, etc. with no space between the figure and the fraction. Other fractions require a hyphen and individual figures, with a space between the whole number and the fraction: *1 3-16, 2 1-3, 5 9-10.*

highway designations   Use these forms, as appropriate in the context, for highways identified by number: *U.S. Highway 1, U.S. Route 1, U.S. 1, Route 1, Illinois 34, Illinois Route 34, state Route 34, Route 34, Interstate Highway 495, Interstate 495.* On second reference only for *Interstate: I-495.*

mile   . . . Use figures for amounts under 10 in dimensions, formulas and speeds: *The farm measures 5 miles by 4 miles. The car slowed to 7 miles per hour. The new model gets 4 miles more per gallon.*

Spell out below 10 in distances: *He drove four miles.*

millions, billions   Use figures with *million* or *billion* in all except casual uses: *I'd like to make a billion dollars.* But: *The nation has 1 million citizens. I need $7 billion.*

Do not go beyond two decimals: *7.51 million persons, $2.56 billion, 7,542,500 persons, $2,565,750,000.* Decimals are preferred where practical: *1.5 million.* Not: *1½ million.*

Do not mix *millions* and *billions* in the same figure: *2.6 billion.* Not: *2 billion 600 million.*

Do not drop the word *million* or *billion* in the first figure of a range: *He is worth from $2 million to $4 million.* Not: *$2 to $4 million,* unless you really mean *$2.*

Note that a hyphen is not used to join the figures and the word *million* or *billion,* even in this type of phrase: *The president submitted a $300 billion budget.*

minus sign   Use a hyphen, not a dash, but use the word *minus* if there is any danger of confusion.

Use a word, not a minus sign, to indicate temperatures below zero: *minus 10* or *5 below zero.*

No.   Use as the abbreviation for *number* in conjunction with a figure to indicate position or rank: *No. 1 man, No. 3 choice.*

Do not use in street addresses, with this exception: *No. 10 Downing St.,* the residence of Britain's prime minister.

Do not use in the names of schools: *Public School 19.*

page numbers Use figures and capitalize *page* when used with a figure. When a letter is appended to the figure, capitalize it but do not use a hyphen: *Page 1, Page 10, Page 20A.*

One exception: *It's a Page One story.*

percentages Use figures: *1 percent, 2.5 percent* (use decimals, not fractions), *10 percent.*

For amounts less than 1 percent, precede the decimal with a zero: *The cost of living rose 0.6 percent.*

Repeat *percent* with each individual figure: *He said 10 percent to 30 percent of the electorate may not vote.*

political divisions Use Arabic figures and capitalize the accompanying word when used with the figure: *1st Ward, 10th Ward, 3rd Precinct, 22nd Precinct, the ward, the precinct.*

proportions Always use figures: *2 parts powder to 6 parts water.*

ratios Use figures and a hyphen: *the ratio was 2-to-1, a ratio of 2-to-1, a 2-1 ratio.* As illustrated, the word *to* should be omitted when the numbers precede the word *ratio.*

Always use the word *ratio* or a phrase such as *a 2-1 majority* to avoid confusion with actual figures.

Roman numerals They use letters (*I, X,* etc.) to express numbers.

Use Roman numerals for wars and to establish personal sequence for people and animals: *World War I, Native Dancer II, King George V, Pope John XXIII, John Jones I, John Jones II, John Jones III.* See the **junior, senior** entry.

Use Arabic numerals in all other cases.

scores Use figures exclusively, placing a hyphen between the totals of the winning and losing teams: *The Reds defeated the Red Sox 4-3, the Giants scored a 12-6 football victory over the Cardinals, the golfer had a 5 on the first hole but finished with a 2-under-par score.*

Use a comma in this format: *Boston 6, Baltimore 5.*

sizes Use figures: *a size 9 dress, size 40 long, 10½B shoes, a 34½ sleeve.*

speeds Use figures. *The car slowed to 7 miles per hour, winds of 5 to 10 miles per hour, winds of 7 to 9 knots, 10-knot winds.*

Avoid extensively hyphenated constructions such as *5-mile-per-hour winds.*

telephone numbers Use figures. The forms: *(212) 262-4000, 262-4000, (212) MU2-0400.* If extension numbers are given: *Ext. 2, Ext. 364, Ext. 4071.*

The parentheses around the area code are based on a format that telephone companies have agreed upon for domestic and international communications.

temperatures Use figures for all except *zero.* Use a word, not a minus sign, to indicate temperatures below zero.

times Use figures except for *noon* and *midnight.* Use a colon to separate hours from minutes: *11 a.m., 1 p.m., 3:30 p.m.*

Avoid such redundancies as *10 a.m. this morning, 10 p.m. tonight* or *10 p.m. Monday night.* Use *10 a.m. today, 10 p.m. today* or *10 p.m. Monday,* etc., as required by the norms in **time element.**

The construction *4 o'clock* is acceptable, but time listings with *a.m.* or *p.m.* are preferred.

weights Use figures: *The baby weighed 9 pounds, 7 ounces. She had a 9-pound, 7-ounce boy.*

years Use figures, without commas: *1975.* Use an *s* without an apostrophe to indicate spans of decades or centuries: *the 1890s, the 1800s.*

Years are the lone exception to the general rule in **numerals** that a figure is not used to start a sentence: *1976 was a very good year.*

Grammar, Spelling and Word Usage

This section lists common problems of grammatical usage, word selection and spelling.

a, an Use the article *a* before consonant sounds: *a historic event, a one-year term* (sounds as if it begins with the letter w), *a united stand* (sounds like you).

Use the article *an* before vowel sounds: *an energy crisis, an honorable man* (the h is silent), *an NBA record* (sounds as if it begins with the letter e), *an 1890s celebration.*

accept, except *Accept* means to receive.
Except means to exclude.

adverse, averse *Adverse* means unfavorable: *He predicted adverse weather.*
Averse means reluctant, opposed: *She is averse to change.*

affect, effect *Affect,* as a verb, means to influence: *The game will affect the standings.*
Affect, as a noun, is best avoided. It occasionally is used in psychology to describe an emotion, but there is no need for it in everyday language.
Effect, as a verb, means to cause: *He will effect many changes in the company.*
Effect, as a noun, means result: *The effect was overwhelming. He miscalculated the effect of his actions. It was a law of little effect.*

aid, aide *Aid* is assistance.
An *aide* is a person who serves as an assistant.

ain't A dialectical or substandard contraction. Use it only in quoted matter or special contexts.

allude, refer *To allude* to something is to speak of it without specifically mentioning it.
To refer is to mention it directly.

allusion, illusion *Allusion* means an indirect reference: *The allusion was to his opponent's record.*
Illusion means an unreal or false impression: *The scenic director created the illusion of choppy seas.*

among, between The maxim that *between* introduces two items and *among* introduces more than two covers most questions about how to use these words: *The funds were divided among Mondale, Hart and Jackson.*
However, *between* is the correct word when expressing the relationships of three or more items considered one pair at a time: *Negotiations on a debate format are under way between the network and the Mondale, Hart and Jackson committees.*
As with all prepositions, any pronouns that follow these words must be in the objective case: *among us, between him and her, between you and me.*

anticipate, expect *Anticipate* means to expect and prepare for something; *expect* does not include the notion of preparation:

They expect a record crowd. They have anticipated it by adding more seats to the auditorium.

anybody, any body, anyone, any one One word for an indefinite reference: *Anyone can do that.*

Two words when the emphasis is on singling out one element of a group: *Any one of them may speak up.*

apposition A decision on whether to put commas around a word, phrase or clause used in apposition depends on whether it is essential to the meaning of the sentence (no commas) or not essential (use commas).

because, since Use *because* to denote a specific cause-effect relationship: *He went because he was told.*

Since is acceptable in a casual sense when the first event in a sequence led logically to the second but was not its direct cause: *He went to the game, since he had been given the tickets.*

blond, blonde Use *blond* as a noun for males and as the adjective for all applications: *She has blond hair.*

Use *blonde* as a noun for females.

boy Applicable until 18th birthday is reached. Use *man* or *young man* afterward.

brunet, brunette. Use *brunet* as a noun for males, and as the adjective for both sexes.

Use *brunette* as a noun for females.

burglary, larceny, robbery, theft Legal definitions of *burglary* vary, but in general a *burglary* involves entering a building (not necessarily by breaking in) and remaining unlawfully with the intention of committing a crime.

Larceny is the legal term for the wrongful taking of property. Its non-legal equivalents are *stealing* or *theft.*

Robbery in the legal sense involves the use of violence or threat in committing larceny. In a wider sense it means to plunder or rifle, and may thus be used even if a person was not present: *His house was robbed while he was away.*

Theft describes a larceny that did not involve threat, violence or plundering.

USAGE NOTE: You *rob* a person, bank, house, etc., but you *steal* the money or the jewels.

collective nouns Nouns that denote a unit take singular verbs and pronouns: *class, committee, crowd, family, group, herd, jury, orchestra, team.*

Some usage examples: *The committee is meeting to set its agenda. The jury reached its verdict. A herd of cattle was sold.*

PLURAL IN FORM: Some words that are plural in form become collective nouns and take singular verbs when the group or quantity is regarded as a unit.

Right: *A thousand bushels is a good yield.* (A unit.)
Right: *A thousand bushels were created.* (Individual items.)
Right: *The data is sound.* (A unit.)
Right: *The data have been carefully collected.* (Individual items.)

compose, comprise, constitute *Compose* means to create or put together. It commonly is used in both the active and passive voices: *He composed a song. The United States is composed of 50 states. The zoo is composed of many animals.*

Comprise means to contain, to include all or embrace. It is best used only in the active voice, followed by a direct object: *The United States comprises 50 states. The jury comprises five men and seven women. The zoo comprises many animals.*

Constitute, in the sense of form or make up, may be the best word if neither *compose* nor *comprise* seems to fit: *Fifty states constitute the United States. Five men and seven women constitute the jury. A collection of animals can constitute a zoo.*

Use *include* when what follows is only part of the total: *The price includes breakfast. The zoo includes lions and tigers.*

contractions Contractions reflect informal speech and writing. Webster's New World Dictionary includes many entries for contractions: *aren't* for *are not,* for example.

Avoid excessive use of contractions. Contractions listed in the dictionary are acceptable, however, in informal contexts or circumstances where they reflect the way a phrase commonly appears in speech or writing.

contrasted to, contrasted with Use *contrasted to* when the intent is to assert, without the need for elaboration, that two items have opposite characteristics: *He contrasted the appearance of the house today to its ramshackle look last year.*

Use *contrasted with* when juxtaposing two or more items to illustrate similarities and/or differences: *He contrasted the Republican platform with the Democratic platform.*

dangling modifiers Avoid modifiers that do not refer clearly and logically to some word in the sentence.

Dangling: *Taking our seats, the game started.* (*Taking* does not refer to the subject, *game*, nor to any other word in the sentence.)

Correct: *Taking our seats, we watched the opening of the game.* (*Taking* refers to *we*, the subject of the sentence.)

either   Use it to mean *one or the other*, not *both*.

Right: *She said to use either door.*

Wrong: *There were lions on either side of the door.*

Right: *There were lions on each side of the door. There were lions on both sides of the door.*

either ... or, neither ... nor   The nouns that follow these words do not constitute a compound subject; they are alternate subjects and require a verb that agrees with the nearer subject:

Neither they nor he is going. Neither he nor they are going.

essential clauses, non-essential clauses   These terms are used instead of *restrictive clause* and *non-restrictive clause* to convey the distinction between the two in a more easily remembered manner.

Both types of clauses provide additional information about a word or phrase in the sentence.

The difference between them is that the essential clause cannot be eliminated without changing the meaning of the sentence — it so "restricts" the meaning of the word or phrase that its absence would lead to a substantially different interpretation of what the author meant.

The non-essential clause, however, can be eliminated without altering the basic meaning of the sentence — it does not "restrict" the meaning so significantly that its absence would radically alter the author's thought.

PUNCTUATION: An essential clause must not be set off from the rest of a sentence by commas. A non-essential clause must be set off by commas.

The presence or absence of commas provides the reader with critical information about the writer's intended meaning. Note the following examples:

— *Reporters who do not read the stylebook should not criticize their editors.* (The writer is saying that only one class of reporters, those who do not read the stylebook, should not criticize their editors. If the *who ... stylebook* phrase were deleted, the meaning of the sentence would be changed substantially.)

— *Reporters, who do not read the stylebook, should not criticize their editors.* (The writer is saying that all reporters should not criticize their editors. If the *who . . . stylebook* phrase were deleted, this meaning would not be changed.)

USE OF WHO, THAT, WHICH: When an essential or non-essential clause refers to a human being or an animal with a name, it should be introduced by *who* or *whom*. (See the **who, whom** entry.) Do not use commas if the clause is essential to the meaning; use them if it is not.

That is the preferred pronoun to introduce essential clauses that refer to an inanimate object or an animal without a name. *Which* is the only acceptable pronoun to introduce a non-essential clause that refers to an inanimate object or an animal without a name.

The pronoun *which* occasionally may be substituted for *that* in the introduction of an essential clause that refers to an inanimate object or an animal without a name. In general, this use of *which* should appear only when *that* is used as a conjunction to introduce another clause in the same sentence: *He said Monday that the part of the army which suffered severe casualties needs reinforcement.*

essential phrases, non-essential phrases These terms are used in this book instead of *restrictive phrase* and *non-restrictive phrase* to convey the distinction between the two in a more easily remembered manner.

The underlying concept is the one that also applies to clauses:

An essential phrase is a word or group of words critical to the reader's understanding of what the author had in mind.

A non-essential phrase provides more information about something. Although the information may be helpful to the reader's comprehension, the reader would not be misled if the information were not there.

PUNCTUATION: Do not set an essential phrase off from the rest of a sentence by commas:

We saw the award-winning movie "One Flew Over the Cuckoo's Nest." (No comma, because many movies have won awards, and without the name of the movie the reader would not know which movie was meant.)

They ate dinner with their daughter Julie. (Because they have more than one daughter, the inclusion of Julie's name is critical if the reader is to know which daughter is meant.)

Set off non-essential phrases by commas:

We saw the 1976 winner in the Academy Award competition for best movie, "One Flew Over the Cuckoo's Nest." (Only one movie won the award. The name is informative, but even without the name no other movie could be meant.)

They ate dinner with their daughter Julie and her husband, David. (Julie has only one husband. If the phrase read *and her husband David*, it would suggest that she had more than one husband.)

The company chairman, Henry Ford II, spoke. (In the context, only one person could be meant.)

Indian corn, or maize, was harvested. (*Maize* provides the reader with the name of the corn, but its absence would not change the meaning of the sentence.)

DESCRIPTIVE WORDS: Do not confuse punctuation rules for non-essential clauses with the correct punctuation when a non-essential word is used as a descriptive adjective. The distinguishing clue often is the lack of an article or pronoun:

Right: *Julie and husband David went shopping. Julie and her husband, David, went shopping.*

Right: *Company Chairman Henry Ford II made the announcement. The company chairman, Henry Ford II, made the announcement.*

every one, everyone   Two words when it means each individual item: *Every one of the clues was worthless.*

One word when used as a pronoun meaning all persons: *Everyone wants his life to be happy.* (Note that *everyone* takes singular verbs and pronouns.)

farther, further   *Farther* refers to physical distance: *He walked farther into the woods.*

Further refers to an extension of time or degree: *She will look further into the mystery.*

fewer, less   In general, use *fewer* for individual items, *less* for bulk or quantity.

flaunt, flout   To *flaunt* is to make an ostentatious or defiant display: *She flaunted her beauty.*

To *flout* is to show contempt for: *He flouts the law.*

flier, flyer   *Flier* is the preferred term for an aviator or a handbill.

Flyer is the proper name of some trains and buses: *the Western Flyer.*

girl   Applicable until 18th birthday is reached. Use *woman* or *young woman* afterward.

good, well *Good* is an adjective that means something is as it should be or is better than average.

When used as an adjective, *well* means suitable, proper, healthy. When used as an adverb, *well* means in a satisfactory manner or skillfully.

Good should not be used as an adverb. It does not lose its status as an adjective in a sentence such as *I feel good.* Such a statement is the idiomatic equivalent of *I am in good health.* An alternative, *I feel well,* could be interpreted as meaning that your sense of touch was good.

hopefully It means in a hopeful manner. Do not use it to mean it is hoped, let us hope or we hope.

Right: *It is hoped that we will complete our work in June.*
Right: *We hope that we will complete our work in June.*

Wrong as a way to express the thought in the previous two sentences: *Hopefully, we will complete our work in June.*

imply, infer Writers or speakers *imply* in the words they use. A listener or reader *infers* something from the words.

in, into *In* indicates location: *He was in the room. Into* indicates motion: *She walked into the room.*

lay, lie The action word is **lay**. It takes a direct object. *Laid* is the form for its past tense and its past participle. Its present participle is *laying.*

Lie indicates a state of reclining along a horizontal plane. It does not take a direct object. Its past tense is *lay.* Its past participle is *lain.* Its present participle is *lying.*

When **lie** means to make an untrue statement, the verb forms are *lie, lied, lying.*

like, as Use *like* as a preposition to compare nouns and pronouns. It requires an object: *Jim blocks like a pro.*

The conjunction *as* is the correct word to introduce clauses: *Jim blocks the linebacker as he should.*

majority, plurality *Majority* means more than half of an amount.

Plurality means more than the next highest number.

marshal, marshaled, marshaling, Marshall *Marshal* is the spelling for both the verb and the noun: *Marilyn will marshal her forces. Erwin Rommel was a field marshal.*

Marshall is used in proper names: *George C. Marshall, John Marshall, the Marshall Islands.*

obscenities, profanities, vulgarities Do not use them in stories unless they are part of direct quotations and there is a compelling reason for them.

Confine the offending language, in quotation marks, to a separate paragraph that can be deleted easily.

In reporting profanity that normally would use the words *damn* or *god*, lowercase *god* and use the following forms: *damn, damn it, goddamn it.* Do not, however, change the offending words to euphemisms. Do not, for example, change *damn it* to *darn it.*

If a full quote that contains profanity, obscenity or vulgarity cannot be dropped but there is no compelling reason for the offensive language, replace letters of an offensive word with a hyphen. The word *damn*, for example, would become d--- *or* ----.

off of The *of* is unnecessary: *He fell off the bed.* Not: *He fell off of the bed.*

On Do not use *on* before a date or day of the week when its absence would not lead to confusion: *The meeting will be held Monday. He will be inaugurated Jan. 20.*

Use *on* to avoid an awkward juxtaposition of a date and a proper name: *John met Mary on Monday. He told Reagan on Thursday that the bill was doomed.*

Use *on* also to avoid any suggestion that a date is the object of a transitive verb: *The House killed on Tuesday a bid to raise taxes. The Senate postponed on Wednesday its consideration of a bill to reduce import duties.*

over It is not interchangeable with *more than.*
Over refers to spatial relationships: *The plane flew over the city*
More than is used with figures: *More than 40,000 fans were in the stadium.*

people, persons Use *people* when speaking of a large or uncounted number of individuals: *Thousands of people attended the fair. Some rich people pay few taxes. What will people say?* Do not use *persons* in this sense.

Persons usually is used when speaking of a relatively small number of people who can be counted, but *people* also may be used:

Right: *There were 20 persons in the room.*
Right: *There were 20 people in the room.*

People is also a collective noun that takes a plural verb and is used to refer to a single race or nation: *The American people are united.* In this sense, the plural is *peoples: The peoples of Africa speak many languages.*

principal, principle   *Principal* is a noun and adjective meaning someone or something first in rank, authority, importance or degree: *She is the school principal. He was the principal player in the trade. Money is the principal problem.*

Principle is a noun that means a fundamental truth, law, doctrine or motivating force: *They fought for the principle of self-determination.*

prior to   *Before* is less stilted for most uses. *Prior to* is appropriate, however, when a notion of requirement is involved: *The fee must be paid prior to the examination.*

reign, rein   The leather strap for a horse is a *rein*, hence figuratively: *seize the reins, give free rein to, put a check rein on.*

Reign is the period a ruler is on the throne: *The king began his reign.*

should, would   Use *should* to express an obligation: *We should help the needy.*

Use *would* to express a customary action: *In the summer we would spend hours by the seashore.*

Use *would* also in constructing a conditional past tense, but be careful:

Wrong: *If Soderholm would not have had an injured foot, Thompson would not have been in the lineup.*

Right: *If Soderholm had not had an injured foot, Thompson would not have been in the lineup.*

spelling   The basic rule when in doubt is to consult the stylebooks followed by, if necessary, a dictionary. . . .

Memory Aid: Noah Webster developed the following rule of thumb for the frequently vexing question of whether to double a final consonant in forming the present participle and past tense of a verb:

— If the stress in pronunciation is on the first syllable, do not double the consonant: *cancel, canceling, canceled.*

— If the stress in pronunciation is on the second syllable, double the consonant: *control, controlling, controlled; refer, referring, referred.*

— If the word is only one syllable, double a consonant unless confusion would result: *jut, jutted, jutting.* An exception, to avoid confusion with *buss,* is *bus, bused, busing.*

Here is a list of commonly misspelled words:

adviser	council	likable
accommodate	counsel	machine gun
Asian flu	drought	percent
ax	drunken	percentage
baby-sit	employee	restaurant
baby sitter	embarrass	restaurateur
baby-sitting	eyewitness	rock 'n' roll
cannot	firefighter	skillful
cave in (v.)	fulfill	subpoena
cave-in (n., adj.)	goodbye	teen-age (adj.)
chauffeur	hanged	teen-ager (n.)
cigarette	harass	under way
clue	hitchhiker	vacuum
commitment	homemade	weird
consensus	imposter	whiskey
consul	judgment	X-ray (n., v. and adj.)
copter	kidnapping	

subjunctive mood   Use the subjunctive mood of a verb for contrary-to-fact conditions, and expressions of doubts, wishes or regrets:

If I were a rich man, I wouldn't have to work hard.
I doubt that more money would be the answer.
I wish it were possible to take back my words.

Sentences that express a contingency or hypothesis may use either the subjunctive or the indicative mood depending on the context. In general, use the subjunctive if there is little likelihood that a contingency might come true:

If I were to marry a millionaire, I wouldn't have to worry about money.
If the bill should overcome the opposition against it, it would provide extensive tax relief.

But:

If I marry my millionaire beau, I won't have to worry about money.
If the bill passes as expected, it will provide an immediate tax cut.

that (conjunction)   Use the conjunction *that* to introduce a dependent clause if the sentence sounds or looks awkward without it. There are no hard-and-fast rules, but in general:

— *That* usually may be omitted when a dependent clause immediately follows a form of the verb *to say: The president said he had signed the bill.*

— *That* should be used when a time element intervenes between the verb and the dependent clause: *The president said Monday that he had signed the bill.*

— *That* usually is necessary after some verbs. They include: *advocate, assert, contend, declare, estimate, make clear, point out, propose* and *state.*

— *That* is required before subordinate clauses beginning with conjunctions such as *after, although, because, before, in addition to, until* and *while: Haldeman said that after he learned of Nixon's intention to resign, he sought pardons for all connected with Watergate.*

When in doubt, include *that.* Omission can hurt. Inclusion never does.

that, which, who, whom (pronouns) Use *who* and *whom* in referring to persons and to animals with a name: *John Jones is the man who helped me.* See the **who, whom** entry.

Use *that* and *which* in referring to inanimate objects and to animals without a name.

See the **essential clauses, nonessential clauses** entry for guidelines on using *that* and *which* to introduce phrases and clauses.

under way Two words in virtually all uses: *The project is under way. The naval maneuvers are under way.*

One word only when used as an adjective before a noun in a nautical sense: *an underway flotilla.*

verbs . . . In general, avoid awkward constructions that split infinitive forms of a verb (*to leave, to help,* etc.) or compound forms (*had left, are found out,* etc.).

Awkward: *She was ordered to immediately leave on an assignment.*

Preferred: *She was ordered to leave immediately on an assignment.*

Awkward: *There stood the wagon that we had early last autumn left by the barn.*

Preferred: *There stood the wagon that we had left by the barn early last autumn.*

Occasionally, however, a split is not awkward and is necessary to convey the meaning:

He wanted to really help his mother.
Those who lie are often found out.

How has your health been?
The budget was tentatively approved.

who, whom   Use *who* and *whom* for references to human beings and to animals with a name. Use *that* and *which* for inanimate objects and animals without a name.

Who is the word when someone is the subject of a sentence, clause or phrase: *The woman who rented the room left the window open. Who is there?*

Whom is the word when someone is the object of a verb or preposition: *The woman to whom the room was rented left the window open. Whom do you wish to see?*

See the **essential clauses, non-essential clauses** entry for guidelines on how to punctuate clauses introduced by *who, whom, that* and *which.*

who's, whose   *Who's* is a contraction for *who is,* not a possessive: *Who's there?*

Whose is the possessive: *I do not know whose coat it is.*

widow, widower   In obituaries: A man *is survived by his wife,* or *leaves his wife.* A woman *is survived by her husband,* or *leaves her husband.*

Guard against the redundant *widow of the late.* Use *wife of the late* or *widow of.*

Glossary

Absolute privilege   The right of legislators, judges and government executives to speak without threat of libel when acting in their official capacities.

Absolutism   The ethical philosophy that there is a fixed set of principles or laws from which there is no deviation. To the absolutist journalist the end never justifies the means.

Actual malice   Reckless disregard of the truth. It is a condition in libel cases.

Ad   An advertisement.

Add   A typewritten page of copy following the first page. "First add" would be the second page of typewritten copy.

Advance   A report dealing with the subjects and issues to be dealt with in an upcoming meeting or event.

Advertising department   The department of the newspaper responsible for advertisements. Most advertising departments have classified and display ad sections.

Anecdotal lead   A newspaper story beginning that uses humor or an interesting incident.

Angle   The focus of, or approach to, a story. The latest development in a continuing controversy, the key play in a football game, the tragedy of a particular death in a mass disaster may serve as an angle.

Antinomianism   The ethical philosophy that recognizes no rules. An antinomian journalist judges every ethical situation on its own merits. Unlike the situation ethicist, the antinomian does not use love of neighbor as an absolute.

525

AP The Associated Press, a worldwide news-gathering cooperative owned by its subscribers.

APME Associated Press Managing Editors, an organization of managing editors and editors whose papers are members of The Associated Press.

Arraignment A court proceeding at which a defendant is informed of the charge. At the proceeding, the defendant is asked to enter a plea, and bail may be set.

Background Information that may be attributed to a source by title, but not by name; for example, a "White House aide said."

Backgrounder Story that explains and updates the news.

Beat A reporter's assigned area of responsibility. A beat may be an institution, such as the courthouse; a geographical area, such as a small town; or a subject, such as science. The term also refers to an exclusive story.

Books Assembled sheets of paper, usually newsprint, and carbon paper on which reporters prepare stories. Books are not used with modern OCR and VDT processes.

Brightener A story, usually short, that is humorous or pleasing to the reader. It is also called a "bright."

Bureau A news-gathering office maintained by a newspaper at other than its central location. Papers may have bureaus in the next county, in the state capital, in Washington, D.C., or in foreign countries.

Business department The newspaper department that handles billing, accounting and related functions.

Byline A line identifying the author of a story.

Chain Two or more newspapers owned by a single person or corporation. Also known as group. The American chain owning the most newspapers is Gannett.

Change of venue An order transferring a court proceeding to another jurisdiction for prosecution. This often occurs when a party in a case claims that local media coverage has prejudiced prospective jurors.

Circulation department The department responsible for distribution of the newspaper.

City editor The individual (also known as the metropolitan, or metro, editor) in charge of the city desk, which coordinates local news-gathering operations. At some papers the desk also handles regional and state news done by its own reporters.

Civil law Statutes under which an individual or group can take action against another individual or group.

Clips Stories clipped from your own or competing newspapers.

Closed-ended question A direct question designed to draw a specific response; for example, "Will you be a candidate?"

Conditional privilege The right to report on the three branches of government if the report is full, fair and accurate, and the reporter does not seriously doubt the truth of the material.

Control The process of structuring an experiment so that the only forces affecting the outcome are the variables you are observing.

Controller The computer that drives a video display terminal or optical character recognition system.

Copy What reporters write. A story is a piece of copy.

Copy desk The desk at which final editing of stories is done, headlines are written and pages are designed.

Copy editor A person who checks, polishes and corrects stories written by reporters. Usually copy editors write headlines for those stories, and sometimes they decide how to arrange stories and pictures on a page.

Cover To keep abreast of significant developments on a beat or to report on a specific event. The reporter covering the police beat may be assigned to cover a murder.

Criminal law Statutes under which a grand jury or an officer of the court can take action against an individual.

Cub A beginning reporter.

Cursor A rectangle of light on a video display terminal that indicates the writer's or editor's position within the text of a story. Changes in text are made with the keyboard and appear on the screen where the cursor is located.

Data base A computerized information bank, usually accessible only on a subscription basis.

Deadline Time by which a reporter, editor or desk must have completed scheduled work.

Deep background Information that may be used but that cannot be attributed to either a person or a position.

Delayed identification lead Opening paragraph of a story in which the "who" is identified by occupation, city, office or any means other than by name.

Desk A term used by reporters to refer to the city editor's or copy editor's position, as in, "The desk wants this story by noon."

Developing story One in which newsworthy events occur over several days or weeks.

Dig To question or investigate thoroughly, as in, "Let's do some digging into those campaign reports."

Directory The index of stories within a video display terminal system.

Documentary In-depth coverage of an issue or event, especially in broadcasting.

Editor The top-ranking individual in the news department of a newspaper, also known as the "editor in chief." The term may refer as well to those at any level who edit copy.

Editorial department The news department of a newspaper, responsible for all content of the newspaper except advertising. At some papers this term refers to the department responsible for the editorial page only.

Editorialize To inject the reporter's or the newspaper's opinion into a news story or headline. Most newspapers restrict opinion to analysis stories, columns and editorials.

Editorial page editor The individual in charge of the editorial page and, at larger newspapers, the op-ed (opposite editorial) page.

Fair comment and criticism Opinion delivered on the performance of anyone in the public eye. Such opinion is legally protected if reporters do not misstate any of the facts upon which they base their comments or criticism, and it is not malicious.

Felonies Serious crimes punishable by death or imprisonment.

Field experiment A research technique in which the reporter deliberately takes some action in order to observe the effects. For example, a perfectly tuned automobile could be taken to several repair shops to find out if the mechanics would invent problems that required fixing.

Follow A story supplying further information about an item that has already been published. "Folo" is an alternate spelling.

Freedom of Information Act A law passed in 1966 to make it easier to obtain information from federal agencies. The law was amended in 1974 to improve access to government records.

Futures file   A collection, filed according to date, of newspaper clippings, letters, notes and other information to remind editors of stories to assign.

General manager   The individual responsible for the business operations of a newspaper. Some newspaper chains award this title to the top-ranking local executive.

Graf   A shortened form of paragraph, as in, "Give me two grafs on that fire."

Handout   See *Press release.*

Hard lead   A lead that reports a new development or newly discovered fact. See *Soft lead.*

Hard news   Coverage of the actions of government or business; or the reporting of an event, such as a crime, an accident or a speech. The time element often is important.

Human-interest story   A piece valued more for its emotional impact or oddity than for its importance.

Hypothesis   In investigative reporting the statement a reporter expects to be able to prove, as in, "The mayor took a bribe from that massage parlor." In an experiment the statement of what a researcher hopes to find.

Immediate identification lead   The opening paragraph of a story in which the "who" is reported by name.

Indictment   A document issued by a grand jury that certifies there is sufficient evidence against a person accused of a crime to warrant holding that person for trial.

Invasion of privacy   Violation of a person's right to be left alone.

Inverted pyramid   The organization of a news story in which information is arranged in descending order of importance.

Investigative reporting   The pursuit of information that has been concealed, such as evidence of wrongdoing.

IRE   Investigative Reporters and Editors, a group created to exchange information and investigative reporting techniques. IRE has its headquarters at the University of Missouri School of Journalism.

Lay out (v.)   The process of preparing page drawings to indicate to the composing room where stories and pictures are to be placed in the newspaper.

Layout (n.)   The completed page drawing, or dummy.

Lead The first paragraph or first several paragraphs of a newspaper story (sometimes spelled "lede"); also, the story given the best display on Page One; also, a tip.

Lead-in An introduction to a filmed or recorded excerpt from a news source or from another reporter.

Lead story The major story displayed at the top of Page One.

Libel Damage to a person's reputation caused by a false written statement that brings the person into hatred, contempt or ridicule, or injures his or her business or occupational pursuit.

Linecaster A device used in hot-metal composition to set type. The cold-type equivalent is a phototypesetter.

Managing editor The individual with primary responsibility for day-to-day operation of the news department.

Misdemeanors Minor criminal offenses, including most traffic violations, which usually result in a fine or brief confinement in a local jail.

More Designation used at the end of a page of copy to indicate there are one or more additional pages.

Morgue The newspaper library, where previous stories, photographs and resource material are stored for reference.

Multiple elements lead The opening paragraph of a story that reports two or more newsworthy elements.

Negligence test The legal standard that requires reporters to use the same care in gathering facts and writing a story as any reasonable individual would under similar circumstances.

News conference An interview session, also called a "press conference," in which someone submits to questions from reporters.

News editor The supervisor of the copy desk. At some newspapers this title is used for the person in charge of local news-gathering operations.

News room The place, sometimes called the "city room," where reporters and editors work.

News value How important or interesting a story is.

Not for attribution Information that may not be ascribed to its source.

OCR Optical character recognition. The process in which reporters write their stories on electric typewriters and a device called an optical character reader translates the typed material into electrical impulses for processing.

Off the record   Usually means, "Don't quote me." Some sources and reporters, however, use it to mean, "Don't print this." Phrases with similar, and equally ambiguous, meanings are "not for attribution" and "for background only."

Op-ed page   The page opposite the editorial page, frequently reserved for columns, letters to the editor and personality profiles.

Open-ended question   One that permits the respondent some latitude in the answer; for example, "How did you get involved in politics?"

Open meetings laws   State and federal laws, often called "sunshine laws," guaranteeing access to meetings of public officials.

Open records laws   State and federal laws guaranteeing access to many — but not all — kinds of government records.

Participant observation   A research technique in which the reporter joins in the activity he or she wants to write about.

Payola   Money or gifts given in the expectation of favors from journalists.

Photo editor   The individual who advises editors on the use of photographs in the newspaper. The photo editor also may supervise the photography department.

Play   A shortened form of "display." A good story may be played at the top of Page One; a weak one may be played inside.

Poll   The measurement of opinion by questioning members of some small group chosen at random so as to be representative of the entire group. A poll is also referred to as a "survey" or "public opinion poll."

Population   In scientific language the whole group being studied. Depending on the study the population may be, for example, voters in St. Louis, physicians in California or all residents of the United States.

Preliminary hearing   A court hearing held to determine whether there is probable cause that a defendant committed a crime and whether the defendant should be bound over for grand jury action or trial in a higher court.

Press   The machine that prints the newspaper. Also a synonym for journalism, as in the phrase "freedom of the press." Sometimes used to denote print journalism, as distinguished from broadcast journalism.

Press agent A person hired to gain publicity for a client. The tactics used, often called "press agentry," might include the staging of interviews or stunts designed to attract the attention of reporters.

Press box The section of a stadium or arena set aside for reporters.

Press conference See *news conference.*

Press release An item, also called a "handout," that is sent out by a group or individual seeking publicity.

Production department The department of the newspaper that transforms the work of the news and advertising departments into the finished product. The composing room and pressroom are key sections of this department.

Profile A story intended to reveal the personality or character of an institution or person.

Public figure A person who has assumed a role of prominence in the affairs of society and who has persuasive power and influence in a community or who has thrust himself or herself to the forefront of a public controversy. Courts have given journalists more latitude in reporting on public figures.

Publisher The top-ranking executive of a newspaper. This title often is assumed by the owner, although chains sometimes designate as publisher the top local executive.

Pulitzer Prize The most prestigious of journalism awards. It was established by Joseph Pulitzer and is administered by Columbia University.

Queue A holding area within a video display terminal system. It is the electronic equivalent of an in-basket.

Quote As a noun, the term refers to a source's exact words, as in, "I have a great quote here." As a verb, it means to report those words inside quotation marks.

Randomization The mathematical process used to assure that every member of a population being studied has an equal chance of being chosen for questioning or observation.

Records column The part of the newspaper featured regularly that contains such information as routine police and fire news, births, obituaries, marriages and divorces.

Reporter A person whose job it is to gather and write the news for a publication or a broadcast outlet.

Rewrite   To write a story again. It also means to take information over the telephone from a reporter in the field and mold it into a story.

Roundup   A story including a number of related events. After a storm, for example, a reporter might do a roundup of accidents, power outages and other consequences of the storm.

Sample   A portion of a group, or population, chosen for study as representative of the entire group.

Sampling error   The allowance that must be made in any survey for the possibility that the sample questioned may not be exactly like the other members of the population.

Scanner   The popular term for an optical character reader.

Scenic lead   A lead that concentrates on a description of an environment.

Second-cycle story   A second version of a story already published, also called a "second-day" story. It usually has new information or a new angle.

Series   Two or more stories on the same or related subjects, published on a predetermined schedule.

Shield laws   Legislation giving journalists the right to protect the identity of sources.

Sidebar   A secondary story intended to be run with a major story on the same topic. A story about a disaster, for example, may have a sidebar that tells what happened to a single victim.

Situation ethics   The philosophy that recognizes that a set of rules can be broken when circumstances dictate that the community will be served better by it. For example, a journalist who believes it normally unethical to deceive a news source may be willing to conceal his or her identity to infiltrate a group operating illegally.

Slug   A word that identifies a story as it is processed through the newspaper plant. It is usually placed in the upper left-hand corner of each take of the story.

Sniff   The preliminary phase of an investigation.

Soft lead   A lead that uses a quote, anecdote or other literary device to attract the reader. See *Hard lead*.

Soft news   Stories about trends, personalities or lifestyles. The time element usually is not important.

Sources People or places from which a reporter gets information. The term often is used to describe persons, as opposed to documents.

Spot news A timely report of an event that is unfolding at the moment.

Story The term most journalists use for a newspaper article. Another synonym is "piece," as in, "I saw your piece on the mayor." A very long story may be called a takeout or a blockbuster.

Stylebook A book of standard usage within newspaper text. It includes rules on grammar, punctuation, capitalization and abbreviation. AP and UPI publish similar stylebooks that are used by most papers. (Portions of the AP and UPI stylebooks are reprinted in the appendix to this book.)

Substantial Truth The correctness of the essential elements of a story.

Summary lead The first paragraph of a news story in which the writer presents a synopsis of two or more actions rather than focusing on any one of them.

Sunshine laws See *Open meetings laws.*

Take A page of typewritten copy for newspaper use.

30 A designation used to mark the end of a newspaper story.

Tie-back The sentence or sentences relating a story to events covered in a previous story. Used in follow-up or continuing stories or in parts of a series of stories. Also, the technique of referring to the opening in the ending of the story.

Tip A fragment of information that may lead to a story; also called a "lead."

Transition A word, phrase, sentence or paragraph that moves the reader from one thought to the next and shows the relationship between them.

TTS Teletypesetter, a system used to produce coded paper tape that is read by an automated typesetter to produce type.

Universal desk A copy desk that edits material for all editorial departments of a newspaper.

Update A type of follow that reports on a development related to an earlier story.

UPI United Press International, a worldwide news gathering organization that is privately owned.

Variable   In an experiment, one of the elements being observed. The independent variable is what is thought to be a cause; the dependent variable is the effect of that cause.

VDT   Video display terminal or visual display terminal, a computer-assisted device with television-like display and attached keyboard for writing stories and headlines and editing copy.

Videoprompter   A mechanical or electronic device that projects the copy next to the television camera lens so that a newscaster can read it while appearing to look straight into the lens.

Index

Acknowledgments (continued from page iv)

pp. 196–197: Excerpted news story reprinted by permission of The Columbia Daily Tribune.

pp. 197–198: Excerpted news story reprinted by permission of the Columbia Missourian.

p. 199: Excerpted news story reprinted by permission of the Columbia Missourian.

pp. 249–250: News story by George Frank reprinted by permission of United Press International.

pp. 255–256: Excerpted news story reprinted by permission of the Columbia Missourian.

p. 256: Excerpted news story reprinted by permission of the Columbia Missourian.

pp. 257–258: Excerpted news story reprinted by permission of the Columbia Missourian.

p. 274: News story reprinted by permission of The Kansas City Star Company.

pp. 275–276: News story reprinted by permission of The Kansas City Star Company.

p. 412: News story reprinted by permission of United Press International.

p. 412: Broadcast story reprinted by permission of The Associated Press.

Photo Credits

Part 1 intro: Eve Arnold, Magnum Photos, Inc.

p. 10: Boston Globe photo.

p. 13: Photo by Eric Kroll.

p. 14: Jacques Tiziou/Sygma.

p. 28: New York Times photo by Bill Aller.

p. 44 (top): Photo by Cliff Schiappa.

p. 44 (bottom): Photo by Cliff Schiappa.

p. 48: © 1984 by Randy Matusow.

p. 91: AP/Wide World Photos.

p. 92: Boulder Daily Camera photo.

p. 93: David Chalk, Omni-Photo Communications.

p. 116: © 1984 by Randy Matusow.

p. 124: Beaver County Times photo.

p. 152: Boston Globe photo.

p. 167: Atlan/Sygma.

p. 175 (top left): Virginia Schau, Wide World.

p. 175 (top right): Stanley Forman, Boston Herald American.

p. 175 (bottom right): George Mattson, Daily News.

p. 215: UPI photo.

p. 221: Waring Abbott/Sygma.

pp. 231–233: Excerpted news stories from the Louisville Courier-Journal, © 1977, reprinted with permission.

p. 236: © Randy Matusow.

p. 243 (top): Courtesy of the Mark Twain Memorial, Hartford, Connecticut.

p. 243 (bottom): UPI photo.

p. 262: Burk Uzzle, Magnum Photos, Inc.

p. 265: Advertisement for Foster Parents Plan, reproduced by permission.

p. 273: Milwaukee Journal photo.

pp. 278–283: Excerpted news story reprinted by permission of the Des Moines Register, copyright 1983.

p. 281: Des Moines Register photo.

p. 285: Miami Herald photo.

p. 291: Photo by Alain Keler.

p. 293: Miami Herald photo.

p. 345: UPI/Bettmann Archive photo.

p. 348: Copyright 1979 by Consumers Union of United States, Inc., Mount Vernon, NY 10550. Reprinted by permission from Consumer Reports (October 1984).

p. 357: David Chalk, Omni-Photo Communications.

p. 358: API/Wide World Photos.

p. 368: Sports Illustrated cover reproduction by permission of the publisher. Photo by Andy Hayt, © 1984 Time Inc.

p. 369: Washington Post photo.

p. 374: Wide World Photos.

p. 384: Photo by Adele Hodge.

p. 388: Courtesy of the Pelletier Library, Allegheny College, Meadville, Pa. 16335.

p. 390: Newsday photo by George Argeroplos.

p. 410: AP/Wide World Photos.

p. 426: © 1984 by Randy Matusow.

p. 459: Photograph by Jim Frost. Reproduced with permission from The Chicago Sun-Times.

p. 464: The Oregonian/Tom Treick.

PN
4781
.N34
1985

News Reporting and
Writing

Salem Academy and College
Gramley Library
Winston-Salem, N.C. 27108